MARRIAGES and DEATHS
from
BALTIMORE NEWSPAPERS,
1796-1816

By
Robert Barnes

CLEARFIELD

NOTICE

This work was reproduced from the original edition. A characteristic of this copy, from which the printer worked, was that the image was uneven. Every effort has been made by the printer to produce as fine a reprint of the original edition as possible.

Reprinted for
Clearfield Company, Inc. by
Genealogical Publishing Co., Inc.
Baltimore, Maryland
2000, 2005

© 1978
Genealogical Publishing Co., Inc.
Baltimore, Maryland
All Rights Reserved
Library of Congress Catalogue Card Number 78-61144
International Standard Book Number 0-8063-0826-5
Made in the United States of America

To P. W. Filby

Introduction

Close to twenty years ago a novice genealogist met the librarian of the Peabody Library in Baltimore, and the librarian showed that genealogist many kindnesses. In the intervening years the librarian has done much to help the art and science of genealogy, first at the Peabody Library and then at the Maryland Historical Society. His revitalization of the Committee on Genealogy and Heraldry and his bibliographies of American and British genealogical sources have earned him the thanks of genealogists across the state and throughout the country. For his kindnesses to this genealogist, and his services to all genealogists, this book is gratefully dedicated.

This book started out to be a compilation of marriages and deaths in the Baltimore *Federal Gazette*, published in an unbroken run from its inception in 1796 through 1816. The compiler soon discovered that deaths and marriages published in one newspaper did not always appear in other newspapers. In order to make the compilation as exhaustive as possible it was decided to include vital records from all Baltimore newspapers for the period 1796-1816. Items from Maryland and the states that border Maryland were included, but items from states any farther from Maryland were not included unless one of the parties or the deceased was stated to have some Maryland connection.

Users of the book will find after each item a coded source designation and a date in parentheses, and they must consult the list of sources to find what paper was used. Entries are arranged alphabetically by the name of the deceased or bridegroom. There is a surname index to brides and others mentioned in the entry. Names of ministers were not included in the index, but following the text there are some identifying notes on many of the clergymen mentioned. All of the newspapers consulted may be found either at the Maryland Historical Society or the Enoch Pratt Free Library in Baltimore.

The compiler of any genealogical work owes a debt of thanks to many people, and I would like to thank the staffs of the two libraries for their interest and support, and I would like especially to thank Mary K. Meyer of the Maryland Historical Society for her assistance and for allowing me to use some items she copied from the Baltimore *Telegraphe*. Thanks are also due to Mr. William Gruhn, formerly of the Maryland Historical Society, for his help in locating some of the copies of the older newspapers. Finally, I want to thank my wife, for her patience, and my son, for his work in helping to prepare the index.

Contents

Introduction — v

List of Newspapers — ix

Marriage and Death Notices — 1

Additions and Corrections — 365

Notes on Maryland Clergy — 367

Index — 373

List of Newspapers

BA —Baltimore American, 1799-1801, 1804-1816.

BAP —Baltimore American Patriot, 1802-1803.

BEP —Baltimore Evening Post, 1805-1811.

BFG —Baltimore Federal Gazette, 1796-1816.

BFR —Baltimore Federal Republican and Commercial Advertiser, 1808-1812.

BI —Baltimore Intelligencer, 1798.

BMG —Baltimore Mechanics' Gazette and Merchants Daily Advertiser, 1815.

BMJ —Baltimore Maryland Journal and Baltimore Advertiser, 1796-1797.

BNA —Baltimore North American, 1809.

BPEA —Baltimore Patriot and Evening Advertiser, 1813-1815.

BRAD—Baltimore Republican or Anti-Democrat, 1802.

BS —Baltimore Scourge, 1810.

BS —Baltimore Sun, 1811-1812.

BT —Baltimore Telegraphe, 1796-1806, 1815.

BW —Baltimore Whig, 1808-1812, 1814.

BWA —Baltimore Wanderer, 1816.

BWM—Baltimore Weekly Museum, 1797.

All copies of these papers were found at the Enoch Pratt Free Library or the Maryland Historical Society Library, both in Baltimore. The letter B is used in each code designation to indicate Baltimore as the place of publication, whether the word *Baltimore* appears as part of the name of the newspaper or not.

MARRIAGES AND DEATHS FROM

BALTIMORE NEWSPAPERS, 1796-1816

-(?)-,. Mrs., mother of the wife of Rev. Mr. Dunham, Brier Creek
settlement, Northumberland Co., Penna., was burnt to death,
along with a young lad of 14 years, on 21st ult. Mrs. Dunham's life is also despaired of. (BFG, 13 May 1803)

ABBITT, John, and Miss Nancy Little, both of Baltimore, were wed
last Thurs. eve., by Rev. Mr. Bend. (BTD, 16 July 1798)

ABERCROMBIE, Miss Charlotte, late of the Baltimore Theatre, died
2nd inst., at Washington, age 16 years and 3 mos. (BFG, 2
Aug. 1813)

ABERCROMBIE, James, son of Rev. Dr. Abercrombie, of Philadelphia,
and Mary Riddell, dau. of the late Robert Riddell, of Baltimore, were married last Tues., by Rev. Kemp. (BFG, 18
Feb. 1814)

ABERCROMBIE, Mrs. Sophia, died Monday morning at Philadelphia, in
her 52nd year. (BA, 13 Nov. 1815)

ABRAMS, Jacob, and Miss Elizabeth Swartzauer, of Baltimore Co.,
were married near Fort McHenry last Thurs. evening by Rev.
Kurtz. (BA, 3 March 1810)

ADAIR, Capt. Abraham, died 4th inst., leaving a widow and several
small children. Interment in Methodist burying ground.
(BFG, 6 July 1803)

ADAMS, Benjamin, and Mrs. Mary Primrose, both of Baltimore, were
married last evening, by Rev. Mr. Rozill. (BFG, 26 Jan.
1809)

ADAMS, Charles, died at New York, second son of the President of
the United States. (BA, 5 Dec. 1800)

ADAMS, Jacob, and Miss Elizabeth Marsden, all of Baltimore, were
married last evening by Rev. Roberts. (BFG, 14 May 1806)

ADAMS, James, merchant of Baltimore, died yesterday in his 27th
year. (BFG, 26 June 1805)

ADAMS, John, and Miss Eliza Robinson, were married last Thurs.,
by Rev. Dr. Rattoone. (BFG, 4 May 1805)

ADAMS, William, of Balto., and Miss Susan Reeder, of St. Marys Co., were married at Boonsborough last Tues., by Rev. Rahauser. (BPEA, 4 Aug. 1815)

ADDISON, Capt. William H., of the U. S. Corps of Sea Fencibles, died Friday. (BFG, 19 Dec. 1814)

ADIEU, Peter, of Balto., and Kitty Estafv, of Alexandria, were married at the latter place last Sat. (BT, 11 Aug. 1797)

AGNEW, Edward, died yesterday, of yellow fever. (BFG, 28 April 1804)

AGNEW, William, and Miss Mary Ann Hague, all of Balto., were married last evening by Rev. Richards. (BA, 31 Jan. 1812)

AIRES, Jacob, and Miss Sedonia C. Sellman, both of Balto., were married last Tuesday evening by Rev. McCane. (BFG, 18 Nov. 1811)

AISQUITH, Edward, of Balto., and Miss Sarah Lyttleton Moore, of Charlestown, Va., were married 29th ult., by Rev. Edward Heath. (BA, 8 Dec. 1804)

AISQUITH, Edward, died yesterday at Ellicott's Mills, in his 36th year, leaving a widow and four small children. (BFG, 24 Feb. 1815)

AISQUITH, Mr. John, died yesterday; son of Major Aisquith of Chatham St. (BFG, 30 May 1804)

AISQUITH, Mrs. Tabitha, died yesterday, in her 76th year; funeral from the residence of Edward Aisquith, Pitt St., Old Town. (BA, 19 March 1814)

AISQUITH, William, died yesterday in his 72nd year. During the Revolutionary struggle for independence, he took an active part. (BFG, 8 May 1804)

AITKEN, Andrew, Jr., died yesterday in his 21st year, eldest son of Dr. Andrew Aitken of Baltimore. (BEP, 7 June 1808)

AITKEN, Dr. Andrew, died yesterday, formerly a surgeon of the U. S. Navy, and since the war, a respectable inhabitant of Baltimore; funeral from his late dwelling in South St. (BFG, 10 April 1809)

AITKEN, Mrs. Elizabeth, relict of Dr. Andrew Aitken, of Balto., died Monday, aged 49 years, 5 mos. (BW, 11 Nov. 1811)

AITKEN, Dr. Hugh, died Wed., 17th inst., aged 31 years; of the U. S. Navy. (BA, 23 Sept. 1806)

ALBERS, L., of the House of Zwisler and Albers, died yesterday, leaving a widow and three small children; interment in the Lutheran burying ground. (BFG, 16 Aug. 1802)

ALBERS, Lueder, merchant, and Miss Eve Diffenderfer, dau. of Mr. Michael Diffenderfer, all of Balto., were married last evening, by Rev. Altenar. (BFG, 5 Jan. 1798)

ALBERS, Solomon G., merchant, and Miss Eliza Kipp, both of Balto., were married last evening by Rev. Mr. Dwyer. (BTD, 21 Nov. 1803)

ALBERTI, Mrs. Hannah, died 24th ult., at Phila., wife of Dr. George F. Alberti, leaving a numerous family. (BRAD, 1 March 1802)

ALBORN, Jacob, barber of Easton, killed himself last Friday. "Easton, Dec. 11." (BFG, 24 Dec. 1798)

ALBRIGHT, Mrs. Anna Maria, consort of John Albright, printer, died in the borough of Lancaster, on Tues., 4th inst., in her 45th year, leaving a husband and ten children. (BFG, 17 Jan. 1803)

ALBRIGHT, Jesse P., and Miss Mary Smallwood, both of Balto., were married last Thurs., by Rev. Hargrove. (BPEA, 16 Sept. 1815)

ALCOCK, Mrs. Elizabeth, died last Wed., in her 67th year. For many years she taught the young ladies of Balto. (BFG, 3 Nov. 1800)

ALCOCK, James, died last Sun., and was buried yesterday. A magistrate, he leaves a wife and several children. (BFG, 28 Aug. 1798)

ALCOCK, William J., merchant of Balto., and Miss Catherine Hughes of Bucks Co., Penna., were married in the latter place on 15th inst., by Rev. Dr. Boyd. (BFG, 22 June 1801)

ALCORN, Capt. James, and Mrs. Margaret Dunlavy. both of Balto., were married yesterday by Rev. Richards. (BFG, 17 June 1812)

ALDEN, Capt. Benjamin, and Miss Mary Mitchell, dau. of Peter Mitchell, all of Balto., were married on Thurs. last by Rev. Mr. Beeston. (BTD, 5 Nov. 1803)

ALDEY, Mr. Perrin, aged 105, and Mrs. Ann Tankeley, aged 90, were married Tues., 30th ult., in Charlotte Co., Va., it being the third marriage for both. (BFG, 17 Aug. 1805)

ALDRIDGE, Andrew, and Miss Ann Eliza Alricks, all of Balto., were married yesterday by Rev. Glendy. (BA, 28 Dec. 1814)

ALDWORTH, John M., and Miss Catherine Dornin, all of Balto., were married last evening by Rev. Dr. Reese. (BS, 4 April 1812)

ALEXANDER, Mr. A., of Balto., died at Cap Francois. (BFG, 18 Sept. 1804)

ALEXANDER, Alexander, of Alexandria, Va., died 31st ult., at Fells Point, aged 44 years. (BEP, 10 Sept. 1807)

ALEXANDER, Mr. Andrew, died last Wed., in his 21st year. (BFG, 3 Nov. 1797)

ALEXANDER, Dr. Ashton, of Balto., and Miss Catherine Thomas of Frederick were married 26th Dec., by Rev. Mr. Bowers. (BFG, 2 Jan. 1800)

ALEXANDER, Joseph, and Miss Mary Wallis, all of Balto., were married yesterday by Rev. Galen Hick, rector of Trinity Church. (BFG, 10 Jan. 1812)

ALEXANDER, Robert, native of Balto., in North American, died yesterday, aged 64. "London paper, 21 Nov. 1805." (BA, 27 March 1806)

MARRIAGES AND DEATHS

ALEXANDER, Robert, architect, late of Washington City, died at New Orleans on 3 Sept.; 1st Lieut. of the Columbian Infantry. (BFG, 4 Oct. 1811)

ALEXANDER, Gen. William, of Carlisle, died last Sun., in his 66th year. "Carlisle, Dec. 31." (BW, 11 Jan. 1814)

ALLEN, Mrs. Christiana, wife of John Allen, died; funeral from her late dwelling near John Chalmers' ropewalk. (BTD, 25 May 1805)

ALLEN, Capt. James, of Cecil Co., and Sally Browning of Kent Co., were married Sun, 27th inst. (BA, 30 July 1806)

ALLEN, James, of Fredericktown, Cecil Co., and Miss Lydia M'Donaugh, of N. Castle Co., Del., were married 10th inst., by Rev. Mr. Davis. (BEP, 18 Jan. 1809)

ALLEN, James, and Miss Mary Barnes, all of Balto., were married last Thurs., by Rev. Glendy. (BFG, 29 Dec. 1815)

ALLEN, James, and Miss Mary Barnfield, both of Balto. Co., were married last Sat. by Rev. Mr. Healey. (BA, 20 July 1816)

ALLEN, John, the mathematical instrument maker, and Miss King, were married Thurs. by Rev. Dashields. (BFG, 9 Nov. 1811)

ALLEN, Capt. John, of the Sassafras Packet, died 20th inst., in his 52nd year. (BMG, 1 Sept. 1815)

ALLEN, Owen, and Miss Margaret Hays, both of Balto., were married last Sat. by Rev. Glendy. (BA, 3 Dec. 1806)

ALLEN, Robert D., and Miss Rebecca Mills, both of Balto., were married last Tues. by Rev. Dr. Roberts. (BA, 5 Feb. 1807)

ALLEN, Samuel, and Miss Elizabeth Edwards, all of Balto., were married last evening by Rev. M'Cain. (BFG, 7 April 1809)

ALLEN, Mr. William, and Miss Hannah Bond, dau. of Thomas Bond, Esq., of Harford Co., were married last Thurs. by Rev. Mr. Allen. (BFG, 17 April 1798)

ALLEN(D)ER, Mr., and Miss Charity Grimes, both of Balto., were married on Thurs. by Rev. Dr. Rattoone. (BFG, 9 Nov. 1803)

ALLENDER, Miss Eliza, died at Fells Point, 17th inst., in her 20th year. (BFG, 22 Sept. 1802)

ALLENDER, Dr. Joseph, and Mary, dau. of Major Joseph Biays, all of Balto., were married last Thurs. by Rev. Dr. Allison. (BFG, 3 Feb. 1800)

ALLENDER, William, died last Tues., aged 57, on Bird River. (BFG, 6 Oct. 1796)

ALFORD, John, and Miss Margaret Austen, all of Balto., were wed 19th ult., by Rev. Roberts. (BFG, 12 May 1812)

ALLIBONE, Thomas, died last Mon., in Philadelphia. (BFG, 12 July 1809)

ALLISON, Rev. Dr. Patrick, senior pastor of the Presbyterian Ch., died last Sat.; interment in the western burying ground. (BFG, 23 Aug. 1802)

ALLISON, Mr. Elisha, of Montgomery Co., and Nancy Sheppard of Balto., were married last Sun., by Rev. Bend. (BFG, 21 June 1796)

ALLSTAN, Charles, Balto. merchant, died yesterday, aged 29 years. (BFG, 10 April 1812)

ALLSTAN(?), Henry, formerly of Balto., and Miss Ann Wilson Jordan, were married Thurs., 13th inst., in St. Marys Co., by Rev. Magrath. (BFG, 19 Dec. 1804)

ALLSTAN, William, died in St. Marys Co., on 30 Sept.; formerly of Balto. (BFG, 10 Oct. 1815)

ALMEDA, Mrs. Ann, consort of Capt. Joseph Almeda, died Sat.; funeral from her late dwelling in Duke St., Old Town. (BA, 21 Feb. 1814)

ALSTAN, James, Balto. merchant, died 12th inst., in his 42nd year. (BA, 16 Sept. 1813)

ALTER, Christian, and Mrs. Elizabeth Clark, both of Balto., were married last Thurs. by Rev. Coats. (BTD, 22 March 1803)

ALTER, Mrs. Elizabeth, wife of Christian Alter of Balto., died at Fredericksburg, Va., while on a visit. (BFG, 9 May 1815)

ALTER, John, died last Fri., in his 36th year; a longtime inhab. of Balto. (BFG, 3 March 1801)

ALTER, Samuel, died at Hagerstown, aged 24. (BPEA, 24 March 1815)

AMBROSE, John, died at the Island of Curracoa on 8th ult., aged 23 years; a resident of Balto. (BFG, 30 Dec. 1799)

AMELUNG, Frederick L., and Mrs. Sophia Seekamp, were married last Thurs. by Rev. Kemp. (BFG, 19 Oct. 1812)

AMELUNG, Frederick M., and Miss Sophia, dau. of Alexander Furnival, of Balto., were married Thurs., 4th inst., at New Bremen. (BFG, 8 May 1797)

AMELUNG, Frederick M., died at Port Elizabeth, leaving a family. (BFR, 9 Sept. 1811)

AMELUNG, John Frederick, died today, aged 57, at the house of Mr. Peter A. Volckman in Bank St. (BFG, 21 Nov. 1798)

AMMORY, Ballard, and Miss Frances Sharpe were married last Tues. by Rev. John Lindsay. At the same time were married Robert Bradley and Miss Sally Sharpe and George Roper and Miss Anna Sharpe; the brides were the only daus. of Mr. Peter Sharpe, dec., of Four Mile Creek. "Richmond Enquirer." (BFG, 15 July 1811)

AMOS, James, skipper of a York craft, was murdered in Cavert Alley, Norfolk. (BA, 19 Feb. 1805)

AMOS, James, of Harford Co., died 21 Feb., aged 63, leaving a wife and several children. (BA, 26 Feb. 1811)

AMOS, John, and Ruth Wilson, were married 14 June, by Rev. Stevenson. (BA, 18 June 1810)

MARRIAGES AND DEATHS

AMOS, John, and Miss Susan Wiseman were married 25th ult. by Rev. Glendy. (BFG, 6 March 1813)

AMOS, John Archer, of Harf. Co., and Saran Wane of Balto. were married 27 Dec. by Rev. Ryland. (BFG, 29 Dec. 1814)

AMOS, Mordecai, and Susanna Sharp, both of Balto., were married 3 Nov. by Rev. Parks. (BA, 6 Nov. 1813)

AMOS, William, died 26th ult. in Harf. Co. in his 97th year, for 76 years a minister of the Society of Friends. In his early life he was an officer in the militia. In 1806, many of his descendants met at Friends Meeting House in Lombard Street. He left 16 children, 92 grandchildren, 133 great-grandchildren, and 6 great-great-grandchildren, totalling 249 descendants. (BFG, 10 March 1814)

AMOS, William H., and Miss Rebecca Young, all of Balto., were married last Thurs. by Rev. Dashiell. (BFG, 5 Oct. 1812)

AMOSS, Thomas, and Caroline Waters, dau. of Edwin Waters, all of Balto., were married at Friends Meeting House, Old Town, 21 Nov. (BA, 22 Nov. 1816)

ANDERSON, Andrew, and Mary Carson, were married last evening by Rev. Dr. Rattoone. (BFG, 16 Jan. 1806)

ANDERSON, Henry, Balto. merchant, and Miss Crawford, dau. of Dr. Crawford of Hanover St., were married yesterday by Dr. Allison. (BTD, 24 Oct. 1799)

ANDERSON, Capt. J., of the schooner Anna and Maria, died at Petit Guave, 4th inst., in his 29th year. (BTD, 25 June 1796)

ANDERSON, John, for several years a merchant of Balto., died last Thurs. (BTD, 24 Jan. 1803)

ANDERSON, John, and Miss Eleanor Ricker, both of Balto., were wed last Mon., by Rev. Roberts. (BFG, 3 April 1807)

ANDERSON, John, died yesterday, leaving a wife and several small children. (BFG, 18 July 1807)

ANDERSON, John, and Miss Mary Bodley, dau. of Capt. Thomas Bodley, all of Balto. Co., were married 27th inst., by Rev. Mr. Roberts. (BEP, 28 Feb. 1810)

ANDERSON, Joshua, and Ruth Towson, all of Balto. Co., were married Thurs. by Rev. Shinn. (BFG, 2 June 1810)

ANDERSON, Lieut. Walter G., U. S. Navy, and Miss Ann Crawford, were married 1 May at Norfolk. (BA, 15 May 1810)

ANDERSON, Capt. William, and Mrs. Mary Roe, were married yesterday at Canton, the seat of Col. O'Donnell, by Rev. Mr. Ireland. (BFG, 12 April 1799)

ANDERSON, Wm., and Ruth White, were married in Balto. Co. (BPE, 26 Aug. 1813)

ANDERSON, William, and Euphemia Jefferson, dau. of Joseph Jefferson, all of the Theatre, were married on 13 Aug. by Rev. Balch, in Washington. (BFG, 16 Aug. 1815)

ANDERSON, William J., and Miss Sybella Parker, all of Balto., were married last Mon. by Rev. Dashiell. (BA, 15 May 1811)

ANDREW, Capt. Alexander, and Miss Louisa Burn, all of Balto., were married yesterday by Rev. Dr. Wyatt. (BFG, 1 Dec. 1815)

ANDREWS, Rev. John, D. D., Provost of the University of Penna., died 29th ult., aged 67. (BFG, 6 April 1813)

ANDREWS, Peter, died at Phila., 11th inst., a worthy minister of the Society of Friends. (BEP, 17 Oct. 1808)

ANGEL, James, formerly a printer, died yesterday. (BTD, 26 Sept. 1797)

ANGLIAN, Zachariah, and Miss Jane Coburn, both of Balto., were married last Thurs., by Rev. Hagerty. (BW, 26 Jan. 1811) (BA, 2 Feb. 1811, gives the bride's name as Cobuner.)

ANNADOWN, Thomas, and Miss Susan Thompson, were married in Phila. (BT, 17 May 1799)

ANNAN, Dr. William, died at Phila., 4 Oct., leaving a widow. (BT, 11 Oct. 1797)

ANNIS, James, shipbuilder, and Mrs. Rachel Hamilton, both of this city, were married last Sun., by Rev. Backsler. (BA, 17 Dec. 1799)

ANSPACH, Mrs. Eliza, died yesterday in her 22nd year, widow of the late Henry Anspach, who died 6 months ago. (BFG, 20 Dec. 1799)

ANSPACH, Frederick, and Mrs. Constant McCabe, were married 1st inst., by Rev. Glendy. (BT, 12 Dec. 1805)

ANSPACH, Henry N., merchant, and Miss Eliza Furnival, dau. of Alexander Furnival, both of Balto., were married last evening, by Rev. Bend. (BFG, 20 Feb. 1799)

ANSPACH, Henry N., merchant of the House of Von Kapf and Anspach, died leaving a widow. (BFG, 20 June 1799)

ANSPACH, Tilman, Balto. merchant, and Miss Belliza Marshall of Cambridge, were married last evening by Rev. Bend. (BFG, 29 July 1805)

ANTHONY, Jacob, musical instrument maker, died Sat., 29th ult., in his 68th year. He was a native of Germany, but resided in Balto. for over 40 years. (BA, 7 Jan. 1805)

ANTHONY, William, and Miss Letitia Brown, all of Balto., were married last Tues., by Rev. Glendy. (BFG, 20 April 1813)

ANTONY, Robert, and Miss Martha Howard, all of Balto., were married last evening by Rev. Roberts. (BFG, 23 Dec. 1808)

APPLETON, William, and Elizabeth Dorsey, were married 27th inst., by Rev. Dr. Rattoone. (BFG, 2 Jan. 1807)

APPLETON, Wm. G., of Balto., and Miss Ann H. Adams, were married at Portsmouth, N. H. (BPE, 10 June 1814)

APPOLD, George, and Miss Margaret Wardell, all of Balto., were married Thurs., 25 Feb., by Rev. Kurtz. (BFG, 6 March 1813)

MARRIAGES AND DEATHS

ARCHER, Dr., and Miss Mary Stump, were married 4th inst. (BFG, 9 April 1805)

ARCHER, Dr. John, Jr., and Miss Nancy Stump, were married at Stafford, Tues., 16th inst., by Rev. Martin. (BFG, 24 Nov. 1802)

ARCHER, Dr. John, a member of Congress, died Fri., 28th ult., at his seat in Harf. Co. (BFR, 11 Oct. 1810)

ARCHER, Dr. Thomas, and Miss Eliza Phillips, both of Harf. Co., were married last Thurs., by Rev. Dr. Allen. (BFG, 11 June 1803)

ARMAT, Christopher, merchant, and Miss Mary E. Hunter, both of Balto., were married yesterday by Rt. Rev. Bishop Carroll. (BFG, 11 March 1808)

ARMISTEAD, Charles Canter, of the House of Armistead and Canter, of Balto., died yesterday in his 26th year. (BFG, 13 Nov. 1803)

ARMISTEAD, Capt. George, U. S. A., and Miss Louisa Hughes, dau. of Christopher Hughes of Balto., were married yesterday by Rev. Bend. (BFG, 27 Nov. 1810)

ARMISTEAD, Mrs. Lucinda, relict of the late John Armistead of Caroline Co., Va., died in Alexandria, 26th ult., in her 71st year. At one time she had four sons in the service of their country; one was a captain in the Rifle Corps, and fell at Fort Erie. (BFG, 2 Dec. 1816)

ARMISTEAD, Theodorick, Navy Agent of the U. S., died Fri., 20th inst., at his residence in Norfolk. (BFG, 30 Nov. 1812)

ARMISTEAD, Col. Walker A., of the corps of engineers, and Miss Elizabeth Stanly, dau. of John Stanly, Esq., of Newbern (N.C.), were married 20th ult. (BFG, 7 Jan. 1815)

ARMITAGE, Mr. Jonas Osborn, died 27th inst. at Fells Point, in his 23rd year. He was a Mason and a member of Capt. Thomas Sheppard's infantry. (BA, 29 Oct. 1814)

ARMONDS, James, and Susan Askew, both of Balto., were married on 21 Dec. by Rev. Burch. (BA, 23 Dec. 1815)

ARMOR, John, and Mary S. Stricker, both of Balto., were married 26 Oct. by Rev. Fechtig. (BA, 27 Oct. 1815)

ARMOUR, David, and Miss Mary Winchester, dau. of Wm. Winchester, were married last Thurs. by Rev. Bend. (BFG, 15 Oct. 1803)

ARMOUR, David, died yesterday in his 42nd year; funeral from his late residence in South St. (BFG, 12 Nov. 1810)

ARMSTRONG, Mrs. Catherine C., wife of Dr. R. W. Armstrong, of Balto., died 29th ult., in her 26th year, leaving her husband and her father. (BA, 4 May 1816)

ARMSTRONG, Major Horatio Gates, U.S.A., and Miss Mary Hughes, dau. of Christopher Hughes of Balto., were married last evening by Bishop Kemp. (BFG, 28 Dec. 1814)

ARMSTRONG, James, merchant, and Miss Mary Crabbin, both of Balto., were married last Wed., by Rev. Richards. (BT, 5 June 1801)

ARMSTRONG, James, bricklayer, aged 40, died last night; funeral
from his late residence, Franklin, near Howard St. (BEP,
12 Sept. 1810)

ARMSTRONG, Mrs. Jane, wife of James Armstrong, Sr., died 6th inst.
in her 52nd year. (BFG, 16 Dec. 1816)

ARMSTRONG, Rev. John, and Miss Ann Yellott, dau. of John Yellott
were married last Tues. at St. Peter's Church, by Rev.
Dashiell. (BFG, 15 Aug. 1805)

ARMSTRONG, John, and Miss Sophia Everhard, all of Balto., were
married Thurs. by Rev. Roberts. (BA, 16 June 1810)

ARMSTRONG, Robert W., M.D., of Cecil Co., and Miss Catherine C.
Jamison, dau. of Major Jamison of Balto., were married on
Tues. by Rev. John Glendy. (BFG, 24 Feb. 1814)

ARMSTRONG, Thomas, of Harf. Co., and Mrs. Sarah Wilcox of Balto.
were married last Thurs. by Rev. Mr. Atterbene (Otterbein?). (BA, 22 Aug. 1801)

ARMSTRONG, Thomas, and Miss Harriet Sherwood, of Easton, were
married last Friday at the latter place. (BA, 8 Feb.
1816)

ARMSTRONG, William, and Miss Elizabeth Fleming, all of Balto.
Co., were married last Thurs. by Rev. Glendy. (BEP, 13
July 1809)

ARNOLD, Capt. John, of Balto., and Mrs. Cralben of the Eastern
Shore were married last Wed. by Rev. Kurtz. (BFG, 5 Nov.
1803)

ARNOLD, John, and Miss Margaret Radel, were married last Sun. (8
Nov.) by Rev. Glendy. (BFG, 14 Nov. 1812)

ARNOLD, William, and Miss Sarah Ann Johnson, all of Fells Pt.,
were married last Thurs. by Rev. Joshua Wells. (BFG, 6
April 1816)

ARTHUR, John, and Miss Clemence Thomson, both of Balto., were wed
last evening by Rev. Richards. (BEP, 21 Nov. 1808)

ARTHURS, Hugh, and Miss Margaret Kithcart, all of Balto., were
married last Thurs., by Rev. Glendy. (BFG, 6 March 1813)

ASBURY, Francis, Bishop of the M. E. Church, died 31 March, aged
72, near Fredericksburg, Va. (BA, 11 April 1816)

ASH, John, and Miss Martha M'Gowan, dau. of Capt. John M'Gowan,
all of Balto., were married last evening by Rev. Annan.
(BFG, 24 Feb. 1809)

ASH, George, and Miss Rebecca Grover, all of Balto., were married
last evening by Rev. Fry. (BFG, 29 May 1812)

ASHBAW, John, died at his residence in A. A. Co., on 27th ult.,
in his 44th year, leaving a wife and two children. (BW,
4 Dec. 1809)

ASHBURN, Capt. John, and Miss Nackey Clarke, both of Balto., were
married last Thurs. by Rev. Glendy. (BW, 31 July 1811)

ASHLEY, Abraham, and Miss Eleanor Scoful, of Balto., were wed on

MARRIAGES AND DEATHS

Sunday, 18th Jan., by the Rev. Kurtz. (BA, 13 March 1807)

ASHLEY, William H., of New Orleans, and Miss Mary Craig, late of Newcastle, Del., were married last evening by Rev. Roberts. (BFG, 27 May 1811)

ASHMAN, Mrs. Ann Greenbury, died 11th inst. (BFG, 12 Feb. 1814)

ASHWORTH, Charles, and Miss Lois M'Kim, all of Balto., were married last Sun. by Rev. Alexander McCormick. (BPEA, 4 Jan. 1815)

ASKINS, Rev. George, died at Fredericktown, on Wed., 28th ult., aged 39. (BWA, 9 March 1816)

ASPLAND, Mathias, Swedish sailor, died at City Hospital, prior to 18 Sept. (BFG, 20 Sept. 1805)

ATHEY, Walter F., of Balto., and Miss Sarah Stone of Mont. Co., were married last Thurs. by Rev. Dashiell. (BEP, 13 Nov. 1810)

ATHOE, Merrichurch Llewhelling, and Miss Doretha Cummins, both of Balto., were married last Sun., by Rev. Bend. (BT, 20 Dec. 1803)

ATKINSON, Mrs. Ann, wife of August Atkinson, died Wed. morning. (BFG, 29 March 1806)

ATKINSON, Anthony, native of Eng., died yesterday in his 68th year. He has lived in this country for 30 years. (BA, 8 Nov. 1811)

ATKINSON, August, and Miss Ann Patrick, all of Balto., were married on Tues. by Rev. Roberts. (BA, 12 June 1805)

ATKINSON, August, died Thurs., in his 29th year; interment in Parson Otterbine's burial ground. (BFG, 23 Feb. 1809)

ATKINSON, George, hatter, of Fells Point, died Sat., aged 32 years. (BA, 2 Sept. 1811)

ATKINSON, Joshua, and Mrs. Ann Brown, all of Balto., were married on last Sun. (BA, 25 Aug. 1801)

ATTERBURY, Lewis, Balto. merchant, and Miss Catherine Boudinot, dau. of the Hon. Elias Boudinot, of Newark, were married at the latter place last Mon. by Rev. Dr. McWhorter. "N.Y. paper." (BFG, 19 Sept. 1803)

ATWOOD, John, and Miss Catherine Logan, both of Fells Pt., were married last Fri., by Rev. Roberts. (BA, 14 March 1808)

AUCHINCLOSS, John, Jr., and Miss Matilda Ingles, both of Balto., were married last evening by Dr. Inglis. (BFR, 9 April 1812)

AUCHINCLOSS, John, Jr., Balto. merchant, died in New York last Sun. in his 23rd year. (BFG, 1 April 1813)

AULD, Sgt. James, a member of the "First Baltimore Volunteers," died at Buffalo on 3rd inst. (BFG, 16 Jan. 1813)

AULLE, James, and Miss Anne Wells were married last evening by Rev. Mr. Reese. (BFG, 4 Dec. 1816)

AUSTEN, Benjamin, and Miss Margaret Shaw were married. (BEP, 22 April 1809)

AUSTIN, Collins, of Conn., and Miss Mary Miller, of Balto., were married last Thurs. by Rev. Burch. (BW, 11 Feb. 1811)

AUSTIN, James, died 11th inst. He lived about 27 miles from Balto. (BFG, 18 Aug. 1806)

AUSTIN, Capt. Purnew, and Miss Amelia Hardister, both of Balto., were married Thurs., 25th ult., by Rev. Ryland. (BA, 4 July 1812)

AUZE, Charles, New York merchant, and Miss Anna L. Martin of Balto., were married last evening by Rev. Beeston. (BFG, 15 June 1808)

AYRES, Samuel, died last Sat., in Elizabeth Town. "Elizabeth Town, 22 Sept." (BA, 29 Sept. 1801)

AYRES, Samuel, and Miss Elizabeth Spier, both of Balto. Co., were married Thurs. evening by Rev. Richards. (BT, 23 Nov. 1805)

BACHE, Benjamin Franklin, editor of the Aurora, has died of the fever at Phila., on 11 Sept. (BTD, 14 Sept. 1798)

BACHE, Richard, Jr., and Miss Dallas, dau. of Alexander J. Dallas, were married at Phila. last Thurs. by Rev. Bishop White. (BA, 10 April 1805)

BACHE, Richard, of Settle, Bucks Co., Penna., died 29th ult. in his 74th year. (BFR, 2 Aug. 1814)

BACHE, Mrs. Sarah, wife of Richard Bache, and dau. of the late Benjamin Franklin, died last Wed., at her house in Phila., aged 64 years. "Aurora." (BW, 12 Oct. 1808)

BACKER, Mr. I. H., merchant, and Miss S. Van Noemer, both of this city, were married last evening by Rev. Dr. Allison. (BFG 30 May 1797)

BACKER, John P., nephew of Adrian Valck of Balto., died yesterday in his 30th year. (BFG, 3 May 1799)

BACON, Edward, and Miss Sally Andrews, both of Balto., were wed last evening by Rev. Glendy. (BEP, 11 April 1806)

BACON, James, and Ann Long, both of Balto., were married last evening by Rev. Dr. Bend. (BA, 8 May 1805)

BACON, Martin, and Miss Elizabeth Lynch, all of Balto. Co., were married 27th inst., by Rev. Mr. Luckey. (BPE, 28 May 1813)

BAER, George, Sr., died at Frederick Town, Md., on 21st ult., in his 79th year. (BEP, 4 Aug. 1807)

BAHLER, John, and Miss Elizabeth Hans, all of Balto., were married last evening by Rev. Kurtz. (BFG, 23 Oct. 1812)

BAHNE, Mrs. Barbara, died last Mon. in her 67th year. (BFG, 17 March 1804)

BAILEY, Mrs. Eliza, consort of Joseph Bailey, druggist of Balto.,

dau. of Joseph Tatnall of Brandywine, died last Thurs. in
Wilmington, Del. (BEP, 2 Nov. 1808)

BAILEY, Enoch, a revolutionary soldier, died last evening. (BFG,
16 April 1808). (BEP, same date, states he was in his
50th year; funeral from his late residence in Market Space)

BAILEY, Enoch Fry, only son of Capt. Enoch Bailey of Balto., died
after an illness of 10 days; aged 7 mos. (BA, 24 Oct.
1800)

BAILEY, Samuel, merchant, and Hannah James, dau. of Joseph James,
all of Balto., were married 17th inst. at Friends Meeting
House, Lombard St. (BA, 22 Jan. 1816)

BAILEY, Thomas, attorney at law, late of Balto., died 4th inst.,
in Savannah. (BFG, 23 Sept. 1799)

BAILIE, John, and Elizabeth Faris, all of Balto., were married on
Sun. by Rev. Glendy. (BT, 1 July 1806)

BAILIE, Thomas, and Miss Mary Campbell of Balto., were married on
last Tues. by Rev. Sinclair. (BT, 28 Oct. 1802)

BAILY, George, druggist, and Miss Elizabeth Gallagher, were married last Thurs. by Rev. Glendy. (BA, 29 June 1805)

BAILY, George W., and Miss Mary Ann Browning of Balto., were wed
last Thurs. by Rev. Fechtig. (BA, 9 Sept. 1816)

BAILY, John, native of Balto. Co., died at Plattsburg, N. Y., on
16th ult., aged 21; member of Capt. Burd's Troop of U. S.
Light Dragoons. (BFG, 15 Dec. 1812)

BAIRD, William, and Miss Mary Graham, all of Balto., were married
on Tues. evening by Rev. Glendy. (BFG, 18 June 1813)

BAKER, Dr., formerly Health Officer of Balto., died last Thurs.
(BFG, 11 Oct. 1800)

BAKER, Alexander, merchant of Portland, Me., died in Balto., on
Thurs., of typhus; aged 38. He had come to Baltimore for
his health, and leaves a wife and several children in
Portland. (BFG, 4 March 1816)

BAKER, Charles, and Miss Mary Coleman, were married 21 May by Rev,
Glendy. (BA, 5 June 1807)

BAKER, Conrad, and Miss Kitty Freshour, were married by Rev. Waggoner. (BAP, 7 June 1803)

BAKER, George S., merchant, and Miss Maria Flanagan, all of Balto., were married last evening by Rev. Otterbein. (BFG,
25 April 1810)

BAKER, Isaac, died Thurs., 26th inst., son of William Baker, merchant of Balto., in his 6th year. (BFG, 1 March 1800)

BAKER, Miss Mary, dau. of Benjamin Baker, of Fells Point, died
yesterday in her 21st year. (BFG, 19 Feb. 1799)

BAKER, Mrs. Mary, wife of Charles Baker, died 13th inst., at
Fells Point, aged 21, leaving a husband and one child.
(BT, 18 Jan. 1804)

BAKER, Nancy, died yesterday in her 19th year; dau. of Benjamin Baker of Fells Point. Another sister died scarcely 12 months ago. (BFG, 15 March 1800)

BAKER, Peter, and Miss Murnier Marshall, both of Balto. Co., were married there 19 March by Rev. Mr. Howard. (BFG, 3 April 1812)

BAKER, Dr. Samuel, of Balto., and Miss Sally Dickins, dau. of the late Rev. John Dickins of Phila., were married at Washington last Thurs. by Rev. Wells. (BFG, 25 Nov. 1808)

BAKER, Thomas B., and Miss Sophia Flanagan, were married last Tues. by Rev. Roberts. (BFG, 7 March 1805)

BAKER, William Jr., and Miss Jane Jones, dau. of Mr. Richard Jones of this county, were married last Tues. by Rev. Mr. Wells. (BFG, 22 March 1804)

BAKER, William, Jr., of Bladensburg, and Miss Ann Marshall of Balto., were married last Wed., 1st inst., by Rev. Bend. (BFG, 6 March 1809)

BAKER, William, and Mrs. Ann Chesney, both of Balto., were married last Thurs. by Dr. Bend. (BEP, 28 Nov. 1809)

BAKER, William, merchant, died Sat. morning, in his 68th year; funeral from the House of Wm. Baker and Son, Market St. (BA, 1 Jan. 1816)

BALDERSTON, Mr. Hugh, and Miss Margaret Wilson, both of Balto., were married this morning at Friends Meeting House. (BFG, 23 Dec. 1802)

BALDERSTON, Jonathan, of Balto., and Miss Elizabeth Yarnall of Easton, Tal. Co., were married at Friends Meeting House on Thurs., (21st?) inst. (BFG, 26 April 1808)

BALDWIN, Henry, Esq., Attorney at Law, and Miss Sally Ellicott, dau. of Andrew Ellicott, Sec'ty of the Penna. Land Office, were married at Meadville, Penna., on 11 June by Rev. Stockton. (BFG, 3 July 1805)

BALDWIN, Mr. Silas, and Miss Charlotte Sterett, dau. of John Sterett of Harf. Co., were married last Thurs. by Rev. Hammon. (BA, 10 Feb. 1816)

BALL, Mr. Henry, and Miss Mary Clark, were married 14th ult., by Rev. Mr. Healey. (BA, 3 June 1815)

BALL, Walter, and Miss Mary Ball, all of Balto., were married on last Thurs. by Rev. Burch. (BFG, 15 Sept. 1815)

BALL, William, and Miss Hannah Jones, both of Old Town, were married last evening by Rev. Kurtz. (BFG, 13 March 1809)

BALL, William, of Phila., died Wed., 30 May, in his 81st year. The long obit gives an account of his Masonic activities and the funeral ceremonies. (BEP, 8 June 1810)

BALL, William, died this morning in his 54th year, leaving a wife and several children. (BPEA, 2 June 1815)

BALLARD, Lieut. Edward J., died on board the frigate *Chesapeake*. (BFG, 7 July 1813)

BALLARD, Lieut. Commandant Henry E., U. S. Navy, and Miss Julianna Maccubbin of A. A. Co., were married 28 May, at Belle Field, near Annapolis, by Rev. Mr. Dashiell. (BA, 31 May 1815)

BALLARD, William, merchant, and Miss Hannah Owings, dau. of Samuel Owings, of Balto. Co., were married last evening by Rev. Wells. (BFG, 26 May 1813)

BALTZELL, Major Charles, died 31st ult., at his farm near Woodsborough, Fred. Co., in his 77th year. A native of Germany, he came to this country over 50 years ago, and served in the Rev. War. He was a member of the Society of the Cincinnati. (BFG, 17 Jan. 1814)

BALTZELL, Lewis, merchant, and Miss Ann Maria Jeames, all of Balto., were married last evening by Rev. Browning. (BFG, 18 Sept. 1811)

BALTZELL, Thomas, and Miss Lydia Welsh, dau. of Adam Welsh, Esq., were married last evening by Dr. Dashiell. (BFG, 13 March 1805)

BANDEL, Michael, and Rachel, dau. of James Grimes, all of Balto., were married last Thurs., by Rev. Kurtz. (BA, 30 March 1805)

BANDELL, Frederick, and Maria Mines, both of Balto., were married on 16 June by Rev. Kurtz. (BA, 18 June 1816)

BANDELL, George, and Miss Maria Strough, all of Balto., were wed last Sun. by Rev. M'Cane. (BW, 1 Jan. 1811). (BEP, 31 Dec. 1810 gives the bride's name as Strahan.)

BANDELL, William, and Miss Polly Clark, both of Balto., were wed last Sun. by Rev. Kurtz. (BA, 10 Dec. 1805)

BANGE, Francis, and Miss Catherine Sahner, both of Balto., were married last Thurs. by Rev. Baker. (BA, 12 Aug. 1809)

BANGE, George, merchant, and Miss Elizabeth Brungart of York Co., Penna., were married last evening by Dr. Baker. (BFG, 23 May 1808)

BANGS, John, and Miss Hannah Phipps, both of Balto., were married last Tues. by Rev. Birch. (BW, 28 Feb. 1811)

BANKS, Allen, and Miss Ann Darnell Mokebee, all of A. A. Co., were married there last Thurs. (BA, 2 Nov. 1807)

BANKS, Major George W., of Essex, Va., and Miss Charlotte Hayward Martin, dau. of the late Col. Thomas Martin, were married last evening by Rev. Duncan. (BFG, 12 June 1816)

BANKSON, Col. John, died yesterday at his late residence in Balto. He entered the army at the start of the Rev., and served in Canada as a Captain. At the end of the war he was adjutant, brigade major and inspector general of the Penna. Line. For many years he was an inhabitant of Balto. (BFG, 6 June 1814)

BANNEKER, Benjamin, a black man, died Sun., 9th inst., at his residence in Balto. Co., in his 73rd year. (Long obit.) (BFG, 28 Oct. 1806)

BANNERMAN, John, of Balto., died last Tues.; an engraver, he was in his 33rd year, and was a native of Scotland. (BFG, 29 June 1809)

BANNING, Jeremiah, Jr., son of Col. Henry Banning, of Tal. Co., died yesterday. (BFG, 2 April 1796)

BANNING, Thomas, Esq., of Tal. Co., and Miss Mary Miller, dau. of Gen. Henry Miller of Balto., were married last Tues. by Rev. Bend. (BFG, 28 April 1808)

BANTZ, Gideon, Balto. merchant, and Miss Ann Maria Sower of Fred. were married at the latter place last Sun. by Rev. Shaffer. (BFG, 25 June 1811)

BANTZ, Jacob, merchant of Newbern, N. C., and Miss Catherine Mackenheimer, dau. of J. Mackenheimer, of Balto., were married last evening by Rev. Kurtz. (BFG, 22 Nov. 1804)

BANTZ, John, died today, aged 50, leaving a widow and one son. (BFG, 27 Oct. 1810)

BANTZ, Miss Margaret, only dau. of Mr. John Bantz, died last Sun. in her 14th year. (BFG, 15 Oct. 1800)

BARBER, Mr. Cornelius, died at his seat in St. M. Co., 25 Jan., aged 86, leaving a wife and children. (BT, 1 March 1800)

BARBER, Mr. Thomas, of the firm of Hand and Barber, died last Mon.; a member of the 5th Regiment. (BFG, 2 Oct. 1799)

BARBIE, A. C., died in the country on 15th inst.; merchant taylor of Balto.; funeral from his res. in Water St. (BA, 17 May 1806)

BARCLAY, Mrs., wife of Rev. Francis Barclay, rector of Wm. and Mary Parish in St. M. Co., died 9th ult. (BFR, 10 Oct. 1809)

BARCLAY, Anthony, and Mrs. Ann Glen, were married at New York on last Thurs. by Rev. Dr. Bowen. (BA, 23 Oct. 1816)

BARCLAY, William, merchant of the firm of Barclay and M'Kean, died yesterday; funeral from his late res. at Mrs. Gordon's, next door above the post office. (BW, 3 Jan. 1814)

BARE, Jacob, merchant of Balto., and Miss Eliza Geiger of Lancaster Co., Penna., were married last Sun. by Rev. Hoffmeyer. (BW, 8 Sept. 1809)

BARGE, Jacob, died at Phila. on Mon., 8th inst., in his 87th yr. (BFG, 10 Aug. 1807)

BARGEN, George, and Miss Elizabeth Hay, were married last Thurs. by Rev. Inglis. (BA, 27 Jan. 1816)

BARKER, Abraham, N. Y. merchant, and Priscilla Hopkins of Balto., were married this morning at Friends Meeting House. (BFG, 17 May 1809)

BARKER, Ephraim, and Miss Ann Maxwell, both of Balto., were wed last Wed. by Rev. Duncan. (BFG, 8 March 1816)

BARKLIE, Thomas, merchant, and Miss Jane M'Cormick, both of Balto. were married last Thurs. by Rev. Allison. (BT, 3 Nov. 1798)

BARKMAN, John, and Miss Elizabeth Gooddens, all of Balto., were
married last Sun. by Rev. George Roberts. (BFG, 17 Nov.
1813)

BARLING, Aaron, died yesterday, in his 41st year. (BFG, 11 Oct.
1800)

BARLING, William, and Miss Sarah Barling, both of Balto., were
married last Tues. by Rev. Richards. (BEP, 15 Dec. 1808)

BARLOW, Jesse, and Miss Elizabeth Moore were married last evening
by Rev. Rattoone. (BFG, 21 Oct. 1805)

BARNABY, Elias, died this morning, an old inhabitant of Balto.
(BFG, 26 June 1812)

BARNES, Miss Ann, dau. of James Barnes of Kent Co.,died; funeral
from the house of Capt. Barnes, corner of Lancaster and
Ann Sts., Fells Point. (BA, 16 July 1811)

BARNES, Barnaby, of Phila., and Christiana Pechin, eldest dau. of
Major William Pechin of Balto., were married 12 Nov. by
Rev. Glendy. (BFG, 13 Nov. 1816)

BARNES, Hiram, printer, died this morning, in his 24th year.
(BFG, 27 Jan. 1798)

BARNES, Capt. James, and Miss Jane Kean, all of Fells Point, were
married last Thurs. by Rev. Glendy. (BA, 16 April 1808)

BARNES, Johnson, son of James Barnes of Peachbottom Ferry, on the
Susquehanna, died. Obit gives account of his symptoms.
(BRAD, 6 Aug. 1802)

BARNES, Leven, of Balto., and Catherine Shorb, dau. of John Shorb
of Balto. Co., were married last Tues. by Rev. Suckey.
(BFG, 28 Dec. 1803)

BARNES, Mrs. Mahala, died last 25 Aug., in her 25th year; funeral
sermon will be preached this Sun. at Christ Church. (BA,
15 Sept. 1804)

BARNES, Mrs. Margaret, died 25 Aug. in her 25th year. A funeral
sermon will be preached from Christ Church. (BFG, 14 Sept.
1804--obviously the same individual as in the previous
entry: RWB)

BARNES, Samuel, printer, and Susan Dobbin, both of Balto., were
married last evening by Rev. Glendy. (BA, 4 Dec. 1807)

BARNES, Thomas, and Mrs. Frances McLane, eld. dau. of Adam McLane
all of Balto., were married last eve. by Rev. Richards.
(BA, 21 Dec. 1804)

BARNES, Whiteley, and Mrs. Frances G. Hughston, all of Balto.,
were wed last Sat. by Rev. Rattoone. (BT, 25 Jan. 1803)

BARNES, Whitely, died, in the 39th year of his age. (BA, 15 June
1814)

BARNES, William, died Thurs., 17th inst., long a res. of Balto.;
he leaves a widow and two children. (BA, 19 March 1808)

BARNES, William, and Miss Deborah Jenkins, were married by Rev.
John Glendy last Sat. (BA, 11 March 1815)

BARNETT, Mrs., wife of William Barnett, died. (BPE, 17 Aug. 1813)

BARNETT, Mr. Manning, son of Thomas Barnett of Dorset Co., died last Sat. morning at Fells Point, aged 21 years. (BFG, 14 Sept. 1802)

BARNETT, William, of Balto., and Miss Elizabeth Lavell of Easton were married last Thurs. by Markland. (BFG, 9 Aug. 1810)

BARNETT, William, and Miss Kitty Copeman were married 19th inst. by Rev. Glendy. (BFG, 28 Nov. 1812)

BARNEY, Mrs. Ann, wife of Commodore Barney, died yesterday; the funeral will be from her house in Charles St. (BFG, 26 July 1808)

BARNEY, Miss Hebe, dau. of John H. Barney, died 19th inst. (BFG, 22 March 1811)

BARNEY, John, and Miss Elizabeth Nicholson Hindman were married at Chesterfield last Thurs. by Rev. Dr. Reed. (BFG, 15 Oct. 1810)

BARNEY, Joshua, and Mrs. Harriet Coale, were married by Rev. Glendy last Mon. (BEP, 26 April 1809)

BARNEY, Mrs. Rebecca, wife of William B. Barney, died Thurs. (BFG, 18 July 1807)

BARNEY, William, and Miss Rebecca Ridgely, all of Balto., were married last eve. by Rev. Ireland. (BFG, 4 May 1799)

BARNEY, William B., of Balto., and Miss Mary Chase, dau. of Hon. Judge Chase, were married at Princeton, N.J., on 9th inst., by Rev. Mr. Comfort. (BEP, 12 Sept. 1808)

BARNHILL, Thomas, of the town of Strabane, northern Ireland, died last Sat. (BT, 5 Dec. 1803)

BARNS, Mrs, Mary, wife of Hosier Barns, died in Harf. Co., last Fri. leaving a number of small children. (BFG, 22 March 1803)

BARON, Mrs. Ann, consort of John Baron, died 1st inst., in her 27th year. (BFG, 4 Nov. 1811)

BARON, John, and Miss Ann Kimmel, both of Balto., were married last Tues. by Rev. Kurtz. (BFG, 2 March 1804)

BAROUX, James Michael, and Miss Eliza Bromfield, both of Balto., were married last eve. by Rev. Rattoone. (BFG, 6 April 1804)

BARR, Mrs. Araminta, wife of William Barr, merchant of Elkton, died at that place on 11th inst. (BFG, 16 Aug. 1803)

BARRETT, John M., and Miss Mary D. Leahy, were married last Tues. by Rev. Beasley. BFG, 1 Nov. 1811)

BARRETT, Miss Maria, of Cecil Co., died last Sat. in the convent of Rockland Farm, Cecil Co. On Mon. her remains were interred in St. Mary Ann's Episcopal burying ground. Her large fortune has fallen into the hands of someone who is "in now wise related to her," while several nephews and nieces are objects of charity. (BEP, 13 March 1806)

BARRETT, Thomas, and Rachel Philips, all of Balto., were married last evening by Rev. Beasley. (BFG, 15 May 1812)

BARRIERE, David, and Charity Fendall Fakes, were married last evening by Rev. Hargrove. (BFG, 8 March 1806) (BA, 8 March 1806 gives the bride's name as Fendall.)

BARRIERE, Capt. Joseph, and Miss Jane Fenby, all of Fells Point, were married last Tues. by Rev. Snethen. (BEP, 8 March 1810)

BARROLL, James, merchant, and Miss Mary Ann Crockett, all of Balto., were married last eve. by Rev. Dashiell. (BFG, 16 Dec. 1812)

BARRON, Mrs. Mary, died Mon., 18th inst., in her 60th year. (BT, 20 March 1801)

BARRON, Commodore Samuel, of U. S. Navy, died 20th ult. in Hampton. (BEP, 4 Nov. 1810)

BARRON, Mrs. Sarah, consort of William Barron of Balto., died yesterday. (BFG, 18 Feb. 1804)

BARRON, William, of Balto., and Miss Sally Brownly of Harf. Co., were wed last Fri. by Rev. Richards. (BFG, 2 July 1799)

BARRON, Capt. William, of Balto., died 25th inst., in his 28th year, of an apoplectic fit. (BT, 27 Dec. 1804)

BARRY, Miss Ann, dau. of the late James Barry, formerly of Balto., died 17th July at Madeira. (BFG, 21 Oct. 1808)

BARRY, Mrs. Catherine, died yesterday, 28th inst., in her 25th year. (BFG, 29 Dec. 1813)

BARRY, Mrs. Elizabeth Rose Duclos, wife of J. Barry of Cayenne, died at that place on 26 Dec. in her 23rd year. (BA, 14 Feb. 1816)

BARRY, Gilbert, formerly of Balto., died in Washington, on 25th inst. (BEP, 29 March 1811)

BARRY, Mrs. Joanna, late of Balto., died at Washington, 18th inst. Her husband and two daughters predeceased her. (BFG, 21 Oct. 1811)

BARRY, Commodore John, died at Phila. on 13th inst. He was one of the little band of naval heroes that first hoisted the American flag in 1775. (BFG, 16 Sept. 1803)

BARRY, Peter, from Denmark, and Miss Mary Carson, native of Ireland, were married Wed. eve. by Rev. Bend. (BEP, 18 April 1805)

BARRY, Redmond, died as a result of a kick from a horse. "Nat. Int." (BFG, 27 Aug. 1803)

BARRY, Robert, formerly of Balto., died 30 Dec. at Pine Grove, Va., aged 61. (BPE, 26 Jan. 1814)

BARRY, Standish, Jr., of Balto., and Miss Matilda Pearce of N. Y., were married 6th inst. in N . Y. (BA, 13 June 1815)

BARRY, William T., late a member of Congress from Ky., and Miss

Catherine Mason, dau. of Stephens Thompson Mason, dec., were married in Va., by Rev. Dunn. (BS, 24 March 1812)

BARTHOLOMEW, Julius, and Miss Susannah Jennings, all of Balto., were married on Tues. by Rev. Glendy. (BS, 21 May 1812)

BARRYMORE, Joseph, formerly an officer in the U. S. Navy, died 14th inst. (BEP, 13 June 1809)

BARTLEMAN, William, merchant, and Margaret Douglass, both of Alexandria, were married Sat. evening. (BT, 19 April 1800)

BARTLETT, Mr., superannuated carpenter of the British navy, died lately at Woolwich, Eng. (Obit gives curious details of his 23 year seclusion.) (BFG, 20 June 1800)

BARTLETT, William E., and Mary James, dau. of Amos James, all of Balto., were married at Friends Meeting House, Old Town, on 20 Nov. (BA, 22 Nov. 1816)

BARTOL, George, and Sophia Gatch, all of Balto., were married 28 Nov. by Rev. Roberts. (BA, 30 Nov. 1816)

BARTON, Dr. Benjamin Smith, prof. of medicine at the Univ. of Penna., died 19 Dec. in Phila. (BA, 21 Dec. 1815)

BARTON, John, and Miss Susannah Duncan, both of Balto., were wed Thurs. by Rev. Richards. (BA, 21 Jan. 1809)

BARTON, Joseph, of Balto. Co., and Aley Small of Balto., were married last eve. by Rev. Bend. (BFG, 28 Sept. 1801)

BARTON, Philip A., of Cecil Co., and Elizabeth Jay of Harf. Co., were married by Rev. Duke. (BA, 26 Feb. 1801)

BARTON, Mrs. Sarah Emerson, consort of Seth Barton, Balto. merchant, died yesterday, aged 28 years, leaving a husband and five infant children. (BFG, 5 Jan. 1796)

BARTON, Seth, and Polly Chew, dau. of John Chew of Fredericksburg., were married there last Thurs. (BFG, 1 May 1804)

BARTRAM, Moses, druggist of Phila., died there suddenly last Mon. in his 78th year. (BEP, 28 Dec. 1809)

BASSETT, Isaac, long a res. of Balto., died yesterday in his 46th year, leaving a widow and seven children. (BFG, 7 July 1809)

BASSETT, Richard, formerly Gov. of Del., died last Fri. at his seat on the Manor in that state. (BPEA, 28 Aug. 1815)

BATEMAN, Mr. Amzi, died 24th inst., in his 40th year, leaving a wife and five children; funeral from his late res. in Eden St. (BA, 25 June 1816)

BATEMAN, Artemas, and Miss Harriet Ensor, all of Balto., were wed last eve. by Rev. Hargrove. (BFG, 6 March 1810)

BATEMAN, Mr. Warren, and Miss Ellen Smith were married last Wed. by Rev. Glendy. (BA, 28 Dec. 1816)

BATES, Jacob, and Miss Rebecca Dunning, all of Balto., were wed last Thurs. by Rev. Glendy. (BA, 2 Dec. 1816)

MARRIAGES AND DEATHS

BATES, William H., and Miss Eliza M. Boyle, dau. of Capt. Thomas Boyle, all of Balto., were married last Mon. by Rev. Bartow. (BA, 30 Aug. 1815)

BATTURS, Richard, and Miss Sophia Shaeffer, dau. of Baltzer Shaeffer, all of Balto., were married last eve. by Rev. Otterbein. (BFG, 6 Sept. 1811)

BAUGE, Francis, and Miss Catherine Sanner, both of Balto., were married last Thurs. by Rev. Baker. (BW, 12 Aug. 1809)

BAUM, Christian, architect and house carpenter, died Fri. in his 26th year; funeral from his late res. in Green St., W. P. (BA, 4 Nov. 1815)

BAUSMAN, Benjamin, of Balto., and Miss Elizabeth Byerly of Frederick Town, were married last Sun. by Rev. Wagner. (BA, 23 Jan. 1807)

BAUSMAN, Capt. Benjamin, died last Wed. aged 27 years. (BW, 4 Feb. 1814)

BAUSWICK, William, and Miss Catherine Wolfington, all of Balto., were married last Sat. by Rev. Glendy. (BFG, 11 May 1813)

BAXLEY, James, and Miss Mary Luke, all of Balto.,were married last Thurs. eve. by Rev. Richards. (BW, 14 April 1810)

BAXLEY, Levi, and Miss Margaret D. Barnes, dau. of Capt. William Barnes, all of Balto., were married last eve. by Rev. Roberts. (BFG, 31 May 1805)

BAXLEY, Mrs. Mary, Sr., died last Sat., at Elisha Peregoy's near Balto.; widow of the late John Baxley, Sr., aged 63 years. (BFG, 6 Aug. 1804)

BAXLEY, Mary, wife of John Baxley, died 20 Nov. in her 44th yr., leaving a husband and six children. (BFG, 3 Dec. 1812)

BAXLEY, Thomas, of Balto., and Miss Rebecca Morrow of Cecil Co., were married last Sun. by Rev. Mr. Kurtz. (BT, 19 Jan. 1802)

BAXTER, Isaac, and Miss Lydia Burches, both of Balto., were wed Sun. by Rev. Bishop Carroll. (BFG, 24 Dec. 1804)

BAXTER, James, and Miss Margaret Roney, all of Balto., were married last Thurs. by Rev. Glendy. (BA, 28 April 1812)

BAXTER, Joseph, late sheriff of Cecil Co., died at Elkton, on 6th inst. He stepped forth to command early in our Revolutionary struggle. (BFG, 16 May 1809)

BAXTER, William, Cashier of the Bank of Elkton, died at Elkton on 25th inst. (BFG, 29 Jan. 1812)

BAYARD, James A., died at Wilmington, Del., shortly after his arrival from Europe, one of our commissioners at Ghent. (BA, 9 Aug. 1815)

BAYER (or Boyer), Dr. Thomas, and Miss Hannah Metcalf of Fred. Co., were married last Tues. by Rev. Mr. Armstrong. (BFG, 18 May 1808)

BAYER, Valentine, victualer, died in Philadelphia Co., on Sat.

13th inst., aged 92 yrs., 6 mos., 2 weeks and 2 days. On Sun. he was buried in the burial ground of the German Reformed Church at Philadelphia. He left 16 children, 48 grandchildren, 61 great-grandchildren, and 4 great-great-grandchildren, totalling 129 descendants. (BFG, 23 July 1799)

BAYLIE, David, of Balto., died last eve. (BEP, 14 April 1809)

BAYLLY, Louis C., of Md., and Miss Anna Gray of the Island of Dominica, were married in Savannah by Rev. Mr. Holcombe. (BT, 1 Sept. 1803)

BAYLY, Henry E., of Balto. Co., and Mrs. Hannah Greer of York Co., Penna., were married at the latter place on 16th inst. by Rev. Cathcart. (BFG, 24 Jan. 1812)

BAYLY, Mrs. Rachel, wife of Edmund Bayly, Esq., of Accomack, died at her res. in Va., 7th inst., in her 46th year. (BFG, 26 Jan. 1816)

BAYLY, Mrs. Sarah, consort of Henry E. Bayly, of Balto. Co., and dau. of the late Charles Rogers, died this morning. (BFG, 10 Oct. 1811)

BAYLY, William, and Miss Sarah Andre, all of Balto., were married last eve. by Rev. Mr. Fry. (BFG, 19 May 1812)

BAYNE, Stephen, blacksmith of Balto., died 7th inst., after a very short illness. (BFG, 9 Feb. 1799)

BEALL, Mr. Evan, and Miss Martha M. Preston, both of Balto., were married last eve. by Rev. Wells. (BFG, 9 March 1804)

BEALL, Evan, of Harf. Co., and Mrs. Mary Presbury of Balto. City, were married last eve. by Rev. Dr. Roberts. (BFG, 8 April 1812) (BA, 9 April 1812 gives the bride's name as Preston.)

BEALL, John W., and Miss Rachael M. Lambert, all of Balto., were married last Tues. by Rev. Roberts. (BFG, 4 Jan. 1810)

BEALL, Mrs. Martha, wife of Evan Beall, died this morning in her 29th year; funeral from her late res. No. 2, N. Liberty St. (BFG, 18 Nov. 1806)

BEALL, Mr. Richard B., merchant, and Miss Mary N. Hannah, dau. of the late Andrew Hannah all of Balto. were married last evening by Rev. Glendy. (BFG, 5 May 1815)

BEAM, Elijah, and Miss Charlotte Christiana Robinson, both of Balto., were married last Thurs. by Rev. Inglis. (BFG, 2 Oct. 1813)

BEAM, George, of Balto. Co., died last Sun., aged 58. (BA, 28 March 1815)

BEANS, Matthew, and Miss Mary Darlington, were married in Phila. (BPE, 23 Jan. 1813)

BEAR, David, died at Frederick Town. (BPE, 24 March 1815)

BEARD, Capt. Alexander, and Miss Mary Ann Blithe, were married last Wed. by Rev. Rattoone. (BFG, 20 Sept. 1803)

BEARD, Capt. Jonathan, and Miss Harriet Hargrove, dau. of Rev.
John Hargrove of Balto., were married last eve. by Rev.
Rattoone. (BFG, 27 Dec. 1805)

BEARD, Mrs. Mary, wife of Capt. Alexander Beard, died at Hooks
Town last eve., aged 28 years. (BFG, 16 Oct. 1802)

BEARD, Matthew, of the brig Susannah, of Balto., died Wed. (BFG,
10 June 1808)

BEATTY, Mrs. Achsah Chamier, died Tues. eve. last in her 19th
year, wife of Thomas I. Beatty of Georgetown, and dau. of
John Robert Holliday of Balto. (BFG, 29 April 1796)

BEATY, Samuel, and Miss Ann Forisdell, all of Balto., were wed
on Sat. by Rev. Hagerty. (BEP, 27 May 1811)

BEATY, William, and Miss Eleanor Murphy, both of Balto., were
wed on last Sun. by Rev. Mr. Beeston. (BT, 3 Dec. 1803)

BEAUCHAMP, Mrs. Mary, died a few days ago in Caroline Co., at the
age of 119 years. (BFG, 24 Dec. 1801)

BECK, Adolph E., and Miss Josephine Cadored, both of Balto., were
married last Tues. eve. by Rev. Fenwick. (BPEA, 30 Nov.
1815)

BECK, John G., and Miss Ann Moody, both of Balto., were married
last Tues. by Dr. Bend. (BFG, 31 Jan. 1806)

BECKER, Simon, of Balto., and Miss Henrietta Hammer, dau. of
Charles Hammer of Adams Co., Penna., were married 11th of
this mo., at Meorallen Twp., that county, by Rev. Hinsch.
(BFG, 16 Oct. 1810)

BECKLEY, John, late clerk of the House of Rep., died last Wed.,
in his 50th year. A native of Britain, he was elected
Mayor of Richmond, Va., during the Rev. War. "Nat. Int."
(BFG, 11 April 1807)

BEDFORD, Hon. Gunning, Judge of the U. S. Dist. Court for Delaware, died at Wilmington last Mon. (BFG, 3 April 1812)

BEDFORD, Gunning S., and Miss Eliza Deady, dau. of Daniel Deady,
all of Balto., were married on Mon. eve. by Rev. Richards.
(BT, 3 March 1803)

BEDFORD, Gunning S., died this morning in his 28th year, leaving
a wife and family. (BFG, 2 May 1809)

BEECK, William, of Capt. Gill's Corps of Sea Fencibles, died 16th
inst. (BA, 19 Feb. 1814)

BEEDLE, Thomas, and Miss Catherine Stewart, were married last
Thurs., by Rev. Beaseley. (BFG, 3 Dec. 1811)

BEELDERMAKER, John, died at Hamburg, Consul of the U. S. at Rotterdam. (BFG, 19 March 1800)

BEESTON, Rev. Francis, rector of St. Peter's (R.C.) Church, died
this morning. (BFR, 22 Dec. 1809) A solemn requiem service will be held at St. Peter's on Fri., 19th inst. (BFG,
18 Jan. 1810)

BEHN, Henry, eld. son of John H. Behn, died yesterday. (BFG, 15
Dec. 1804)

BEHN, John H., of Lubeck, and Violet Bryden, dau. of James Bryden of Balto., were married last eve. by Rev. Allison. (BFG, 19 Sept. 1798)

BELL, Amos, and Miss Sarah Murray, all of Balto., were married last eve. by Rev. Hargrove. (BA, 20 July 1812)

BELL, Andrew, late Custom House Officer of Balto., died yesterday. Members of the Tammany Society are requested to attend his funeral from his late res., 10 Philpot St., Fells Point. (BA, 27 May 1811)

BELL, Edward, and Nancy Kennedy, both of Fells Point, were married last eve. by Rev. Mr. Richards. (BA, 5 Aug. 1799)

BELL, Jacob, and Mrs. Elizabeth Mayns, both of Balto., were wed at Fells Point on Thurs. eve. by Rev. Dr. Rattoone. (BFG, 9 April 1808)

BELL, Jehu, and Miss Keturah Mason, both of Balto. Co., were wed last Thurs. by Rev. Grice. (BFG, 1 March 1811)

BELL, John, died last Mon. night, in his 25th year, a "genuine son of Scotland." (BFG, 10 April 1811)

BELL, John, died Sun. in his 50th year. (BA, 27 Aug. 1816)

BELL, Samuel, and Miss Rachel Goulding, all of Balto., were wed last Mon. by Rev. Healey. (BA, 6 March 1816)

BELL, Thomas, died Sun., 5th inst., at Mr. James Robertson's in Amelia (Co.). About ten mos. ago he married a young lady of Amelia, who lived only a few months. Mr. Bell was a united Irishman. (BA, 23 Oct. 1800)

BELOND, Pascol, and Miss Ruth Quay, all of Balto. Co., were wed 9th inst., by Rev. Glendy. (BA, 29 July 1807)

BELSCHES, John S., Lieut., U. S. Navy, and Miss Margaret Aldridge of Balto., were married last eve. (BPEA, 10 March 1815)

BELT, Mrs. Anna, wife of James Belt, Jr., died Sat. eve. in her 23rd year. (BFG, 12 March 1810)

BELT, James, Jr., and Miss Ann Chase, dau. of Capt. Thorndick Chase, were married last eve. by Rev. Mr. Glendy. (BFG, 13 June 1806)

BELT, Thomas Hanson, and Miss Eliza Key Heath, all of Balto., were married last eve. by Dr. Kemp. (BFG, 8 Oct. 1813)

BELT, Capt. Tobias, J., and Miss Sarah Heath, both of Balto., were married last Thurs. at Harlam, by Rev. Sinclair. (BT, 28 May 1802)

BELT, Capt. Walter, died last Mon., at his house on Fells Point, one of the customs officers. Interment was on Tues. in St. Pauls Churchyard, attended by members of the Ancient and Honorable Society of Free Masons. (BFG, 15 Feb. 1798)

BEN, negro, died at Gesham Hall, Kent Co., a few days ago, aged between 90 and 100 years. (BFG, 24 Feb. 1807)

BEND, Rev. Joseph, D.D., and Mrs. Elizabeth Claypoole, were wed last Wed. by Rev. Whitehead at the seat of Col. Nathaniel Ramsay in Cecil Co. (BFG, 27 April 1807)

MARRIAGES AND DEATHS

BEND, Rev. Joseph J. G., rector of St. Pauls Church, died this morning in his 51st year. He had been rector for over 20 years. (BFG, 15 Sept. 1812)

BEND, Mrs. Mary Boudinot, wife of Rev. Joseph J. G. Bend, died yesterday. (BFG, 30 Oct. 1804)

BENDER, Jacob, died; funeral will be tomorrow from his late res. in Franklin St. (BFG, 14 Sept. 1813)

BENDER, William, and Miss Eliza Ulrick, were married in Phila. (BPE, 4 Jan. 1813)

BENEZET, Samuel, died in Bucks Co., Penna., aged 26. (BPE, 4 Jan. 1813)

BENICUE, Peter, innkeeper near the Fort, committed suicide yesterday during the races at Whetstone Point. (BA, 5 June 1799)

BENNER, George, and Mrs. Sophia Wright, both of Balto., were wed last Thurs. by Rev. Hagerty. (BT, 24 Aug. 1805)

BENNET, Amos, died in Towanda Twp., Penna., aged 78, leaving 12 children, 93 grandchildren, and 23 great-grandchildren. (BPE, 11 Sept. 1813)

BENNET, Mrs. Elizabeth, wife of Patrick Bennet of Fells Point, died this forenoon. (BFG, 16 July 1804)

BENNET, Matthew, Esq., and Miss Harriet Skerett, both of Balto., were married last Tues. by Archbishop Carroll. (BW, 24 April 1811)

BENNET, Thomas, and Nelly Ratlin, both of Balto., were married Sat. by Rev. Rattoone. (BFG, 14 May 1804)

BENNET, Thomas, and Mrs. McKinzie, both of Balto., were married 20 Nov. by Rev. Glendy. (BA, 27 Nov. 1810)

BENNETT, Fielding T., and Miss Ann Sophia Shurley, all of Balto., were married last eve. by Rev. Moranville. (BFG, 12 Oct. 1812)

BENNETT, Mrs. Mary, wife of Patrick Bennett of Fells Point, died last Sat. in her 56th year. (BFG, 23 June 1800)

BENNETT, Patrick, and Mrs. Elizabeth McCay both of Balto. were married last eve. by Rev. Beeston. (BFG, 10 July 1801)

BENSON, Mrs. Harriott, wife of Robert Benson, died yesterday in her 25th year, leaving her husband and a mother. (BFG, 23 March 1812)

BENSON, Isaac, son of Benjamin Benson of Cecil Co., died Sun., 20th inst., at his father's dwelling in Sassafras Neck; in his 20th year. (BEP, 24 April 1806)

BENSON, John, and Miss Mary Grady, all of Balto., were married last Thurs. by Rev. Neale. (BFG, 14 March 1812)

BENSON, Mrs. Rebecca, wife of Peter Benson, died last Wed., aged 50 (or 30) years. (BFG, 15 Feb. 1813)

BENSON, Robert, and Miss Harriet Bevan were married last eve. by Rev. Dashiell. (BFG, 21 Jan. 1807)

BENSON, Robert, and Miss Ketura Keyser, both of Balto., were wed on last Tues. by Rev. Mr. Stier. (BFG, 18 Nov. 1815)

BENTALOU, Mrs. Catherine, died this morning in her 54th year. (BFG, 11 Jan. 1813)

BENZANT, John, and Mrs. Rhody Cruse, all of Balto., were married last eve. by Rev. Dr. Roberts. (BS, 1 Aug. 1812)

BERGER, John, of Balto. Co., and Miss Mary Fryer of Balto. were married last Thurs. by Rev. Dr. Baker. (BA, 31 May 1810)

BERNABEU, Don Juan Joseph, son of Don Juan Bautista Bernabeu, Consul of His Catholic Majesty, Ferdinand VII, for the State of Md., and Ellen Moale, dau. of the late John Moale of Balto., were married yesterday by Bishop Carroll. (BFG 4 Aug. 1813)

BERNARD, John, of Fells Point, died Sun. se'ennight; interment in the Episcopal burying ground. (BT, 13 June 1803)

BERRET, Joseph, and Mary Elliot O'Donnell, all of Balto., were married last Thurs. by Rev. Inglis. (BFG, 11 March 1809)

BERRY, Dr. Benjamin, of Balto., died last Sun. eve. at the seat of Dr. A. Dorsey, in Elk Ridge, leaving a widow and seven children. (BFG, 19 July 1815)

BERRY, Benjamin F., and Elizabeth W. Constable, dau. of Charles Constable, all of Balto., were married last Tues. by Rev. Roberts. (BA, 8 Nov. 1816)

BERRY, Mrs. Catherine, died yesterday in her 25th year. (BA, 30 Dec. 1813)

BERRY, Mr. Horatio, and Miss Polly Pawson, both of Balto., were married Thurs. by Rev. John Hagerty. (BFG, 30 Jan. 1804)

BERRY, Mr. Horatio, and Miss Sarah Godman, both of Balto., were married last eve. by Rev. Roberts. (BFG, 6 Sept. 1805)

BERRY, John, of Balto. and Miss Sarah C. Jackson of P. G. Co., were married last Thurs. by Rev. Brackenage. (BW, 4 Jan. 1812)

BERRY, Mrs. Mary, wife of Horatio Berry of Balto., died last Thurs. (BFG, 14 Jan. 1805)

BERRY, Thomas, and Miss Ann Foreman, both of Balto., were married on Sun. eve. by Rev. Roberts. (BW, 1 Feb. 1809)

BERRY, Thomas L., of Balto., and Miss Christiana D. Jackson, dau. of the late William Jackson of P. G. Co., were married last Thurs. by Rev. Mr. Searle. (BA, 23 July 1816)

BESSE, Capt. Claude, an active officer in the late Chesapeake Flotilla, died a few days ago at an advanced age. (BA, 24 June 1816)

BETS, Mrs. Anna, wife of James Bets., Jr., died Sat. in her 23rd year. (BA, 12 March 1810)

BETSWORTH, Peter C., and Miss Elizabeth Shyrack, all of Balto., were married last Tues. by Rev. Sneethen. (BA, 3 Jan. 1811)

BETTS, Solomon, and Miss Araminta Alexander, both of Balto., were married last Thurs. by Rev. Bend. (BMJ, 26 Nov. 1796)

BETZ, George W., and Miss Eleanor Pindle, both of Balto., were wed last Thurs. by Rev. Richards. (BFG, 13 April 1811) (BW 13 April 1811 fives the groom's name as Betts).

BEVAN, Mr. Samuel, died Thurs. (BFG, 4 March 1797)

BEVAN, Capt. Thomas S., and Miss Priscilla Dallas both of Balto., were married last eve. by Rev. Roberts. (BFG, 16 Aug. 1811)

BEVANS, George, and Miss Mary Ogle, dau. of former Gov. Benjamin Ogle of Md. were married in Annapolis last Sun. by Rev. Mr. Duke, rector of St. Ann's parish. (BT, 31 July 1804)

BEVERLY, Stafford, and Miss Lydia Campbell, all of Balto., were married last Saturday by Rev. Mr. Dashiell. (BA, 12 Aug. 1805)

BEVINS, James, and Miss Priscilla Andrews of Balto. Co. were married by Rev. Mr. Riley. (BA, 25 Dec. 1812)

BIAYS, Mrs. Elizabeth, wife of Maj. Joseph Biays of Fells Point, died last Tues., aged 42. (BFG, 7 March 1800)

BIAYS, James, and Miss Trimble, both of Fells Point, were wed last Thurs. (BMJ, 14 May 1796)

BIAYS, Col. Joseph, and Mrs. Hannah Gartner, both of Balto., were married last eve. by Rev. Mr. Kurtz. (BFG, 23 Oct. 1801)

BIAYS, Mr. Joseph, Jr., died last Fri., in his 22nd year; a member of a volunteer company attached to the 6th Regt.; Capt. Shepherd was commander. (BA, 4 Oct. 1814)

BIAYS, William, died today, in his 20th year; at the house of his father in the Point. (BFG, 21 Sept. 1797)

BICKERTON, B. Fitzrandolph, printer, and Miss Mary Parker, all of Phila., were married there on 2nd inst. (BT, 9 July 1806)

BICKHAM, Mrs. Elizabeth, consort of the late John Bickham, Balto. merchant, died yesterday in her 48th year. (BEP, 3 May 1810)

BICKHAM, Herman H., of Balto., and Miss Ann Dorsey Burgess, dau. of Capt. Vachel Burgess, of A. A. Co., were married last Thurs. evening by Rev. Linthicum. (BEP, 21 May 1806)

BICKHAM, James, and Miss Mary C. Thornton, all of Balto., were married last Sun. by Rev. Roberts. (BFG, 28 April 1812)

BIDDISON, Thomas, and Hannah Lucas, both of Balto., were married last Sun. by Rev. Richards. (BA, 19 Sept. 1801)

BIDDISON, William, and Sarah Knowles, were married 12 Jan. by Rev. Greenfield. (BA, 15 Jan. 1808)

BIDDLE, Capt. Augustine, of Cecil Co., and Miss Sarah Killum, of Balto., were married Thurs. eve. by Rev. Bartow. (BA, 26 Oct. 1816)

BIDDLE, Edward, midhsipman, son of Charles Biddle, Esq., of
Phila., died on board the President, Commodore Truxton,
in his 18th year. (BFG, 26 Dec. 1800)

BIDDLE, Nicholas, and Miss Jane Craig, dau. of the late John
Craig, were married at "Andalusia," the seat of Mrs. Craig,
by Rev. Dr. Abercrombie. "Phila. paper." (BFR, 7 Oct.
1811)

BIER, Jacob, and Sarah Ann Briscoe, dau. of S. Briscoe, of Balto.,
were married 9 Nov. by Rev. Kemp. (BA, 11 Nov. 1815)

BIER, John George, merchant, and Miss Jane Augusta Wilson Cunningham, all of Balto., were married Thurs. by Rev. Glendy.
(BFG, 18 Dec. 1813)

BIER, Philip, Jr., of Balto., and Miss Polly Miller, dau. of Major
Miller, of Fred. Town, were married last Sun. evening by
Rev. Schneider. (BT, 16 Nov. 1798)

BIER, Philip, died 10th inst., in his 70th year. (BFG, 12 July
1806)

BIGELOW, Henry, merchant, late of Boston, died 10th inst., in
Balto., aged 31. (BPEA, 21 Aug. 1815)

BIGELOW, Rufus, Balto. merchant, died Tues., 21st inst. (BFG,
22 Dec. 1813)

BIGGER, Gilbert, watchmaker, native of Ireland, died 6 Nov. in
his 66th year. (BFG, 8 Nov. 1816)

BILLINGTON, James, and Mrs. Matilda Auld, both of Balto., were
married last Thurs. by Rev. Roberts. (BA, 12 Oct. 1813)

BILLUPS, Robert, and Miss Louisa Wynn, both of Balto, were married last Sat. by Archbishop Carroll. (BFG, 30 July
1810)

BILSON, William, and Miss Ruth Murray, all of Balto. Co., were
married last Thurs. by Rev. Greenfield. (BEP, 15 March
1806)

BINGHAM, Henri, and Eleanor Chavenes, both of St. Dominique,
were married Jeudi dernier par Rev. Dr. Rattoone. (BFG,
20 Sept. 1804)

BINGHAM, John, and Mary Ann Carr, were married 12 Oct. by Rev.
Healey. (BA, 31 Oct. 1815)

BINGHAM, William, Esq., of Phila., died at Bath, Eng., last 7
Feb. (BFG, 19 March 1804)

BINNIX, Henry, and Miss Eleanor Rigby, were married 24th ult. by
Rev. Healey. (BA, 30 Sept. 1812)

BIRCH, George, and Miss Rebecca Mears, of Balto. Co., were wed
last Thurs. by Rev. Dr. Baker. (BA, 9 Nov. 1816)

BIRCKHEAD, Matilda, youngest dau. of Dr. Birckhead, died yesterday in her 14th year. (BFG, 14 Sept. 1813)

BIRCKHEAD, Pollard E., formerly of Balto., and Miss Ella Kintzing
dau. of Abraham Kintzing of Phila., were married at that
place on Thurs. by Dr. Janeway. (BT, 14 Feb. 1815)

BIRD, Empson, died yesterday in his (29th?) year, of a pulmonary complaint. (BFG, 10 Nov. 1808)

BIRD, Thomas, native of England, and lately in the service of the U. S. Naval Agency at Syracuse, died Wed., 18th inst., in his 37th year. (BA, 30 Sept. 1811)

BIRD, Lieut. William C., U.S.N., and Miss Susanna Cochran, dau. of Hiram Cochran, Esq., were married last eve. at Mt. Pleasant, Balto. Co. (BFG, 24 Sept. 1813)

BISCOE, Major George Washington, and Miss Hannah Sophia Oden, dau. of Benjamin Oden, Esq., of Belle Field, P. G. Co., were married 1st inst. by Rev. Claggett. (BS, 23 Oct. 1812)

BISCOE, James, merchant, and Miss Ann Farnandis, both of Balto., were married last eve. by Rev. Rattoone. (BFG, 28 Jan. 1807)

BISHOP, Mr., and Miss (Fuller?), both of Balto. Co., were wed last Thurs. eve. by Rev. Mr. Richards. (BA, 4 April 1801

BISHOP, Eleazer, and Miss Elizabeth Page, were married in Phila. (BPE, 23 Jan. 1813)

BISHOP, Capt. Richard, and Miss Elizabeth Young, both of Fells Point, were married last eve. (BFG, 10 Oct. 1796)

BISSELL, James, and Phebe Maxwell, all of Balto., were married Wed., 4th inst. (BT, 12 Dec. 1805)

BLACK, John, of Balto. Co., and Miss Ann Divers of Balto., were married last Thurs. eve. by Rev. Griffith. (BA, 16 Sept. 1815)

BLACK, Mrs. Mary, died last Fri., in her 38th year. (BA, 29 Jan 1816)

BLACK, William G., of Penna., and Miss Sarah Bailey, of Charlestown, Cecil Co., were married 24 Feb. by Dr. Hendy. (BA, 12 March 1807)

BLACKBURN, Edward, died in this city, aged 71. Columbia, S. C. papers please copy. (BW, 1 Feb. 1814)

BLACKESTON, James, died last Sept. at his farm in Kent Co., leaving a wife and children. (BA, 7 Oct. 1816)

BLACKFORD, James, and Mary Rains, were married Christmas day by Rev. Dr. Rattoone. (BFG, 16 Jan. 1806)

BLACKFORD, John, merchant, and Miss Sally Swearingen, both of Sheppards Town, Va., were married in that place on 19th inst., by Rev. Wilson. (BFG, 24 Aug. 1797)

BLACKISTON, George, merchant, died in Balto., 12th inst., aged 49 years. (BFG, 14 March 1814)

BLACKISTONE, Mrs. Mary, consort of Thomas Blackistone, died 8th inst., in St. M. Co., in her 25th year; a wife and mother. (BFR, 26 Jan. 1810)

BLAGGE, John, Balto. merchant, and Miss Elizabeth Holmes Clapp, eld. dau. of late Capt. Elkanah Clapp, were married at Bath, Mass. (BA, 21 June 1816)

BLAGROVE, Sarah, dau. of Wm. Blagrove, died at Ellicotts Mills, 24th inst., aged 10 mos. (BPE, 27 Aug. 1813)

BLAINE, Col. Ephraim, died at his seat near Carlisle, 16th inst., in his 63rd year; an active agent in securing American independence. (BT, 2 March 1804)

BLAIR, James, Balto. merchant, and Miss Eliza Gibson, dau. of John Lee Gibson, of Harf. Co., were married last Tues. by Rev. Mr. Pasquit. (BFG, 13 Oct. 1806)

BLAIR, Matthew, merchant, died last Sat. at Port Tobacco. (BFG, 26 Dec. 1798)

BLAIR, William, merchant, and Miss Eliza Dukehart, both of Balto., were married last Thurs. by Rev. Glendy. (BA, 22 May 1809)

BLAKE, James, Esq., commercial agent of the U. S. for the city of Antwerp, and Alphonsa Carmichael, only child of the late William Carmichael, of Kent Co., were married last eve. by Rev. Mr. Beeston. (BFG, 9 Oct. 1801)

BLAKE, James, died 7th inst., at Violet Hill, near Chestertown, Kent Co. The dec. was a native of Ireland, but had long been a res. of the Eastern Shore. (BFG, 21 Sept. 1816)

BLAKELY, David, of Keady, Co. Armagh, Ire., died in Balto., on 29th ult.: interment in Second Presbyterian Burial Ground. (BW, 4 March)

BLAKELY, Matthew, and Miss Ann Brown, all of Balto., were married last Thurs. by Rev. John Glendy. (BA, 23 May 1815)

BLAMIRE, Dr. James, died Wed., at his dwelling in Portsmouth, Va. "Norfolk, Oct. 13." (BFG, 28 Oct. 1806)

BLISSETT, Mrs. Elizabeth, wife of Francis Blissett of the New Theatre, died in Phila., last Wed. (BEP, 5 May 1810)

BLOCK, Andrew, for many years a res. of Balto., died last Sun. (BPE, 12 May 1814)

BLOODGOOD, Rev. John, and Miss Ann Inloes, of Balto., were married last eve. by Rev. George Smith. (BA, 26 Feb. 1808)

BLOODGOOD, Rev. John, died Sat. eve.; funeral from his late res., 69 Bond St., Fells Point. (BA, 29 Oct. 1810)

BLOUNT, Thomas H., son of John Gray Blount, of N. C., and Miss Eleanor Margaret Brown, of Chas. Co., Md., were married Tues. eve. in Washington. (BA, 17 Nov. 1810)

BLOUNT, William, died at Knoxville, Fri., 26th ult., aged 56; former Gov. of Tenn., of a bilious fever. (BFG, 16 April 1800)

BLYDEN, John, and Mrs. Sarah Muir, all of Balto., were married last Wed. by Rev. Glendy. (BA, 25 Sept. 1810)

BOASH, James, died Wed., 18 June; a lieut. in the U. S. Navy. (Norfolk paper, 21 June). (BA, 28 June 1800)

BOEHM, Charles G., and Miss Elizabeth Capito, all of Balto., were married last Thurs. eve. by Rev. Kurtz. (BEP, 4 May 1811)

BOGGS, Hermanus, and Miss Margaret Parks were married on Wed. eve. by Rev. Mr. Glendy. (BT, 17 March 1806)

BOGGUZ, Robert, and Miss Eliza King, all of Balto., were wed on last Thurs. by Rev. Roberts. (BA, 11 Sept. 1809)

BOLAND, Alexander, printer, died last eve. in his 48th year; a native of Ireland. (BFG, 2 Nov. 1808)

BOLLMAN, Wm., died this morning, aged 27; native of Bremen, and bro. of Thomas Bollman of Balto. (BEP, 28 Dec. 1808)

BOLTE, John, and Miss Charlotte Focke, both of Balto., were wed last Thurs. by Rev. Dreyer. (BFG, 16 July 1805)

BONAPARTE, Mr. Jerome, and Miss Elizabeth Patterson, eld. dau. of William Patterson, Esq., of Balto., were married last Sat. by Bishop Carroll; the groom was the ygst. bro. of the First Consul of the French Republic. (BFG, 27 Dec. 1803)

BOND, Edward F., and Miss Frances Hawkins, both of Balto., were married last Thurs. by Rev. Birch. (BW, 28 Jan. 1811)

BOND, Mrs. Elizabeth, of Balto. Co., died last Fri., in her 87th year. (BFG, 1 Sept. 1806)

BOND, Frances, died Tues., 13th ult., at Phila., in the prime of life, ygst. dau. of Dr. Phineas Bond, and sister of H.B.M. Consul General. (BMJ, 3 Jan. 1797)

BOND, James, merchant, and Juliana M'Hard, both of Balto., were married Thurs. eve. (BA, 15 July 1799)

BOND, James, and Mrs. Stewart, both of Balto., were married last Tues. (BT, 13 June 1803)

BOND, John, and Miss Polly Richardson, both of Harf. Co., were married in Harf. Co. last Thurs. (BFG, 1 June 1802)

BOND, Joshua, son of Rev. Nicodemus Bond of Balto. Co., dec.; and Sophia, dau. of Benjamin Beeks, were married last 14th May, in Indiana Territory. (BA, 5 Sept. 1804)

BOND, Phineas, died in London, last 29 Dec., for many years consul general of H.B.M. for the middle and eastern states of America. (BWA, 16 March 1816)

BOND, Polly, dau. of Jacob Bond of Gunpowder Neck, Harf. Co., died 3rd inst. (long obit). (BFG, 8 Jan. 1802)

BOND, Mrs. Rachel, consort of Benjamin Bond of Balto., died 21st inst., in her 36th year. (BA, 23 July 1816)

BOND, Richard, carpenter, died yesterday. (BA, 18 Sept. 1800)

BOND, Shaderick, and Nancy Tobel, both of Balto. Co., were wed on 13 April by Rev. D. E. Reese. (BA, 15 April 1815)

BOND, Thomas, died last Tues., 2nd inst., at his seat in Balto. Co., aged 69 years. He left children. (BA, 6 Sept. 1800)

BOND, Thomas, son of John, died Thurs., 2nd inst., at his res. in Harf. Co., in his 63rd year. (BFG, 8 May 1805)

BOND, Dr. Thomas E., and Christiana Birckhead, dau. of Dr. S. Birckhead, all of Balto., were married last eve. by Rev. Bend. (BFG, 29 June 1808)

BOND, Thomas W., and Miss Sarah Y. Scott, all of Harf. Co., were married Thurs., 3rd Jan., by Rev. Allen. (BT, 12 Feb. 1806)

BOND, Thomas W., and Miss Sarah Y. Slett, all of Harf. Co., were married 3rd inst. by Rev. Allen. (BFG, 11 Feb. 1806)

BOND, William, and Miss Martha M'Brune, both of Balto. Co., were married Thurs., 19 Oct., by Rev. Chambers (BW, 24 Oct. 1809)

BONSTEAD, James, died last Fri. of "an early decay;" a native of Co. Cumberland, Eng. (BFG, 27 Sept. 1802)

BOOTH, William, and Miss Mary Gardiner, all of this city, were married 6th inst., by Rev. Richards. (BEP, 8 Dec. 1810)

BORDER, Samuel of Balto. City, and Miss Dorcas Clarke, of Balto. Co., were married last Thurs. by Rev. John Glendy. (BA, 21 Sept. 1815; BFG, 18 Sept. 1815 gives the groom's name as Borden.)

BORDLEY, Maj. John, of Kent Co., and Miss Catherine Starck, dau. of John Starck of Balto., were married last eve. by Rev. Mr. Bend. (BFG, 3 Aug. 1798)

BORDLEY, William C., Esq., of Chestertown, Q. A. Co., and Miss Margaret Keener of Balto., were married last eve. by Rev. Ireland. (BFG, 11 July 1798)

BORIN, John, and Miss Elizabeth Rose, both of Balto., were married last Sat. by Rev. Richards. (BT, 11 June 1803)

BORLAND, John, merchant, of Balto., and Sophia, dau. of Englehard Yeiser of Balto. Co., were married last Tues. eve. by Rev. Glendy. (BFG, 24 Jan. 1806)

BORLAND, Mrs. Sophia F., consort of John Borland, Balto. merchant, died yesterday in her 19th year, at the seat of Englehard Yeiser of Balto. Co. (BFG, 7 Feb. 1807)

BOSLEY, Greenbury, of Balto. Co., died 1 April in his 76th year; for many years he had been afflicted. (BFG, 18 April 1814)

BOSLEY, Joshua, of Balto., died at the Havana, 8th ult., aged 26. (BFG, 9 Oct. 1809)

BOSLEY, Nicholas M., and Eleanor Addison Smith, were married Sat. eve. by Dr. Bend. (BFG, 21 Nov. 1808)

BOSLEY, William, son of John, and Miss Elizabeth Parks of Balto. Co., were married last Thurs. eve. by Rev. Healey. (BA, 15 Jan. 1816)

BOSS, Mrs. Margaret, died yesterday in her 19th year; funeral from her late res., 57 Strawberry Alley. (BA, 5 April 1815)

BOSTON, Jesse, and Mrs. Cassandra Stewart, both of Balto., were married last Thurs. eve. by Rev. Mr. Guest. (BW, 7 Feb. 1814)

BOTNER, Mrs. Elizabeth, died on the Eastern Shore in her 56th
    year. (BFG, 24 Sept. 1804)

BOTNER, Capt. John, and Elizabeth Sherwood, were married on last
    Thurs. at Fells Point. (BT, 9 April 1796)

BOUGHAN, Mrs. Eleanor, consort of Augustine Boughan, merchant of
    Balto., died Fri., 21st inst., in her 28th year. (BFG,
    26 June 1805)

BOUGHMAN, Christopher, died last Sun. in his 22nd year. (BS, 4
    Sept. 1812)

BOUIS, John, and Miss Martha Mitchell, both of Balto., were wed
    last Thurs. eve. (BFG, 6 Dec. 1800)

BOUIS, Capt. Silas, and Miss Matilda Johnston, all of Balto.,
    were married last Mon. by Rev. Mr. Burns. (BFG, 6 Nov.
    1816)

BOULDIN, Richard, hay-weigher of Balto., died last Sat. (BFG,
    20 Feb. 1804)

BOUNDS, Capt. Joseph, and Mrs. Ann Maria Danniels, both of Balto.,
    were married last eve. by Rev. Glendy. (BFG, 1 Jan. 1807)

BOURNE, John, of Calvert Co., and Miss Elizabeth Dalrymple, of
    Balto. City, were married Thurs., 19th inst., by Rev. Mr.
    Bartow. (BA, 23 Dec. 1816)

BOURNE, Sylvanus, and Miss Rebecca Haslett, were married last
    eve. (BFG, 18 Oct. 1797)

BOUSMAN, William, and Miss Rebecca Jacobs were married last Sat.,
    2nd inst., at Alexandria, by Rev. Balch. (BFG, 6 May
    1807)

BOUVART, Mme. Eulalie, widow of late M. de Donjeur, died at Nor-
    folk, in her 50th year. (BFG, 5 Sept. 1811)

BOWEN, Benjamin C., and Miss Matilda Wheeler of Balto. Co., were
    married Thurs., 25th ult., by Rev. Healey. (BA, 3 Feb.
    1816)

BOWEN, John, and Miss Ann Evans, of Balto. Co., were married on
    Thurs. eve. by Rev. Mr. Kane. (BA, 17 Aug. 1811)

BOWEN, John B., and Sarah Marshall, both of Balto., were married
    last eve. (BA, 8 July 1799)

BOWEN, Josias, of Balto. Co., died yesterday in his 52nd year.
    (BT, 2 Oct. 1805)

BOWEN, Pitt E., and Miss Mary Bailey, were married last eve. by
    Dr. Roberts. (BA, 30 Nov. 1810)

BOWEN, Richard P., and Miss Mary Askew, dau. of Joshua Askew of
    Kentucky, were married last Thurs. at the res. of Mr.
    Barry by Rev. Mr. Neale. (BA, 11 Feb. 1811)

BOWEN, Capt. Sabritt, died yesterday in his 53rd year. He took
    part in the Rev. War. He was wounded at the charge on the
    Savannah Line under Gen. Wayne. (long obit). Interment
    will be from his late res., High St., Old Town. (BA, 12
    Nov. 1811)

BOWEN, Solomon, died last Wed. at his seat in Balto. Co. in his
    81st year. (BFG, 15 June 1804)

BOWEN, Mrs. Temperance, wife of Solomon Bowen, died 25th ult.,
    aged 79. (BA, 3 June 1811)

BOWERS, John, and Sarah Binnix, were married last Sat. eve. by
    Rev. Mr. Hargrove. (BFG, 14 Jan. 1805)

BOWERS, John, of Balto., died last night of the prevailing fever.
    "N. Y. Com. Adv." (BEP, 26 Oct. 1805)

BOWERS, John, and Mrs. Harriet Green, both of Balto., were wed
    last Sun. eve. by Rev. Kurtz. (BW, 21 May 1811)

BOWERSOX, George A., and Miss Sarah Mohler, both of Balto., were
    married last eve. by Rev. Kurtz. (BT, 11 Jan. 1804)

BOWIE, Capt. James, and Miss Ann Christie, of Balto., were married
    on Thurs. eve. by Rev. Rattoone. (BFG, 7 Jan. 1809)

BOWIE, Osburn Sprigg, brother of Robert Bowie, Gov. of Md., died
    last Mon. (BFG, 2 April 1806)

BOWIE, Rubin S., of Alexandria, and Miss Eliza Young of Balto.,
    were married last eve. by Rev. Glendy. (BA, 23 Oct. 1816)

BOWIE, Thomas C., died last Tues. at his seat near Queen Anne,
    P. G. Co.; leaving a large family. (BFG, 2 May 1812)

BOWIE, Walter, died 19th inst., at his seat in P. G. Co., in his
    62nd year. (BEP, 23 Nov. 1810)

BOWIE, Mr. Washington, and Mrs. Chew, were married 17th inst. at
    Georgetown, by Rev. Mr. Gantt. (BFG, 20 Sept. 1799)

BOWLEY, Daniel, Esq., of Furley, died last Thurs. (BFG, 14 Nov.
    1807)

BOWLY, Samuel H., and Miss Sarah Hollins, were married last Tues.
    eve. by Bishop Kemp. (BA, 27 Dec. 1816)

BOWLY, W. L., and Miss Mary Hollins, dau. of Wm. Hollins, both
    of Balto., were married last Thurs. eve. by Rev. Bend.
    (BA, 1 May 1809)

BOYCE, William, native of Eng., died yesterday aged 25 years.
    (BFG, 13 April 1801)

BOYD, Capt., of Fells Point, who commanded Major Biays' ship
    Ritson, on her late voyage to Cork, died in that city last
    Feb. (BA, 16 April 1811)

BOYD, Alexander, and Mary Ann Bowen, both of Fells Point, were
    married last Sun. eve. by Rev. Moranville. (BA, 17 March
    1807)

BOYD, Alexander, and Miss Eleanor Slubey, both of Balto., were
    married last Thurs. in Harf. Co. by Rev. Mr. Stevenson.
    (BS, 25 Aug. 1812)

BOYD, Alexander H., and Miss Mary J. Hollingsworth, dau. of Zebu-
    lon Hollingsworth, all of Balto., were married last eve.
    by Rev. Kemp. (BFG, 14 May 1813)

BOYD, James P., and Ann McHenry, dau. of James M'Henry, were wed last eve. by Rev. Inglis. (BFG, 5 Feb. 1808)

BOYD, John, and Miss Lydia Moran, of Balto. Co., were married last Tues. by Rev. Healey. (BPE, 23 Sept. 1813)

BOYD, Mary, wife of Andrew, died last Mon. in her 76th year. (BFG, 4 Sept. 1813)

BOYD, Samuel, and Miss Catherine Dewitt, all of Balto., were wed last Thurs. by Rev. Glendy. (BA, 11 May 1809)

BOYER, Mr. David, and Mrs. Ann Kincaid, of Balto., were married last eve. by Rev. Mr. Hargrove. (BA, 9 Dec. 1800)

BOYER, Eleanor, committed suicide by throwing herself from the third story window of Godfrey Horton's house on Howard's Hill yesterday. She leaves a 5 month old child. (BA, 17 May 1799)

BOYER, Jacob, and Miss Margaret Nants, were married last eve. by Rev. Richards. (BA, 1 June 1814)

BOYER, Stephen, and Miss Maria Semans, both of Kent Co., Md., were married 18th inst. by Rev. Wilmer. (BFG, 24 April 1809)

BOYER, Valentine, victualler, died 13th inst., in Philadelphia Co., aged 96 years, 6 mos., and 16 days; interment in the burial ground at German Ref. Church, Phila. He leaves 16 children, 48 grandchildren, 61 great-grandchildren, and 4 great-great-grandchildren. (BA, 23 July 1799)

BOYLE, David, and Miss Jane Neale, both of Balto., were married last Wed. eve. by Rev. Glendy. (BA, 24 Jan. 1807)

BOYLE, Edward, and Mrs. Mary Willey, both of Balto., were married last Fri., by Rev. Hagerty. (BA, 11 June 1813)

BOYLE, Mr. Frederick, merchant, of Balto., died at Fort Republican on the 1st inst. (BFG, 4 Nov. 1799)

BOYLE, James, and Miss Susan Maccubbin were married Thurs., 12th inst. at South River in A. A. Co., by Rev. Nind. (BW, 19 May 1812)

BOYLE, John, and Miss Catherine Hager, both of Balto., were married last eve. by Rev. Kurtz. (BT, 4 June 1802)

BOYLE, Joseph, and Louisa Hoyes, both of Balto., were married last Sun. eve. by Rev. Mr. Kurtz. (BFG, 28 Jan. 1806)

BRACKE, Ferdinand, and Hannah Cornwall of Balto., were married 2nd inst., by Rev. Dr. Allison. (BFG, 8 April 1799)

BRACKENRIDGE, Hon. Henry Hugh, one of the Judges of the Penna. Supreme Court, died 25 June at Carlisle, Penna., aged 67. (BFG, 29 June 1816)

BRADEN, Samuel, son of Mr. Braden of Wilmington, Del., died in Baltimore Hospital on 12th inst., aged 32. (BPEA, 19 May 1815)

BRADENBAUGH, John, Jr., Balto. merchant, and Miss Priscilla Pew, of Ashton, Penna., were married last April 7. (BFG, 23 Dec. 1803)

BRADFORD, Mrs., wife of Thomas Bradford, editor of the True American, died. (BFG, 21 Nov. 1805)

BRADFORD, Dr. John, died at his seat in Balto. Co., on 28 Jan., in his 44th year. (BA, 9 Feb. 1814)

BRADFORD, Samuel, editor of the True American, and Miss Abby Inskeep, dau. of John Inskeep of Phila., were married 7th inst. at that city by Rev. Blackwell. (BFG, 12 March 1799)

BRADIN, James, merchant, of Carlisle, Penna., and Miss Ann Magaurin, of Balto., were married last Thurs. by Rev. Glendy. (BA, 16 Dec. 1815)

BRADNER, Rev. Benoni, died at Blooming Grove, 29 Jan. in his 71st year. (BT, 22 Feb. 1804)

BRADSHAW, James, died in Kent Co., Md., last Fri., in his 63rd year. (BPE, 22 June 1813)

BRADSHAW, Thomas Crausling, and Miss Eleanora Deal, both of Balto., were married last Sun. by Rev. Jacob Grouber. (BT, 24 Jan. 1815)

BRADY, Jason, and Mrs. Ann Graham were married 20 Sept. by Rev. Glendy. (BFG, 6 Oct. 1814)

BRAHANEY, Major James, and Miss Caroline Blackney, both of Balto., were married last Thurs. by Bishop Carroll.

BRANCH, William, of Va., and Miss Louisa Magruder, dau. of Patrick Magruder, were married in Washington. (BPE, 19 Jan. 1814)

BRAND, Daniel, and Mary Ann White, all of Balto., were married Wed., 6 Feb., by Bishop Carroll. (BFG, 7 Feb. 1805)

BRANDON, Noah, and Miss Catherine Hanner, both of Balto., were married last Thurs. by Rev. Bend. (BEP, 20 Oct. 1810)

BRANDT, Jacob, and Ann, dau. of Charles Mankin, all of Port Tobacco, were married there on 5th inst. by Rev. Weems. (BFG, 11 Jan. 1800)

BRANE, Job, of Fred. Co., died 13th inst., aged 84 years, 6 mos., and 6 days. (BEP, 24 May 1811)

BRASHEARS, Richard Wells, died 26th ult., at his res. in Upper Marlborough, P. G. Co. (BA, 11 Nov. 1806)

BRAY, Capt. Edward, and Miss Catherine Mullen, both of Balto., were married last Sun. by Rev. Moranville. (BA, 24 Oct. 1810)

BRAY, John, and Miss Sally Hunt, both of the Balto. Theatre, were married last Thurs. at Washington by Rev. M'Cormick. (BW, 28 Sept. 1808)

BRAYTON, Isaac, died last Tues., leaving a wife and three small children. (BFG, 21 Sept. 1805) (BEP, 19 Sept. 1805, gives his name as Israel.)

BRECKENRIDGE, Rev. John, pastor of St. Andrews Church, City of Washington, and Miss Nelly White of P. G. Co., were wed Tues., 15th inst. by Rev. Balch. (BT, 24 March 1796)

BREEZE, John M., and Miss Harriot Beall, were married at Mount Royal on last Mon. by Rev. Ryland. (BFG, 10 June 1813)

BREIDENHART, George, merchant, and Miss Elizabeth Stein, dau. of Abraham Stein, all of Balto., were married at Phila. on Tues., 24th ult. by Rev. Frederick Smith. (BFG, 19 Nov. 1806)

BREITENODER, Adam, of Fells Point, died last eve., aged 57 years of age. (BEP, 12 Jan. 1810)

BRENAN, Capt. William, died yesterday at his late res., Fells Point; a member of Washington Lodge. (BFG, 22 Jan. 1806)

BRENT, Daniel, of Washington, and Miss Eliza Walsh, dau. of Robert Walsh of Balto., were married last eve. by Archbishop Carroll. (BFG, 28 April 1813)

BRENT, Daniel Carroll, died last Fri., on his 55th birthday in Stafford Co., Va.; bro. of Richard Brent who died two weeks earlier. (BPEA, 21 Jan. 1815)

BRENT, Mrs. Eliza, wife of Daniel Brent of Wash., and dau. of Robert Walsh, of Balto., died at the former place yesterday. (BFG, 9 May 1816)

BRENT, Robert, died at his res. in Chas. Co., Sat., 2nd inst., in his 52nd year; interment at Mount Carmel. (BEP, 11 March 1811)

BRENT, Robert Y., of Washington, and Miss Eliza L. Carrere, dau. of John Le Carrere of Balto., were married last eve. by Bishop Carroll. (BFG, 5 Jan. 1814)

BRENTON, Miss Louisa, dau. of James Brenton, Esq., late Judge of the Vice Admiralty Court at Halifax, N. S., died 9th inst., at the seat of James M'Culloch, Esq., near Annapolis, in her 20th year. (BFG, 15 Jan. 1807)

BREVITT, Dr., of Balto., and Cassandra Webster Woodland, of Harford Co., were married at Abingdon last Thurs. by Rev. Dr. Allen. (BFG, 1 Dec. 1798)

BREWER, John, and Elizabeth Gaston, both of Annapolis, were wed there on last Sun. by Rev. Higginbotham. (BT, 2 July 1800)

BREWER, Nicholas, and Mrs. Sarah Maccubbin, both of Annap., were married there last Sun. by Rev. Higginbotham. (BFG, 27 June 1800)

BREWER, Nicholas, and Miss Mary Stansbury, of Balto. Co., were married 24th inst., by Rev. Green. (BPE, 29 June 1813)

BREWER, William, and Miss Jane Boyd, all of Balto., were married last Sun. by Rev. Dr. Roberts. (BW, 30 Oct. 1811)

BREYAN, Charles, and Harriot Hopkins, dau. of Johns Hopkins, all of Balto. Co., were married last Tues. eve. by Rev. Roberts. (BFG, 18 April 1807)

BRIAN, James, died 17 Dec. in his 89th year, a native of Balto. Co. At one time the dec. said he knew Baltimore when it contained one small brick house, 16 x 20, one story high, and three or four small frame (houses.). (BFG, 21 Dec. 1812)

BRICE, Henry, of Balto., and Miss Harriot Tilghman, dau. of
Richard Tilghman, IV, of Chestertown, were married last
Mon. at the latter place. (BFG, 10 May 1804)

BRICE, Joseph W., and Miss Ann Maria Tilden, both of Kent Co.,
were married 1 Feb. by Rev. Smith. (BFG, 11 Feb. 1814)

BRICE, Mrs. Mary, consort of John Brice of Annap., died last
Thurs. in her 57th year. (BFG, 4 Feb. 1806)

BRICE, Nicholas, Esq., and Miss Anna Maria Tilghman, the 4th dau.
of Richard Tilghman of Chestertown, were married last
Tues. at that place. (BFG, 11 Dec. 1797)

BRIDE, Mrs. Mary, died this morning at Fells Point, aged 73 years;
a native of Ireland; funeral will be from the res. of
Capt. M. S. Bunbury, 59 Market St. (BFG, 29 April 1811)

BRIDENBAUGH, Mr. Valentine, and Miss Mary Willey, both of Balto.,
were married Sun. by Rev. Kurtz. (BT, 25 May 1802)

BRIDGES, John S., of Georgetown, D. C., and Miss Catherine Capito
of Balto. were married last eve. (BPEA, 7 Dec. 1815)

BRIERLY, Anthony M., and Miss Sally Willis, both of Balto., were
married last Sun. by Rev. Kurtz. (BFR, 16 May 1810)

BRIGGS, James, and Miss Temperance Ensor, both of Balto., were
married last eve. by Rev. Dr. Allison. (BFG, 6 Dec. 1797)

BRIGHT, Mrs. Elizabeth, consort of Gen. Michael Bright, died at
Phila. last Tues. eve. (BA, 14 July 1810)

BRIGHT, Brig.-Gen. Michael, Inspector of Flour for the port of
Phila., died yesterday in his 51st year. "Another soldier
of the Revolution has descended into the tomb." "Phila.-
12 Feb." (BFG, 14 Feb. 1812)

BRISCOE, Alexander, of Balto., and Miss Mary Wilson of Balto. Co.
were married Tues., 15th inst., by Rev. Roberts. (BFG,
19 Aug. 1809)

BRISCOE, Mrs. Ann, consort of Peregrine Briscoe, of Cecil Co.,
died lately and was buried in the Welsh Tract, Newcastle
Co. (BFG, 26 Oct. 1802)

BRISCOE, Brig.-Gen. John Hanson, died Wed., 7th inst., at his res.
near Chaptico, St. M. Co., in his 44th year, leaving a
widow and several small children. (BMJ, 26 Sept. 1796)

BRISCOE, Samuel, merchant, and Miss Elizabeth Craig, all of Balto., were married last Thurs. by Rev. Dr. Whitehead.
(BFG, 8 Jan. 1808)

BRISCOE, Samuel H., of St. M. Co., died this morning, about 60
years of age; funeral from the house of Peter Carnes, at
Pratt and Eutaw Sts. (BFG, 21 Nov. 1815)

BRISTOW, Samuel, and Miss Margaret Peters, both of Balto., were
married last Thurs. by Rev. Richards. (BEP, 2 Nov. 1807)

BRITNELL, Theophilus P., died Mon. morning, 21st inst.; a native
of Devonshire, Eng.; interment in the Prot. Ep. graveyard.
(BFG, 23 Nov. 1803)

BRITTON, -(?)-, aged about 13 years, died yesterday from a wound caused by the accidental discharge of a fowling piece. "American." (BFG, 23 Nov. 1802)

BRITTON, John, and Miss Hetty Patterson, all of Balto., were wed last Sun. by Rev. Healey. (BA, 3 April 1816)

BROADFOOT, James, and Miss Cassandra Cole, all of Balto., were married on Sun. by Rev. Glendy. (BT, 4 June 1805)

BROADHURST, Miss Dorothea, of Phila., died 1st inst. at Charleston, aged 25 years; survived by her mother. (BT, 18 Oct. 1802)

BROBSON, Miss Sarah, died at Wilmington, Del., dau. of James Brobson; in her 23rd year. (BEP, 3 July 1806)

BROMWELL, William, Jr., and Miss Eliza Coulson, all of Balto., were married last Mon. by Rev. M'Cain. (BFR, 19 June 1811)

BROOK, William, and Miss Nancy Walker, were married yesterday evening. (BFG, 28 May 1802)

BROOKE, Basil, of Mont. Co., and Miss Maria Patrick, of Balto., were married last Fri. at Joshua Hervey's. (BFG, 27 Nov. 1797)

BROOKE, James, and Miss Esther Boone, both of Mont. Co., were married Wed. at the Friends Meeting House in that county. (BFG, 26 June 1797)

BROOKE, John James, and Miss Juliet Duke, dau. of Capt. James Duke, all of Cal. Co., were married 23 Oct. by Rev. Mr. Eadling. (BFR, 9 Nov. 1810)

BROOKE, Robert, late Governor of Va., died 27th ult. at Petersburg, Va. (BFG, 5 March 1800)

BROOKE, Roger, and Miss Maria Pleasant Younghusband, both of Mont. Co., were married 22nd inst. at the Friends Meeting House in that county. (BFG, 29 Aug. 1804)

BROOKS, Benjamin, major in the U. S. artillery, and veteran of the Rev. War, died at Upper Marlborough, Md. (BA, 21 Jan. 1800)

BROOKS, Charles, aged 68, and Miss Eleanor Thomas, 70, both of Balto. Co., were married last Thurs. by Rev. McCombs. (BFG, 30 June 1804)

BROOKS, Daniel T., and Miss Barbara Limes, all of Balto., were married last eve. by Rev. Pitt. (BFG, 12 May 1806)

BROOKS, John, and Miss Elizabeth Weaver, both of the Northern Liberties, were married in Phila. (BT, 4 Oct. 1800)

BROOKS, Thomas, and Miss Rachel Underwood were married last Friday evening by Rev. Dr. Roberts. (BEP, 23 Oct. 1807)

BROOM, Mrs. Ann, wife of James M. Broom, Esq., of this city, died yesterday. (BFG, 10 Aug. 1808)

BROOM, Daniel, and Miss Mary Deale, were married last Thurs. by Rev. Healey. (BPE, 1 Dec. 1813)

BROOM, John, died recently; funeral discourse will be preached
by Rev. John Healey at Second Baptist Church, Fells Point,
on the first Sabbath in June. (BA, 31 May 1814)

BROOME, Daniel, died this morning; funeral from his late res.
in Argyle Alley near Wilks St. (BFG, 18 July 1816)

BROOME, Lieut. James M., commander of the marines of the frigate
Chesapeake, native of Maryland, died on board ship. (BFG,
7 July 1813)

BROOME, Thomas, and Miss Eliza Todd, were married on Thurs. at
Fells Point by Rev. Rattoone. (BFG, 25 May 1805)

BROUGHTON, Isaac W., and Miss Henrietta Morrison, both of Balto.,
were married last eve. by Rev. Mr. M'Cain. (BW, 31 Jan.
1812)

BROSIUS, Michael, merchant, and Miss Mary Foy, all of Balto.,
were married yesterday eve. by Rev. Moranville. (BFG, 22
June 1807)

BROUGHAN, Aquilla, and Miss Elizabeth Meads, both of Balto.,
were married Sat., 26th inst., by Rev. Parks. (BA, 30
Oct. 1816)

BROUGHTON. See above, following Broome.

BROWN, Amos, Balto. merchant, and Miss Sarah Griffith of Mont.
Co., were married Thurs., 20th, at the res., of Mrs. Griffith near Mont. Court House, by Rev. Linthicum. (BFG,
25 Jan. 1808)

BROWN, Miss Ann Demillon, died last Sat., in her 18th year; dau.
of Dixon Brown of Fells Point; interment in the Episcopal
burying ground. (BFG, 22 Jan. 1798)

BROWN, Charles B., editor of the Semi-annual Register, died 21
Feb. at Phila., in his 40th year, of pulmonary consumption.
(BW, 5 March 1810)

BROWN, David, member of the Society of Friends, died suddenly
last night at his country seat. (BFG, 4 Nov. 1807)

BROWN, David, of Balto., and Ann B. Troth, dau. of William
Troth of Tal. Co., were married at Friends Meeting House
near Easton, 20th inst. (BFG, 26 Sept. 1810)

BROWN, Mr. Elias, died last Sun.; of Balto. Co. (BFG, 24 Sept.
1800)

BROWN, Mrs. Elizabeth, wife of Valentine Brown, died yesterday,
aged about 60 years. (BFG, 25 May 1809)

BROWN, G. R. A., of Prince William, Va., and Miss Caroline Esminard of Balto., were married last eve. by Rev. Roberts.
(BFG, 25 Nov. 1812)

BROWN, George I., and Miss Esther Allison, all of Balto., were
married yesterday eve. by Rev. Inglis. (BFG, 8 March
1810)

BROWN, Dr. Gustavus R., died 27th ult. at his seat near Port
Tobacco; an eminent physician. He was one of three doctors who attended Gen. Washington in his last illness.
(BFG, 11 Oct. 1804)

MARRIAGES AND DEATHS

BROWN, Henry, and Miss Mary Boulogne, both of Balto., were wed last Sat. by Rev. Fenwick. (BW, 10 Sept. 1811)

BROWN, Henry, died 16th Sept. at Lexington, Ky., where he had lately removed from Balto. (BW, 1 Oct. 1811)

BROWN, Henry, and Maria Martin, all of Balto., were married last Thurs. eve. by Rev. Glendy. (BFG, 18 Dec. 1812)

BROWN, Dr. Jacob, died yesterday in his 26th year. (BPE, 23 Sept. 1813)

BROWN, James, died yesterday, a member of the Society of Friends in Old Town. (BFG, 1 Feb. 1811)

BROWN, James, and Miss Ann Tippins, all of Balto., were married last eve. by Rev. Dr. Roberts. (BS, 19 June 1812)

BROWN, Mrs. Jane, consort of John Dixon Brown, died Tues., 26th inst. at her mother's res. in Balto. Co. (BFG, 29 March 1811)

BROWN, Joel, of Washington, and Miss Nancy Hamer of Kent Co., Md. were married Tues., 19th inst. by Rev. Walker. (BFG, 28 Nov. 1799)

BROWN, John, and Miss Mary Rosensteel, both of Balto., were married last eve. by Bishop Carroll. (BFG, 26 Nov. 1798)

BROWN, John, and Miss Mary Read, both of A. A. Co., were wed last Mon. by Rev. Richards. (BT, 2 Aug. 1799)

BROWN, John, a member of the Society of Friends, died Thurs. (BFG, 4 Feb. 1802)

BROWN, John, of Balto., and Miss Ann Smith of the Northern Liberties, were married 18th inst., at Phila., by Rev. Green. (BT, 24 Jan. 1804)

BROWN, Capt. John, formerly master of the ship William Bingham, died 20 Sept. at Port-au-Prince. (BA, 23 Nov. 1810)

BROWN, John, and Miss Ann Wilson, all of Balto. Co., were married last eve. by Rev. Healey. (BA, 12 March 1811)

BROWN, Dr. John, and Frances R. Walter, both of Balto., were wed on Tues. by Rev. Dashiell. (BFG, 9 Dec. 1813)

BROWN, John, and Miss Elizabeth Merriken, both of Balto., were married last Tues. by Rev. Kemp. (BFG, 16 Nov. 1815)

BROWN, John D., and Miss Margaret C. Mitchell, both of Fells Point were married last Thurs. by Rev. Glendy. (BT, 24 Sept. 1804)

BROWN, John Dixon, and Miss Jane Orrick, were married last Thurs. by Rev. Wells, at the seat of John Orrick, of Balto. Co. (BFG, 5 May 1804)

BROWN, John Dixon, died Sun., 28 July, in the prime of life; interment at Beach Hill Burying Ground. (BFG, 31 July 1811)

BROWN, Joseph, and Miss Fanny Davis, both of Balto., were wed on Thurs. by Rev. Richards. (BFG, 23 April 1802)

BROWN, Joseph, of N. H., and Miss Mary Shilling of Balto., were married Sun. by Rev. Rattoone. (BEP, 27 Jan. 1808)

BROWN, Joseph, merchant tailor, and Miss Ellen Lenaghan, all of Balto., were married last Wed. by Rev. Kurtz. (BA, 15 Dec. 1809)

BROWN, Justus, printer of Balto., died yesterday at a very advanced age; funeral from the house of Mr. Hugh Stewart, Duke St., Old Town. (BFG, 26 Sept. 1809)

BROWN, Lewis Randolph, and Miss Susan Bickham, 3rd dau. of Geo. Bickham, were married last Wed. at St. James Church, Phila., by Rev. Bishop White. (BEP, 9 May 1810)

BROWN, Mrs. Mary, consort of Henry Brown, died last Sun. in her 18th year, leaving a husband and child. (BFG, 9 June 1812)

BROWN, Mrs. Mary Ann, died 7th inst., at her mother's res. in Harf. Co.; in her 30th year, leaving a husband and two small children. (BFG, 11 Sept. 1812)

BROWN, Moses, late a captain in the American navy, died at sea, aged 62 years. (BFG, 26 Jan. 1804)

BROWN, Robert, and Miss Sarah Elder, all of Balto. Co., were married last Sun. by Rev. Mr. Sinclair. (BT, 16 Aug. 1803)

BROWN, Miss Sally, died last Tues., 8th inst., Elk Ridge, aged 74, a member of the Society of Friends. (BFG, 14 Sept. 1802)

BROWN, Samuel, and Miss Polly Whealer of Harf. Co., were married last Tues. by Rev. Pasket. (BFG, 13 Nov. 1800)

BROWN, Samuel, and Miss Mary Sugars, were married by Rev. Glendy 14th ult. (BA, 4 Dec. 1809)

BROWN, Capt. Samuel Montgomery, formerly of Alexandria, died at Ky. (BA, 21 Jan. 1800)

BROWN, Mrs. Sarah, consort of Dixon Brown, died 7th inst., in her 63rd year, leaving a husband and son. (BFG, 9 Nov. 1809)

BROWN, Mrs. Sarah, consort of Fulford Brown of Balto., died on Wed., leaving her husband and children. (BFG, 2 March 1811)

BROWN, Mrs. Sarah, wife of Stewart Brown, died last Fri., 23 Aug., aged 34; interment in the West Burying Ground of the First Presbyterian Church. (BFG, 26 Aug. 1811)

BROWN, Solomon, died 17th inst., in his 42nd year. (BA, 19 April 1813)

BROWN, Stewart, Balto. merchant, and Miss Harman of Twit'nam, were married Tues., 18th inst., at Phila. by the Rev. Mr. Abercrombie. (BFG, 22 April 1797)

BROWN, Sylvester, and Miss Sarah Sparks, all of Balto., were married on Tues. by Rev. Glendy. (BFG, 6 Oct. 1814)

BROWN, Thomas, a native of Ireland, died yesterday in Balto., in his 43rd year. (BW, 17 March 1810)

BROWN, Thomas Cockey, and Miss Susannah Snowden, dau. of Col. Francis Snowden, all of Balto. Co., were married at Branton Hall on Tues., 23 April by Rev. Ralph. (BFG, 27 April 1811)

BROWN, Valentine, died yesterday in his 78th year. (BFG, 4 Oct. 1810)

BROWN, William, currier of Balto., and Miss Ann Loughbridge, dau. of Abraham Loughbridge, merchant of Carlisle, were married 12th inst. (BFG, 23 Jan. 1797)

BROWN, William, Jr., merchant, and Miss Susanna Biays, dau. of Col. Joseph Biays, all of Balto., were married last eve. by Rev. Glendy. (BFG, 22 June 1810)

BROWNE, John, clerk of Q. A. Co., died Wed., 13th inst., at Centreville; formerly a member of Congress. (BPEA, 28 Dec. 1815)

BROWNE, Mrs. Margaret, wife of Dr. M. Browne, died 6th inst. at Chester Town (long obit). (BFR, 13 Nov. 1810)

BROWNE, Thomas, and Mrs. Frances Lewis, both of Balto., were wed last Tues. by Rev. Toy. (BEP, 27 Oct. 1808)

BROWNING, Mr. P. G., died Sat., 20th inst., at his late res. in Sharp St.; long an inhab. of Balto., leaving a wife and seven children. (BA, 23 April 1816)

BROWNING, Mrs. Rebecca, wife of Jeremiah Browning, and dau. of Mrs. Providence Lane, died last Fri. week near Chestertown. (BA, 17 Aug. 1808)

BROWNING, Ritson, and Miss Mary Ann Lee, both of Balto., were married last Thurs. by Rev. George Roberts. (BW, 12 June 1813)

BROWNLEY, James S., and Miss Martha Snowden of Balto., were wed Thurs. by Rev. Glendy. (BA, 9 Dec. 1815)

BRUCE, Richard Barrow, a native of Eng., died last Sun., after a short illness. (BFG, 1 Oct. 1800)

BRUCKMAN, Mr. Gerret, and Miss Christina Myer, both of Balto. City, were married Thurs. eve. by Rev. Mr. Kurtz. (BFG, 3 March 1804)

BRUFF, Joseph, merchant, and Mrs. Mary Rice, all of Balto., were married last eve. by Rev. Wells. (BFG, 15 July 1813)

BRUFF, Richard, eldest son of William Bruff, Balto. merchant, died at Point Petre, Guadaloupe, on 18 Jan.; of yellow fever. (BFG, 16 Feb. 1802)

BRUFF, William, and Miss Sarah Norris, all of Balto., were wed last Sat. by Rev. Richards. (BFG, 21 Nov. 1804)

BRUNE, Frederick William, and Anne, dau. of Ambrose Clarke, all of Balto., were married Sat. by Rev. Bend. (BFG, 1 Oct. 1805)

BRUNTON, Mrs., died in Eng.; mother of Mrs. Wignell of the Balto. and Phila. Theatres. (BA, 9 Aug. 1804)

BRYAN, John, and Miss Isabella Montgomery, both of Balto., were married 13th inst. by Rev. Rattoone. (BFG, 26 Dec. 1806)

BRYAN, Mrs. Mary, wife of James Bryan, died last Wed. at her res. in Balto. Co., aged 74. (BFG, 31 March 1806)

BRYAN, Nathan, Esq., member of Congress from N. C., died 4th inst., at his lodgings in Phila. (BT, 7 June 1798)

BRYCE, John R., died Sat., 4th inst., at Annapolis in his 34th year. (BFG, 13 May 1805)

BRYDENODER, Martin, and Miss Susan Myers, both of Balto., were married Fri. eve. by Rev. Dr. Rattoone. (BFG, 6 March 1806)

BRYSON, John, and Miss Peggy Bond, both of Balto., were married Sun. by Rev. Inglis. (BT, 17 Aug. 1802)

BRYSON, Nathan G., merchant, and Mrs. Susanna Perkins, both of Balto., were married 20th inst., by Rev. Dr. Allison. (BA, 25 Oct. 1799)

BUCHANAN, Andrew, Balto. merchant, and Miss Ann M'Kean, dau. of Thomas M'Kean, Chief Justice of the state of Penna., were married last Thurs. in Phila. (BFG, 10 April 1797)

BUCHANAN, Andrew, Balto. merchant, and Miss Carolina Virginia Maryland Johnson, of Boston were married in Boston 23 July. (BFG, 29 July 1807)

BUCHANAN, Andrew, died yesterday, formerly a merchant of Balto.; leaving a widow and five children. (BFG, 4 Oct. 1811)

BUCHANAN, Ann, wife of Andrew Buchanan, and dau. of Thomas Mc-Kean, Gov. of Penna., died last Sun., leaving her husband "four pledges of domestic happiness." (BFG, 31 May 1804)

BUCHANAN, Archibald, died last Thurs. (BFG, 29 Sept. 1800)

BUCHANAN, Mrs. Elizabeth, wife of James A. Buchanan, died yesterday. (BFG, 22 Aug. 1815)

BUCHANAN, Dr. George, Lazaretto physician for the port of Phila., died 9th inst. For many years he was a magistrate in Balto., and moved to Phila. in 1806. (Long obit gives additional biog. data) (BFG, 30 July 1808)

BUCHANAN, Capt. George, died last Mon., at his seat in Balto. Co., aged 70 years. (BFG, 17 Nov. 1810)

BUCHANAN, George A., and Miss Sarah P. Nesbitt, were married last Thurs. by Rev. Kurtz. (BA, 8 Dec. 1815)

BUCHANAN, Lloyd, and Catherine Isabella Stewart, second dau. of Mr. D. Stewart, all of Balto., were married last Thurs. by Rev. Bend. (BFG, 26 Jan. 1802)

BUCHANAN, Mrs. Susan, died last Fri., in her 38th year, leaving a husband and seven children; interment in St. Pauls burying ground. (BFG, 15 July 1805) (BEP, 15 July 1805 states she was the wife of James Buchanan.)

BUCHANAN, William, Esq., of Balto. Co., and Mrs. H. Prian of
    Balto., were married last eve. (BFG, 11 Nov. 1799)

BUCHANAN, William, Sr., died this morning in his 78th year.
    (BFG, 19 Sept. 1804)

BUCHANAN, William, late Consul of the U. S., and formerly of Balto., died last 27 June at Isle of France. (BFG, 3 Nov. 1815)

BUCK, John, Jr., of Fells Point, and Sophia Winks of Balto. Co.,
    were married 29 Aug. (BA, 30 Aug. 1799)

BUCK, John, and Mrs. Catherine Green, both of Balto. Co., were
    married 12 March. (BA, 13 March 1801)

BUCK, John, Jr., and Miss Ann Foster, both of Balto. Co., were
    married last Thurs. by Rev. Andrew Hoffman. (BPE, 21
    Dec. 1814)

BUCK, John, Jr., and Mary Weeks of Fells Point, were married 24
    Jan. by Rev. Wells. (BA, 27 Jan. 1816)

BUCK, or BURK, Nathan, and Mrs. Elizabeth Johnson, both of Balto., were married last Sun. by Rev. Dashiell. (BFG, 29
    Oct. 1804)

BUCK, Samuel, and Sarah Curran, both of Fells Point, were married
    last Sun., by Rev. Mr. Otterbein. (BEP, 26 Oct. 1808)

BUCKLER, John, late of London, merchant, died last Tues., from
    severe bruises he received as a result from a fall at the
    race ground. (BFG, 6 June 1799)

BUCKLEY, Lieut. Joseph, and Miss Eliza Sumwalt, both of Balto.,
    were married last eve. by Rev. Hargrove. (BFG, 7 July
    1815)

BUCKLEY, Robert, and Miss Julia Carter, second dau. of late Col.
    Carter of Balto., were married last Thurs. by Rev. Rattoone. (BFG, 8 June 1804)

BUDD, Miss Mary Araminta, died 8th inst., in her 24th year in
    Harford Co. (BFG, 21 Sept. 1816)

BUEL, Albert D., and Miss Catherine Maria Hall, all of Balto.,
    were married last eve. by Rev. Dr. Roberts. (BPE, 12
    March 1813)

BUELL, Mrs. Maria, died last Thurs. morning. (BW, 31 Jan. 1814)

BUFFUM, John, merchant, and Jane Keys, dau. of Richard Keys, merchant, all of Balto., were married last eve. by Rev. Dr.
    Inglis. (BFG, 24 June 1807) (BA, 25 June 1807 gives his
    name as Bossom.)

BULFINCH, Samuel, died in Phila., aged 76, a patriot of the Rev.
    (BEP, 4 March 1813)

BULL, Albert D., and Miss Catherine Maria Hall, of Balto., were
    married Thurs. by Rev. Roberts. (BFG, 13 March 1813)

BULL, Rev. George S., of Balto., and Miss Rebecca A. Jordan of
    St. M. Co., were married 25 May in Alexandria, by Rev.
    Waugh. (BA, 1 June 1815)

BULL, John, and Miss Eliza Wisotzky, all of Balto., were married last eve. by Rev. Glendy. (BA, 17 Aug. 1816)

BULLOUGH, Richard, and Miss Ruth Ridgely, were married 1st inst. by Rev. Glendy. (BA, 10 Nov. 1814)

BUNKER, Capt. Moses, and Miss Margaret Franciscus, were married last Tues. by Rev. Dr. Allison; both parties were of Balto. (BFG, 10 May 1798)

BURCH, William, and Miss Rachel Hanes, both of Balto., were married Thurs. eve. by Rev. Kurtz. (BA, 20 July 1816)

BURCHINELL, William, and Miss Martha Kendall, dau. of the late William Kendall, all of Kent Co., were married at Langford's Neck, on Wed., 28th ult. by Rev. Wilmer. (BFG, 5 March 1810)

BURGESS, Barnabas, and Mrs. Lydia Launders, both of Balto., were married by Glendy last Sun. (BW, 7 Aug. 1811)

BURGESS, John B., of Fred. Co., and Miss Margaret Morrison of Balto., were married last eve. by Rev. Roberts. (BFG, 19 Oct. 1812)

BURGESS, William P., of Balto., and Miss Lydia Plummmer, of Fred. Co., were married Thurs., 30th ult., by Rev. Mr. Higgens. (BFG, 3 June 1816)

BURK, Alexis, and Miss Eliza Langenfelter, both of Balto., were married last Thurs. by Rev. Richards. (BT, 12 Oct. 1803)

BURK, Greenbury, and Miss Rhoda Davis, both of Fells Point, were married last eve. by Rev. Bend. (BMJ, 18 Aug. 1796)

BURK, Nathan, and Mrs. Elizabeth Johnson, both of Balto., were married last Sun. eve. by Rev. Mr. Dashiell. (BT, 30 Oct. 1804)

BURKE, Elizabeth, died Tues. eve. in her 15th year. (BA, 2 Nov. 1805)

BURKE, Francis, printer, and Miss Sarah Hands, both of Balto., were married last eve. by Rev. Fry. (BFR, 16 Aug. 1817)

BURKE, Rev. Dr. John, pastor of St. Marys Church, Phila., died in that city. (BT, 24 Sept. 1799)

BURKE, John, of Balto., and Miss Mary P. Wheaton, of Washington were married last Sat. by Rev. Mr. Breckenridge. (BW, 14 Jan. 1812)

BURKE, Nicholas, and Miss Sarah Wright, both of Balto., were married last Thurs. by Rev. Carroll. (BEP, 26 April 1805)

BURKE, Patrick, died 20th ult., aged 104 years, at Norfolk, a native of Ireland, and a res. of that borough for 16 years. (BEP, 4 April 1807)

BURKE, William, lately from Dublin, died 5th ult., at the Havana. He sailed from this port in the sloop Delight belonging to Burke and Mitchell. (BFG, 7 Sept. 1799)

BURNET, Richard and Miss Ann McCullough, were married last Thurs. eve. by Rev. Glendy. (BA, 19 May 1808)

BURNET, Thomas, and Ann Roe, were married last Tues. eve. by Rev. Glendy. (BA, 4 Sept. 1806)

BURNETT, Charles, of Fells Point, died Sun. eve. last in his 46th year, leaving a wife and eight children. (BFG, 25 May 1812)

BURNETT, Garland, of Hanover Co., Va., and Miss Susan McComas of Harf. Co., were married last Sun. by Rev. Mr. Healy. (BA, 8 Aug. 1815)

BURNETT, Mary, widow, died in Balto., yesterday, aged 52 years a native of New Town, L. I. (BA, 26 Oct. 1816)

BURNETT, Richard, and Miss Mary Riley, were married 1 June by Rev. Glendy. (BA, 19 Aug. 1814)

BURNS, Kennedy, N. Y. merchant, and Miss Charlotte Crensa Rowe, were married in Washington, at the house of John B. Colvin. (BPE, 27 March 1813)

BURNS, William, and Miss Sarah Rediar, both of Harf. Co., were married last Thurs. by Rev. Reese. (BA, 6 July 1816)

BURNSIDES, Mr., clerk in the auditor's office, died at Washington, on 26th ult. (BT, 4 Oct. 1800)

BURRIER, John, and Miss Temperance Winks, all of Balto., were married last Sun. by Rev. M'Cain. (BA, 25 Sept. 1810)

BURROUGHS, Thomas, died yesterday at Fells Point, and was buried with Masonic honors. (BA, 24 March 1801)

BURROWS, Edward, and Miss Mary Zane, were married on Sun. eve. vy Rev. Rattoone. (BFG, 21 April 1808)

BURROWS, Hugh, and Miss Maria Ross, both of Balto., were wed last eve. by Rev. Glendy. (BT, 22 March 1804)

BURROWS, Col. William W., died 6th inst., in Washington, late Col. Commandant of the Marine Corps. (BA, 11 March 1805)

BURTON, Charles A., merchant, and Miss Ann Stockett, both of Williamson Co., Tenn., were married Tues., 30 Oct. 1804 by Rev. Daniel Perkins. (BT, 2 Feb. 1805)

BURTON, Myers, of Del., and Miss Esther Button, of Balto. Co., were married Thurs. eve. by Rev. Richards. (BFG, 10 April 1805)

BURWELL, Hon. John, of Va., and Miss Letitia McCreary, were wed yesterday at Clover Hill, the seat of William McCreery. (BFG, 4 Jan. 1809)

BUSH, James, Lieut. in the U. S. Navy, died Wed. "Norfolk, 21 June." (BA, 28 June 1800)

BUSH, William, and Miss Sarah Bartley, all of Balto., were married by Rev. Glendy last Thurs. (BPEA, 17 Jan. 1815)

BUSK, Mrs. Barbara, died last eve.; funeral from the house of Nicholas Leake, Ann St., Fells Point. (BA, 28 July 1813)

BUSSEY, Bennett, of Harf. Co., and Mrs. Elizabeth Slade, of Balto., were married last Mon. by Bishop Carroll. (BFG, 10 July 1806)

BUSSY, Thomas D., of Balto., and Mrs. Peggy Bennett of A. A. Co., were married last eve. (BFG, 5 Feb. 1796)

BUTLER, Capt., of Phila., died at Norfolk from lockjaw caused by a ball lodged in the back of his hand in a duel, which was the result of a political dispute. (BI, 18 May 1798)

BUTLER, Dr., of Shepherdstown, and Miss Priscilla Robinson of Balto. were married 21st inst. by Rev. Inglis. (BFG, 23 April 1814)

BUTLER, Amon, Jr., died 4th inst., in his 60th year, a res. of Balto. Co., leaving a wife, nine children, and an aged mother and father. (BFG, 11 Aug. 1804)

BUTLER, Clement, and Miss Harriot Wells, were married last Thurs. by Rev. Coco. (BFR, 4 March 1811)

BUTLER, James, and Mrs. Ann Green, both of Balto., were married last Sun. eve. by Rev. Wells. (BT, 30 Nov. 1802)

BUTLER, John, and Miss Sally McAtee, both of Harf. Co., were wed last eve. by Rev. Mr. Beaston. (BT, 11 Jan. 1804)

BUTLER, John, and Miss Sarah Mason, all of Balto. Co., were wed last Thurs. by Rev. Armstrong. (BFG, 6 Jan. 1808)

BUTLER, John West, Balto. printer, and Miss Margaretta Elliot, dau. of Samuel Elliot of Phila., were married at that place last Wed. eve. by Rev. Jacob Janeway. (BFG, 25 May 1807)

BUTLER, Major Lawrence, a veteran of the Rev. War, died at Soldier's Retreat, Frederick Co., Va., aged 58 years. (BA, 8 May 1811)

BUTLER, Mrs. Mary, Sr., died Sun., 21st inst., aged 71 years and 1 month. (BFG, 22 March 1802)

BUTLER, Mrs. Susan Maria, died last Sun., in her 45th year, wife of Capt. David West Butler of Fells Point; leaving a husband, dau. and aged parents. (BFG, 22 July 1812)

BUTLER, William, tailor, died Fri., 11th inst., at Mr. James M'Kean's, Westmoreland Co., Penna. Prior to his death he and his father, Elijah Butler, lived in Balto. (BFG, 28 March 1808)

BUTTON, Robert, and Miss Susanna Sapp were married last Sat. by Rev. Bloodgood. (BEP, 28 June 1810)

BYERLY, Christopher, a young man, died last Sat. (BFG, 4 Nov. 1800)

BYRNE, Mr. B. C., of the Federal Circus, and Mrs. Hamilton of Balto., were married Sat. by Rev. Richards. (BI, 9 April 1798)

BYRNE, Columbus J., long an inhab. of Balto., died last Sat. (BPE, 15 June 1814)

BYRNE, Columbus John, and Margaret Hankey, both of Balto., were married last eve. by Rev. Mr. Beeston. (BA, 18 Jan. 1800)

BYRNE, Mrs. Eleanor, wife of C. I. Byrne of Balto., and late of Dublin, died last night. (BFG, 13 Oct. 1798)

MARRIAGES AND DEATHS

BYRNE, Patrick, native of Ireland, and 40 years a res. of Balto., died Fri., 1 July, aged 74, of apoplexy. (BEP, 9 July 1808)

BYRNE, Patrick, eminent bookseller of Phila., and formerly of Dublin, died 20th inst. in his 73rd year. (BW, 24 Feb. 1814)

BYRNE, Patrick, of Phila., and Miss Isabella Stewart, dau. of Dr. William Stewart of Balto., were married last eve. by Rev. Glendy. (BA, 12 Sept. 1815)

BYRNE, William, Balto. bookseller, and son of Patrick Byrne, a bookseller of Phila., and late of Dublin, Ire., died yesterday. (BFG, 21 Dec. 1805)

BYRNES, Daniel, and Rachel Bull, both of Balto., were married last eve. by Rev. Richards. (BFG, 13 April 1804)

BYRNES, Mrs. Rachel, wife of Daniel Byrnes, cashier of the Wilmington and Brandywine Bank, died at Wilmington last Thurs. (BEP, 31 Dec. 1810)

BYUS, Mrs. Ellen, died last Tues. in her 25th year, dau. of the late Gilbert Hamilton Smith, and niece of John Kilty of this place. (BFG, 20 Jan. 1800)

CABLE, Jacob, and Miss Mary Ann Tinges, both of Balto., were married last eve. by Rev. Kurtz. (BFG, 8 June 1812)

CADUC, John, and Miss Mary Ann Maillet Lacoste, all of Balto., were married Mon., 27th inst., by Rev. Enoch Fenwick. (BFG, 28 April 1812)

CAHILL, Hugh, died yesterday of a liver complaint, aged 25 years; a native of Co. Wexford, Ire., which he left almost 5 years ago; for a while he lived in New York. (BAP, 30 June 1803)

CAIN, Alexander, of the New Theatre, died last Sun. at Bristol, Penna., in his 28th year, leaving a wife and two children. (BFG, 15 June 1808)

CAIN, John, of Harf. Co., and Jane Holmes of Balto., were wed at My Lady's Manor on 28 May by Rev. Smith. (BA, 6 June 1816)

CALDCLEUGH, Robert, late of Balto., and Miss Poyntell, dau. of Mr. Poyntell of Phila., were married last Thurs. by Right Rev. Bishop White. (BFG, 11 June 1805)

CALDER, George, died Sun. morning, aged 32, son of the late Capt. Calder of Balto. Co. (BFG, 13 April 1809)

CALDER, James, a native of Scotland, died 11th inst. at his seat in Balto. Co., in his 79th year, leaving a wife and children. (BFG, 26 Aug. 1808)

CALDWELL, John, cabinet-maker, and Mary Puel, both of Balto., were married last eve. by Dr. Allison. (BT, 12 Feb. 1796)

CALDWELL, John, N. Y. merchant, and Miss Higginbothom of Annapolis, Md., were married last Tues. at N. Y. by Right Rev. Bishop Provost. (BFG, 23 April 1803)

CALDWELL, Joseph, and Mrs. Mary King, all of Balto., were wed last eve. by Rev. Inglis. (BA, 18 May 1816)

CALHOUN, Mrs. Ann, wife of James Calhoun, Mayor of Balto., died last eve. in her 53rd year. (BFG, 5 March 1799)

CALHOUN, James, (first mayor of Baltimore), died this morning, aged 73; funeral tomorrow from his late res. in Baltimore St. (BFG, 14 Aug. 1816)

CALHOUN, William, eldest son of James Calhoun of Balto., died last Sun. eve. at Summer Hill, the seat of James Buchanan. The dec. was aged 40 and leaves a widow and four children. For many years he lived in S. C., but returned to his native state in 1803. (BFG, 29 June 1808)

CALLAHAN, John, Register of the Land Office for the Western Shore, died last Sat. in his 50th year. (BFG, 31 Oct. 1803)

CALLENDER, James, and Miss Rebecca Parks, both of Balto., were married Thurs. eve. by Rev. Glendy. (BA, 11 Aug. 1807)

CALLENDER, Major John, died last Mon. in Alexandria, an old and respectable officer in the American War; interment on Tues. morning at the Episcopal Church. (BFG, 9 Oct. 1797)

CALLENDER, John A., and Sarah Evans, both of Balto., were married 21 Dec. by Rev. Glendy. (BA, 23 Dec. 1815)

CALLOPY, Timothy, and Mrs. Sarah Adreon were married last eve. by Rev. Hargrove. (BFG, 18 Nov. 1803)

CALWELL, Thomas, and Miss Ann Kelso, all of Balto., were married last Thurs. by Rev. Glendy. (BFG, 19 March 1813)

CAMBY, Benjamin, and Miss Mary Lord, both of Balto., were wed last eve. by Rev. Linthicum. (BEP, 29 Oct. 1810)

CAMP, Mrs. Sarah, wife of William Camp, of 26 Water St., died yesterday eve. (BFG, 10 Dec. 1814)

CAMPBELL, Mrs. Ann, wife of William Campbell of Balto., died Sat. morning. (BW, 30 Jan. 1809)

CAMPBELL, Archibald, died Sat. in his 58th year. (BFG, 22 April 1805)

CAMPBELL, Archibald, and Mrs. Ann Crozier, all of Balto., were married last Thurs. by Rev. Glendy. (BW, 6 April 1811)

CAMPBELL, Gen. Donald, died at Washington; he resigned his commission in the British army to fight for our freedom in the Rev. War. (BAP, 5 April 1803)

CAMPBELL, Mrs. Eleanor, widow of John Campbell of Mine Bank, died 15th inst. (BW, 24 Oct. 1810)

CAMPBELL, Mrs. Elizabeth, died this morning. (BFG, 10 Sept. 1805)

CAMPBELL, G. W., Senator from Tenn., and Miss Hannah Stoddert, dau. of Benjamin Stoddert of Bladensbergh, were married a few days ago in this vicinity. (BA, 3 Aug. 1812)

CAMPBELL, Dr. Gustavus Brown, formerly of Alexandria, died in Va. (BA, 12 Dec. 1799)

CAMPBELL, Hugh, and Miss Maria Death, both of Balto., were wed on Thurs. eve. (BPEA, 4 April 1815) (BPEA, 26 May 1815 gives the bride's name as Mariah T. Death, and states the marr. was perf. by Rev. Inglis.)

CAMPBELL, James, negro, was killed by Samuel Cromwell, negro, last Mon. night near the ropewalk of John Chalmers. (BT, 28 Sept. 1804)

CAMPBELL, James, merchant, and Miss Rebecca Winchester, dau. of W. Winchester of Balto., were married last Tues. by Rev. Bend. (BFG, 17 Nov. 1808)

CAMPBELL, John, manager of the works, died at the Mine Bank on Sat., 29th ult. (BW, 3 Oct. 1810)

CAMPBELL, John C., died Sat., 21st inst., at Cedar Point, near Elkton. (BA, 26 Feb. 1801)

CAMPBELL, Miss Mary Ann, dau. of William Campbell of Balto., died last Sun. at New York in her 17th year. (BA, 14 June 1816)

CAMPBELL, Rebecca, wife of James Campbell, Balto. merchant, died Sun. (19 July). (BFG, 22 July 1812)

CAMPBELL, Samuel, of Balto., and Miss Ann Buford of Charleston were married lately in the latter place by Rev. Mr. Frazer. (BFG, 19 March 1804)

CAMPBELL, Capt. Samuel, merchant of Balto., died last night, aged about 35 years. (BFG, 31 Jan. 1807)

CAMPBELL, Thomas, and Miss Ellen Peregoy, both of Balto. Co., were married last Sat., 4 Dec., by Rev. Glendy. (BFG, 8 Dec. 1813)

CAMPBELL, William, died. (BFG, 10 Aug. 1802)

CANNADY, Hugh, and Miss Elizabeth Coke, all of Balto., were married. (BFG, 21 Oct. 1805)

CANNON, William, and Miss Mary M. Smith, both of Balto., were married last Tues. by Rev. Dashiell. (BFG, 10 April 1807)

CANOT, Mrs. Mary, died last Fri., in her 46th year. (BFG, 1 June 1813)

CANTWELL, Joseph, and Miss Mary Dudley, all of Balto., were wed Sun. eve. by Rev. Bartow. (BA, 19 March 1816)

CAPPEAU, Joseph, and Miss Sarah Galloway, both of Balto., were wed on Thurs. by Rev. Pitts. (BA, 29 June 1811)

CARD, Capt. John R., native of New Jersey, died 1st inst. (BT, 3 April 1805)

CAREY, Capt. Edward, and Miss Mary Basse, all of Balto., were married Tues. eve., 22 Sept., by Rev. Glendy. (BFG, 25 Sept. 1812)

CAREY, Eleanor, dau. of Matthew Carey, died in Phila., aged 15. (BPE, 20 Feb. 1813)

CAREY, James, printer, died last Mon. (BT, 9 Feb. 1801)

CAREY, James, Jr., son of James Carey, of Balto. Co., died at
    Ballstown Springs, N. Y., 8th inst. (BFG, 18 Aug. 1813)

CARLISLE, Mrs. Mary, died, aged 68. (BA, 20 Jan. 1800)

CARMAN, Henry, and Mrs. Maria Banker, all of Balto., were wed
    last eve. by Rev. Dr. Rattoone. (BEP, 24 June 1808)

CARNADY, Hugh, and Miss Eliza Cole, were married Wed. eve. by
    Rev. Rattoone. (BA, 22 Oct. 1805)

CARNAL, Mr. Joseph, died Mon., 29th ult., aged 29; native of Eng.
    (BFG, 1 Oct. 1800)

CARNAN, Charles, died yesterday morning at his res. in Garrison
    Forest, an old inhab. of Balto. Co. (BFG, 20 Jan. 1809)

CARNAN, Mr. Christopher, and Miss Christiana Sim Holliday, both
    of Balto. Co., were married last Tues. by Rev. Pitts.
    (BFG, 12 March 1802) (BT, 13 March 1802 gives the minister's
    name as Potts.)

CARNIGHAN, James, and Miss Kitty Miller, both of Balto., were
    married Thurs. eve. by Rev. Richards. (BFG, 28 Oct. 1797)

CARPENTER, Dr. John, died 19th ult., in his 61st year, of Lan-
    caster Co.; a husband and parent. (Long obit follows.)
    (BFG, 7 April 1798)

CARPENTER, Lewis, late mariner in the private armed schooner
    Chasseur, and Miss Rachel Leydingham, both of Fells Point
    Balto., were married on Tues. eve. by Rev. Guest. (BT,
    30 March 1815). (BPEA, 29 March 1815 gives the bride's
    name as Lowderman.)

CARPENTER, Nathaniel, and Miss Margaret Barnes, all of Balto.,
    were married. (BFG, 31 July 1807)

CARR, Mrs. Elizabeth, of Fells Point, died yesterday from her
    68th year; funeral from the house of Mrs. B. Stockett, No.
    47 Bond St. (BFG, 1 Feb. 1812)

CARR, Emanuel, and Miss Mary Ann Read, all of Balto., were wed
    last eve. by Rev. Dr. Burch. (BA, 26 Jan. 1816)

CARR, Mrs. Martha, widow of Dabney Carr, and sister of former
    Pres. Thomas Jefferson, died Tues., 3rd inst., at Dunlora,
    the seat of Samuel Carr of Albemarle, in her 64th year.
    (BW, 18 Sept. 1811)

CARR, Mrs. Mary, died this morning at Bolton, the seat of George
    Grundy, in her 79th year. (BFG, 14 March 1803)

CARR, Mrs. Mary, wife of Joseph Carr, died Wed., 8th inst., aged
    about 76 years; a wife and mother. (BPEA, 14 Nov. 1815)

CARR, Major Robert, of Phila., and Miss Ann M. Bartram, dau. of
    John Bartram, botanist, of Kingsetting, Phila. Co., were
    married 4 March by Rev. Nathan Jones. (BEP, 9 March 1809)

CARR, Thomas, of Balto., and Miss Milcah Merryman of Balto. Co.,
    were married last Thurs. by Rev. Coleman. (BFG, 5 March
    1806)

CARR, William, and Miss Catherine Ostend, both of Balto., were
    married last eve. by Rev. Fenwick. (BA, 15 April 1814)

CARROLL, Aquila, of Balto., and Miss Ruth Bowen, of Balto. Co., were married last eve. by Rev. Hemphill. (BFG, 5 April 1816)

CARROLL, Charles, Jr., and Harriet, dau. of Benjamin Chew of Phila., were married Thurs. eve. The groom is a son of the Hon. Charles Carroll of Carrollton. (BFG, 21 July 1800)

CARROLL, Charles, Esq., of Washington, and Miss Mary Ann Carroll, dau. of Henry H. Carroll of Balto. Co., were married at Sweet Air, 4th inst., by Rev. Edene. (BFG, 5 Feb. 1812)

CARROLL, Daniel, died last Sat. at Rock Creek. (BFG, 14 May 1796)

CARROLL, Col. Daniel, of Mount Dillon, and Miss Nancy Maccubbin dau. of the late Zachariah Maccubbin of Balto. Co., were married a few days ago. (BFG, 28 Jan. 1799)

CARROLL, Harry D. G., and Miss Eliza Ridgely, dau. of Gen. Chas. Ridgely of Hampton, were married Thurs., 19th inst., by Rev. Dashiell. (BFG, 23 Jan. 1815)

CARROLL, Henry Hill, died at his res., Sweet Air, Balto. Co., on 26th Oct., after a tedious indisposition; a husband and a father. (BFG, 1 Nov. 1804)

CARROLL, James, Jr., and Miss Achsah Ridgely, dau. of Gen. Chas. Ridgely of Hampton, were married. (BFG, 8 Nov. 1811)

CARROLL, John, Archbishop of Baltimore, of the R. C. Church, died 2 Dec., aged 80. (Long obit.) (BFG, 4 Dec. 1815)

CARROLL, Mr. Matthew, and Miss Mary Ann Burnett, of Balto., were married Thurs. eve. by Rev. Wells. (BA, 20 July 1816)

CARROLL, Nicholas, an old inhab. of Annapolis, died last Fri. "Annap. - May 26." (BFG, 27 May 1812)

CARROLL, Richard, and Mrs. Judith C. Riddell, all of Balto., were married 21st inst., by Rev. Kemp. (BFG, 27 Aug. 1813)

CARROLL, Mrs. Sarah, died last Sat. eve., in her 33rd year, leaving a husband and 5 small children. (BFG, 8 Oct. 1804)

CARROLL, Thomas King, of Somerset, and Miss Julianna Stevenson, of Balto., were married last Thurs. by Rev. Dr. Kemp. (BA, 27 June 1814)

CARROLL, William, and Mrs. Rose McCormick, were married 20th inst., by Rev. Hargrove. (BA, 22 Dec. 1815)

CARSON, Mrs., consort of Nathan Carson of Fells Point, died on Sun. (BFG, 27 May 1800)

CARSON, David, and Miss Sarah T. Hynson, all of Balto., were married last Thurs. eve. by Rev. Mr. Hunt. (BA, 9 Nov. 1816)

CARSON, John, and Miss Elizabeth Bryan, both of Balto., were wed last Fri. by Rev. Coats. (BEP, 28 Aug. 1807)

CARSON, Capt. John, was shot 20 Jan. in Phila., by Lieut. Smith, and died last Mon. (BWA, 10 Feb. 1816)

CARSON, Nathaniel, for a long time an inhab. of Fells Point, died at Lower Marlborough, Md., in his 47th year. (BFG, 19 Oct. 1811)

CARSON, Nehemiah, merchant of Alexandria, and Rachel Bull, of Balto., were married Thurs. by Rev. Richards. (BA, 25 Sept. 1806)

CARTEE, Benjamin, a native of New Eng., died last Sun. at his res. in Market St. (BFG, 28 April 1812)

CARTEE, Robert E., and Miss Eliza C. Mitchell, both of Balto., were married at Phila. last Tues. by Rev. Abercrombie. (BA, 2 Nov. 1812)

CARTER, Clement, and Miss Eliza Tittle both of this city, were married Thurs. by Rev. Roberts. (BFG, 7 May 1810)

CARTER, George, auctioneer, died last eve. (BFG, 22 Oct. 1811)

CARTER, Henry, drowned Wed., 1st inst., when a squall of wind overturned the schooner of Capt. John Morling from Wye River. (BFG, 3 May 1799)

CARTER, John, died 5th inst., at his late dwelling in Rock Run, Harford Co., leaving a widow and children. (BFG, 11 Sept. 1805)

CARTER, John S., and Miss Elizabeth Ensor, both of Balto., were married last Sun. by Rev. Mr. Shote. (BA, 21 June 1814)

CARTER, Josias, and Miss Elizabeth Miles, dau. of Thomas Miles, all of Harf. Co., were married last Tues. by Rev. Lucky. (BEP, 17 Oct. 1808)

CARTER, Robert, died yesterday morning, an old inhab. of Balto. During the Rev. War he was a member of the executive council of Va. (BFG, 12 March 1804)

CARTER, Miss Sally, died at The Park, Stafford Co., Va., in her 23rd year, eld. dau. of George Carter of Williamsburg. (BEP, 3 March 1809)

CARTER, Capt. William, and Miss Maria Gibbon, youngest dau. of Major Gibbon of Richmond were married at that city on 2nd inst. (BA, 20 July 1816)

CARTMELL, Mrs. Sarah, died in Frederick Co., Va., aged 83 years. She lived to see the 5th generation of her descendants. (BPEA, 20 April 1815)

CARVER, Mr. John H., and Miss Sarah Ann Clemment, all of Balto., were married Thurs., 11th inst., by Rev. D. E. Reese. (BA, 19 July 1816)

CARY, John D., died at Frederickstown, 13th inst., a soldier at the time that "tried men's souls." (BA, 23 Oct. 1804)

CASENAVE, Peter, died last Sun., in Phila.; merchant of Georgetown, a husband and father. (BFG, 10 Sept. 1796)

CASENAVE, Stephen, died last 27 July, at St. Thomas in the West Indies; partner of the house of Casenave and Walker, merchants of Balto. (BFG, 4 Sept. 1797)

CASEY, John, and Miss Mary Vickers, both of Balto., were wed on Tues. eve. by Rev. Roberts. (BFR, 9 April 1812)

CASEY, Robert, and Elizabeth Davis, both of Balto., were married last Wed. by Bishop Carroll. (BT, 1 April 1796)

CASEY, Robert, and Miss Eliza Hammond, were married last eve. by Rev. Dr. Bend. (BFG, 10 Nov. 1808)

CASEY, William, died this morning; funeral from his late res., 34 High St., Old Town. (BA, 28 Feb. 1816)

CASKERY, Mrs. Anastasia, wife of Bernard Caskery, died Sat., 7th inst., aged 45 years. (BFG, 11 Sept. 1811)

CASLE, Josias, and Mrs. Nancy Scott, both of Balto., were married last Wed. by Rev. Mr. Allison. (BT, 19 March 1796)

CASPER, David, German, employee of a Mr. Butler, drowned Fri. at the mouth of Curtis Creek. He lived at North Frederick St. (BFG, 13 May 1805)

CASSARD?, Gilbert, and Miss Sarah Inloes, all of Balto., were married last Sun. by Rev. Richards. (BEP, 16 March 1811)

CASSARD, Luke, of Balto., and Miss Jane Allison of Phila. were married last Thurs. (BT, 15 Sept. 1797)

CASSAT?, Peter, and Miss Susanna Stansbury, all of Balto., were married last Thurs. by Rev. Ireland. (BFG, 6 Jan. 1798)

CASSAT, Peter, Balto. merchant, died Fri. (BFG, 22 Dec. 1806)

CASSELL, Mrs. Ann, wife of Joseph Cassell, of Western Precincts, died Thurs., 22nd inst., in her 34th year, leaving a husband and 6 small children. (BA, 25 Oct. 1816)

CASSEL, Rev. Leonard, and Miss Elizabeth Chambers, dau. of Rev. Daniel Chambers, all of Balto. Co., were married at Mt. Prospect last Thurs. eve. by Rev. Mr. McCain. (BFG, 5 May 1808)

CASSELL, Rev. Leonard, pastor of the M. E. Church at Fells Point, died Mon., 26th inst., in his 24th year; interment in the Meth. burying ground. (BFG, 1 Oct. 1808)

CASTLE, Mr. Joseph, of Pipe Creek, Fred. Co., and Miss Nancy Matthews of Balto., were married last eve. by Rev. McCombs. (BT, 10 May 1802)

CASWELL, Capt. Josiah, late of Conn., died in his 28th year, at Aux-Cayes. (BFG, 22 Jan. 1798)

CASY, Mr., and Miss Zane, were married Sun. by Rev. Rattoone. (BFG, 21 Dec. 1804)

CATHELL, Capt. Clement, and Miss Mathilda B. Mitchel, both of Fells Point, were married last eve. by Rev. Rattoone. (BFG, 13 March 1805)

CATHELL, William, and Miss Sarah McDonald, both of Balto., were married Mon. by Rev. Duncan. (BW, 16 March 1814)

CATTS, George, of Balto., and Miss Liticia Paden, of Dor. Co., were married last eve. by Rev. Fechtig. (BA, 7 Nov. 1815)

CAUGHEY, Michael, and Dorcas Walker were married 5 Dec. by Rev. Reese. (BA, 12 Dec. 1816)

CAULFIELD, Mrs. Phebe, died Mon. in her 54th year. (BA, 17 Aug. 1805)

CAULFIELD, Thomas, comedian, died 22 April at Cincinnati, Ohio, in his 49th year. (BA, 8 May 1815)

CAUSIN, Jenny Pope, wife of Gerrard Blackiston Causin, of Chas. Co., died Mon., 24th ult., in her 58th year, leaving a husband and children. (BFG, 3 Nov. 1803)

CAUSTEN, Isaac, and Mrs. Susanna Cassat, all of Balto., were wed last eve. by Rev. Shinn. (BFG, 2 Nov. 1812)

CAUSTEN, James H., merchant, and Miss Eliza Myer, were married 9th inst., by Rev. Glendy. (BFG, 19 Nov. 1813)

CAUSTEN, Mrs. Jane, consort of Isaac Causten, died yesterday after a short illness. (BFG, 9 Sept. 1807)

CAUSTEN, John Hyman, son of Isaac Causten, Balto. merchant, died yesterday, aged 20. (BFG, 29 Oct. 1801)

CAVENAUGH, Peter, and Miss Ruth Jane Staples, all of Balto., were married last Sat. eve. by Rev. Glendy. (BW, 8 Nov. 1811)

CHALMERS, David, and Mary Clark, both of Balto., were married last Thurs. by Rev. Dr. Bend. (BA, 21 Oct. 1806)

CHALMERS, James, and Miss Prudence Gough Holliday, both of Balto. Co., were married last eve. by Rev. Lee. (BRAD, 22 Jan. 1802)

CHALMERS, John, Jr., and Mrs. Mary Gilder, both of Balto., were married Sun. eve. by Bishop Asbury. (BT, 4 July 1797)

CHALMERS, John M., and Miss Matilda Picket, both of Balto., were married last Tues. eve. by Rev. Birch. (BPEA, 8 Sept. 1815)

CHALMERS, Capt. Timothy, and Miss Jerusha Harlow, all of Balto., were married last Mon. by Rev. Richards. (BFG, 19 Feb. 1811)

CHALMERS, William, and Sarah R. Wilson, dau. of James Wilson, all of Balto., were married last Tues. by Rev. Roberts. (BA, 16 Sept. 1811)

CHALTER, Walter S., Esq., of Georgetown, and Miss Rogers, dau. of the late Chancellor of Md., were married at Annapolis last Thurs. by Rev. Higginbothom. (BA, 26 Sept. 1799)

CHAMBERLAIN, J. G., Phila. merchant, and Miss Maria Mitchell of Yorktown, Va., were married at the latter place on 20th ult., by Rev. Bracken. (BT, 3 Jan. 1804)

CHAMBERLAINE, Mrs. Margaret, relict of the late John Chamberlaine of Long Green, Balto. Co., died Sun., 22nd ult., aged 80 years. Her descendants number upwards of 180 persons. (BFG, 1 April 1801)

CHAMBERS, Gen. Benjamin, Rev. officer, died at Charleston, 10 Jan., in his 67th year. (BA, 22 Jan. 1816)

CHAMBERS, Campbell, merchant, and Sarah Clarkson, dau. of Levinus Clarkson, all of Balto., were married last Thurs. by Rev. Bend. (BFG, 19 Jan. 1807)

CHAMBERS, Campbell, died last Sun. in his 28th year. (BW, 9 Jan. 1812)

CHAMBERS, Mrs. Hannah, died last Thurs., consort of John C. Chambers of Cecil Co. (BFG, 25 Aug. 1806)

CHAMBERS, John C., died last Thurs. at his farm on Cecil Co., an old inhab. of that place. (BFG, 9 Oct. 1806)

CHAMBERS, Matthew, Balto. merchant, and Miss Kitty Mummy of Balto Co., were married last eve. by Rev. Kurtz. (BA, 21 Nov. 1800)

CHANDLER, Mrs., wife of Dr. Thomas B. Chandler, dec., died last Sun. "Elizabeth-Town, 22 Sept." (BA, 29 Sept. 1801)

CHANDLER, Mrs. Eliza, died, after an illness of five days, wife of Capt. Ebenezer Chandler of Balto., and dau. of William Masters of Boston. (BFG, 11 Oct. 1800)

CHANDLER, Rev. Jno., rector of St. Marks and Zion Parishes, died at Oakland, Fred. Co. (BPEA, 24 March 1815)

CHANDLER, Walter S., of Georgetown, and Miss Rogers, dau. of the late Chancellor of Md., were married at Annapolis last Thurs. by Rev. Mr. Higginbothom. (BFG, 24 Sept. 1799)

CHAPMAN, Amos, merchant, and Miss Maria Ann Beebe, all of Balto., were married by Rev. Glendy last Sun. (BA, 28 May 1812)

CHAPMAN, Henry H., Speaker of the House of Delegates, and Miss Mary Davidson of Annapolis, were married at Annapolis last Tues. (BFG, 3 Jan. 1799)

CHAPMAN, Jonathan, and Miss Margaret Lee, dau. of Major John Lee, all of Balto., were married last eve. by Rev. M'Cain. (BFG, 22 April 1811)

CHAPMAN, Joseph, died 20th inst., of the prevailing fever, of the House of Waters and Chapman of Balto., aged 35 years; a native of Ireland, from which he emigrated about 15 years ago. (BFG, 22 Sept. 1800)

CHAPMAN, William, died last Sat., of a pulmonary complaint in his 40th year, leaving a wife and several children; interment in the M. E. burying ground; dec. was a member of the journeymen tailors and the Fells Point Columbian Blues. (BEP, 7 Nov. 1809)

CHAPPELL, William L., and Miss Mary M. Rickard, both of Balto., were married last Thurs. by Rev. Mr. Hunt. (BA, 9 Oct. 1816)

CHARLES, Richard, and Miss Elizabeth Benson, both of Balto., were married last eve. by Rev. Mr. Lyle. (BFG, 22 April 1799)

CHARPENTIER, Mrs. Louisa, widow of the late John Baptist Reynaud de Chateaudun, died last Fri., 31 March in her 45th year. (BA, 6 April 1815)

CHASE, Capt. Basil, and Miss Mary Everson, both of Balto., were married last Thurs. by Rev. Kurtz. (BT, 25 Dec. 1802)

CHASE, Richard Moale, and Miss Matilda Green, dau. of Frederick Green, all of Annapolis, were married there last Tuesday eve. by Rev. Gibson. (BFG, 29 Nov. 1806)

CHASE, Hon. Samuel, Associate Judge of the U. S. Supreme Court, a patriot of 1776, died the night of 17th inst. (BFR, 21 June 1811)

CHASE, Thomas, of Balto., and Miss Matilda Chase, dau. of Hon. Jeremiah T. Chase, were married at Annapolis by Rev. Mr. Davis. (BA, 25 Sept. 1816)

CHASE, Capt. Thorndick, and Miss Jane M'Nelty, both of Balto., were married last eve. by Rev. Glendy. (BT, 9 June 1804)

CHASE, William J., and Miss Elizabeth Besse, both of Fells Point, were married last Thurs. eve. by Rev. Mr. Glendy. (BW, 8 Oct. 1808)

CHATTAM, John, and Mrs. Jane Herron, all of Balto., were married last Thurs. eve. by Rev. Glendy. (BA, 17 Feb. 1816)

CHATTEL, Samuel, and Miss Julia Delavet, both of Balto., were wed last eve. by Rev. Dr. Rattoone. (BFG, 18 April 1804)

CHATTLES, John, and Miss Ann Fernandis, all of Balto., were wed 28th ult. by Rev. Hargrove. (BA, 2 April 1816)

CHAUNCEY, Elihu, of Phila., and Miss Henrietta Teackle, of Georgetown, were married last Sat. eve. at the res. of John Teackle, in D. C., by Rev. Addison. (BFG, 15 Oct. 1810)

CHAYTOR, Capt. Daniel, and Miss Sarah Sewell, all of Fells Point, were married last Thurs. by Rev. Ryland. (BA, 6 March 1813)

CHEDAL, John, and Mrs. Mary Duncan, both of Fells Point, were married last Tues. eve. by Rev. Mr. Glendy. (BT, 5 Jan. 1804)

CHEESEBOROUGH, Naboth, native of New England, and steward of the ship Eutaw of Balto., died at St. Thomas. (BFG, 13 March 1807)

CHENOWETH, Mrs. Ann, dau. of Joseph Clark, died last eve. aged 24. (BPE, 2 Oct. 1813)

CHENOWITH, Arthur, tobacconist, and Miss Ann Clark, dau. of Joseph Clark, Sr., auctioneer, all of Balto., were married last eve. by Rev. Bend. (BFG, 5 April 1811)

CHESELDINE, Mr. Biscoe, eldest son of Mr. Seneca Cheseldine, of St. Marys Co., died yesterday in his 19th year. (BFG, 30 Sept. 1799)

CHESLEY, John, late of Md., died 1 Aug., at his seat in Prince William Co., Va., leaving a wife and many children. (BFG 6 Aug. 1805)

CHESLEY, William F., and Miss Jane Dare, both of Balto., were married last Thurs. by Rev. Dashiell. (BFG, 4 March 1815)

CHESNEY, Thomas E., and Mrs. Rebecca Gamble, of A. A. Co., were married last eve. by Rev. Hargrove. (BFG, 5 July 1815)

CHESTER, Capt. Samuel, died last eve., well known during and since our Rev. as a recruiting officer in this place; funeral will be on Sun., with the honors of war. (BFG, 4 Dec. 1801)

CHESTON, Daniel, and Mrs. Isabella Colver, relict of Capt. Stephen Colver, all of Balto., were married last Thurs. by Rev. Glendy. (BA, 16 Oct. 1809)

CHESTON, James, and Miss Mary Ann Hollingsworth, both of Balto., were married last eve. by Rev. Bend. (BFG, 2 June 1803)

CHEW, Benjamin, died at Phila., aged 87. The deceased was born in Md., and was a son of Samuel Chew, Esq., who held high judicial office before the Rev. (BFG, 23 Jan. 1810)

CHEW, Bennett, died this morning after a short illness, son of late Samuel Chew of Calvert Co. (BFG, 3 Dec. 1806)

CHEW, Philemon, merchant, and Miss Anna Maria Bowie Brooke, dau. of the late Benjamin Brooke of P. G. Co., were married last Sat. eve. by Rev. Mr. Handy at the seat of S. L. Chew of A. A. Co. (BPE, 25 Feb. 1813)

CHICK, Peregrine, died lately at Chicksville, Cecil Co. In our revolutionary struggle, he was found in the ranks of his countrymen at an early age, and as a soldier took part of the laurels of those days. (BFG, 7 June 1806)

CHILD, Samuel C., and Miss Mary Jenning, both of Balto., were married last eve. by Rev. Mr. M'Cain. (BFG, 17 Feb. 1812) (BFR, 18 Feb. 1812 gives the bride's name as Jenny.)

CHILDS, Nathaniel, and Miss Ann Jessop, dau. of Wm. Jessop, all of Balto., were married last eve. by Rev. Richards. (BFG, 15 June 1803)

CHILDS, Thomas, and Miss Temperance Inloes, all of Balto., were married last eve. (BT, 12 Feb. 1802)

CHILTON, Mrs. Sarah, died this morning at Lansdowne, at the seat of John E. Dorsey. The dec. was 76 years old. (BFG, 11 Nov. 1808)

CHINOWETH, Mrs. Ann, dau. of Mr. Joseph Clark, auctioneer, died last eve., aged 24; funeral from No. 18, Balto. St. (BFG, 2 Oct. 1813)

CHISMAN, Mount Edward, collector of the customs of the port of Norfolk, died last Mon., leaving a wife and 5 children. "Hampton, 1 Aug." From the Norfolk Herald. (BT, 14 Aug. 1804)

CHITTENDEN, Capt. Nathaniel, and Miss Harriet Smith, were married last Sun. eve. by Rev. Griffith. (BA, 30 March 1815)

CHOATE, Capt. Job, of Boston, and Miss Margaret Adams, of Balto., were married last eve. by Rev. Bend. (BW, 15 Sept. 1808)

CHOATE, Capt. Job, died yesterday; funeral from his late dwelling 65 Albemarle St. (BA, 8 Dec. 1813)

CHRISTFIELD, Absolom, and Miss Mary Sligh, all of Balto., were married last eve. by Rev. Mr. Kurtz. (BA, 9 Nov. 1804)

CHRISTIE, Gabriel, Collector of the Port of Baltimore, died yesterday in his 51st year, of a pulmonary complaint. Vessels in the port honored his memory by wearing their colours at half-mast. (BFG, 2 April 1808)

CHRISTIE, Napier Burton, second son of Gabriel Christie, died 17 Jan. at St. Vincents, in his 19th year. He had gone to the West Indies for a few years. (BFG, 25 April 1804)

CHULL (commonly called SHOALS), Philip, died 16 Nov. 1813 at his res. in Fairfax Co., Co., Va., in his 155th year. He was born in Germany in 1699, and came to America in 1721. (BFG, 5 Jan. 1814)

CHUNN, Zachariah, merchant, and Miss Eliza Speake, both of Port Tobacco, were married Tues., 9th inst., by Rev. Whems. (BEP, 13 Feb. 1808)

CHURCH, Capt. Gilbert, died in Alexandria, Va., aged 40. (BPE, 6 March 1813)

CHURCH, John, member of the Society of Friends, died last Tues.; lately from Dublin, leaving a wife and six small children (obit gives causes of death). (BFG, 22 Oct. 1801)

CHURCH, John, and Mrs. Jane Church, all of Balto., were wed on last Sat. by Rev. Kurtz. (BFG, 13 Aug. 1811)

CHURCHILL, Simeon, and Miss Catherine Hunt, dau. of Joshua Hunt, all of Balto., were married last eve. by Rev. William McPherson. (BA, 8 Aug. 1810)

CHURCHMAN, Micajah, of Balto. Co., and Miss Eliza Sinclair, dau. of John Sinclair of Balto., were married 20th inst., at Lombard St., Friends Meeting House. (BA, 22 Dec. 1815)

CIST, Charles, printer, of Phila., died 1st inst., at the home of Philip Weis. Dec. was a native of Petersburg, Russia, and left a widow and 7 children. (BFG, 12 Dec. 1805)

CIST, Jacob, of the city of Washington, and Miss Sarah Hollenback, dau. of Matthias Hollenbacke of Wilkesbarre, Penna., on 27th ult., by Rev. Hoyt. (BEP, 3 Sept. 1807)

CLACKNER, Capt. Joseph, and Mrs. Rebecca Travers, dau. of Matthew Travers, all of Fells Point, were married last Tues. by Rev. Kurtz. (BFG, 22 Jan. 1806)

CLAGETT, Mrs., wife of Hezekiah Clagett, of Balto., died last Wed. (BFG, 14 Jan. 1803)

CLAGETT, Horatio, died last Dec. in London, a native of Md., and an officer in the Rev. War. Since 1783 he has been a merchant and an underwriter in London. (BFG, 23 Sept. 1816)

CLAGETT, Mrs. Janet, died 16th inst., in her 31st year, at her father's house in Balto., and wife of Mr. Benjamin Clagett of Hagerstown. She leaves a husband and 3 daus., as well as her aged parents. (BFG, 22 July 1806)

CLAGETT, John, eld. son of Hezekiah Clagett, of Balto., died last Sat. (BFG, 9 Oct. 1805)

CLAGETT, Rev. Dr. Thomas John, Bishop of the Prot. Ep. Church in Md., died 2 Aug., aged 73. He had been ordained more that 40 years ago. (BFG, 5 Aug. 1816)

MARRIAGES AND DEATHS

CLAGETT, William, Esq., Assoc. Judge of the 5th Judicial Dist., died at Hagerstown, 25th ult. (BFG, 2 April 1810)

CLAGETT, William K., merchant, and Miss Cecilia Brown Briscoe, dau. of the late Gen. John H. Briscoe, were married in St. M. Co., on Sun., 29th ult., by Rev. Magrath. (BFG, 3 Oct. 1805)

CLAIBORNE, Dr. John, died 9th inst., in Brunswick Co., Va.; member of Congress. (BW, 25 Oct. 1808)

CLAIR, Isaac, and Mrs. Mary Lynch, both of Balto., were married Sun. eve. by Rev. Rattoone. (BFG, 3 April 1809)

CLAP, Enoch, merchant, and Mary Tyson, dau. of Elisha Tyson, all of Balto., were married last eve. by Rev. Roberts. (BFG, 12 June 1812)

CLARE, Benjamin, of Calvert Co., and Charlotte Bevans, were wed last eve. by Rev. Bend. (BA, 24 May 1799)

CLARIDGE, Solomon, of A. A. Co., and Mrs. Elizabeth Barnett, of Balto., were married Fri. eve. by Rev. Rattoone. (BFG, 30 June 1806)

CLARK, Charles, drowned yesterday, when a gust of wind overturned a sailboat. (BFG, 25 July 1803)

CLARK, George, died, age 67. (BA, 20 Jan. 1800)

CLARK, George, died Sun., 5th inst. He lived within 19 miles of Balto.; funeral sermon will be preached the 12th inst. by Rev. WilliamParks. (BEP, 8 Oct. 1806)

CLARK, George, merchant, and Miss Ann Susanna Cobb were married last eve. by Archbishop Carroll. (BFG, 22 March 1811)

CLARK, Henry H., and Miss Elizabeth Speak, all of Balto., were married 16th inst., by Rev. Fenwick. (BWA, 25 May 1816)

CLARK, Hooper, and Miss Rebecca Ingram, both of Balto., were wed last Thurs. by Rev. Pitt. (BFG, 15 June 1811)

CLARK, Isabella, dau. of Stephen Clark, died 8th inst., aged 19 years. (BFG, 14 Jan. 1814)

CLARK, James, printer, and Miss Nancy M'Millan, of Fells Point, were married last eve. by Rev. Glendy. (BA, 8 May 1805)

CLARK, James, of Jefferson Co., Va., and Miss Elizabeth Head, dau. of William Head of Fred. Co., were married last Tues. near Creagerstown, by Rev. Dubois. (BFG, 24 Nov. 1807)

CLARK, James, lumber merchant, and Miss Elizabeth Herring, both of Balto., were married last Thurs. eve. by Rev. Bartow. (BA, 22 July 1816)

CLARK, James M., and Mrs. Nancy Tier, all of Balto., were wed last eve. by Rev. Hargrove. (BFG, 18 May 1813)

CLARK, John, and Miss Abigail Green, were married in Phila. (BT, 17 May 1799)

CLARK, John, and Polly Cassins, were married last Mon. by Rev. Glendy. (BA, 2 May 1806)

CLARK, John, merchant, and Martha Thomas, dau. of John Thomas, of Balto., were married last eve. by Rev. Richards. (BA, 14 Nov. 1806)

CLARK, John, a native of Ireland, and long a res. of Balto.,died last eve., aged 55 years; funeral from his late res., No. 56 Cumberland Row. (BA, 26 Jan. 1813)

CLARK, John Chesley, died yesterday, aged 36, leaving a sister and brother-in-law. (BFG, 26 July 1805)

CLARK, Joseph, and Miss Elizabeth Lyon, both of Balto., were wed last eve. by banns. (BFG, 12 Jan. 1807)

CLARK, Joseph, Jr., died this morning in his 24th year; funeral from No. 11 Market Space. (BFG, 3 June 1812)

CLARK, Samuel, and Miss Jane Mitchell, both of Balto., were wed last Thurs. eve. by Rev. Roberts. (BFG, 30 Aug. 1806)

CLARK, Sam'l, and Miss Margaret Dannie, both of Balto., were married Tues. eve. by Rev. Mr. Nicholas Smeethen. (BA, 8 Sept. 1810)

CLARK, William, died at Carlisle, on Thurs., 29th ult., in his 64th year. (BT, 13 April 1804)

CLARK, William, and Miss Hannah St. Clair, all of Balto., were married last Thurs. by Rev. Mr. Glendy. (BFG, 4 Aug. 1804)

CLARKE, Ambrose, native of Ireland, and long an inhab. of Balto., died last Wed. morning. (BFG, 8 Sept. 1810)

CLARKE, Elijah, Esq., died 15 Dec. 1799; late a major-general in the service of the state of Georgia. (BA, 18 Jan. 1800)

CLARKE, George, and Nancy Thompson, were married last Thurs. by Rev. Glendy. (BA, 4 Sept. 1806)

CLARKE, George, Balto. merchant, died last Sat. (BFG, 15 Dec. 1812)

CLARKE, George W., and Amelia Jane, dau. of William Hughes of Washington Co., were married at Antietam Forge by Rev. B. Kurtz on 26th ult. (BFG, 2 Oct. 1816)

CLARKE, Isaac, of Balto., and Miss Mary Smith, dau. of John Smith of Alexandria, were married at that place last Tues. by Rev. Dr. Muir. (BPEA, 13 Oct. 1815)

CLARKE, James, died last Sat., aged 80, a native of Leeds, Yorkshire, Eng.: born 5 July (24 June, o.s.) 1734. He came to this state in 1779, and has lived in Md. ever since. (BW, 2 May 1814)

CLARKE, James H., and Miss Hannah Hammond, of Fells Point, were married Thurs. eve. by Rev. Mr. Riggen. (BA, 17 Aug. 1799)

CLARKE, Joseph, architect, died this morning; formerly grand master of the Free Masons in Md. (BFG, 26 April 1798)

CLARKE, Joseph, Jr., and Miss Mary Ann Fanse, both of Balto., were married at Fells Point last eve. by Rev. Rattoone. (BFG, 2 June 1809)

MARRIAGES AND DEATHS

CLARKE, Mrs. Margaret, wife of George Clarke, Esq., of Green
Castle, Penna., died 12th inst. (BA, 22 Feb. 1810)

CLARKE, Michael W., and Miss Phoebe Creek, were married on Mon.
last by Rev. Dashiell. (BFG, 28 May 1808)

CLARKE, Nicholas, of Ky., and Miss Amelia Hall, dau. of Caleb
Hall of Balto. were married last Mon. by Rev. Rattoone.
(BFG, 12 June 1804)

CLARKSON, Levinus, died 18th ult. at the res. of William Graves,
Esq., in Kent Co., in his 50th year. (BFR, 6 Feb. 1812)

CLARKSON, Matthew, former Mayor of Phila., died last Fri. (BFG,
8 Oct. 1800)

CLASSEN, John, and Elizabeth Gallispy, both of Balto., were wed
last Thurs. eve. by Rev. Rattoone. (BA, 9 Aug. 1806)

CLASSON, Christian, was found dead yesterday on the shore of the
Ferry Branch, evidently shot with a pistol. He was from
Germany. (BT, 22 July 1797)

CLAY, Joseph, cashier of the Farmer's and Mechanics Bank, died
Tues., aged 41; he was also a rep. in Congress for Phila.
"Phil. Press. (BA, 30 Aug. 1811)

CLAY, Matthew, member of Congress, died Sat., 27th ult. at Halifax Court House. (BFG, 14 June 1815)

CLAYLAND, Samuel, died last Tues. at Annap., in his 35th year.
(BT, 22 Sept. 1797)

CLAYLAND, Mrs. Sarah, died 23 April in her 79th year. (BA, 25
April 1816)

CLAYLAND, Mrs. Susannah, died 26th ult., consort of Major James
Clayland in her 37th year, leaving a husband and 6 children. (BEP, 2 March 1811)

CLAYLAND, Thomas E., one of the proprietors of the Baltimore
Telegraphe, died today in his 26th year. (BFG, 4 Dec.
· 1797)

CLAYPOOLE, Septimus, one of the proprietors of the American Daily
Advertiser, and Miss Elizabeth Polk, were married 8th inst.
at the seat of Col. Nathaniel Ramsay, Carpenter's Point,
Cecil Co. (BFG, 12 June 1797)

CLAYPOOLE, Septimus, proprietor of the Daily Advertiser, died
15 Oct., at Elk, on his return from Phila. to Md.; he
leaves a widow. (BFG, 17 Oct. 1798)

CLAYTON, John, Associate Judge of the Supreme Court, died at his
house near Dover, Del. (BFG, 18 Dec. 1802)

CLAYTON, Dr. Joshua, Senator of the United States from the state
of Delaware, died the morning of the 11th inst., at his
dwelling house on Bohemia Manor; a husband and a father.
(BFG, 17 Aug. 1798)

CLEMENT, Dr. Evan, druggist, of Balto., died at Haddonfield last
Sat. (BT, 20 Oct. 1797)

CLEMENT, Joseph R., of Salem, N. J., and Miss Mary Levering of
Balto., were married Tues. by Rev. Richards. (BFG, 19
April 1804)

CLEMENT, Nicholas, and Elizabeth Mercer, both of Balto., were married last Mon. by Rev. M'Cain. (BA, 10 Sept. 1801)

CLEMENTS, Josias, Balto. merchant, and Sarah McSherry, of Littlestown, were married last Tues. (BT, 31 March 1796)

CLEMM, Mrs. Harriet, wife of William Clemm, and only dau. of George Poe, died 6th inst., in her 31st year, leaving a husband, 5 children, a father and brothers. (BFG, 9 Jan. 1816)

CLEMM, John, and Miss Maria Eichelberger, dau. of M. Eichelberger of Balto., were married last Thurs. by Rev. Otterbein. (BS, 11 Aug. 1810)

CLEMM, William, Jr., and Miss Harriot Poe, dau. of George Poe, all of Balto., were married last eve. by Rev. Inglis. (BFG, 2 May 1804)

CLEMMENS, Jacob, formerly of Detroit, and Miss Sarah Woodrow of Germantown, were married at the latter place, Thurs. eve. by Rev. Schaeffer. (BA, 16 June 1807)

CLEMMENS, John, and Miss Ruth Mitchel, all of A. A. Co., were married Thurs., 24th inst., by Rev. Mr. Forster. (BEP, 29 Dec. 1807)

CLEMSTEAD, Jabed, and Miss Sally Kelly, of Fells Point, were married on Tues. (BT, 13 Sept. 1804)

CLENDENIN, Dr. William H., and Miss Eliza Belt, all of Balto., were married Thurs. eve. by Rev. Glendy. (BFR, 13 Oct. 1818)

CLIFFORD, Nathaniel H., and Miss Eamorison, of Balto. Co., were married Thurs. eve. by Rev. Bartow. (BA, 27 July 1816)

CLINE, David, and Catherine Shakes, both of Fells Point, were married last eve. by Rev. Mr. Bend. (BA, 29 July 1799)

CLINGMAN, John, of Balto., and Miss Sarah Richardson of Balto. Co., were married last eve. by Rev. Coats. (BT, 19 March 1803)

CLYMER, George, Pres. of the Bank of Philadelphia, died last Sat. eve. at the res. of his son in Morrisville, Bucks Co. (BFG, 28 Jan. 1813)

CLOPPER, Andrew, and Miss Ann Torrence, all of Balto., were wed Tues. eve. by Rev. Glendy. (BFG, 31 May 1804)

CLOPPER, Edward N., and Mrs. Grace M'Curdy, all of Balto., were married last Wed. eve. by Rev. Glendy. (BEP, 14 May 1811)

CLUNET, Mr., and Miss Alice Lannoy, were married Thurs. eve. by Rev. Bend. (BFG, 3 March 1810)

CLYMER, Daniel, formerly of Phila., died at his country seat, Caernarvon Twp., Berks Co., Penna., on 26 Jan. (BEP, 12 Feb. 1810)

CLYMER, George. See above, following Clingman, John.

COALE, Anna Maria, dau. of Dr. Samuel Stringer Coale, of Balto., died Sun., 3rd inst. (BFG, 9 Jan. 1813)

COALE, Charles Ridgely, died in Jamaica, 18 May last in his 18th year, eldest son of Mrs. Sarah Coale, relict of Thomas Coale. (BT, 8 Aug. 1800)

COALE, Edward J., of Balto., and Miss Mary Ann Buchanan, dau. of late Dr. George Buchanan, formerly of Balto., were married last Tues. in Phila., by Bishop White. (BFG, 22 April 1815)

COALE, Mrs. Elizabeth, wife of Philemon Coale, of Balto. Co., died 21st inst., in her 29th year. (BA, 24 May 1811)

COALE, Dr. Samuel Stringer, died Wed. eve. (BFG, 21 Sept. 1798)

COALE, William, of the firm of Smith and Coale, of Balto., died 3rd inst., at Point-Petre in Guadeloupe. (BFG, 24 Sept. 1805)

COATES, Jonathan, aged 80, member of the Society of Friends, died last Tues. (BA, 30 May 1807)

COATS, Samuel, merchant, and Miss Roxanna Wayman, all of Balto., were married last eve. by Rev. Glendy. (BFG, 23 Dec. 1803)

COBB, George, and Miss Harriet Barnes, both of Balto., were wed Thurs. eve. last by Rev. Richards. (BFG, 27 Sept. 1816)

COCHRAN, Robert, and Adelle Percey, were married 21 Sept. by Rev. Inglis. (BA, 26 Sept. 1816)

COCHRAN, Samuel, and Miss Tamer Fouks, all of Balto., were married last Thurs. by Rev. Glendy. (BS, 17 April 1812)

COCHRAN, Mrs. Susannah, wife of Hiram Cochran of Balto., died 9th inst., in her 38th year, leaving a husband and children. (BEP, 10 Sept. 1807)

COCHRAN, William, Esq., and Miss Debby Adams, were married last Thurs. eve. by Rev. Bend. (BFG, 22 Dec. 1804)

COCHRAN, William, late a merchant of Balto., died near Bridge-Town, Ireland. (BA, 27 May 1807)

COCHRAN, William G., and Miss Susanna McCannon, dau. of James McCannon, of Balto., were married last eve. by Rev. Roberts. (BFG, 17 April 1805)

COCHRAN, William G., died on Tues., 28th inst., Secretary of the Balto. Insurance Co., in his 40th year, leaving a wife and five children. (Long obit.) (BFG, 31 March 1815)

COCKE, Dr. James, of Balto., and Miss Eliza B. Smith, of Kent Co., Md., were married Sun., 14th inst. (BFG, 19 Oct. 1810)

COCKE, Dr. James, professor of anatomy at the University of Md., died Mon., 25th inst. (BFG, 29 Oct. 1813)

COCKEY, John, Jr., and Miss Mary Fishpaw, both of Balto. Co., were married last Thurs. (BFG, 19 Nov. 1814)

COCKEY, Thomas B., and Miss Mary Ann Worthington, dau. of John Worthington, of Thos., of Balto. Co., were married Tues., 9th inst., by Rev. Fechtig. (BFG, 12 April 1816)

COCKEY, Thomas Deye, died at his res. in Balto. Co., on Sat., 3rd inst., in his 51st year. (BFG, 7 April 1813)

COCKRILL, Mrs. Sarah, wife of Thomas Cockrill, of Fells Point, died last Thurs., in her 27th year. (BA, 2 Aug. 1805)

COCKRILL, Thomas, and Miss Rebecca Veazey, both of Fells Point, were married last eve. by Rev. Mr. Robert Roberts. (BFG, 23 March 1810)

COE, Samuel, and Mrs. Mary Fowler, both of Annapolis, were wed there. (BFG, 15 April 1796)

COFFEE, Mr. John, and Miss Elizabeth Jamima Woodward, were wed last eve. by Rev. Mr. Hagerty. (BI, 18 May 1798)

COFFEE, Mrs. Susannah, female superintendent of a juvenile academy, died last Sat. (BFG, 27 Jan. 1813)

COFFIELD, Miss Eliza, eldest dau. of Capt. Thomas Coffield of Havre de Grace, died last Tues., 16th inst. (Long obit) (BFG, 20 Feb. 1802)

COFFIELD, John, son of Thomas Coffield, of Cecil Co., died at Port-au-Prince. (BA, 23 Nov. 1810)

COFFIELD, Thomas, son of John Coffield, of N. C., died in Cecil Co., on 25 June, aged 30 years. (BA, 1 Aug. 1816)

COFFIN, Mr. Charles, and Miss Mary McCormick, both of Balto., were married by Rev. Glendy. (BFG, 22 Nov. 1803)

COFFIN, Capt. James, of the state of Mass., died yesterday morning. (BT, 3 Nov. 1797)

COFFIN, Reuben, and Miss Polly Butt, both of Norfolk were married there on Tues. evening by Rev. Mr. Grisby. (BEP, 28 June 1806)

COFFMAN, Mr., and Miss Thrift, were married lately in Harf. Co., by Rev. Mr. Wilmer. (BFG, 4 Jan. 1803)

COHEN, Dr., and Mrs. Margaret Quisic, both of Balto., were married last eve. (BT, 10 Aug. 1797)

COKE, Rev. Dr., died on his passage from England to India. (BA, 22 April 1815)

COLE, Mrs. Elizabeth, late consort of Jacob Cole, died yesterday morning. (BFG, 7 Sept. 1799)

COLE, Frederick, and Miss Sarah Turner were married 2nd inst. by Rev. Turner. (BS, 7 Feb. 1812)

COLE, Mr. Godfrey, died yesterday, in his 48th year; of an apoplectic fit. (BFG, 30 Nov. 1803)

COLE, James Alexander, and Mrs. Charlotte Sear, both of Balto., were married last Sat. by Rev. Dr. Rattoone. (BFG, 4 March 1807) (BA, 3 March, gives her name as Tear.)

COLE, John, merchant, and Mary, dau. of John M'Donough, both of Balto., were married last Sat., by Rev. Dr. Patrick Allison. (BMJ, 7 Feb. 1797)

COLE, Joshua, apprentice to Thomas Jewett, currier, Cumberland Row, died on the 12th. (BFG, 22 July 1802)

COLE, Samuel, and Miss Eliza Nind, were married last eve. by Rev. Nind. (BFG, 15 Feb. 1803)

COLE, Thomas, of West River, A. A. Co., and Miss Elizabeth Dorsey, of Balto. Co., were married last eve. at John Battery's, Patapsco Neck, by Rev. Richards. (BFG, 29 Dec. 1798)

COLE, Thomas, and Elizabeth Welsh, were married Fri. eve. by Rev. Richards. (BA, 21 April 1800)

COLE, Thomas, Balto. Co. farmer, died a few days ago. (BFG, 6 Sept. 1800)

COLE, Thomas B., merchant, and Miss Elizabeth Smith, dau. of Wm. Smith, of Balto., were married Wed. eve. by Rev. Ireland. (BFG, 15 Nov. 1799)

COLE, Thomas B., died yesterday, a Balto. merchant. (BFG, 13 Sept. 1800)

COLE, William, and Miss Ann Guffy, both of Balto. Co., were wed last eve. by Rev. Armstrong. (BFG, 12 April 1806)

COLE, William, of Havre de Grace, and Miss Susan Nicoll of Balto. were married last Sun. eve. by Bishop Kemp. (BA, 17 Dec. 1816)

COLEBY, Nicholas, and Miss Elizabeth Buntz, all of Balto., were married last Wed, eve. by Rev. D. E. Reese. (BA, 27 Dec. 1816)

COLEGATE, Major John, died yesterday at his seat near Balto., one of the associate justices of the county. (BFG, 18 Jan. 1803)

COLEHOUSE, Frederick, and Mrs. Margaret Silverdore, all of Balto. were married last Sun. eve. by Rev. Healey. (BA, 26 March 1812)

COLEMAN, John, of Delaware, and Miss Mary Joiner, of Annapolis, were married at Fells Point, Thurs. eve. by Rev. Rattoone. (BT, 6 Aug. 1806) (BFG, 5 Aug. 1806 gives the bride's name as Gorner.)

COLEMAN, Capt. John, and Mrs. Julia Gardner, were married in Balto. last eve. by Rev. Glendy. (BPE, 5 Feb. 1813)

COLEMAN, Rev. John, died at his seat in Harf. Co., on 21st inst., in his 59th year. (BA, 26 Jan. 1816)

COLGATE, Dr. George, and Miss Mary M'Cannon, all of Frederick Co. were married 12th inst., at the seat of James M'Cannon. (BFG, 16 April 1810)

COLLINGS, John, and Mrs. Mary Connary, both of Fells Point, were married last Sun. eve. by Rev. Mr. Hagerty. (BS, 8 Dec. 1812)

COLLINS, Benjamin, and Mrs. Sarah Ennis, both of Balto., were married last Thurs. by Rev. Glendy. (BW, 31 Dec. 1811)

COLLINS, George, and Miss Eliza Pickever, all of Balto., were married last Thurs. by Bishop Kemp. (BFG, 12 Aug. 1816)

COLLINS, Josias, son of Richard Collins of A. A. Co., dec., died last Mon. in his 27th year. (BFG, 18 May 1816)

COLLINS, Mrs. Mary, wife of Mr. G. Collins, died Sat., 13th inst. in her 31st year, leaving a husband and 3 children. (BFG, 20 Jan. 1816)

COLLINS, Peter, His Swedish Majesty's Vice Consul for the State of Maryland, died yesterday at Fells Point in his 57th year. (BFG, 26 March 1810)

COLLINS, Mrs. Rebecca, died yesterday morning, aged 33, consort of Benj. Collins, leaving a husband and two small children. (BA, 17 March 1815)

COLLINS, Mrs. Sarah, wife of George C. Collins of Balto. Co., died Tues. last, aged 34. (BFG, 16 Nov. 1801)

COLLINS, Thomas, and Mrs. Mary Tyler, were married last Thurs. by Rev. Glendy. (BA, 10 Dec. 1816)

COLLINS, William, died Sun., 9th inst., in his 69th year, a native of Ireland, over 30 years an inhab. of Balto. He bequeathed the whole of his property, except for legacies to his housekeeper and to orphans, to Right Rev. Bishop Carroll for building a Cathedral Church in Balto. (BA, 19 Sept. 1804)

COLLINS, William, of Balto., and Miss Jane Harkins of Harf. Co., were married last Thurs. in Harf. Co. by Rev. Mr. Richardson. (BW, 29 July 1811)

COLLOPY, Timothy, and Miss Sarah Adreon, were married Thurs. by Rev. Mr. Hargrove. (BT, 19 Nov. 1803)

COLLOPY, William, and Miss Mary Fitzpatrick, all of Balto. Co., were married by Rev. Moranville. (BW, 10 Jan. 1811)

COLT, Robert L., of New York, and Miss Oliver of Phila., were married last eve. by Rev. Dr. Inglis. "Phila. paper." (BFR, 7 Oct. 1811)

COLVER, Capt. Stephen, died of a stroke of the palsy on 9th inst. at Washington, long an inhab. of Balto., where he benefited the navigation by freeing the harbor of obstructions. (BFG, 14 Feb. 1809)

COLVIN, Dr. Daniel, died yesterday after an illness of several days. (BFG, 11 April 1803)

COLVIN, John B., and Miss Adeline S. Attwood, were married last Mon. eve. by Rev. John Hargrove. (BFG, 8 May 1801)

COLVIN, Mrs. Margaret, died this morning in his 63rd year. (BFG, 21 July 1806)

COLVIN, Patrick, died 3 Dec. in his 75th year. (BFG, 5 Dec. 1796)

COLVIN, Mrs. Rachel, died Wed., 12th inst., at her family res. in Old Town. (BA, 13 Aug. 1807)

COLVIN, Samuel, Sr., died suddenly yesterday morning; funeral from his res. in Bridge St. (BFG, 11 Jan. 1815)

COMBES, Lewis of Balto., and Margaret D., dau. of Philip Ford, were married 6th inst. in St. M. Co. by Rev. Fenwick. (BA, 14 Feb. 1805)

COMBS, Thomas, and Miss Ann Bahan, both of Balto., were married last eve. by Right Rev. Bishop Carroll. (BFG, 13 Feb. 1801)

COMEGYS, Mrs. Ann, consort of William Comegys, of Balto., died yesterday; interment in Friends Burying Ground. (BEP, 4 Feb. 1809)

COMEGYS, Benjamin, Balto. merchant, died at sea, 15th inst., off Cape Hatteras, on his passage from Havana. His body was returned to his native Kent Co. for interment. He leaves an orphan son. (Long obit.) (BFG, 22 June 1809)

COMEGYS, Cornelius, and Miss Mary Smith, all of Balto., were married Tues. eve., 3rd inst., by Rev. Mark Moore. (BA, 6 Dec. 1816)

COMEGYS, Cornelius P., of Balto., and Ann Blakiston, of Del., were married Thurs., 16th inst., by Rev. Mr. Whitby. (BA, 17 Aug. 1801)

COMEGYS, John, died Sat., 9th inst., at his father's res. in Kent Co.; for many years a merchant in Balto. (BPE, 15 July 1814)

COMEGYS, John G., of Balto., and Mlle. Sophie Labbaddee of St. Louis, Upper Louisiana, were married Tues., 17th Feb., by Rev. Goradeau. (BFG, 11 April 1807)

COMEGYS, William, and Elizabeth Kinsey, both of Balto., were wed yesterday at Friends Meeting House. (BFG, 21 Sept. 1810)

COMER, John, and Miss Hannah Norris all of Balto., were married on 20 Sept. by Rev. Mr. Richards. (BFG, 2 Oct. 1810)

COMPTON, John, and Miss Mary Jackson, both of Balto., were wed last eve. by Rev. Wells. (BT, 13 April 1804)

COMPTON, William H., constable, died last Wed., aged 32. (BA, 11 Sept. 1813)

CONAWAY, Adderson, and Miss Eleanor Hyatt, both of P. G. Co., were married Thurs. by Rev. Ridgely. (BT, 7 Jan. 1804)

CONAWAY, Thomas, of Fells Point, died yesterday; funeral from his late res. in Wilk St. (BA, 17 Aug. 1810)

CONDON, Joseph, and Miss Margaret S. Biddle, both of Cecil Co., were married last Thurs. by Rev. William Duke. (BW, 25 June 1811)

CONKLING, Lieut. Solomon G., of the U. S. Regt. of Artillerists, died at Fort McHenry, on Thurs., 9th inst. (BFG, 10 April 1810)

CONNALLY, Thomas, and Miss Mary Weeks, both of Balto., were wed Thurs. eve., 7th inst., by Right Rev. Bishop Carroll. (BFG, 9 June 1804)

CONNARD, Frederick, and Miss Priscilla Trapnell, both of Balto., were married Tues. eve. by Rev. Mr. Kurtz. (BA, 31 Aug. 1815)

CONNELL, Capt. Timothy, native of Ireland, was drowned in the Basin on Wed. eve., 22nd inst., after helping to rescue a man who fell off a vessel. (BFG, 28 Aug. 1804)

CONNOR (or CORNER), James, and Miss Sarah Johnson, both of Balto., were married last Thurs. eve. by Rev. Budd. (BFG, 14 Dec. 1807)

CONNOR, John, and Miss Hannah Norris, all of Balto., were married on 20 Sept. by Rev. Richards. (BEP, 3 Oct. 1810)

CONNOR, Rebecca, wife of Daniel Connor, died last eve. in her 38th year, leaving a husband and four children; funeral from her late dwelling, 113 Sharp St., to the Catholic Church. (BFG, 16 Oct. 1810)

CONSTABLE, George, merchant, died this morning; funeral from his res., 53 Market Space. (BFG, 29 July 1799)

CONSTABLE, Thomas, for many years a res. of Balto., died at Norfolk on 26th inst., aged 65 years, leaving a wife and family. (BFG, 29 April 1805)

CONTEE, Alexander, Esq., died suddenly in Chas. Co., Md., on 21st ult., in his 56th year, at the res. of Rev. Dr. B. Contee. (BFG, 9 March 1810)

CONWAY, Mrs. Elizabeth, sister of August Atkinson, died Fri., aged 40 years, of a pulmonary complaint. Her brother, August Atkinson, died 10th ult., of the same disease. (BW, 4 March 1809)

CONWAY, John, and Miss Margy Jordan, all of Balto., were wed last eve. by Rev. Richards. (BT, 26 Oct. 1804)

CONWAY, Robert, and Mary Langdon, all of Balto., were wed last Thurs. by Rev. Moranville. (BW, 21 Oct. 1809)

COOK, Capt., died 18th inst.; formerly of the ship *Defense*, which was fitted out in Balto. at the time of the Rev. War. (BA, 28 Dec. 1799)

COOK, Abigail, died at Benjamin Tracey's, near Balto., on 29 Dec. aged 110. She professed to be converted in her 95th year. (BT, 9 June 1802)

COOK, Isaac, merchant of Phila., and Charlotte Amanda Pollock, dau. of Mr. Elias Pollock of Balto., were married on Wed. by Rev. Mr. Wilf. (BFG, 29 Dec. 1810)

COOK, Rev. James, aged 60, and Miss Rebecca Chambers, aged 16, all of Cecil Co., Md., were married 22nd inst., by Rev. Nicholas Chambers. (BW, 29 Sept. 1808)

COOK, John, Balto. merchant, died this morning in his 75th year; funeral from his late res. in Howard St. (BFG, 17 March 1804)

COOK, John F., printer, and Miss Delia Carroll, both of Balto., were married last eve. by Rev. Glendy. (BFG, 3 April 1807)

COOK, Capt. William, of Patapsco Neck, and Mrs. Elizabeth Stansbury, of Back River Neck, were married last Thurs. eve. by Rev. Richards. (BA, 26 Oct. 1816)

COOKE, Caleb, and Miss Ann Maria Swann, both of Balto., were wed last Thurs. by Rev. Fechtig. (BA, 7 Sept. 1816)

COOKE, George, and Miss Ellen A. Dall, were married last eve. by Rev. Dr. Kemp. (BFG, 22 June 1814)

COOKE, Richard, son of William Cooke, and Miss Elizabeth Van Wyck, dau. of William Van Wyck, of Balto., were married on Mon. eve. by Rev. Ireland. (BT, 26 Nov. 1800)

COOKE, William, Jr., Esq., of Balto., and Elizabeth Tilghman, dau. of Edward Tilghman, of Phila., were married at Phila., on Tues., 24th inst. by Right Rev. Bishop White. (BFG, 28 Jan. 1804)

COOKE, William, and Mrs. Rebecca Weary, were married at Fells Point, by Rev. Rattoone. (BFG, 14 June 1804)

COOMBS, Robert, and Miss Rebecca Stiles, sister of Capt. George Stiles, all of Balto., were married on Wed. by Rev. Glendy. (BA, 25 Jan. 1811)

COOPER, Alice, died Wed., 29 Oct., at Northumberland in Md., the wife of Thomas Cooper of that place: she was aged 42 years. (BA, 18 Nov. 1800)

COOPER, Edward Oaks, and Miss Mary Bishop, both of Balto., were married by Rev. Moranville on the last Thurs. eve. (BFG, 9 March 1816)

COOPER, John M., and Miss Ann B. Deaver, all of Balto., were married last eve. by Rev. Pitts. (BFG, 12 Dec. 1806)

COOPER, Samuel, and Miss Margaret Aderson (sic), both of Balto., were married last evening by Rev. Robert R. Roberts. (BFG, 26 May 1810)

COOPER, Thomas, and Miss Catherine West, both of Balto., were wed last eve. by Rev. Rattoone. (BFG, 7 Dec. 1805)

COOPER, Thomas, and Mrs. Nancy Peers, both of Balto., were married 18th inst., by Rev. Dr. Rattoone. (BFG, 24 May 1806)

COOPER, Wells, and Miss Catherine Sitler, all of Balto., were married last Thurs. by Rev. Roberts. (BW, 12 Aug. 1809)

COPE, Jasper, Balto. merchant, and Rebecca Shoemaker, dau. of Joseph Shoemaker of Balto., were married at Friends Meeting House for the northern dist. of Phila., on 14th inst. (BFG, 23 Oct. 1800)

COPE, John, a member of the Society of Friends, died in Fayette Co., Penna., aged 82. (BPE, 20 Feb. 1813)

COPELAND, John, Balto. merchant, and Eliza Bowyer, were married on 12th inst., by Rev. Mr. Osburn in Greenbriar, Va. (BA, 31 Oct. 1806)

COPP, Mrs. Elizabeth, of Phila., died 26th ult., in her 83rd year. "Phila., 3 Dec." (BFG, 4 Dec. 1812)

COPPUCK, William, and Mrs. Mary Shields, both of Balto., were married last Tues. eve. by Rev. Dashiell. (BEP, 4 May 1810)

CORBALLY, Nicholas, teacher in this country for over 30 years, died Sat., 20th inst., in Balto. Dec. was a native of Ireland. (BFG, 27 Feb. 1808)

FROM BALTIMORE NEWSPAPERS   71

CORBLY, Nicholas, Esq., and Mrs. E. Burk, of Balto., were married 17th inst., by Rev. John Baxley. (BA, 18 March 1806)

CORD, Mrs. Jane, consort of Joseph Cord, member of the Society of Friends, died 11th Oct., at her res. in Coolspring Neck in Sussex Co., Del., in her 84th year. (BA, 25 Oct. 1816)

CORDERAY, Henry, and Miss Elizabeth Furlong, both of Balto., were married last Thurs. by Rev. Beasley. (BA, 1 Oct. 1812)

CORKER, Capt. Benjamin, died Sat., 22nd inst. (BW, 27 July 1809)

CORNELIUS, Nicholas, merchant tailor, both of Balto., were wed last eve. by Rev. Roberts. (BFG, 18 Sept. 1801)

CORNTHWAIT, John, and Elizabeth Wilson, dau. of David Wilson, of Balto., were married yesterday at Friends Meeting House. (BFG, 20 Nov. 1807)

CORNTHWAIT, Robert, merchant, and Miss Alisanna Wilson, dau. of John Wilson, late of Harf. Co., were wed last Tues. at Deer Creek Friends Meeting. (BFG, 8 Oct. 1805)

CORNTHWAIT, Thomas, and Miss Eliza Tharp, all of Fells Point, were married last eve. by Rev. Richards. (BFG, 9 Nov. 1810)

CORNTHWAIT, William, and Miss Ann Hill were married yesterday at Friends Meeting House. (BFG, 19 Dec. 1806)

CORRICK, Mrs. Catherine, died last Wed. morning. (BT, 3 June 1803)

CORRIE, James, died this morning: funeral from St. Peter's Church. (BFG, 9 May 1805)

CORRIE, Mrs. Mary, wife of James Corrie of Balto., died this morning; funeral from her res., 47 Pratt St. tomorrow. (BFG, 28 Jan. 1803)

CORSE, Barney, and Miss Rebecca Houston, both of Chestertown, were married 19th inst. by Rev. John Smith. (BFR, 27 Oct. 1810)

CORSE, John, one of the editors of the Alexandria Herald, and Miss Julia G. Talbot of Alexandria, were married there last Thurs. by Rev. Wilmer. (BFG, 15 Nov. 1813)

COSDEN, William Henry, died 9th inst., at Newark, Del., the ygst. son of Jeremiah Cosden in his 19th year. He died by his own hand after receiving a letter from his father ordering him to return to school. (BPE, 19 Dec. 1814)

COSLIN, John J. N., and Mrs. Kitty Pine, both of Balto., were married last Mon. by Rev. Hayley. (BA, 23 Sept. 1807)

COSTELLO, Andrew, and Miss Mary Scource, both of Balto., were married Sunday eve. by Rev. Moranville. (BPEA, 24 Oct. 1815)

COSTELO, James J., and Miss Ann Bull, all of Balto., were wed last Sun. (BMG, 22 Aug. 1815)

COSTIN, Henry, of Tal. Co., and Mrs. Elizabeth Turner of the same county, were married last Thurs. by Rev. Rigg. (BA, 29 Sept. 1801)

COTTOM, Richard, Esq., of Petersburg, Va., and Miss Charlotte M. Cochran, of Balto., were married last eve. by Right Rev. Bishop Kemp. (BFG, 30 May 1815)

COTTON?, W. B., and Miss Susan Levely, all of Balto., were wed last eve. by Rev. Abner Neale. (BT, 15 July 1802)

COTTRELL, Capt. Henry W., and Miss Jane Devrickson, all of Balto., were married. (BS, 9 Nov. 1812)

COUDON, Samuel, died at Elkton, Cecil Co., on 25 Oct.; late High Sheriff of Cecil Co., aged about 56 years. (Long obit.) (BA, 31 Oct. 1806)

COULSON, George, and Miss Margaret Inloes, all of Balto., were married last Tues. by Rev. MacCain. (BEP, 2 May 1811)

COULSON, John, died last Sun.,; of the firm of Hutton and Coulson of Balto. (BFG, 23 Sept. 1800)

COULSON, William, and Mrs. Hannah Underwood, both of Balto. Co.. were married last Tues. by Rev. Inglis. (BA, 15 June 1807)

COULTER, Mrs. Elizabeth, of Balto., died last Tues. in her 21st year. "Md. Gaz." (BA, 2 Aug. 1805)

COULTER, Henry, and Miss Ann Clarke, both of Annap., were married Thurs., 23rd inst., in that city. (BT, 27 Sept. 1802)

COULTER, Mrs. Margaret, of Balto., died yesterday. (BFG, 24 Jan. 1798)

COURSEY, Edward H., and Miss Winifred Allen, all of Balto., were married Sun., 25th inst., by Rev. Griffith. (BA, 27 Dec. 1814)

COURTENAY, Henry, and Miss Isabella Purviance were married last eve. by Rev. Allison. (BT, 11 Jan. 1799)

COURTENAY, Henry, and Miss Elizabeth I. Purviance, were wed on last eve. by Rev. Inglis. (BFG, 21 Feb. 1811)

COURTENAY, Hercules, died yesterday at his res. in Balto. Co., in his 89th year. (BFG, 22 Aug. 1816)

COURTENAY, Mrs. Isabella, died last Sat., wife of Henry Courtenay, of Balto. (BFG, 12 July 1804)

COURTENAY, William, and Miss Maria Weatherburn, were married Tues. eve. by Rev. Mr. Wyatt. (BFG, 15 March 1815)

COURTNEY, Robert, merchant, died this morning in his 44th year; funeral from his late res. in Pitt St., near Friends Meeting House. (BFG, 3 July 1807)

COUSENS, George Barlin, and Miss Margaret M'Connell, all of Balto Co., were married last Sun. by Dr. Sinclair. (BA, 30 April 1816)

COWAN, Boyce, and Miss Sarah Chauncey, dau. of John Chauncey, were married last Thurs. in Harf. Co., by Rev. Mr. Allen. (BFG, 12 April 1802)

COWAN, Mrs. Eleanor, died 10th inst., at Havre de Grace, Harf. Co., aged 59 years. (BFG, 14 Sept. 1811)

COWAN, Peter, and Mrs. Margaret Proctor, all of Balto., were wed last Fri. by Rev. Glendy. (BEP, 10 Oct. 1810) (BA, 11 Oct. 1810 gives the bride's name as Rector.)

COWARD, Mrs. Elizabeth, consort of Capt. Thomas Coward, died yesterday, aged about 28 years, leaving 5 children. (BA, 20 July 1816)

COWARD, Capt. Thomas, Jr., and Mrs. Elizabeth Dashiell, all of Balto., were married last Wed. eve. by Rev. Dr. Sayer. (BFG, 23 Feb. 1810)

COWDEN, Robert, and Jane Donnell, were married 19th inst. by Rev. Glendy. (BEP, 27 Dec. 1810)

COWOOD (sic), Stephen, aged 70, and Miss Jennie Haydon, aged 15, both of near Chaptico, were married last week. (BFG, 21 Dec. 1798)

COX, Mr., and Miss Wilson, were lately married in Harf. Co. by Rev. Mr. Wilmer. (BFG, 4 Jan. 1803)

COX, James, and Miss Catherine Fulford were married last eve. by Rev. Bend. (BFG, 9 Dec. 1796)

COX, Joseph, of Marietta, and Miss Christy Gould, of Balto. Co., were married last Thurs. eve. by Rev. Kurtz. (BT, 22 Oct. 1802)

COX, Larkin, and Miss Jane Hardenbrook, both of Balto., were married last Thurs. by Rev. Lewis Richards. (BFG, 13 May 1811)

COX, Luther I., of Balto., and Miss Maria C. Keener, dau. of Christian Keener, of Balto. Co., were married last eve. by Rev. Hanson. (BFG, 25 Feb. 1814)

COX, Peter, merchant, and Mrs. Margaret Minchin, all of Balto., were married last Sun. by Bishop Carroll. (BFG, 3 Feb. 1807)

COX, Samuel C., of Md., and Miss Eliza Truxton, dau. of Capt. Thomas Truxton, were married 22nd inst., at Phila., by Bishop White. (BFG, 27 Dec. 1798)

COXE, Mrs. Catherine, late consort of James Coxe, died last Sun.; interment in St. Pauls Burial Ground. (BFG, 12 Feb. 1799)

COZINE, Peter, and Miss Elizabeth Augustus, both of Balto., were married last Thurs. eve. by Rev. Mr. Otterbine. (BFG, 17 April 1801)

CRABB, Brig.-Gen. Jeremiah, died at his seat, Ashley Farm, in Mont. Co., on 18th ult., leaving a widow and seven children. (BFG, 24 March 1800)

CRACKLOW, Nathaniel, and Miss Catherine Howard were married last Thurs. by Rev. Glendy. (BT, 3 Dec. 1805)

CRADDICK, Joseph N., and Catherine Williamson, all of Balto., were married last Tues. eve. by Rev. Mr. Duncan. (BA, 2 Nov. 1815)

CRAFT, Abner, merchant, died yesterday in his 23rd year. (BFG, 9 Oct. 1797)

CRAGGS, George, and Elizabeth Stansbury, were married 3 Dec. by Rev. Glendy. (BA, 10 Dec. 1816)

CRAGGS, John, died at Hammond's Ferry, on 20th inst., an old citizen of this state. (BFG, 25 Nov. 1805)

CRAGGS, John, and Miss Fanny Westberry, all of Balto., were wed last Thurs. by Rev. Glendy. (BA, 11 Nov. 1809)

CRAGGS, Mrs. Mary, died Sat., 5th Aug., at Hammonds Ferry, in her 67th year. (BFG, 14 Aug. 1815)

CRAIG, William, and Miss Betty Gibbons, both of Balto., were wed last Thurs. (BPE, 23 Oct. 1813)

CRAIK, George W., late postmaster, died last Wed. at his farm near Alexandria. (BEP, 2 Jan. 1809)

CRAIK, William, late a member of Congress, died last Mon. at Alexandria. (BFG, 12 Feb. 1807)

CRALL, Jacob, of Balto., and Miss Mary Statzell, of the Northern Liberties, were married at Phila. last Tues. eve. by Rev. Dr. Helmuth. (BT, 25 Nov. 1803)

CRAMES?, Nathaniel, and Miss Barbara Harkins, were married 19th inst. by Rev. Glendy. (BA, 6 March 1810)

CRANE, Joseph S., and Catherine Sopp, both of Balto., were wed by Rev. Kurtz. (BW, 27 Oct. 1808)

CRAVE, the Earl of, and Miss Brinton, sister of Mrs. Warren of the Baltimore Theatre, were married recently in Brighton. (BFG, 27 Feb. 1808)

CRAVER, Nathaniel, and Mrs. Barbara Haskins, both of Balto., were married 19th inst., by Rev. Glendy. (BW, 22 Feb. 1810)

CRAWFORD, James, of Phila., merchant, died at that city, 19th inst. (BFR, 21 Sept. 1810)

CRAWFORD, Dr. John. M. D., Right Worshipful Grand Master of the Masons of Md., died yesterday in his 68th year. (BFG, 10 May 1813)

CRAWFORD, Thomas S., son of Dr. Crawford of Balto., died at Montpelier, France on 11 May, while studying medicine at the university there. (BFG, 9 Aug. 1803)

CRAWFORD, William B., Balto. merchant, and Miss Elizabeth Cook, dau. of Alexander Cook of Phila., were married in the latter place last Tues. by Rev. Robert Roberts. (BPE, 11 Dec. 1813)

CREAMER, Joshua, and Miss Margaret Smith, both of Balto., were married last Thurs. eve. by Rev. Birch. (BFG, 31 July 1810)

CREERY, John, and Miss Welthe Ann Crabbin, all of Balto., were married last Thurs. by Rev. Dashiell. (BFG, 11 June 1807)

CREERY, Jonathan, and Miss Margaret Duncan, all of Balto., were married last Thurs. (17 Feb.) by Rev. Dashiell. (BFG, 9 Feb. 1811)

CREIGHTON, John, and Ann M 'Colley, both of Balto., were wed last eve. by Rev. Glendy. (BA, 3 Oct. 1806)

CREIGHTON, Capt. William, and Minny Weary, both of Fells Point, were married last eve. by Rev. Bend. (BT, 22 Aug. 1800)

CRESAP, Mrs. Sarah, wife of Joseph Cresap, of Allegany Co., Md., died 16th ult., in her 54th year, a member of the Meth. Ep. church for 30 years. (BFR, 1 April 1812)

CRESSWELL, John, and Miss Mary Ninde, were married last eve. by Rev. Rattoone. (BFG, 21 April 1808)

CRIDER, Benjamin, and Miss Elizabeth Lyon, all of Balto., were married last Fri. by Rev. Glendy. BA, 16 July 1816)

CRIDER, Mrs. Elizabeth, died at Fort McHenry, aged 21 years. (BA, 18 Sept. 1816)

CROCKER, Bernard, and Miss Elizabeth Taylor, all of Balto., were married Sun. eve. by Bartow. (BFG, 9 Jan. 1816)

CROCKET, George, merchant of Gallatin, Tenn., and Miss Mary Fulton, dau. of David Fulton, of Balto., were wed last Thurs. by Rev. Inglis. (BT, 25 April 1815)

CROMER, John, of Balto., and Mary Elizabeth Magaurin, dau. of Edward Magaurin, of Carlisle, were married on Thurs., 11th inst. by Rev. Dr. Campbell. (BT, 18 Sept. 1806)

CROMWELL, Mrs. Elizabeth, died Sat., 13th inst., aged 71 years, native of Md.; interment in the Meth. burying ground. Her husband William Cromwell died the ev. of her interment. (BFG, 19 Feb. 1802)

CROMWELL, George, and Miss Mercy Pitcher, of A. A. Co., were wed Thurs. eve. at Curtis Creek, by Rev. Parker. (BEP, 1 March 1806)

CROMWELL, Jacob, and Miss Ellen Greenfield, both of Balto., were married last Sun. by Rev. Roberts. (BT, 23 Sept. 1806)

CROMWELL, Nathaniel, Jr., and Miss Susannah Walker, dau. of Charles Walker, of Balto. Co., were married last Tues. by Rev. Butler. (BT, 19 Jan. 1799)

CROMWELL, Richard, died last Sat. in Annapolis, member of the House of Delegates from Wash. Co. His remains were interred the following day. He leaves a widow and a large family of children. "Annap., Dec. 30." (BFG, 4 Jan. 1803)

CROMWELL, Richard, died 25 Aug., in his 53rd year, at his res. on Patapsco. (BFG, 27 Aug. 1804)

CROMWELL, Thomas, and Miss Deborah White, all of Balto., were married last Thurs. by Rev. Birch. (BFR, 28 April 1810)

CROOK, Capt. Alexander, died this morning in his 33rd year; funeral from his late res. on Briton St., Old Town. (BFG, 2 Sept. 1813)

CROOK, Charles merchant, and Miss Charlotte Sellman, eld. dau. of Johnzee Sellman, all of Balto., were married last eve. by Rev. Bend. (BFG, 19 Dec. 1804)

CROSBY, Josiah, of Balto., died of the prevailing sickness at New
  Orleans, in his 22nd year. (BFG, 12 Oct. 1804)

CROSDALE, George, and Harriott Gibson, dau. of William Gibson,
  Esq., were married at Rose Hill by Rev. Bend. (BFG, 26
  Nov. 1806)

CROSGROVE, Levi W., and Mrs. Ann Maxwell, all of Balto., were
  married last eve. by Rev. Hagerty. (BFG, 18 Oct. 1805)

CROSS, Andrew, of the House of Andrew and John Cross & Co., died
  Sat., 23rd inst., aged 43 years. He leaves a wife and two
  children. (BA, 26 Sept. 1815)

CROSS, James, and Margaret Meek, were married 5th inst., at
  Charleston. (BFG, 21 Jan. 1802)

CROSS, John, and Miss Sarah Booth, both of Balto., were married
  last Sun. by Rev. Richards. (BA, 7 Oct. 1813)

CROUCH, Samuel M'Gowan, died yesterday in his 24th year. (BFG,
  13 April 1815)

CROUT, John, and Miss Fetterling, were married by the Rev. Mr.
  Green. (BEP, 20 May 1811)

CROW, James B., merchant of the firm of Aldridge & Crow, died at
  sea, of a pulmonary complaint, on a voyage from Lisbon to
  Madeira. He leaves a widow and two small children, one of
  whom, Jane R. Crow, died 2 Dec., having survived him but
  a few days. (BFG. 12 Feb. 1812)

CROW, Richard B., and Miss Rebecca Garrett, all of Balto., were
  married last Tues. by Rev. Duncan. (BA, 4 Jan. 1816)

CROW, William, for many years an inhab. of Fells Point, died
  last Sat. in his 49th year. (BFG, 28 Aug. 1806)

CROWL, Henry, of Balto., and Miss Mary Hiss of Balto. Co., were
  married last Tues. eve. by Rev. Shin. (BA, 2 Oct. 1809)

CROWL, Mrs. Mary, wife of H. Crowl, of Balto., died 13th inst.,
  in her 24th year, leaving a husband and three children.
  (BEP, 19 Dec. 1808)

CROXALL, Mrs. Eleanor, died 14th inst., at her seat in Balto. Co.,
  in her 75th year. (BFG, 16 Feb. 1805)

CROXALL, James, died Sat., aged 58. (BFG, 24 July 1809)

CROXALL, Thomas, died yesterday in his 39th year. (BFG, 28 Oct.
  1802)

CRUIKSHANK, Joseph, printer, and Rachel Saunders, dau. of Joseph
  Saunders, late of Balto., were married last Wed., at the
  Friends Meeting House in Pine Street. (BMJ, 16 Jan. 1797)

CRUMP, Alfred, and Miss Margaret Waters, dau. of Peter Waters,
  all of Peter Waters, were married last eve. by Rev. Mertz.
  (BFG, 7 Aug. 1816)

CRUSE, Christopher, and Miss Margaretta Bricker, both of Balto.,
  were married last Sun. eve. by Rev. Otterbein. (BT, 30
  July 1799)

CRUSE, Henry, died yesterday morning. (BA, 23 Nov. 1810)

CRUSE, Jacob, Balto. grocer, died last Sat., aged 36, leaving a
widow and three children; interment in the German Ref.
burying ground, Howard's Hill (BFG, 22 April 1799)

CRUSE, Mrs. Rosina, wife of Christopher Cruse, died yesterday,
in her 62nd year; interment in the German Ref. burying
ground, Howard's Hill. (BFG, 28 June 1799)

CUDDY, Rev. Michael, of St. Patrick's R. C. Church, died 5th inst.
in the 2nd year of his priesthood and the 29th year of his
age. (BFG, 6 Oct. 1804)

CULLIDEN, George, native of Ireland, res. of Balto. for 20 years,
died last Sat., aged 60 years; funeral from his late res.
in Harrison St. (BT, 9 Jan. 1815)

CULVERWELL, Stephen, and Miss Griffith, both of Balto., were wed
last Wed., by Rev. Roberts. (BA, 30 Oct. 1801)

CUMMING, John, and Elizabeth Webb were married 11th inst. by
Rev. Glendy. (BFG, 19 Nov. 1813)

CUMMING, Mrs. Mary, wife of William Cumming, merchant of Petersburg, Va., died last Fri. at the house of Alexander Brown
of Balto., in her 24th year. (BFG, 1 May 1815)

CUMMINGS, Thomas, Balto. grocer, and Miss Polly Maxfield of Kent
Co., were married last Sun. (BA, 11 July 1800)

CUMMINS, William, died last Sat.; interment in the Meth. burying
ground. (BT, 10 July 1797)

CUNNINGHAM, Patrick, and Mrs. Ann Morrow, were married. (BA, 26
Aug. 1809)

CUNNINGHAM, Capt. Thomas, and Miss Ann Harrison, both of Fells
Point, were married Thurs. by Rev. Bend. (BFG, 17 Jan.
1801)

CURLEY, James, and Miss Barbara Roach, all of Balto., were married
last eve. by Rev. Hagerty. (BFG, 20 Jan. 1809)

CURLIT, John, and Miss Ann Rusk, both of Balto., were married
last Thurs. eve. by Rev. Kurtz. (BW, 4 April 1812)

CURRAN, Barney, merchant, of Annapolis, died Tues. (BA, 25 Dec.
1816)

CURRAN, Michael, Annapolis merchant, died 3rd inst., after falling
from his horse; leaving a widow and one child. (BEP, 10
Nov. 1808)

CURSON, Richard, an old inhab. of Balto., died Monday night aged
80. (BFG, 10 July 1805)

CURSON, Richard, Jr., died 14th June, in his 45th year, in Balto.; a husband and a father. (BFG, 23 June 1808)

CURTAIN, Thomas, of Fells Point, and Miss Jane Graves were married
Fri. by Rev. Richards. (BWM, 26 Feb. 1797)

CURTAN, Miss Sally, died 2nd inst., in her 22nd year, dau. of
James Curtan of Fells Point; interment in the New English
burying ground. (BT, 5 Nov. 1800)

CURTIN, James, died last Thurs. at Fells Point, aged 67; the funeral sermon will be preached at Christ Church by Rev. Bend. (BFG, 9 Oct. 1802)

CURTIS, Capt. Jacob, of Conn., and Elizabeth Deagan, were wed on Thurs. eve. by Dr. Allison. (BA, 15 Feb. 1800)

CUSHMAN, Isaac, and Miys Margaret Cafrin, were married by Rev. Glendy on Sat. (BPEA, 20 Nov. 1815)

CUSTIS, George Washington Parke, and Miss Molly Fitzhugh of Alexandria, were married at that place on Sat. by Rev. Thomas Davis. (BFG, 14 July 1804)

CUTHBERT, James L., merchant, and Miss Frances E. Lowerslyer, all of Phila., were married on Sat. by Bishop White. (BA, 6 Dec. 1804)

CUYLER, William Howe, and Miss Eleanor Shekell, dau. of Samuel Shekell, late of P. G. Co., were married Fri., 11th ult., at Bellair, Ontario Co., N. Y. (BFG, 14 April 1803)

DAFFT, Edward, and Miss Margaret Cunningham, both of Balto., were married last eve. by Rev. Rattoone. (BFG, 19 Dec. 1805)

DAIL, Daniel, and Miss Elizabeth Block, all of Balto., were wed on last Thurs. by Rev. Wiat. (BMG, 10 July 1815)

DAILY, Peter, of Norfolk, and Mrs. Elizabeth Savington of Balto., were married last eve. by Rev. M'Kean. (BFG, 18 Nov. 1801)

DAKIN, James, died suddenly at Barton, aged 35. (BA, 22 Jan. 1800)

DALEY, Peter, and Miss Elizabeth Daley, both of Balto., were wed 8th inst. by Rev. Dr. Rattoone. (BFG, 22 April 1806)

DALEY, Peter, formerly of Dublin, died Tues., 9th inst. (BT, 15 Sept. 1806)

DALL, James, and Mrs. Eleanor Laming, both of Balto., were wed Thurs. eve. by Rev. Bend. (BFG, 19 Feb. 1803)

DALL, James, merchant, died 18 Sept., in his 54th year, at his country seat, Catalpa Hill. (BFG, 20 Sept. 1808)

DALL, Mrs. Sarah, wife of James Dall of Balto., and dau. of John R. Holliday of Balto. Co., died Sun., aged 25; leaving children. (BT, 14 May 1799)

DALLAM, Francis J., and Mrs. Sarah P. Phillips, were married last Thurs. at Dr. William Dallam's, Harf. Co., by Rev. Mr. Hammond. (BA, 9 March 1815)

DALLAM, Josias W., Esq., of Harf. Co., and Henrietta Jones, dau. of Hon. Thomas Jones of Balto. Co., were married last eve. by Rev. Mansfield. (BFG, 16 Jan. 1800)

DALLAM, William, and Sarah Webster, both of Balto., were married at Friends Meeting House for the Western District on 25th inst. (BFG, 30 March 1813)

DALRYMPLE, William, of William, and Mary S. Augustine, all of Balto., were married 4 June by Rev. Hoffman. (BA, 7 June 1816)

DALRYMPLE, William P., of Balto., and Miss Eleanora Clagett, dau. of Alexander Clagett of Hagerstown, were wed at the latter place last Thurs. by Rev. Jackson. (BFG, 13 Nov. 1816)

DALTON, Margaret, died Thurs., 10th inst., at the house of Charles Magillin in Derry Twp., Mifflin Co., Penna. Born at Newton Steward, Co. Tyrone, Ireland, she claimed to be 116 years, 8 mos., 10 days; she never married. (Long obit.) (BFG, 30 Oct. 1805)

DALY, Elizabeth, died. (BFG, 10 Aug. 1802)

DALY, Jacob, and Miss Elizabeth Pocock, both of Balto., were wed by Rev. M'Combs. (BFG, 17 Sept. 1802)

DALY, William, and Miss Elizabeth Fenby, both of Balto., were married last eve. by Rev. McCane. (BFG, 8 Jan. 1812)

DAME, Richard U., cabinet maker, died Thurs., 16th inst.; native of Augusta, Ga., late a res. of Balto. (BPEA, 20 Nov. 1815)

DAMPSEY, John, and Mrs. Elizabeth Wiley, were married last Sun. by Rev. Moranville. (BA, 26 Oct. 1813)

DANDRIDGE, Adam Stephen, and Miss Sally Pendleton, both of Martinsburg, Va., were married there the 1st day of the present year. (BFG, 8 Jan. 1805)

DANIEL, Mrs. Margaret, consort of John M. Daniel, and eld. dau. of the late Hon. Thomas Stone, of Md., died Thurs., 9th inst., at her res. in Falmouth, Va. leaving a husband and six small children. (BFG, 16 March 1809)

DANIELS, Capt. Anthony, died yesterday, long an inhab. of Fells Point. (BFG, 17 March 1803)

DANIELSON, Richard, and Miss Eleanor Miller, both of A. A. Co., were married last eve. by Rev. Ridgely. (BA, 29 April 1808)

DANNAMAN, C. H., and Miss Olivia Sophia Yeiser, both of Balto., were married last Wed. by Rev. Kurtz. (BA, 27 Nov. 1812)

DANNEMANN, Mrs. Olivia Sophia, wife of Mr. C. A. Dannemann of Balto., died Mon., aged 26 years. (BFG, 15 May 1816)

DANNENBERG, Mrs. Dorothy, died yesterday, aged 33, wife of Mr. Dannenberg. Her father, A. Konig, died three weeks ago. She leaves her husband and an infant dau. (BFG, 30 Dec. 1800)

DARBY, John B., and Miss Harriot Milbourne of the New Theatre, were married last Sun. by Rev. Hargrove. (BFG, 22 Jan. 1799)

DARCOURT, Francis L., and Mrs. Ann G. Renaudet, both of Balto., were married. (BT, 25 Jan. 1803)

DARDEN, Stephen, died 9th inst., aged 61 years, the father of 27 children. "Easton, April 16." (BFR, 22 April 1811)

DARE, Ephraim, and Miss Mary Hay, both of Balto., were wed last eve. by Rev. Kurtz. (BA, 24 March 1808)

DARE, Jacob, merchant of Balto., and Miss Eliza Geiger of Lancaster, Penna., were married last Sun. by Rev. Hoffmyer. (BFG, 7 Sept. 1809)

DARE, Mrs. Jane, wife of Jeremiah Dare, formerly of Balto., died 14 Jan. at Marietta, in her 27th year, leaving numerous small children to mourn her. (BW, 3 Feb. 1812)

DARE, Mrs. Jane, wife of Nathaniel Dare, now a res. of Balto., but formerly of Calvert Co., died 15th inst. in her 73rd year, leaving a husband and ten children. (BFG, 20 Jan. 1813)

DARE, Thomas C., of Calvert Co., and Eliza Snowden of Balto., were married yesterday at Friends Meeting. (BFG, 20 May 1803)

DARRELL, Capt. Sampson, and Miss Mary Anne Ganteaume, both of Fells Point, were married last Thurs. eve. by Rev. Moranville. (BA, 27 Nov. 1815)

DASHIELD, Capt. Benjamin, died Sun. at Fells Point. (BT, 1 Oct. 1799)

DASHIELL, Rev. Alfred H., and Miss Ann Ridgely, dau. of Richard Ridgely of Elk Ridge, were married at the latter place on Thurs., 26th ult., by Rev. Thomas Horrell. (BFG, 1 Nov. 1815)

DASHIELL, Capt. Henry, and Miss Mary Leeke, dau. of Nicholas Leeke of Fells Point, were married last Thurs. by Rev. Ireland. (BFG, 26 Jan. 1799)

DASHIELL, Cp. Levin, and Miss Elizabeth Snyder, all of Balto., were married Wed. eve. by Rev. Mr. Healy. (BAP, 14 July 1803)

DASHIELL, Thomas B., of Washington, and Miss Mary B. Beall of P. G. Co., were married by Rev. Burch on 5 Nov. (BA, 14 Nov. 1816)

DASHIELLS, Mrs. Mary Magdalen, died 17th inst., in her (64th?) year, long an inhab. of Balto. (BFG, 19 Sept. 1816)

DAUGHADAY, Dr. Johnsey, died Mon. at Fells Point. (BA, 6 Aug. 1800)

DAUGHADAY. Mrs. Rachel, widow of the late John Daughaday, of Balto., died Tues. in her 64th year. (BFG, 19 Jan. 1804)

DAUGHERTY, John, died yesterday; funeral from his late res. next door to Chase's Auction Rooms, South Frederick Street. (BA, 10 Sept. 1813)

DAUGHERTY, John, and Miss H. Young, were married last eve. by Archbishop Carroll. (BFG, 31 Oct. 1810)

DAVEY, Capt. Hugh, and Miss Elizabeth Weary, both of Fells Point, were married last eve. by Rev. Glendy. (BA, 4 March 1808)

DAVID, Davidson, died 26th inst. at Elkton; one of the Council of Md. (BFG, 30 July 1804)

DAVIDS, John, and Miss Rachel Bateman, were married last eve. by Rev. Dr. Roberts. (BFG, 17 May 1811)

DAVIDS, Walter C., printer, of Phila., and Elizabeth Harper of
Md., were married at the former place, on Wed. (BA, 15
Sept. 1804)

DAVIDSON, Alexander Tucker, and Mrs. Elizabeth Hilman, were wed
last eve. by Rev. Rattoone. (BFG, 11 Sept. 1804)

DAVIDSON, Charles, Esq., of Balto., and Miss Ann Dyce, dau. of
Alexander Dyce, merchant of Aberdeen, were married at
Rosebank, near Aberdeen, Scotland. (BFG, 11 Oct. 1802)

DAVIDSON, Daniel, and Miss Sarah McCormick, both of Balto., were
married last eve. by Rev. Sinclair. (BT, 10 Feb. 1802)

DAVIDSON, George, Balto. merchant, and Miss Catherine Thomas,
eld. dau. of Philip Thomas, Esq., were married last Tues.
by Rev. Rattoone, at Rockland, near Havre de Grace. (BFG,
4 May 1804)

DAVIDSON, James, of Balto., died Sun., 21 Sept. aged 57; funeral
sermon will be preached at Christ Church. (BFG, 4 Oct.
1806)

DAVIDSON, James, Jr., and Miss Mary Higinbothom of Balto. were
married last eve. at Daniel Delozier's, by Dr. Bend.
(BFG, 6 Nov. 1807)

DAVIDSON, James, and Fanny Fizzrand, both of Balto., were wed
last Thurs. eve. by Rev. Healey. (BFG, 16 Aug. 1808)

DAVIDSON, John, died yesterday in his 78th year. A native of
Ireland he had lived in Balto. only a short time. (BFG,
30 Aug. 1802)

DAVIDSON, Mrs. Margaret, wife of Rev. Dr. Davidson, of Carlisle,
died on Mon., 27th ult., in her 29th year. (BA, 8 April
1809)

DAVIDSON, Mrs. Mary, wife of James Davidson of the Office of Discount and Deposit of Washington, died Thurs., 16th inst.
at that city. (BFG, 20 Oct. 1806)

DAVIDSON, Samuel of Annap. and Polly Bird of Balto. were married
last Sat. by Rev. Bend. (BT, 27 Sept. 1805)

DAVIDSON, Samuel, died yesterday, aged 63; for many years an inhab. of Georgetown. "Georgetown, Aug. 1." (BFR, 3 Aug.
1810)

DAVIDSON, Samuel, of Balto., died at Annap. on 2nd inst. in his
39th year. (BFG, 4 Sept. 1816)

DAVIDSON, Capt. William, and Mary B. Gardner, dau. of Timothy
Gardner of Balto., were married last eve. by Rev. Glendy.
(BA, 25 Jan. 1805)

DAVIES, Mrs., relict of the late Rev. Jacob Davies, Presb. clergyman from the North of Ireland, died Sat., 22nd inst., in
her 74th year. (BA, 23 Aug. 1813)

DAVIES, John, of the house of Davies and Fulton, merchants of
Balto., died yesterday. (BFG, 9 Nov. 1798)

DAVIES, Samuel, and Sally, dau. of Rev. John Chalmers, were wed
last Thurs. by Rev. Hagerty. (BA, 24 Dec. 1805)

DAVIS, Capt., and Miss Amelia Travers, both of Balto., were wed last eve. by Rev. Rattoone. (BFG, 27 April 1805)

DAVIS, Capt., of Phila., and Miss Margaret Matilda Haley of St. M. Co. were married Sat., 13th inst., by Rev. Bowman. (BA, 22 Sept. 1810)

DAVIS, Amos, of Balto. Co., and Miss Elizabeth Fitz of Balto. were married Sat., 9th inst., by Rev. Lewis Richards. (BFG, 12 Jan. 1813)

DAVIS, Mrs. Anna M., consort of Gideon Davis of Washington, died 17th inst., in her 22nd year. (BPEA, 23 Nov. 1815)

DAVIS, Dr. Ashley, of Va., and Miss Eliza B. Dunant , dau. of Edward Dunant of Phila., were married 26th ult. at the latter place. (BFG, 1 May 1811)

DAVIS, Charles F., M. D., and Miss Eliza Stansbury of Balto. Co. were married last Thurs. by Rev. Mr. Healey. (BA, 3 June 1815)

DAVIS, Daniel, and Mrs. Rhodia Thomas (?) were married last eve. by Rev. Hargrove. (BFG, 18 March 1805)

DAVIS, David, and Miss Esther Evans, all of Balto., were wed last Thurs. eve. by Rev. Dr. Roberts. (BPE, 1 May 1813)

DAVIS, Gaither, and Miss Elizabeth Brumingham, were married on Thurs. eve. by Rev. Mr. Kurtz. (BFG, 8 Dec. 1800)

DAVIS, Gaither, died Thurs., 20th inst.; innkeeper; a veteran of '76; leaves a widow and 8 daus. (BEP, 22 July 1809)

DAVIS, Mr. Hughes, Alexandria merchant, and Mrs. Sarah Long of Balto. were married 2nd June by Rev. Glendy. (BA, 19 Aug. 1814)

DAVIS, Mr. John, and Miss Frances Armistead, all of Balto., were married last Thurs. by Rev. Wells. (BA, 21 May 1816)

DAVIS, John, of Abel, of the Navy Yard, and Miss Sarah Walker of Washington, were married in that city last Sun. by Rev. M'Cormick. (BT, 13 June 1805)

DAVIS, John, and Miss Rebecca Linsdid, both of Fells Point, were married Tues. eve. by Rev. M'Caine. (BW, 27 March 1812)

DAVIS, Luke, house carpenter of Balto., died at Chambersburg, Penna., at the house of Robert Peebles, 6th inst. (BFG, 18 Nov. 1815)

DAVIS, Miss Mary, died last Thurs. in A. A. Co. (BFG, 1 March 1804)

DAVIS, Mrs. Mary, wife of Moses Davis, of Richmond, Va., died at the Fountain Inn, Balto., last night. (BFG, 24 May 1811)

DAVIS, Mrs. Mary, wife of Dr. Elijah Davis, died at Belle Vue, Harf. Co., on 12th inst. (BPEA, 17 April 1815)

DAVIS, Capt. Robert, and Catherine Trenton, both of Balto., were married last eve. by Rev. Beeston. (BFG, 12 Feb. 1802)

DAVIS, Samuel, carpenter, and Miss Mary Baker, both of Balto., were married last eve. by Rev. Morrell. (BT, 3 Oct. 1799)

DAVIS, Samuel, and Miss Sarah Bond, both of Balto. Co., were wed at John Hambleton's last Thurs. by Rev. Fuller. (BT, 14 Jan. 1804)

DAVIS, Mrs. Sarah, wife of William S. Davis of Fells Point, died yesterday morning. (BEP, 23 March 1809)

DAVIS, Thomas, and Keziah Richards, both of Balto., were married Sun. by Rev. Rattoone. (BFG, 10 March 1807)

DAVIS, Thomas, of A. A. Co., and Miss Anne Davis of Balto. were married by Rev. Richardson on the 20th inst. (BEP, 28 Nov. 1810)

DAVISON, Daniel, and Miss Sarah M'Cormick, both of Balto., were married last night by Rev. Sinclair. (BFG, 19 Feb. 1802)

DAVISON, Capt. Richard, and Mrs. Elizabeth P. Marsh, all of Balto., were married last Sat. by Rev. John Glendy. (BEP, 4 May 1811)

DAVISON, Thomas, and Miss Isabella M'Kerlie, all of Balto., were married last eve. by Rev. Hargrove. (BFG, 26 May 1815)

DAWES, Mr., bricklayer, was found dead this morning lying in the mud at the head of Cheapside Dock. (BFG, 3 Jan. 1804)

DAWES, Edward Morgan, merchant, and Jane C. Linville, both of Balto., were married 11 April by Rev. Bartow. (BA, 17 April 1816)

DAWES, Mrs. Hetty, wife of James Dawes, died last Mon. in her 31st year. (BFG, 19 May 1813)

DAWES, James, and Miss Susan Lusby, both of Annap., were wed in that city on Thurs. eve. (BFG, 13 Oct. 1801)

DAWES, James, of Balto., and Miss Hetty Martin, of Snow Hill, were married last Sat. by Rev. Dashiell. (BFG, 9 Nov. 1807)

DAWES, James, late Cashier of the Franklin Bank of Balto., died Sun. in his 33rd year. (BFG, 14 March 1815)

DAWES, James Greenleaf, son of Judge Dawes of Boston, died in that city. The dec. was formerly of the House of Dawes & Hastings of Balto., and was one of the United Volunteers at North Point. (BMG, 25 July 1815)

DAWES, Mrs. Jane, wife of Edward Dawes of Balto., died last Sun. aged 18 years. (BFG, 10 Dec. 1816)

DAWSON, Mrs. Jane, wife of Capt. Philemon Dawson, died Thurs., 31 Aug., leaving a husband and a large family. (BFG, 2 Sept. 1815)

DAWSON, John, member of Congress from Va., died in Washington on Thurs., aged about 52 years. (BFG, 4 April 1814)

DAWSON, Capt. Philemon, died at sea 12 Aug., aged 56; on board the ship <u>Emily</u> from London, bound for Balto. (BFG, 20 Sept. 1816)

DAWSON, Thomas, and Miss Catherine Sumwalt, both of Balto., were married last Thurs. by Rev. Hagerty. (BFG, 8 March 1816)

DAY, Edward, and Miss Rebecca Joyce were married in A. A. Co. on last Thurs. by Rev. Ryland. (BA, 6 July 1805)

DAY, Israel, died yesterday; funeral from his late res., 23 Ann St., Fells Point. (BA, 9 Oct. 1812)

DAY, John Young, died at his res. opposite Joppa, Balto. Co., last Wed., in his 33rd year. (BFG, 12 Oct. 1805)

DAY, Miss Rebecca Young, died 1st inst., in her 19th year, leaving a mother and three brothers. (BFG, 2 Aug. 1813)

DAY, Dr. William Fell, of Gunpowder Forks, Balto. Co., died 20th inst., leaving a wife and several children. Rev. Wilmer will deliver a funeral oration at the seat of John Day, Esq., on Sun., 1st Feb. (BFG, 27 Jan. 1801)

DAYMAN, Jacob, died in Fred. Co., aged 94 years, 1 mo., and 30 days. (BFG, 1 Sept. 1806)

DAYTON, Major-Gen. Elias, died last Thurs. of the gout in the stomach in his 71st year, a venerable patriot of '76. A funeral sermon was preached Sat. in the Presb. Church by Rev. John McDowell. From Elizabeth-Town paper. (BFG, 7 Nov. 1807)

DEADY, Mr. Daniel, died last Tues., 1st inst., in his 51st year, for many years an inhab. of this place. (BFG, 4 Nov. 1803)

DEAGAN, Patrick, Balto. merchant, and Miss Polly M'Comas of Harf. Co., were married last eve. (BFG, 25 Oct. 1799)

DEAGEN, Henry, and Miss Charlotte Pierpoint, both of Balto., were married last eve. by Rev. Bend. (BT, 26 March 1799)

DEAGEN, Patrick, merchant, died 28 Feb. at his country res. near Balto. (BEP, 4 March 1808)

DEAGEN, Peter, died Sun., 30 Aug., aged 13, son of George Deagen. (BFG, 11 Sept. 1801)

DEAGLE, Capt. Simon, for thirty years commander of a line of packets from Norfolk to Baltimore, died 21 Aug., aged 53, leaving a wife and four children. (BFG, 24 Aug. 1812)

DEAKINS, Col. Francis, of Washington, died Sun., 28th inst., in his 67th year. (BFG, 1 Nov. 1804)

DEAKINS, William, Jr., died in Georgetown, 3rd inst.; for many years an eminent merchant of that place. (Long obit.) (BFG, 8 March 1798). He was in his 55th year. (Long obit.) (BFG, 9 March 1798)

DEAL, Christopher, died last Sun. eve., aged 54 years and 9 mos.; funeral from his late res., Market Space, Fells Point. (BS, 24 Nov. 1812)

DEALE, Mrs. Mary, consort of Capt. James Deale of Balto., died Wed., 25th inst. (BFG, 30 March 1812)

DEAN, Capt. Henry, and Miss Isabella Orr, both of Balto., were wed on Thurs. by Rev. Bartow. (BA, 27 Jan. 1816)

DEAVER, John, died Fri. eve. in his 55th year. (BFG, 2 Sept. 1813)

DEAVER, John T., son of John Deaver of Balto., died 7th inst. at Zanesville, Ohio, in his 23rd year, of pulmonary consumption. He had recently married and settled at Zanesville. (BFG, 22 Aug. 1810)

DE BENNEVILLE, Dr. George, Jr., died 7th inst. in his 24th year at his father's house in Phila. Co. (BEP, 17 March 1809)

DEBET, Cornelius, and Mrs. Ann Caswell were married on 25 Oct. by Rev. Glendy. (BFG, 7 Nov. 1807)

DE BLOCK, Francois, died Sat.; a native of Zealand of the United Provinces. He came to this country about 36 years ago. He leaves a widow. (BA, 4 Aug. 1801)

DE BUTTS, James, merchant, died last Wed.; of the House of McCormick and De Butts, of Balto. (BA, 4 Oct. 1799)

DE BUTTS, John, died Mon., 2nd inst., at Trent place, his seat on Patuxent River. (BFG, 7 May 1796)

DE BUTTS, Richard, and Miss Louisa Dulany, dau. of Benjamin Dulany were married 18th inst. at Shuter's Mill, Fairfax Co., Va., by Rev. Dr. Muir. (BFR, 29 April 1812)

DE CARNAP, Jasper, died in Washington, on Thurs. morning on 12th inst. in his 40th year. (BFG, 20 Nov. 1801)

DECATUR, Capt. Stephen, and Susan, only dau. of Luke Wheeler, Mayor of Norfolk, were married last Sat. by Rev. Grigsby. (BA, 18 March 1806)

DECATUR, Capt. Stephen, died on Mon. at Frankfort near Phila. (BFG, 17 Nov. 1808)

DECHAND, Rev. William, and Miss Rebecca Andreee, were married on Tues. by Rev. Baker. (BW, 27 Oct. 1808)

DECKER, Frederick, died last Tues. in his 64th year; funeral from his late res., North Howard St. (BFG, 10 Oct. 1804)

DEEMS, Jacob, and Miss Susan Grub, both of Balto., were married last eve. by Rev. Kurtz. (BEP, 14 Aug. 1807)

DEEMS, Joshua, and Miss Mary Ann Payne, all of Balto., were married last eve. by Rev. Hargrove. (BFG, 12 May 1815)

DEEMS, Richard, and Mary Wolf, all of Balto., were married 2 July by Rev. Roberts. (BA, 3 July 1816)

DEGRAFF, Lewis, and Miss Elizabeth Lowman, all of Balto., were married last eve. by Rev. Hargrove. (BFG, 19 Oct. 1803)

DEGRAFF, Richard, died 9th inst.; long a respectable mechanic of Balto. (BPEA, 13 Feb. 1815)

DEGROFF, Richard, and Miss Ann Gooden, both of Balto., were wed last Thurs. by Rev. Dr. Roberts. (BW, 2 March 1811)

DE JONGH, Michael, and Miss Mary Hall, both of Balto., were wed last Thurs. by Rev. Glendy. (BW, 3 Feb. 1810)

DE KRAFFT, Charles, died at Washington, 24th inst., Surveyor and
draftsman of the Treasury Dept. (BA, 27 July 1804)

DELACOUR, David, and Balto. City, and Miss Elizabeth Patten of
Balto. Co. were married last Thurs. (BS, 11 Jan. 1812)

DELANEY, John William, died yesterday morning; merchant; formerly of New York City. (BFG, 22 Nov. 1800)

DELANY, Samuel, and Miss Margaret Mackenheimer, all of Balto.,
were married last Thurs. by Rev. Kurtz. (BPE, 9 Oct. 1813)

DELANY, Sharp, died lately at Phila.; formerly member of the
state assembly, and for many years collector customs of
the port. (BFG, 18 May 1799)

DELAPORTE, Elizabeth H., widow of Frederick Delaporte, died 27
July in her 68th year at her seat in Harf. Co. Her husband had been a French merchant in Balto. (BFG, 2 Aug. 1803)

DELAPORTE, Frederick, Esq., died 2nd inst., at his estate in
Harf. Co., in his 55th year; for many years a respectable
merchant in Balto., leaving a widow. (BFG, 9 Feb. 1797)

DE LA ROCHE, George F., and Miss Anna Maria McNulty, of Balto.,
were married last Sat. by Rev. Dr. Inglis. (BA, 27 March 1816)

DELCHER, John, and Miss Eliza Kelley, both of Balto., were wed
last Thurs. eve. by Rev. Fry. (BPE, 3 April 1813)

DELCHER, William, and Miss Sally Williams, both of Balto., were
married last Sun. eve. by Rev. Healey. (BA, 10 Jan. 1812)

DELEHAY, William, and Mrs. Jane Amos, all of Balto., were wed
last eve. by Rev. Hargrove. (BFG, 5 April 1811)

DELISLE, Dr. F. G., and Miss Elizabeth Waren DelaRoche, both of
Balto., were married last Sat. by Rev. Bean. (BFG, 8 May 1797)

DELOZIER, Daniel, late surveyor of the port of Balto., died last
Sat. at his res. in the Western Precincts in his 53rd
year. (BFG, 8 Nov. 1813)

DELUCE, Mr. F., a res. of Balto., died last Wed. (BT, 4 Feb. 1803)

DEMANGIN, Charles, and Miss Elizabeth Caldwell, all of Balto.,
were married last Thurs. by Rev. Inglis. (BPE, 31 Jan. 1815)

DEMING, John, died in his 76th year. (BMJ, 3 May 1797)

DEMMITT, Mr. Burch, deposit clerk in the office of Discount and
Deposit, died last night; funeral from his late dwelling
5 North Gay. (BFG, 1 Aug. 1799)

DEMMITT, Elisha, and Miss Delilah Jessop of Gunpowder Forest
were married yesterday afternoon by Rev. Mr. Hargrove.
(BFG, 12 Dec. 1798)

DE MONTALIBOR, Grippiere, died last Sun., aged 72, formerly of
the Island of Santo Domingo. (BA, 9 Dec. 1807)

DEMPSEY, John, and Miss Rebecca Gibson, all of Balto., were married last eve. by Rev. Richards. (BA, 17 Dec. 1805)

DENISON, Mrs. Anne, died last eve., in her 32nd year, wife of John M. Denison. (BFG, 6 Nov. 1797)

DENISON, Mrs. D., wife of Edward Denison of Balto., died 31st ult., aged 23 years and 11 mos. (BFG, 7 May 1807)

DENISON, Edward, and Deborah, dau. of Joseph Thornburgh, were wed 20th inst. by Dr. Bend. (BFG, 21 Feb. 1806)

DENISON, Edward, and Miss Elizabeth Wilson both of Balto. were married 26th ult. by Rev. Inglis. (BFG, 3 Dec. 1812)

DENISON, John M., merchant, died last Sun., aged 51. (BFG, 10 Aug. 1813)

DENNIE, Joseph, editor of the Port Folio, died 7th inst., at Phila., in his 45th year. (BFG, 10 Jan. 1812)

DENNIS, John, of Som. Co., Md., died at Phila. aged 34 last Sun.; Member of the House of Rep. (BFG, 20 Aug. 1806)

DENNIS, John W., son of Littleton Dennis, Sr., and Miss Elizabeth Dashiell, dau. of Benjamin Dashiell, all of Som. Co., Md., were married Wed., 14th July, by Rev. Wm. M. Stone. (BFG, 27 July 1813)

DENNISON, Richard, and Miss Jemima Parks, both of Fells Point, were married last Tues. eve. by Rev. Webb. (BA, 11 Jan. 1816)

DENNISTON, Mr. David, founder of the American Citizen, and late partner of the present editor, died last Thurs. of an inflammation of the lungs. (BFG, 20 Dec. 1803)

DENNY, Capt. Robert, Auditor General of the State and Auditor of the Court of Chancery, died Sat., 23rd inst., in his 65th year. A soldier of the Rev., he was Secretary of the Cincinatti. (BA, 2 Nov. 1812)

DENOS, Augustine Rouxelin, Chevalier of the Order of St. Louis, died 7th inst. at the house of his son-in-law, Mr. De Caindry, near this city, in his 65th year. He was a captain in the Saintonge Regiment, and served under Gen. Rochambeau at the siege and taking of York. He leaves a widow and two children. (BFG, 16 Jan. 1806)

DENT, George, died last eve., Balto. merchant; funeral from his late res., Bank St. (BFG, 3 Oct. 1798)

DENYS, James, died Thurs., 18th inst., when he fell from the roof of a house, leaving a father, wife and four children. (BFG, 25 Aug. 1814)

DE RONSERAY, Charles, and Miss Margaret Donnelly, were married last Tues. by Rev. Moranville. (BA, 18 April 1816)

DERRICK, Capt. William of Fells Point, died last Fri. aged 28. (BA, 5 June 1816)

DERRICKSON, Kendal, and Miss Rebecca Biddle, both of Newcastle Co., Del., were married 14th inst., by Rev. Henry L. Davis of Sassafras Neck, Cecil Co. (BEP, 24 Feb. 1806)

DERRS, Daniel, and Mrs. Rhodia Thomas, all of Balto., were wed Sun. eve. by Rev. Hargrove. (BT, 19 March 1805)

DESHIELDS, Capt. Joseph, of Balto., and Miss Mary Martin of Alexandria, were married 30th ult. at the latter place, by Rev. James Griffin of the R. C. Church. (BFG, 14 Dec. 1798)

DESHON, James, and Miss Ann Roache, all of Balto., were married Tues. by Rev. Hargrove. (BFG, 19 Sept. 1816)

DESHON, Capt. John, and Mrs. Elizabeth Ray, both of Balto., were married last Thurs. by Rev. Beeston. (BFG, 13 June 1801)

DE SOUCHE, Mrs. Rose Xousse, native of St. Domingo, died, an aged lady. (BFG, 17 Nov. 1801)

DESPEAUX, Elie, and Miss Eliza Harwood, all of Balto., were married last eve. by Rev. Hargrove. (BFG, 8 Oct. 1813)

DESPEAUX, Mrs. Rachel, died 18th inst., leaving a husband and one child. (BFG, 22 March 1816)

DE TILLY, Count Joseph Alexander, and Maria Matilda Bingham, were married at Phila. on last Wed. night by Rev. Dr. Jones, minister of the Universal Church of that city. (BFG, 15 April 1799)

DEVER, Major Henry, died Wed., 3rd inst., in A. A. Co., in his 39th year. (BFG, 5 April 1815)

DEVEREUX, William, clerk in the Balto. Custom House, died last Sat. (BFG, 25 Oct. 1802)

DEVILBISS, Charles, and Miss Elizabeth Stevens, all of Fred. Co., were married last eve. by Rev. Nelson. (BEP, 8 Jan. 1811) (BA, 9 Jan. 1811 gives the bride's name as Stevenson.)

DEVON, Frederick, and Miss Mary Romney, all of Balto., were wed Thurs., 23rd inst., by Rev. Roberts. (BFG, 25 April 1812)

DEVOSS, William, and Miss Margaret Blunt, all of Balto., were married Sun., 22nd inst., by Rev. Dr. Roberts. (BEP, 23 July 1810)

DEW, Capt. Edward, and Miss Maria Gorsuch, all of Balto., were married last Thurs. by Rev. Glendy. (BFG, 1 Oct. 1813)

DEW, Frederick, and Miss Sarah Gorsuch, all of Balto., were wed last Tues. by Rev. Glendy. (BA, 10 Nov. 1815)

DEW, James C., Balto. merchant, and Henrietta Stansbury, dau. of Tobias E. Stansbury, of Balto. Co., were married last Tues. by Rev. Roberts. (BFG, 3 Oct. 1807)

DEW, Mrs. Mary, consort of Robert Dew, Sr., died yesterday in Balto. (BFG, 23 March 1802)

DEW, Robert, Sr., died last Thurs., aged 75. (BFG, 17 Nov. 1804)

DEW, William, and Miss Jane Long, dau. of Samuel L. Long, all of Balto., were married last eve. by Rev. Dr. Roberts. (BA, 12 May 1815)

DEWEY, Silas, and Mrs. Elizabeth Dowell, both of Balto., were wed last eve. by Rev. Inglis. (BW, 14 Sept. 1810)

DEWITT, Thomas, died yesterday, aged 68. (BA, 29 July 1807)

D'HAPPART, J. L., and Elizabeth, dau. of the late Gen. William
    Thompson, were married at Newcastle on Thurs., 24th inst.
    by Rev. Robert Clay. (BT, 30 April 1800)

DICKEHUT, George, and Miss Hannah Altherr, both of Balto., were
    married yesterday by Rev. Kurtz. (BFG, 31 July 1807)

DICKENSON, Mrs. Mary, died at Wilmington, on 23rd ult., aged
    63, wife of John Dickenson of that place. (BFG, 30 July
    1803)

DICKEY, John, and Mary Quirk, were married Sun. eve. at the Little
    Hotel, Washington, by Rev. George Ralph. (BT, 2 May 1796)

DICKEY, Robert, of New York, and Miss Ann Brown, dau. of Dr.
    Brown of Balto. were married Thurs. eve. by Rev. Inglis.
    (BFG, 20 March 1807)

DICKINS, Rev. John, of the Meth. Church, died at Phila., 26th
    inst., of yellow fever. His eldest dau., aged 15, died a
    few hours earlier. (BFG, 1 Oct. 1798)

DICKINSON, Capt. Brittingham, died Fri., 24th inst. at Fells Pt.,
    aged 74, leaving a widow and a dau. (BFG, 28 June 1808)

DICKINSON, Charles, formerly of Md., was killed in a duel by Gen.
    Andrew Jackson of Tenn. on 30 May. (BFG, 2 July 1806)

DICKINSON, John, died Sun. morning at Wilmington, Del.; author of
    tracts signed "A Pennsylvania Farmer." (BEP, 17 Feb. 1808)

DICKSON, Thomas, died yesterday morning, President of the Franklin Bank, and one of the judges of the Orphans Court.
    (BFG, 9 July 1810)

DICKSON, Thomas, of Balto., died Sun.; a native of Ireland, he
    migrated to this country at an early period of life. (BS,
    14 July 1810)

DICTER, Capt. John, and Miss Mary Ann Fitz Poe were married on
    Wed. by Rev. Dashiell. (BFG, 4 Feb. 1814)

DIDIER, Henry, Jr., and Miss Maria Gibson, were married last eve.
    at Rose Hill by Rev. Beasley. (BFG, 20 Nov. 1812)

DIDIER, William P., died Tues., 18th inst., in his 27th year.
    (BFG, 22 April 1815)

DIEHL, Mrs. Christian, wife of Charles Diehl, late of this county,
    died Fri., 5th inst., near Gettysburg, Penna., in her 63rd
    year. (BFG, 15 May 1809)

DIETZ, George, and Miss Rachel Clark, all of Balto., were married
    last Sun. eve. by Rev. Pitts. (BEP, 19 April 1811)

DIFFENDAL, John, and Miss Catherine Sheeler, both of Balto., were
    married last Tues. by Rev. Mr. Mertz. (BA, 27 Sept. 1811)

DIFFENDERFER, Charles, and Ann Millimon, were married 12 Dec. by
    Rev. Richards. (BA, 14 Dec. 1816)

DIFFENDERFER, John, of Balto. City, and Miss Catherine Rogers of
    Balto. Co., were married last eve. by Rev. Richards. (BEP,
    27 March 1807)

DIFFENDERFER, Michael, died yesterday in his 65th year; funeral
from his late res., No. 3, Market Space. (BFG, 10 April
1809)

DIFFENDERFER, Philip, died Sun., 15th inst., at Lancaster. (BFG,
25 Feb. 1806)

DIGGES, Mrs. Ann, died at Warburton, P. G. Co., 28th ult., in
her 53rd year. (BFG, 25 Jan. 1805)

DIGGS, Mr. Beverly, and Miss Martha Ross, all of Balto., were wed
last Thurs. by Rev. Roberts. (BA, 30 June 1810)

DILLON, James, and Miss Elizabeth Sinners, both of Balto., were
married last eve. by Rev. Richards. (BEP, 17 Jan. 1806)

DILLON, John, merchant, and Edith Hussey, of Balto., were married
last Sun. by Rev. Baxley. (BFG, 6 Oct. 1801)

DILLON, Capt. John, died last Sat., at his res. on Cedar Point in
his 45th year. (BT, 17 April 1804)

DIMMITT, James, and Elizabeth Ford, all of Balto., were married
on Thurs. by Rev. Glendy. (BA, 18 April 1807)

DINSMORE, Henry W., Balto. merchant, died last eve. in his 25th
year, leaving a widowed mother and three sisters. (BA, 4
July 1814)

DIPPLE, Michael, and Miss Betsy Bell, both of Balto., were wed
last Thurs. by Rev. Mr. M'Combs. (BT, 24 April 1802)

DIRICKSON, Mrs. Jane Bell, wife of Dr. James Dirickson, died at
Laurel Town, Del., on 21 Oct. Her twin children, Maden
Bell and Frederick Bell also died, aged 4 weeks. (BEP,
10 Nov. 1808)

DISNEY, James, and Miss Martha Sprigg, all of Balto., were wed
last eve. by Rev. Robert R. Roberts. (BFG, 18 May 1810)

DISNEY, John, and Miss Eliza Watts, all of Balto., were wed on
last Thurs. by Rev. Dr. Roberts. (BA, 21 Oct. 1815)

DISNEY, Mordecai, and Miss Sarah Tudor, all of Balto., were wed
last eve. by Rev. Ryland. (BFG, 14 May 1813)

DISNEY, William, Esq., and Mrs. Rosella Herman, all of Elk Ridge
were married Thurs., 8th inst., by Rev. Mr. Pumphrey. The
groom was 68 and the bride 53. (BFG, 16 Feb. 1810)

DITMORE, Jacob, and Miss Charlotte Barker, both of Balto., were
married last Sun. by Rev. Dr. Roberts. (BFR, 19 May 1812)

DIVERS, John, and Miss Charity Onion, were married Tues., 3rd
inst., in Harf. Co., by Rev. Mr. Richardson. (BFG, 11 Jan.
1804)

DIVEY, Samuel, and Hannah Connor, all of Balto., were married
last Mon. by Rev. Hargrove. (BFG, 28 May 1808)

DIXON, Benjamin, of Balto., and Miss Matilda Smith (?) of Caroline
Co., were married last eve. by Rev. Dashiell. (BA, 27 Nov.
1804)

DIXON, Mrs. Eliza, wife of George Dixon and dau. of George Taylor
of Balto., died 21 inst. at York, Penna., in her 17th
year. (BA, 28 Oct. 1816)

DIXON, George, and Miss Eliza D. Taylor, dau. of George Taylor of Balto., were married 22nd inst. in York, Penna., by Rev. G. Hyde. (BFG, 25 Sept. 1816)

DIXON, Capt. John, printer of Richmond, died there on Wed., 24th inst. (BA, 29 May 1805)

DIXON, John, of Balto., and Miss Polly Douglass, late of Snow Hill, were married last eve. by Rev. Hagerty. (BA, 28 Jan. 1808)

DIXON, John, and Mrs. Elizabeth Dyer, were married last Sun. eve. by Rev. Glendy. (BEP, 26 April 1809)

DIXON, John, and Mrs. Collins were married last Thurs. eve. by Rev. Dashiells. (BW, 29 April 1811)

DIZARD, Miss Elizabeth, died 5th inst., in her 24th year. (BFG, 8 Dec. 1803)

DOBBIN, Archibald, Sr., died last Thurs. in his 72nd year, a native of Ireland. (BFG, 23 May 1808)

DOBBIN, George, and Miss Catherine Bose, all of Balto., were wed last eve. by Rev. Glendy. (BFG, 16 Sept. 1805)

DOBBIN, George, joint owner of the American, of the firm of Geo. Dobbin and Murphy, died this morning. (BFG, 3 Dec. 1811)

DOBBIN, Capt. Robert, and Hester Henderson, both of Balto., were married last eve. by Rev. Mr. Sinclair. (BA, 24 Oct. 1804)

DOBBIN, Thomas, printer and editor of the Telegraphe died. The journeymen printers agreed to wear crepe on their left arm for two months. (BFG, 15 Feb. 1808)

DOBBINS, Catherine, dau. of Catherine and the late George Dobbins, died 25 Dec. in her 6th year. (BA, 27 Dec. 1816)

DOBBINS, James H., midshipman, U. S. Navy, was blown off the yard-arm of the brig Swanwick , Capt. Owens, and died 23 March in his 22nd year. (BA, 18 June 1816)

DOBBINS, William, and Elizabeth Allan, both of Balto., were wed Sat. eve. by Rev. Roberts. (BFG, 8 Dec. 1806)

DOBEL, Dr. Benger, died 6th inst., leaving a wife to whom he had been married only a few months. (BT, 11 Oct. 1797)

DODD, Capt. John, of Balto., and Miss Isabel Tipton, of Chesnut Ridge, Balto. Co., were married last Thurs. eve. by Rev. Mr. Butler. (BFG, 9 March 1801)

DODDRELL, James C., of Balto., and Miss Sarah W. Coale, of Deer Creek, Harf. Co., were married at the latter place last Thurs. (BFG, 9 Sept. 1809)

DODGE, Capt. Samuel, a worthy of the Rev., died yesterday. For seven years he was at his post among "the embattled ranks of his country's defenders." (BFG, 13 July 1803)

DOLE, Robert M., and Sarah Donnally, were married by Rev. Dr. Rattoone. (BA, 8 Oct. 1806)

DONAHUE, Patrick, and Sarah Thornsbury, both of Balto., were wed last Sun. (BA, 26 Feb. 1806)

DONALDSON, Francis, died Sat. last in his 28th year. (BFG, 7 Feb. 1814)

DONALDSON, James Lowrey, and Miss Jane Stewart, dau. of Dr. Wm. Stewart, all of Balto., were married last eve. by Rev. Glendy. (BFG, 6 July 1804)

DONALDSON, James Lowrey, was killed in the late action near North Point, 12th inst.; a native of Ireland. He had lived in this country since he was 11 years old. He was the 3rd son of Col. William Lowry of Balto., but changed his name to comply with the wishes of a relative. A delegate to the General Assembly, he leaves a widow and 5 small children. He was Adjutant to the 27th Regt. (BFG, 24 Sept. 1814)

DONALDSON, John, of P. G. Co., and Miss Caroline Dorsey of Balto. were married Tues. eve. at the seat of Cle't Dorsey, Chas. Co., by Rev. Weems. (BFG, 21 Nov. 1812)

DONALDSON, John, of Balto., died at York, Penna., 6th inst. (BFG, 9 May 1815)

DONALDSON, Joseph, died 10 June at his res. in Hanover St. (BFG, 18 June 1799)

DONALDSON, Samuel I., Attorney-at-Law, and Miss Camilla A. Hammond, both of Balto., were married last eve. by Rev. Bend. (BFG, 9 Nov. 1808)

DONALDSON, Dr. William, and Miss Catherine Weatherburn, both of Balto., were married last eve. by Bishop Kemp. (BFG, 12 April 1815)

DONELLAN, Thomas, died Tues., (11 Sept.) in his 84th year, an inhabitant of Balto. for more than 40 years. (BFG, 14 Sept. 1810)

DONNELL, John, Balto. merchant, and Anna F. Smith, dau. of Isaac Smith, of Northampton, Va., were married in that place on Mon., 15th inst. (BFG, 25 Oct. 1798)

DONNELL, Joseph, died yesterday eve. at the house of his bro. John Donnell, merchant of Balto. (BFG, 12 Nov. 1798)

DONNELLY, Master Patrick, son of Hugh Donnelly, late from Ireland, died 10 Oct., scarcely 18 years old. (BEP, 11 Oct. 1808)

DONOHUE, James, and Miss Margaret Locke, both of Balto., were married last Tues. by Rev. John Healey. (BFG, 2 June 1802)

DONOVAN, John, of Balto., and Miss Sally E. Pattison, dau. of Major Thomas Pattison of Dor. Co., were married the latter place on 26th ult. by Mr. Seward. (BA, 3 June 1812)

DOP, George, died Mon., 29th inst,: funeral from his late res. near Mr. McCausland's Brewery. (BA, 31 March 1813)

DORAN, Thomas, died 3 July last, aged 40 years on his way from Natchez to his res. in Washington Co., Ky. (BFG, 16 April 1808)

DORNIN, Mrs., wife of Bernard Dornin, bookseller, died in North Howard St. (BA, 9 Aug. 1814)

DORSET, Col. Fielder, of P. G. Co., and Miss Amelia T. Beall of Washington, D. C., were married there on 2nd inst., by Rev. McCormick. (BPE, 5 Feb. 1813)

DORSEY, Mrs. Ann, wife of John Hammond Dorsey of Harf. Co., died last Mon.; funeral rites by Rev. Wilmer. (BFG, 9 June 1802)

DORSEY, Caleb, died last Wed. at Elk Ridge. (BFG, 15 Sept. 1798)

DORSEY, Edward, and Miss Elenor Pue, both of Elk Ridge were wed last Thurs. by Rev. Mr. Lyle. (BFG, 12 Dec. 1798)

DORSEY, Edward, of Caleb, died 24th ult. at his seat on Elk Ridge in his 41st year. (BFG, 22 April 1799)

DORSEY, Mrs. Elizabeth, died last eve. at her country seat in A. A. Co.; widow of Edward Dorsey. (BFG, 25 Aug. 1802)

DORSEY, Mrs. Elizabeth, relict of Col. Thomas Dorsey, died Wed., 1 March, at the farm of her dau., Mrs. Norwood, in her 76th year. (BFG, 4 March 1815)

DORSEY, Capt. Ely of Fredericksburg, and Araminta Cummins of A. A. Co., were married last 27 Jan. by Rev. Jones. (BA, 6 Feb. 1801)

DORSEY, Ely, Jr., Balto. merchant, and Miss Sarah Johnson of Fred. Co., Md., were married last Tues. by Rev. Chandler. (BFR, 22 Dec. 1810)

DORSEY, Greenbury, died Fri., 3rd inst.; of Harf. Co., aged 70. (BI, 16 April 1798)

DORSEY, Hammond, of Md., and Miss Elizabeth Pickering, dau. of Hon. Timothy Pickering, were married at Wenham by Rev. Dr. (Prince?) of Salem. (BFG, 20 Aug. 1816)

DORSEY, Henry K., and Miss Susan Hammond, both of Balto., were married last eve. by Rev. Sergent. (BFG, 22 Nov. 1805)

DORSEY, Dr. Hill, died at Thurs. at his seat near Balto., in his 24th year. Interment at Belmont, the res. of A. C. Hanson. (BFG, 10 May 1816)

DORSEY, Col. John, died 2nd inst. in his 76th year, at his res. near Balto. (BFG, 6 Jan. 1810)

DORSEY, John E., and Mrs. Margaret Hudson, both of Balto. were married last Sat. eve. by Rev. Mr. Bend. (BFG, 16 Dec. 1799)

DORSEY, Mrs. Kitty, wife of Lloyd Dorsey of Elk Ridge, died last Wed. in her 45th year, leaving a husband and 8 children. (BFG, 12 Dec. 1809)

DORSEY, Larkin, and Miss Jane Allison all of Balto. were married last eve. by Rev. Glendy. (BFG, 27 Nov. 1805)

DORSEY, Lloyd, died at his farm on Elk Ridge last Tues. in his 49th year. For the last 10 years he had been a member of the Md. Senate. (BFG, 15 May 1812)

DORSEY, Lloyd, died last Sun., at his farm in Mont. Co., in his
    42nd year, leaving a wife and eight children. (BFG, 12
    May 1815)

DORSEY, Mrs. Lydia, wife of Dr. Archibald Dorsey, died last Wed.
    leaving three infant children. (BFG, 24 Aug. 1805)

DORSEY, Mrs. Lydia, dau. of late Nicholas Dorsey, of Elk Ridge,
    died last Sat. in her 25th year. (BFG, 22 Sept. 1807)

DORSEY, Michael, died at his farm on Elk Ridge, aged 67. (BFG,
    28 Feb. 1812)

DORSEY, Nicholas, died at Fells Point, on the ev. of Wed., 10th
    inst., in his 24th year. (BFG, 12 Oct. 1804)

DORSEY, Owen, of Balto., and Miss Henrietta Dorsey of A. A. Co.,
    were married last Sun. at the farm of Mrs. Dorsey by Rev.
    Hargrove. (BFG, 17 Oct. 1797)

DORSEY, Mrs. Rebecca, wife of Dr. Ezekiel John Dorsey, died yes-
    terday, aged 62 years. (BFG, 19 Feb. 1813)

DORSEY, Richard, an old and respectable inhab. of Balto., died
    last Wed. eve. (BFG, 17 May 1799)

DORSEY, Mrs. Ruth, died yesterday in her 75th year; a member of
    the Methodist Society for over 40 years. (BA, 14 Feb.
    1816)

DORSEY, Mrs. Sarah, died Thurs., 29th March at Linganore, the
    consort of Capt. Ely Dorsey, leaving a husband and a num-
    erous family of children. (BFG, 4 April 1798)

DORSEY, Mr. Theodore, and Miss Elizabeth Dorsey, all of Elk
    Ridge, were married last eve. by Rev. Wells. (BFG, 25
    March 1803)

DORSEY, Thomas B., Esq., and Miss Milcah Goodwin, dau. of William
    Goodwin, of Balto., were married last Thurs. by Rev. Geo.
    Dashiell. (BFG, 30 Jan. 1808)

DORSEY, Vachel, and Miss Elizabeth Dorsey, were married at Elk
    Ridge last Thurs. eve. by Rev. Bend. (BT, 9 April 1798)

DORSEY, William, of Elk Ridge, died last 27 Sept. on his passage
    from Balto. to Boston. (BT, 9 Oct. 1802)

DOSH, John Michael, a native of Germany, died Thurs. eve., 25th
    inst., in his 49th year; funeral from his late res., 41
    South Charles St. (BA, 27 Jan. 1816)

DOTTER, Adam, and Miss Susan Langford, both of Balto., were wed
    3rd inst. by Rev. Rattoone. (BEP, 7 April 1809)

DOUGHERTY, Bernard, died 2nd inst., aged 38, a native of Ireland.
    (BWA, 11 May 1816)

DOUGHERTY, John, and Mrs. Ann Donnally, were married. (BA, 26
    Aug. 1809)

DOUGHERTY, Dr. Johnsey, and Miss Susanna Owings, dau. of Caleb
    Owings of Balto. Co., were married last Thurs. by Rev.
    Richards. (BT, 13 Dec. 1798)

DOUGHERTY, William, and Miss Milky Wheeler, all of Balto. were
married on Sat. by Rev. Beaston. (BT, 19 Jan. 1802)

DOUGLAS, Gen. Hugh, died in Loudon Co., Va., 2nd inst. in his 55th
year. He led a brigade of Virginia militia at the late
British attack on Balto. (BA, 13 July 1815)

DOUGLASS, George, and Miss Mary McElderry, were married on Tues.
by Rev. Glendy. (BA, 18 May 1815)

DOVE, Gilson, and Miss Mary Drugan, all of Balto. were married
last Thurs. by Rev. Dr. Roberts. (BA, 6 Nov. 1810)

DOWELL, Allen, printer, died last eve. aged 27, native of Ireland;
he married in Phila., and moved to this city a few years
ago. He leaves a wife and three children. His res. was
opp. Mr. McElderry's, Old Town. (BFG, 19 May 1808)

DOWIG, Mrs. Catherine, died yesterday in her 82nd year; funeral
from her late res. in Fells St. (BA, 18 March 1807)

DOWNES, Mrs. Anna E., wife of Dr. Richard C. Downes, died 11th
inst., at South East, Q. A. Co. (BPEA, 21 Oct. 1815)

DOWNES, Joshua, and Miss Ann Shaw, both of Balto., were married
last Thurs. by Dr. Roberts. (BA, 19 July 1816)

DOWNING, Howell, and Miss Harriet Gorsuch, were married last Wed.
by Rev. Glendy. (BA, 9 Dec. 1815)

DOWSON, Mrs. Elizabeth, wife of Capt. Henry Dowson, died 20th
inst., aged 26 years. (BA, 23 April 1814)

DOWSON, Mrs. Elizabeth, of Washington City, died 15th inst., in
her 50th year. (BFG, 24 Sept. 1816)

DOWSON, Capt. Joseph, died 23 April at sea, aged 46; long an inhab. of Balto. (BA, 27 May 1816)

DOWSON, Thomas H., of Tal. Co., and Miss Edith Matthews of Balto.
Co., were married 3rd inst. at Gunpowder Friends Meeting.
(BFG, 5 Oct. 1810)

DOYLE, John, cabinet maker, died Sat., 18th inst., aged 25, native of Dublin, Ire.: late of N. Y. (BA, 21 Sept. 1813)

DOYLE, Patrick, and Margaret Murray, both of Balto., were married
last eve. by Rev. Dr. Rattoone. (BFG, 8 Oct. 1805)

DRAINE, John, and Mrs. Margaret Kelhouse, were married Sun. eve.
by Rev. Healey. (BMG, 1 Aug. 1815) (BA, 1 Aug. 1815)

DRAWBAUGH, Valentine, of Balto., and Miss Mary Trumbo, dau. of
Adam Trumbo, near Ellicotts Lower Mills, were married 6th
inst., by Rev. Kurtz. (BT, 14 Dec. 1804)

DREW, Miss Kitty, of Q. A. Co., was killed in a carriage accident on Easter Monday while returning home from a visit
to George Town Cross Roads. (BEP, 3 April 1807)

DRIGGS, Nathaniel, and Miss Elizabeth Smith, of Balto. Co.,
were married last Thurs. eve. by Rev. Glendy. (BT, 23
April 1805)

DROUND, Jobe, and Sophia North were married last Tues. by Rev. Richardson. (BA, 31 Oct. 1799)

DRUE, Capt. Nehemiah, of Boston, and Miss Mary Essendon of Balto. were married last eve. by Rev. Dashiell. (BFG, 5 Dec. 1806)

DRUGAN, Michael, merchant of Fells Point, died last Tues. in his 28th year. (BFG, 18 Aug. 1807)

DRUMMOND, W., of Fredericksburg, and Miss Johnson, were married last Fri. at Port Royal, Va. (BFG, 12 Jan. 1798)

DRUMMOND, William, died at Fredericksburg, Va., on Sun., 14th inst. (BA, 27 Oct. 1804)

DRYDEN, Mylby, and Polly Patrick, both of Balto., were married Tues. eve. by Rev. Morsell. (BT, 12 Feb. 1800)

DRYDEN, Milby, died 21st inst., aged 38, leaving a wife and six children. (BS, 24 Jan. 1812)

DUANE, P., died in Balto., last Sat. aged 22; interment in the new burying ground of Rev. Glendy's church. (BW, 20 March 1809)

DUANE, William, editor of the "Aurora," and Mrs. Margaret Hartman Bache, widow of Benjamin Franklin Bache, were married at Phila., Sat., 28th inst., by Bishop White. (BFG, 2 July 1800)

DUANE, William J., eldest son of the editor of the "Aurora," and Miss Deborah Franklin Bache, sister of the late Benjamin Franklin Bache, were married last Tues. by Rev. William White of the Northern Liberties. (BT, 7 Jan. 1806)

DUBOIS, Nicholas, and Miss Agnes M'Kim, dau. of Alexander M'Kim, of Balto., were married last eve. by Rev. Rattoone. (BFG, 13 May 1808)

DUCATEL, Miss Emma, died last Mon. in Balto. Co., of a severe Whooping Cough, dau. of Dr. Germain Ducatel of Balto.; aged 2 years and 6 days. (BA, 14 Aug. 1812)

DUCATEL, Dr. Germain, and Miss Clemence Muloniere, both of Balto., were married 1st inst. by Rev. Beeston. (BEP, 7 April 1807)

DUCKETT, Baruch, died 2nd inst., at his seat in P. G. Co., in his 66th year. (BFG, 11 Oct. 1810)

DUCKETT, John B., attorney-at-law of P. G. Co., died 10th inst. at the seat of his father on Patuxent. (BA, 23 April 1805)

DUER, John, cashier of the Farmers and Merchants Bank, and Miss Susan Norris of Harf. Co., were married last Thurs. in Harf. Co. (BFG, 24 Sept. 1811)

DUFF, Adam, died yesterday; native of Scotland. He was clerk to the Baltimore Insurance Co. (BFG, 3 Nov. 1800)

DUFFEY, John, merchant, and Miss Mary Kinsell of Balto., were married in Alexandria, 14th inst., by Rev. Dr. Muir. (BA, 23 Sept. 1808)

DUFFY, Henry, and Miss Rachel James, were married last Tues. by
    Rev. Dr. Kemp. (BA, 7 Oct. 1814)

DUGAN, George, Esq., and Miss Eliza Chase, dau. of the Hon. Samuel Chase, were married last eve. (BFG, 9 Nov. 1804)

DUGAN, George, died last eve. (BFG, 2 Oct. 1813)

DUGAS, Louis J., Balto. merchant, and Miss Louisa Morris of Frederick, were married there last Tues. by Rev. John Dubois.
    (BFG, 2 Dec. 1805)

DUKEHART, Henry, an old inhab. of this place, died yesterday.
    (BEP, 19 Sept. 1807)

DUKEHART, John, and Parthena Balderston, both of Balto., were
    married yesterday at Friends Meeting. (BFG, 16 Dec. 1796)

DUKES, Christopher, aged 21, and Mrs. Jane Dukes, aged 76, both
    of Back River Neck, were married last Thurs. eve. by Rev.
    Richards. (BWM, 26 March 1797)

DULANY, Daniel, Esq., Barrister at Law, died last Sun., in his
    76th year. He had been Secretary of Md. His remains were
    interred in St. Pauls burial ground on Tues. (BFG, 23
    March 1797)

DULANY, Mrs. Elizabeth, consort of Walter Dulany, late of Annap.,
    died 19th ult., at Windsor, the seat of George Fitzhugh,
    in her 47th year. (BA, 8 Sept. 1804)

DULANY, William, died yesterday; interment in the Methodist burying ground after the funeral at his father's house. (BT,
    2 June 1803)

DUMOURET, Victor Champel, died 6th inst. of apoplexy. He was
    born in Jan. 1755 at Albene, near Grenoble, France, of a
    noble family, and was a son of Andre Champel Dumouret,
    who was at the siege of Philipsburg, and was a grandson
    of a Knight of the Order of St. Louis. Interment was in
    the R. C. graveyard. (Long obit.) (BFG, 13 Aug. 1808)

DUNBAR, George T., and Miss Frances McCannon, both of Balto.,
    were married last eve. by Rev. Mr. Sargent. (BFG, 30 Nov.
    1804)

DUNBAR, Henry, and Miss Eliza Farmer, both of this county, were
    married last Sat. by Rev. Glendy. (BEP, 27 Jan. 1808)

DUNCAN, Andrew, coach-maker of Balto., died Fri. in his 33rd
    year. (BEP, 17 April 1809)

DUNCAN, Mrs. Harriot, wife of Joseph Duncan of Balto., died yesterday in her 20th year. (BEP, 25 Oct. 1808)

DUNCAN, James, died last eve. in his 20th year. (BT, 7 Aug.
    1802)

DUNCAN, John, and Miss Ann Dyer, were married Sun., 26th ult.,
    by Rev. Glendy. (BT, 5 Nov. 1805)

DUNCAN, John, and Catherine King, both of Balto., were married
    last eve. by Rev. Rattoone. (BFG, 31 July 1806)

DUNCAN, Capt. Joshua, of Balto., was married at Charleston on

MARRIAGES AND DEATHS

Wed., 1st inst., by Rev. Mr. Munds, to Miss Elizabeth Brown of that city. (BFG, 20 Oct. 1806)

DUNCAN, Mrs. Martha, wife of William Duncan of Balto., died 6th inst. aged 45 years. (BFG, 10 Aug. 1806)

DUNCAN, Mrs. Rebecca, died early yesterday morning. Her dau., Mrs. Deborah Ford (q.v.) died 6th inst. (BA, 9 March 1813)

DUNCAN, William, died yesterday morning after a long illness in his 40th year. (BFG, 3 May 1802)

DUNCAN, William, and Miss Debbie Robinson, both of Balto., were married last eve. by Rev. Bend. (BEP, 4 Dec. 1807)

DUNDAS, William, died last Sun. at Reading, Penna., son of the late Thomas Dundas. (BEP, 13 Aug. 1808)

DUNKEL, Dr. George A., and Mrs. Catherine Stinnecke, both of Balto., were married 30th ult. by Rev. Otterbein. (BFG, 8 Feb. 1812)

DUNKIN, William, died near Fincastle, Va., at the advanced age of 124 years, and in full possession of her faculties. (BFG, 2 Feb. 1805)

DUNLAVY, Levi, and Margaret Carnigham, both of Balto., were wed last eve. by Rev. Healey. (BFG, 25 April 1806)

DUNN, John, and Miss Milcah Courtenay, both of Harf. Co., were married last Thurs. eve. (BT, 6 Nov. 1802)

DUNN, Mr. Joseph, and Miss Mary M'Gowan, both of Balto., were married last eve. by Rev. Mr. Richards. (BFG, 12 Oct. 1801)

DUNNEHEN, Henry, and Miss Bridget Dougherty, all of Balto., were married last Sun. by Rev. Fenwick. (BMG, 3 June 1815)

DUNNEMANN, C. H., and Miss Olivia Sophia Yeiser, of Balto., were married last Wed. by Rev. Kurtz. (BFG, 27 Nov. 1812)
(Ed. note - see Dannemann.)

DUNNEVIN, Jeremiah, and Miss Sarah Maxwell, both of Balto., were married last Thurs. by Rev. Glendy. (BT, 31 Aug. 1805)

DUNNINGTON, William P., merchant, and Ann G. Reynolds, both of Balto., were married 14 Nov. by Rev. Dashiells. (BA, 17 Nov. 1815)

DUNOTT, Justus, an inhab. of Wilmington, was killed Fri., 19th ult., in Sassafras Neck, Md., by his wagon running over his head. (BFG, 4 May 1805)

DUNSIMORE, Thomas, and Mrs. Hannah Dods, both of New York, were married last Tues. by Rev. Dr. Allison. (BTD, 12 Jan. 1798)

DU PAN, Mallet, died at Richmond (E.) of consumption, editor of Mercure Britannique. He left a wife and several children. (BT, 14 July 1800)

DURAND, John, and Mary Wise were married last Thurs. by Rev. Rattoone. (BFG, 11 May 1807)

DURANG, F., and Miss Jane Petit, both of the Theatre, were married Sun. eve. by Rev. Kurtz. (BFR, 19 May 1812)

DURANG, Mrs. Jane, of the Phila. Theatre, died yesterday, aged 19 years. (BFG, 9 March 1814)

DURBEN, Capt. William, and Miss Elizabeth Reese, were married Thurs., 25th ult. in Fred. Co. (BEP, 20 May 1811)

DURETT, Capt. William, of Caroline Co., Va., died 25th ult.,leaving a wife and children. (BT, 22 Feb. 1804)

DURHAM, Lloyd, merchant, and Susanna Kipp, both of Balto., were married last eve. by Rev. Dashiells. (BFG, 29 Nov. 1805)

DURHAM, Zacharias, and Miss Mary Dabou, all of Balto., were wed last Thurs. eve. by Rev. Healey. (BA, 18 Dec. 1811)

DURKEE, Mrs. Mary, died Sun.; funeral from her late res., George St., Old Town. (BA, 7 Feb. 1809) (BW, 7 Feb. 1809, states the dec. was the consort of Capt. Pearl Durkee.)

DURKEE, Capt. Pearl, and Miss Charlotte Rose, all of Balto., were married last Tues. by Rev. Glendy. (BA, 10 Nov. 1814)

DUSHANE, John, and Miss Harriet Ann Wilson, all of Balto., were married Tues. eve. by Rev. Dr. Roberts. (BA, 11 Feb. 1813)

DUVAL, Anthony, and Mary Obey, both of Balto., were married on last Mon. by Rev. Kurtz. (BA, 12 Nov. 1806)

DUVAL, Frederick, and Miss Mary Hyatt, all of P. G. Co., were wed last week by Rev. Mr. Ralph. (BFG, 10 Jan. 1800)

DUVALL, Mr. Benjamin, died 11th inst., in P. G. Co., aged 103 years. (BFG, 27 Dec. 1803)

DUVALL, Mareen H., of P. G. Co., aged 17, and Mrs. Dorothy Allen, aged 50, widow of the late Zachariah Allen of Balto., were married last Thurs. by Rev. Ralph. (BT, 14 May 1801)

DUVALL, Capt. Marsh M., and Miss Mary Ann Taylor, dau. of James Taylor, all of Balto., were married Thurs. by Rev. Mr. Wyland. (BPE, 11 Dec. 1813)

DUVALL, Samuel, of Severn, and Miss Mary Duvall, dau. of Mareen Duvall of P. G. Co., were married last Tues. by Rev. Scott. (BEP, 29 Oct. 1808)

DUVALL, Samuel, surveyor of Fred. Co., died at Frederick Town. (BA, 23 Jan. 1811)

DUVANCY, John, of Phila., and Mrs. Elizabeth Cole, of Balto., were married at Lancaster, by Rev. Henry Hoffman. (BFG, 7 July 1814) (BA, 9 July gives the groom's name as Durang.)

DWERHAGEN, George, died 15th inst. at Hagerstown, in his 26th year; a native of Bremen. (BFG, 20 Oct. 1797)

DWYER, Catherine, drowned yesterday. (BFG, 26 July 1803)

DWYER, Mrs. Dennis, of Second Street, died last Sat. when she fell into a fire. (BFG, 21 Feb. 1797)

DYER, Elijah, and Miss Amelia March, both of Balto., were wed last Sat. by Rev. Glendy. (BT, 30 Oct. 1804)

DYKEN, John, Esq., His Britannic Majesty's commissary for Cape-Nichola-Mole, died last Thurs. at Gray's, where he had retired for his health. (BFG, 11 Sept. 1797)

D'YRUJO, Chevalier Don Carlos Martinez, Minister Pleniopotentiary from the Court of Spain to the United States, and Miss Sarah M'Kean, dau. of Thomas M'Kean, Chief Justice of the state of Penna., were married Wed. at Phila. (BFG, 13 April 1798)

DYSART, Mr. Marcus, died yesterday at 7:00 P. M., aged 25 years. (BFG, 16 Sept. 1800)

EAGEN, Anthony, and Mrs. Lydia French, both of Balto., were wed last Sun. by Rev. Richards. (BPE, 4 Nov. 1813)

EAGLESTON, Abraham, died yesterday in his 40th year; funeral from his late res. in Eden St. (BA, 25 Oct. 1813)

EAGLESTON, Abraham, and Miss Mary Crawford, both of Fells Point, were married on Wed. by Rev. Wells. (BFG, 1 Dec. 1815)

EAGLESTON, Henry, and Esther Wright, were married last Sun. by Rev. Dodge. (BFG, 18 Nov. 1801)

EAGLESTONE, Mrs. Jane, consort of Capt. Abraham Eaglestone, died last Sat., aged 32. (BA, 4 Nov. 1800)

EARLE, James, clerk of the Court of Appeals and cashier of the Branch Bank at Easton, died Wed., 2nd inst. (BW, 16 March 1814)

EARLE, Thomas C., Balto. merchant, and Miss Henrietta M. Hemsley, dau. of Wm. Hemsley, Esq., of Wye, were married Thurs., 4th inst. by Rev. Mr. Rigg. (BFG, 12 Nov. 1802)

EARNEST, Charles, died 31 Aug., after lingering two years and ten days from wounds received in the Battle of Bladensburg, in his 26th year. (BA, 11 Sept. 1816)

EARRICKSON, Thomas, of Balto., and Paulina Susan Cook, of Balto. Co., were married 26 Dec. by Rev. Glendy. (BA, 27 Dec. 1816)

EASTON, John, and Mrs. Eliza Ferguson, both of Balto., were married Thurs. by Rev. Roberts. (BFG, 26 Dec. 1807)

EATON, William, Balto. merchant, and Miss Mary Keys, dau. of Richard Keys of Govans Town, were married there by Rev. Inglis. (BFG, 20 Nov. 1812)

ECCLESTON, Hugh, second son of Dr. John Eccleston of Dor. Co., died 15 Jan. in his 19th year. (BA, 17 Jan. 1816)

ECCLESTON, Capt. Samuel, died 29th ult. in Kent Co., aged 33 years leaving a widow and four children. (BFG, 9 Nov. 1802)

ECKEL, Mrs. Mary, wife of Philip P. Eckel, died last eve. (BPE, 18 July 1814)

ECKLES, Mr. Andrew, of Balto., and Miss Eliza Nagle of Phila., were married there on 31st ult. by Rev. Dr. Smith. (BFG, 8 Feb. 1799)

EDDS, John, and Jane Hogg, both of Balto., were married last Thurs. by Rev. Inglis. (BA, 4 March 1806)

EDELEN, Dr. Philip R., of St. M. Co., who graduated in 1815 with highest honors, died 7 Oct. (BA, 12 Oct. 1816)

EDELEN, William, and Mrs. Sarah Scarf, both of Balto., were married by Rev. Parks. (BA, 26 Oct. 1816)

EDES, Benjamin, and Miss Mary Ann Cumming, both of Balto., were married last eve. by Rev. Glendy. (BFG, 25 Oct. 1809)

EDES, Benjamin, infant son of Maj. Benjamin Edes of Balto., died last Sat., aged about three years and six months. (BFG, 10 April 1816)

EDES, William, Boston merchant, and Catherine Pennell of Fells Point were married on Thurs. by Rev. Richards. (BA, 22 June 1799)

EDGAR, Dr. Thomas, native of Ireland, died last eve. in his 52nd year. (BFG, 8 April 1815)

EDGER, David, Balto. merchant, and Miss Mary Muclay of Franklin Co., Penna., were married 1st inst. ny Rev. John Moody. (BA, 12 Oct. 1811)

EDMONDS, James, and Miss Susan Bowers, dau. of Major C. Bowers, all of Fred. Co., were married last Tues. (BA, 26 Jan. 1811)

EDMONDSON, Franklin, and Sarah Ann Wray, both of Balto., were married 31 Oct. by Rev. Richards. (BFG, 7 Nov. 1816)

EDMONDSON, John, of Tal. Co., and Susan Howard, dau. of Samuel H. Howard, were married in Annapolis last Thurs. by Rev. Higgenbothom. (BT, 1 April 1799)

EDMONSON, Edward, of Mont. Co., and Mrs. Crowner, widow of the late Dr. Crowner of P. G. Co., were married last week. (BFG, 19 Sept. 1800)

EDWARDS, Aquilla, and Miss Mary Ann Clark Foster, both of Balto., were married 11th inst. by Rev. Wells. (BWA, 20 April 1816)

EDWARDS, James, and Mrs. Elizabeth Brown, were married last eve. by Rev. Bend at Edwards' res. in Balto. Co. (BFG, 30 Oct. 1805)

EDWARDS, James, died last eve. at his res. near Balto. (BFG, 26 July 1811) (BW, 26 July 1811 gives the name as Jacob Edwards.)

EDWARDS, Jesse, of Phila., and Miss Sally Claxton were married last Wed. by Bishop White. (BA, 20 June 1805)

EDWARDS, Philip, lieut. of marines, and proprietor of the Maryland Journal, died this morning in his 28th year; funeral from his house near Chatsworth Gardens. (BFG, 16 Oct. 1800)

EDWARDS, Mrs. Ruth, consort of James Edwards, died 2nd inst. in her 61st year, leaving four children. (BFG, 4 June 1804)

EDWARDS, Thomas, and Miss Ann Gordon, both of Balto., were wed last Thurs. by Rev. Dr. Allison. (BFG, 15 Sept. 1798)

EDWARDS, Midshipman William W., son of Lewis Edwards of Washington City, died on the U. S. brig Argus, Capt. Allen, last 14 Aug. after being wounded in action against the Pelican. (BA, 15 Jan. 1814)

EGAN, Right Rev. Dr. Michael, first R. C. Bishop of Phila., died there on 22nd inst., in his 53rd year. (BPE, 3 Aug. 1814)

EGERTON, Bennett, died at Martinique on 17th March in his 31st year, a native of St. M. Co. (BA, 23 April 1807)

EGERTON, Charles Calvert, of Balto., and Miss Jane Dubois of Phila., were married last eve. at Edward Ireland's, by Rev. Rattoone. (BFG, 6 Feb. 1807)

EICHELBERGER, Jacob, died last Mon. in his 42nd year, leaving four children. (BFG, 18 Jan. 1804)

EICHELBERGER, Martin, of Balto., and Mrs. Elizabeth Eichelberger of York were married Tues., 2nd inst. by Rev. Geistwide. (BW, 11 March 1814)

EICHELBERGER, Mrs. Mary, wife of Martin Eichelberger, tanner, died this morning leaving ten children, the youngest two months old. (BFG, 5 Oct. 1810)

EIKEN, Capt. John, died yesterday, aged about 22 years, a native of Del.; funeral from the house of John Rea, 20 Pratt St. extended. (BA, 28 Sept. 1810)

EISELEN, Capt. Conrad, died yesterday at his seat near Balto., aged 55 years. (BFR, 11 Oct. 1809)

ELDER, Basil S., merchant, and Elizabeth Snowden, dau. of Col. Francis Snowden, were married last Wed. by Rev. Beeston. (BFG, 20 Nov. 1801)

ELDER, Hilary, and Miss Patience Stansbury were married on Sun. eve. by Rev. Beeston. (BFG, 7 Oct. 1807)

ELDER, James, and Mrs. Mary Dunn, all of Balto., were married last eve. by Rev. Dashiell. (BFG, 2 Oct. 1812)

ELDER, John, employee of Mr. Butler, drowned on Fri. at the mouth of Curtis Creek. He lived on the east side of Jones Falls and left 4 or 5 small children. (BFG, 13 May 1805)

ELDER, Joseph, and Miss Lucy Head were married 26th ult. near Creagerstown, by Rev. Dubois. (BEP, 4 May 1808)

ELDER, Mrs. Mary, wife of James Elder, died last Mon. in her 32nd year. (BFG, 22 April 1813)

ELDER, William P., aged 21 years, died yesterday at William Spalding's in Fayette St. (BFG, 24 Aug. 1799)

ELDERKIN, William G., and Miss Margaret Maggs, both of Balto., were married last eve. by Bishop Kemp. (BMG, 20 July 1815)

ELLHALL, Mr. Henry, and Miss Rebecca Stewart, both of A. A. Co., were married yesterday by Rev. Rattoone. (BFG, 2 March 1804)

ELLICOTT, Andrew, Sr., died this morning, aged about 74; funeral from his late res., Ellicotts Mills, Patapsco. (BFG, 20 June 1809)

ELLICOTT, Andrew, Balto. merchant, and Hannah Tunis, dau. of
Richard Tunis, late of Phila., were married yesterday at
Friends Meeting, Pine St. "Phila., 5 March." (BFG, 6
March 1812)

ELLICOTT, Augustus, of Md., and Sally Williams of Rahway, were
married at Elizabeth Town, N. J., on Sat., 5th inst., by
Rev. Henry Hollock. (BFG, 12 Sept. 1801)

ELLICOTT, James, Balto. merchant and Henrietta Thomas, dau. of
Philip William Thomas of London (or Loudon?), were married
yesterday at Friends Meeting, Balto. (BFG, 19 Feb. 1807)

ELLICOTT, John, and Miss Mary Mitchell, both of Balto., were wed
yesterday at Friends Meeting. (BT, 21 Jan. 1803)

ELICOTT, John? of John, and Miss Mary Kirk, of Balto. Co., were
married on Wed., 19th inst., at Friends Meeting, Elk Ridge.
(BFG, 24 Jan. 1814)

ELICOTT, John, Jr., died 27 Jan.; interment at Ellicott's Patapsco. Mills. (BFG, 27 Jan. 1814)

ELLICOTT, Mrs. Judith, died Sun., aged 79 years, consort of Joseph Ellicott, late of Ellicotts Upper Mills. (BFG, 13 July 1809)

ELLIOT, Thomas, died Wed., 19th inst. in his 67th year; for many
years a magistrate in Md. (BFG, 20 Aug. 1807)

ELLIOTT, George, and Miss Harriet Rusk, both of Balto., were wed
last eve. by Rev. McCain. (BW, 25 May 1812)

ELLIOTT, Henry, died at Wyalusing, Penna., on 22nd Dec., in his
97th year. A native of Stonington, Conn., he emigrated
to this country in 1776, and experienced the horrors of
an Indian war. (BEP, 13 Jan. 1809)

ELLIOTT, James, died; funeral from his late res. in Aisquith St.,
near Capt. McElderry's, Old Town. (BEP, 6 May 1809)

ELLIOTT, John, and Miss Margaret Fearle, both of Balto., were
married last Tues. by Rev. Bend. (BEP, 24 Oct. 1810)

ELLIOTT, John Hartman, and Mrs. Troltener, all of Balto., were
married last eve. by Rev. Dreiser. (BT, 26 Nov. 1802)

ELLIOTT, Joseph B., merchant, and Miss Margaret Schultz, both of
Balto., were married last Thurs. by Rev. Kurtz. (BMG, 10
July 1815)

ELLIS, George, of Norfolk, Va., and Martha M'Clevery, of Balto.,
were married yesterday by Rev. Rattoone. (BFG, 23 June
1806)

ELLIS, John, died Wed., 9th inst., aged 62 years. (BA, 15 Dec.
1807)

ELLIS, Mr. Reuben, died yesterday, 23rd inst., in his 44th year.
He had been an itinerant Meth. minister for 20 years, and
leaves a widow. Interment will be in the Meth. burying
ground. (BFG, 24 March 1796)

ELLIS, Robert, late clerk in the Dept. of War, Washington, died
4th inst. at Phila. (BEP, 7 Dec. 1809)

ELLMS, Benjamin, and Miss Betsy Lenum, all of Balto., were wed on 17th ult. by Rev. Richards. (BA, 18 Feb. 1813)

ELVERSON, Mr., died. (BEP, 3 Jan. 1809)

ELWIN, Francis, native of Germany, had relatives in Phila.,where he was about to return after two years' absence. He was killed last Fri. when he walked into the dock and was drowned. (BA, 10 Feb. 1806)

EMANUEL, Augustus, and Miss Elizabeth Milliman, both of Balto., were married last eve. by Rev. Richards. (BFG, 30 April 1802)

EMBLETON, William, Esq., died lately at his res. in Kent Co. on the Eastern Shore; a native of Eng. He emigrated at an early period of his life. (BFG, 12 June 1806)

EMMERSON, Arthur, and Miss Sarah Purdin, all of this place, were married last Tues. by Rev. Roberts. (BFR, 26 March 1812)

EMORY, Peregrine, and Mrs. Kitty E. Higson, both of the Eastern Shore, were married last eve. by Rev. Rattoone. (BFG, 9 May 1806)

EMORY, Robert, Jr., died in Q. A. Co. (BFG, 27 May 1809)

EMORY, Thomas L., and Miss Eliza H. Grant, were married last eve. by Bishop Kemp. (BFG, 14 June 1815)

ENGLAND, John, and Mrs. Sarah Mackey, both of Harf. Co., were married last Tues. by Rev. Healey. (BA, 10 Dec. 1816)

ENGLEBRIGHT, John, and Miss Susanna Starr, both of Balto., were married last Sun. by Rev. Kurtz. (BEP, 2 Aug. 1808)

ENGLISH, Lieut. Marshall, was accidentally shot and killed at Fort McHenry last Wed., a member of Capt. Buffum's Artillery Co. He leaves a widow and several small children. (BFG, 23 April 1813)

ENGLISH, Maxwell, and Miss Eliza Davidson, both of Balto., were married last Thurs. by Rev. Coats. (BT, 26 March 1803)

ENNALLS, Henry, died last month at his res. in Dor. Co. (BFG, 9 Feb. 1803)

ENNALLS, Mrs. Leah, relict of Andrew S. Ennalls, Esq., formerly of Balto., died yesterday at Beech Hill, the seat of Robert Gilmor, in her 63rd year. (BFG, 11 Oct. 1806)

ENSOR, Abraham, and Miss Rebecca Cole, all of Balto. Co., were married 6th inst. by Rev. Mr. Green. (BFG, 11 Feb. 1813)

ENSOR, William, and Nancy Herrington, all of Balto., were married last eve. by Rev. Richards. (BT, 3 March 1800)

ENSOR, William, Jr., died last Sat.; a partner of the firm of James G. Ensor and Co.; interment in Meth. burial ground. (BFG, 23 June 1800)

ENSOR, William, died last Thurs. at his res. in Fells Point, in his 59th year, leaving a widow and nine children. (BA, 25 April 1801)

EPES, Col. Peter, of P. G. Co., died 15th ult., at the age of 80 years. He was one of the earliest defenders of his country's independence. (BA, 2 Dec. 1807)

EPPES, Mrs., second dau. of Thomas Jefferson, Esq., died at Monticello on 3rd inst. (BT, 27 April 1804)

EPPES, John W., member of Congress from Va., and Miss Martha Jones, dau. of the late Willie Jones, were married 5th inst., in Halifax, N.C. (BW, 1 May 1809)

EPPS, John, of Chesterfield, Va., and Miss Polly Jefferson, ygst. dau. of the Hon. Thomas Jefferson, were married on Wed., 23rd ult. at Monticello. (BT, 2 Nov. 1797)

ERWIN, James, and Miss Sally Cunningham, both of Balto., were married last Tues. by Rev. Allison. (BT, 7 Feb. 1799)

ERWIN, John, and Rachel Lee Preston, all of Balto., were married last Thurs. by Rev. Roberts. (BA, 3 May 1806)

ESCAVILLE, James, and Polly Hargrove, eld. dau. of John Hargrove, were married last eve. by Bishop Carroll. (BFG, 9 Sept. 1799)

ESCAVILLE, Mrs. Mary, died last Dec. on the Island of Martinique; eld. dau. of Rev. John Hargrove of Balto. Her mother died in Oct. 1800, and when she left for Martinique last April she took with her an only child who died four months later. She leaves a father, brother, and six sisters. (BFG, 15 Feb. 1803)

ESMENARD, Mrs. Henrietta, died last Sat., aged 34 years. (BA, 13 March 1816)

ESMENARD, John B., and Miss Zelia Bergeral of Bedford, Penna., were married by Rev. Dr. Gallitzin on Mon., 12th inst. at Loretto. (BA, 22 Aug. 1816)

ESMENARD, John Francis, died last eve.; funeral from his dwelling just above Dr. Stevenson's and near the Penitentiary. (BFG, 14 May 1813)

EULER, Jacob, and Miss Rachael Porter, all of Balto., were wed last Sun. by Rev. Roberts. (BFG, 31 Aug. 1813)

EUNICK, Mrs. Margaret, died Sun., 3rd inst., aged 27 years. (BFG, 9 Feb. 1816)

EVALT, Mr. Edward, and Miss Ann Lagge, both of Balto., were wed 16th inst. by Rev. Rattoone. (BFG, 19 Aug. 1803)

EVANS, Miss Catherine, ygst. dau. of the late John Evans of Balto., died last Sat. (BFG, 18 June 1813)

EVANS, Charles, merchant, and Miss Esther Walker, both of Balto., were married last Tues. by Rev. Roberts. (BFG, 2 Aug. 1809)

EVANS, Daniel, and Miss Ann Wollar, both of Fells Point, were married last eve. by Rev. M'Kean. (BFG, 14 Oct. 1808)

EVANS, David, son of Henry Evans, died Fri. at Eden St., Fells Point, aged 24 years. (BFG, 31 May 1802)

MARRIAGES AND DEATHS

EVANS, David, and Miss Maria Paints, were married last eve. by Rev. Dr. Roberts. (BPEA, 25 Jan. 1815)

EVANS, Edward Augustus, midshipman in the U. S. navy, died last Fri. Capt. Evans, bro. of the dec., thanks those who attended the funeral. (BA, 18 Sept. 1808)

EVANS, Evan Rice, died at Sunbury, Penna., on 3rd inst., for over 19 years a lawyer of that district. In his 40th year he left a widow and three children. (BFR, 28 Dec. 1811)

EVANS, George W., and Miss Rebecca Shaw, all of Balto., were wed last eve. by Rev. Hanson. (BPE, 3 Dec. 1813)

EVANS, Henry, long a res. of Fells Point, died in his 64th year; funeral from his late res., Eden St. (BA, 9 Aug. 1814)

EVANS, Isaac, Jr., and Miss Caroline C. Onion, all of Balto., were married Thurs. by Rev. Oliver Norris. (BFG, 16 June 1809)

EVANS, James, and Mrs. Mary Flax, of Balto. Co., were married last Thurs. by Rev. Healey. (BA, 25 May 1816)

EVANS, Jeremiah, and Miss Margaret Phillips, were married last Thurs. by Rev. Glendy. (BS, 9 Nov. 1812)

EVANS, Job, and Miss Ruth Ensor, all of Balto., were married last eve. by Rev. M'Cain. (BFG, 4 Oct. 1811)

EVANS, John, and Mrs. Jonned Jones, all of Balto., were married 5th inst., by Rev. Mr. Healey. (BFG, 12 June 1804)

EVANS, John, died Tues., 2nd inst., leaving a wife and six children; funeral sermon will be preached in St. Peter's Church next Sun. by Rev. George Dashiell. (BFG, 6 Oct. 1804)

EVANS, John, and Miss Eliza Hopkins, all of Balto., were married last Tues. by Rev. Dashiell. (BFG, 30 Nov. 1812)

EVANS, John, of Balto., died Thurs. (BFG, 4 Dec. 1813)

EVANS, Lewis E., and Miss Miriam Hunt, all of Balto. Co., were married last Thurs. by Rev. Roberts. (BFG, 31 Oct. 1807)

EVANS, Mrs. Mary, wife of William Evans, died yesterday morning; funeral from her late res. in Fleet St. (BA, 18 Sept. 1816)

EVANS, Capt. Samuel, of U. S. Navy, and Mrs. Jane Norris of this place, were married last Mon. eve. by Rev. Bend. (BFG, 5 Oct. 1810)

EVANS, William, and Margaret Randall, both of Balto., were wed last eve. by Rev. Dashiell. (BFG, 9 Jan. 1807)

EVANS, William, proprietor of the Indian Queen Tavern in Balto., died yesterday, aged 56. He was a revolutionary soldier and fought under Gen. Sam. Smith at Long Island. (BA, 29 June 1807)

EVANS, William, and Mrs. Mary Salsbury, both of Balto., were married last eve. by Rev. Rattoone. (BFG, 5 Oct. 1808)

EVATT, Mrs. Mary Ann, wife of Edward Evatt of Balto., died Tues. in her 44th year. (BA, 26 Aug. 1816)

EVERARD, William, Balto. merchant, and Eliza Ann Mills, dau. of John Mills of N. Y. state, were married Sat. by Rev. Richards. (BFG, 3 June 1800)

EVERETT, Rev. Joseph, died at Cambridge, Md., 16th inst., in his 78th year, and in the 30th year of his ministry in the Meth. church. (BFG, 20 Oct. 1809)

EVERETT, Thomas, merchant, and Miss Rebecca Myring, all of Balto., were married last eve. by Rev. Richards. (BFG, 14 Dec. 1802)

EVERITT, James, of Fells Point, died 25 March in his 42nd year, leaving a wife and six children. (BW, 28 March 1814)

EVERLY, Mrs. Margaret, died last Thurs. in Balto. Co., in her 71st year, leaving ten children, 55 grandchildren, and 25 great-grandchildren, all residing in Md. (BW, 9 March 1814)

EVERSON, Capt. Nicholas, and Mrs. Catharina Carlbon, all of Balto., were married yesterday eve. ny Rev. Kurtz. (BT, 13 Jan. 1800) (BA, 13 Jan. 1800 gives the bride's name as Carlson.)

EVES, Joseph Bennett, and Miss Maria Kucher, dau. of John Peter Kucher, all of Phila., were married there 16th inst. by Rev. Philip F. Mayer. (BEP, 23 June 1808)

EWALDT, Henry, and Miss Dorothea Raab, both of Balto., were wed last eve. by Rev. Kurtz. (BFG, 14 Feb. 1812)

EWING, Samuel W., and Miss Mary Clayton, all of Balto., were wed last eve. by Rev. Hargrove. (BA, 15 Nov. 1816) (BA, 20 Nov. 1816 states that the bride was a dau. of Samuel Clayton of Tal. Co., dec.)

FABURELLE, Francis, and Miss Hester Mortimore, were married 9th inst. by Rev. Glendy. (BFG, 13 June 1816)

FADREY, Joseph, aged 36, a native of Phila., died at Liverpool on 6 Jan., on board the ship Bellona. (BFG. 22 March 1816)

FAHERTY, Patrick, and Miss Mary Cloherty, both of Balto., were married by Rev. Fenwick. (BPEA, 13 Feb. 1815)

FAIR, Charles, of Fred. Co., and Miss Elizabeth Marr of Balto., were married Thurs., 28th inst. by Rev. Roberts. (BFG, 1 March 1809)

FAIRBAIRN, Thomas H., and Miss Maria Eliza Henry, both of Balto., were married last eve. by Bishop Carroll. (BEP, 8 Nov. 1809)

FAIRBANK, William, and Miss Elizabeth Amey, both of Balto., were married Thurs. eve. by Rev. Dr. Roberts. (BA, 21 Oct. 1816)

FAIRBANKS, Mrs. Blanche, died Fri., 18th inst., in A. A. Co., in her 29th year. (BFG, 28 Nov. 1803)

FAIRBANKS, William, and Miss Amelia Beckley, both of Fells Point, were married last eve. by Rev. Bend. (BA, 2 Dec. 1799)

FAIRCHILD, Robert, and Mrs. Julia Ann Kirk, all of Balto., were married by Rev. Glendy last Mon. (BFG, 13 June 1816)

FAIRFAX, Mrs. Jane, relict of the late Bryan (Lord) Fairfax, died Mon. at Alexandria. (BFG, 5 July 1805)

FAITHFULL, William, Phila. printer, and Miss Margaret Burke of Balto., were married last eve. by Rev. Bend. (BFG, 6 June 1803)

FALCONAR, Abraham, died at Georgetown on Sassafras River, Tues., 31st ult., in his 54th year. He was a merchant in Balto. several years previous to his return to the Eastern Shore. (BFG, 9 Feb. 1804)

FALCONAR, Peregrine, merchant, and Mrs. Elizabeth Levy, both of Balto., were married last Tues. eve. by Rev. Bend. (BFG, 3 Nov. 1808)

FALES, Benjamin, and Miss Eliza Clarke, all of Balto., were wed by Rev. Rattoone. (BA, 28 July 1807)

FALKNER, Samuel, and Mrs. Mary Brown, both of Balto., were wed last Sat. by Rev. Bend. (BT, 7 Oct. 1799)

FALLS, Jacob, and Miss Susanna Waters, were married in Portsmouth. (BPE, 20 Aug. 1813)

FALLS, Dr. Moor, and Mrs. Rebecca Wilson, both of Balto., were married last Sat. by Rev. Allison. (BMJ, 26 Sept. 1796)

FARIS, Robert, of Balto., was found dead in his bed on Sat. (BA, 29 April 1805)

FARRALL, Capt. Jeffery, and Miss Sarah Isaacke, both of Balto., were married last eve. by Rev. Glendy. (BFG, 20 Oct. 1809)

FARRALL, Capt. Jeffery, died 23 Feb. in his 32nd year, leaving a widow and two small children. (BPEA, 3 March 1815)

FARRELL, James, and Mrs. Eleanor Donnelly, both of Fells Point, were married last Sat. by Rev. Mirandula. (BEP, 4 Aug. 1807)

FARRELL, James W., and Miss Mary Ann Ennis, both of Balto., were married last Mon. by Rev. Marouville (sic; prob. Moranville). (BPEA, 11 Feb. 1815)

FARRELL, William, and Miss Polly Wilson, both of Balto. Co., were married last Thurs. by Rev. Glendy. (BA, 21 Sept. 1811)

FARRON, James, of Balto., died Mon., 3rd inst., leaving a widow and two children. (BA, 7 July 1809)

FAUBLE, Jacob, and Miss Margaret Hoffleigh, were married last Sun. (BFG, 24 May 1796)

FAUCET, Michael, died a few days ago at the house of James Armitage near Great Gunpowder Falls; a native of Ireland, he arrived 11th inst., in the *Arden* from Londonderry. (BAP, 20 July 1803)

FENBY, Peter, Jr., and Miss Ally Davis, were married Thurs., 14th inst. by Rev. M'Caine. (BFG, 16 Jan. 1813)

FENNELL, Elijah, and Miss Rachel Lusby, were married by Rev. D. E. Reese last Thurs. (BA, 19 Oct. 1816)

FENNELL, James, professor of elocution, died yesterday. Phila.,
June 15. (BFG, 17 June 1816)

FENNELL, John, city guager, and Miss Jordan, both of Balto., were
married Sunday eve. by Bishop Carroll. (BFG, 31 May 1803)

FENNER, Capt. Darius, and Mrs. Sarah Brown, both of Balto., were
married last eve. by Rev. Hargrove. (BFG, 11 July 1810)

FENNO, John, editor of the Gazette of the United States, died
last eve., of the prevailing fever, in his 47th year. The
paper will be conducted in the future by his son John Ward
Fenno. From the Phila. Gaz. (BFG, 18 Sept. 1798)

FENTON, John, and Miss Sarah Gumms, both of Fells Point, were wed
16th ult. by Rev. Glendy. (BT, 5 Jan. 1804)

FENTON, John, and Miss Nancy Hay, were married 8th inst., by Rev.
Glendy. (BEP, 20 Dec. 1808)

FENWICK, Dr. Martin, and Miss Anna Louisa Ghequiere, dau. of
Chas. Ghequiere, of Balto., were married Tues. 22nd inst.,
by Archbishop Carroll. (BA, 24 Aug. 1815)

FERGUSON, David B., and Miss Mary Buchanan, all of Balto., were
married last Tues. by Rev. Fechtig. (BFG, 12 July 1816)

FERGUSON, Mrs. Dinah, wife of James F. Ferguson, schoolmaster of
Chatham St., died this morning, leaving three small children. (BFG, 5 March 1811)

FERGUSON, John, and Elizabeth Hamilton, both of Balto., were married last Fri. by Rev. Glendy. (BT, 17 April 1804)

FERGUSON, Mrs. Sarah, died last Wed., aged 20 years; she had been
married only nine weeks. (BFG, 13 Oct. 1810)

FERGUSSON, James, and Miss Catherine Robb, all of Balto., were
married last Tues. by Rev. Inglis. (BFG, 14 Oct. 1813)

FERGUSSON, John, Balto. merchant, and Miss Eliza Turner, of Chas.
Co., were married at Friendly Hall, Chas. Co., 3rd inst.
by Rev. Weems. (BFG, 14 Dec. 1805)

FERGUSSON, Robert, died 1st inst. at his res., Mulberry Grove,
near Port Tobacco, in his 73rd year. He was a native of
Dumfries, Scot., and came early to Md. For many years he
was Chief Justice of the Orphans Court of Chas. Co. (BFG,
25 Sept. 1812)

FERNANDIS, Walter, Balto. merchant, and Miss Mary E. Dorsey, dau.
of Col. Henry Dorsey of Harf. Co., were married 30th inst.,
at Bel Air by Rev. Mr. Stevens. (BFG, 24 June 1816)

FERNANDIS, Samuel, merchant, and Miss Ann Bowly Stewart, dau. of
John Stewart, all of Balto., were married last Tues. by
Rev. Bend. (BFG, 8 Oct. 1808)

FERREE, Joseph, died last Tues. at Phila., in his 76th year; formerly of Lancaster Co., Penna. (BA, 6 Aug. 1804)

FICKE, Herman, of Balto., and Miss Nancy Cain of Harf. Co., were
married last eve. by Bishop Carroll. (BT, 5 Dec. 1799)

FIDLER, Rev. Daniel, and Sarah Larsh, dau. of Abraham Larsh, Sr.,
were married last eve. by Rev. Sargent. (BFG, 3 Jan. 1806)

FIELDS, Josiah, of Boston, and Miss Margaret M'Fadon of Balto., were married last eve. by Rev. Glendy. (BEP, 10 Sept. 1807)

FILBERT, Peter, of Alexandria, Va., and Mrs. Hannah Green of Balto., were married last Fri. (BA, 11 Nov. 1805)

FIMISTER, Alexander, Balto. merchant, and Miss Roday Ridgely of Elk Ridge, were married last eve. by Rev. Ridgely. (BA, 1 May 1805)

FINIGAN, Capt. John P., and Miss Rosanna Nearey, all of Balto., were married last eve. by Rev. Moranville. (BT, 11 Jan. 1806)

FINLATER, Alexander, native of Aberdeen, Scot., died yesterday in his 66th year. (BA, 3 May 1809)

FINLEY, Capt. James, and Miss Catherine Gantz, all of Balto., were married last eve. by Rev. Curtis. (BFG, 20 Sept. 1798)

FINLEY, Jane, wife of Ebenezer Finley of Balto., died Sun., 26th March, aged 43 years; interment in the West burying ground. (BEP, 29 March 1809)

FINLEY, Dr. Michael A., and Miss Eliza Vanlear, dau. of Matthew Vanlear of Wash. Co., were married there on last Tues. by Rev. King. (BFR, 17 Oct. 1809)

FINLEY, Michael L., merchant of St. Francisville, and Miss Ann H. Griffith of Westminster, Md., were married Tues., 7th inst., at the latter place. (BFG, 11 Sept. 1813)

FINLEY, William, and Miss Ann Finley, both of Fells Point, were married last Thurs. by Rev. Dr. Bend. (BFG, 15 March 1805)

FINLY, Capt. James, and Miss Catherine Gantz, both of Balto., were married last eve. by Rev. Curtis. (BFG, 20 Sept. 1798)

FINOUS, Charles, and Margaret Maxwell, both of Balto., were wed last Tues. by Bishop Carroll. (BA, 7 March 1801) (BT, 9 March 1801 gives the groom's name as Finour.)

FISCHER, Mrs. Margaret, died at Frederick Town on Fri., 1st inst. relict of the late Dr. Adam Fischer, upwards of 60 years of age. (BFG, 8 Nov. 1799)

FISHER, Mrs. Elizabeth, died last eve., wife of John Fisher, in her 52nd year. (BFG, 12 March 1803)

FISHER, Henry M., and Susannah Swann, both of Balto., were married Wed. eve. by Rev. Roberts. (BA, 31 Jan. 1801)

FISHER, Henry M., and Miss Polly M'Caskey, all of Balto., were married last Tues. by Rev. Glendy. (BFG, 13 June 1807)

FISHER, James, died last Sun. (BFG, 11 Oct. 1800)

FISHER, John, merchant, and Miss Ann Robinson, all of Balto., were married last Tues. by Rev. Inglis. (BFG, 21 Nov. 1811)

FISHER, Joshua, merchant, died last week in Phila. (BEP, 6 Nov. 1806)

FISHER, Robert, and Miss Amelia Alexander, both of Balto., were married Sat. eve. by Rev. Rattoone. (BA, 26 March 1807)

FISHER, Thomas, and Miss Elizabeth Yates, both of Balto., were married last eve. by Rev. Ireland. (BFG, 15 Nov. 1799)

FISHER, William, and Miss Elizabeth Dick, all of Balto., were married last Fri. by Rev. Glendy. (BFG, 27 Sept. 1813)

FISHPAW, Elijah, and Miss Ketura Bond, all of Balto. Co., were married Thurs. last by Rev. Grice. (BFG, 17 Jan. 1815)

FISHPAW, Thomas, and Miss Ann Potter, both of Balto. Co., were married last Thurs. (BT, 19 March 1804)

FISSOUR, John M., native of France, and long a Balto. merchant, died 8th inst., aged 52 years. (BFG, 15 Nov. 1816)

FITCH, Gideon, of Balto., and Miss Mary Anne Lynch of Balto. Co., were married last eve. by Dr. Roberts. (BA, 10 Nov. 1815)

FITCH, John, and Miss Pleasant Chamberlain, both of Balto. Co., were married yesterday morning by Rev. Daniel Dodge. (BFG, 16 Oct. 1801)

FITE, Henry, and Miss Mary Owings Worthington, dau. of Thomas Worthington, all of Balto. Co., were married Tues., 10th inst. (BFG, 13 Oct. 1815)

FITE, Jacob, Balto. merchant, died yesterday in his 35th year. (BFG, 10 March 1806)

FITZE, William, and Mrs. Jane Larere, were married last eve. at Fells Point by Rev. Rattoone. (BFG, 30 Nov. 1802)

FITZGERALD, Col. John, of Alexandria, died. (BA, 12 Dec. 1799)

FITZGERALD, Joshua C,, cabinet maker, died a few days ago of the nervous fever. He came to Balto. about four weeks ago and said he was from Frankfort, Ky. He recently joined the Second Baptist Church in Balto. (BA, 11 Sept. 1811)

FITZHUGH, Daniel Dulany, of Balto. Co., and Miss Margaret Murray Maynadier of A. A. Co., were married 4th inst. at Belvoir, the seat of Henry Maynadier, by Rev. Judd. (BFR, 24 Jan. 1810)

FITZHUGH, George, Jr., and Miss Harriet Richardson, both of Balto., were married last eve. by Rev. Whitebread. (BEP, 4 Dec. 1807)

FITZHUGH, John, died Thurs. last at his seat in Stafford Co., Va., near the commencement of his 83rd year. (BFG, 16 May 1809)

FITZHUGH, Walter, eldest son of George Fitzhugh, died at his father's res. in Balto. Co., last Thurs., in his 22nd year. (BFG, 2 Oct. 1802)

FITZHUGH, Washington, son of George Fitzhugh of Balto. Co., died in P. Co., in his 19th year. (BFG, 25 April 1807)

FITZJEFFREY, Richard, and Miss Eleanora Lowry, both of Balto., were married last eve. by Rev. Rattoone. (BFG, 9 March 1805)

FITZSIMMONS, Thomas, died at Phila., late President of the Chamber of Commerce. (BFG, 28 Aug. 1811)

FLAHERTY, John R., and Miss Catherine Bhaner, all of Balto., were married last Tues. by Archbishop Carroll. (BFG, 9 Feb. 1815)

FLAKSKOM, William, and Miss Margaret Craig, all of Balto., were married last Thurs. by Rev. Dr. Becker. (BA, 20 June 1812)

FLAXEN, Michael, and Miss Sarah Halfpenny of Balto. Co., were wed last eve. by Rev. Richards. (BT, 9 July 1802)

FLEESON, John Glen, printer, grandson of Plunket Fleeson, died 20th ult., in Phila. in his 28th year. Born in South Carolina, he was buried in the cem. of the First Baptist Ch., Second St. (BFG, 2 Aug. 1810)

FLEMING, Capt. Mathias, native of Ireland, and late of New York, died yesterday. Funeral from # 14 Harrison St. (BA, 14 Aug. 1810)

FLETCHER, Edward, merchant, and Miss Margaret Flora, both of Balto., were married last Thurs. by Rev. Beeston. (BFG, 31 May 1809) (BEP, 29 May 1809 gives the bride's name as Florey.)

FLITCHEL, Anthony of Balto., and Miss Barbary Koopson of Phila., were married last Tues. by Rev. Beard. (BT, 29 June 1805)

FLOOD, Thomas, and Mrs. Elizabeth Murray, were married 5 Oct. by Rev. Glendy. (BW, 21 Nov. 1808)

FLOYD, Andrew, died last Wed. at Fells Point. (BT, 24 Feb. 1798)

FLOYD, Jesse, Sr., died at his res. in St. M. Co., 14th inst. in his 67th year. (BPE, 23 March 1813)

FLOYD, Rev. John, of the Catholic Church, died yesterday about 30 years of age. (BFG, 9 Sept. 1797)

FLOYD, Thomas, of Balto. Co., and Miss Lydia Hunt of Balto. were married last Thurs. by Rev. Duncan. (BFG, 21 Feb. 1814)

FOARD, Capt. Jeremiah, died 9 March at his res. in Balto. Co., "one of the worthies of '76." (BFG, 14 March 1812)

FOLEY, Mr. Prestley, and Miss Sarah Fleming, both of Fells Point, were married Monday. (BFG, 9 Nov. 1803)

FOLTZ, Mrs. Margaret, died yesterday in her 61st year; funeral from her late res., corner of Pratt and Eutaw St. (BFG, 17 Jan. 1815)

FOLTZ, William, died this morning, an old inhab. of Balto.; funeral from his late res. at Pratt and Eutaw Sts.; interment in the burying ground at Mr. Otterbein's church. (BFG, 1 March 1810)

FOLTZ, William, of Balto., and Miss Catherine Birely of Frederick Town, were married at the latter place last Tues. by Rev. Schaeffer. (BPEA, 8 April 1815)

FONERDEN, James M., of Balto., and Eliza Murry Spingler, dau. of Henry Spingler of N. York, were married last Thurs. at the latter place by Bishop Moore. (BFG, 15 Aug. 1809)

FONERDEN, Mrs. Martha, consort of Adam Fonerden, died last Tues., aged 45 years. (BFG, 11 Oct. 1797)

FONERDEN, William, and Miss Keziah Marshall, were married last Fri. by Rev. Glendy. (BS, 8 Jan. 1812)

FORBES, Capt. James, and Miss Harriet Burke, both of Balto., were married on Wed. by Rev. Glendy. (BFG, 24 Feb. 1814)

FORBES, John, and Miss Peggy Fisher, both of Balto., were married last Wed. by Rev. Mr. Hagerty. (BFG, 6 Feb. 1801)

FORBES, Thomas, drowned Tues., 27th ult., in his 21st year, while trying to cross the ice on Swanson's Creek, a branch of Patuxent. His body was found last Thurs. He was the son of the late J. Forbes of Benedict, Chas. Co. (BFG, 5 Feb. 1807)

FORBUS, John, and Peggy Fisher, both of Balto., were married on Thurs. eve. by Rev. Hagerty. (BA, 7 Feb. 1801)

FORD, Daniel, died 16th inst., near Dumfries, of hydrophobia, in his 20th year; bro. of John Ford. "Alexandria, Aug. 23." (BA, 27 Aug. 1799)

FORD, Mrs. Deborah, wife of William Ford, died 6th inst., in her 18th year. Her mother was Mrs. Rebecca Duncan. (BA, 9 March 1813)

FORD, George W., and Miss Eliza Ann Dorsey, all of Balto., were married Tues., 22nd inst., by Rev. Roberts. (BFG, 24 Nov. 1814)

FORD, John Edward, delegate to the General Assembly of Md., died at his seat in Chas. Co., 23rd ult. (BWA, 6 April 1816)

FORD, Capt. Joseph, died 23rd ult., at his seat in St. M. Co., aged 60 years. He was a father and husband. (BFG, 7 Feb. 1812)

FORD, Nicholas J., and Miss Elizabeth Ford, all of Balto., were married last eve. by Dr. Roberts. (BEP, 24 Aug. 1807)

FORD, Philip, Esq., of St. M. Co., died 12th inst., in his 59th year. (BA, 22 June 1807)

FORD, Stephen H., merchant, and Mrs. Grace Hammond, all of Balto., were married last Wed. by Rev. Bend. (BFG, 27 Sept. 1811)

FORD, William, of Balto., and Miss Eliza Byus of Dor. Co., were married Sun., 22nd inst., by Rev. Kemp. (BT, 31 July 1804)

FORD, William, and Miss Deborah Duncan, all of Balto., were wed last eve. by Rev. Glendy. (BW, 18 Sept. 1811)

FOREMAN, Mr. Elijah, died yesterday, aged 33 years; funeral from his late res., 94 Dugan's Wharf. (BA, 21 Feb. 1816)

FOREMAN, Joshua, and Miss Mary Philips, both of Balto. City, were married last eve. by Rev. Richards. (BFG, 22 June 1807)

FORMAN, Charles, of Balto., and Miss Sarah Wolf of Phila., were married there last Sat. by Rev. Dr. Smith. (BFG, 26 June 1799)

FORMAN, Francis, merchant, and Miss Ann Elizabeth Immel were married Tues., 9th inst., near Chambersburg, Penna., by Rev. Miller. (BFG, 18 Dec. 1806)

FORMAN, William L., died yesterday morning, leaving a widow and orphans. (BFG, 5 Oct. 1804)

FORMWALT, Jacob, and Miss Rebecca Grammer, both of Fred. Co., were married last eve. by Rev. Mr. Kurtz. (BFG, 7 April 1815)

FORREST, General, clerk of the Circuit Court, of the Dist. of Columbia, died last Sat. (BFG, 12 July 1805)

FORREST, Alexander, and Elizabeth Sampson, both of Balto., were married last Thurs. eve. (BA, 7 March 1801)

FORRESTER, James, and Rachel Burgain, all of Balto. Co., were married last Thurs. by Rev. Healey. (BW, 29 Aug. 1809)

FORREST, Leonard, and Miss Sarah Stuart, both of Balto., were married last Thurs. by Rev. Dr. Roberts. (BA, 27 July 1816)

FORRESTER, Ralph E., of Phila., and Miss Sarah Gantz, dau. of Adam Gantz, of Balto., were married on last Mon. by Rev. M'Clain. (BEP, 5 Nov. 1807)

FORSTER, Francis, and Sarah Askew, both of Balto., were married last eve. by Rev. Rattoone. (BFG, 23 June 1806)

FORSTER, Francis, and Miss Mary H. Miller, were married at Govans Town, last Sat. by Rev. Mr. Allen. (BFG, 18 April 1808)

FORSTER, Vilas, native of Phila., aged 21, belonging to the privateer Atlas, died at the Poor House and Hospital in Savannah, Ga., on 16th ult. (BA, 14 Nov. 1812)

FORSTER, William, and Mrs. Elizabeth McKnight, all of Balto., were married last eve. by Rev. Hargrove. (BA, 29 Aug. 1812)

FORSYTH, Mr. Jacob, and Miss Sally Cooper, both of Balto., were married last Thurs. by Rev. Mr. Parrott. (BFG, 25 Nov. 1797)

FORSYTH, William, and Miss Lydia Everson, both of Balto. Co., were married Thurs. by Rev. Hargrove. (BFG, 11 June 1802)

FORT, Mr. Benjamin, and Miss Airey Caney, were married last eve. by Rev. Fort. (BT, 19 Jan. 1803)

FORTUNE, Capt. James, of Fells Point, died yesterday, in his 57th year. (BFG, 6 Nov. 1797)

FOSS, Daniel, died Thurs., 17th inst., aged 22. (BA, 19 Nov. 1814)

FOSS, George, and Miss Mary Pouder, dau. of Mr. Leonard Pouder, all of Balto., were married last eve. by Rev. Otterbein. (BFG, 11 April 1806)

FOSS, Jacob, and Miss Margaret Detmar, all of Balto., were wed last eve. by Rev. Otterbein. (BFG, 3 June 1808)

FOSSE, Mr. John, and Miss Elizabeth Mitchell, both of Fells Pt., were married last eve. by Rev. Passmore. (BFG, 25 Jan. 1798)

FOSTER, Barton, a native of Ireland, and late of Balto., died on Sat. "New Orleans, Sept. 19." (BFG, 31 Oct. 1811)

FOSTER, Caleb, died Sun.; a cut nail manufacturer. (BA, 25 Sept. 1804)

FOSTER, Emilia Louisa, infant dau. of Francis and Sarah Foster, died Fri., 2nd inst., aged 4 mos., 12 days. (BFG, 5 Aug. 1816)

FOSTER, Capt. James, and Mrs. Rebecca Shehanasey, both of Balto., were married last eve. by Rev. Ireland. (BFG, 23 Sept. 1799)

FOSTER, John M., and Louisa Dimmitt, all of Balto., were married last eve. at Christ Church, by Rev. Wyatt. (BA, 22 Oct. 1816)

FOSTER, Louisiana Foster, and James Winn Foster, children of Anthony Foster, died last Wed. when their father's house caught fire. (BA, 28 March 1814)

FOSTER, Mrs. Sarah, wife of Francis Foster, died 2nd inst., leaving a husband and three small children. (BFG, 5 Aug. 1816)

FOULCONER, Capt. Nathaniel, died suddenly on Fri., at Phila., master warden, one of the oldest captains of that port, aged 77. (BA, 11 Nov. 1806)

FOULK, Lewis, merchant, and Miss Susanna Fonerden, dau. of Adam Fonerden, all of Balto., were married last Wed. by Rev. Dashiells. (BFG, 20 Dec. 1805)

FOWBLE, Daniel, and Miss Ann Buck, all of Balto., were married last Thurs. by Rev. Otterbein. (BA, 14 Sept. 1811)

FOWBLE, Peter, and Miss Rebecca Hardester, all of Balto., were 20th inst., by Rev. Fechtig. (BWA, 30 March 1816)

FOWLE, Jacob, died Wed., aged 22. (BA, 17 Aug. 1799)

FOWLER, Mr., of Hawkins Point, was supposedly murdered last Thurs. by three of his negroes. (BFG, 19 March 1805)

FOWLER, Benjamin, merchant of Pittsburgh, and Miss Mary Hughes, of Balto., were married Thurs. eve. by Rev. Richards. (BMJ, 26 March 1796)

FOWLER, John, of Patapsco, had been murdered by three of his negroes, Dennis, Ned, and Kate, who were executed yesterday. "Annap., 9 May." (BA, 13 May 1805)

FOWLER, John, and Miss Esther Sagassar, both of Balto., were wed Thurs. by Rev. Kurtz. (BPE, 11 Dec. 1813)

FOWLER, William, of Fells Point, died a few weeks ago in Balto. Co. (BA, 20 Oct. 1800)

FOWLER, William, and Miss Catherine Deale, all of Balto., were married on Thurs., 20th inst., by Rev. Healey. (BA, 28 July 1815)

FOWNES, John, merchant of London, and Mrs. Sarah Thomas, of Fells Point, were married last week at Phila., by Bishop Butler. (BFG, 7 Jan. 1799)

FOWNES, John, merchant, formerly of Fells Point, died Fri., 24th inst., at Washington. (BFG, 28 Sept. 1802)

FOX, Jonathan, of Balto., died 28th ult, aged 19. (BPEA, 13 Jan. 1815)

FOX, Justus, type founder and printer, died 26th inst., in his 69th year; a native of Germany. (BFG, 4 Feb. 1805)

FOX, Thomas, merchant of Petersburg, Va., died there on Sat., 14th inst. (BFG, 19 June 1806)

FOXALL, Mrs. Elizabeth, died last Sat., wife of Thomas Foxall, aged 38 years. (BFG, 24 April 1810)

FOXALL, Thomas, and Miss Mary Cox, all of Balto., were married last eve. by Rev. Richards. (BFG, 13 July 1810)

FOZEUR, Thomas R., and Miss Christiana Hydorne, both of Balto., were married last Thurs. by Rev. Baxley. (BA, 16 March 1816)

FRAILEY, Adeline, dau. of L. Frailey, printer, died last eve. aged 1 year, 1 mo., 17 days. (BFG, 12 Oct. 1808)

FRAILEY, Edward J., died Tues. eve., infant son of Leonard Frailey of Balto. (BA, 11 Sept. 1806)

FRAILEY, Leonard, co-editor of the American, and Miss Elizabeth Stitcher, of Balto., were married last eve. by Rev. Mr. Kurtz. (BFG, 11 March 1803)

FRANCIS, Mrs. Anne, relict of the late Tench Francis of this city, died at Phila., 2nd inst., in her 79th year. (BFR, 7 Jan. 1812)

FRANCIS, Tench, died at Phila. on Thurs. He was Purveyor of the U. S. Navy. (BA, 7 May 1800)

FRANCIS, Thomas Willing, died yesterday morning in his 48th year. "Phila., June 3." (BFG, 5 June 1815)

FRANCISCUS, John, and Miss Mary Thompson, all of Balto., were married last eve. by Rev. Richards. (BFG, 3 Feb. 1804)

FRANKLIN, Mrs. Elizabeth Ann, consort of Capt. Samuel Franklin, of Balto., died 6th inst., at West River, A. A. Co., in her 21st year. (BFG, 22 Feb. 1816)

FRANKLIN, George, and Miss Juliet Essex, both of Balto., were married last Thurs. by Rev. Roberts. (BPEA, 10 March 1815)

FRANKS, Samuel D., and Miss Sarah May were married at Reading on
Wed., 8th inst. (BA, 15 Aug. 1804)

FRASER, Thomas, merchant, native of Scotland, died this morning
of apoplexy. (BFG, 18 Oct. 1802)

FRASIER, James, and Mrs. Coatney (sic) Berry, were married by
Rev. Rattoone. (BFG, 1 March 1806)

FRAZER, Richard, purser of the Navy Yard in Wash., died last
Sun. "Nat. Int." (BT, 31 March 1804)

FRAZIER, Charles, late Speaker of the House of Delegates, died
3rd inst. at his farm in Q. A. Co. (BFG, 5 Sept. 1805)

FRAZIER, Mr. E., and Miss Porter, both of Fells Point, were wed
on Thurs. (BFG, 3 Dec. 1804)

FRAZIER, Jeremiah, and Miss Susanna Margaret M'Kenzie, were wed
by Rev. Rattoone. (BEP, 13 June 1808)

FRAZIER, Levin, and Miss Margaret Bradenhouse, were married on
6th inst. by Rev. Glendy. (BFG, 11 Feb. 1814)

FRAZIER, Miss Maria, dau. of Capt. Frazier of the U. S. Navy,
died in Balto., on 6th inst., in her 16th year. (BPE, 9
June 1813)

FREANER, Henry, and Mrs. Mary Miller, both of this county, were
married last Mon. by Rev. Glendy. (BA, 20 March 1806)

FREEMAN, Ezekiel, of Balto., and Miss Rebecca Price of Balto.
Co. were married on Tues. by Rev. Frederick Beasley. (BA,
13 May 1813)

FRENCH, Bennett, died this morning, aged 32; funeral will be tomorrow from his late res. 9 Conawago St. (BEP, 7 Feb.
1809)

FRENCH, Ebenezer, printer, and Caroline Hargrove were married in
Balto. by Rev. Mr. Hargrove. (BFG, 21 Feb. 1814)

FRENCH, Mrs. Hannah, wife of the publisher of the Patriot, died
yesterday. (BFG, 10 Nov. 1813)

FRENCH, Rev. John C., and Mary Paul, both of Balto., were married
9 Nov. by Rev. Hemphill. (BA, 21 Nov. 1816)

FRENCH, Nathaniel, and Miss Rachel Baldwin, all of Balto., were
married 17th inst. by Rev. Hargrove. (BFG, 27 Aug. 1812)

FRENCH, Samuel, of the Office of Discount and Deposit, died yesterday aged 38 years; funeral from his res., Greene St.,
Old Town. (BFG, 14 April 1808)

FRENCH, Mrs. Urith, died last Sun., aged 72 years. (BFG, 2 May
1805)

FRENCH, William, Balto. merchant, and Miss Ann R. Halverson of
Phila., were married at the latter place last Thurs. by
Rev. Blackwell. (BFG, 18 April 1812)

FREY, Miss Ann, dau. of Samuel Frey, of Balto., died last Sat.,
in her 17th year. (BFG, 19 March 1816)

MARRIAGES AND DEATHS

FREY, Mrs. Elizabeth, died; funeral from her father's res. in Sharpe St. (BA, 8 Aug. 1811)

FREY, George, of Somerset Co., Penna., and Mary Hampshire of Balto., were married 12 June by Rev. Hoffman. (BA, 13 June 1816)

FREY, Samuel, of Balto., and Miss Susan Shriver, dau. of David Shriver of Little Pipe Creek, Fred. Co., were married on 22nd inst. by Rev. Glendy. (BA, 31 Aug. 1809)

FREY, Samuel, Jr., son of Samuel Frey, died yesterday in his 18th year. Funeral will be from his father's res. corner of Barre and Sharpe Sts., and interment will be in Otterbein's burial ground. (BA, 5 May 1809)

FREY, Susan, dau. of Samuel, of Balto., died yesterday in her 16th year. (BEP, 16 Nov. 1810)

FRICK, William, Esq., Attorney-at-Law, and Miss Mary Sloan were married last Thurs. by Rev. Glendy. (BFG, 8 June 1816)

FRIESE, John F., and Miss Rebecca Prince of Balto., were married last eve. by Rev. Kurtz. (BFG, 16 Dec. 1814)

FRIEZE, Philip R. I., and Miss J. G. Avenaux, all of Balto., were married Sun. eve. by Rev. Kurtz. (BFG, 18 Dec. 1805)

FRISBY, George, of Kent, and Miss Elizabeth Brown of Balto. Co., were married last eve. at Oxford, the seat of James Edwards, by Rev. Bend. (BFG, 13 Aug. 1811)

FRISBY, James, Jr., planter of the Eastern Shore of Md., died on Tues. in the Penna. Hospital, having resided therein over twelve years. (BFG, 6 Feb. 1797)

FRISBY, R'd., and Miss Sally Barroll, both of Chestertown, Kent Co., were married 11th inst., by Rev. William H. Wilmer. (BFR, 27 Oct. 1810)

FROST, Capt. Thomas, died yesterday; funeral from his late res., Mrs. Lauderman's, 21 Bond St., Fells Point. (BA, 18 June 1816)

FRY, Conrad, of Windsor Twp., York Co., Penna., died Mon., 17 Feb., aged 85. His wife Catherine died Sat., 15 Feb., aged 90. They had been married for 63 years. (BA, 6 March 1800)

FRY, Mrs. Elizabeth, of Fells Point, died last Tues. in her 67th year. (BA, 26 Aug. 1816)

FRYER, George, printer, and long an inhab. of Balto., died last Sun. (BA, 15 Sept. 1812)

FRYER, Henry, and Miss Elizabeth Renshaw, all of Balto., were married last Tues. by Rev. Dr. Roberts. (BFG, 19 July 1810)

FULFORD, Mrs. Eleanor, died Wed. in her 78th year. (BFG, 2 Nov. 1815)

FULFORD, Thomas, of Balto., died 19th ult., at Vera Cruz, after a short illness. (BFG, 21 May 1799)

FULFORD, William, and Miss Mary Frances Patterson of Miles Mill, Harf. Co., were married Mon., 18th inst., by Rev. Allen. (BFG, 26 June 1804)

FULLEN, Daniel, and Mrs. Honora McCormick, both of Balto., were married 1st inst. by Rev. Glendy. (BA, 12 Oct. 1811)

FULLER, Alexander, merchant, died in Phila. (BA, 4 Oct. 1799)

FULLER, Horace, and Mrs. Nicey Whitelsy, both of Balto., were wed last Thurs. (BW, 23 March 1814)

FULLER, Mrs. Mary, formerly of Phila., died in Balto., on last Wed., in her 70th year. (BFG, 9 Jan. 1801)

FULLER, Oliver, Balto. merchant, and Rebecca Chase of Salem, Mass., were married 20th inst. at the latter place. (BA, 31 Aug. 1801)

FULLERTON, Campbell, and Miss Jane Miller, were married last Thurs. by Rev. Glendy. (BT, 14 Jan. 1804)

FULLERTON, James, ship joiner, died Mon. in Phila., as a result of an accident during the launching of the ship Franklin. (BFG, 24 Aug. 1815)

FULTON, David, bro. of Alexander and James Fulton, Balto. merchants, died yesterday in his 17th year. (BT, 4 Oct. 1802)

FULTON, James, merchant, and Mary Neilson, second dau. of Mrs. Neilson, all of Balto., were married last eve. by Rev. Mr. Sinclair. (BFG, 3 March 1802)

FULTON, James, of Balto., and Miss Eliza Mayo, second dau. of Col. William Mayo of Henrico Co., Va., were married Sun., 25th inst. at Richmond. (BFG, 30 Sept. 1803)

FULTON, Thomas, and Miss Margaret Furnor, were married last Fri. by Rev. John Glendy. (BFG, 19 Aug. 1814)

FULTON, William, and Mrs. Mary Davison, consort of the late Andrew Davison, of Balto., were married 6th inst. (BA, 14 Nov. 1800). (BT, 13 Nov. 1800 gives the bride's name as Davidson.)

FURLONG, Nicholas, and Miss Dorothy Bayly, both of Balto., were married last Thurs. by Rev. Glendy. (BA, 29 June 1805)

FURNACE, William, and Miss Phebe Sprague, all of Balto., were married last Mon. by Rev. D. E. Reese. (BA, 24 July 1816)

FURNIVAL, Alexander, died last Mon. at "Harmony," Balto. Co., in his 55th year; interment was in Balto. yesterday. (BFG, 17 Sept. 1807)

FURNIVAL, Mrs. Elizabeth, wife of Alexander Furnival, died yesterday morning. (BFG, 4 Nov. 1801)

FUSELBAUGH, John, died 19th inst.; native of Germany, aged 46 years. (BFG, 22 Jan. 1814)

FUSSELBAUGH, John, and Barbara Zigler, both of Balto., were wed last eve. by Rev. Kurtz. (BT, 23 June 1800)

FYLEA?, Frederick, and Miss Juliet Murray, both of Balto., were married Thurs., 29th inst. by Rev. Dr. Baker. (BFG, 31 Oct. 1807)

GABER, Daniel, died at Frederick Town, an old inhab. of that county. (BA, 28 Dec. 1799)

GADE, John, died last Sun. (BPE, 12 Jan. 1814)

GADSBY, Mrs. Margaret, died this morning, leaving a husband and six children. (BFG, 10 Feb. 1812)

GAINES, Maj.-Gen. Edmund Pendleton, and Miss Barbara B. Blount, dau. of Wm. Blount, dec., were married in Knoxville, Tenn., on 7 Aug. by Rev. Thomas Nelson. (BMG, 24 Aug. 1815)

GAITHER, Col. Henry, died 22nd inst., in his 61st year (Long obit gives details of his Rev. career.) "Georgetown, 25 June." (BFR, 28 June 1811)

GAITHER, Henry C., and Miss Eliza Worthington, dau. of William Worthington, all of Mont. Co., were married Tues., 28th ult. by Rev. Mr. Read. (BFR, 5 Feb. 1812)

GAITHER, James, and Mrs. Patience Hall, both of A. A. Co., were married last eve. by Rev. Mr. Hargrove. (BFG, 6 Dec. 1798)

GALAND, John B., and Miss Catherine Kurnrich, both of Balto., were married last Thurs. by Rev. Kurtz. (BA, 8 June 1807)

GALBRAITH, George, and Mrs. Ann Beggs were married by Rev. Glendy. (BW, 16 Feb. 1809)

GALBRAITH, Thomas, and Mrs. Rosanna Willis, all of Balto., were married last eve. by Rev. Hargrove. (BFG, 15 Dec. 1806)

GALE, John, and Miss Martha Hudgins were married by Rev. Glendy last Mon. (BEP, 26 March 1811)

GALE, Gen. John, died 25th ult., at Annamessex, Som. Co., a revolutionary hero, taken prisoner at Long Island; he represented his country in the State Legislature. (BFG, 10 Feb. 1813)

GALE, William, late an officer in the U. S. Army, died; funeral from his late res., 200 1/2 Market St. (BA, 14 Nov. 1815)

GALES, Joseph, editor of the National Intelligencer, and Miss Juliana Lee, dau. of Theodorick Lee, were married on 13th inst. at Woodsville, near Winchester, Va., by Rev. A. Balmain. (BA, 20 Dec. 1813)

GALLAGHER, Mrs. Jane, died this morning aged 77 years; a native of Ireland and for the last 7 years a res. of Balto.; funeral from her late res., Frederick and Water Sts. (BFG, 16 March 1816)

GALLAHER, James, printer, died of the prevailing fever on 25th ult. (BFG, 13 Oct. 1800)

GALLAWAY, James, and Mrs. Priscilla Strain, both of Fells Point, were married last Sun. eve. by Rev. Rattoone. (BAP, 7 July 1803)

GALLAWAY, Thomas, and Miss Mary Minee, both of Balto., were wed Thurs. eve. by Rev. Alexander M'Caine. (BFR, 25 May 1811)

GALLIGHER, Richard, and Miss Hannah Peters, both of Balto., were married last eve. by Rev. Glendy. (BFG, 4 April 1811)

GALLOWAY, John, died at West River, at Tulip Hill, last Wed. (BFR, 28 May 1810)

GALLOWAY, William, Esq., died Sat., 15th inst., in Balto. Co., at his seat in Middle River Neck, in his 52nd year. (BFG, 18 Aug. 1801)

GALT, Mr. Peter, and Miss Araminta Patton, both of Balto., were married Thurs. eve. (BT, 29 March 1802)

GALT, Peter, of Balto., and Miss Eliza Murray, dau. of John Murray of Balto. Co., were married last eve. by Rev. Hagerty. (BFG, 3 Nov. 1809)

GAMBLE, Joseph, sailing master, died 23 Feb. in Washington, leaving a family in Balto. (BA, 4 March 1814)

GAMBRILL, William, of A. A. Co., and Martha Peach of P. G. Co., were married last Thurs. by Rev. Ridgely. (BT, 12 Nov. 1803)

GANTT, Capt. Christopher L., and Miss Mary Newburn, all of Balto., were married last Tues. by Rev. Bend. (BA, 21 Sept. 1809)

GARDENER, Capt. Samuel, and Miss Elizabeth Merin, both of Balto., were married last eve. by Rev. Inglis. (BFG, 2 Jan. 1808)

GARDINER, Edward T., of Wood Co., Va., died on 3rd inst., of consumption on board the *Western Trader*, bound for Phila. (BFG, 27 May 1808)

GARDINER, Mr. James, and Miss Margaret Hassin, both of Balto., were married Thurs. eve. by Rev. Mr. Beaston. (BT, 13 March 1802)

GARDINER, John M., and Miss Sophia Gassaway, of Balto., were wed on Fri. last at Annapolis. (BT, 11 Nov. 1805)

GARDINER, Samuel, and Miss Eleanor Hillen, both of Balto., were married last Sat. by Rev. Rattoone. (BFG, 20 Aug. 1805)

GARDINER, William C., merchant of Newport, R. I., and Miss Eliza F. Casenove, dau. of Anthony Casenove of Alexandria, were married 16th inst. by Rev. James Muir. (BWA, 25 May 1816)

GARDNER, Capt., and Miss Juliana Larea, both of Fells Point, were married on Tues. by Rev. Rattoone. (BFG, 12 July 1803)

GARDNER, Mrs. Elizabeth, consort of Capt. Joseph Gardner, died last night; funeral from her late res. in Philpott St., Fells Point. (BFG, 15 Jan. 1803)

GARDNER, George, and Miss Sarah Stretch, all of Balto., were wed last eve. by Rev. Richards. (BFG, 12 May 1806)

GARDNER, John E., only child of Mr. H. Gardner, died Sun. on Fells Point. (BFG, 31 Oct. 1803)

GARDNER, Capt. Joseph, and Miss Elizabeth Weatherly, dau. of Capt. Joseph Weatherly, were married last eve. by Rev. Richards. (BT, 7 June 1802)

GARDNER, Capt. Joseph, and Miss Sophia Aldredge, were married last eve. by Rev. Glendy. (BFG, 31 Oct. 1806)

GARDNER, Peter, of Washington, and Mrs. Margaret Green of Balto. Co., were married last Mon. eve. by Rev. Richards. (BA, 5 June 1811)

GARDNER, Capt. Thaddeus, late master of the schooner Argo of this port, died 26 Sept. at Kingston, Jamaica. (BFG, 14 Nov. 1798)

GAREY, Jeremiah, of Easton, and Miss Elizabeth Burke, of Balto. Co., were married last Mon. by Rev. Reese. (BA, 29 March 1810)

GARNES, Capt. John, and Miss Lydia Champlin, all of Balto., were married last Sun. by Rev. Glendy. (BEP, 20 Dec. 1808)

GARRAUD, E., and Miss Elizabeth Long, both of Balto., were wed last Sat. by Rev. Glendy. (BFG, 1 Feb. 1813)

GARRET, Andrew, aged 88 years, died Sun. from wounds received from a gang of villains who robbed him the night of the 19th ult. "Phila., 3 Dec." (BFG, 4 Dec. 1812)

GARRET, Robert, and Miss Martha Hanna, all of Balto., were married last eve. by Rev. Glendy. (BFG, 22 Feb. 1811)

GARRETSON, Richard W., and Miss Elizabeth F. Osborne, all of Balto., were wed Thurs. by Rev. M'Caine. (BW, 8 Jan. 1814)

GARRETT, Martha, wife of Robert Garrett, and dau. of A. B. Hanna, died this morning in her 21st year; funeral from her late res., Dutch Alley, near Howard St. (BFG, 2 Oct. 1812)

GARRETTSON, Freeborn, and Mrs. (?) Eliza Richardson of Harf. Co. were married 1 Jan. by Rev. Guest. (BFG, 4 Jan. 1812)

GARRETTSON, George, died Tues., 24th inst., at his late res. in Harf. Co., aged 64; a member of the Methodist Society for almost 30 years. (BFG, 1 Dec. 1807)

GARRETTSON, Ruthen, and Miss Polly Gallion, were married at Mr. George Garrettson's in Harf. Co. (BFG, 27 Nov. 1797)

GARRETTSON, Mrs. Susanna, relict of George Garrettson, died Mon., 6th inst., in her 72nd year. (BFG, 11 May 1811)

GARRISON, John, and Miss Mary Brumridge, were married by Rev. Rockland. (BA, 3 April 1812)

GARTS, Charles, died this morning, an old merchant of Balto. (BFG, 24 Aug. 1811)

GARTS, John, son of the late Charles Garts of Balto., died 21st inst. in his 38th year. (BA, 23 July 1816)

GARTS, Mr. Peter, eldest son of Mr. Charles Garts of Balto., died last eve. (BEP, 18 June 1808)

GATES, Hon. Horatio, died 10th inst., in his 78th year; a lieut.-gen. in the service of the U. S. in the late Rev. War (long obit.). (BA, 15 April 1806)

GAULINE, John B., and Miss Mary Thryack, both of Balto., were married last Thurs. by Rev. Richards. (BT, 27 Aug. 1804)

GAVET, Capt. John, and Miss Maria Morgan, all of Balto., were married by Rev. Glendy. (BA, 20 Oct. 1810)

GEARY, William, died yesterday, aged 24 years; funeral from the house of James Gould, No. 31 N. Howard St. (BA, 22 Jan. 1816)

GEAUTHROP, Thomas, and Miss Sarah S. Spence, all of Balto., were married last eve. by Dr. Roberts. (BA, 17 Aug. 1816)

GEBHARDT, John F., died 24th inst., in his 52nd year, an old inhab. of Balto. (BS, 25 May 1812)

GEDDES, Capt. David, an old inhab. of Fells Point, died yesterday. Members of the different lodges are requested to attend his funeral from his late res., Fleet and Market Sts. (BFG, 7 March 1807)

GEDDES, James L., son of Mr. Geddes of Newport, Del., died yesterday at the Globe Inn, as a result of having taken too large quantity of laudunum. (BA, 15 Aug. 1806)

GEDDES, Mrs. Mary, widow of the late William Geddes, Esq., of Md., died at Wilmington, Del., on 2nd inst.: interment in the Presbyterian burying ground, Arch St., Phila. (BFG, 8 June 1803)

GEDDES, William, native of Md., died 15th ult. in Phila., at an advanced age. (BFG, 6 Feb. 1801)

GEIGER, John, of Lancaster Co., Penna., and Miss Catherine Uhlring of Balto. were married last eve. by Rev. Dashiell. (BA, 2 July 1805)

GEIGER, John, Esq., died at Hagerstown on Mon., 14th inst., aged 52 years. (BFG, 18 Oct. 1805)

GELBACH, Christian, and Miss Sarah Richards, both of Balto., were married last Thurs. by Rev. Kurtz. (BA, 2 Sept. 1809)

GEORGE, Archibald, merchant, and Isabella Knox, dau. of Rev. Samuel Knox of Balto., were married last Thurs. by Rev. Glendy. (BFG, 1 Feb. 1806)

GEORGE, John, died yesterday in his 65th year, a native of London, and a respected attendant in the family of William Trimble. (BFG, 30 July 1802)

GEORGE, Lucas, and Miss Margaret Ferral, all of Balto., were wed last eve. by Rev. Mr. Du Bourg. (BEP, 28 Dec. 1807)

GEORGE, Lucas, A. M., professor of belles lettres at St. Marys College, died this morning in his 30th year. His friends are invited to attend his funeral service at the College tomorrow. (BFG, 2 Nov. 1808)

GEORGE, William E., Balto. merchant, and Sarah Ellicott, were married at Friends Meeting House, Elk Ridge. (BFG, 24 Dec. 1812)

GERMAN, Philip, died Mon., 11th inst., in his 66th year; funeral from his late res., 98 N. Howard St. (BPE, 13 July 1814)

GETCHER, Mr. Francis, and Miss Mary Etchberger, all of Balto., were married last Thurs. by Rev. Kurtz. (BPEA, 28 March 1815)

GHEQUIERE, Bernard, died yesterday. (BPE, 17 Jan. 1814)

GHEQUIERE, Francis W., member of the Baltimore United Volunteers, died. Members of the brigade will assemble tomorrow in full uniform with side arms, and crape for left arm, to attend his funeral. (BFG, 15 Feb. 1808)

GHISELIN, Dr. Reverdy, and Miss Margaret Bowie, dau. of His Excellency the Governor, were married at Annapolis on Tues. by Rev. Mr. Duke. (BA, 31 Dec. 1804)

GHOLSON, Thomas, member of Congress from Va., died at Maj. William Gholson's house in Brunswick Co., Va., last Thurs. (BFG, 12 July 1816)

GHORMEY (?), Richard, and Miss Elizabeth Ann Hodgers (?), both of Balto., were married last Thurs. by Rev. Healey. (BA, 7 Oct. 1816)

GIBBONS, William, died Sun., 5th inst. (BS, 11 Aug. 1810)

GIBBS, John, and Miss Elizabeth Gordon, all of Balto., were married last eve. by Rev. Mr. Dashiell. (BFG, 14 Nov. 1808)

GIBNEY, Mrs. Elizabeth, wife of John Gibney, a native of St. Martins, died Tues., 6th inst., aged 52. (BA, 9 Aug. 1816)

GIBSON, James, and Miss Emily Ann Grundy, dau. of George Grundy of Balto., were married Wed. eve. at Bolton, by Rev. Dr. Kemp. (BA, 29 Dec. 1815)

GIBSON, John, and Eliza C., dau. of Geo. Grundy, were married last eve. at Bolton, by Rev. Dr. Bend. (BFG, 19 Sept. 1806)

GIBSON, Joshua, and Miss Sarah Brown, both of Balto., were wed on Thurs. eve. by Rev. Mr. Roberts. (BA, 7 Feb. 1814)

GIBSON, Samuel, died yesterday of a pulmonary complaint, in his 27th year. Funeral from his late res., South Frederick, near Water St. (BA, 16 April 1810)

GIBSON, Dr. William, and Miss Sarah C. Hollingsworth were married last Thurs. by Rev. Bend. (BFG, 14 Dec. 1811)

GILCHRIST, Capt. Alexander, and Miss Elizabeth Smith, were married last Thurs. by Rev. John Duncan. (BFG, 15 June 1816)

GILES, Edward, of New York, and Cordelia Phillips, dau. of the late James Phillips, were married in Abingdon, Harf. Co., on 24th inst. by Rev. Handy. (BFG, 31 Dec. 1808)

GILES, Jacob W., and Miss Martha Phillips, both of Bush River Neck, Harf. Co., were married 30th ult. by Rev. Allen. (BFG, 4 Jan. 1803)

GILES, Mrs. Martha, wife of Jacob W. Giles, of Harf. Co., died Fri., 24th inst., of typhus. (BFG, 30 March 1815)

GILES, Mrs. Rebecca, formerly of Harf. Co., died Mon., in her 57th year, leaving four orphan children. (BFG, 7 Sept. 1814)

GILES, Thomas, died Sun. at his res. near Havre de Grace in his 45th year. (BFG, 30 Oct. 1798)

GILES, Thomas, of Cecil Co., died at Elkton last Fri.; a faithful public servant during the Rev. War. (BS, 7 Feb. 1812)

GILES, Hon. William B., U. S. Senator, and Miss Frances Ann Gwynn, eld. dau. of the late Thomas Peyton Gwynn of Va., were married in Georgetown on 22 Feb. by Rev. Dr. Gantt. (BW, 7 March 1810)

GILL, Absalom B., and Ann Taylor, were married last Tues. by Rev. Dashiells. (BFG, 29 Sept. 1806)

GILL, John, and Miss Actious Perigo, both of Balto., were wed last Sat. by Rev. Richards. (BW, 22 Sept. 1810)

GILL, Stephen, died 29 Nov. at his farm in Balto. Co., aged 71 years. Any information regarding his son Benjamin Gill will be thankfully rec'd by his bro. William Gill. (BFG, 30 Nov. 1811)

GILLERAN, L., and Miss Catherine Hegerty, all of Balto., were married last Thurs. by Rev. Beeston. (BT, 9 July 1806)

GILLETT, Wheeler, and Miss Marybah? Russell were married last Sun. by Rev. Healey. (BS, 1 Dec. 1812)

GILLINGHAM, Mr., of the theatre, and Miss Anne Heislit, of A. A. Co., were married last Mon. by Rev. Rattoone. (BT, 7 Dec. 1803) (BFG, 7 Dec. 1803 gives the bride's name as Hazel.)

GILLINGHAM, George, and Miriam James, were married this day at Friends Meeting, Lombard St. (BFG, 18 Sept. 1811)

GILLINGHAM, William, and Jane M'Pherson, were married this morning at Friends Meeting, Lombard St. (BFG, 18 March 1812)

GILMAN, John H., native of Winthrop, Mass., died last Thurs., aged 25. (BFG, 12 March 1811)

GILMOR, Robert, Jr., and Miss Elizabeth S. Cooke, dau. of Wm. Cooke, Esq., were married last eve. (BFG, 2 June 1802)

GILMOR, Robert, Jr., and Miss Sarah Reeve Ladson, dau. of Major James Ladson of Charleston, were married there on 11th inst. by Rev. Mr. Simons. (BFG, 27 April 1807)

GILMOR, Mrs. Robert, Jr., died last Sun. (BT, 5 May 1803)

GILMOR, William, Balto. merchant, and Mrs. Mary Ann Drysdale, were married last Tues. in Northampton Co., Va. (BFG, 22 April 1799)

GILPIN, George, died at Alexandria, in his 73rd year. In 1776 he was a champion of his country's cause, commencing his career at Bunker Hill. (BPE, 12 Jan. 1814)

GILPIN, Capt. Samuel, son of Col. George Gilpin of Balto., died Tues. at Alexandria, in his 30th year. (BT, 2 Nov. 1805)

GILPIN, Vincent, died at his seat near the borough of Wilmington, in his 35th year. (BEP, 15 Aug. 1810)

GINAPHIN, Michael, and Miss Elizabeth Welsh, both of Balto., were married Wed. by Rev. Richards. (BEP, 23 Dec. 1808)

GINNODO, Capt. Samuel H., and Miss Eliza Skinner, all of Balto., were married last Wed. by Rev. Glendy. (BEP, 16 March 1809)

GIST, Basil, and Jane Stansbury, were married last Thurs. in Back River Neck by Rev. John Welch. (BEP, 16 Jan. 1808)

GIST, Charles, and Jemima Wesby, all of Balto., were married last Tues. by Rev. Roberts. (BEP, 3 Jan. 1807)

GIST, Independent, and Miss Gest, dau. of Col. Gest, near Winchester, were married last Thurs. by Rev. Armstrong. (BFG, 12 Jan. 1807)

GIST, Gen. Nathaniel, died at his seat at Bourbon, on Fri., 30th ult. "Lexington, Oct. 11." (BMJ, 21 Nov. 1796)

GIST, Col. Thomas, died 22 Nov. at his res. in Balto. Co., in his 73rd year. (BFG, 1 Dec. 1813)

GIST, Capt. Thomas, and Miss Harriot Dorsey, both of Fred. Co., were married last Thurs. by Rev. James Higgins. (BT, 15 April 1815)

GITCHELL, Increase, of the House of Pearce and Gitchell, and Miss Cassandra Barton, were married Sat. by Rev. Rattoone. (BFG, 29 May 1804)

GITTINGS, Archibald, son of James Gittings, Esq., and Miss Elizabeth Bosley, dau. of Elijah Bosley, all of Balto. Co., were married. (BT, 14 March 1799)

GITTINGS, Thomas, Esq., and Miss Polly Williams, both of Balto. Co., were married Thurs., 10th inst. (BFG, 16 Dec. 1801)

GITTINGS, Thomas, Esq., died this morning at the res. of Mrs. Eleanor Croxall, in his 43rd year. (BFG, 26 Sept. 1804)

GLASGOW, Dr. James, and Miss Eliza Schaeffer, both of Balto., were married Tues., 9th inst. (BFG, 11 June 1807)

GLASSGO, William, and Miss Elizabeth Russel, dau. of Alexander Russel, all of Balto., were married last Thurs. by Rev. George Roberts. (BA, 18 Dec. 1810)

GLASSON, Mr. Christian, was found dead last Fri. on the shore of the Ferry Branch (of Patapsco). He was from Germany, with "very respectable connections," and had been very melancholy for some time past. (BFG, 24 July 1797)

GLENDY, Miss Eliza, dau. of Rev. John Glendy, died last Fri. (BFG, 4 May 1813)

GLENDY, Mrs. Elizabeth, died Wed., 13th inst.; consort of Rev. John Glendy; interment in the Presbyterian burying ground. (BFG, 19 June 1804)

GLENN, Mrs. Eliza. wife of John W. Glenn, merchant, died last Fri. in her 24th year. (BFG, 5 Sept. 1805)

GLENN, Harrison W., and Miss Martha, both of Balto., were wed 28th ult. by Rev. Beasley. (BEP, 1 Jan. 1810)

GLENN, John W., merchant, and Mrs. Eliza Watts, both of Balto., were married last eve. by Rev. Rattoone. (BFG, 15 April 1803)

GLENN, Samuel, late of Cecil Co., died in Balto., 24th inst., aged 63 years. (BT, 1 July 1802)

GLISAN, Charles, and Miss Mary Boyer were married in Liberty Town. (BPE, 8 Feb. 1814)

GLOVER, Mr. Josias, and Miss Sarah Hall, all of Balto., were married last eve. by Rev. Coats. (BFG, 17 June 1803)

GNAT, William, and Nancy Flin, of Balto. Co., were married last Thurs. by Rev. Dr. Davis. (BFG, 26 March 1806)

GOARHAM, Capt. John, and Mrs. Sarah Manning, both of Balto., were married 24th inst. by Rev. Bartow. (BPEA, 27 Dec. 1815)

GOBRIGHT, William, of Georgetown, Potomac, and Miss Louisa Norman of Balto. were married last eve. by Rev. Bend. (BEP, 26 Sept. 1806)

GODDARD, Mary Katherine, late of the Maryland Journal, died 12th inst., aged 80 years. (BFG, 14 Aug. 1816)

GODMAN, Mrs. Anne, wife of Capt. Samuel Godman, of Annapolis, and eld. dau. of Capt. Robert Henderson of Phila., died on Mon., having been married for 20 years, and bearing 10 children, 8 of whom still are living. (BT, 29 Nov. 1799)

GOLD, Capt. Joseph, and Miss Harriet Landy, all of Balto., were married 21st by Bishop Carroll. (BA, 25 July 1807)

GOLDER, Archibald, and Miss Mary Jane Butler, both of Balto., were married in Phila. last Mon. eve. by Rev. Pillmore. (BFG, 3 April 1815)

GOLDSBOROUGH, Mrs. Elizabeth, wife of Charles Goldsborough of Dor. Co., and dau. of the Hon. Robert Goldsborough, died Tues., 4th inst., in her 23rd year; interment in St. Pauls burying ground. (BFG, 16 Aug. 1798)

GOLDSBOROUGH, Hawes, and Miss Mary Rodgers, all of Harf. Co., were married Tues., 13th inst., at Havre de Grace by Rev. Mr. McGraw. (BFG, 15 Oct. 1812)

GOLDSBOROUGH, Mrs. Mary, relict of the late Hon. Robert Goldsborough, one of the Judges of the General Court, died 30 Oct. "Easton paper." (BFR, 25 Nov. 1811)

GOLDSBOROUGH, Miss Mary Ann Turbutt, died Thurs., 18th inst., in Tal. Co. (BFG, 6 May 1811)

GOLDSBOROUGH, Dr. Richard, died 11th inst. at his res. in Cambridge. (Long obit.) (BFG, 18 Nov. 1815)

GOLDSBOROUGH, Robert, of Md., and Miss Sally Potter, dau. of the late John Potter of Phila., were married last Mon. by Rev. Abercrombie. (BFG, 29 March 1799)

GOLDSBOROUGH, Robert, of Cambridge, Md., and Miss Mary Nixon, of Del., eld. dau. of Charles Nixon, dec., were married at Dover 9th inst. by Rev. Keene. (BFR, 16 Jan. 1810)

GOLDSBOROUGH, Thomas, of Caroline Co., and Maria, dau. of James Thomas of Annapolis were married there last Sun. by Rev. Higginbothom. (BFG, 1 Oct. 1801)

GOLDTHWAIT, Mrs. Amey, consort of Samuel Goldthwait, merchant of Balto., died Sun.; interment in St. Paul's Churchyard. (BFG, 25 July 1797)

GOLDTHWAIT, Miss Amey, dau. of Samuel, of Balto., died last eve. (BFG, 13 July 1803)

GOLDTHWAIT, Capt. Ezekiel, and Miss Sally Evans, both of Balto., were married 4th inst. by Rev. Glendy. (BEP, 16 Jan. 1811)

GOLDTHWAIT, Joseph, and Sarah Gordon, both of Balto., were wed on last Sun. by Rev. Glendy. (BA, 23 May 1806)

GOLDTHWAIT, Joseph, merchant, and Miss Mary Dorsey, of Elk Ridge, were wed last Thurs. at that place by Rev. Bend. (BFG, 24 Sept. 1808)

GOLDTHWAIT, Samuel, merchant, and Mrs. Mary Jamison, both of Balto., were married last eve. by Rev. Bend. (BFG, 16 Oct. 1801)

GOLDTHWAIT, Samuel, died Sat. in his 73rd year; long an inhab. of Balto. (BFG, 30 Sept. 1806)

GOLDTHWAIT, Mrs. Sarah, wife of Joseph Goldthwait, died Wed., 2 July. (BFG, 11 July 1806)

GOLDTHWAIT, Thomas, son of Samuel, died last Oct. on his passage from St. Thomas to Curracoa, in his 22nd year. (BFG, 25 Nov. 1799)

GOLDTHWAIT, William, died last eve. in his 39th year. (BFG, 11 Aug. 1806)

GOLDTHWAIT, Winkles, druggist of Balto., died this morning. (BFG, 16 July 1806)

GOOD, Frederick, was found yesterday in the canal of the Lower Mills on the Falls with his throat cut. (BFG, 2 Oct. 1799)

GOODALE, Mrs. Margaret, wife of N. Goodale, died. (BA, 20 Jan. 1800)

GOODALE, Mr. Samuel W., Balto. merchant, died 15th inst., aged 22 years. (BFG, 19 Feb. 1798)

GOODMAN, Richard, mate, was drowned Sat., 28th inst., when he was swept overboard from the Rock Hall Packet, Capt. Humphreys. (BA, 30 Sept. 1805)

GOODRICH, Eli, and Miss Susan Sinners, both of Balto., were wed last Tues. eve. by Rev. Mr. Curtis. (BA, 11 March 1813)

GOODWIN, James, son of the late Dr. Goodwin of this place, died yesterday in his 17th year. (Long obit.) (BFG, 27 Aug. 1810)

GOODWIN, Dr. Lyde, died last Wed., in his 47th year. (BFG, 22 Aug. 1801)

GOODWIN, Lyde, and Miss Elizabeth Augusta Campbell, both of Balto., were married last eve. by Dr. Kemp. (BA, 22 Dec. 1813)

GORDON, John, and Miss Dickey of Balto. were married Mon. by Rev. Sinclair. (BFG, 11 March 1802)

GORDON, Joshua, and Miss Charlotte Shisler were married last eve. by Rev. Hargrove. (BFG, 31 July 1807)

GORDON, Capt. Lewis, of Balto., and Miss Esther Osmon, dau. of Capt. John Osmon of Tacony, near Frankford, Penna., were married at that place by Rev. Dr. Blackwell. (BFG, 16 Dec. 1805)

GORDON, Ross, of Tarlborough, N. C., died last Wed. in this city. (BFG, 14 Sept. 1799)

GORDON, William, died Mon., an old inhab. of Balto. (BFG, 12 Dec. 1798)

GORDON, William, died at Jeremie, St. Domingo, brother of John Gordon of Balto. (BEP, 9 May 1811)

GORE, Samuel, and Teresia Harden, both of Balto. Co., were wed yesterday in Balto. by Rev. Beeston. (BEP, 25 Oct. 1807)

GORGES, Gustavus, and Miss Josephine Maloniere, all of Balto., were married 6th inst., by Rev. Fenwick. (BA, 8 July 1811)

GORLEY, Norval, the "crazy, noisy, drinking" schoolmaster, died at Carlisle, 14th inst. "Carlisle, June 21." (BEP, 2 July 1810)

GOROSZ, Adam, died in Phila., 28th ult., aged 92 years, 6 mos., and 9 days. He was born at Rosenthal, Germany, on 19 May 1712, and lived in Phila., 64 years. (BFG, 5 Dec. 1804)

GORSUCH, Mrs. Ann, died 10th inst., after an illness of 11 days, consort of Capt. Joshua Gorsuch, aged 35 years. (BFG, 12 Feb. 1803)

GORSUCH, John, and Miss Mary Ann Slocum, all of Balto., were wed last Thurs. by Rev. Richards. (BS, 11 April 1812)

GORSUCH, Nicholas, and Miss Jane Ensor, all of Balto. Co., were married last Thurs. by Rev. Green. (BPE, 14 Sept. 1813)

GORSUCH, Thomas, of Balto., and Miss Sarah Wheeler, of Balto. Co., were married last Thurs. by Rev. Rockwell. (BFG, 21 Dec. 1811)

GORSUCH, Thomas, and Miss Mary Edwards, all of Balto., were wed married 10th inst. by Rev. M'Cain. (BA, 12 April 1813)

GORTON, Capt. Wanton, and Miss Mary Pentz, all of Balto., were married last eve. by Rev. Kurtz. (BFG, 13 Jan. 1807)

GOSICK, Thomas, and Elizabeth Lauder, were married Tues. eve. by Rev. Richards. (BA, 21 April 1800)

GOTT, James, and Mrs. Sarah Helld were married 27th ult., by Rev. Glendy. (BFG, 6 April 1813)

GOTT, Robert, and Mrs. Mary Randall, all of Balto., were married last Mon. by Rev. Hargrove. (BFG, 10 July 1811)

GOUGH, Benjamin, died Sat., 18th inst., aged about 30 years, a native of Wiltshire, Eng. (BFG, 23 Aug. 1810)

GOUGH, Harry Dorsey, of Perry Hall, Balto. Co., died last Wed. (BFG, 9 May 1808)

GOULD, Ignatius, late of Balto., died at Norfolk, 2nd inst. (BT, 11 Sept. 1797)

GOULD, James, hatter, died Sun., in his 35th year. (BFG, 8 Aug., 1809)

GOULD, Mrs. Susannah, wife of Alexander Gould, died yesterday in her 30th year, leaving a husband and five children.; her funeral will be from her late res., Federal Hill. (BA, 20 Feb. 1816)

GOULDING, Mrs. Arabella, died Thurs., 8th inst. (BFG, 12 June 1809)

GOULDING, James, and Miss Rachel Wright were married last Thurs. by Rev. Healey. (BA, 18 Dec. 1811)

GOULDSMITH, William Copeland, died yesterday at his country res. in his 57th year. (BFG, 27 Sept. 1811)

GOUVERNET, Charles, and Miss Margaretta Wells, both of Balto., were married last eve. by Bishop Carroll. (BFG, 29 Nov. 1799)

GOUVERNEUR, Isaac, of Gouverneur, Kemble and Co., New York, died at Albany, 28th ult. (BA, 11 March 1800)

GOVANE, William James, Attoryney at Law, died yesterday in his 27th year. (BFG, 8 Oct. 1807)

GOVER, Mrs. Hannah, consort of Samuel Gover, died Sat., 18th inst., at her late res., Rock Run, Harf. Co., leaving a husband and a large family. (BFG, 25 July 1812)

GOVER, Mr. Nathaniel, and Miss Sarah Jolly, both of Balto., were married last Thurs. by Rev. Glendy. (BFG, 28 Feb. 1803)

GOVER, Capt. Samuel, and Miss Mary Wilson, were married last Sun. at Fells Point by Rev. Roberts. (BFG, 17 Dec. 1804)

GOVINE, Peter, and Miss Elizabeth Augustus, both of Balto., were married last Thurs. by Rev. Otterbein. (BT, 18 April 1801)

GOWAN, John, of Balto., and Miss Mary Smith of Norfolk, were wed at the latter place on Sat. by Rev. Halstead. (BEP, 13 Sept. 1808)

GOWEN, John, son of Dr. Joseph Gowen of Boston, died this morning in his 20th year. (BFG, 17 Jan. 1803)

GRABLE, William, and Miss Blachley, both of Fells Point, were married last Thurs. by Rev. Mr. Hagerty. (BFG, 9 Feb. 1801)

GRACE, John, and Miss Priscilla Hook, both of Balto. Co., were married last eve. at Hookstown by Rev. Ralph. (BFG, 7 Oct. 1811)

GRACE, John J., and Miss Margaret Caughey, both of Balto., were married last Sun. by Rev. Bartow. (BFG, 6 June 1815)

GRAFF, C., Balto. merchant, and Miss Hannah Boller, dau. of the late Mr. F. Boller, Phila. merchant, were married in the latter city on 18th inst. by Rev. Zaeslein. (BFG, 21 Nov. 1810)

GRAHAM, David, merchant, died 8th inst. in Alexandria, in his 42nd year, of the prevailing fever, leaving a widow and four small children. (BT, 12 Oct. 1803) His widow died 12th inst. (BT, 14 Oct. 1803)

GRAHAM, David, and Miss Elizabeth M'Coy were married 29th ult. by Rev. Glendy. (BA, 7 Nov. 1807)

GRAHAM, James, of Balto., and Miss E. Holliday, dau. of William Holliday, were married 24th ult. at Winchester, Va., by Rev. Mr. Hill. (BA, 15 March 1814)

GRAHAM, John, died 3rd ult., in Ky., aged 27 years, formerly of Phila.; a Mason. (BT, 13 Feb. 1800)

GRAHAM, Thomas, and Miss Mary Gaddis, all of Balto., were wed last Thurs. by Rev. Glendy. (BA, 31 Oct. 1809)

GRAHAM, Thomas, nephew of Hamilton Graham of Balto., died last Sat. in his 22nd year. (BEP, 20 May 1811)

GRAHAM, William, formerly an instructor of youth in Balto., died 3rd inst. at his farm in Elk Ridge in the 70th year of his age. (BFG, 10 Jan. 1815)

GRAHAM, Dr. William T., and Miss Matilda J. Myers, were married last eve. at Hamstead by Rev. Glendy. (BW, 12 April 1811)

GRAHAME, Ann Rebecca, only dau. of Major John Grahame, of Frederick Town, died yesterday, at the res. of her aunt, Mrs. Nichols, in the Western Precincts, aged 18 years. (BFG, 17 Feb. 1816)

GRAHAME, Mr. George, of Alexandria, and Miss Mary Harris of Balto. were married last Mon. by Rev. Roberts. (BFG, 4 March 1813)

GRAMMAR, Frederick, Jr., died at Annapolis, Wed., 5th inst. in his 21st year. (BA, 11 Feb. 1806; BFG, 13 Feb. 1806)

GRANGER, William, a native of Eng., died this morning. (BFG, 25 Sept. 1802)

GRANT, Daniel, died Sat. in his 83rd year, one of the oldest inhabitants of Balto. (BFG, 2 July 1816)

GRANT, Daniel, Jr., died Tues., 4th inst., in his 24th year; a husband and father. (BFG, 6 Oct. 1796)

GRANT, James, merchant late of Phila., died at New York. (BA, 26 Sept. 1799)

GRANT, James, of Allegany Co., Md., died at Charleston, S. C., in his 40th year. (BFG, 4 Dec. 1804)

GRANT, Joseph, and Miss Nancy Griffin, all of Balto., were wed last Tues. by Rev. Glendy. (BA, 14 March 1816)

GRANT, Patrick, and Jane Gilmor, dau. of Robert Gilmor of Balto., were married last Sat. (BFG, 5 Jan. 1803)

GRAPEVINE, Mrs. Catherine, mother of Frederick Grapevine, of Balto., died yesterday in her 90th year. (BFG, 9 Sept. 1808)

GRAPEVINE, Frederick, Jr., and Miss Mary Ryland, both of Balto., were married last eve. by Rev. M'Combs. (BT, 18 Jan. 1802)

GRATZ, Barnet, formerly a merchant of Phila., died last Mon. in Balto. at an advanced age, and was buried in the Jews' burying ground. (BFG, 22 April 1801)

GRAVES, Basil, an old inhab. of Phila., died there and was buried in St. Augustine's Church. (BA, 13 Dec. 1816)

GRAVES, John, of Harf. Co., died recently at his res. on Bush River. (BT, 27 Jan. 1802)

GRAVES, Mrs. Margaret, wife of J. Graves, died. The funeral will be from her late res., corner of Thames and Bond Sts. (BA, 20 June 1814)

GRAVES, Matthew, Balto. merchant, and formerly of Providence in New England, died yesterday. He had lived in Balto. for about two years. (BFG, 11 Jan. 1797)

GRAVES, Robert, and Miss Catherine Rusk, all of Balto., were wed last eve. by Rev. Kurtz. (BFG, 1 July 1805)

GRAY, Alexander, of Penna., and Rebecca, dau. of Col. John Rodgers of Havre de Grace, were married Tues. by Rev. Wilmer. (BFG 25 Feb. 1802)

GRAY, Andrew, of Del., and Becky, youngest dau. of the late Col. Rodgers of Havre de Grace, were married Tues. eve., 23rd inst. by the rector of St. Johns Parish. (BFG, 3 March 1802)

GRAY, Edward, and Miss Bathula Patterson, were married at Balto. (BFG, 14 June 1804)

GRAY, Enoch, of Penna., aged 74, and Mary Hicks, of Balto., aged 72, were married this morning at Friends Meeting. (BFG, 17 April 1811)

GRAY, George Lewis, formerly of Balto., died at St. Helena in his 31st year, leaving a young family and a mother. (Long obit.) (BFG, 26 May 1808)

GRAY, Henry W., and Miss Sarah Eliza Churchman, both of Balto., were married last Thurs. by Bishop Kemp. (BFG, 4 Nov. 1815)

GRAY, John, Sr., died this morning at Chatsworth in his 51st yr., leaving a widow and a numerous family of children. (BFG, 22 April 1799)

GRAY, Capt. John, of Georgetown, and Miss Araminta Forman of Balto., were married last Sat. eve. in Balto. (BT, 16 Dec. 1799)

GRAY, John, and Miss Sophia Gould, all of Balto., were married last eve. by Bishop Carroll. (BA, 23 Jan. 1807)

GRAY, Walton, merchant, and Miss Ann Ferguson, dau. of Benjamin Ferguson, all of this place, were married last Thurs. by Rev. Glendy. (BA, 30 Oct. 1815)

GRAY, William, and Miss Catherine McSherry, both of Balto., were married last Thurs. eve. by Bishop Carroll. (BEP, 4 March 1809)

GRAY, William, and Miss Martha Arnold, all of Balto., were married Thurs. by Rev. Bartow. (BFG, 8 March 1816)

GRAYSON, Capt. Alfred, of U. S. Marine Corps, and Miss Eliza Coulter, dau. of Dr. Coulter of Balto., were married last eve. by Rev. Glendy. (BFG, 13 May 1816)

GRAYSON, John, and Miss Martha Wray, dau. of John Wray of Balto., were married last Thurs. by Rev. Inglis. (BA, 13 May 1816)

GREEN, Mrs. Abigail, wife of Isaac Green of Balto. Co., died last Sat. in her 52nd year. (BFG, 24 June 1806)

GREEN, Benjamin, Sr., died Sat., 16th inst., at his seat on Deer Creek, Harf. Co., aged 79 years. (BFG, 21 April 1808)

GREEN, Frederick, printer to the State, and brother to Samuel Green, postmaster, died Sat., 12th inst. Thus have two brothers who were never separate in life, been united in death in one short week. "Annap.-Jan. 19." (BFG, 21 Jan. 1811)

GREEN, Gardiner, of Boston, Mass., and Miss Copley, eld. dau. of J. S. Copley of George St., Hanover Square, London, were married there. (BFG, 12 Sept. 1800)

GREEN, George, and Elizabeth Perigo, both of Western Precincts, were married 12 May by Rev. Richards. (BFG, 18 May 1810)

GREEN, Miss Harriet, dau. of Clement Green, died yesterday at Deer Creek, Harf. Co., in her 19th year. (BFG, 7 April 1815)

GREEN, Jeremiah, of New York, and Miss Louisa Cook, of Balto., were married last Thurs. by Rev. E. J. Reese. The groom was formerly a lieut. in the U. S. Army. (BPEA, 21 Nov. 1815)

GREEN, Mr. John, and Miss Hannah Bryan, both of Balto., were wed 10th inst. by Rev. Ruchards. (BT, 20 Jan. 1801)

GREEN, John, and Miss Rebecca Sinners, all of Balto., were wed last eve. (BEP, 16 Nov. 1810)

GREEN, John, and Miss Elizabeth Drury, all of Balto., were married last Sat. by Rev. Glendy. (BA, 2 Nov. 1816)

GREEN, Joseph, and Miss Mary Isgrig, all of Balto., were married last Sat. by Rev. Glendy. (BA, 4 July 1810)

GREEN, Capt. Josiah, and Miss Mary Batteem both of Balto. Co., were married last Thurs. by Rev. Fidler. (BA, 2 March 1811)

GREEN, Peter, and Miss Lydia Trimble, both of Fells Point, were married on Sun. by Rev. Richards. (BT, 19 Oct. 1803)

GREEN, Peter, died this morning in his 36th year. Interment in Friends burying ground; funeral from his late res., Ann and Alisanna Sts. (BFG, 10 Oct. 1815)

GREEN, Samuel, died at New Haven, aged 56, printer and late co-editor of the Connecticut Journal. (BFG, 6 March 1799)

GREEN, Samuel, postmaster of Balto., and one of the editors of the Maryland Gazette, died last Sat. "Annap. Jan. 12." (BFR, 14 Jan. 1811)

GREEN, Wilfrid, and Miss Isabella Carson, eld. dau. of Nath'l Carson, were married on Tues. by Rev. Dr. Bend. (BEP, 16 Feb. 1810)

GREENE, Henry, Balto. printer, and Miss Ann Walker, dau. of Capt. James Walker of A. A. Co., were married last eve. in that county by Rev. Bend. (BFG, 6 Sept. 1799)

GREENE, Thomas D., and Miss Ann Kergin, all of Balto., were wed last eve. by Rev. Duncan. (BFG, 17 Dec. 1813)

GREENFIELD, Jacob, of Harf. Co., died 17th inst., leaving a widow and a number of small orphan children. (BFG, 24 June 1802)

GREER, Mr. George, and Miss Mary Hall, both of Balto., were married last Wed. eve. by Rev. Bend. (BFG, 13 May 1803)

GREER, Mrs. Sarah, wife of William Greer of Balto., died last Fri. leaving a husband, mother, sister, and three small children. (BW, 22 Jan. 1810)

GREETHAM, William, merchant, and Miss Margaret Weatherburn, all of Balto., were married Thurs. eve. by Rev. Bend. (BT, 1 Dec. 1804)

GREGG, Mr. John, and Miss Harriet Hall, dau. of Caleb Hall, were married last Mon. by Rev. Bend. (BFG, 12 June 1804)

GREIST, Mrs. Mary, widow of the late Major Isaac Greist, died 29th Nov. in her 92nd year. (BA, 12 Dec. 1814)

GRESHAM, Richard M., of Kent Co., and Margaret Richards of Balto. were married last Thurs. eve. by Rev. Parkinson. (BFG, 28 Sept. 1805)

GREW, Henry, and Nancy Pierrepont, all of Balto., were married last Wed. by Rev. Hargrove. (BFG, 16 Oct. 1812)

GRICE, Major Isaac, died yesterday morning at Fells Point, in his 73rd year, who served his country during our revolution; funeral from his dwelling in George St.; interment in the Baptist burying ground. (BFG, 6 Dec. 1802)

GRIDLEY, Horace, merchant, and Miss Susan Smith, both of Balto. Co., were married by Rev. Glendy last Tues. at the res. of Samuel Smith. (BA, 21 Sept. 1811)

GRIEVES, James, and Mrs. Catherine Jephson, were married 25th inst. by Rev. Glendy. (BA, 28 Dec. 1815)

GRIFFIN, Cyrus, Judge of the Federal Court for the District of Va., died at Yorktown on 14th ult. at an advanced age. (BW, 4 Jan. 1811)

GRIFFIN, George, and Miss Ann Nichols, both of Balto. Co., were married by Rev. Dr. Rattoone last Thurs. (BFG, 9 Sept. 1808)

GRIFFIN, Henry, and Miss Mary Taylor, all of Balto., were married on Tues. by Rev. Griffith. (BA, 15 Dec. 1814)

GRIFFIN, James S., of Balto., and Miss Eliza Little, of Balto. Co., were married 20th ult. by Rev. Dr. Roberts. (BS, 1 Sept. 1810)

GRIFFISS, Osborn, of Balto. Co., died this morning; funeral from his late res. on Reisterstown Turnpike. (BEP, 11 April 1809)

GRIFFITH, Dr. Alexander L., died in Harf. Co. on 9th inst. in his 23rd year, a pupil of the late Dr. Rush. (BA, 15 April 1815)

GRIFFITH, Henry B., and Maria Dennis, both of Balto., were married on Thurs. eve. by Rev. Dashiell. (BFG, 17 May 1806)

GRIFFITH, Henry B., merchant, and Maria C. Ashman, all of Balto., were married last Tues. by Rev. Hammond. (BA, 1 Dec. 1815)

GRIFFITH, John, and Miss Mary Miller, all of Kent Co., were wed last Tues. by Rev. Browning. (BEP, 27 April 1810)

GRIFFITH, Matthew, and Mrs. Nancy Herbert, all of Balto., were married last eve. by Rev. Hargrove. (BFG, 20 Aug. 1808)

GRIFFITH, Nathan, died Sun. in his 67th year. (BFG, 14 Oct. 1806)

GRIFFITH, Samuel G., and Mary Leypold, dau. of Frederick Leypold, all of Balto. were married 2nd inst. by Rev. Kurtz. (BFG, 4 June 1807)

GRIFFITHS, Jonathan Camp, New York merchant, and Mary Harvey Ellicott, dau. of Andrew Ellicott the geographer of the U. S., were married at Phila. last Thurs. by Rev. Green. (BFG, 16 April 1800)

GRIFFITHS, Thomas, of New York, and Miss Rachel Nealy of Phila. were married last Tues. by Rev. Mr. Pitts. (BEP, 2 April 1807) (BA, 7 April gives the bride's name as Rachel Neaves.)

GRIGGS, Mr., printer, died at Phila. of hydrophobia. (BW, 30 March 1811)

GRIMES, John, died 29 Oct. at Govanstown, formerly of Phila. (BFG, 3 Nov. 1807)

GRISWOLD, Mr. Levi, and Miss Mary Ann Mitchell, were married last eve. by Rev. Glendy. (BFG, 28 June 1816)

GRONAU, Christian, printer, and Miss Peggy Commer, both of Balto., were married last eve. by Rev. Trottenier. (BT, 18 Nov. 1799)

GROOMBRIDGE, William, died in Balto., 24th inst. in his 63rd yr., a native of Tunbridge, Eng. (BFG, 29 May 1811)

GROSH, Capt. John, and Miss Elizabeth Pamphilion, both of Fells Point, were married last eve. by Rev. Dashiell. (BA, 4 Sept. 1812)

GROSS, James, Lieut., of the U. S. Frigate Constellation, and Miss Ann Job, dau. of Mr. Morris Job of Fells Point, were married last Thurs. by Rev. Allison. (BT, 29 Jan. 1798)

GROSVENOR, Mrs. Mary Jane, wife of Thomas P. Grosvenor, died Mon., aged 25, at the seat of her bro., Alexander C. Hanson. (Long obit). (BFG, 6 Dec. 1815)

GROSVENOR, Thomas P., and Miss Mary J. Hanson, were married last Thurs. by Bishop Kemp at the res. of Chas. W. Hanson. (BFG, 20 March 1815)

GROSS, Mrs. Margaret, died yesterday in her 86th year. (BPEA, 29 March 1815)

GROVE, Henry, of Balto., and Miss Catherine Hage of York Co., Penna., were married 12th inst. by Rev. Smuckey. (BFG, 23 June 1810)

GROVE, Stephen, merchant, and Miss Sally Forney, both of Balto., were married last eve. by Rev. Dashiell. (BA, 14 March 1807)

GROVER, Abraham, of Balto., died last Sat. in his 24th year. (BFG, 24 April 1797)

GROVER, George, and Mrs. Mary Chamberlaine, all of Balto., were married last Sun. by Rev. Beeston. (BFG, 10 Nov. 1807)

GROVERMAN, Anthony, merchant, and Miss Henrietta Delius, both of Balto., were married last eve. by Rev. Kurtz. (BFG, 2 Nov. 1798)

GROVES, Capt. John, and Miss Ann Carroll, both of Fells Point, were married last Sat. by Rev. Bend. (BI, 20 April 1798)

GRUB, Andrew, cooper, died Mon.; an honest and industrious man who has left a wife and 14 children. (BFG, 18 Sept. 1800)

GRUMPACKER, Jonas, and Miss Deborah Hubbs, both of Fred. Co., were married yesterday afternoon. (BEP, 11 May 1809)

GRUNDY, Mrs., wife of George Grundy, Balto. merchant, died last Sat. (BFG, 15 May 1797)

GRUNDY, Thomas Byrom, and Miss Mary Jane Bend, dau. of the late Rev. Bend., were married at Burlington, N. J., last Mon., by Rev. Dr. Wharton. (BA, 13 May 1814)

GUERIN, Bertrand, formerly professor at Baltimore College, but now in Transylvania University, and Miss Frances Hickey were married at Lexington, Ky., on 10 Feb. (BA, 23 July 1812)

GUIRE, John, died last Sat., an old inhab. of (Annapolis?). (BFG, 15 Dec. 1812)

GUISHARD, Mark, and Catherine M'Cabe, both of Balto., were married last eve. by Rev. Allison. (BT, 23 Feb. 1796)

GUN, John, merchant, died 22nd inst., at his res. Last Sat. he was buried in the Presb. burying ground. (BFG, 26 Feb. 1799)

GUNBY, Elisha, of Som. Co., and Miss Jemima Gunby of Balto., were married last Sun. by Rev. Mr. Wells. (BA, 13 Dec. 1816)

GUNBY, Stephen, and Miss Eliza Ann Hague, all of Balto, were wed last Tues. by Rev. Richards. (BA, 19 March 1813)

GUNN, Mrs. Elizabeth, consort of James Gunn, died last Fri. at the country res. of Mr. Charles Garts. in her 31st year. (BFG, 14 Oct. 1806)

GUNN, James, and Mrs. Elizabeth Robb, dau. of Charles Garts, were married on Tues. by Rev. Inglis. (BFG, 28 Nov. 1805)

GUNN, James, of Balto., and Miss P. Ford, dau. of the late Philip Ford, of St. M. Co., were married at Society Hill in St. M. Co., on 20th ult. by Rev. Malvoy. (BFG, 14 Oct. 1808)

GUNN, Mrs. Sarah, wife of James Gunn of Balto., died in Calvert Co., on 3rd inst. (BFG, 13 March 1804)

GUTHROW, Stephen, and Miss Julian Deagle, all of Balto., were wed last eve. by Rev. Beeston. (BFG, 24 April 1804)

GUTTRE, Joseph, of Balto., died last Sun., 18th inst., aged 23, leaving an aged mother. "Charleston, Sept. 17." (BFG, 3 Oct. 1801)

GUTTRY, Joshua, died last Fri. at Chesterfield, seat of William Bordley. (BFG, 23 Oct. 1800)

GUYTON, Abraham, and Miss Polly Sheffy, all of Fred. Co., were married at Frederick by Rev. Samuel Knox. (BAP, 7 June 1803)

GWINN, Charles, Balto. merchant, and Miss Eliza Phillips, dau. of Thomas Phillips of Christiana, Del., were married on Tues. eve. (BFG, 4 April 1811)

GWINN, Edward, Elk Ridge merchant, died there last Thurs. (BFG, 30 Sept. 1797)

GWINN, Capt. John M., late of Balto., died 28th ult., on his passage from Havanna to Phila., aged 20 years. (BFG, 16 June 1809)

GWYNN, Caleb D., of Balto., and Miss Adelaide E. L. Hawkins, of Fauquier Court House, were married there last Wed. by Rev. M. Reynolds. (BT, 19 April 1815)

GWYNN, Samuel, died last Sun. at Monkton Mills, in his 23rd year. (BS, 1 Sept. 1810)

HAAS, George, Howard St. merchant, died last Sat., leaving a widow and three children. (BFG, 23 Sept. 1799)

HACKEMAN, Herman Henry, died last Sun. morning in his 45th year, a native of Germany. (BFG, 13 June 1815)

HACKEMAN, Mrs. Mary, died yesterday in her 25th year. (BFG, 15 March 1805)

HACKEMAN, Thomas H., died last Sun. in his 45th year, a native of Germany. (BPEA, 14 June 1815)

HACKETT, James, and Miss Hannah Jane Sheldon, all of Balto., were married last Thurs. by Rev. Dashiell. (BPEA, 10 June 1815)

HAD?, Capt. William, and Miss Sarah Barrett, all of Balto., were married last Sat. by Rev. Glendy. (BA, 5 Aug. 1809)

HADDAWAY, Capt. William, and Miss Margaret Flannegin, all of Balto., were married on Tues. eve. by Rev. Roberts. (BFG, 20 Dec. 1806)

HADLEY, John, and Miss Deborah Barnes, all of Balto., were wed last Tues. by Rev. Dr. Wells. (BWA, 9 March 1816)

HADWAY, Daniel, and Miss Clemency Hughes, were married on Thurs. by Rev. Rattoone. (BEP, 3 Jan. 1807)

HAGE, Hiram, and Elizabeth Murray, both of Balto., were married last Thurs. by Rev. Healey. (BT, 24 March 1806)

HAGEDORN, John, died yesterday; funeral from Eagle and Harp Inn. (BFG, 8 June 1802)

HAGERTY, George, of the House of John Hagerty and Nephew, died yesterday in his 24th year; of consumption. (BFG, 22 Oct. 1804)

HAGERTY, John, Jr., died today. (BFG, 28 Sept. 1797)

HAGERTY, Rev. John, and Sarah Dean, were married last Thurs. eve. by Rev. Coats. (BFG, 6 Feb. 1808)

HAGERTY, John, of Georgetown, and Miss Ann Deaver, dau. of John Deaver of Balto., were married last Thurs. by Rev. Roberts. (BFR, 6 June 1812)

HAGERTY, Mrs. Sarah, wife of John Hagerty, died 1st inst. in her 57th year. (BFG, 6 Oct. 1807)

HAGNER, Peter, of Washington, and Miss Frances Randall, were wed at Annap. on 22nd inst., by Rev. Higinbothom. (BT, 30 April 1806)

HAILEN, John, late of Phila., died 13th inst.; funeral from his late res., Bond St., Fells Point. (BA, 15 March 1809) (BW, 15 March 1809, gives his name as Hailer.)

HAINES, Reuben, of Phila., and Jane Bowne, dau. of Robert Bowne of New York, were married at Friends Meeting, N. Y., 13th inst. (BFG, 18 May 1812)

HALE, Capt., and Susan, dau. of Aquila Hall, were married Thurs., 11th inst. by Rev. Wilmer at Long Green, Balto. Co. (BFG, 15 Sept. 1800)

HALES, Charles, and Miss Mary Allen, both of Balto., were married last eve. by Rev. Hagerty. (BFG, 12 July 1802)

HALES, Randal, of Balto., and Miss Anna Taylor of Balto. Co., were married last Thurs. by Rev. Wells. (BFG, 6 Nov. 1802)

HALEY, Henry, and Miss Ann Holland, both of Balto., were married last eve. by Rev. Stansbury. (BA, 29 May 1813)

HALL, Andrew, of Balto., and Miss Ann Gray, dau. of Samuel Gray, were married in Boston last Sun. by Rev. Frothingham. (BPEA, 15 April 1815)

HALL, Mrs. Ann, wife of Andrew Hall of Balto., died at Medford, Mass., near Boston, while visiting friends. (BPEA, 27 Dec. 1815)

HALL, Col. Aquila, died yesterday at his late res. in Long Green, in his 67th year. (BFG, 23 Feb. 1815)

HALL, Benedict William, and Miss Mary Calhoun, all of Balto., were married last eve. by Rev. Inglis. (BFG, 10 June 1812)

HALL, Edward, and Nancy Shaw, both of Fells Point, were married last eve. by Rev. Riggen. (BA, 26 Aug. 1799)

HALL, Edward, died 8th inst. at his res. in Harf. Co. (BFG, 19 Sept. 1801)

HALL, Francis C., of Q. A. Co., and Miss Mary Louisa Van Wyck, dau. of William Van Wyck, of this place, were married last eve. by Rev. Beaseley. (BFG, 27 July 1813)

HALL, Harry W., of Balto. Co., and Miss Elizabeth Ann Hall, dau. of William Hall, of the same place, were married Mon., 14th inst. by Rev. Job Guest. (BFG, 16 Nov. 1814)

HALL, Mr. J. W., merchant, and Miss Grace Craig, both of Alexandria, Va., were married last eve. by Rev. Allison. (BMJ, 27 Jan. 1797)

HALL, Dr. Jacob, died 7th inst., at his seat in Harf. Co.; aged 65, a patriot of the Revolution. (BFG, 11 May 1812)

HALL, James White, died last Thurs. at Havre de Grace, in his 53rd year, for many years an inhab. of that place. (BFG, 14 March 1808)

HALL, Dr. John, died at Phila., 24th ult., in his 44th year. (BFG, 5 Feb. 1801)

HALL, Capt. John, died in Harf. Co., last Tues. (Long obit.) (BFG, 17 Feb. 1804)

HALL, John, died at Long Green, Balto., Co., on Sat., 15th June in his 45th year; long an inhab. of Harf. Co., and lately of Fells Point. (BFG, 17 June 1805)

HALL, Capt. John, and Miss Susan Hawkins, were married Thurs., 14th inst. at the country res. of William Hawkins, by Rev. M'Caine. (BFG, 16 Jan. 1813)

HALL, Capt. Joseph, and Miss Elizabeth Levely, were married on Thurs. eve. by Rev. Bend. (BFG, 4 Oct. 1806)

HALL, Mrs. Josias Carvil, died yesterday in her 60th year. (BFG, 2 March 1812)

HALL, Mrs. Margaret, died last eve. at Fells Point, far advanced in age. Funeral from the res. of John Boyer, 23 Market St., Fells Point. (BFG, 16 April 1803)

HALL, Richard, and Miss Eleanor Blake, both of Q. A. Co., were married last 10 Jan. (BFG, 3 Jan. 1802)

HALL, Richard W., M. D., and Miss Eliza Taylor, dau. of Mr. W. W. Taylor, of Balto., were married last eve. by Rev. Inglis. (BFG, 15 May 1815)

HALL, Robert L., second son of Col. Aquila Hall of Balto. Co., and Miss Blanche Lee, dau. of Parker H. Lee, were married last Thurs. at the latter's res. on Deer Creek, by Rev. Handy. (BFG, 3 Nov. 1808)

HALL, Thomas, died last Thurs. at his res. in Harf. Co., aged 52 years, leaving a widow and several children. (BFG, 14 Aug. 1804)

HALL, Thomas B., of Hagerstown, and Miss Ann B. Pottenger of Balto., were married Thurs. by Rev. Bend. (BFG, 29 Oct. 1808)

HALL, Mr. W. J., merchant of Alexandria, and Miss Grace Craig, were married Wed. at Capt. George Hunter's by Rev. Allison. (BFG, 27 Jan. 1797)

HALL, Walter, merchant, and Miss Charlotte Hall, eld. dau. of the Hon. Benedict E. Hall, were married 6th inst. at Havre de Grace, by Rev. Wilmer. (BFG, 10 Jan. 1801)

HALL, Washington, and Miss Ann Gwinn, all of Balto., were wed last Thurs. by Rev. Roberts. (BFG, 19 Sept. 1809)

HALL, William, and Miss Mary Davis, both of Balto., were married last eve. by Rev. Bend. (BFG, 3 July 1807)

HALL, William White, and Miss Elizabeth Hall Presbury, both of Harf. Co., were married last eve. by Rev. Duncan. (BA, 26 Oct. 1815)

HALLAM, Lewis, father of the American Theatre, died at Phila., last Tues. in his 75th year. (BEP, 4 Nov. 1808)

HALLER, George William, and Miss Wilhelmina Zinstack, all of Fred. Co., were married 4th inst. by Rev. D. F. Schaeffer. (BPEA, 12 April 1815)

HALLOCK, Mrs. Elizabeth, died this morning in her 63rd year, widow of the late Capt. William Hallock; interment in the Baptist burying ground. (BFG, 31 Dec. 1802)

HALSEY, Edward, of Caroline Co., died Sun. eve. "Easton, 22 Sept." (BA, 29 Sept. 1801)

HALWADT, Charles, and Sarah Frazer, both of Balto., were married this morning at Friends Meeting, Lombard St. (BFG, 20 Nov. 1811)

HAMBLETON, James, and Martha Brooks, were married yesterday at Friends Meeting. (BFG, 18 July 1811)

HAMBLETON, Mrs. Peggy B., consort of John Hambleton,, and dau. of Thomas Bond, of Harf. Co., died at Pipe Creek, Fred. Co., 26th inst. (Long obit.) (BFG, 2 March 1812)

HAMEL, Charles, and Miss Anne Davidson, were married on Thurs. by Rev. Glendy. (BA, 23 Sept. 1806)

HAMILL, Robert, and Mrs. Jane Smith, all of Balto., were married last Fri. by Rev. Glendy. (BW, 13 Jan. 1812)

HAMILL, William, of Fells Point, died Sun. (BA, 28 July 1813)

HAMILTON, Archibald, merchant, and Miss Eliza Adams, ygst. dau. of John Adams, all of Balto., were married last eve. by Rev. Glendy. (BFG, 30 Aug. 1805)

HAMILTON, Mr. Archibald, died this morning; funeral from his res.
No. 48 North St. (BFG, 2 Sept. 1809)

HAMILTON, Mrs. Avarina, consort of Pliny Hamilton, died this morning, aged 41; funeral from her res. on Dugan's Wharf.
(BFG, 4 Feb. 1815)

HAMILTON, Charles, and Anne Davidson, were married Thurs. eve.
by Rev. Glendy. (BFG, 20 Sept. 1806)

HAMILTON, George, and Miss Sarah Cunningham, both of Balto., were
married on Mon. by Rev. Glendy. (BA, 10 April 1805)

HAMILTON, James, Balto. merchant, died last eve., aged 32; funeral from his late res., Frederick and Water Sts. (BPEA,
10 March 1815)

HAMILTON, John, an old officer of the Rev. War, and the oldest
revenue officer of the port of Balto., died yesterday;
funeral from the res. of Capt. Samuel Poor, Prince St.,
Old Town. (BA, 17 May 1815)

HAMILTON, Capt. John Agnew, died last Thurs., aged upwards of 50
years. He was an officer in our struggle for independence.
(BFG, 13 Aug. 1803)

HAMILTON, Mrs. Margaret, wife of Capt. John Hamilton, of Fells
Point, died yesterday in her 62nd year. (BA, 1 April
1813)

HAMILTON, Capt. Robert M., and Miss Mary Ann Armitage, all of
Balto., were married last eve. by Rev. Hicks. (BFG, 7
May 1813)

HAMILTON, William, pilot, and Mrs. Maria Sullivan, both of Fells
Point, were married Sun. by Rev. Bend. (BA, 28 May 1799)

HAMILTON, William, died at the Woodlands, on 5 June in his 68th
year; interment at the family burial ground at Bush Hill.
"Phila., June 8." (BFG, 9 June 1813)

HAMMEL, Thomas R., and Miss Jane R. Preston, all of Balto., were
married last Mon. by Rev. Glendy. (BEP, 15 Feb. 1809)

HAMMER, August, and Miss Jane Munday, all of Balto., were married
last eve. by Rev. Kurtz. (BFG, 14 April 1815)

HAMMER, Jacob, and Miss Ann Robinson, all of Balto., were married
Thurs. by Rev. Roberts. (BFG, 14 Sept. 1816)

HAMMOND, Andrew, and Miss Anritta Thomas, both of A. A. Co., were
married Tues., 29th inst., by Rev. Rattoone. (BFG, 30 Nov.
1808)

HAMMOND, Henry, and Miss Evelina Truxton, dau. of Commodore Truxton, were married last Thurs. at Phila. by Bishop White.
(BFG, 16 Dec. 1805)

HAMMOND, James, formerly of Balto., died last Mon. at his res.
in Va. (BFG, 14 Sept. 1803)

HAMMOND, James, and Miss Grace Anderson, were married Mon. eve.
by Rev. Rattoone. (BFG, 3 Nov. 1803)

HAMMOND, James, Balto. merchant, died last Sun. (BEP, 3 Jan.
1809)

HAMMOND, John, son of Charles, died 13th inst. at Patapsco in his 28th year. (BMJ, 21 April 1796)

HAMMOND, John, died 7th inst., in his 53rd year. (BFG, 10 April 1805)

HAMMOND, John B., died this morning in his 19th year: funeral from his late res., 34 Market St. (BFG, 2 Feb. 1808)

HAMMOND, John L., and Miss Charlotte MacCubbin, all of A. A. Co., were married 18th inst. by Rev. Welch. (BFG, 24 Feb. 1812)

HAMMOND, Mrs. Mary, died near Liberty Town, Md. (BPE, 1 Feb. 1814)

HAMMOND, Mrs. Matilda, consort of Thomas Hammond, died at her res. in Charlestown, Va. (BFG, 14 Dec. 1804)

HAMMOND, Philip, and Miss Sarah Brown, both of Balto. Co., were married last Sat. by Rev. Bend. (BFG, 10 April 1797(

HAMMOND, Philip, and Miss Julian Hammond, both of A. A. Co., were wed on Fri. by Rev. Daniel Stansbury. (BW, 7 March 1814)

HAMMOND, Rezin, of P. G. Co., and Miss Ann Mewburn, of Balto., were married last Thurs. by Rev. Bartow. (BA, 17 Aug. 1816)

HAMMOND, Thomas, merchant, and Miss Milly Washington, dau. of Col. Charles Washington, both of Charlestown, Berkley Co., Va., were married Thurs., 20th inst. (BWM, 30 April 1797)

HAMON, Wm., died 17th inst., native of France, and formerly an inhab. of Leogane, St. Domingo; interment in Wilmington, Del., on the 18th. (BA, 25 Oct. 1816)

HANCOCK, Jonathan, formerly of Hartford, Conn., and Miss Sophia Stutson of Balto., were married by Rev. Inglis. (BA, 16 Jan. 1816)

HANCOCK, William, printer, and Ann Gavin, both of Balto., were married last eve. by Rev. Ustick. (BT, 7 Aug. 1797)

HAND, Mr. John, and Miss Margaret Barton, both of Phila., were married last Tues. eve. by Rev. Rattoone. (BFG, 15 May 1806)

HAND, Mrs. Patience, wife of Moses Hand, near Grays Gardens, died yesterday, in her 41st year, leaving a husband and children. (BFG, 26 June 1804)

HANDS, William G., and Miss Tabitha Spurrier, both of Balto., were married on Sat. by Rev. Hagerty. (BT, 17 April 1804)

HANDY, George Day Scott, and Mary Frisby Tilden, dau. of M. Tilden, of Kent Co., were married 2nd inst., by Rev. Armstrong. (BFG, 12 Sept. 1804)

HANDY, Dr. Hast, died at Goree, Africa, last Dec., formerly of the Eastern Shore of Md. (BFG, 13 Feb. 1806)

HANDY, Samuel, Jr., and Miss Maria Chase, dau. of Capt. Thorndick Chase, were married last eve. by Rev. Glendy. (BFG, 20 March 1807)

HANDY, Dr. William W., and Elizabeth Tyson, all of Balto., were married this morning at Friends Meeting, Lombard St. (BFG, 27 Nov. 1811)

HANFORD, Dr. Cary H., died at Norfolk on 29th ult., an eminent physician and magistrate; a husband and a father. (BFG, 12 Nov. 1801)

HANKEY, Joseph, and Miss Rebecca Pearce, both of Balto., were married Mon. by Rev. Hargrove. (BT, 21 April 1802)

HANKS, Thomas, and Miss Sarah Adams, were married on Thurs. eve. by Rev. Mr. Guest. (BA, 21 Feb. 1814)

HANNA, Andrew, of the House of Warner and Hannah, booksellers of Balto., died this morning, leaving a widow and five children; funeral from his late res. in Great York St. (BW, 26 March 1812)

HANNA, James, Balto. druggist, and Miss Sarah Deas, dau. of Capt. James Deas of N. J., were married 1st inst. by Rev. Dr. Miller. (BA, 7 March 1807)

HANNA, Mrs. Jane, died yesterday; funeral from her late res. in the North St., near the Dutch Roman Catholic Church. (BA, 29 April 1812)

HANNA, John, merchant, and Miss Eliza Cooper, both of Fells Point, were married Tues. eve. by Rev. Glendy. (BFG, 30 Jan. 1806)

HANNA, John, of the Baltimore Volunteers, died 11th Jan. at Buffalo. (BA, 27 Jan. 1813)

HANNA, Gen. John Andre, died 30th ult. at Harrisburg, Pa., in his 44th year; for several years a member of Congress. (BA, 6 Aug. 1805)

HANNA, Mrs. Mary, died 21st inst. at Cecil Co., in her 51st year. (BTD, 29 Sept. 1798)

HANNA, Mrs. N., died Tues. in her 34th year, consort of Mr. Thomas Hanna, merchant. She leaves a husband and children. (BFG, 19 June 1806)

HANNA, Thomas, and Mrs. Hetty Leahy, all of Balto., were married on Fri. by Rev. Glendy. (BT, 7 July 1806)

HANNA, William, and Miss Ann C. Betsworth, both of Fells Point, were married last eve. by Rev. Glendy. (BFG, 9 Jan. 1807)

HANNAH, Mrs. Grizelda, died suddenly, 4th inst., aged 60, a native of Ireland. (BFG, 8 Dec. 1815)

HANNAN, James, and Miss Eliza Thomas, both of Balto., were married on Sun. by Bishop Carroll. (BMJ, 20 Jan. 1796)

HANSE, George, seaman of Md., died last month at the New York Hospital of hydrothorax. (BS, 20 July 1812)

HANSON, Mr., Chancellor of Maryland, died suddenly last Thurs., of a stroke. (BA, 19 Jan. 1806)

HANSON, Alexander C., Jr., and Miss Priscilla Dorsey, were wed last Mon. by Rev. Higinbothom. (BA, 2 July 1805)

HANSON, Alexander Contee, late Chancellor of Md., died last Thurs. of an apoplectic fit. (BT, 18 Jan. 1806)

HANSON, Charles W., and Miss Rebecca Ridgely, dau. of Gen. Charles Ridgely, were married last Thurs. at Hampton by Rev. Dashiell. (BFG, 6 Oct. 1807)

HANSON, Henry, and Miss Mary Rutter, both of Balto., were married Tues. by Rev. Fenwick. (BA, 16 Sept. 1815)

HANSON, Mrs. Jane, relict of John Hanson, died this evening in her 85th year. Her husband was President of the Continental Congress in Phila., 1781-1782. She was a native of P. G. Co. Her husband died 30 years ago. Her youngest son Lieut. Peter Contee Hanson, died at Fort Washington in 1776. Her oldest son was Alexander Contee Hanson, late Chancellor of Md. (BFG, 24 Feb. 1812)

HANSON, William, and Miss Ruth Peters, both of Balto., were married last eve. by Rev. Mr. Coates. (BA, 30 April 1808)

HARBISON, Robert, merchant, and Miss Mary Heslip, were married last eve. by Rev. Glendy. (BA, 30 Nov. 1810)

HARDCASTLE, Robert, of Caroline Co., and Miss Elizabeth Bayard, were married 8 Jan. at Middletown, by Rev. William Shelley. (BA, 14 Jan. 1800)

HARDEN, Mrs. Frances, died 23rd inst., in her 45th year. (BA, 26 Nov. 1816)

HARDESTY, Mr. Henry, and Miss Stracey Susanna Brevitt, were wed last Thurs. by Rev. George Roberts. (BFG, 3 May 1806)

HARDY, George, native of Eng., died Fri., 22nd inst., at Dunkerstown, Penna., aged 19. (BFG, 25 March 1816)

HARDY, Joseph, of Phila., died Fri., 15th inst. in that city. (BA, 18 Feb. 1805)

HARE, James, of Fells Point, died last Tues. (BFG, 29 Oct. 1802)

HARE, Jesse, and Miss Catherine Welsh, both of Balto., were wed last Thurs. eve. by Rev. Kurtz. (BA, 13 Oct. 1810)

HARE, Robert, Esq., formerly Speaker of the Penna. Senate, died at Germantown. (BFG, 12 March 1811)

HARE, William, and Miss Jane Bell, both of Balto., were married on Sun. by Rev. Roberts. (BA, 7 May 1805)

HARGROVE, Mrs. Hannah, died this morning, consort of Rev. John Hargrove of Balto., aged near 49 years, leaving eight children. (BFG, 2 Oct. 1800)

HARGROVE, Rev. John, pastor of the New Jerusalem Church, and Mrs. Mary Mather, widow of the Rev. Mr. Mather, formerly of Balto., were married yesterday by Rev. Rattoone. (BT, 16 June 1804)

HARGROVE, Thomas, inn-keeper, and grocer of Balto., died last Thurs.; interment in the R. C. burying ground. (BFG, 13 Oct. 1804)

HARKMAN, John, and Miss Elizabeth Goodden, all of Balto., were wed last Sun. by Rev. Geo. Roberts. (BPE, 17 Nov. 1813)

HARLAND, Samuel D., and Miss Ann Fifer, both of Balto., were married last Thurs. by Rev. Coats. (BFG, 25 June 1808)

HARLEY, Joseph, and Miss Sarah M'Kenzie, both of Fells Point, were married last Sat. by Rev. Richards. (BW, 8 Aug. 1809)

HARLOW, Capt. Winslow, from Conn., and Mrs. Rebecca Osborne of Fells Point, were married last Mon. (BFG, 27 Dec. 1805)

HARMAN, Henry, and Miss Ann Brown, both of Balto., were married last Wed. by Rev. Kurtz. (BFG, 11 May 1816)

HARMAN, Thomas L., and Miss Charlotte Gorham, all of New Orleans, were married at that city 18 April. (BFG, 11 June 1812)

HARMAN, William, drowned Sunday. (BFG, 26 July 1803)

HARNEY, Joshua, merchant, and Miss Eliza Patrick, both of Balto., were married Fri., 21st inst. by Rev. Willis. (BWM, 30 April 1797)

HARPER, Mrs. Mary, died 19th inst., at Phila., in her 53rd year; interment in the cemetery of the 1st Baptist Church. (BT, 25 Sept. 1804)

HARPER, Robert Goodloe, and Miss Carroll, dau. of Charles Carroll of Carrollton, were married last Thurs. by Bishop Carroll. (BFG, 11 May 1801)

HARPER, Richard Caton, second son of Gen. Harper, died yesterday in his 10th year. (BFG, 29 July 1815)

HARRAN, John, and Nancy Hill, all of Balto., were married on Wed. eve. by Rev. Hargrove. (BFG, 24 Jan. 1806)

HARRICK, John, died last Mon., aged 74, long an inhab. of Balto. (BFG, 11 May 1816)

HARRIMAN, Mrs. Ann, died 19 Feb., aged 89 years, for over 40 years a strict member of the Methodist Society. (BWA, 2 March 1816)

HARRIS, David, Cashier of the Office of Discount and Deposit in Balto., died yesterday. He joined the army under Gen. Washington in 1775. (BFG, 17 Nov. 1809)

HARRIS, Mrs. Eleanor, died Tues., 8th inst., at Annap., wife of Thomas Harris of that city. (BFG, 22 Feb. 1802)

HARRIS, Mrs. Johanna, wife of John Harris of Balto., died Sat. (BFG, 16 July 1804)

HARRIS, John F., and Ruth Trunstell, both of Balto., were married last Sat. at Mr. Hewitts, by Rev. Dr. Whitehead. (BFG, 1 Oct. 1807)

HARRIS, John F. W., and Miss Sophia Douglass Abercrombie, both of the theatre, were married in Washington on 11 Aug. by Rev. McCormick. (BFG, 16 Aug. 1815)

HARRIS, Joseph, actor, died 16th inst., in his 25th year, of the Balto. and Phila. theatre. He was a volunteer in the defense of Fort McHenry. (BFG, 18 Oct. 1816)

HARRIS, Peter, of Easton, died 3rd inst. (BWA, 16 March 1816)

HARRIS, Samuel, and Miss Eliza Story Conkling were married last eve. by Rev. Inglis. (BFG, 12 Oct. 1810)

HARRIS, Capt. Samuel, and Mrs. Mary Warner, all of Balto., were married last eve. by Rev. Geo. Roberts. (BFG, 2 Dec. 1811)

HARRIS, Samuel, a native of Co. Derry, Ireland, who distinguished himself at the battles of Bladensburgh and North Point, died yesterday; funeral from his late res., No. 40, corner of Frederick and Water Sts. (BA, 5 Oct. 1814)

HARRIS, Capt. Thomas, of Balto., and Henrietta Ringgold, dau. of William Ringgold of Kent Co., were married 20th inst. at Eastern Neck by Rev. Dashiell. (BFG, 22 Oct. 1801)

HARRIS, W. C., editor of the York Gazette, and Miss Mary Goering, dau. of the late Rev. Goering of York, Pa., were married 28th ult. by Rev. Schmucker. (BFG, 20 June 1816)

HARRISON, Capt. Alexander, of the U. S. Navy, and Miss Catherine Owings, all of Fred., were married 26th ult. at Liberty Town. (BEP, 4 May 1808)

HARRISON, Mrs. Ann, consort of Richard Harrison, Treasurer of the U. S., died at Washington. (BEP, 4 Aug. 1808)

HARRISON, Benjamin K., and Miss Maria Inloes, both of Fells Pt., were married last Tues. by Rev. Dr. Roberts. (BFG, 7 May 1812)

HARRISON, Daniel, and Miss Illingworth, both of Fells Point, were married last eve. by Dr. Bend. (BFG, 5 March 1796)

HARRISON, Francis, of Phila., and Sally Cook of Balto., were wed last Tues. by Rev. Kurtz. (BFG, 12 June 1807)

HARRISON, Mr. Hall Caile, and Eliza Galt, both of Balto., were married last eve. by Rev. Ireland. (BFG, 18 March 1800)

HARRISON, Jonathan, of Kent Island, Q. A. Co., and Mrs. Ann Bloodgood, of Balto., were married last Thurs. by Rev. Gist. (BFG, 18 Dec. 1813)

HARRISON, Joseph, native of Eng., and for 40 years a res. of Kingston, Jamaica, died Tues., 2nd inst., at his brother's house in Balto., in his 73rd year. (BFG, 4 June 1807)

HARRISON, Samuel, and Mrs. Jane Murray, both of Balto., were wed last eve. by Rev. Sneethen. (BFG, 21 Jan. 1811)

HARRISON, Thomas, and Miss Elenor Hargrove, all of Balto., were married last eve. by Rev. Glendy. (BFG, 25 July 1803)

HARRISON, Thomas, merchant, and Miss Ann Maria Fowler, all of Balto., were married by Rev. Glendy last Thurs. (BA, 29 April 1816)

HARRISON, William, son of James, of Tal. Co., and Miss Martha Dent of Balto., were married last Tues. by Rev. Richards. (BA, 14 Dec. 1805)

HARRISON, William, died last Fri., in his 69th year. A native of Eng., he lived in Balto. for almost 32 years. He was unmarried and leaves a widowed sister. (BFG, 15 Nov. 1815)

HARROD, Clement, and Mrs. Sarah Collins, all of Balto., were wed last Wed. by Rev. Glendy. (BFG, 17 July 1813)

HARROD, Henry, and Mrs. Ann Mounticue, were married last eve. at Fells Point, by Rev. Rattoone. (BA, 10 Dec. 1805)

HARROD, John, and Hannah Dodds, all of Balto., were married last Tues. by Rev. Dr. Roberts. (BA, 8 Aug. 1806)

HARROD, Mrs. Margaret, matron of the Female Humane Asssociation Charity School, died Thurs. in her 46th year. (BFG, 12 Aug. 1806)

HARROD, William, of Balto., and Martha Huff, only dau. of Abraham Huff of Harf. Co., were married last eve. by Rev. Dr. Roberts. (BA, 24 June 1806)

HARROW, James, and Miss Rebecca Ellis, both of Balto., were wed last eve. by Rev. Rattoone. (BFG, 14 July 1809) (BW, 14 July 1809 gives his name as Harlow.)

HARRYMAN, William, and Miss Mary M. Yeiser, both of Balto. Co., were married last eve. by Rev. Richards. (BA, 28 April 1814)

HART, James, and Mrs. Elizabeth Cyser, all of Balto., were married last eve. by Rev. Fidler. (BEP, 22 June 1810)

HART, Capt. Robert, and Miss Margaret Murphy, both of Balto., were married on Sat. by Rev. Rattoone. (BFG, 10 April 1804)

HARTLY, Thomas, died at Yorktown, Penna., 21st inst., aged 52 years, for a long time a member of Congress for Penna. (BFG, 26 Dec. 1800)

HARTMAN, Mrs. Elizabeth, consort of Paul Hartman, died yesterday about noon. (BFG, 14 Aug. 1799)

HARTMAN, Paul, Balto. merchant, and Mrs. Margaret Pryce of Annap., were married last eve. by Rev. Richards. (BFG, 6 March 1800)

HARTMAN, Paul, died yesterday, aged 45; funeral from his res., corner of South and Water Sts. (BFG, 1 Nov. 1800)

HARVEY, Jonathan, Balto. merchant, and Miss Jane Steward, of Londontown, P. G. Co., were married last eve. at Geesborough, res. of Dr. Shaaf. by Rev. Addison. (BA, 30 March 1815)

HARVEY, Joshua, merchant, and Miss Eliza Patrick, both of Balto., were married last eve. by Rev. Willis. (BFG, 22 April 1797)

HARVEY, Joshua, of Balto., died 24 Aug. at St. Thomas, leaving a wife and children. (BFG, 23 Sept. 1806)

HARVEY, Mrs. Margaret, wife of Samuel D. Harvey of Balto., died today, aged 36 years; funeral from the dwelling of Mr. Harvey, North Calvert St. (BFG, 9 Aug. 1813)

HARVEY, Samuel, Esq., of Phila., and Mrs. Margaret McMechen, dau. of D. Carroll, Esq., of Mt. Dillon, Balto. Co., were married Thurs., 6th inst., by Rev. Bend. (BFG, 7 Aug. 1812)

HARVIE, Lewis, of Balto., died at Norfolk last Wed.; he was one
of the Privy Council. (BA, 24 April 1807)

HARWOOD, Henry, aged 71, and Miss Susan Chandley, aged 75, both
of Harf. Co., were married last Sun. by Rev. Stephenson.
(BA, 3 March 1808)

HARWOOD, Jacob, formerly a preacher of the Gospel in Great Britain, died this morning on Fells Point, leaving a widow and
six children. (BFG, 30 Oct. 1802)

HARWOOD, James, and Miss Mary Elder, were married on last Thurs.
by Rev. Inglis. (BA, 12 Aug. 1815)

HARWOOD, John, died 9th inst., at Easton, Cashier of the Easton
Branch of the Farmer's Bank of Md. (BFG, 19 July 1813)

HARWOOD, John Edmund, of Norwich, Great Britain, and Eliza Franklin Bache, eld. dau. of Richard Bache, of Phila., were
married Thurs., 9th inst. by Rev. Schaeffer. (BA, 16 Jan.
1800)

HARWOOD, Nicholas, died last Thurs. at Annapolis, in his 65th
year; clerk of the county court. (BA, 8 Oct. 1810)

HARWOOD, Thomas, merchant, and Miss Elizabeth Wall, dau. of Mr.
Michael Wall, were married last Thurs. by Dr. Roberts.
(BFG, 3 June 1815)

HARWOOD, William, clerk of the House of Delegates, died 4 July
in his 56th year. (BFG, 17 July 1804)

HASENCLEVER, Mr. Caspar, died last Sat. in his 26th year, when
his gun accidentally went off. A native of the Duchy of
Berg, he had planned to travel there to claim a handsome
estate. (BFG, 12 March 1810)

HASH, Samuel, and Miss Mary Ann Lary, both of Balto., were married last Sun. by Rev. Roberts. (BEP, 29 March 1808)

HASKINS, Joseph, Balto. merchant, and Miss Henrietta Sullivane
of Dorset, were married 10th inst., at New Market, Kent
Co. (BFG, 14 Oct. 1802)

HASKINS, Mrs. Leah, wife of Mr. Govert Haskins of Balto., died
Thurs., 29th ult. at Easton, Tal. Co. (BFG, 4 Oct. 1803)

HASLET, Mr. Alexander, and Mrs. Elizabeth High, both of Balto.,
were married last eve. by Rev. Allison. (BFG, 16 Feb.
1798)

HASLETT, Dr. Moses, died Mon., well known in Balto. as a physician
long established. (BFG, 2 March 1796)

HATCH, Rev. F. W., of Balto., and Miss Frances L. Robertson of
Norfolk, were married last eve. by Rev. Beasley. (BFG,
9 Sept. 1811)

HATCH, Mrs. Frances, consort of Rev. Hatch, and a native of Balto., died 9th inst. at Edenton, N. C., in her 20th year.
(BFG, 22 July 1812)

HATCH, Frederick W., of Edenton, N. C., and Miss Mary Ann Weatherburn, dau. of the late John Weatherburn, were married
last eve. by Rev. Kemp. (BFG, 10 Aug. 1814)

HATCHESON, R., for several years a delegate to the state legislature, from Kent Co., was drowned Sat., 28th inst., when swept overboard from the Rock Hall Packet, Capt. Humphreys. (BA, 30 Sept. 1805)

HATTIER, Jacob, and Miss Anna Norwood, 3rd dau. of William Norwood of Balto. Co., were married Tues. by Rev. Reed. (BA, 14 Dec. 1805)

HATTON, John, of Balto. Co., and Miss Anna Maria Bond, dau. of James Bond of Balto., were married last Sun. by Rev. Bunn. (BFG, 20 Jan. 1807)

HAUBERT, Frederick, and Mrs. Eliza C. Rawlings, all of Balto., were married last Sun. by Rev. Dr. Roberts. (BW, 27 June 1810)

HAUBERT, Michael, and Miss Eliza Smith, both of Balto., were wed last eve. by Rev. Dashields. (BFG, 28 June 1811)

HAUBERT, Capt. Michael, died yesterday, aged 35 years of age. (BA, 19 Oct. 1814)

HAUPT, George, and Miss Mary Dorney, both of Balto., were married last Thurs. by Rev. Kurtz. (BA, 4 May 1816)

HAUPTMAN, H., and Miss Susanna Barkman, both of Balto., were wed last eve. by Rev. Kurtz. (BT, 27 June 1806)

HAWES, Frederick, and Miss Catherine Youse, all of Balto., were married Thurs. by Rev. Kurtz. (BA, 16 Sept. 1815)

HAWES, Luke, of Boston, Mass., and Miss Ann B. Crow, of P. G. Co., were married in the latter place by Rev. Mr. Searl. (BA, 13 Dec. 1816)

HAWKEN, Nicholas, of Elizabeth-Town, Md., became the father of three sons delivered by his wife at one birth, on Tues., 15th inst.: they were named Abraham, Isaac, and Joseph. (BFG, 25 April 1800)

HAWKINS, Mrs. Frances, died last Sat., wife of William Hawkins, a member of the Meth. Church. (BFG, 7 Oct. 1799)

HAWKINS, George, merchant of Phila., and Miss Gertrude P. Moore, dau. of Bishop Moore of Richmond, were married at the latter place on Thurs., 4th inst., by Rev. Buchanan of the Monumental Church. (BA, 20 July 1816)

HAWKINS, James L., Balto. merchant, and Miss Elizabeth Clagett, dau. of Alexnader Clagett of Hagerstown, were married on Thurs., 14th inst., at Hagerstown. (BFG, 21 Oct. 1802)

HAWKINS, John, and Mrs. Margaret Kirby, both of Balto., were wed 7th inst., by Rev. Roberts. (BA, 18 June 1812)

HAWKINS, Mrs. Juliet, of Balto., died last Fri., in her 26th year. (BFG, 22 Dec. 1806)

HAWKINS, Matthew, of Hartford, and Mrs. E. Hatcheson, of Kent Co., were married in Balto. on Tues. by Rev. Dashiell. (BA, 24 Jan. 1807)

HAWKINS, Matthew, and Miss Martha Ann Perryman, dau. of Isaac Perryman, all of Harf. Co., were wed last Thurs. by Rev. John Allen. (BPEA, 31 July 1815)

HAWKINS, William, Sr., and Miss Mary H. Smith, both of Balto., were married last eve. by Rev. Thomas Lyle. (BFG, 27 March 1801)

HAWKINS, William B., and Miss Juliet Dorsey, both of Balto., were married last eve. by Rev. Lytle. (BFG, 16 Jan. 1801) (William B. Hawkins, late of Balto. Co., dec.: Juliet Hawkins, admnx. BA, 16 Oct. 1806)

HAWLEY, Freeman, died last Thurs., having arrived here on 14th ult. on the schooner Perseverance, Capt. Young, from Balto. "Nassau, Sept. 14." (BFG, 3 Oct. 1804)

HAY, George, of Balto., and Miss Margaret Bateman, of A. A. Co., were married Tues. eve. by Rev. Roberts. (BEP, 25 Aug. 1808)

HAY, George, of Richmond, and Miss Eliza Monroe, dau. of James Monroe, late minister to Great Britain, were married in Albemarle Co., Va. (BW, 12 Oct. 1808)

HAYES, Mrs. Frances, died last Mon. (BFG, 9 Aug. 1804)

HAYES, Isaac, and Elizabeth M'Comas, both of Harf. Co., were wed on Sun. by Rev. Davis. (BA, 27 Aug. 1801)

HAYES, John, and Miss Mary Simmons, all of Balto., were married last Thurs. by Rev. Guest. (BPE, 18 Aug. 1814)

HAYES, William, and Mrs. Anna Goulding, all of Balto., were married last eve. by Rev. Hargrove. (BFG, 15 Jan. 1800)

HAYES, William, merchant, and Miss Catherine Armstrong, dau. of James Armstrong, all of Balto., were married last Tues. by Rev. Glendy. (BFG, 20 Dec. 1811)

HAYNEY, John, and Miss Eliza Yandell, both of Fells Point, were married 27th ult., by Rev. Beesley. (BS, 8 Sept. 1812)

HAYS, Alexander, and Miss Elizabeth Hamilton, both of Balto., were married last eve. by Rev. Bend. (BAP, 11 June 1803)

HAYS, Thomas A., and Miss Betsy Jones, only dau. of Gilbert Jones, were married Thurs. eve. in Belle Air, by Rev. Wilmer. (BFG, 12 April 1802)

HAYWARD, Mrs. Harriet, dau. of John H. Barney, died at her father's res., 14th inst., in her 40th year. (BA, 17 April 1815)

HAYWARD, Isaac, merchant, and Elizabeth Balderston, dau. of Ely Balderston, all of Balto., were married yesterday at the Friends Meeting House, Old Town. (BFG, 21 June 1816)

HAYWARD, William, died 12th inst., in his 77th year, for many years a minister of the Society of Friends. (BW, 14 Jan. 1814)

HAZARD, William, merchant, and native of Ireland, died Tues., 20th inst., in his 81st year. (BW, 23 Sept. 1808)

HAZLEHURST, Alexander, and Frances, dau. of Robert Purviance, all of Balto., were married last Thurs. by Rev. Inglis. (BFG, 8 Jan. 1805)

HAZLET, Robert, and Sophia Mills, both of A. A. Co., were married 4th inst. by Rev. Glendy. (BEP, 6 April 1808)

HEAD, Mr., merchant, and Mrs. Margaret Stitcher, were married on Thurs. (BT, 13 June 1803)

HEADINGER, Michael, died yesterday; funeral from his late res., corner of Caroline and Slay's Lane. (BA, 21 April 1812)

HEAGEN, Michael, died. (BS, 18 Aug. 1810)

HEALD, William, and Miss Hannah Hannaman, both of Balto., were married last Tues. by Rev. Duncan. (BA, 13 May 1815)

HEALEY, Mrs. Mary Martha, died yesterday. (BFG, 23 Dec. 1803)

HEATH, Mrs., wife of Jesse Heath of Balto., died Sat., 28th inst., in her 36th year; a loving wife and mother. (BFG, 30 April 1798)

HEATH, Daniel C., son of the late Daniel C. Heath of Del., and Miss Eliza McKim, dau. of Alexander McKim, of Balto., were married last eve. by Rev. Rattoone. (BFG, 3 July 1807)

HEATHCOTE, John, merchant, died this morning, about 64; funeral from his late res. in Paca St. (BFG, 6 April 1814)

HEBBARD, Dr. William B., and Miss Ann Robinson, dau. of the late Andrew Robinson of York, Penna., were married last eve. by Rev. Dashiell. (BFG, 19 April 1809)

HEBERT, Mrs. Susan, consort of H. O. Hebert, aged 45, died yesterday eve. (BFG, 19 March 1814)

HEDCALF (sic), Abraham P., and Miss Jemima Houlton, all of Balto., were married Thurs., 3rd inst. by Rev. Dashiell. (BT, 12 May 1804)

HEDGES, Peter, and Hetty Hook, dau. of Capt. Joseph Hook, all of Balto., were married last Tues. by Rev. Dashiells. (BA, 12 Dec. 1805)

HEDRICK, Richard, and Miss Julyann Edwards, all of Balto., were married on the 26th by Rev. Roberts. (BA, 1 Dec. 1812)

HEISTER, Dr. Isaac, of Phila., and Miss Hetty Muhlenberg, dau. of late Gen. Peter Muhlenberg, dec., were married at Norristown, on 3rd inst. (BA, 11 April 1810)

HELLEN, Mrs. Susannah, died Sun., on Fells Point; consort of Mr. David Hellen, aged 56 years. (BFG, 12 May 1802)

HELM, Capt. James, died last eve. in his 44th year. (BS, 13 May 1812)

HELMS, Thomas, and Mary Mags, both of Balto., were married last eve. by Rev. Bend. (BFG, 20 Nov. 1801)

HENCK, F. W., and Miss Sarah Pugh of Balto. were married last Thurs. by Rev. Kurtz. (BFG, 15 Feb. 1809)

HENDERSON, Archibald, died this morning in his 39th year, a native of Kilmarnock, Scotland, and an inhab. of Balto. for the last 15 years. (BFG, 9 Oct. 1813)

HENDERSON, David, and Miss Sophia Jones, all of Balto., were wed last Sat. by Rev. Fenwick. (BMG, 22 May 1815)

HENDERSON, James, and Miss Jane Herley were married last eve. at Fells Point by Rev. Rattoone. (BFG, 16 Dec. 1803)

HENDERSON, John, died Sun., 18th ult., in Accomac Co., Va., in his 33rd year. (BEP, 10 March 1810)

HENDERSON, Nathaniel, and Miss Jane McCullough, all of Balto., were married last Thurs. by Rev. Glendy. (BS, 11 April 1812) (BW, 10 April 1812 gives his name as Nathaniel Anderson.)

HENDERSON, Peter, and Miss Mary Booth, all of Balto., were wed last Sun. by Rev. Richards. (BA, 4 Nov. 1815)

HENDERSON, Mrs. Phoebe, wife of Robert Henderson, of Fells Pt., died yesterday, aged 23, a wife and mother. (BEP, 4 Feb. 1809)

HENDERSON, Robert, Balto. merchant, and Miss Lucy Irving, dau. of John Irvin of Lewistown, Penna., were married there on Thurs., 24th inst. by Rev. Johnston. (BFG, 31 March 1803)

HENDON, Henry, an old inhab. of Balto. Co., died 2 Oct. (BFG, 8 Oct. 1810)

HENDRICKSON, Daniel, and Mrs. Sophia Jones, all of Harf. Co., were married last Thurs. by Rev. Glendy in Balto. (BFG, 12 April 1815)

HENDRICKSON, Joseph, and Miss Susannah Cochran, all of Balto., were married last eve. (BFG, 16 Dec. 1796)

HENLEY, Mrs. Mary, died yesterday, aged 72; funeral from Mr. Jas. Summers, Old Town. (BA, 10 April 1810)

HENLEY, Robert, of U. S. Navy, and Miss Mary Rothery, of Balto., were married last Thurs. by Rev. Dr. Whitehead. (BFG, 16 May 1808)

HENNAMANN, Isaac, and Miss Hannah Jones, all of Balto., were wed last Thurs. by Rev. D. E. Reese. (BA, 19 Oct. 1816)

HENNEMAN, Joseph, died 15th inst., in his 30th year. (BA, 19 Jan. 1814)

HENNICK, Samuel, of Boston, Mass., and Miss Amelia Bramble of Balto., were married last eve. by Rev. Waugh. (BPE, 17 Aug. 1813)

HENRICKS, Isaac, and Miss Mary Pollock, were married in Balto., on 18th inst. (BAP, 6 Aug. 1803)

HENRY, Daniel, Balto. merchant, died in Norfolk on 13th inst.; a hubsand and parent. (BT, 19 Sept. 1797)

HENRY, James, died last 9 Dec. at his res., Fleetby, Northumberland Co., Va., aged 73; member of the old Congress, and a judge of the general court of that state. (BFG, 1 Feb. 1805)

HENRY, John, late Governor of Md., died a few days ago. "Easton, 11 Dec." (BFG, 24 Dec. 1798)

HENRY, John, died yesterday, grandson of Dr. Henry Stevenson of Balto. (BFG, 3 July 1813)

HENRY, John C., and Miss Mary Steele were married at Cambridge last Thurs. by Rev. Kemp. (BFG, 26 April 1808)

HENRY, Patrick, died 6th inst. (BA, 18 June 1799)

HEPBURN, Mrs. Elizabeth, died last Tues. in her 50th year. (BFG, 25 April 1806)

HERBERT, John, of Balto., died last Wed. (BFG, 15 April 1805)

HERBERT, John, died last Wed.; long an inhab. of Balto.; funeral from his res. in Market Space. (BA, 15 April 1808)

HERBERT, John, merchant, and Eleanor Jenkins, both of Balto., were married last eve. by Bishop Carroll. (BFG, 26 Aug. 1801)

HEROLD, Dietrich, died yesterday in his 39th year, leaving a wife and several small children; funeral from his late res., Fleet St., Fells Point. (BA, 27 Sept. 1811)

HERON, James, printer, and Miss Mary Cooper, all of Balto., were married last Sat. by Rev. Glendy. (BFG, 19 Dec. 1803)

HERRING, Henry, and Miss Eliza Poe, all of Balto., were married last Thurs. by Rev. Glendy. (BA, 22 Nov. 1804)

HERRING, Thomas, and Miss Hannah Burnett, both of Balto., were married last Sun. by Rev. Beasley. (BA, 8 April 1813)

HERRON, Edward, born in Kent Co., Md., near Chester Town, Quaker Neck, has been impressed by the British. (BFG, 9 Feb. 1807)

HERRON, James, died 29th ult. at Richmond. (BFG, 6 Oct. 1801)

HERRON, Capt. John, and Miss Ann Powell, all of Balto., were wed last eve. by Rev. G. Hicks. (BA, 1 Jan. 1813)

HERRON, Robert, native of Ireland, but lately from Balto., died this morning; funeral from his late res. in Duke St., Old Town. (BS, 1 May 1812) (BW, 1 May 1812, gives his name as Herring and adds he left a wife and a family of young children.)

HERRON, Mrs. Susanna, wife of Robert Herron, died yesterday in her 29th year; funeral from the res. of Mrs. Levely, Gay St. (BT, 15 Jan. 1803)

HERRON, William, and Miss Rebecca Gordon, all of Balto., were wed last Wed. by Rev. Sinclair. (BT, 4 Dec. 1802)

HERSH, Martin, and Miss Elizabeth Shore, all of Balto., were wed last Tues. by Rev. Kurtz. (BFG, 10 Feb. 1812)

HERSHBERGER, Mrs. Catherine, died Friday, 27th ult. in her 66th year; a native of Carlisle, but a res. of Balto. for the last 17 years. She leaves three children. (BW, 1 May 1810)

HERSTONS, Charles, merchant of Polar Springs, and Miss Delilah Sprigg, dau. of Capt. Thomas Sprigg, were married last eve. by Rev. Richards. (BFG, 6 Nov. 1797)

HERTICH, Jacob, committed suicide last Fri., while in jail. (BT, 21 Aug. 1797)

HERWIG, Dr. C. P., a native of Germany, died this morning in his 45th year; funeral from his late res. in Bank St. (BFG, 16 Aug. 1810) (BEP, 16 Aug. 1810, gives his name as Dr. Philip Christopher Herwig.) (BS, 18 Aug. 1810, states the dec. was a member of the Baltimore Yagers.)

HESLIP, Jesse, and Miss Henrietta Grimes, were married last Thurs. by Rev. Hanson. (BPE, 7 Dec. 1813)

HESLIP, Samuel, died 31st ult., in his 24th year; a tutor in the Baltimore College, and nephew of Rev. Samuel Knox. (BFG, 1 Feb. 1811)

HESTON, Joseph, and Miss Ann Evans, both of Balto. Co., were wed last eve. by Rev. Dr. Roberts. (BFG, 2 Jan. 1807)

HEWES, Abram, of the House of Hewes and Miller, merchants, died at Alexandria on Wed., in his 37th year. (BT, 2 Nov. 1805)

HEWES, John, proprietor of the Federal Gazette, and Rachel T. Ellicott, dau. of Elias Ellicott, were married this morning at Friends Meeting House in Lombard St. (BFG, 15 Jan. 1812)

HEWIT, Caleb, and Polly Moreton, both of Balto., were married on Sat. (BA, 27 Aug. 1799)

HEWITT, Caleb, tobacconist, died last Mon., aged 47; interment in the Meth. burial ground. (BFG, 23 Jan. 1805)

HEWITT, Caleb, died 24th inst. in his 18th year. (BA, 29 Dec. 1814)

HEWITT, William, of Balto. Co., and Miss Henrietta White of Q. A. Co., were married last Tues. by Rev. Richard Thomas. (BPEA, 31 July 1815)

HEWLETT, Richard S., and Miss Elizabeth Riley, all of Balto., were married Thurs. by Rev. Baker. (BA, 9 Nov. 1816)

HEYDEN, James, and Miss Elizabeth Nussear, dau. of Jacob Nussear, Jr., both of Balto., were wed last eve. by Bishop Carroll. (BFG, 21 Dec. 1798)

HEYL, William, of Phila., merchant, and Mary Louisa Martin of Balto. were married Sun., 15th inst. by Rev. Francis Beeston. (BA, 18 June 1806)

HEYLAND, Mr. Marcus, formerly of Balto., died at Cadiz, 14 Oct. (BA, 11 Dec. 1813)

HEYSER, William, Jr., and Miss Sally Artz, dau. of Peter Artz, a Hagerstown merchant, were married there. (BPE, 8 Jan. 1813)

HICKLEY, Robert, of Balto., and Miss Eleanor Porter, were wed 24 Aug. at Samuel Silly's, Mount Pleasant Twp., Adams Co., Penna., by Rev. Debart. (BEP, 3 Sept. 1807)

HICKLEY, Thomas James, and Mrs. Barbara Rosensteel of Balto. were married on Sun., 23 Aug., at John Steiger's, Berwick Twp., Penna., by Rev. Debart. (BEP, 3 Sept. 1807)

HICKMAN, John, and Miss Ann Everett, both of Balto. Co., were wed last Thurs. by Rev. Healey. (BA, 1 Aug. 1810)

HICKS, Charles G., and Sarah Cole, both of Balto. Co., were wed 24th inst. by Rev. Green. (BW, 2 March 1814)

HICKS, Elijah, of Balto., and Sarah B. Watts, of Patapsco Neck, were married 14 Nov. (BA, 20 Nov. 1816)

HICKS, George, cordwainer, and Miss Sally Matthews, both of Balto., were married last eve. by Rev. Dunken. (BT, 21 Oct. 1799)

HICKY, William, member of Washington Lodge, No. 3, and res. of Fells Point, died. (BA, 2 May 1805)

HIESTER, Gen. Daniel, died last Wed. at the seat of government, late a rep. in Congress for the State of Md.; interment will be at Hagerstown. (BFG, 12 March 1804)

HIGENBOTHAM, Mr. Ralph, Jr., and Miss Isabella Presbury, niece of George G. Presbury, were married last Thurs., by Rev. John Allen. (BFG, 2 March 1799)

HIGGINBOTHOM, William, and Margaret Turner, both of Balto., were married last eve. by Rev. Rattoone. (BFG, 20 Oct. 1804)

HIGGINS, Mrs., and her child drowned yesterday when a gust of wind overset a sailboat. (BFG, 25 July 1803)

HIGGINS, Edward, and Susanna Grubb, both of Balto., were married Wed. eve. by Rev. Richards. (BT, 5 May 1804)

HIGINBOTHOM, Lieut. James S., of U. S. Navy, died Sat., in his 25th year. (BEP, 19 Oct. 1807)

HIGINBOTHOM, R., and Miss Sophia Hall, all of Balto., were married Thurs. by Rev. Kemp. (BA, 21 Oct. 1815)

HIGINBOTHOM, Mrs. Isabella, wife of Ralph Higinbothom, cashier of the Union Bank of Md., died 18th inst., in her 32nd year. (BFG, 18 Sept. 1813)

HIGINBOTHOM, Rev. Ralph, Vice Principal of St. Johns College in Annap., died there 21st inst. (BFG, 24 April 1813)

HIGINBOTHOM, Thomas, and Susanna Blundell, both of Balto., were married last eve. by Rev. Bend. (BT, 22 Jan. 1800)

HIGSON, George, and Miss Judith H. Ferguson, all of Balto., were married last Sat. by Rev. Hargrove. (BFG, 5 June 1810)

HIGSON, James, and Miss Kitty Eden Hutchings, all of Balto., were wed last eve. by Rev. Hargrove. (BT, 6 April 1804)

HIGSON, James, a native of Lancashire, Eng., but for many years a res. of Balto., died of yellow fever on 11 June in Kingston, Jamaica. (BFG, 12 Aug. 1805)

HILDEBRAND, Jacob, Sr., died yesterday in his 79th year; funeral from his late res., 42 Market Space. (BA, 6 Aug. 1807)

HILL, Aaron, of Harf. Co., and Miss Martha Browning of Balto. were married last eve. by Rev. Gruber. (BPE, 27 Jan. 1815)

MARRIAGES AND DEATHS

HILL, Mrs. Ann, died last Sat., aged 55 years, wife of John Hill.
(BFG, 30 April 1804)

HILL, George, Jr., of Balto., and Miss Matilda Bryant of Wilmington, Del., were married last Thurs. by Rev. Annan. (BFG, 3 Jan. 1812)

HILL, George, bookseller, died Sun., in his 46th year; a native of Edinburgh, Scot., he had lived in Balto. for the last 15 years. (BFG, 13 July 1813)

HILL, James W., died at Phila. last Fri., 27th inst., aged 35 years. (BFG, 30 Nov. 1809)

HILL, Richard, and Ann Willis, both of Balto., were married last eve. by Rev. Bend. (BT, 27 June 1800)

HILL, Stephen, and Miss Eleanor Shannon, both of Balto. Co., were married last eve. by Rev. Hargrove. (BFG, 8 May 1815)

HILL, Thomas G., and Mary Slubey, all of Balto., were married last eve. by Rev. Dr. Roberts. (BFG, 1 May 1816)

HILL, Sgt. William, of the corps of artillerists and engineers, died last Wed. at Fort McHenry. (BFG, 28 Nov. 1797)

HILL, Dr. William, and Miss Ann Smith, eld. dau. of Dr. Clement Smith, all of P. G. Co., were married there on 3rd ult., at Poplar Hill, by Rev. Vergnes. (BFR, 11 Dec. 1811)

HILLEGAS, Michael, died at Phila. last Sat., in his 76th year, formerly one of the aldermen. (BA, 3 Oct. 1804)

HILLEN, Solomon, died yesterday in his 64th year; interment will be in the family burying ground of Balto. Co. (BFG, 28 March 1801)

HILLEN, Solomon, Jr., merchant, and Miss Frances Woodyear, dau. of Edward Woodyear of Balto., were married last eve. (BFG, 24 July 1807)

HILTON, James G., and Miss Elizabeth Hagerty, both of Balto., were married Tues. eve. by Rev. Hagerty. (BPEA, 17 March 1815)

HILYARD, Benjamin R., and Miss Harriet M'Neir, all of Balto., were married Sun., 25th inst. by Rev. Dr. Roberts. (BA, 28 Feb. 1816)

HINCK, Joseph, formerly of Balto., died 13th inst., in A. A. Co. (BPE, 16 May 1814)

HINCKS, Mrs. Mary, of Balto., died last Mon., aged 58; interment in St. Pauls churchyard. (BFG, 4 April 1798)

HINDES, Moses, and Miss Mary Hanaman, of Balto., were married last Thurs. by Rev. Glendy. (BS, 23 June 1810)

HINGSTON, Nicholas, botanist and merchant of Alexandria, and Elizabeth Bloomfield, sister of the author of "Farmers Boy," etc., were married in Georgetown by Rev. Balch. (BA, 30 Jan. 1806)

HINKLE, Baltzel, of Fred. Co., died last Sat., in his 65th year. (BT, 28 Feb. 1804)

HINKS, Joseph, and Miss Eliza M. Oliver, all of Balto., were wed last eve. by Rev. Hargrove. (BFG, 31 Oct. 1808) (BW, 1 Nov. 1808, gives bride's name as Olivier.)

HINTON, Capt. Abijah John, and Mrs. Jane Mastin, both of Balto., were married Sun. by Rev. Rattoone. (BFG, 19 Dec. 1808)

HIPKINS, Capt. Leroy, U. S. Navy, died 1 Oct., in his 35th year, leaving a wife and infant. (BA, 18 Oct. 1808)

HIZER, John, and Miss Margaret Johnson, all of Balto., were married last eve. by Rev. Dashiell. (BFG, 16 April 1813)

HOBBY, John, of Balto., and Mary Stansbury of Balto. Co., were married by Rev. Richards. (BA, 9 March 1801)

HOBURG, John, and Miss Elizabeth Wright, all of Balto., were wed last eve. by Rev. Kurtz. (BFG, 3 July 1811)

HOBURG, Richard, of Balto., and Miss Elizabeth Rice of Georgetown, Ca., were married last eve. by Rev. Kurtz. (BFG, 7 Dec. 1810)

HODGE, Robert, and Mrs. Sarah Everett were married last Thurs. by Rev. Glendy. (BFG, 18 Dec. 1812)

HODGES, Mrs. Susan, wife of Benjamin Hodges of Queen Anne Town, P. G. Co., died Fri., 24th inst.; interment was in the family burying ground, at the res. of Mr. Hodges' father. (BA, 4 Feb. 1806)

HODGKINS, Thomas B., died last eve. in his 67th year; funeral from his late res., King George and Granby Sts. (BFG, 28 Feb. 1805)

HODGSON, John, Jr., merchant of Birmingham, died at that place last 15 Sept., aged 23 years. (BFG, 31 Dec. 1805)

HODGSON, Joseph, of the Federal City and Miss Rebecca Hersey, near Elk, were married last Thurs. eve. by Rev. Mr. Kinkey at Isaac Hersey's, near Elk. (BFG, 14 May 1798)

HODGSON, Joseph, member of the City Council, died at Washington on 20th inst.; a husband and father. The funeral sermon will be preached by Rev. John Chalmers on 2 June at the Meth. Meeting House in Georgetown. (BFG, 25 May 1805)

HODGSON, Robert, of Md. and Miss Ann Houston of Kensington were married at Phila. 18th inst. by Rev. Joseph Turner. (BFG, 1 Nov. 1806) (BA, 3 Nov. 1806 gives the groom's name as Hodgston.)

HOEY, Thomas, and Mrs. Catherine Dunagan were married Sat. by Rev. Rattoone. (BFG, 1 May 1805)

HOFFMAN, Mrs., wife of the late Peter Hoffman of Balto., died this morning; funeral from her late res. on Market St. (BFG, 6 April 1811)

HOFFMAN, David, of Balto., and Miss Mary M'Kean, dau. of the late Robert M'Kean of Balto., were married 8th inst. at Phila. by Bishop White. (BFG, 10 Jan. 1816)

HOFFMAN, Frederick G., died yesterday. Funeral from his late res., Pitt and High Sts. (BA, 6 Sept. 1815)

HOFFMAN, George, Balto. merchant, and Miss Margaret Eliza Tilghman, dau. of Richard Tilghman, IV, of Chestertown, were married there last Tues. (BFG, 26 April 1799)

HOFFMAN, George, and Henrietta Rogers were married last eve. (BFG, 27 Feb. 1805)

HOFFMAN, Jacob, of Bridge St., died and was found dead in his own cellar last Sat. "Balto., Jan. 10" A letter to the editor states that this item was copied from an Eastern paper and the writer wants to know if it came from any Balto. papers. (BFG, 31 Jan. 1810)

HOFFMAN, John, died this morning in his 21st year; funeral from his father's res., 46 Hanover St. (BFG, 25 Nov. 1815)

HOFFMAN, John, Jr., died 10th inst., aged nearly 26 years, son of John Hoffman, Sr., of Frederick; of the House of Hoffman and Baltzell. (BFG, 12 May 1804)

HOFFMAN, Mrs. Mary Eliza, died Tues., 12th inst., aged 19 years; interment yesterday in St. Pauls yard. (BFG, 14 Nov. 1799)

HOFFMAN, Peter, Jr., Balto. merchant, and Deborah Owings, dau. of Samuel Owings of Balto. Co., were married last Thurs. by Rev. Coleman. (BFG, 18 May 1799)

HOFFMAN, Peter, Sr., died; funeral will be today. (BFG, 14 Sept. 1810)

HOGAN, Dennis, formerly an officer in the British army, died yesterday in Phila. (Long obit gives details of his military career) (BEP, 15 June 1810)

HOGG, Charles, and Miss Arey Eagleston, of this county, were wed last Thurs. by Rev. Richards. (BFG, 30 Oct. 1807)

HOGG, Charles, and Miss Margaret Bowers, both of Balto., were married last eve. by Rev. J. Fry. (BFG, 20 Nov. 1812)

HOGG, John, and Miss Martha Bready, all of Balto., were married last Sat. by Rev. Dashiell. (BEP, 4 April 1808)

HOGGARD, Capt. Thomas, died at Gibraltar of a wound received in action with several privateers off Algeria; of the ship *Louisa*, of Phila. (BA, 25 Nov. 1800)

HOLLAND, Littleton, of Balto., and Hester, dau. of William Ringgold of Eastern Neck, Kent Co., were married last Mon. on the Eastern Shore, by Rev. Ferguson. (BA, 20 Oct. 1804)

HOLLIDAY, Mrs. Eleanor A., wife of John R. Holliday, died 4th inst. (BFG, 7 July 1798)

HOLLIDAY, John Robert, and Miss Mary Burrows Stone, all of Balto. Co., were married last Thurs. by Rev. Pitts. (BRAD, 25 Feb. 1802)

HOLLIDAY, Capt. Thomas, and Mrs. Ann Hall of Norfolk were married at that place. (BT, 4 Oct. 1800)

HOLLINGSWORTH, Mrs. Cassandra, wife of Isaac Hollingsworth, died 18th ult. at Onion's Old Works, mouth of Little Gunpowder Falls, leaving a husband and two infants. Her father died two months ago. (BFG, 21 March 1812)

HOLLINGSWORTH, Col. Henry, died 29th ult. at Elkton, one of the
senators of this state, and an active Whig from the start
to the end of the Rev. War. (BFG, 4 Oct. 1803)

HOLLINGSWORTH, Isaac, and Miss Cassandra Divers of Balto. Co.
were married last Tues. by Rev. Coleman. (BFG, 21 April
1804)

HOLLINGSWORTH, Isaac, of Harf. Co., and Miss Ruth James Edwards
Stansbury, of Balto. City, were married last Tues. by Rev.
Ryland. (BPE, 27 Jan. 1815)

HOLLINGSWORTH, Jacob, died at Elkton, on 28th inst., in his 61st
year. He was born on the spot where he died. He has no
children, but leaves a wife, mother, eight bros. and two
sisters. (BFG, 7 March 1803)

HOLLINGSWORTH, Jacob, and Miss Nancy Gooding both of Balto. were
married last eve. at Pike Creek by Rev. Dashiell. (BFG,
6 May 1812)

HOLLINGSWORTH, Jesse, died. Long obit gives details of service
in the Rev. War. (BFG, 8 Oct. 1810)

HOLLINGSWORTH, Levi, of Balto., and Miss Ann Dorsey of New Castle
Delaware, were wed at the latter place on 13th inst. by
Rev. Mr. Clay. (BFR, 17 Feb. 1812)

HOLLINGSWORTH, Pascal, and Miss Mary Wilson, dau. of the late
Hon. James Wilson, Assoc. Judge of the U. S. Supreme
Court, were married at Christ Church, Phila., on Sun., 31
May by Bishop White. (BFG, 6 June 1812)

HOLLINGSWORTH, Samuel, Jr., and Miss Ellen Moale, eld. dau. of
Samuel Moale, all of Balto., were married Tues. eve. by
Bishop Kemp. (BA, 17 Oct. 1816)

HOLLINGSWORTH, Thomas, died 30th inst., at his father's res. in
South St. (BFG, 31 July 1813)

HOLLINGSWORTH, Thomas, merchant, died yesterday in his 69th year.
(BFG, 6 Sept. 1815)

HOLLINGSWORTH, William, and Ann Black, both of Elkton, were wed
there by Rev. Reed. (BA, 11 March 1806)

HOLLINS, John Smith, and Miss Rebecca Dugan, dau. of Cumberland
Dugan, were married 18th inst. by Rev. Glendy. (BFG, 20
May 1809)

HOLLINS, Mary, died 8th inst., leaving five children. Her husband, William, died 19th ult. (BFG, 12 Nov. 1810)

HOLLINS, William, died 19th ult. in his 55th year. (BFG, 12 Nov.
1810)

HOLLINS, William, Jr., and Miss Eliza Bowly, all of Balto., were
married last Tues. by Rev. Bend. (BFR, 11 Jan. 1810)

HOLLIS, James, of Harf. Co., and Rebecca Ridgely Risteau, were
married at Cool Spring, Balto. Co. on 9th inst. by Rev.
Dr. Keene. (BA, 13 Dec. 1813)

HOLMES, Miss Ann, dau. of John Holmes of Balto., died in Carlisle,
on Mon., 26th inst. (BFG, 4 March 1816)

HOLMES, James, Balto. merchant, and Miss Sarah Button of Balto. Co. were married on Thurs. eve. by Rev. Roberts. (BEP, 26 March 1808)

HOLMES, Jonathan, died at Carlisle the 22nd ult., in his 80th year; for over 60 years a res. of that neighborhood. (BFG, 8 July 1803)

HOLMES, Mrs. Juliana, wife of John Holmes of Balto., died Wed.; interment in St. Pauls churchyard. (BFG, 3 March 1798)

HOLMES, William, of Md., midshipman, died 21st last Sept. in his 18th year, on board the U. S. Frigate Adams, Capt. Campbell, in the Mediterranean. (BFG, 26 Nov. 1802)

HOLMES, William, and Miss Maria Crow, both of Balto., were wed 17th inst. by Rev. Rattoone. (BFG, 23 Nov. 1803)

HONEYWELL, Stephen, and Miss Mary Magdalen Carre, all of Balto., were married last eve. by Rev. Fenwick. (BFG, 17 July 1812)

HONICOMBE, Mrs. Rachel, aged 57, wife of Jno. Honicombe of Balto., died yesterday. (BEP, 19 Oct. 1807)

HOOD, James, of Balto. Co., and Miss Sarah Howard of A. A. Co., were married last Tues. by Rev. Dashiell. (BFG, 20 Dec. 1806)

HOOD, John, died 16th ult. at Concord, his res. in A. A. Co. in his 40th year. (BA, 1 Jan. 1816)

HOOE, Abraham Barnes, of Va., and Miss Sarah Norwood Johnson, dau. of the late Horatio Johnson of Elk Ridge, were wed 22nd ult. at Aquasco, seat of Rinaldo Johnson, by Bishop Claggett. (BFG, 9 Sept. 1809)

HOOE, Bernard, Jr., of Prince William Co., Va., died 14th inst. in his 40th year as a result of a duel between him and James Kempe of the same county. He leaves a wife and family. (BFR, 19 Oct. 1809)

HOOE, Robert Townsend, died at Alexnadria, 16th inst. In our struggles for independence he bore an early and conspicuous part. (BFG, 22 March 1809)

HOOGLA, John, and Miss Nancy Radel were married 9th inst. by Rev. Glendy. (BA, 17 Nov. 1812)

HOOK, Conrad, native of Balto., died at Charleston, S. C., on 10th ult. in his 38th year, leaving a widow and two daus. (BFG, 4 April 1805)

HOOK, Jacob, died Fri., 5th inst., at Hookstown, in his 76th year. A native of Basle, Switzerland. His wife, aged 82, is now separated from the husband with whom she lived in the bonds of union for 53 years. (BFG, 8 Dec. 1800)

HOOK, Capt. Joseph, and Miss Ann Conn, dau. of Capt. Daniel Conn, were married Sat., 11th inst., by Rev. Dr. Roberts. (BA, 15 Nov. 1815)

HOOK, Michael, and Miss Elizabeth Stagers, all of Balto., were married last Thurs. by Rev. Fenwick. (BS, 16 Oct. 1812)

HOOK, Mrs. Ursula, relict of the late Jacob Hook, died at Hookstown near Balto. on Thurs. last in her 85th year. (BFG, 25 June 1803)

HOOPER, Mrs. Mary, consort of Nicholas Hooper, died 12th inst. in her 32nd year. (BA, 16 Sept. 1815)

HOOPER, William C., and Miss Margaret Wells, all of Balto., were married last eve. by Rev. Fenwick. (BFG, 3 June 1812)

HOOVER, Daniel, and Miss Catherine Lemott both of Balto. Co. were wed Sat., 11th inst., by Rev. Kurtz. (BFG, 13 Feb. 1815)

HOPE, James, native of Gretna Green, Scot., died in Balto., on 5th inst. aged 37 years. (BFG, 29 Aug. 1806)

HOPKINS, Mr., and Miss Morgan, were married lately in Harf. Co. by Rev. Wilmer. (BFG, 4 Jan. 1803)

HOPKINS, Charles D., formerly of the Balto. Theatre, died 27th ult. at Washington; one of the performers in the Virginia Company. (BT, 2 Nov. 1805)

HOPKINS, Major David, Marshal of Md., and Miss Isabella Ford, a young lady lately from Jamaica, were married on Sun. at Washington by Rev. Mr. McCormick. (BFG, 19 March 1801)

HOPKINS, Mrs. Elizabeth, wife of John Hopkins, Sr., of Balto. Co., died 26th inst., in her 59th year; member of the Society of Friends. (BFG, 27 Sept. 1806)

HOPKINS, Gerard, died Fri. evening; a cabinet maker; funeral from his late res. in Gay St. He was buried in the Friends Burial Ground. (BFG, 19 and 21 April 1800)

HOPKINS, Col. Henry, died at New Orleans the latter end of October, adjutant general of the militia. He was a native of Baltimore. (BW, 5 Dec. 1811)

HOPKINS, James, and Rachel Groundfield, both of Balto., were wed Tues. eve. by Rev. Rattoone. (BFG, 17 April 1806)

HOPKINS, John, Jr., of Balto. Co., and Miss Sally Wilson of Harf. Co., were married Thurs., 1st inst., at Deer Creek by Rev. Mr. Allen. (BFG, 5 June 1809)

HOPKINS, Joseph, who lived in the counting house of Messrs. Pollard and Cornthwait, Bowly's Wharf, died on the 7th. (BFG, 22 July 1802)

HOPKINS, Joseph, of Balto. Co., died last Mon. aged 47 years; a husband and a father. (BFG, 2 June 1808)

HOPKINS, Joseph R., of Phila., and Anna Maria Snowden, dau. of the late John Snowden of Md., were married at Birmingham House on 3rd inst. by Rev. Dashiell. (BA, 9 Nov. 1814)

HOPKINS, Levin, of Balto. Co., and Miss Elizabeth Pervail of Balto. City were married in Balto. last Thurs. by Rev. Dashiell. (BPE, 6 Feb. 1813)

HOPKINS, Miss Mary, eld. dau. of Major David Hopkins, died Sun. at Greenwood, the country res. of Mr. P. Rodgers. (BFG, 21 July 1812)

HOPKINS, Capt. Samuel, aged 22 years, son of John Hopkins of Balto Co., died 1st inst. on his passage from St. Iago to this port. (Long obit.) (BFG, 16 Sept. 1801)

HOPKINS, Mrs. Sarah, consort of John Hopkins, Jr., died 8th inst. aged 22 years. (BFG, 19 March 1812)

HOPKINS, Thomas C., died at sea the 16th of July on his passage from Aquin to Balto.; son of John Hopkins of Balto. Co. (BFG, 1 Sept. 1798)

HOPKINSON, Francis, and Mrs. Mary Hewit, were married last Sat. by Rev. Bend. (BFG, 10 May 1808)

HOPKINSON, Mrs. Jane, sister of the late Judge Hopkinson of Phila., and for many years a res. of Balto., died 6th inst., in her 72nd year. (BFG, 8 Aug. 1811)

HOPPE, Daniel, and Miss Catherine Cain, both of Balto., were wed last eve. by Rev. M'Cain. (BFG, 11 Nov. 1808)

HOPPE, Justus, and Anna Eliza Wadsack, both of Balto., were wed last Wed. by Rev. Kurtz. (BFG, 26 March 1813)

HOPPER, Philemon B., Attorney-at-Law, of Centreville, and Miss Rebecca G. Carter of Miles River, Tal. Co., were married 21 Jan. by Rev. Emory. (BPE, 11 Feb. 1813)

HORENSIE?, Dr. William, and Catherine, dau. of the late David Sutherland all of Balto. Co., were married last Thurs. by Rev. Armstrong. (BA, 12 March 1806)

HORNE, John S., and Miss Mary Ridgely, all of Balto., were wed last eve. by Rev. Ireland. (BFG, 4 May 1799)

HORNE, Thomas, and Miss Rachel Chamberlain, were married by Rev. Glendy. (BS, 7 Feb. 1812)

HORSEY, Outerbridge, U. S. Sen. from Del., and Miss Eliza Lee, dau. of Thomas S. Lee of Georgetown, were married Thurs. eve. (BFG, 20 April 1812)

HORSEY, William, and Henrietta Langford, both of Balto., were wed last eve. by Rev. Rattoone. (BA, 9 Aug. 1806)

HORSNEPE, Dr. William, and Hetty (sic), dau. of David Sutherland, were married. (BFG, 10 March 1806) (See HORENSIE, Dr. William, above)

HORTON, James, merchant, and Miss Eliza Diffenderfer, dau. of Peter Diffenderfer, all of Balto., were married last Thurs. by Rev. Richards. (BEP, 19 Dec. 1808)

HOSKINS, Joseph, of Balto., and Miss Henrietta Sullivan of Dorset, were married at New Market, Kent Co., 10th inst. (BT, 15 Oct. 1802)

HOUBERT, Mrs. Mary, wife of Frederick Houbert of Balto., died last Sat. in her 33rd year, leaving a husband and four children. (BFG, 1 Nov. 1804)

HOUGH, John, Balto. merchant, and Miss Rebecca Thompson of Phila. were married last Thurs. (BFG, 27 Nov. 1797)

HOUGH, Robert, of Balto., died yesterday; funeral from his late res. in Sharp St. (BFG, 17 Jan. 1810)

HOULTEN, William, and Miss Ann Starchen, all of Balto., were wed last Thurs. by Rev. M'Cain. (BW, 25 Dec. 1810)

HOULTON, David, died 8th inst. at his res. in Balto. Co., aged 76. (BPEA, 10 March 1815)

HOULTON, Mrs. Mary, wife of David Houlton, died yesterday in her 58th year. (BT, 28 March 1804)

HOUSTON, Capt. Benjamin, died at his res. in Kent Co. near Rock Hall on 15th inst. (BS, 21 Oct. 1812)

HOVER, Dr. Francis, of N. J., and Miss Ann Anthony of Phila. were married there on Wed., 8th inst. by Rev. Smith. (BA, 17 May 1805)

HOVER, Henry, and Miss Eleanor Brody, all of Balto., were wed last eve. by Rev. Kurtz. (BA, 8 Oct. 1804)

HOVEY, Dominicus, and Mrs. Ann Johnson, were married last eve. by Rev. Rattoone. (BFG, 16 Dec. 1808)

HOVEY, Capt. Ebenezer, died Thurs. eve. in his 24th year. (BFG, 13 Nov. 1798)

HOWARD, Dr., and Miss Rebecca Bond, were married Tues. eve. by Rev. Snethen. (BFG, 14 April 1803)

HOWARD, Miss Ann M., ygst. dau. of Samuel Harvey Howard, died at Annap. 23rd ult. in her 15th year. (BA, 2 Oct. 1811)

HOWARD, Benjamin, Governor of Louisiana Terr., and Miss Mary Thompson Mason, dau. of Stephen Thompson Mason, dec., were married 14th inst. at the seat of Mrs. Mason in Loudon Co. Va. (BA, 26 Feb. 1811)

HOWARD, Edward A., and Mrs. Agnes Day were married 24th ult. in Balto. Co. (BFG, 1 June 1814)

HOWARD, Dr. Ephraim, of Balto., died at Elk Ridge 1st inst. aged 27 years. (BFG, 7 Aug. 1811)

HOWARD, George, and Prudence, dau. of Gen. Ridgely of Hampton, were married Thurs. by Rev. Beasley. (BFG, 27 Dec. 1811)

HOWARD, Harriet Louisa, died last Sat., aged 10 years and 2 mos., 2nd dau. of Henry Howard of Balto. (BFG, 5 Feb. 1816)

HOWARD, Henry, and Miss Rachel Hargrove, were married last eve. by Rev. Richards. (BFG, 12 March 1802)

HOWARD, Jacob, and Rachel, dau. of Tephenia Prather, all of P. G. Co., were married last Tues. (BT, 11 Feb. 1800)

HOWARD, James, was murdered on the Ohio River on 27th Oct. by some negroes. All were caught and two have been sentenced to death. (BFG, 20 Dec. 1803)

HOWARD, James Govane, merchant, and Miss Mary Woodward Govane, both of Balto., were married last Thurs. by Rev. Lyell. (BFG, 27 Oct. 1798)

HOWARD, John, ygst. son of Thomas Gasway Howard of Balto. Co., and Miss Maria Sewell, eld. dau. of Capt. John Sewell, were married at the latter's res., Harf. Co., on Thurs., 8th inst., by Rev. Richardson. (BFG, 16 April 1802)

HOWARD, Capt. John, died 18 Feb., in his 96th year, at the res. of the late Thomas G. Howard, Sr., Balto. Co. (BFG, 25 Feb. 1805)

HOWARD, Joshua, died last Sat. in his 49th year, of a stroke of palsy; long an inhab. of Balto. (BEP, 14 Jan. 1811)

HOWARD, Capt. Lewis, artillery commander at Fort Michillimakinac, died on that island last 13 Jan. (BFG, 5 April 1811)

HOWARD, Louisa Maria, dau. of Dr. Henry Howard of Balto., died 2nd inst., aged 12 mos. (BPE, 3 Aug. 1813)

HOWARD, Mrs. Martha, died 11 June at her late res. in A. A. Co., in her 66th year. (BPEA, 19 June 1815)

HOWARD, Robert, and Miss Sarah Patterson, all of Balto., were married Thurs. eve. (BA, 25 Nov. 1815)

HOWARD, Samuel Harvey, died 24th inst., Register of the Court of Chancery of Md., aged 57. (Long obit.) (BFG, 30 April 1807)

HOWARD, Thomas Gassaway, of Balto. Co. died 9th inst. in his 64th year. (BFG, 12 Aug. 1803)

HOWARD, Thomas Worthington, of Elk Ridge and Miss Ruthy Dorsey of Balto. Co. were married last Thurs. by Rev. Pills. (BT, 5 March 1803)

HOWEL, Arthur, died 25th inst. at his house in Chest..(?) St., Phila., a minister in the Society of Friends. (BFG, 1 Feb. 1816)

HOWELL, Abraham P., and Miss Mary Weddrington all of Balto. were married last Thurs. by Rev. Griffith. (BA, 6 Jan. 1816)

HOWELL, William, and Miss Abigail Smith, all of Balto. were wed last Thurs. by Rev. Glendy. (BFG, 29 Feb. 1812)

HOWELL, William, Jr., and Miss Frances Hall, dau. of Caleb Hall, all of Balto. were married Tues., 26th inst., by Rev. Beasley. (BFG, 30 Oct. 1812)

HOWLAND, John M., and Miss Maria H. Livingston, dau. of John Livingston of Balto., were married last Sat. by Rev. Dr. Roberts. (BA, 4 Dec. 1816)

HOWMAN, Matthias, died 18th ult., near Winchester, Va., aged 100 years. (BFG, 5 Aug. 1801)

HOY, John, of Fells Point, porter for William James of Shakespeare St., died yesterday after drinking a glass of raw brandy. (BA, 7 June 1799)

HUBBALL, Ebenezer, and Miss Sarah Broome were married last eve. by Rev. John Healey. (BFG, 22 March 1813)

HUBBARD, William, Balto. merchant, died yesterday in his 34th year, leaving a wife and children. (BFG, 13 June 1804)

HUBBARD, William, and Mrs. Frances Harwood, all of Balto. were married last Sat. by Rev. Hargrove. (BFG, 28 April 1806)

HUBER, Henry, and Eleanor Brody all of Balto. were married last eve. by Rev. Kurtz. (BFG, 9 Oct. 1804)

HUBLEY, Bernard, died at Lancaster on Wed., 19th ult., in his
84th year, after living in that place for almost 70 years.
(BFG, 6 July 1803)

HUBLEY, Michael, died 17th inst. at Lancaster in his 83rd year.
A native of Germany, he arrived at Phila. with his father
in 1732, and in May 1740 he settled in Lancaster. (BFG,
23 May 1804)

HUDSON, George, died 12th inst., in his 38th year. (BFG, 17
Dec. 1813)

HUDSON, George, and Miss Seraphina Maria Carolina Matilda Juliana
Sophia Ann Mansfield were married in Washington, Va. (BEP
2 June 1808)

HUELL, Samuel, and Miss Deborah Miles, were married Tues. by Rev.
Rattoone. (BFG, 31 March 1803)

HUFF, Abraham, died in Fred. Co. aged 40. (BPE, 12 Jan. 1814)

HUFFINGTON, Jesse, sailing master of the U. S. Navy, and Miss
Mary R. Guiterr, all of Balto., were married Thurs. eve.
by Rev. Dashiell. (BA, 21 Jan. 1814)

HUFNAGLE, George, died at Lancaster on 3rd inst. in his 68th
year. (BEP, 16 March 1809)

HUGER, Lieut., quartermaster of the Marine Corps, died last Fri.
at Phila., aged 25 years. (BT, 14 Nov. 1799)

HUGG, Jacob, died this day in his 40th year, a res. of Fells
Point. He leaves a widow and six children. (BFG, 7 Aug.
1800)

HUGGETT, Sigismund, late of Balto., died at Newark, N. J., on
Thurs. (BEP, 23 July 1810)

HUGHES, Christopher, Jr., and Miss Laura Smith, dau. of Gen.
Samuel Smith of Balto., were married last eve. (BA, 19
Dec. 1811)

HUGHES, Edward, and Miss Mary Luttz both of Balto. were married
3rd inst. by Rev. Alex M'Laine. (BW, 6 Sept. 1809)

HUGHES, James, died Tues., 7th inst., as a result of a duel he
fought recently with Mr. Tasker at Petersburgh. (BT, 22
June 1803)

HUGHES, James, Balto. merchant, and Miss Rosanna Fetter, dau. of
Daniel Fetter, merchant of Allegany Co., were married on
Tues. in Old Town by Rev. Jacobs. (BFG, 2 Dec. 1807)

HUGHES, James, American seaman from Md., died 26 April at Gottenburg, about 22 years of age. (BFG, 10 Sept. 1811)

HUGHES, John, and Miss Julian S. B. Weisenthal, dau. of the late
Dr. Weisenthal of Balto., were married last Tues. by Rev.
Bend. (BT, 9 Oct. 1806)

HUGHES, Thomas, died of lockjaw, in New Bedford. (BFG, 1 March
1804)

HUGHLETT, Mrs. Elizabeth S., wife of William Hughlett, died at
Portland Farm, near Greensborough, Caroline Co., 24 March
in her 37th year. (BFR, 3 April 1810)

HULBERT, Nathan, and Miss Elizabeth White, all of Balto., were married by Rev. Birch. (BEP, 13 Nov. 1810)

HULL, Edward, and Ann Clarke, both of Balto., were married on Thurs. by Rev. Dashiell. (BFR, 6 June 1812)

HULL, Isaac, of U. S. Navy, and Miss Ann M. Hart, dau. of Elisha Hart of Saybrook, Conn., were married last Sat. at St. Michael's Church, Bloomingdale. (BFG, 9 Jan. 1813)

HULL, Capt. William, and Mrs. Sarah Barnett, both of Fells Point, were married last Sat. by Rev. Glendy. (BFG, 1 Aug. 1809)

HULL, Capt. William, died 31 May at his house in Fells Point, a husband and father. (BFG, 2 June 1810)

HUMPHREYS, James, printer and bookseller, died at Phila., last Fri., aged 63 years. (BEP, 7 Feb. 1810)

HUMPHREYS, Kerr, and Miss Elizabeth Weir, both of Balto., were married Thurs., 11th inst., by Rev. Glendy. (BW, 19 Oct. 1810) (BA, 15 Oct. 1810, gives the bride's name as Weaver.)

HUMPHREYS, Mrs. Vitale, wife of Kerr Humphreys, died. (BFG, 27 Sept. 1810)

HUNN, Capt. John, died last Sun. at the seat of C. A. Rodney, near Wilmington, Del. He served in the navy during the Rev. War. (BEP, 25 April 1810)

HUNT, Benedict, and Prudence Cockey, were married 11th inst. (BA, 20 Sept. 1806)

HUNT, Jesse, and Margaret, dau. of Leonard Yundt, all of Balto. Co., were married last eve. by Rev. Hoffman. (BA, 9 Sept. 1815)

HUNT, Job, died last Sat., 18th inst., at his res. in Balto. Co. in his 62nd year. (BFG, 20 Feb. 1809)

HUNT, John H., and Miss Susanna Bosley, both of Balto. Co., were married last Tues. by Rev. Snethen. (BFG, 3 Aug. 1809)

HUNT, Walter S., of Balto. Co. and Mrs. Barbara Nichols of Balto. were wed 18 Sept. by Rev. Roberts. (BA, 18 Sept. 1815)

HUNTER, Capt. George, Balto. merchant, died this morning. He was in his 67th year. Interment in the Presbyterian burying ground. (BFG, 10 and 12 June 1797)

HUNTER, James, and Miss Elizabeth Glover all of Annap. were wed there last Thurs. by Rev. Judd. "Annap. - May 23." (BFR, 28 May 1810)

HUNTER, John, and Mrs. Rebecca Stephens, both of Balto., were married last eve. by Rev. James Inglis. (BT, 7 Nov. 1806)

HUNTER, John, and Miss Martha Hillen, dau. of John Hillen, all of Balto., were married last eve. by Bishop Carroll. (BFG, 29 Nov. 1809)

HUNTER, Narsworthy, died at Washington 11th inst., delegate from the Mississippi Territory. (BRAD, 18 March 1802)

HURXTHAL, Ferdinand, and Miss Dorothea Karthaus both of Balto. were wed last Thurs. by Rev. Kurtz. (BFG, 10 March 1808)

HURXTHALL, Lewis, and Miss Caroline Karthaus, all of Balto., were married Mon. by Rev. Richards. (BPE, 16 June 1813)

HUSBAND, Joseph, of Balto. and Sally G. Brown of Harf. Co. were married Thurs. at Friends Meeting House at Deer Creek. (BFG, 10 Jan. 1801)

HUSBAND, Samuel, Balto. merchant, and Miss Rachel Snowden of Balto Co. were married last eve. by Rev. Ireland. (BFG, 17 Oct. 1801)

HUSBANDS, Robert, and Miss Flora Foreman all of Balto. were wed last Mon. by Rev. Healy. (BPE, 18 Sept. 1813)

HUSH, William, and Miss Mary Ann Boughen all of Balto. were wed last eve. by Rev. Martse. (BA, 31 Jan. 1816)

HUSSEY, Asahel, merchant, and Sarah Keyser, dau. of Derick Keyser of Balto., were married last Tues. by Rev. Roberts. (BA, 25 Jan. 1805)

HUSSEY, George, Jr., and Miss Sarah Preston both of Balto. were married last eve. by Rev. Geo. Roberts. (BFG, 22 Sept. 1812)

HUSSEY, Joseph, and Miss Eleanor League all of Balto. were married last eve. by Rev. M'Caine. (BFG, 29 Jan. 1813)

HUTCHINGS, John, and Miss Elizabeth Gorsuch, dau. of Robert Gorsuch of Balto. were married last eve. by Rev. Dashiell. (BFG, 2 Jan. 1807)

HUTCHINS, John, late sheriff of Balto. Co., died this morning at the farm of Robert Gorsuch in his 29th year; interment in the family burial ground. (BFG, 15 July 1813)

HUTCHINS, Capt. Samuel, and Mrs. Meareb Johnson both of Balto. were married last eve. by Rev. Richards. (BEP, 30 June 1808)

HUTCHINS, Thomas F., died in Balto. Co. on 19th inst. aged 83 years. (BA, 27 Dec. 1816)

HUTSON, John, and Mrs. Martha Glass both of Balto. were married Thurs. eve. by Rev. Glendy. (BA, 24 Jan. 1807)

HUTTON, Samuel, died in Annap. last Fri. in his 53rd year. "Annap. - May 23." (BFR, 28 May 1810)

HYATT, Aquilla D., and Miss Rachel Hyatt both of P. G. Co., were married a few evenings ago by Rev. Ridgely. (BFG, 24 Jan. 1798)

HYATT, William, of Balto., and Miss Rebecca Miller, dau. of the late Richard Miller of Kent Co., were married last Thurs. near Chestertown by Rev. Dr. Shields. (BFG, 22 Nov. 1800)

HYATT, William, clerk in the custom house, died Sat., 30th ult., in his 24th year leaving a wife and infant. (BFG, 2 Nov. 1802)

HYDE, Samuel G., merchant, and Miss Catherine Smith, all of Balto., were married by Glendy last Tues. (BFG, 25 April 1816)

HYLAND, John, son of Col. Stephen Hyland of Cecil Co., and Miss Ann Johnson, dau. of Thomas Johnson of Va., were married last eve. by Rev. Bend. (BFG, 1 Nov. 1799)

HYMES, Mrs. Mary, died at Frederick Town, last Tues., aged 103 years, a native of Germany. (BFG, 17 March 1806)

IJAMS, John, and Miss Catherine Barnes, all of Balto., were wed by Rev. Glendy last Thurs. (BFG, 24 April 1813)

IKLER, John, and Miss Mary Brown, were married last Sun. by Rev. Richards. (BA, 25 July 1816)

ING, Edward, and Miss Ann Hadley, all of Balto., were married on Thurs. by Rev. Hagerty. (BA, 30 Nov. 1816)

INGLES, Abraham, and Miss Catherine Fit, all of Balto., were wed Mon. by Rev. Glendy. (BT, 17 Jan. 1806)

INGLIS, Rev. James, pastor of the Presbyterian Church, and Jane Johnson, dau. of Christopher Johnson of Balto., were wed last Thurs. by Rev. Muir. (BFG, 29 Nov. 1802)

INGLIS, Mrs. Jane, wife of Dr. James Inglis of First Presbyterian Church, died yesterday. (BFG, 3 Sept. 1816)

INGRAM, Hugh, and Miss Catherine Ryan, both of Balto. were married last eve. by Rev. Kain. (BS, 4 May 1812)

INLOES, John, and Mrs. Elizabeth Glenn all of Balto. City were married last Sat. by Rev. Rattoone. (BFG, 27 July 1807)

INLOES, Joshua, of Fells Point, died this morning aged 35; funeral from his late res. in Bond St., Fells Point. (BFG, 5 Feb. 1806)

INLOES, William, and Miss Mary Sewell of Fells Point were married Thurs. by Rev. Dashiell. (BFR, 6 April 1810)

IRELAND, Edward, died Wed. in his 80th year, a native of Barbadoes; for many years an inhab. of Balto. (BFG, 20 July 1816)

IRELAND, Mrs. Johanna Giles, consort of Rev. John Ireland, late of Balto., died in London, last 25 April. (BFG, 26 Aug. 1803)

IRVIN, Jacob, hatter, and Sarah Lane both of Winchester, Va., were married 21st inst. there by Rev. B. Neilson. (BA, 23 Feb. 1805)

IRVINE, Maj. Gen. William, died Sat. eve. of cholera morbus, a distinguished officer in the Rev. War, and president of the Society of Cincinnati of Md. "from the Aurora." (BA, 4 Aug. 1804)

IRWIN, Capt, Mark H., of the custom house, died last Sun. in his 52nd year. (BW, 18 and 19 Sept. 1810)

ISAACS, Mrs. Henrietta, wife of Capt. Isaac Isaacs, died Tues. in her 22nd year. (BA, 6 June 1799)

ISAACS, Capt. Isaac, and Henrietta Mulakin both of Balto., were married last eve. by Rev. Bend. (BFG, 8 Oct. 1798)

ISRAEL, Fielder, of Balto. and Miss Sally Simpson were married
last Thurs. at Elk Ridge by Rev. Linthicum. (BFG, 2 Nov.
1816)

JACK, Negro, died Sun., 20th inst. at the plantation of George
Calvert in P. G. Co., in his 120th year. (BFR, 28 May
1810)

JACK, Hugh, and Miss Margry Strowbridge all of Balto. were wed
14th inst. by Rev. Sinclair. (BFG, 15 May 1810)

JACK, John, native of Ireland, died last Fri., in his 21st year.
(BFG, 15 Oct. 1800)

JACKSON, Mrs., wife of Henry Jackson, formerly of the city of
Dublin, died last Mon.; a wife and mother. (BFG, 17 Aug.
1805)

JACKSON, David, and Miss Elizabeth Ducate all of Balto. were wed
last Sun. by Rev. Glendy. (BFG, 3 Nov. 1812)

JACKSON, Edward, merchant, and Miss Harriot Myers, dau. of Jacob
Myers, Balto. merchant, were married last eve. by Rev.
Roberts. (BFG, 13 Jan. 1809)

JACKSON, Dr. Elijah, of St. M. Co., died 25 Aug. 1805, leaving a
wife and infant dau. (BFG, 2 Sept. 1805)

JACKSON, Col. George W., of Somerset Co., Md., and Mrs. Louisa
Evans, dau. of Peter Bowdoin, were married 14 July at the
latter's res. in Northampton Co., Va., by Rev. Sims.
(BFG, 29 July 1816)

JACKSON, Gen. Henry, died last Wed. at his lodgings in Common St.
aged 62. (BNA, 10 Jan. 1809)

JACKSON, Mrs. Jane, died last Tues. at the house of her bro. Mr.
Cochran, leaving two orphan children. (BFG, 17 Sept. 1808)

JACKSON, Joseph, and Miss Mary Robinson both of Balto. were wed
last eve. by Rev. Wells. (BT, 15 Feb. 1804)

JACKSON, Nathaniel, died Thurs., 31st ult. in his 34th year.
(BA, 11 April 1809)

JACKSON, Richard, of Va., and Miss Jane Donaldson of Balto. were
married last Tues. by Archbishop Carroll. (BFG, 9 April
1812)

JACKSON, Capt. Thomas, of Balto. and Miss Elizabeth Reilly of
Phila. were married last eve. by Rev. Bend. (BT, 9 Sept.
1797)

JACKSON, Dr. William, and Miss Margaret Douglass, all of Dor.
Co., were married Wed., 28th ult., by Dr. Kemp. (BFR, 10
Dec. 1810)

JACKSON, William B., and Miss Elizabeth B. Lowndes, dau. of the
late Benjamin Lowndes, were married in Baldensburg last
Tues. by Rev. Norris. (BFG, 27 Dec. 1813)

JACOB, Miss Achsah, dau. of Daucy Jacob of A. A. Co., dec., died
12th inst. at Henry Evans in A. A. Co., leaving two sisters. (BA, 16 Oct. 1815)

MARRIAGES AND DEATHS

JACOB, William, of Fells Point, died yesterday. (BFG, 10 July 1804)

JACOB, Zachariah, died last Wed. in his 29th year, leaving three sisters; interment in the family burying ground in A. A. Co. (BEP, 19 June 1811)

JACOBI, George, and Miss Sarah Anna Reese both of Balto. were married last eve. by Rev. Dr. Becker. (BA, 4 Sept. 1807)

JACOBS, George, and Mrs. Mary Myers all of Balto. were married last eve. by Rev. Hargrove. (BFG, 5 April 1805)

JACOBS, John, and Miss Ann Pettit both of Balto. were married last Thurs. by Rev. Armstrong. (BA, 2 June 1809)

JACOBS, Meyers, died 22nd inst. in his 24th years. (BFG, 25 Sept. 1804)

JACOBS, Samuel, and Ann S. Pennington both of Balto. were married 5 March by Rev. Bartow. (BA, 8 March 1816)

JACOBS, Capt. Wilson, and Miss Susanna Carrick both of Fells Point were married last Thurs. eve. by Rev. Kurtz. (BFG, 3 Nov. 1807)

JACQUETT, J. P., and Mrs. Rebecca Stran both of Fells Point were married last eve. by Rev. Ireland. (BT, 19 Oct. 1798)

JALLAND, John, died last Wed.; long an inhab. of Balto. (BT, 29 Aug. 1800)

JAMART, Michael, of A. A. Co., and Mrs. Elizabeth Bray of Balto. were married last Tues. by Rev. Dr. Roberts. (BA, 19 May 1813)

JAMES, Capt., and Sarah Legard both of Balto. were married on Tues. by Rev. Bruce. (BFG, 14 May 1800)

JAMES, James W., of Balto., and Miss Mary Ann Britten or Butten of Balto. Co. were married yesterday eve. by Rev. Roberts. (BA, 18 Oct. 1811)

JAMES, Jesse, and Miss Mary Murphy both of Balto. were married last Sat. by Rev. Roberts. (BPE, 9 May 1814)

JAMES, John, and Jane Taylor both of Balto. were married 2nd inst. by Rev. Richards. (BFG, 10 June 1799)

JAMES, Levi, and Miss Elizabeth Story of Balto. were married on last Wed. by Rev. M'Caine. (BT, 5 Oct. 1802)

JAMES, Mrs. Mary, wife of Amos James died yesterday; funeral from his res., South Hanover St. (BA, 13 Jan. 1810)

JAMIESON, Dr. Jesse, died at Bryantown, Chas. Co., 18 July. (BA, 1 Aug. 1816)

JAMISON, Mrs. Ann, wife of Major Joseph Jamison, died yesterday. Funeral from her late res. in Frederick St. (BA, 6 Feb. 1815)

JAMISON, James, the murderer of Eshelman, was executed at Harrisburg on Sat. (BA, 20 Jan. 1807)

JAMISON, Major Joseph, and Miss Catherine Wallace all of Balto. were married last Thurs. by Rev. Glendy. (BA, 2 Dec. 1815)

JAMISON, Col. William, and Miss Catherine Maria Mackelfresh, dau. of John Mackelfresh of Reisterstown, were married on Thurs. at the latter place by Rev. Davis. (BA, 6 July 1815)

JANNEY, Aquilla, died yesterday, aged 45, merchant. "Alexandria, Jan. 17." (BFG, 18 Jan. 1805)

JANNEY, George F., merchant, and Sarah H. John, both of Balto., were married yesterday at Friends Meeting east of Jones Falls. (BA, 17 May 1816)

JANNEY, Jonathan, of Va., and Elizabeth M'Pherson of Balto. were married this morning at Lombard St. Friends Meeting. (BFG, 16 May 1810)

JANNEY, Joseph, Alexandria merchant, and Elizabeth Hopkins of A. A. Co. were married at the Friends Meeting in that county on 2nd inst. (BFG, 11 July 1812)

JANNEY, Mahlon, Sr., died last Sat. at his res. near Waterford, Va., in his 85th year, a member of the Quaker Society. (BFR, 19 May 1812)

JANNEY, Dr. P., and Mrs. Isabella Carback all of Balto. were married Thurs., 10th inst., by Rev. Healey. (BFG, 12 Nov. 1814)

JAQUETT, John P., died last eve. in his 37th year. (BFG, 14 Feb. 1812)

JARRET, Abraham, and Mrs. Elizabeth Stump were married 19th inst. at Mount Friendship, Harford Co. (BFG, 21 Nov. 1804)

JARRETT, Samuel, merchant, and Miss Amelia Simpson both of Balto. were married last Thurs. by Rev. Roberts. (BA, 31 July 1809)

JARVIS, Nathan, printer, died at Annap. 15th inst., in his 39th year. (BFG, 23 April 1810)

JAY, Anthony, and Mrs. Mary Winkes or Wintkles both of Balto. were married last Sun. by Rev. Healey. (BMG, 1 Aug. 1815)

JAY, Sir James, Knight, formerly of Md., died 12th ult. at his res. in New Jersey. (BPEA, 11 Nov. 1815)

JAY, Samuel, Esq., and Miss Sarah Griffith were married Sun. eve. at Swansbury, Harf. Co. (BFG, 10 April 1810)

JAY, Samuel, and Mrs. Martha Smith were married in Harf. Co. on 9th inst. by Rev. Stevenson. (BFG, 12 Feb. 1812)

JAY, Mrs. Sarah, consort of Samuel Jay, died at Havre de Grace 8th inst. in her 34th year. (BFG, 14 Dec. 1810)

JEAN, George, and Miss Sarah A. Bowen, all of Balto. Co. were married there on Thurs., 31st Oct., at the res. of Mrs. Susanna Bowen, by Rev. Dr. Hall. (BW, 7 Nov. 1811)

JEDFORD, William, and Miss Elizabeth McMaster all of Balto. were married 26th inst. by Rev. Glendy. (BFG, 28 Feb. 1815)

JEFFERIES, G. M., bookseller, and Ann Yundt, dau. of Leonard Yundt, were married last eve. by Rev. Otterbein. (BA, 11 Oct. 1805)

JEFFERIS, Mrs., wife of Samuel Jefferis, bookseller, of Balto., died last Tues. (BFG, 23 Oct. 1807)

JEFFERIS, Samuel, bookseller, and Miss Hannah Townsend, dau. of Joseph Townsend, all of Balto., were married yesterday at Friends Meeting. (BFG, 17 April 1807)

JEFFERIS, Samuel, Balto. bookseller, and Miss Lydia Cope of York Co., Penna., were married at the Friends Meeting at the latter place on Wed., 13th inst. (BFG, 20 Sept. 1809)

JEFFERS, George, mariner, and Miss Catherine Robinson, were wed last eve. at Fells Point by Rev. Dr. Allison. (BMJ, 29 Jan. 1796)

JEFFERSON, George, late American consul at Lisbon, and a relation of the late Pres., died at sea on 20th inst. on his way home in the *Diana*. (BFG, 31 July 1812)

JEFFREY, Francis, editor of the *Edinburgh Review*, and Charlotte Wilkes of Balto., dau. of Chs. Wilkes, cashier of the Bank of New York, were married Tues. by Rev. Bowen. (BA, 20 Oct. 1813)

JENKINS, Mrs. Ann, wife of William Jenkins of Balto., died last eve. in her 26th year. (BFG, 10 Aug. 1799)

JENKINS, Mr. Edward, sadler, and Ann Spalding, dau. of William Spalding, Balto. merchant, were married last eve. by Rev. Beeston. (BFG, 16 Feb. 1803)

JENKINS, Felix, and Miss Martha Croskery, dau. of B. Croskery of Balto., were wed last Tues. by Archbishop Carroll. (BFG, 13 May 1814)

JENKINS, Henry, and Miss Ann Harrison all of Balto. were married last Sun. by Bishop Carroll. (BA, 19 Sept. 1809)

JENKINS, Josias, of Long Green and Elizabeth Ann Hillen, dau. of John Hillen, merchant, were married last eve. by Bishop Carroll. (BFG, 9 Oct. 1805)

JENKINS, Michael, and Mrs. Ann Worthington all of Balto. were married last Thurs. by Bishop Carroll. (BA, 11 Jan. 1806)

JENKINS, Oswald, and Miss Sarah Pearce both of Balto. Co. were married last Tues. by Rev. John Coleman. (BFG, 13 April 1804)

JENKINS, Thomas, and Eliza Gold both of Balto. were married last Thurs. by Bishop Carroll. (BA, 25 Jan. 1806)

JENKINS, Thomas, and Miss Margaret Crist all of Balto. were wed on Sun. by Rev. Glendy. (BA, 10 Dec. 1816)

JENKINS, Walter, merchant, and Miss Catherine Gillmeyer both of Balto. were wed last Tues. by Rev. Beeston. (BFG, 2 July 1801)

JENKINS, William, of Balto., and Miss Ellen Wilcox, dau. of Mark Wilcox of Chester Co., Penna., were married last Tues. by Rev. Wheland. (BFG, 6 June 1801)

JENKINS, William V., and Miss Ann M. Wells, dau. of Cyprian Wells of Balto., were married Mon. eve. by Rev. Beeston. (BA, 12 Nov. 1807)

JENNE, Capt. Benjamin, of Balto. died Fri., 31st ult., leaving a wife and dau. (BA, 4 Sept. 1804)

JENNINGS, James, died yesterday in his 38th year; funeral from his late res. in Duke St. (BFG, 4 Aug. 1812)

JENNINGS, John, and Miss Harriet Keith, all of Balto., were wed last Thurs. by Rev. D. E. Reese. (BA, 1 Aug. 1816)

JENNINGS, Solomon, blacksmith, died 7th inst., at Fells Point. (BT, 9 Sept. 1800)

JENNY, Capt., and Miss Conway, dau. of Robert Conway, were wed last eve. at Fells Point by Bishop Carroll. (BA, 7 March 1800)

JEPHSON, John, died yesterday aged 47 years of a wound he received at North Point. His funeral from his late res. in Franklin St., near Gray's Gardens. (BA, 8 Oct. 1814)

JESSON (?), John, and Mrs. Theresa M. Overstreet all of Balto. were married last Tues. by Rev. Moranville. (BFG, 10 June 1813)

JESSOP, Charles Jr., of Balto., and Miss Jemima S. Buck, of Balto Co. were married last Tues. by Rev. Roberts. (BFG, 13 May 1813)

JESSOP, Dominic B., Balto. merchant, and Anne Owings, dau. of R'd. Owings, were married at Elk Ridge, 12th inst., by Rev. Norris. (BFG, 15 Jan. 1813)

JESSOP, Nicholas, and Miss Lydia Borley (Bosley?) both of Balto. Co. were married last eve. by Rev. Richards. (BT, 17 Jan. 1799)

JESSOP, Nicholas, and Mrs. Ruth Welsh both of Balto. Co. were wed yesterday by Rev. Hargrove. (BT, 16 Dec. 1803)

JESSOP, William, merchant, and Mrs. Ann Dodge all of Balto. were married last eve. by Rev. Dashiell. (BFG, 14 Oct. 1805)

JESTER, William H., died 2nd inst. at Head of Chester, Kent Co., in his 26th year; only son of Mr. Jonathan Jester. (BFG, 20 Oct. 1800)

JEWEL, George, and Miss Mary Ridgaway both of Balto. were married last eve. by Rev. Wells. (BFG, 19 Nov. 1802)

JEWITT, John, of Harf. Co., and Miss Susanna Judge, dau. of Hugh Judge of Balto., were married last Thurs. at Friends Meeting House in this city. (BEP, 18 June 1808)

JILLARD, John, and Eliza Dillon both of Balto. were married Sun. eve. by Rev. Dr. Rattoone. (BFG, 23 Oct. 1804)

JOB, Nicholas, died 3rd inst. in his 89th year, a native of Germany and a long time res. of Lancaster, Penna.; lately he had lived in Balto. (BA, 5 Nov. 1816)

JOHNS, Miss Elizabeth, died yesterday morning in her 20th year; consort of Isaac Johns of Balto. (BT, 18 April 1796)

JOHNS, Mr. Isaac, of Balto. died last eve. in his 58th year. (BFG, 16 Aug. 1803)

JOHNS, James, and Miss Mary Clarke all of Balto. were married last eve. by Rev. Roberts. (BFG, 12 Oct. 1812)

JOHNS, James, and Miss Ann M. Gardiner all of Balto. were wed 23rd inst. by Rev. Roberts. (BPEA, 27 July 1815)

JOHNS, Mrs. Mary, wife of James Johns of Balto. died Sun., 2nd inst. in her 25th year. (BW, 11 Jan. 1814)

JOHNS, Col. Richard, died at seat four miles from Reisterstown on 6th inst. aged 53 years. (BFG, 9 Jan. 1806)

JOHNS, Stephen S., of Cal. Co. and Miss Susannah Waters of Balto were married 24th inst. by Rev. Dashiells. (BW, 25 Feb. 1814)

JOHNSON, Mrs. Ann, died last Thurs. at her res. in Garrison Forest. (BFG, 21 June 1802)

JOHNSON, Baker, Jr., of Fred. Co. and M iss Sophia Grundy, dau. of George Grundy, Esq., were married at Bolton last eve. by Rev. Beasley. (BFG, 3 Oct. 1810)

JOHNSON, Col. Baker, died 16th inst. at Frederick Town; another patriot of the Revolution. (BFG, 26 June 1811)

JOHNSON, Barnett, of Harf. Co. died eve. of 16th inst. leaving a wife and three children. (BA, 24 Feb. 1812)

JOHNSON, Capt. Cecilius, of the ship *Louisa*, and bro. of Dr. Thomas Johnson, of Balto., died yesterday. (BT, 27 Sept. 1797)

JOHNSON, Dr. Edward, died last Sun., for many years an eminent practitioner of the art of physic; first of Lower Marlborough, and later of Balto. (BFG, 26 Sept. 1797)

JOHNSON, Edward, of Balto. and Miss Mackubin, dau. of William Mackubin, were married last eve. by Rev. Ireland. (BI, 1 June 1798)

JOHNSON, Dr. Edward, and Miss Eliza Gray all of Balto. were wed last eve. by Rev. Bend. (BA, 15 Sept. 1809)

JOHNSON, Mrs. Eleanor, wife of Henry Johnson, of Balto., died 16 Nov. at her father's home in Westmoreland, Eng. (BFG, 12 April 1806)

JOHNSON, Capt. Francis, U. S. Army, died at the Cantonment, Columbian Spring, near Fort Adams. (BFG, 20 May 1809)

JOHNSON, Horatio, Sr., died at Chantilly on Elk Ridge, 2nd inst., aged 47 years. (BFG, 6 Jan. 1804)

JOHNSON, James, and Miss Ann Hall both of Balto. were married yesterday by Rev. Reid. (BT, 26 March 1798)

JOHNSON, James, Jr., of Fred. Co. and Miss Ann M. Richards, dau. of Rev. Lewis Richards of Balto. were married last Thurs. by Rev. Wydown. (BFG, 30 May 1807)

JOHNSON, Mrs. Johanna, wife of Dr. Thomas Johnson of Balto. Co. died on Wed. (BFG, 29 May 1807)

JOHNSON, Mrs. Margaret, relict of the late James Johnson, died
Sun., 5th inst., at Springfield, Fred. Co. (BFG, 15 Sept.
1813)

JOHNSON, Rinaldo, of Aquasco, P. G. Co., died in Balto. on Tues.,
aged 56 years; interment was in the family vault at Pleasant Green in his native county on Thurs. (BFG, 18 Nov.
1811)

JOHNSON, Samuel, of Balto. died 30th ult. in his 84th year; for
more than 20 years a member of the Maryland Bar. (BS, 11
Aug. 1810)

JOHNSON, Samuel, and Miss Elizabeth Orrick, dau. of John Orrick,
both of Balto. Co., were married last Thurs. by Rev. Goslin. (BW, 14 Jan. 1812)

JOHNSON, Dr. Steven W., and Mrs. Eleanor Hall were married 26th
ult., by Rev. Healy. (BA, 18 Nov. 1812)

JOHNSON, Thomas, died at Frederick, aged 38. (BPEA, 4 March
1815)

JOHNSON, William, and Mrs. Eleanor Aiskey were married last eve.
by Rev. Ireland. The groom was a sailmaker of Fells Pt.
(BFG, 24 Aug. 1797)

JOHNSON, William, and Miss Lucy Baptist all of Balto. were wed
last Thurs. by Rev. Hargrove. (BT, 4 Sept. 1802)

JOHNSON, William, and Miss Mary Fleehart both of Harf. Co., were
married last Sun. by Rev. Richardson. (BT, 30 March 1803)

JOHNSON, William, and Miss Eliza Worthington, ygst. dau. of Mr.
Charles Worthington, were married Thurs. by Rev. Glendy.
(BFG, 13 April 1804)

JOHNSON, William, and Mrs. Mary Stevenson both of Balto. were
married last Sun. by Rev. Chambers. (BFG, 15 April 1807)

JOHNSON, William, and Miss Elizabeth Hunter all of Balto. were
married last Thurs. by Rev. Glendy. (BA, 21 March 1810)

JOHNSON, William F., of Balto., and Miss Ellender Pumphrey of
A. A. Co., were married last Sat. by Rev. Roberts. (BW,
15 Oct. 1808)

JOHNSON, William M., eld. son of Edward Johnson of Balto., died
yesterday in his 21st year. (BFG, 27 Nov. 1813)

JOHNSON, William Stewart, and Miss Margaret Hooper, were married
1st inst. by Rev. Glendy. (BFG, 13 June 1816)

JOHNSTON, Charles, and Miss Sarah Shoate both of Balto. Co. were
married 26 Dec. by Rev. Glendy. (BA, 8 Jan. 1808)

JOHNSTON, Mrs. Elizabeth, consort of Samuel Johnston of Balto.,
died last eve. in her 75th year. (BFG, 3 Jan. 1806)

JOHNSTON, George, of Balto. and Miss Burnham, dau. of the late
Robert Burnham of New York, were married last eve. by Rev.
Ireland. (BT, 23 July 1800)

JOHNSTON, James, and Miss Prudence Lowry, both of Balto., were
married last Thurs. by Bishop Kemp. (BA, 12 Aug. 1815)

JOHNSTON, Capt. John, of Balto., died last Fri. at Mr. Towson's in the county, in his 40th year. (BFG, 19 Aug. 1799)

JOHNSTON, Peter, and Miss Elizabeth Funk formerly of Balto. were married last Sun. at Steepback by Rev. Mr. Funck. (BA, 16 Nov. 1801)

JOHNSTON, Samuel, died Mon. in his 84th year, a member of the bar for over 20 years. (BFG, 1 Aug. 1810)

JOHNSTON, Samuel, and Miss Eleanor Auld all of Balto. were wed last Tues. by Rev. Glendy. (BEP, 27 Dec. 1810)

JOHNSTON, Thomas, of N. Y. and Miss Susan Buchanan, dau. of the late Gen. Buchanan of this county, were married last Tues. at Benjamin Lowndes, near Bladensburg. (BEP, 29 May 1807)

JOHNSTON, William, and Miss Elizabeth Weatherington both of Balto. were married last Thurs. by Rev. Glendy. (BT, 18 April 1804)

JOICE, Night, and Miss Peggy Langford of Patapsco Neck were wed last Thurs. (BA, 1 Jan. 1810)

JOICE, Stephen, and Miss Rebecca Shipley were married last Sun. by Rev. Shane. (BA, 24 Nov. 1812)

JOLLEY, Mrs. Sarah, wife of William Jolley, merchant, died yesterday in her 29th year. (BFG, 15 March 1800)

JONES, Mrs., the actress, died at New York, 11th inst., a few weeks after her husband died in Charleston. (BA, 17 Nov. 1806)

JONES, Abraham, and Miss Honor M'Kenzie both of A. A. Co., were married yesterday by Rev. Hargrove. (BFG, 13 Oct. 1802)

JONES, Abraham, and Miss Charity Stansbury both of Fred. Co. were married Sun. by Rev. Bend. (BT, 10 April 1804)

JONES, Awbray, and Miss Peggy Doran were married last eve. by Bishop Carroll. (BFG, 28 Jan. 1801)

JONES, Bennet, and Miss Susanna Wilson were married last Thurs. at Chester by Rev. Bolton. (BFG, 28 Oct. 1797)

JONES, David, Balto. merchant, and Miss Maria Thomas, dau. of Richard Snowden Thomas, were married at the latter's res., Hopewell, in Kent Co., on Thurs., 18th inst. by Rev. Wilmer. (BFG, 20 May 1809)

JONES, Dennis, and Susannah Rubert were married last Thurs. by Rev. Rattoone. (BA, 5 June 1805)

JONES, Dorsey James, and Miss Mary Fisher both of Balto. were wed last eve. by Rev. Beeston. (BEP, 10 April 1807)

JONES, Mrs. Frances, wife of Nicholas S. Jones, died yesterday in her 30th year; funeral from her late res. in Bridge St. (BFG, 20 March 1815)

JONES, Gabriel, Esq., died 18th ult. at his seat in Rockingham Co., Va., in his 86th year. he was one of the oldest men in the state bred to the law. (BFG, 6 Nov. 1806)

JONES, George, and Miss Amelia Dunbar both of Fells Point were married last Sun. by Rev. Kurtz. (BEP, 20 March 1809)

JONES, Gilbert, died in Belle Air on 25th ult. aged 66 years. (BWA, 4 May 1816)

JONES, Henry, died at Soldiers Delight aged 69. (BT, 14 Feb. 1809)

JONES, James, was murdered about two months ago on Fells Point by Dominic Cloris, who has just been found guilty of the crime. (BFG, 30 July 1802)

JONES, James B., and Miss Elizabeth Simmons both of Balto. were married last Sun. by Rev. Dashiell. (BA, 25 Dec. 1810)

JONES, John, and Miss Sarah Cole both of Balto. were married last Thurs. by Rev. Dr. Fry. (BW, 6 Jan. 1812)

JONES, Joseph, and Miss Sophia Wallis all of Balto. were married last Thurs. by Rev. Birch. (BEP, 30 March 1811)

JONES, Lewis, and Miss Mary Baldwin all of P. G. Co. were wed last Thurs. by Rev. Ridgely. (BT, 11 Dec. 1802)

JONES, Mrs. Mary, wife of Samuel G. Jones of Balto., died this morning in her 34th year; late res. on Market St. (BFG, 17 Aug. 1814)

JONES, Meriwether, died 9th inst., near Warm Springs, Va., formerly editor of the Richmond Examiner, and since commissioner of loans for Va. (BFG, 26 Aug. 1806)

JONES, Morris, sheriff of Fred. Co., died 24th ult. at Frederick in his 35th year, leaving a widow; interment in the Baptist burying ground. (BPEA, 7 March 1815)

JONES, Nicholas S., merchant, and Frances Brown both of Balto. were married last eve. at the res. of James Edwards by Rev. Dashiell. (BFG, 5 Sept. 1806)

JONES, Richard, Sr., died Tues. 5th inst. in his 61st year. (BFG, 10 June 1811)

JONES, Robert, and Miss Sarah Jenkins of Balto. Co. were married last Sun. by Rev. Healey. (BA, 19 Nov. 1816)

JONES, Robinson, and Miss Mary Etchberger both of Balto. were wed last eve. by Rev. Roberts. (BFG, 11 Sept. 1816)

JONES, Maj.-Gen. Samuel, member of the Gen. Assembly for Charles Co. died 15th ult. at Port Tobacco in his 49th year. He served as an officer until the end of the Rev. War. (Long obit.) (BT, 7 Feb. 1804)

JONES, Miss Susan C., died last Thurs., 9th inst., at "Clean Drnking," the res. of Charles C. Jones, Esq. (BFR, 17 April 1812)

JONES, Mrs. Susanna, died last Thurs., 14 Dec., aged 76. (BA, 18 Dec. 1815)

JONES, Talbot, and Miss Helen Mattison both of Balto. were wed last Thurs. by Rev. Samuel Knox. (BT, 4 Feb. 1804)

MARRIAGES AND DEATHS

JONES, Thomas, and Nancy Connally all of Balto. were married last eve. by Rev. Roberts. (BFG, 13 Sept. 1805)

JONES, Hon. Thomas, died last Sun. at Fort McHenry in his 77th year. (BFG, 29 Sept. 1812)

JONES, Thomas D., of Som. Co. and Miss Olevia? Edmonston of Balto. were married last eve. by Rev. Richards. (BFG, 19 Oct. 1812)

JONES, Thomas S., and Miss Susanna Trotten both of Balto. Co. were married last Thurs. by Rev. Guest. (BPE, 19 Jan. 1814)

JONES, William, merchant of Granada, and Elizabeth Leary of Balto. were married last Sun. by Rev. Allison. (BFG, 12 Feb. 1800)

JONES, William, and Miss Maria Miller all of Balto. were married last eve. by Rev. Bend. (BFG, 7 March 1810)

JONES, William, and Miss Catherine Britain all of Balto. were wed 10th inst. by Rev. Glendy. (BFG, 21 Jan. 1813)

JONES, William, died; funeral from his late res. in Great York St. (BA, 20 April 1816)

JORAY, John, and Eliza Hammond both of Balto. were married Sun. eve. by Rev. Rattoone. (BFG, 13 March 1806)

JORDAN, Augustus C., died at Norfolk on Wed., 21st ult., in his 33rd year. (BEP, 2 April 1810)

JORDAN, Dr. Dominick, son of Mr. D. Jordan of Balto., died 21st ult. in Fayetteville, N.C., in his 23rd year. (BT, 15 Aug. 1803)

JORDAN, Dominick, died at Emmittsburgh on 24 Sept. in his 77th year; long a merchant of Balto. A native of Ireland he went to the West Indies and then came to Balto. (BFG, 2 Oct. 1816)

JORDAN, James, and Miss Eliza Hambleton of Balto. were married on Thurs. eve. by Rev. Glendy. (BA, 24 June 1815)

JORDAN, John, Esq., Associate Judge of the Court of Common Pleas of Cumberland Co., Penna., died at Phila. (BA, 26 Dec. 1799)

JORDAN, John, and Miss Wilhelmina Landeryoung both of Balto. were married last Thurs. by Rev. Dr. Baker. (BA, 2 Feb. 1811)

JORDAN, Richard, died this morning in his 40th year. "At. Marys Co. - Aug. 13." (BFG, 1 Sept. 1804)

JORDAN, William, and Miss Martha Culverwell both of Balto. were married last eve. by Rev. M'Combs. (BFG, 19 March 1802)

JOYCE, John, and Miss Ann Biddison all of Balto. were married on Thurs. by Rev. Glendy. (BPEA, 20 Nov. 1815) (BA, 20 Nov. 1815, gives the groom's name as Choice.)

JUNCA, Bernard, of the House of Junca and Lebon, died Sun. aged 49. He had been a captain of artillery in the French army and at the start of the French Rev. brought his family to Balto.; leaves a wife and two children. (BFG, 6 Dec. 1808)

KALBFUS, William, and Miss Catherine Bare both of Balto. were
married 19th inst. by Rev. Dashields. (BFG, 23 Jan. 1812)

KAMINSKY, J. C., and Miss Martha Bayles, both of Balto., were
married last Sun. by Rev. Beasley. (BFG, 21 Oct. 1812)

KAR, John, and Mrs. Catherine Pebeto both of Fells Point were
married 30th inst. by Rev. M'Kane. (BA, 2 Dec. 1807)

KARTHAUS, Mrs. A. C. Magdalen, wife of P. A. Karthaus, Balto.
merchant, died 3rd inst. (BPEA, 5 April 1815)

KAUFFMAN, John, and Miss Sarah Grubb both of Balto. were married
Tues. by Rev. Kurtz. (BFG, 18 June 1812)

KAY, James, died at Fells Point, Sun., 17th inst., in his 25th
year. (BFG, 19 Oct. 1802)

KEAN, Charlotte, died last Mon. in her 11th year, eld. dau. of
Zacharia Kean of Fells Point; interment in the Episcopal
burying ground. (BFG, 7 Sept. 1803)

KEAN, Mr. Edmund, died last Fri., for many years an inhab. of
Balto. (BFG, 12 Sept. 1803)

KEAN, Mrs. Eleanor, died 25th ult. in the Merryland tract in
Fred. Co., aged 101 years, 7 mos. and 11 days, leaving a
son Thomas Kean. (BFG, 14 Aug. 1804)

KEAN, Sarah, aged 11 years, drowned yesterday when a gust of
wind overset a sailboat. (BFG, 25 July 1803)

KEAN, William, died in Washington, in his 35th year; native of
Belfast, Ireland. He came to this country after the strug-
gle which took place in Ireland in 1796-1798. (BA, 26
Aug. 1813)

KEANE, John M., Balto. merchant, and Miss Ann King of Phila. were
married last Tues. at Phila. by Rev. Mr. Potts. (BT, 16
Dec. 1803)

KEARBY, Clawsberry, and Miss Heaster Buckman all of Balto. were
married Thurs. by Rev. Roberts. (BA, 8 Aug. 1812)

KEARNY, Richard, a native of Ross, Ireland, but long an inhab.
of Balto., died last 8 Nov. at St. Marys. (BA, 10 Feb.
1813)

KEATING, George, of Balto., and Ann Simonson of Phila. were wed
in Phila. last Tues. by Rev. White. (BA, 7 Nov. 1806)

KEATING, Mrs. Elizabeth, wife of George Keatinge, Balto. bookseller, died yesterday. (BFG, 13 March 1802)

KEATINGE, George, native of Ireland and Balto. bookseller, died
last Mon. (BA, 23 Jan. 1811)

KEDRICK, Thomas, and Miss Eliza Myers, both of Balto., were wed
last Thurs. by Rev. Roberts. (BA, 11 Aug. 1807)

KEEFER, David, and Miss Nancy Brown were married last Tues. by
Rev. Cromwell. (BEP, 20 May 1811)

KEEMLE, Samuel, of Phila. and Miss Anna Maria Mather of Balto.
were married last eve. by Rev. Hargrove. (BPEA, 29 March
1815)

KEEN, Mrs. Ablona, wife of William Keen of Balto. died 18th inst. in her 47th year. (BFG, 22 April 1812)

KEENE, Mr. Benjamin, merchant of Dor. Co., died 26 June in his 57th year when a gun accidentally went off. (BFG, 6 July 1812)

KEENE, Mrs. Catherine, wife of Zachariah Keene of Balto., died Sat., 18th inst., in her 33rd year. (BA, 21 Oct. 1800)

KEENE, Mrs. Eleanora, wife of Richard Raynall Keene, and dau. of Luther Martin, died 16 Nov., aged 21, at the seat of Hector Scott, Greenwich, N. Y. She was born 8 Oct. 1786 and leaves one child, a boy a little over four years old. (BFG, 21 Nov. 1807)

KEENE, Jesse L., of Phila., late of the U. S. Navy, and Miss Jennett Bryden, dau. of J. Bryden, Keeper of the Fountain Inn, were wed last eve. by Rev. Inglis. (BFG, 26 Aug. 1807)

KEENE, Lawrence, of U. S. Navy, and Maria Martin, eld. dau. of Luther Martin, Esq., of Balto., were married last Fri. by Rev. Inglis. (BFG, 13 April 1808)

KEENE, Marcellus, of Cecil Co. and Mrs. Sarah Hodgson of Kent Co. were married last Wed. in the latter place by Rev. M'Combs. (BA, 4 Dec. 1809)

KEENE, Richard Raynall, and Eleanora Martin, both of Balto., were married 27th ult. by Rev. Ireland of Brooklyn. (BFG, 11 Feb. 1802)

KEENER, Jacob, and Nancy Jones, both of Balto. were married last eve. by Rev. Rattoone. (BFG, 25 May 1804) (BT, 29 May 1804 gives the bride's name as Johns.)

KEENER, John, and Miss Mary Griffith both of Balto. were married Sat., 22 Nov. by Rev. Kurtz. (BEP, 10 Dec. 1807)

KEENER, John, and Miss Susan Yeiser, dau. of the late Frederick Yeiser, all of Balto. were married last eve. by Rev. Mr. Kurtz. (BFG, 22 Sept. 1809)

KEENER, John, and Mrs. Margaret Griffith, all of Balto., were wed last eve. by Rev. Richards. (BA, 30 Sept. 1815)

KEENER, Mrs. Mary, wife of John Keener, died this morning in her 27th year; funeral from her late res., North Green St., Old Town. (BFG, 31 March 1809)

KEENER, Melcher, died yesterday in his 79th year, one of the oldest settlers of Balto.; interment will be in the German Presbyterian burying ground. (BFG, 27 Aug. 1798)

KEENER, Peter, died Sun., 24th inst., in his 70th year. (BFG, 27 July 1803)

KEERL, Mrs. Mary, wife of Dr. Henry Keerl, died last eve. in her 37th year, leaving four children; funeral from her late res. on German St. near Howard. (BFG, 28 Nov. 1799)

KEERL, William, and Mrs. Mary Hill, were married Thurs. by Rev. Glendy. (BFG, 27 Sept. 1813)

KEERLE, Dr. Henry, of Balto. and Miss Margaret Candle of Frederick were married Sun. eve. (BFG, 8 Nov. 1803) (BT, 9 Nov. 1803, gives the bride's name as Kendall.)

KEITH, Thomas, died 19th inst. in his 26th year; a native of Pomona, one of the Orkneys. (BFG, 22 Aug. 1804)

KELL, Mrs. Alisanna, died 25th ult. in her 71st year at the res. of Dr. Thomas E. Bond. (BA, 1 March 1814)

KELL, Mrs. Elizabeth, of Harf. Co. died 17 Dec., aged 26 years. (BA, 22 Dec. 1812)

KELL, Nathaniel, late of Balto. died in Harf. Co. on 15th inst. (BFG, 23 Aug. 1804)

KELLAND, John, late of Great Britain, died in Phila. last Thurs. (BA, 5 Sept. 1799)

KELLER, Christian, and Miss Mary Kraber, dau. of Martin Kraber of Balto., were married last Mon. by Rev. Kurtz. (BA, 15 Dec. 1815)

KELLER, Conrad, of Phila. and Miss Catharina Jordan of Balto. were married last eve. by Rev. Fenwick. (BFG, 1 April 1815)

KELLER, John, and Miss Catherine Allbright, dau. of John Allbright, all of Balto. were married last eve. by Rev. Roberts. (BA, 22 Aug. 1804)

KELLER, John, long an inhab. of Balto. died 26 Dec. in his 62nd year. (BFG, 28 Dec. 1812)

KELLY, ---, was found drowned last Sat. near Capt. Fortune's wharf. (BMJ, 1 March 1796)

KELLY, Bartholomew, and Miss Mary Ann Kelly both of Balto. were married last Thurs. by Rev. Glendy. (BA, 18 June 1816)

KELLY, John, of Thames St., Fells Point, died the 7th. (BFG, 22 July 1802)

KELLY, Joshua, and Rebecca Elliott both of Balto. were married 12 Oct. by Rev. Healey. (BA, 20 Oct. 1812)

KELLY, Capt. Matthew, and Miss Harriot Wells all of Balto. were married last Sun. by Rev. Moranville. (BA, 23 June 1812)

KELLY, Patrick, of Balto. and Miss Jane Young late of Ireland, now of Fells Point, were married last Sun. (BT, 12 Feb. 1799)

KELLY, Patrick, and Miss Catherine Liddy all of Balto. were wed last Tues. by Rev. O'Brien. (BA, 13 March 1810)

KELLY, Thomas, who lived on Carroll's Manor, Balto. Co., was killed when his house was struck by lightning on Sat. He leaves a wife and 12 children. (BA, 21 July 1815)

KELMAN, John, and Miss Mary Grubb both of Balto. were married last eve. by Rev. Otterbein. (BFG, 10 May 1802)

KELPY, George, and Miss Betsy Todd were married last Thurs. by Rev. Bend. (BAP, 12 July 1803)

KELSO, George, long an inhab. of Balto. died yesterday in his
43rd year. (BFG, 22 Oct. 1807)

KELSO, James, of A. A. Co., died yesterday aged 63 years. (BFG,
14 April 1797)

KELSO, John, merchant of James Town, Va., and Rebecca Neilson,
dau. of Mrs. Neilson of Balto., were married last eve.
by Rev. Sinclair. (BFG, 16 Oct. 1801)

KELSO, Thomas, of A. A. Co., died yesterday as a result of a
shooting accident; funeral from his late res. at Patapsco
Lower Ferry to Hammonds Ferry. (BFG, 2 Jan. 1800)

KEMP, Thomas, of Tal. Co. and Miss Sophia Horstman of Balto.
were married last eve. by Rev. Rattoone. (BFG, 19 Aug.
1803)

KENDALL, James, of Balto. died this morning. (BFG, 28 May 1810)

KENDALL, Mr. Sylvanus, of Westminster, Worcester Co., Mass., died
18th inst. in his 26th year, at Mr. Hariton's res., 25
Bond St. (BA, 22 Oct. 1814)

KENEAG, Jacob, died at Frederick-Town at an advanced age. (BPEA,
4 March 1815)

KENLY, Edward, and Miss Maria K. Reese both of Balto. were married last eve. by Rev. Dr. Roberts. (BW, 16 Feb. 1814)

KENNARD, George, died 19th inst. at Phila. aged 49 years. (BFG,
26 Oct. 1812)

KENNARD, Samuel, and Miss Henny Banks all of Balto. were married
last Thurs. by Rev. M'Cain. (BFG, 3 Feb. 1812)

KENNEDY, Arthur, died last Sun.; Balto. merchant. (BFG, 6 Sept.
1796)

KENNEDY, Dennis, and Mrs. Rachel Savage all of Balto. were wed
last eve. by Rev. Mr. Fenwick. (BFG, 28 May 1813)

KENNEDY, James, and Miss Ann Williams all of Balto. were married
last eve. by Rev. Fechtig. (BFG, 31 May 1815)

KENNEDY, John, and Miss Mary Somers both of Balto. were married
on Thurs. eve. (BFR, 25 Jan. 1812)

KENNEDY, John F., and Miss Marcy Gray all of Balto. were married
last eve. by Rev. Bend. (BFG, 30 Dec. 1801)

KENNEDY, Robert J., of Phila. and Miss Elizabeth Lambden of Balto. were married on Sun. by Rev. Dashiells. (BA, 10 Dec.
1811)

KENNEDY, Thomas S., of Balto. and Sophia Meissen, dau. of Joseph
Meissen of New Orleans, were married at the latter place
on 1 March. (BFG, 2 April 1806)

KENNEDY, William, and Sally Bouldin all of Balto. were married
last Thurs. by Rev. Bend. (BA, 19 Aug. 1801)

KENNER, Charles, and Miss Elizabeth Green all of Balto. were wed
last eve. by Archbishop Carroll. (BMG, 30 Aug. 1815)

KENNY, William M., Chestertown merchant, died 10th inst. at his
    farm in Kent Co. in his 46th year. (BEP, 28 Dec. 1808)

KENT, Robert, merchant, and Miss Margaret Myers all of Balto.
    were married last Sat. by Rev. Kurtz. (BFG, 9 Jan. 1798)

KENTER, Mr. C. F., merchant, and Miss Eliza Griffith both of
    Balto. were married last eve. by Rev. Richards. (BFG,
    30 Oct. 1799)

KERMER, Godfrey, and Miss Polly Barry were married 19th ult. by
    Rev. Glendy. (BA, 4 Dec. 1809)

KERNS, John, and Mrs. Susanna Robb both of Balto. were married
    last Thurs. by Rev. Richards. (BA, 4 Oct. 1806)

KERR, Alexander, and Ann, fourth dau. of William Whetcroft of
    Annap., were married at Phila. last Sat. by Rev. Dr.
    White. (BT, 20 April 1796)

KERR, David, Jr., and Miss Maria Perry, dau. of the late William
    Perry, all of Easton, were married at that place last
    Thurs. by Rev. Jackson. (BFG, 7 Nov. 1804)

KERR, Hugh, slater, died yesterday when the tie rope gave way
    and he fell from the roof of a house in Gay St. He leaves
    a wife and family. (BFG, 18 Dec. 1812)

KERSNER, Jacob, innkeeper, died at Hagerstown, aged 58. (BPEA,
    24 March 1815)

KESSLER, David, and Miss Araminta Mercer both of Balto. were wed
    last Mon. by Rev. Rozell. (BFG, 18 Aug. 1808)

KEY, Philip, of St. M. Co., and Miss Sophia Hall of Balto. were
    married Thurs. eve. at Col. Ramsay's by Rev. Bend. (BFG,
    11 June 1796)

KEY, Philip Barton, died at his seat near Georgetown on 28 July,
    aged 58 years. A native of Cecil Co. he served in the Md.
    legislature and in Congress. (Long obit.) (BFG, 8 Aug.
    1815)

KEYS, James, Balto. merchant, and Miss Jane Barr of Shippensburg,
    Penna., were married at the latter place last Thurs. by
    Rev. Mr. Moody. (BFG, 8 Dec. 1807)

KEYS, John, merchant, and Elizabeth Hardester both of Balto. were
    married 6th inst. by Rev. Alexander M'Kean. (BW, 12 April
    1809)

KEYS, Richard, Jr., youngest son of Richard Keys of Woodville,
    Balto. Co., died yesterday in his 15th year. (BFG, 4 Jan.
    1812)

KEYSER, Ann Maria, eld. dau. of Major George Keyser of Balto.,
    died last Mon. in her 10th year. (BS, 28 Aug. 1812)

KEYSER, Eliza Caroline, dau. of Capt. George Keyser of Balto.,
    died yesterday aged 4 years. (BFG, 14 Jan. 1811)

KEYSER, George of Balto. and Elizabeth Chenoweth, dau. of Rich-
    ard Chenwoeth of Balto. Co., were married last Tues. by
    Rev. Butler. (BFG, 26 Feb. 1802)

KEYSER, Mrs. Mary, wife of Samuel Keyser, Balto. merchant, died yesterday. (BFG, 27 Feb. 1805)

KEYSER, Samuel, and Miss Polly Stouffer both of Balto. were wed last eve. by Rev. Kurtz. (BT, 31 Dec. 1802)

KEYSER, Samuel, merchant, and Mrs. Hetty Polk, both of Balto., were wed last eve. by Rev. Richards. (BFG, 1 Jan. 1806)

KIDD, Samuel, Norfolk merchant, and Miss Pamela A. Simpson of Balto. were married 7th inst. (BFG, 20 Jan. 1808)

KIDDAW, Capt. John, and Mrs. Eliza M. Chase all of Balto. were married last Thurs. by Rev. Glendy. (BFG, 13 March 1813)

KIER, Richard, and Miss Isabella Murray were married last Thurs. by Rev. Parks. (BA, 12 Feb. 1814)

KIERLE, Matthew, and Miss Charlotte Pindell both of Balto. were married Thurs. eve. by Rev. Richards. (BA, 28 Nov. 1815)

KIERNAN, Mr. Hugh, died at Phila. 7th inst. aged 45 years. (BFR, 30 Nov. 1810)

KIESTARD, Luke, and Miss Amelia Kelburn both of Fells Point were married last Thurs. by Rev. Glendy. (BA, 3 Sept. 1807)

KILLEN, John, Balto. merchant, died yesterday after a long illness. (BTD, 10 Sept. 1798)

KILLEN, John, died yesterday aged 22. (BFG, 12 July 1808)

KILTY, Mrs. Elizabeth, wife of the Hon. William Kilty, died at Annap. on 21st inst. (BFG, 26 Oct. 1807)

KILTY, Capt. John, died at Annap. on Mon., 27th inst., in his 55th year; late register of the land office for the western shore, and adjutant general of the state of Md.; "Another revolutionary hero gone!" (BFG, 6 June 1811)

KIMMEL, Liss Lydia, youngest dau. of Anthony Kimmel of Balto., died last Fri. in her 24th year. (BFG, 15 Jan. 1816)

KIMMEL, Mrs. Margaret, wife of Anthony Kimmel, died Thurs. in her 58th year. (BFG, 19 May 1810)

KIMMEL, Michael, and Miss Kitty Stouffer were married last eve. by Rev. Hargrove. (BFG, 12 March 1802)

KINCAID, James of Balto. and Miss Barbara Kendal of Fred. Town were married this morning by Dr. Roberts. (BPE, 2 Sept. 1813)

KINDEL, James, and Miss Mary Ewing all of Balto. were married by Rev. Glendy last Thurs. (BA, 17 Sept. 1816)

KING, Edward, and Miss Mary Williams all of Balto. were married last eve. by Rev. Roberts. (BFG, 11 May 1809)

KING, Mrs. Eleanor, wife of William King, died yesterday aged 27 years. (BA, 27 July 1807)

KING, Mrs. Elizabeth, wife of Jacob King, died Wed. in her 61st year. (BWA, 17 Feb. 1816)

KING, Fitz, and Miss Nancy Tilden both of Balto. were married last Thurs. by Rev. Glendy. (BA, 9 Aug. 1815)

KING, Gideon F., and Louisa H. W. Busch both of Balto. were wed last Thurs. by Rev. Kurtz. (BFG, 17 Oct. 1816)

KING, Jacob, and Mrs. Hart all of Balto. were married 8th inst., by Rev. McJilton. (BA, 23 April 1816)

KING, James, and Miss Elizabeth Jones, were married on Wed. by Rev. Dr. Rattoone. (BFG, 21 Dec. 1804)

KING, Mrs. Letitia, wife of Josias W. King of Washington, died at Phila. in her 42nd year. (BA, 27 Sept. 1813)

KING, Thomas, of Balto., and Miss Jane Wilson of Balto. Co. were married last Thurs. by Rev. Luckey. (BA, 16 Dec. 1816)

KING, William, and Mrs. Martha Campbell, both of Balto., were wed on Sun. by Rev. Rattoone. (BFG, 14 Dec. 1808)

KING, William, long a res. of Balto., died last night in his 50th year. (BPE, 3 Sept. 1813)

KINGKART, Robert, and Miss Grace Auld all of Balto. were married last Thurs. by Rev. Glendy. (BA, 15 Dec. 1806)

KINGSMORE, Richard Sex, and Rebecca Yeiser both of Balto. were married last eve. by Rev. Hargrove. (BFG, 20 Sept. 1804)

KINGSTONE, George, died in East St. of the prevailing fever, on Fri., aged 12 years. (BFG, 23 Sept. 1800)

KINKEAD, James, died this morning in his 22nd year, son of Mr. Kinkead of Elkton. (BFG, 6 Oct. 1804)

KINNAMOND, Henry, and Miss Betsy Crosier all of Balto. were wed last Fri. by Rev. Glendy. (BFG, 1 May 1813)

KIPP, John, and Mrs. Mary Wolslager of Balto. were married last eve. by Rev. Kurtz. (BFG, 16 June 1800)

KIRBEY, James, and Miss Jane Harvey all of Balto. were married last Thurs. eve. by Rev. Pitts. (BA, 7 Sept. 1811)

KIRBY, Mrs. Mary, consort of Jno. Kirby of Jones St. died Mon., in her 34th year. (BS, 5 May 1812)

KIRBY, Capt. Nicholas, died yesterday at Fells Point. (BFG, 3 March 1800)

KIRK, Bennett, of Balto. died last Jan. at St. Bartholomew's. (BA, 17 Jan. 1810)

KIRKLAND, Alexander, and Agnes Quail, eld. dau. of Robert Quail, were married 11 April by Rev. Hemphill. (BA, 13 April 1816)

KITHCART, Robert, and Miss Nancy Maxwell were married last Thurs. by Rev. Glendy. (BFG, 11 May 1813)

KITTEN, John, died last Mon., aged 22. (BFR, 18 July 1808)

KLASSEN, Charles, and Margaret Smith, both of Balto., were wed last Thurs. by Rev. Hoffman. (BPEA, 18 Nov. 1815)

KLOCKGETHER, Mr. Deadrick, and Miss Charlotte Stanley all of Balto., were married 13th inst. by Rev. Kurtz. (BA, 17 Feb. 1816)

KNIGHT, Isaac, merchant, and Julianna M. Thomas, dau. of Samuel Thomas of Roxbury Mills, were married at Friends Meeting House, Sandy Spring, on 25th inst. (BFG, 28 Sept. 1811)

KNIGHT, James M., and Miss Elizabeth M'Garven, all of Balto., were married last Thurs. by Rev. Beeston. (BAP, 23 Aug. 1803)

KNIGHT, Joshua, merchant of Mont. Co., and Mrs. Mary Falconer of Balto. were married last Mon. by Rev. Robert R. Roberts. (BFG, 5 Dec. 1810)

KNIGHT, Michael, and Miss Patty Van Horn were married by Rev. Glendy on 9th inst. (BFG, 13 June 1816)

KNIGHT, Mr. Nathaniel, and Miss Elizabeth Hoyle all of Balto. were married last eve. by Rev. Hargrove. (BFG, 9 May 1803)

KNIGHT, Peregrine, of Balto. and Miss Sarah G. Forrest of A. A. Co., were married last Tues. in A. A. Co. by Rev. Inglis. (BA, 1 Feb. 1816)

KNIGHTON, Thomas, and Miss Margaret Patton, all of Balto., were married 9th inst. by Rev. Griffith. (BA, 12 Dec. 1815)

KNOTT, James, died last Thurs. in his 31st year, leaving a wife and two children. (BFG, 5 Sept. 1803)

KNOWER, John, of Balto., died 26th inst., aged 37; formerly of Worcester, Mass., leaving a wife and three children. Dec. was a member of the Sea Fencibles. (BW, 6 Jan. 1814)

KNOWLES, James S., and Miss Ann McConnell both of Balto. were married last Thurs. by Rev. Rattoone. (BFG, 13 March 1807)

KNOX, Gen., died at Warren, 25th ult. (BA, 10 Nov. 1806)

KNOX, Mrs., wife of Rev. Samuel Knox of Balto., died Wed., 11th inst. (BA, 13 Nov. 1812)

KOHLSTADT, Benjamin, and Miss Elizabeth Keener all of Balto. were married last Thurs. by Rev. Kurtz. (BA, 13 July 1814)

KONECKE, Richard N., merchant, and Miss Rebecca Y. Sewell of Balto. were married last Thurs. by Rev. Duncan. (BFG, 23 Dec. 1815)

KONICKE, Nicholas, native of Bremen, died in Balto. on Fri., 1st inst., in his 61st year. (BA, 5 Jan. 1813)

KONIG, August, merchant, native of Hanover, and for the last 12 years a res. of Balto., died last Fri. of an apoplectic fit; in his 63rd year. Interment in the Lutheran burying ground. (BFG, 9 Dec. 1800)

KONSTADT, Benj., and Miss Elizabeth Keener all of Balto. were wed last Thurs. by Rev. Kurtz. (BPE, 13 July 1814)

KOOG, Martin, and Miss Nancy Radal all of Balto. were wed last Mon. by Rev. Glendy. (BFG, 14 Nov. 1812)

KOONE, Daniel, and Miss Mary W---k, all of Balto. were married last eve. by Rev. Roberts. (BFG, 25 Nov. 1808)

KRACHT, Frederick, merchant, and Hannah Amelung, both of Balto., were married last eve. by Rev. Kurtz. (BFG, 4 Nov. 1801)

KREBS, George, and Miss Maria Loudenslager all of Balto. were married last Thurs. by Rev. Glendy. (BA, 4 May 1816)

KREEMER, Henry, clerk in the Treasury Dept., died last Thurs. at Washington, D. C. (BEP, 11 June 1808)

KREMS, Mr. Joseph, died last eve. aged 48 years, long an inhab. of Balto. Funeral from his late res., corner of Franklin and Union Sts., W. P. (BA, 23 Aug. 1816)

KROUSE, George G., died 8th inst. at his res. in Balto. Co., in his 64th year. Interment in the Lutheran burying ground in the Western Precincts of Balto. (BA, 9 Nov. 1811)

KUNIUS, John, native of Penna., belonging to the privateer Matilda, died 15th ult., aged 29 years, at the Poor House and Hospital in Savannah, Ga. (BS, 13 Nov. 1812)

KUNTZ, Mrs. Maria, wife of Jacob Kuntz of Balto., and dau. of John Selve of Mont. Co., died this morning aged 31 years and 3 weeks. (BA, 30 Aug. 1811)

KURTZ, Jacob, died. Funeral will be from the res. of John Shultz, his father-in-law, No. 5, German St. (BFG, 22 Jan. 1810)

KURTZBERGER, Peter, died in his 34th year. (BEP, 3 Jan. 1809)

KYLE, Adam B., and Miss Charlotte Dinsmore, were married last Tues. eve. by Rev. Glendy. (BA, 27 Oct. 1815)

KYSER, John, and Miss Catherine Greenwood, were married last Thurs. by Rev. Beeston. (BA, 25 Aug. 1804)

LABE, Mr., died at Frederick. (BPEA, 4 March 1815)

LABLY, Lewis, and Ann Lewis were married on Sun. at Fells Point, by Rev. Dr. Rattoone. (BFG, 9 May 1806)

LACAZE, William, M. D., of Balto. died last Sat. (BT, 28 Jan. 1801)

LACEY, Capt. Stephen, died yesterday in his 40th year. (BFG, 18 Oct. 1806)

LAFFETHY, William, and Miss Ann Kelly, both of Balto., were married last Thurs. by Rev. Hagerty. (BA, 15 June 1807)

LAFITTE, William, and Miss Ann Kelly both of Balto. were married last eve. by Rev. Hagerty. (BFG, 12 June 1807)

LAIDLER, Mrs. Catherine, wife of John Laidler of Rose Hall, Chas. Co., died 25 June in her 40th year. (BFG, 8 July 1809)

LAIRD, James, died 26th ult.; rector of Great Choptank Parish, and Pres. of the Academy in Cambridge. (BWA, 6 April 1816)

LAKENAN, John, and Miss Juliana M'Rea, were married 30th inst. by Rev. Dr. Elliott, Chaplain, U. S. Army, N.D. (BA, 31 Dec. 1816)

MARRIAGES AND DEATHS

LAMBERT, Robert, and Miss N. Apsley were married. (BEP, 22 April 1809)

LAMBRECHT, Henry, Sr., died at Frederick Town on 3rd inst., an old inhab. of Balto. (BA, 9 April 1805)

LAMDEN, Thomas, and Miss Ann Davey were married last Thurs. by Rev. Moranville. (BA, 28 May 1816)

LAMDIN, Robert, of Tal. Co., died 25th ult. in his 55th year. (BWA, 9 March 1816)

LAMMOT, Daniel, Jr., Balto. merchant, and Miss Susan P. Beck, dau. of Paul Beck, Jr., of Phila., were married there last Thurs. by Rev. Bishop White. (BFG, 20 May 1806)

LAMMOT, Daniel, and Mrs. Mary Evans all of Balto., were married last eve. by Rev. Hargrove. (BFG, 9 July 1810)

LAMMOT, Daniel, died this morning, an old inhab. of the Western Precincts of Balto.; funeral from his mansion house below the Market House precincts to the Dunkers burying ground. (BFG, 2 May 1812)

LAMOTTE, Mrs. Elizabeth, wife of Daniel Lamotte, Sr., of the west suburbs of Balto., died Fri. (BFG, 1 March 1803)

LANCASTER, John H., of Chas. Co., and Miss Juliet Trenton of Balto., were married last eve. by Bishop Carroll. (BFG, 6 Feb. 1807)

LANCASTER, Moses P., late of Boston, and Miss Betsy Miller of Balto., were married last eve. (BFG, 20 March 1801)

LANCASTER, Moses P., attached to the sheriff's office of Balto. City and Co., died yesterday, leaving a wife and three children. (BEP, 23 April 1808)

LANDMAN, Nicholas, and Miss Ann Hugg, all of Balto., were wed last Thurs. by Rev. Wells. (BPEA, 30 June 1815)

LANDSTREET, John, and Miss Belinda Ore, both of Balto., were wed last Thurs. by Rev. Dr. Roberts. (BEP, 22 April 1811)

LANE, Mrs. Providence Dorsey, died this morning in her 70th year. Funeral from John Brice's res. near the Court House. (BFG, 18 April 1809)

LANGSTRETH, John G., Phila. merchant, and Miss Rebecca Amelia Dunn, dau. of the late James Brown Dunn, of Kent Co., were married 7th inst. at Phila. by Rev. Dr. Kewley. (BFG, 16 Aug. 1808)

LANGTON, Sylvester, of Farmington, Conn., and Miss Eliza Kilpatrick of Balto., were married Mon., 19th inst., by Rev. Birch. (BPEA, 19 Sept. 1815)

LANGTON, Thomas, died yesterday in his 43rd year; formerly a merchant in Balto. (BFG, 6 Sept. 1799)

LANGWORTHY, Edward, died yesterday in his 64th year, deputy naval officer of the Port of Balto. (BFG, 2 Nov. 1802)

LANGWORTHY, James E., formerly teller in the Office of Discount and Deposit in Balto. died yesterday. (BFG, 19 Oct. 1804)

LANGWORTHY, James Edward, and Miss Providence Norris of Harf. Co. were married last Thurs. by Rev. Richards. (BFG, 26 May 1804)

LANGWORTHY, Miss Nancy, died yesterday in the bloom of life. (BFG, 5 Nov. 1800)

LANSDALE, Major Thomas, of Queen Ann, P. G. Co., died Wed., 19th inst. (BFG, 21 Jan. 1803)

LA REINTREE, John Louis Roy, and Miss Catherine Neilson, all of Balto., were married last eve. by Rev. Inglis. (BFG, 27 Dec. 1811)

LARY, Peter, and Miss Eliza Hagerman, both of Balto. were wed 31st Jan. by Rev. Kurtz. (BA, 11 Feb. 1813)

LARSH, Abraham, Balto. merchant, and Miss Catherine Worthington, dau. of Samuel Worthington of Balto. Co. were married last Thurs. by Rev. Armstrong. (BEP, 7 March 1810)

LARSH, Isaac, of Reisterstown, died 9th inst., aged 24 years. (BA, 15 Jan. 1805)

LATHERBURY, Peregrine, died at Chester Town, Md. (BA, 1 Sept. 1801)

LATIMER, Sergt. Charles, died this morning at Fort McHenry; of the artillerists and engineers of the U. S. (BFG, 4 March 1799)

LATIMER, James, of Phila., and Miss Sophie Hoffman were married last Thurs. by Rev. Bend. (BFG, 11 Nov. 1809)

LATIMER, Capt. James, died last Wed. at Mill Creek in Elizabeth City Co. (BFG, 5 Sept. 1811)

LATIMER, Randolph W., and Miss Catherine B. Griffith, both of Balto. were married last Thurs. by Rev. Richards. (BA, 20 May 1816)

LAUDAMAN, Fred'k, and Miss Jane Maria Harrison all of Balto. were married Thurs. by Rev. Bartow. (BA, 6 April 1816)

LAUDER, Alexander, died yesterday. (BFG, 12 Jan. 1803)

LAUGHLIN, James, and Miss Jane Lown, all of Balto., were married last Wed. by Rev. Glendy. (BFG, 6 April 1813)

LAURENSON, Philip, and Margaret Whelan, daughter of Capt. Ricnard Whelan of Balto., were married last eve. by Rev. Beeston. (BFG, 13 Oct. 1803)

LAWDER, Benjamin, of Balto., and Miss Mary Burton of Balto. Co. were married 29th inst. by Rev. Rilen. (BPE, 7 Dec. 1814)

LAWLESS, Michael, of Balto. was drowned 29th ult. in Currituck Sound. (BT, 8 Dec. 1798)

LAWRENCE, Charles, and Mrs. Barbara Webb, both of Havre de Grace were married there on 26th ult. by Rev. J. J. Wilmer. (BS, 8 Dec. 1812)

LAWRENCE, John, late of London, and Mrs. Mary Marshall of Balto. were married Sat., 27 April by Rev. Dr. Staughton. (BFG, 6 May 1805)

LAWRENCE, Richard. and Miss Ellen Scott all of Balto. were wed last eve. by Rev. Smith. (BFG, 8 Jan. 1813)

LAWRENCE, Lieut. Thomas John, of U. S. Regt. of Infantry, died at Fort McHenry last Sun. (BFG, 24 Sept. 1799)

LAWSON, Mrs. Elizabeth, relict of the late Alexander Lawson of Balto., died at her late res. on 11th inst. in her 69th year. (BA, 26 Jan. 1814)

LAWSON, Richard, of Balto. died last eve. in his 54th year; the funeral will be from his late res. in Albemarle St. (BFG, 25 Oct. 1803)

LAWSON, Robert, and Miss Elizabeth M'Allister, both of Balto., were married last eve. by Rev. Bishop Carroll. (BFG, 13 Feb. 1798)

LAYMAN, Nicholas, and Miss Elizabeth Gibb, both of Balto. Co., were married last Sun., 6th inst. by Rev. Mr. Baker. (BFG, 8 Dec. 1812)

LEA, Isaac C., merchant, and Mrs. Rebecca Pinney, all of Balto., were married 3rd ult. at Frankfort, Penna., by Rev. Mr. Docke. (BA, 6 April 1816)

LEA, Thomas, Jr., of Wilmington, Del., and Eli(za)beth Ellicott were wed 18th inst. at Friends Meeting House, Elk Ridge. (BFG, 20 Nov. 1812)

LEACH, Richard Henry, of Savanna, Ga., attorney-at-law, and Mrs. Joharina Loeffler (nee Marsello) of Amsterdam were married in Balto. Thurs., 2nd inst. by Rev. Dr. Ireland. (BFG, 3 Jan. 1800)

LEAGDE, William W., and Miss Elizabeth Emmerson both of Balto. were married last Sun. by Kurtz. (BWA, 20 April 1816)

LEAHY, John, cooper, died yesterday in his 43rd year. (BFG, 10 July 1805)

LEAKIN, Frederick, died yesterday in his 22nd year; recently arrived from the West Indies, he leaves an aged mother. (BFG, 15 Jan. 1812)

LEAKIN, Jesse, died last Fri. on his passage from Havanna in his 17th year. (BA, 10 Dec. 1816)

LEAKIN, Sheppard C., and Miss Margaret Dobbin, both of Balto., were married last eve. by Rev. Glendy. (BW, 13 April 1812)

LEAKIN, Thomas J., and Miss Mary L. Little, both of Balto., were married last Sun. by Rev. Inglis. (BA, 8 May 1813)

LEAMAN, Thomas Jefferson, eld. son of Thomas Leaman of Cumberland Row, died Thurs. (BA, 1 Aug. 1801)

LEAR, Col. Tobias, accountant of the Dept. of War, died in Washington on 11 Oct. (BFG, 15 Oct. 1816)

LEARY, John, cooper, died last eve. in his 43rd year. (BT, 10 July 1805)

LEASE, Abraham, and Mrs. Margaret Foster, all of Balto. were wed 7th inst. by Rev. Wells. (BWA, 20 April 1816)

LEATHERBOROUGH, William, and Mrs. Deborah Thompson all of Balto. were married Sat. by Rev. Allison. (BT, 20 April 1801)

LEATHERBOROW, William, of Balto., died 8th inst. at the house of William Taylor of Wash., D. C., leaving a widow. (BT, 14 Oct. 1803)

LECKY, John, of Fells Point, and Miss Isabella Beard, dau. of Capt. Alexander Beard of Price's Town were married last eve. by Rev. Glendy. (BFG, 28 Dec. 1807)

LECLAIRE, ---, child of Mr. Leclaire, apothecary of Balto., was killed in a carriage accident on Mon. (BA, 29 Aug. 1807)

LEDLIE, Thomas, printer, and Miss Sarah Armstrong both of Balto. were married last eve. by Rev. Byrch. (BEP, 16 Jan. 1807)

LEE, Charles, died at his seat in Fauquier Co., Va., last Sat., aged about 58 years. He held public offices during the administrations of Washington and Adams. (BA, 30 June 1815)

LEE, David, member of the Soc. of Friends, died 16th ult. at his res. in Harf. Co. (BFG, 20 Dec. 1815)

LEE, George, and Miss Sarah Wilson, both of Balto., were married Sun. eve. by Rev. D. Roberts. (BA, 29 May 1811)

LEE, Capt. George, for many years an inhab. of Balto., died Thurs. 2nd inst. (BWA, 11 May 1816)

LEE, James, and Miss Evy Spedden, both of Balto., were married last eve. by Rev. Roberts. (BEP, 12 Sept. 1806)

LEE, James, of Balto. and Miss Dealy Poteet of Harf. Co. were wed last Thurs. by Rev. Davis. (BFG, 12 Jan. 1807)

LEE, James A., and Miss Catherine M. Coskery, second dau. of Bernard Coskery, all of Balto. were married last Tues. by Rev. Fenwick. (BFG, 27 April 1816)

LEE, Rev. Jesse, late chaplain to Congress, and for 33 years an itinerant Methodist minister, died 12th inst. at Hillsborough on the Eastern Shore, in his 59th year. At his own request he was interred in the Methodist burying ground in Balto. (BA, 21 Sept. 1816)

LEE, Joseph, and Miss Elizabeth Ramsey were married 16th inst. by Rev. Dr. Rattoone. (BFG, 25 April 1804)

LEE, Mrs. Mary, lady of Thomas Sim Lee, died yesterday after a short illness. "Georgetown, Jan. 22." (BFG, 26 Jan. 1805)

LEE, Mrs. Mary, wife of Capt. George Lee, died last Thurs. aged 24 years. (BA, 25 Jan. 1808)

LEE, Michael, died Tues., aged 34. (BS, 1 Sept. 1810)

LEE, Nathaniel, aged 78, already married three times, having 11 children, 49 grandch., and 10 gr.-grand ch., and Elizabeth Tucker, aged 25, both of P. G. Co., Va., were married last Thurs. (BA, 12 Feb. 1806)

LEE, Nicholas, and Miss Mary Clark, were married last eve. at Fells Point by Rev. Richards. (BFG, 7 Dec. 1803)

LEE, Parker Hall, of Harf. Co. and Mrs. Mary Munickhuysen of Balto. Co. were married last Sun. by Rev. Richardson. (BA, 26 Sept. 1809)

LEE, Richard, died this morning in his 64th year; funeral from his late res. Philadelphia Road. (BFG, 3 Nov. 1809)

LEE, Robert C., clerk of the superior court of Jefferson Co., Va., and Miss Mary Ann Roberts, dau. of the late George Roberts of Balto., were married 28th ult. at Winchester, Va. (BFG, 8 June 1811)

LEE, Lieut. Samuel M., of U. S. Light Dragoons, a native of Harf. Co., Md., died 20 Aug. at New Orleans. (BFG, 20 Sept. 1811)

LEE, Thomas, and Miss Honora Shipley, dau. of Robert Shipley of Balto. Co., were married last Tues. by Rev. Joshua Wells. (BW, 27 Feb. 1810)

LEE, William, of Georgetown, and Miss Mary L. Holliday of Balto. were married last Mon. by Bishop Carroll. (BFR, 10 Oct. 1809)

LEEF, Jacob, and Miss Elizabeth Taylor of Balto. Co. were married last Thurs. by Rev. Rozewell. (BFG, 24 Jan. 1809)

LEFAVER, Abraham, printer of Balto., and Miss Eliza Hannaman of Balto. Co. were married 26 March. (BEP, 9 April 1805)

LEFAVER, Nicholas, died Sat., 30 Nov., in his 81st year. (BFG, 3 Dec. 1811)

LE FORT, George Louis Francois Isidore, and Mrs. Frances Deschamps both of Balto. were married last eve. by Rev. Carroll. (BFG, 13 July 1799)

LEGRAND, William T., artist, and Mrs. Mary Tull all of Balto. were married last Tues. by Rev. Dr. Roberts. (BA, 15 Nov. 1816)

LEIB, Gen. Michael, and Miss Susan Kennedy both of Phila. were married there 9th inst. (BW, 22 Nov. 1808)

LEIPER, George G., of Phila. and Miss Eliza S. Thomas, dau. of John Chew Thomas, were married last Thurs. at Farmland, by Rev. Janeway. (BFG, 7 May 1810)

LE MARR, Mr., a young man, died when he fell from the roof of a high building. (BFG, 16 Oct. 1802)

LEMMON, Capt. John, and Mrs. Esther Lawrence both of Fells Point were married Sun. by Rev. Richards. (BT, 12 Nov. 1799)

LEMMON, Capt. John, of Fells Point died yesterday in his 49th year; funeral from his late res., No. 27 Bond St. (BA, 12 Feb. 1805)

LEMMON, Joshua, of the House of Lemmon and Campbell, died this morning. (BFG, 29 Sept. 1802)

LEMMON, Moses, and Mary Wheeler, were married 25 Feb. by Rev. Armstrong. (BFG, 10 March 1806)

LEMOINE, Peter, Va. merchant, and Miss Elizabeth Mongee of Balto. were married last Tues. by Bishop Carroll. (BT, 23 Feb. 1798)

LEMONIER, Mr. A. L., merchant, and Miss M. Sophia Waters all of
Balto. were married last eve. by Rev. Bend. (BFG, 8 Feb.
1809) (BA, 9 Feb. gives the groom's name as Lemontier)

LENNEWAY, Miss Sally, died 22nd ult., aged 33 years. (BWA, 6
April 1816)

LENOX, James, and Mrs. Mary Ackinson were married 6th inst. by
Rev. Glendy. (BFG, 25 Sept. 1812)

LENOX, William, died 25th inst. at Charleston, aged 74 years, an
old inhab. of that city. (BAP, 14 June 1803)

LEPPER, William D., and Miss Esther Oyster both of York Co., were
married last Tues. at Hanover, Penna., by Rev. Melzheimer.
(BFG, 7 Feb. 1798)

LEREW, James, and Miss Elizabeth Kantz, both of Balto., were wed
last Tues. by Rev. Bend. (BT, 17 Oct. 1799)

LESTER, John, son of the late Benjamin Lester of York Co., Va.,
and Mrs. Elizabeth Courtnay, all of Balto., were married
last Sun. by Rev. Beasley. (BFG, 16 Nov. 1812)

LESTER, William, cabinet maker, and Miss Elizabeth Johnson both
of Fells Point were married Tues. eve. by Rev. Bend. (BT,
12 Aug. 1797)

L'ESTRANGE, Joseph, of the Balto. and Phila. theatres, died last
Sat. in his 78th year. (BFG, 22 May 1805)

LETTER, Mrs., consort of Thomas Letter of the Bank of Balto.,
died last Fri. in her 37th year. (BFG, 26 Oct. 1802)

LEUTY, Charles, and Miss Margaret Nevets all of Balto. were wed
last Sun. by Rev. Kurtz. (BEP, 3 Jan. 1809)

LEVELY, George, clockmaker, died yesterday at his house in Balto.,
aged 46 years. (BFG, 30 April 1796)

LEVELY, John S., and Miss Phebe Ann Skelton, all of Balto. were
married last Thurs. (BPE, 17 Nov. 1813)

LEVER, Jonathan, of Balto., died yesterday evening. (BT, 30 Jan.
1798)

LEVERING, Capt., formerly of Md., last of Marietta, Ohio, died
at Kaskaskia. "Western Spy." (BW, 2 Nov. 1811)

LEVERING, Mrs. Ann, died Sun., leaving a husband and children.
(BFG, 22 Oct. 1799)

LEVERING, Enoch, and Miss Hannah Brown were married last eve. by
Rev. Dr. Allison. (BT, 29 Jan. 1800)

LEVERING, Mrs. Mary, wife of A. Levering, Balto. merchant, died.
(BS, 18 Aug. 1810)

LEVILLAIN, Mr. James, consul of the French Republic to this state,
died yesterday. (BFG, 30 July 1803)

LEVRING, Francis, and Miss Charlotte Elliott, both of Balto.,
were married 6th inst. by Rev. Rattoone. (BFG, 13 Nov.
1806)

LEVY, Benjamin, died yesterday in his 76th yr. (BFG, 4 Feb. 1802)

LEVY, Miss Hetty, died 18th inst. aged 52 years. (BA, 23 Jan. 1816)

LEVY, Isaac Jacob, Phila. merchant, and Miss Hester Pollock, dau. of Elias Pollock of Balto. were married by Rabbi Wolf of Phila. (BFG, 13 Feb. 1809)

LEVY, Jacob F., and Miss Ann Maggs both of Balto. were married last eve. by Rev. Bend. (BA, 20 Nov. 1804)

LEVY, Joseph, son of Levy Andrew Levy, died last Sun. in his 35th year. (BFG, 5 Oct. 1813)

LEVY, Mrs. Susanna Scott, wife of Levy Andrew Levy of Balto., died 29 July in her 62nd year. (BFG, 31 July 1807)

LEWIS, Capt., of Boston, and Miss Eliza Hertick of Balto. were married Tues. by Rev. Rattoone. (BFG, 5 April 1804)

LEWIS, Charles, of Conn., and Miss Margaret Barron of Balto. were married last Thurs. (BFG, 20 Nov. 1797)

LEWIS, Charles, Balto. merchant, died Mon., 29th inst. in his 24th year. (BT, 9 Oct. 1800)

LEWIS, Edward, Ensign, 38th Regt., U. S. Inf., and Miss Ann Maria Britain, were married 25th inst. by Rev. Glendy. (BA, 30 Dec. 1814)

LEWIS, Henry, of Alexandria, and Mrs. Mary Hager, widow of the late John Hager, were married at Hagerstown on 20th inst. by Rev. Bowers. (BFG, 25 May 1802)

LEWIS, Dr. J. W., died yesterday. (BFG, 16 Sept. 1800) (BFG, 17 Sept. 1800, contains long obit.)

LEWIS, John, died this morning, aged 19. (BEP, 4 Sept. 1810)

LEWIS, John D., of Balto., and Miss Sophia Hall, dau. of J. White Hall of Harf. Co., were married at Halls Park on Tues. by Rev. Mr. Allen. (BFG, 6 Nov. 1806)

LEWIS, John D., of Balto., died at Abingdon, Harf. Co., on Wed., aged 29 years. (BFG, 15 Sept. 1809)

LEWIS, Joseph, of Balto., died in the marine hospital at Brest, seaman belonging to the ship Ceylon. (BA, 29 Oct. 1812)

LEWIS, Lewis D., and Miss Catherine McGowan, both of Balto., were married Thurs. by Rev. Roberts. (BFG, 20 June 1812)

LEWIS, Mrs. Mary, consort of Dr. Philip Lewis, died last Sat., aged 33, leaving seven children. On Sunday her remains were interred in the Baptist burying ground. (BFG, 17 Dec. 1799)

LEWIS, Mrs. Mary, died last Fri. in her 41st year. (BFG, 28 May 1811)

LEWIS, Mary Clementina, dau. of William Young Lewis of Balto., died this morning aged three years. (BFG, 23 Jan. 1807)

LEWIS, Mordecai, Balto. merchant, died Wed. in his 51st year. (BT, 19 March 1799)

LEWIS, Philip, and Sally Barton both of Balto. were married Mon. by Rev. Hagerty. (BA, 30 April 1800)

LEWIS, Samuel W., and Miss Eliza C. Holliday both of Balto. were married Mon. by Rev. Rattoone. (BFG, 14 Dec. 1808)

LEWIS, Willeby, and Miss Martha Sprole all of Balto. were married by Rev. Glendy last Sat. (BA, 12 April 1810)

LEWIS, William, and Mrs. Mary Sidwell both of Balto. were married last Fri. by Rev. John Healey. (BT, 16 Aug. 1802)

LEWIS, William Barron, elder son of the late Charles Lewis of Balto., died yesterday aged 5 years. (BT, 5 Jan. 1803)

LEWIS, William Peter, of Balto. and Miss Susanna Mary Mashaw of this place were married in Charleston on Tues., 13th inst. by Rev. Munds. (BFG, 27 Nov. 1806)

LEWIS, William Young, and Miss Stewart, dau. of Dr. William Stewart, lately from Europe, were married last Tues. by Rev. Ireland. (BT, 15 May 1798)

LEWTHWAITE, Capt. Christopher, died 5 May at sea on his passage from the Isle of May. (BT, 13 June 1801)

LEYPOLD, John, died last Sat. in his 80th year, long an inhab. of Balto. (BFG, 2 July 1810)

LEYPOLD, Samuel F., and Miss Breidenbaugh both of Balto. were wed last eve. by Rev. Kurtz. (BT, 19 Oct. 1798)

LIDDIE, John, and Miss Catherine Foy both of Fells Point were married last (?) eve. by Rev. Beeston. (BMJ, 30 May 1796) (The original notice in BMJ 27 May erroneously gave the groom's name as Doolittle.)

LIGGETT, George, died last Mon. in his 72nd year, a native of Chester Co., Penna., but for many years a res. of Balto. (BA, 2 May 1814)

LIGHTNER, George, aged 60, died yesterday. (BA, 27 Jan. 1815)

LIGHTNER, George W., and Miss Eliza Rice Springer both of Cecil Co. were married Thurs., 29th Oct., at the country seat of Jas. Springer by Rev. Grahame. (BA, 11 Nov. 1809)

LINDENBERGER, Frederick, Balto. merchant, and Miss Rebecca Hebb, dau. of the late Col. Vernon Hebb, were married last Thurs. at St. M. Co. (BFG, 16 Dec. 1801)

LINDENBERGER, George, of Balto. died Tues. in his 66th year, an inhab. of Balto. for 37 years. In the late revolution he proved himself a friend to the principles of American liberty. (BMJ, 28 July 1796)

LINDENBERGER, Jacob, and Miss Anne Emory, dau. of Thomas L. Emory of Q. A. Co., were married last Thurs. by Rev. Barclay. (BFG, 17 June 1805)

LINDENBERGER, Mrs. Susanna, died yesterday in her 80th year. (BA, 8 Aug. 1812)

LINE, George, and Miss Webe Koahl all of Balto. Co. were married last Thurs. by Rev. Glendy. (BA, 19 May 1808)

LINGAN, Nicholas, died at Georgetown last Fri., an old inhab. of
that town. (BFR, 7 Nov. 1811)

LINGENFELTER, Jacob, and Miss Eliza Freeman both of Balto. were
married Sun. by Rev. Roberts. (BFG, 19 May 1807)

LINGFORD, Mrs. Ann, consort of John Lingford of Balto. died 27th
inst. in her 25th year. (BFG, 29 Oct. 1808)

LINGFORD, John, and Ann Mattocks, all of Balto., were married on
last Thurs. by Rev. Bend. (BA, 26 April 1806)

LINN, Rev. J. B., pastor of the First Presb. Church in Phila.,
died last Thurs. in his 27th year. (BA, 3 Sept. 1804)

LINTHICUM, Amasa, of A. A. Co., died last Sun. in his 19th year.
(BEP, 11 Sept. 1810)

LINTON, Miss Elizabeth, of Balto. died yesterday in her 18th year.
(BT, 29 May 1800)

LINVILLE, John, comb-maker, died last Fri., aged 47; resided at
70 Market St. (BFG, 14 Sept. 1801)

LION, Mr., and Miss Bull all of Balto. were married last Thurs.
by Rev. Roberts. (BA, 19 May 1814)

LIONI, Gasper, and Miss Cecilia Richards both of Balto. were wed
last Thurs. by Rev. Moranville. (BFG, 12 Oct. 1811)

LISHMAN, Capt. William, and Miss Ruth Humphreys both of Balto.
were married Sun. (BA, 20 Jan. 1807)

LIST, John, and Miss Deborah Jackson both of Balto. were married
last Thurs. by Rev. Addison. (BPE, 4 Nov. 1813)

LISTEMANN, Charles Frederick, native of Magdeburg, died yesterday
in his 25th year. (BFG, 13 Oct. 1800)

LITTLE, Francis, and Miss Rosanna Thompson, all of Balto., were
married Wed., 2nd inst. by Rev. Wm. Sinclair. (BFG, 3
May 1810)

LITTLE, Henry, and Miss Elizabeth Neafe all of Balto. were married
last Thurs. by Rev. Dashiell. (BEP, 10 April 1810)

LITTLE, John, Balto. druggist, and Sarah Sinclair, dau. of Robert
Sinclair of Balto., were married yesterday at Friends Meeting House in Lombard St. (BA, 21 June 1816)

LITTLE, Joseph, and Miss Elizabeth Spicer both of Balto. were
married last eve. by Rev. Roberts. (BFG, 11 Nov. 1808)

LITTLE, Peter, and Miss Arabella Hughes all of Balto. were wed
last eve. by Rev. Richards. (BFG, 25 Aug. 1797)

LITTLE, Col. Peter, and Miss Catherine Levely all of Balto. were
last Sun. by Rev. Hargrove. (BFG, 21 May 1816)

LITTLE, Thomas, and Miss Mary Calder all of Balto. Co. were wed
last Fri. by Rev. Glendy. (BA, 10 Aug. 1810)

LITTLEJOHN, Mrs. Catherine, died last Sat. aged 80 years. (BFG,
27 Sept. 1802)

LITTLEJOHN, Dr. Miles, died 23 Dec. aged 57. (BPEA, 27 Dec. 1815)

LIVERS, Arnold, of Balto. died last Sat. in his 44th year, leaving a wife, five small children and a mother. (BFG, 1 Oct. 1804)

LIVERS, Miss Elizabeth, died at Emmittsburgh on Sat. se'ennight in her 18th year, dau. of the late Arnold Livers of Balto. (BEP, 4 May 1808)

LIVERS, James, and Miss Sarah Wheeler both of Balto. were married last eve. by Rev. Beeston. (BT, 11 June 1802)

LIVESAY, Mrs. Martha, died last eve. consort of William Livesay, Balto. merchant; res. in Pratt St. (BFG, 26 Feb. 1807)

LIVESAY, William, merchant, and Miss Rebecca Hynson, dau. of John C. Hynson of Kent Co., Md., were married 24th inst. by Rev. Spry. (BFG, 28 Nov. 1807)

LIVINGSTON, Hon. Robert Le Roy, member of Congress from New York, and Miss Anne Maria Diggs, dau. of the late George Diggs of P. G. Co., Md., were married at Green Hill on Tues., 22nd inst. by Archbishop Carroll. (BFR, 6 July 1811)

LLOYD, Edward, died Fri., 8th inst., at his res. in Tal. Co. (BMJ, 16 July 1796)

LLOYD, Henry, and Miss Isabella Howard all of Balto. were married last eve. by Rev. Richards. (BFG, 25 Oct. 1803)

LLOYD, Peregrine, died yesterday of the prevailing disease; a hatter; an inoffensive, deserving man. (BFG, 24 Sept. 1800)

LLOYD, William A., merchant of Frederick Town, Md., and Mrs. S. H. Young, dau. of Gen. John Bull of Penna., were married 26 Dec. at Washington by Rev. James Lowery. (BT, 7 Jan. 1815)

LOAMAN, Thomas Jefferson, son of Thomas Loaman of Cumberland Row, died Thurs. (BA, 1 Aug. 1801)

LOCK, Edward, and Miss Rhoda Gun, were married at Westminster. (BA, 22 July 1801)

LOCKWOOD, Aquila, Balto. merchant, and Miss Cassandra M. Dallam, dau. of Josias U. Dallam of Harf. Co., were married last Thurs. by Rev. Hammond. (BA, 18 Sept. 1815)

LOGAN, Rev., died Sun., 19th ult. in Mifflin Co., Penna. (BA, 7 June 1805)

LOGAN, Albanus C., son of Dr. Logan of Stenton, and Miss Maria Dickenson, dau. of John Dickenson of Wilmington, Del., were married at the Friends Meeting there. (BEP, 3 May 1808)

LOGAN, John, of Balto., and Mary Maria Kennedy of Lancaster Co., Penna., were married last Thurs. by Rev. Arthur. (BA, 5 Nov. 1801)

LOGAN, John B., and Miss Mary Ann Bryson, all of Balto., were married last eve. by Rev. Hargrove. (BFG, 27 Aug. 1813)

LOGAN, Michael, of Fells Point, died yesterday in his 65th year. (BFG, 16 July 1813)

LOMAX, Thomas Lunsford, died at Fredericksburg, Va., on 29 ult., in his 25th year. (BFG, 1 June 1805)

LONG, Capt., and Susanna Brown, both of Balto., were married last eve. (BFG, 9 April 1802)

LONG, Abraham, and Miss Mary Thomas, dau. of Capt. Amos Thomas of Taneytown, were married last Sat. by Rev. Richards. (BEP, 15 Sept. 1806)

LONG, George Hunter, son of Col. Long of Balto., died Sat., 24th inst. in his 16th year; a student at Baltimore College. (BFG, 26 June 1815)

LONG, Henry, of Balto., and Miss Eliza Ann Gittings of Long Green, Balto. Co., were married Thurs. eve. last by Rev. Coleman. (BA, 29 Aug. 1809)

LONG, James, died yesterday, a res. of Balto. for the last 44 years. (BFG, 11 May 1807)

LONG, Kennedy, Balto. merchant, and Miss Eliza Kennedy, dau. of Andrew Kennedy of Phila., were married 16th inst. by Dr. Green, at Phila. (BT, 20 Nov. 1797)

LONG, Robert, died last Fri., aged 76, leaving a wife and three children. (BEP, 9 June 1808)

LONG, Robert, ensign in the 14th Regt., U. S. Infantry, died in Balto., on Tues. (BA, 11 March 1813)

LONG, Robert Carey, and Miss Sarah Carnighan, both of Balto., were married on Thurs. by Rev. Richards. (BT, 11 Oct. 1797)

LONG, Robert Cary, and Miss Anna Hamilton, all of Balto., were married 24th inst. by Bishop Carroll at the house of Chas. Ghequiere. (BFG, 25 Jan. 1809)

LONG, Samuel, and Miss Sally Dawson were married Wed. by Rev. Glendy. (BA, 1 Dec. 1810)

LONG, Capt. Seth, of Balto., and Sally M. Harper of Alexandria were married at the latter place last Thurs. by Rev. Muir. (BFG, 11 Oct. 1806)

LONG, Capt. Seth, of Balto., master of the private armed schooner The Comet, died last 10 Jan. at sea, off Pernambuco. (BA, 23 April 1813)

LONGBOTTOM, Richard, and Miss Christiana Love, all of Balto., were married last Wed. by Rev. Glendy. (BA, 24 May 1816)

LOOCKERMAN, Mrs. Frances, relict of Thomas Loockerman of Dor. Co., died Sun. in her 49th year. (BA, 1 Dec. 1812)

LOOCKERMAN, Jacob, and Miss Mary Harrison of Dorset were married 10th inst. by Rev. Wilmer. (BFG, 14 Oct. 1802)

LORD, Maria, wife of Joseph L. Lord, died yesterday, aged 22. (BA, 15 May 1816)

LORMAN, William, and Miss Amelia Jane Spear both of Balto. were married last Sun. by Rev. Glendy. (BMG, 18 July 1815)

LOUIS, Domingo, convicted of murdering Mr. Jones, was executed yesterday in the prison yard. (BRAD, 8 Sept. 1802)

LOUIS, Pierre Henry, agent of the French Republic in Balto., died last Thurs. His remains were interred yesterday. (BFG, 21 March 1801)

LOURINON, Mathew, and Miss Jane Johnston, all of Balto., were married last Tues. by Rev. Sinclair. (BT, 25 Nov. 1802)

LOVE, Dr. John, and Miss Apolonia Walter, both of Balto., were married last Sat. by Rev. Mertz. (BFG, 2 Oct. 1810)

LOVE, Dr. Thomas, and Mrs. Martha Ridgely, all of Balto. Co., were married last eve. by Rev. Lucky. (BFG, 3 Sept. 1802)

LOVELL, John, died at the Natchez, aid-de-camp of Gen. Wilkinson, son of the Hon. James Lovell (or Lowell?) of Boston. (BFG, 20 Feb. 1800)

LOVELL, William, and Miss Lilly Meekins both of Balto. were wed last Sat. by Rev. Dr. Rattoone. (BA, 15 Oct. 1806)

LOVELL, William, and Miss Mahala Woollen all of Balto. were married last eve. by Rev. Dashiell. (BA, 13 Sept. 1811)

LOVERING, Mr. Francis, coachmaker, died this morning in his 36th year; funeral from his late res. in Duke St. (BFG, 5 Sept. 1816)

LOVRING, Francis, and Charlotte Elliott all of Balto. were married last eve. by Rev. Rattoone. (BT, 7 Nov. 1806)

LOW, Henderson P., and Miss Rebecca Patterson both of Balto. were married last Thurs. by Rev. Pitts. (BFG, 11 May 1807)

LOWE, Mrs. Solomon, died in Easton. (BPE, 17 Aug. 1813)

LOWE, John, Phila. organ builder, died yesterday in his 23rd year, in New York where he was setting up an organ in St. Johns Church. "N. Y. paper." (BA, 18 Dec. 1813)

LOWE, Jonas, died last 17 July at the Havanna, late master of the schooner *Felicity* of this port. (BFG, 18 Sept. 1799)

LOWERY, Robert, and Miss Eliza Holmes all of Balto. were married Tues. by Rev. Fenwick. (BA, 6 Oct. 1815)

LOWNDES, Benjamin, of Bladensburg, died Sun., 15th inst. in his 60th year. (BFG, 20 Jan. 1809)

LOWRY, Mrs., wife of Col. Lowry of Balto., died Sat. (BW, 5 Sept. 1808)

LOWRY, Edward B., died Wed., 9th inst., in his 37th year; funeral from his res. in Great York St. (BA, 10 March 1814)

LOWRY, James, merchant, and Miss Rebecca Parker, both of Balto., were married last eve. by Rev. Glendy. (BEP, 23 April 1804)

LOWRY, Robert K., Balto. merchant, and Miss Henrietta Wager, dau. of the late Philip Wager, Esq., of Phila., were married at Phila. on Tues. eve. by Bishop White. (BFG, 17 March 1815)

LOWRY, Capt. Samuel, and Mrs. Agnes Cooper of Fells Point, were married last eve. by Rev. Hargrove. (BFG, 13 Sept. 1798)

LUCAS, Mr., discharged soldier from the U. S. Army who had been wounded at New Orleans, died last Sun. at Fort McHenry. (BA, 15 Dec. 1815)

LUCAS, Basil, died last Fri. at Ellicotts Mills, in his 32nd year. (BFG, 11 April 1803)

LUCAS, Fielding, Jr., of Balto., and Miss Eliza Carrell of Balto. were married at Phila. last Tues. by Rev. Hurley. (BFG, 18 May 1810)

LUCAS, John, millwright, died 1 Nov., aged 51 years. (BA, 4 Nov. 1814)

LUCENA, Thomas, Savannah merchant, and Miss Hester Rour of Balto. were married last Thurs. by Rev. Glendy. (BA, 2 Sept. 1809)

LUCKETT, Dr. Mountjoy B., son of Col. William Luckett of Fred. Co., Md., died at Baton Rouge, on 26 Feb. in his 23rd year. (BFG, 9 April 1812)

LUCKIE, William, of Harf. Co., and Miss Jane Ward were married last eve. at Montpelier, the res. of Henry Didier by Rev. Hargrove. (BFG, 31 March 1807)

LUCKY, William, of Harf. Co., died 13th inst. on his farm when a piece of timber fell on him; he leaves a wife and family. (BFG, 17 Oct. 1798)

LUDDEN, Lemuel, Jr., merchant, and Miss Margaret McDonogh, dau. of the late John McDonogh of Balto., were married last eve. by Dr. Inglis. (BFG, 7 June 1815)

LUDLOW, Robert C., of U. S. Navy, and Miss Ann C. Wethered, dau. of John Wethered of Wilmington, Del., were married at Prospect Hill, near Wilmington, on 23rd inst. by Rev. William Price. (BFG, 27 July 1812)

LUSBEY, Mrs. Rebecca, wife of Robert Lusbey, died Sun., 10th inst. at Frederick Town, Cecil Co., leaving a husband and four children. (BFG, 18 Aug. 1806)

LUSBY, Henry, and Miss Ann Cook, all of Balto. were married last Thurs. by Rev. Wm. M'Ferson. (BW, 1 May 1811)

LUTHER, Capt. Christopher, and Mrs. Agnes Carlisle both of Balto. were married last Sun. by Rev. Alison. (BT, 12 July 1797) (BFG, 10 July 1797, gives the groom's name as Lewthwaite.)

LUTTIG, John C., merchant, and Miss Sally Prestt, both of Balto. were married last eve. by Rev. Bend. (BFG, 22 Jan. 1798)

LUTZE, George, merchant, and Miss Henrietta Hapke both of Balto. were married last eve. by Rev. Kurtz. (BFG, 6 May 1801)

LUX, Darby, and Miss Mary Nicholson both of Balto. Co. were married last Wed. eve. by Rev. Richards. (BTm 23 Feb. 1798)

LUX, Darby, of Balto. Co. died last Sun. within a few days of completing his 40th year, and just three weeks after the death of his eldest dau. (BA, 17 Sept. 1812)

LUX, Miss Elizabeth Ann, died last Sat. at the res. of Mrs. Rachel Lux, Balto. Co., in her 15th year. (BA, 26 Aug. 1812)

LUX, George, died last Wed. in his 43rd year. (BT, 5 Aug. 1797)

LUX, Mrs. Rachel, died Sun. in her 79th year. (BFG, 12 Jan. 1813)

LYASON, John, of Washington Co., Tenn., and Miss Mary Cole of Balto. Co. were married last Thurs. by Rev. Cullerson. (BFG, 13 Dec. 1802)

LYLES, Mrs. Ann, wife of William Henry Lyles of Alexandria, and dau. of Col. William Lowry of Balto., died at the former place 23rd ult. in her 23rd year. (BT, 14 Dec. 1804)

LYLES, Col. William, died 27th ult. at his res. in P. G. Co., an officer in the Rev. War. (BA, 2 Jan. 1816)

LYLES, William H., Alexandria merchant, and Miss Ann Lowry of Balto. were married Wed. by Rev. Sinclair. (BFG, 6 Nov. 1801)

LYNCH, Abraham, and Mrs. Elizabeth Jones both of Balto. were wed last eve. by Rev. Rattoone. (BFG, 23 July 1806)

LYNCH, Ann, of Balto., late of Kent Co., died Thurs. (BFG, 5 Aug. 1811)

LYNCH, Major John, died Sun., 4 Dec., in his 44th year. He took an active part in our struggle for independence. (BFG, 8 Dec. 1796)

LYNES, James, and Eliza Church, all of Balto., were married last Sun. by Rev. Dashiell. (BFG, 31 March 1806)

LYNN, Col. John, died in Allegheny Co., one of the bravest of patriots. "Georgetown, March 29." (BFG, 30 March 1813)

LYON, Mrs. Abigail, of Worcester, Mass., died 5th inst., aged 58 years, at her son's house in Balto. (BEP, 7 June 1808)

LYON, Andrew, and Mary Massey, formerly of St. M. Co., were wed at Alexandria last Wed. by Rev. Muir. (BA, 2 March 1805)

LYON, George, of Carlisle, Penna., and Miss Ann G. Savage were married 14th June by Rev. Thomas Davis. (BFG, 5 July 1815)

LYON, Peter, and Miss Elizabeth Foster, all of Balto., were married last Mon. by Rev. Glendy. (BA, 13 Nov. 1815)

LYON, Samuel, Balto. merchant, and Hetty, dau. of Jacob Brown of Wilmington, were married at the latter place on 3rd inst. (BFG, 14 March 1800)

LYONS, Bartholomew, and Miss Elizabeth Coulson, all of Balto., were married Thurs. by Rev. Glendy. (BEP, 26 March 1811)

LYTLE, James, died 18th inst. at his res. in Harf. Co. in his 63rd year. Formerly a member of the State Legislature, he leaves a wife. (BPE, 22 Oct. 1814)

MARRIAGES AND DEATHS

LYTLE, Thomas. and Miss Mary Gover all of Balto. were married on Tues. by Rev. Beasley. (BA, 17 Dec. 1812)

M'ALLISTER, Christopher, and Miss Margaret Morton were married yesterday by Rev. Rattoone. (BFG, 11 July 1805)

McALLISTER, James, Balto. merchant, died yesterday. (BFG, 23 Jan. 1796)

M'ALLISTER, Lloyd, and Miss Elizabeth Fite all of Balto. Co. were married last Thurs. by Rev. Lynch. (BFG, 7 June 1806)

M'ALLISTER, Mrs. Mary, wife of John M'Allister of Balto., died last Sun. in her 27th year. (BEP, 21 Feb. 1809)

McALLISTER, William, one of the masters of the Balto. Academy, died yesterday. (BT, 6 Sept. 1797)

M'BLAIR, Miss Isabella, died last Sun. in her 17th year. (BFG, 18 Nov. 1802)

McCABE, John, and Miss Jane Fitzgerald, were married in Balto. last Mon. (BAP, 6 Aug. 1803)

M'CALLISTER, John, and Miss Sarah Mallett were married last Wed. by Rev. Rattoone. (BA, 26 Aug. 1809)

McCANDLESS, James, and Miss Margaret March, both of Balto., were married last Sun. (BFG, 27 Dec. 1803)

M'CANN, James, and Mrs. Ann Roach, were married 13th inst. by Rev. Hargrove. (BA, 22 Dec. 1815)

McCANNON, James, died last night at his farm in Fred. Co., near Westminster in his 62nd year; for many years a res. of Balto. (BFG, 26 April 1815)

M'CARTER, Alexander, and Miss Esther Pasley both of Balto., were married last eve. by Rev. Otterbein. (BT, 18 Dec. 1804)

M'CARTY, John, and Miss Peggy Elvard, both of Balto. were married last Sun. by Rev. Inglis. (BFG, 28 Nov. 1802)

M'CASHIN, Mark, and Miss Mary Everson all of Balto. were married last Tues. by Rev. Glendy. (BS, 7 Feb. 1812)

M'CASKEY, Alexander, died yesterday in his 59th year; a res. of Fells Point. He was an officer in the Revolutionary army, a husband and parent. His remains were interred in the Friends burying ground. (BFG, 15 March 1798)

M'CAULEY, James, and Jane Glenn Bird of Balto. were married 19th inst. by Rev. Bend. (BA, 22 April 1806)

M'CAUSLAND, Emily Jane, third dau. of Marcus M'Causland of Balto., died Sun., 10th inst., in her 15th year. (BFG, 12 March 1811)

M'CAUSLAND, Frederick William P., son of Marcus M'Causland, died this morning in his 23rd year. (BFG, 25 Oct. 1813)

M'CIEU, Edward, and Mrs. Sarah Seger both of Balto. were married last eve. by Rev. Dr. Roberts. (BFG, 20 Oct. 1809)

MACILLIER, Louis Lambert, formerly of Alexandria, Va., died at Guadeloupe; a husband and father. (BA, 4 Feb. 1811)

M'CLAIN, John, and Miss Eleanor Holland both of Balto. were married last Tues. by Rev. Roberts. (BW, 28 Sept. 1809)

McCLASKEY, Charles, and Mrs. Elizabeth McBride were married last Thurs. by Rev. Healey. (BA, 4 May 1816)

M'CLASKEY, George, died suddenly in his 28th year; employed at the Office of Discount and Deposit. (BFG, 11 July 1804)

MACLAY, Samuel, died Thurs., 5th inst. at his farm in Northumberland Co., Penna., in his 70th year. He served in the state legislature and that of the nation. (BW, 27 Sept. 1811)

M'CLEAN, Col. Moses, died at Chilicothe, Ohio, 25th ult. in his 73rd year; formerly of Adams Co., Penna. He entered the Rev. War at an early period as captain. (BFG, 20 Sept. 1810)

M'CLEARY, William, and Miss Sarah Osborn, both of Balto., were married Thurs., 30th ult. by Rev. Mr. Sinclair. (BT, 2 July 1803)

M'CLEESTER, Henry, and Miss Agness Fleming both of Balto. were married Wed. by Rev. Glendy. (BW, 9 Feb. 1810) (BA, 16 Feb. 1810, gives the bride's name as Herring.)

M'CLELLAN, Andrew, and Miss Mary Danskin both of Balto. were wed by Rev. Roberts. (BEP, 2 March 1810)

McCLELLAN, John, and Miss Mary Neale were married 27th ult. by Rev. Glendy. (BA, 11 May 1809)

McCLELLAN, Mrs. Mary, of Balto. Co., died last Tues. in her 69th year, consort of John McClellan, Sr. (BFG, 5 Dec. 1811)

M'CLELLAN, Samuel, and Miss Eliza Raborg, dau. of Christopher Raborg, all of Balto. were married last Thurs. by Rev. Dashiell. (BFG, 28 Dec. 1812)

M'CLOSKEY, Daniel, drowned Sunday. (BFG, 26 July 1803)

M'CLURE, John C., and Miss Mary Ann Thornburgh both of Balto. were married last eve. by Rev. Dr. Allison. (BFG, 7 Dec. 1798)

M'CLURE, Francis, printer, died 28th inst. in Washington. (BT, 4 Sept. 1804)

M'CLURE, William G., and Miss Mary T. Finch all of Balto. were married last eve. by Rev. Dr. Roberts. (BFG, 20 Feb. 1811)

McCLUSTER, Henry, and Miss Agnes Hemings were married 8th inst. by Rev. Glendy. (BEP, 15 Feb. 1810)

M'COLM, Duncan, blacksmith, for many years a res. of Fells Point, died; his body was taken up at one of the wharves on the Point on 18th inst. He was a native of Scotland. (BFG, 20 March 1806)

M'COMAS, Josiah, of Harford Co., and Mrs. Charity Divers of Balto. Co. were married Tues., 25th inst. by Rev. Mr. Handy. (BFG, 30 May 1808)

MACOMB, John N., late of Balto., merchant, died at Falmouth on H. B. M. packet *Princess Charlotte*. He died from wounds received while helping to defend the ship from a French attack. (BEP, 21 Jan. 1811)

McCONKEY, John, and Mrs. Mary Bailey all of Balto. were married last Thurs. by Rev. Glendy. (BFG, 8 June 1816)

McCONKLE, Joseph P., druggist, and Mrs. Maria Morrell Hahn both of Phila. were married in that city on Tues. by Rev. Ezra Stiles Ely. (BA, 3 Dec. 1813)

M'CONKY, Jesse, merchant of Yorkhaven, and Miss Priscilla Bull of Balto. were married last Tues. by Rev. Roberts. (BFG, 26 March 1812)

McCONNELL, Mrs. Elizabeth, died this morning in her 73rd year, leaving three daughters. (BFG, 15 Oct. 1803)

McCONNELL, John, and Miss Sarah Leret both of Balto. were married last eve. by Rev. Ireland. (BFG, 17 June 1799)

McCONNELL, John, died suddenly last Tues. of Balto., aged 26 yrs. (BFG, 9 April 1802)

M'CONNELL, Capt. Robert, and Miss Eleanor Burn, dau. of James Burn, all of Fells Point were married Sun., 8th inst. by Rev. Inglis. (BEP, 10 Jan. 1809)

McCORKLE, Capt. Archibald, and Miss Elizabeth Moore, of Cecil Co., were married Tues., 30th inst. by Rev. Wm. Duke. (BA, 3 June 1815)

M'CORMICK, James, Jr., and Miss Rachel Ridgely Lux of Balto. Co. were married last Thurs. at Mt. Airy. (BI, 18 April 1798)

M'CORMICK, John Montgomery, son of Mrs. M'Cormick, died last Fri., aged about 13 years. (BEP, 23 Jan. 1809)

M'CORMICK, Thomas, and Miss Ellen Gardner, all of Balto., were married yesterday by Rev. Glendy. (BFG, 1 Jan. 1816)

McCORMICK, William, and Mrs. Elizabeth Montgomery both of Balto. were married last Sun. (BA, 11 March 1801)

M'CORMICK, William, Balto. stone-cutter, died last Wed. in his 43rd year. (BA, 1 June 1807)

M'COY, Daniel, and Miss Mary Hendricks, both of Balto., were wed Tues. eve. by Rev. Morainville. (BEP, 23 April 1807)

McCOY, John, and Miss Mary Fuller, both of Balto. were married last eve. by Rev. Kurtz. (BFG, 22 April 1803)

M'COY, Samuel, and Mrs. Kileholtz both of Balto. were married last eve. by Rev. Dr. Inglis. (BA, 18 June 1816)

M'COY, Stephen, and Miss Ruth Ryan were married by Rev. Glendy, on 27th ult. (BFG, 19 April 1816)

McCOY, Thomas, and Miss Mary Willis, were married last Thurs. by Rev. Glendy. (BA, 7 May 1812)

M'CRA, Edward, and Jane Porter all of Balto. were married by Rev. Dr. Rattoone. (BA, 8 Oct. 1806)

M'CREA, Samuel, printer, died this morning, aged 38, formerly of Strabane, Ireland, and a res. of Balto. for over ten years. (BEP, 12 Aug. 1807)

McCREERY, Thomas, late of Balto. died 20 Feb. at Dublin. (BMJ, 27 April 1796)

McCREERY, William, died 28th inst. at his res. Clover Hill near Reisterstown, in his 84th year. A native of Ulster, Ireland, he was a member of Congress. (BW, 2 April 1814)

McCRERY, Miss Mary, died at Elkton, Cecil Co., on Sun., 15th inst., in her 23rd year. (BEP, 20 Feb. 1807)

M'CUBBIN, William, and Miss Catherine Grimes, dau. of Mrs. Mary Grimes, all of Balto., were married last Sun. by Rev. Bend. (BFR, 18 Nov. 1809)

M'CUBBIN, Wm., died yesterday in his 36th year; res. at Head of Frederick St. (BA, 28 April 1814)

McCUBBIN, William Henry, of Balto., died last Sun. eve. in Norfolk of consumption. He leaves a wife. (BA, 11 Nov. 1815)

MacCUBBIN, Major Zachariah, died at his farm in Balto. Co. on 18th inst. in his 64th year. (BFG, 23 Nov. 1809)

M'CULLA, John, and Miss Margaret Logan, late from Ireland, now all of Balto., were married Thurs. by Rev. Richards. (BT, 4 March 1800)

M'CULLOH, Hugh, second son of James H. M'Culloh, died yesterday in his 14th year, when a bean he had been eating passed into his windpipe. (BA, 29 Aug. 1807)

M'CULLOH, Mrs. Isabella, wife of Dr. Samuel M'Culloh of Balto. Co., died on 10th inst. in her 41st year. (BFG, 13 Feb. 1815)

M'CULLOH, James W., and Miss Abby H. Sears, only dau. of the late George Sears of Balto. (BPE, 20 May 1814)

M'CULLOUGH, Hugh, and Mrs. Betty Stockard all of Balto. were married Mon. eve. by Rev. Glendy. (BA, 21 March 1807)

McCULLOUGH, James, and Miss Elizabeth White of Balto. Co. were married last eve. by Rev. Inglis. (BEP, 16 Sept. 1808)

M'CULLY, Henry, and Miss Mary Kerr, both of Southwork, were married at Phila. by Rev. Milledollar. (BT, 16 Feb. 1804)

McCURDY, Hugh, merchant, died 14th inst. at his res. in Calvert St. (BFG, 15 March 1805)

McCURDY, John, and Mrs. Jane Duffie both of Balto. were married last Thurs. eve. by Rev. Glendy. (BMG, 10 July 1815)

M 'DANIEL, Mrs. Mary, wife of Hugh McDaniel of Fells Point, died yesterday; res. in George's St. (BEP, 29 Aug. 1810)

M'DANIELD, James, died this morning in his 47th year; res. in Short Alley near New Market. (BFG, 11 Oct. 1816)

M'DAVID, Peggy, res. at Lombard and South Sts., died. (BFG, 10 Aug. 1802)

McDERMOT, Mrs. Esmy, died at Charleston, of consumption; dau. of Mrs. Diminic Jordan. (BFG, 5 Feb. 1799)

MARRIAGES AND DEATHS

M'DERMOTT, Henry, and Miss Esmy Jordan, both of Balto., were wed last Tues. by Bishop Carroll. (BFG, 7 Dec. 1797)

McDERMOTT, Henry, and Miss Susan M'Ilvaine, late of Co. Tyrone, Ireland, were married last Tues. by Rev. Fenwick. (BA, 4 March 1813)

M'DERMOTT, Capt. Thomas, and Jane Cunningham, were married Sun. by Rev. Ellison (sic). (BA, 28 May 1799)

M'DOLE, Robert, and Miss Sarah Donnally were married by Rev. Rattoone. (BEP, 7 Oct. 1806)

McDONALD, Charles, and Elizabeth Fisher, all of Balto. were married last Sun. by Rev. Bend. (BT, 11 May 1803)

McDONALD, Mrs. Elizabeth, wife of Alexander McDonald of Lancaster St., Fells Point, died this morning; interment in the Presb. burial ground attached to Rev. Inglis' church. (BFG, 17 Aug. 1813)

M'DONALD, Henry, and Miss Catherine Roche both of Balto. were wed last Sun. by Rev. Moranville. (BPE, 1 Feb. 1815)

M'DONALD, John, apprentice, was killed last Wed. when lightning struck the printing office of Mr. Way in Washington. (BFG, 25 Aug. 1804)

M'DONALD, John, native of Ireland, died yesterday at the house of William Morrow. (BT, 23 May 1805)

M'DONALD, John, and Miss Kitty Miller, both of Balto. were married last eve. by Rev. Neal. (BEP, 25 May 1808)

M'DONALD, Mrs. Mary, wife of Hugh M'Donald, died last eve.; res. at George St., Fells Point. (BFG, 29 Aug. 1810)

McDONAUGH, Patrick, and Miss Catherine Timons both of Balto. were married 15th inst. by Rev. O'Brian. (BA, 26 March 1810)

McDONNELL, John, and Miss Margaret Pickering all of Balto. were married by Rev. Glendy. (BA, 28 Dec. 1816)

McDONOGH, Elizabeth, late wife of John McDonogh, died yesterday aged 62 years. (BFG, 17 June 1808)

McDONOGH, John, died last Sun., after a long illness, a patriotic veteran, aged 75. Under Washington he witnessed the terrible defeat of Braddock in 1755. Under the same immortal hero he fought for the liberty of these states. He enlisted under Capt. Cox, whom he saw die at Brandywine. (BFG, 21 March 1809)

McDONOGH, Joseph, and Mrs. Rabecca Hagemen both of Balto. were married Sun. eve. the 3rd by Rev. Richards. (BFG, 5 July 1808)

McDONOUGH, John, and Mrs. Elizabeth Barten all of Balto. were wed by Rev. Glendy last Tues. (BA, 31 May 1816)

M'DOWALL, Mr. Thomas and Miss Catherine Clisroe, both of Fells Point, were married last Sun. eve. by Rev. Kurtz. (BFG, 27 Feb. 1798)

M'DOWELL, Hugh, and Miss Eleanor Clark all of Balto. were wed 1st inst. by Rev. Richards. (BA, 3 Aug. 1807)

M'DOWELL, Miss Martha, dau. of James M'Dowell, died lately at the family res. in Chester Co., Penna. (BFG, 6 Nov. 1809)

M'DOWELL, Thomas, tallow chandler, died Sun. at his res. on Fells Point. (BFG, 20 Aug. 1799)

M'DOWLAND, Henry, of N. Y., and Mrs. Sarah Johnston of Balto. were married Mon. by Rev. Rattoone. (BT, 17 Nov. 1802)

M'ELDERRY, Mr. Hugh, and Miss Margaret Alricks all of Balto. were married by Rev. Glendy on Tues. ((BA, 17 Nov. 1814)

M'ELDERRY, John, of Balto. and Miss Ann West Evans of Lancaster were married at that place last Thurs. by Rev. Clarkson. (BS, 9 March 1812)

M'ELDERRY, Thomas, died yesterday; one of the senators in the state legislature. (BFG, 29 May 1810) (BS, 2 June 1810, states he was a member of the Levy Court of Balto. Co.)

M'ELDERRY, Thomas, died 5th inst. in his 25th year, son of the late Thomas M'Elderry. (BPEA, 10 May 1816)

M'ELROY, William Jedford, and Miss Elizabeth McMaster all of Balto. were married 26th inst. by Rev. Glendy. (BT, 28 Feb. 1815)

M'EVERS, David, of Frederick, merchant, and Mrs. Ursula Otto of Balto. were married last eve. by Rev. Sinclair. (BT, 18 Jan. 1802)

M'EVOY, James, and Mary Anne Hickley both of Balto. were married last Thurs. (BFG, 5 July 1800)

M'FADON, John, and Miss Priscilla Wilson both of Balto. were wed last eve. by Rev. Allison. (BFG, 21 Dec. 1798)

M'FADON, Mrs. Rebecca, died 2nd inst., aged 46 years. (BFG, 9 Feb. 1816)

McGARMAN, Robert, and Mrs. Mary McNamara, both of Balto., were married Mon. by Rev. Rattoone. (BFG, 10 May 1804)

M'GARRETTY, Thomas, and Miss Elizabeth Gray, both of Balto. were married last eve. by Rev. Allison. (BFG, 28 Feb. 1798)

M'GILL, Mrs. Ann, wife of Archibald M'Gill of Winchester, Va. (BFG, 13 Dec. 1815)

M'GOWAN, John, died this morning in his 25th year; res. at northeast corner of Pratt St. and Market Space. (BFG, 6 Dec. 1805)

M'GOWAN, John, died Fri., 15 Feb., aged 64; res. in King George St. near Granby. (BFG, 17 Feb. 1810)

McGOWAN, Mrs. Judith, died Sat. in her 60th year, leaving children. (BFG, 5 Nov. 1804)

M'GOWAN, Terence, Balto. merchant, and Miss Margaret Baltzell of Frederick were married Sun., 26 Oct., by Rev. Mallavay. (BA, 10 Nov. 1810)

McGREGON, Patrick, of Fells Point, died last Sun. aged 31 years. (BA, 8 April 1801)

M'GREW, Charles, and Nancy Floyd, dau. of Joseph Floyd, all of Balto. Co., were married last Tues. by Rev. Hagerty. (BA, 21 Dec. 1805)

M'GUIRE, John, and Miss Aeley M'Guire both of Balto. were married in Balto. last eve. by Rev. Cuddy. (BAP, 9 Aug. 1803)

M'GUIRE, Philip, and Mrs. Susanna Bannerman all of Balto. were married last Sun. by Rev. Glendy. (BW, 16 Feb. 1810)

M'GURR, John, and Miss Martha Dixon were married Sat. by Rev. Fenwick. (BPE, 6 Sept. 1813)

M'HARD, Miss Mary, of Balto. died last Mon. (BEP, 1 Oct. 1807)

McHENRY, Daniel, died a few days ago near Balto. aged about 27 years, son of James McHenry who was Secretary of War under Washington. His death was a result of a fall from his horse. He leaves a widow, an infant, and parents, and a brother and sister. (BFG, 9 July 1814)

McHENRY, Daniel W., and Miss Sophia Ramsay, eld. dau. of Col. Nathaniel Ramsay, were married last Thurs. by Rev. Inglis. (BFG, 25 June 1812)

McHENRY, Mrs. Frances, wife of F. D. McHenry, died yesterday; res. on Bernard St. (BFG, 27 Jan. 1814)

McHENRY, Francis D., merchant, and Miss Frances Moren both of Balto. were married Sat. by Rev. Rattoone. (BFG, 3 Dec. 1804)

McHENRY, James, died 3rd inst. in his 63rd year, at his res. near Balto. (BFG, 15 May 1816)

McHENRY, John, and Miss Martha Hall, all of this place, were wed last Sun. by Rev. Dr. Kemp. (BFG, 16 Nov. 1813)

M'ILVAIN, Andrew, died in Adams Co., Penna., on 1 March 1811 in his 74th year. He was born in Lancaster Co., Penna. in 1737. (BFG, 5 March 1811)

M'ILVAIN, Andrew, died 28th ult. in his 18th year. (BFG, 2 Oct. 1813)

M'ILVAIN, Robert, oldest son of Alexander M'Ilvain, merchant of Balto., died 20th inst. (BFG, 30 Nov. 1812)

M'ILVAINE, Alexander, died last Sun. in his 48th year. (BA, 9 Nov. 1814)

M'INTIRE, Alexander, and Miss Nancy Campbell all of Balto. were married last Mon. by Rev. Glendy. (BFG, 16 June 1813)

M'INTIRE, Patrick, drowned Wed., 1st inst., when a squall of wind overturned the schooner of Capt. John Morling between the Fort and Fells Point. (BFG, 3 May 1799)

MACKALL, Walter, native of Cal. Co., died Sat., 3rd inst. He had recently married. (BT, 20 March 1804)

M'KANNA, Anthony, died yesterday in his 55th year, a native of Co. Tyrone, Ireland, leaving a widow and six children. The funeral will be from No. 4 Cheapside. (BA, 9 March 1814)

MACKAY, Robert, and Mrs. Mary Gabriel were married 22nd ult. by Rev. Glendy. (BFG, 3 Nov. 1812)

M'KEAN, Joseph Kirkbride, son of Joseph B. M'Kean, died yesterday in his 24th year. (BFG, 29 Feb. 1816)

McKEE, Hugh, and Ann Campbell both of Balto. were married 23 May by Rev. Glendy. (BA, 28 May 1816)

M'KEIL, Thomas, aged 32 years, native of Balto., and late carpenter of the ship Hope, died 10 Oct. (BEP, 25 Oct. 1807)

MACKENHEIMER, Peter, died this morning aged 50 years; res. Bridge St., Old Town. (BFG, 22 Sept. 1801)

MACKENHEIMER, Mrs. Susanna, consort of Col. John Mackenheimer of Balto., died yesterday in her 46th year, leaving a husband and a large family of children and relatives. (BA, 4 July 1810)

McKENNA, Francis, died this afternoon, of the house of Paskin and McKenna. (BT, 3 July 1797)

M'KENZEY, John D., of New York and Miss Elizabeth Flanagan of Balto. were married last eve. by Rev. Toy. (BFG, 1 May 1801)

MacKENZIE, Mr., foemrly of the Balto. Theatre, was found in the Charles River, Boston, on 24th ult. He is supposed to have killed himself in a fit of insanity owing to pecuniary embarrassments. (BA, 4 May 1815)

McKENZIE, Alexander, and Miss Frances Hazell both of Balto. were married Thurs. eve. by Rev. Rattoone, at Fells Point. (BA, 6 April 1805)

MacKENZIE, Dr. Colin, of Balto., and Miss Sally Pinkerton of Chester Co., Penna., were married Thurs. eve. by Rev. Dr. Allison. (BFG, 25 May 1799)

MacKENZIE, Normand, and Miss Susanna Burrows all of Balto. were married last eve. by Rev. Hargrove. (BFG, 11 Sept. 1805)

MacKENZIE, William, wine cooper, native of Rossshire, Scot., aged 59 years, died last eve.; res. at No. 16, North Liberty St. (BFG, 11 Aug. 1810)

M 'KERLEY, Alexander, and Mrs. Sarah Nicholson all of Balto. were married last eve. by Rev. Mr. Hargrove. (BFG, 7 May 1813)

M'KESACK, Mrs., died last Sun. aged 90 years, a native of Ireland, for many years a res. of Phila. She died in Frederick. "Frederick Town - 18 Feb." (BFG, 1 March 1802)

M'KEY, John, and Miss Bethune both of Balto. were married last eve. by Rev. Dr. Dashields. (BFG, 24 Jan. 1806)

MACKEY, Michael, and Miss Elizabeth Eiselen, both of Balto. were married last Sun. by Rev. Beeston. (BA, 18 Aug. 1801)

MACKIE, Ebenezer, cashier of the Bank of Maryland, died, in his 56th year. Interment was on Sat. in the Presb. Burying Ground. (BFG, 11 July 1796)

M'KIM, Daniel, and Miss Eliza Harps all of Balto. were married last Sun. by Rev. D. E. Reese. (BA, 2 Oct. 1816)

McKIM, Isaac, and Miss Ann Hollins, dau. of William Hollins, were married last Thurs. by Rev. Bend. (BEP, 17 Dec. 1808)

M'KIM, John, and Miss Augusta Porter all of Balto. were married last Sun. (BPEA, 4 Jan. 1815)

M'KIM, William D., merchant, and Miss Susanna Haslett all of Balto. were married last Tues. by Rev. Glendy. (BFG, 19 Dec. 1806)

M 'KIVAN, Charles, and Mrs. Elizabeth Thompson late of Balto. Co. were married 8th inst. by Rev. Rattoone. (BFR, 21 Aug. 1809)

M'KNIGHT, James, and Miss Elizabeth McGarvin all of Balto. were married last Thurs. by Rev. Beeston. (BFG, 22 Aug. 1803)

M'KNOW, Nathaniel, and Mrs. Maria Thompson were married last Sat. by Rev. Kurtz. (BA, 25 Aug. 1801)

MacKUBIN, Frederick, was killed last Tues. on his farm on the north side of Severn, A. A. Co., when a tree fell on him leaving a widow, two children, and his parents. (BA, 3 Feb. 1816)

MACKY, Dr. Robert, a native of Penna., was struck by lightning on 8th ult., in Halifax Co., Va., leaving a wife and six children. (BFG, 16 July 1805)

M'LANE, John, and Maria Thornton, both of Balto., were married last Thurs. by Rev. Dashiell. (BFG, 13 April 1806)

M'LANE, Louis, and Miss Catherine M. Milligan, dau. of Robert Milligan, were married at Wilmington, Del., on Tues., 29th ult., by Bishop White. (BFG, 4 Jan. 1813)

M'LAUGHLIN, Andrew, of Balto. died at Cap Francois on 5th inst. (BFG, 21 Dec. 1805)

McLAUGHLIN, Charles, of Georgetown, died in Balto. last Sat. (BFG, 17 March 1806)

M 'LAUGHLIN, John, and Miss Catherine Morrow both of Balto. were married last eve. by Rev. Sinclair. (BT, 30 Dec. 1803)

M'LAUGHLIN, Mathew, and Mrs. Sidney Revely, all of Balto., were married by Rev. Glendy on 16th inst. (BA, 29 July 1809)

M'LAUGHLIN, W. F., printer, and Miss Sarah Fromberger, dau. of John Fromberger of Germantown, were married at Phila. on Wed. eve. by Rev. Potts. (BT, 24 July 1802)

M'LEAN, Archibald, printer, and Miss Jane Murphy both of Balto. were married last eve. by Rev. Mr. Fecta. (BMG, 16 Aug. 1815)

M'LEAN, Cornelius, of New York, and Miss Eliza Espey of Phila. were married in the latter city. (BT, 17 May 1799)

M'LEAN, Col. Samuel, a Rev. patriot, died in Phila. (BPE, 4 Sept. 1813)

M'MANUS, Mrs. Mary, died at Carlisle, Penna., aged 103. (BFG, 13 Oct. 1803)

McMECHEN, Alexander, and Miss Mary Bond all of Balto. were married last Thurs. by Rev. M'Kean. (BA, 18 June 1810)

McMECHEN, David, and Miss Margaret Carroll were married last Sat. at the res. of Daniel Carroll near Baltimore. (BFG, 25 Oct. 1803)

McMECHEN, David, died yesterday at his res. in Balto. Co. aged 56 years. (BFG, 16 July 1810)

McMECHEN, William, and Eleanor B. Armistead of Balto. were wed last eve. by Rev. Ireland. (BFG, 21 Feb. 1800)

M'NEAL, James, and Miss Sarah Quin, both of Balto., were married last eve. by Rev. Robert Annon. (BW, 25 June 1811)

M'NEAL, James, and Miss Eliza Quay both of Balto. were married last Thurs. by Rev. Glendy. (BA, 6 July 1816)

McNEAL, Capt. John, and Miss Sarah Childs were married last eve. by Rev. Richards. (BT, 12 Feb. 1802)

M'NEAL, John, and Miss Eliza Wilson were married Tues. at Falls Hill, the res. of Dr. Moor Falls by Rev. Inglis. (BFG, 3 July 1806)

M'PHERSON, Jonas, Balto. merchant, and Miss Margaret James of Sharpsburg, Wash. Co., were married at Hagerstown on 21st inst. by Rev. Bower. (BT, 29 Aug. 1806)

MACHEN, Mrs. Cynthia, wife of Lewis H. Machen, late of Washington, died at her husband's res. in P. G. Co. on her 24th year. (BPEA, 29 June 1815)

MacPHERSON, Gen. William, distinguished officer in the American army, died in Phila. 5th inst. in his 58th year. (BPE, 23 Nov. 1813)

McTAVISH, John, Esq., of Lower Montreal, Canada, and Emily, youngest dau. of Richard Caton, Esq., were married at Doughregan Manor on Thurs., 15th inst. (BA, 19 Aug. 1816)

MACTIER, Mrs. Dorcas, wife of Henry Mactier of Balto., and dau. of Roger Johnson, Esq., of Md., died Mon., aged 22 years in New York. (BPEA, 8 Dec. 1815)

MACTIER, Henry, and Miss Dorcas Johnson, dau. of Major Roger Johnson of Bloomsbury, Fred. Co., were married last Tues. by Rev. Gibson. (BFG, 3 June 1815)

MADCAP, John, and Miss Mary M'Cumsey were married Thurs., 13th inst. by Rev. B. Nelson. (BEP, 18 Dec. 1810)

MADDEGON, Paul, and Mrs. Campbell, all of Balto., were married on Sun. by Rev. Bishop Carroll. (BT, 5 Feb. 1805)

MADDOCK, John George, died 15th inst. in his 32nd year, a native of St. Kitts. (BPE, 17 Jan. 1814)

MADISON, Capt. Andrew Lewis, native of Va., member of the 4th Regt., U. S. Infantry, died lately at Fort Johnson, S. C. (BA, 5 June 1816)

MAELLER, Adolphus, merchant, and Miss Eliza M'Glathery of Balto. were married at New Bremen on 5th inst. (BT, 14 April 1798)

MARRIAGES AND DEATHS

MAGAFFIN, Joseph, Phila. merchant, died last Wed. in his 71st year. (BEP, 17 March 1806)

MAGAUREN, James C., and Miss Margaret Fox both of Balto. were wed last eve. by Bishop Carroll. (BFG, 29 Nov. 1811)

MAGAW, Rev. Dr., died on Wed. "Phila. - 3 Dec." (BFG, 4 Dec. 1812)

MAGILL, Mr., and Miss Macrahon, were married lately in Harf. Co. by Rev. Wilmer. (BFG, 4 Jan. 1803)

MAGILL, Samuel, of Cumberland, Md., and Miss Christiana Mischa Myer of Washington were married 10th inst. by Rev. McCormick. (BFG, 15 Nov. 1816)

MAGILL, William, died this morning, aged 36; res. in Albemarle St. (BFG, 4 Sept. 1813)

MAGRAIN, Thomas, and Miss Mary Conroy both of Balto. were married last Sun. by Rev. Beeston. (BT, 27 Jan. 1804)

MAGRUDER, Alexander C., of Annap., and Miss Rebecca Thomas, dau. of Dr. P. Thomas, were married at Frederick last Tues. by Rev. Bower. (BFG, 25 Nov. 1805)

MAGRUDER, Miss Ann H., consort of J. R. Magruder, of Brooke Grove, P. G. Co., died Thurs., 31st ult., aged 26 years. (BEP, 9 June 1808)

MAGRUDER, Miss Christina, of Balto. died yesterday in her 81st year. (BFG, 15 March 1813)

MAGRUDER, Dennis F., and Miss Rebecca Claggett, dau. of Hezekiah Claggett all of Balto., were married last Thurs. by Dr. Kemp. (BFG, 9 May 1814)

MAGRUDER, Mrs. Rebecca B., wife of Alexander C. Magruder, died 27 Oct. in her 37th year. (BFG, 3 Nov. 1814)

MAGRUDER, Mrs. Rebecca B., wife of Dennis P. Magruder, and dau. of Hezekiah Claggett, died last Sat. in her 23rd year. (BFG, 12 June 1815)

MAGRUDER, Richard B., and Miss Maria Stricker, dau. of Gen. John Stricker, were married Thurs. eve. by Rev. Inglis. (BFG, 28 April 1809)

MAGRUDER, Thomas, and Mary Clark, all of P. G. Co., were married last week by Rev. Ralph. (BFG, 14 Jan. 1800)

MAGUIRE, Mrs., wife of John Maguire of Balto., died last Sat. (BA, 15 Nov. 1809)

MAGUIRE, John, and Miss Kitty Condle all of Balto. were married on Sun. eve. by Archbishop Carroll. (BA, 21 Nov. 1810)

MAGUIRE, Joseph, printer, formerly of Balto., died 27 Nov. in Washington. (BFG, 1 Dec. 1815)

MAHA, Samuel, and Miss Sarah Stall all of Balto. were married last eve. by Rev. Hargrove. (BFG, 18 June 1804)

MAINSTER, Jacob, and Miss Sally Wilkinson all of Balto. were married last Thurs. by Rev. Hargrove. (BEP, 9 Jan. 1808)

MAINSTER, Mrs. Lucy, consort of Jacob Mainster of Balto., died last Wed. in her 46th year. (BA, 9 Sept. 1807)

MALCOLM, John, died in Bristol, Penna., aged 90, late an officer in the British Navy. (BFG, 20 Dec. 1803)

MALLORY, Mrs. Mary, wife of Capt. John Mallory, died Sun. (BFR, 10 Sept. 1811)

MALOY, ---, a young man, fell from the attic window of a house in Water St. yesterday and instantly expired. He was a member of Capt. Grafflin's Co., 27th Regt. of Militia and was buried last eve. with military honors. (BFG, 28 July 1800)

MALTBY, George, died last eve.; Balto. merchant. (BFG, 16 Sept. 1807)

MAN, Mr., and Miss Campbell both of Balto. were married last eve. by Rev. Kurtz. (BMJ, 24 April 1797)

MAN, George, died 9 July; had enlisted as a common soldier in the U. S. Army. (BA, 23 July 1813)

MANDEVEL, Tobias, and Miss Teresa Trippolet both of Balto. were married last eve. by Rev. Rattoone. (BFG, 12 Sept. 1805) (BEP, 13 Sept. 1805, gives the groom's name as Manaciel.)

MANKIN, Mrs. Ann, wife of Isaiah Mankin of Balto., died Sat., 9th inst., in her 32nd year. (BFG, 15 Oct. 1813)

MANKIN, Isaiah, and Mrs. Martha Gautier, dau. of Abraham Bininger, all of Balto., were married in New York by Rev. Benjamin Mortimer. (BPE, 17 Oct. 1814)

MANN, Mr. Frederick, and Miss Campbell, both of Balto., were wed last eve. by Rev. Mr. Kurtz. (BFG, 24 April 1797)

MANNING, William, of Norfolk, Va., and Miss Betsy Ritter of Elkton, Md., were married Wed., 4th inst., by Rev. Glendy. (BA, 6 July 1810)

MANON, Dennis, and Mrs. Bridget Kabol, all of Balto. Co., were married last Sun. by Rev. Kurtz. (BPE, 23 Nov. 1813)

MANRO, James C., died last Sun. in his 19th year; eldest son of Jonathan Manro. (BA, 6 Sept. 1815)

MANSFIELD, John, of London, and Mary B., dau. of Gen. Smith, were married last Sun. by Rev. Bend. (BEP, 30 Nov. 1809)

MANSFIELD, John, and Miss Jane McCausland, all of Balto. were wed last eve. by Rev. G. Hicks. (BPE, 29 Oct. 1813)

MANTZ, Miss Caroline, dau. of M. Francis Mantz of Frederick, died there 23rd ult. in her 18th year. (BFG, 7 March 1815)

MANTZ, Mrs. Christiana, died at Frederick Town aged 76. (BA, 28 Nov. 1804)

MAREAN, Mrs., widow of Jonas Marean late of Balto., died at York, Penna., on 28th ult. (BFG, 1 Sept. 1809)

MAREAN, Jonas, Balto. merchant, died Sat., 21st inst., leaving a wife and children. Interment in the Presb. burying ground. (BFG, 25 April 1804)

MARKELL, Jacob, and Miss Sophia Schley all of Frederick were wed 28th ult. by Rev. Helfenstein. (BPEA, 12 April 1815)

MARKELL, Samuel, and Miss Amelia Schley, all of Frederick Co., were married 6th inst. by Rev. J. Helfenstein. (BPEA, 12 April 1815)

MARKWOOD, Mr. John, and Miss Mary Ford, both of Marple Twp., Delaware Co., were married last Thurs. 5th inst. by Rev. Mr. Collin. (BA, 16 Nov. 1801)

MARLOW, Capt. Winslow, from Conn. and Mrs. Rebecca Osborn of Fells Point were married last Mon. by Rev. Dr. Rattoone. (BA, 28 Dec. 1805)

MARPOOL, David, and Miss Martha Dillon, dau. of Moses Dillon, all of Zaneville, Ohio, were married 10th inst. at Zaneville (sic) by Rev. Jones. (BFG, 23 Oct. 1810)

MARR, Charles, merchant, formerly of Balto. died on his passage from New Orleans on last 19 June. (BFG, 20 July 1810)

MARRD(?), Thomas, and Miss Eleanor Kirkpatrick all of Balto. were married last Thurs. by Rev. Glendy. (BFG, 17 Aug. 1813)

MARRIOTT, John H., and Miss Hetty Pumphrey all of Balto. were wed Thurs., 21st inst. by Rev. Roberts. (BFG, 2 Oct. 1815)

MARSH, Lloyd, of Balto. and Miss Mary Chenoweth, dau. of Richard Chenoweth of Balto. Co. were married Thurs. by Rev. Armstrong. (BFG, 24 Dec. 1808)

MARSH, Mrs. Mary, wife of Lloyd Marsh of Balto., died Thurs. at her father's in Balto. Co. in her 23rd year. (BA, 12 Dec. 1810)

MARSHALL, John, of Md., commander of Gun Boat No. 2, died recently at New Orleans. (BEP, 30 Nov. 1809)

MARTIN, Alexander, printer, a native of Boston and former editor of the Baltimore American, died in New York aged 33. (BFG, 13 Oct. 1810)

MARTIN, Major Daniel, Tal. Co., and Miss Mary C. Maccubbin of Balto. Co. were married Tues., 6th inst., by Rev. Ryland. (BWA, 17 Feb. 1816)

MARTIN, Eliza, died Thurs., dau. of Mrs. Mary Martin of Wor. Co., sister of Capt. George Martin of Balto. Interment in the Presbyterian burying ground. (BFG, 24 Aug. 1799)

MARTIN, Capt. George, died 10th inst. at his res. on Fells Point in his 39th year. (BFG, 14 April 1806)

MARTIN, George H., son of Col. Thomas Martin of Cedar Grove Springs, died 19th ult. at St. Iago de Cuba, in his 16th year. (BA, 17 Nov. 1810)

MARTIN, James, and Miss Jane Eugenia Vallette of Balto. were wed last eve. by Rev. Fenwick. (BA, 22 Dec. 1815)

MARTIN, Capt. James Blair, of the brig Venus of Balto., died at New Orleans last 13 Sept. (BFG, 19 Oct. 1810)

MARTIN, John, and Miss Maria M'Conkey both of Balto. were wed last eve. (BFG, 21 March 1812)

MARTIN, John J., died yesterday after a lingering disease, a native of France, and for the last 12 years a res. of Balto. (BA, 22 Jan. 1806)

MARTIN, John S., of Snow Hill, Md., and Miss Rebecca Duffield, dau. of the late Dr. Benjamin Duffield of Phila., were married there. (BFG, 21 March 1805)

MARTIN, Mrs. Maria, wife of Luther Martin, died last eve. (BFG, 3 Nov. 1796)

MARTIN, Peter, and Catherine Allender both of Balto. were married. (BEP, 29 March 1808)

MARTIN, Mrs. Sally, died yesterday, aged 20, wife of Alexander Martin, editor of The American; niece of the Hon. Benjamin Hitchborn of Boston. (BFG, 25 Aug. 1800)

MARTIN, Samuel, son of Capt. John Martin, late of Balto., died yesterday morning aged 27. (BFG, 30 March 1809)

MARTIN, Samuel B., and Miss Ann Fisher all of Balto. were wed on last Thurs. by Rev. Glendy. (BFG, 19 Nov. 1813)

MARTIN, Thomas, of Cedar Grove, Balto. Co., died last Tues., leaving a wife, four daus and a son.; funeral from the res. of William Norris, Jr. (BFG, 8 Feb. 1815)

MARTIN, Mrs. William, of Balto. died last Sun. (BFG, 20 Jan. 1807)

MARTIN, William, merchant, and Miss Ann Carrick, both of Balto., were married last Thurs. eve. by Rev. Dr. Roberts. (BFR, 18 April 1812)

MARYE, Vincent A., aged 72, and Miss Nina Chateaudun, aged 16, both of Balto. were married last Fri. by Archbishop Carroll. (BA, 14 Nov. 1809)

MASLIN, Michael M., of Balto., and Miss Eliza Sarah Mohler of Hanover were married at York, Penna., on 13th inst. by Rev. Armstrong. (BFG, 15 Sept. 1810)

MASON, Abraham Barnes Thompson, died 12th inst. in Loudon Co., Va., in his 52nd year. (BPE, 21 Jan. 1813)

MASON, David, and Miss Ann Fitzgibbon both of Balto. were married last Sun. by Rev. Richards. (BA, 14 May 1805)

MASON, George, of Fairfax Co., Va., and Miss Eliza Mason of the same county were lately married by Rev. Mr. McCormick. (BPE, 20 Feb. 1813)

MASON, John, and Miss Sophia Slaughter were married last eve. by Rev. Dr. Bend. (BFG, 23 Oct. 1807)

MASON, Gen. Stephens Thomson, U. S. Senator from Va. died at Phila. on Mon. night. (BT, 12 May 1803)

MASON, Stephen Thompson, youngest son of the late Gen. Stephen T. Mason, died 17 Nov. at Raspberry Plain, Loudon Co., Va. (BA, 2 Dec. 1815)

MASSEY, Mr., and Miss Burkhead, were lately married in Harf. Co. by Rev. Wilmer. (BFG, 4 Jan. 1803)

MASSEY, Joshua, of Q. A. Co., and Miss Pamela Massey, dau. of
Benjamin Massey of Kent Co., were married 3rd inst. in
Kent Co. (BPE, 17 Aug. 1813)

MASSEY, Mrs. Mary, wife of Joshua Massey, died near Sadler's
Cross Roads, Q. A. Co., in her 21st year. (BPE, 15 Feb.
1813)

MASSY, Caleb G., attorney at law from the State of Del., died
yesterday, as a result of the indiscriminate use of opium.
(BFG, 7 April 1804)

MASTIN, Michael M., of Balto. and Miss Eliza Sarah Mohler of Balto. were married at York, Penna. on 13th inst. by Rev. Dr.
Armstrong. (BA, 15 Sept. 1810)

MATCHET, George, carpenter, and Mrs. Streimel were married Sun.
se'ennight by Rev. Otterbein. (BEP, 1 Feb. 1808)

MATCHETT, Richard J., and Miss Ann Woods all of Balto. were wed
last eve. by Rev. Dr. Roberts. (BFG, 14 Sept. 1812)

MATHER, Ralph, died 24th ult. at Portsmouth, Va., formerly a
Methodist preacher, but for several years past a minister
of the New Jerusalem Church, both in Liverpool, Eng., as
well as in Balto. He leaves a widow and an only child.
(BFG, 27 Oct. 1803)

MATHERS, James, Segt.-at-Arms and Door Keeper to the U. S. Senate,
died last Mon. aged 67. A native of Ireland he came to
this country before the Rev., in which he took an early
and active part. (Long obit.) (BA, 9 Sept. 1811)

MATHERS, William, and Anna Farris both of Balto. were married
last Thurs. eve. by Rev. Richards. (BFG, 7 June 1799)

MATHIAS, Mr. F., from Germany, and Miss Elizabeth Miller from
Frederick Town were married last eve. by Rev. Baker.
(BEP, 23 May 1810)

MATHIETT, George, and Mrs. Elizabeth Strimall all of Balto. were
married last Sat. by Rev. Otterbein. (BFG, 27 Jan. 1808)

MATHIOT, Christian, died Sun. in his 69th year, having served in
the Penna. Line during our Rev. struggle. (BA, 20 Feb.
1816)

MATLACK, Mason, and Miss Mary Baily both of Balto. Co. were wed
Tues., 5th Nov., by Rev. Parson Davis. (BFG, 12 Nov. 1816)

MATTHEWS, Mr., of Pitt St., died on the 5th. Mrs. Matthews died
on the 4th, and her sister had died on the 3rd. (BFG, 9
Aug. 1802)

MATTHEWS, George, died this morning in his 82nd year; res. near
Friends Meeting House East of Jones Falls. (BFG, 7 Feb.
1811)

MATTHEWS, Thomas, and Miss Harriet Bussey all of Balto. were wed
Thurs. by Rev. Roberts. (BEP, 15 May 1811)

MATTISON, Mrs. Helen, died last eve. aged 60 years, wife of Aaron
Mattison. (BFG, 5 Nov. 1803)

MATTISON, William, hatter, originally from N. J., shot and killed
himself last eve. (BFG, 28 March 1812)

MAULSBY, Israel, and Miss Jane Hall, dau. of the late John Hall, were married in Harf. Co. last Sun. by Rev. John Coleman. (BA, 21 Feb. 1806)

MAXCY, Virgil, of Balto. and Miss Mary Galloway of West River were married at Phila. on 22nd inst. by Bishop White. (BFG, 27 Feb. 1811)

MAXWELL, Hugh, bookbinder, died Wed. (BFG, 18 March 1803)

MAXWELL, Moses, and Mrs. Nancy McGraw all of Balto. were married by Rev. Glendy last Sat. (BA, 14 March 1811)

MAXWELL, Nathaniel G., of Washington, and Miss Ann Proud, dau. of John Proud of New Bedford, were married at the latter place on 24th ult. (BFG, 5 Oct. 1811)

MAXWELL, Robert, and Miss E. Rogers both of Balto. Co. were wed yesterday by Rev. Coleman. (BT, 20 April 1803)

MAXWELL, Robert, of Balto. died 28th inst. in his 49th year. (BFG, 29 Dec. 1812)

MAXWELL, Thomas, and Miss Elizabeth Boone all of Balto. were wed last Thurs. by Rev. Glendy. (BA, 4 Dec. 1809)

MAY, Mrs. Catherine, consort of Dr. Adam May, died 18th inst. (BA, 26 Aug. 1801)

MAY, Jonas, and Mary Hall both of Balto. were married last eve. by Rev. Dr. Roberts. (BA, 18 Nov. 1806)

MAY, Thomas, and Miss Ann Auiler both of Penna. were married yesterday by Rev. Baker. (BFG, 12 July 1813)

MAYBURY, Thomas, and Miss Elizabeth Sands both of Balto. were married last Wed. by Rev. Grice. (BA, 20 March 1816)

MAYER, Capt., an old officer of the Rev., and long an inhab. of Balto., died yesterday. (BFG, 5 March 1807)

MAYER, Christopher, died 11th ult. in his 59th year. (Long obit.) "Lancaster Journal." (BFG, 23 Aug. 1815)

MAYER, Mr. George C., and Miss Elizabeth Wagner both of Balto. were married last Thurs. night by Rev. Kurtz. (BFG, 21 April 1804)

MAYES, Robert, and Miss Eve Wagner were married 28th ult. by Rev. Glendy. (BT, 14 Jan. 1804)

MAYLAND, Samuel, and Miss Ann Dewlin all of Balto. were married last Wed. by Rev. Moore. (BEP, 6 May 1808)

MAYNARD, Mrs. Asenath, wife of Foster Maynard of Balto., died yesterday afternoon; funeral from corner of Eutaw St. and Brandy Alley. (BFG, 9 March 1815)

MAYNARD, Foster, of Balto. and Miss Rachel Forister of A. A. Co. were married 27 July in A. A. Co. by Rev. Dashiell. (BA, 4 Aug. 1815)

MAZZEI, Philip, died at Pisa, Tuscany, 19 March in his 86th year, formerly a citizen of the U. S., and author of a political and historical work on North America. (BA, 21 June 1816)

MEACHER, Timothy D., and Miss Nyomea Boyce all of Balto. were married Thurs., 22nd inst., by Rev. Morainville. (BA, 24 April 1813)

MEADS, Daniel, and Martha Magee both of Balto. were married last eve. by Rev. Dr. Glendy. (BA, 30 Nov. 1805)

MEASON, Gen. Thomas, of Union Town, Penna., died at George Town, D. C., on 10th inst., from a violent cold. (BFG, 17 March 1813)

MEDTART, Joshua, and Miss Mary Ann Schultz all of Balto. were married Thurs. eve. by Rev. Dr. Kurtz. (BFG, 23 March 1816)

MEDYGER, Daniel, of Balto. and Miss Milly Harryman of Balto. Co. were married Thurs. eve. by Rev. Budd. (BA, 5 Jan. 1808)

MEEKS, Aquila, Jr., merchant, died last Wed. when the schooner Betsy, Capt. Thomas Cumming, sank on her passage to Still Pond, Kent Co. James Cann, farmer, and co-owner with Meeks, John Taylor, former owner, and Charles Lias, mulatto, were found lashed to the quarter rail and frozen. Thomas Cumming, Robert Worrell of Balto., and a black boy are still missing. (BFG, 28 Feb. 1812)

MEEKS, James, died; funeral will be today. (BA, 30 Jan. 1816)

MELCHER, Frederick, and Mrs. Margaret Courtenay both of Fells Point were married last eve. by the Rev. Dr. Rattoone. (BFG, 21 March 1804)

MELMOTH, Mrs., celebrated actress of the theatre in this city, died at New Brunswick, N.J., from an injury received when the stage overturned. (BW, 27 May 1812)

MENDENHALL, James, member of the Society of Friends, and a minister of the Gospel for 40 years, died 26th inst. at his farm near Martinsburg, Va. (BA, 31 Aug. 1816)

MENDENHALL, Thomas, Sr., cashier of the U. S. Branch Bank of Savannah, Ga., died Sun., 2ns inst. at that city. BFG, 21 Oct. 1808)

MENEUR, William, and Polly Fry, both of Fells Point, were married Fri. by Rev. Richards. (BA, 21 April 1800)

MENIER, Francis, native of Cap,Francois, died 11th inst., aged 37 years. For several years he had been a res. of New York. (BFG, 16 May 1808)

MERCER, Mr. Bartholomew, and Miss Temperance Darrington were wed last Sun. eve. (BFG, 15 Nov. 1803)

MERCER, Benjamin James, master of the Balto. Lodge, died in his 42nd year; interment in the Meth. burying ground. (BFG, 9 Dec. 1799)

MERCER, James, and Elizabeth Money both of Cecil Co. were married Thurs., 29th ult., by Rev. Dr. Jones. (BEP, 11 Oct. 1808)

MERCER, John, and Mrs. Elizabeth Pearpoint both of this county, were married last eve. by Rev. Mr. Bend. (BT, 12 June 1799)

MERCER, Mrs. Sophia, wife of John Francis Mercer, died Fri., 25th
ult., at West River Farm, where her family had lived for
generations. (BFG, 3 Oct. 1812)

MERCER, Thomas, and Miss Matilda Griffith both of Balto. were
married Tues. by Rev. Dashiell. (BEP, 23 April 1807)

MEREDITH, Benjamin, and Miss Sally Martin both of Balto. were
married last eve. by Rev. Wells. (BT, 31 Dec. 1802)

MEREDITH, Jonathan, died 20 Aug. in his 71st year, at Jenkintown,
near Phila. His remains were interred the next day at
Christ Church burial ground. (BFG, 26 Aug. 1811)

MEREDITH, Mrs. Mary, died 1st inst. at Plumstead, Penna., aged
100 years, relict of the late William Meredith. (BW, 15
Nov. 1808)

MEREDITH, Thomas, merchant, and Miss Maria Spalding all of Balto.
were married last Mon. by Bishop Carroll. (BFG, 8 March
1810)

MEREDITH, Capt. William, died 24th ult. at the Havana in his 33rd
year. An inhab. of Balto., he leaves a wife and two small
children. (BFG, 16 Sept. 1808)

MERIDETH, William, Esq., died at his res. in Lancaster Co., Va.,
in his 58th year; a husband and father. (BFG, 7 April
1808)

MERRIAM, Joseph, and Miss Harriot G. C. Locke, dau. of Nathaniel
Locke all of Balto. were married Thurs., 23rd inst. by
Rev. Hagerty. (BFG, 28 Feb. 1809)

MERRIDETH, Jonathan, and Hannah Haslett were married last eve. by
Rev. Inglis. (BFG, 31 Oct. 1806)

MERRIKEN, James, and Miss Catherine Foreman both of Balto. were
married last Thurs. by Rev. Bend. (BFG, 18 June 1808)

MERRIKEN, John, and Miss Elizabeth Sleppy all of Balto., were
married last eve. by Rev. Bend. (BFG, 3 Oct. 1806)

MERRIKEN, William, and Miss Elizabeth Chancy (Chaney?) both of
A. A. Co., were married last Thurs. by Rev. Rattoone.
(BFG, 3 Dec. 1803)

MERRIWETHER, Thomas B. D., of A. A. Co., and Miss Maria Handy,
dau. of the late Col. Levin Handy were married. (BEP, 20
Feb. 1810)

MERRY, Robert, formerly of Eng., died Mon. in a fit of apoplexy.
(BFG, 26 Dec. 1798)

MERRYMAN, Miss Ann, dau. of Nicholas Merryman of Balto. Co., died
last Sun. (BFG, 15 Dec. 1796)

MERRYMAN, Benjamin, Jr., Balto. merchant, died last Mon. (BFG, 1
June 1796)

MERRYMAN, Benjamin, died last Mon. at his res. in Balto. Co., aged
75. (BPE, 7 June 1814)

MERRYMAN, Elijah, died Wed., 3rd inst., aged 46; a rep. of this
county in the legislature. (BFG, 5 July 1799)

MERRYMAN, Mr. Elijah, and Miss Cassandra Harvey both of Balto. Co. were married last eve. by Rev. Richards. (BFG, 21 Sept. 1804)

MERRYMAN, John, of Balto. Co., died 13th ult. at the Havana. (BT, 16 Aug. 1800)

MERRYMAN, John, died Mon., aged 77; res. on Calvert St. Interment in St. Pauls burying ground. (BFG, 15 Feb. 1814)

MERRYMAN, Mrs. Mary, wife of Dr. Merryman, died yesterday at Mrs. Cockey's in Balto. Co., in her 29th year; interment at Sater's meeting house. (BFG, 25 Feb. 1809)

MERRYMAN, Mrs. Mary, wife of Caleb Merryman, died 23rd inst. in Balto. Co. in her 44th year, leaving a husband and children. (BFG, 27 April 1809)

MERRYMAN, Nicholas, Sr., died last Tues. at his res. in Balto. Co. in his 76th year. (BA, 20 July 1801)

MERRYMAN, Nicholas, Jr., and Dorcas Buck, dau. of John Buck all of Balto. Co. were married 20 Jan. by Rev. Stevens. (BA, 25 Jan. 1814)

MERRYMAN, Nicholas, of E., and Miss Charlotte Worthington, dau. of Samuel Worthington of Balto. Co., were married Thurs. by Rev. Coleman. (BT, 11 Dec. 1802)

MERRYMAN, Nicholas, and Miss Ann Merryman, both of Balto. Co., were married Sat., 16th inst. (BFG, 25 Nov. 1805)

MERRYMAN, Samuel, died last Mon., at his late res. in Balto. Co. in his 88th year. A prominent Methodist for over 30 years, he was a great-grandfather. (BFG, 28 Sept. 1809)

MERRYMAN, Samuel, and Miss Elizabeth Schannaman, were married last Sun. at Hampstead, Balto. Co., by Rev. Green. (BPE, 25 Nov. 1813)

MERRYMAN, Sarah, died 21st Aug. at Hereford Farm in Balto. Co. in her 74th year, wife of the late John Merryman. (BFG, 23 Aug. 1816)

MERRYMAN, Thomas, and Miss Priscilla Briton, dau. of Richard Briton, all of Balto. Co., were married 17th inst. at Blathania by Rev. Grimes. (BFG, 26 Sept. 1812)

MERRYMAN, William, merchant, and Miss Ann Presbury, dau. of George G. Presbury, all of Balto. were married Thurs. eve. by Rev. Ireland. (BFG, 8 Feb. 1800)

MESSECK, Capt. Joshua, and Miss Charlotte Hall, dau. of George Hall, were married last eve. by Rev. M'Kane. (BFG, 7 Oct. 1807)

MESSERSMITH, Elizabeth, consort of Samuel Messersmith, died last eve. in her 68th year. Interment in the Lutheran burying ground. (BFG, 16 Oct. 1802)

MESSERSMITH, Samuel, an old inhab. of Balto., died yesterday in his 71st year. Interment will be in the Lutheran burying ground. Funeral will be from his res. in Gay St. (BFG, 26 Sept. 1803)

MESSONIER, Francis, died last night in his 30th year, Librarian
to the Baltimore Library Co. Funeral from the res. of his
uncle, Mr. H. Messonier, S. Charles St. (BFG, 14 Jan.
1813)

METYR, Joseph, and Miss Mary Conner, both of Balto., were wed
last Thurs. by Rev. Roberts. (BFG, 12 March 1810)

METZGER, William, and Miss Rebecca Kraber all of Balto. were wed
Tues., 15th inst., by Rev. Dr. Roberts. (BA, 18 Nov. 1814)

MEWBURN, James, late of the House of Mewburn and Wilkinson, died
last Sun. (BFG, 8 Jan. 1806)

MEWSHAW, David, aged 81 and a widower for 3 mos., and Elizabeth
Mitchell, aged 71, and the mother of 10 children, all of
of A. A. Co., were married last Sat. by Rev. Hagerty.
(BEP, 1 Sept. 1808)

MEYER, Charles J., of Balto. and Miss Ann Davidson of Cambridge
were married. (BFG, 12 Sept. 1805) (BA, 9 Sept. 1805,
gives the bride's name as Davis.)

MEYER, John C., and Catherine Ann Shugart were married last eve.
by Rev. Bend. (BFG, 3 Nov. 1801)

MEYERS, Jacob, of Phila., formerly American Consul at Cap Francois, died yesterday. (Phila. paper.) (BT, 24 May 1802)

MEYERS, Mrs. Margaret, died 20 June in her 64th year at Hampstead
Hill. (BFG, 22 June 1804)

MEZICK, Capt. Baptist, and Miss Mary Johnson, were married Thurs.,
14th inst., by Rev. McCombs. (BFG, 23 Oct. 1802)

MICKLE, John, died last Sun., 9 May; an old inhab. of Balto.
(BFG, 11 May 1813)

MICKLE, Mrs. Sarah, died Sun. in her 78th year. (BFG, 15 Feb.
1815)

MIDDLETON, Capt. Moses, and Mrs. Mary Kennedy, both of Fells Pt.,
were married last Tues. by Rev. Rattoone. (BEP, 15 Nov.
1805)

MIDDLETON, Richard, and Miss Sarah A. Reynolds, all of Balto.,
were married last Tues. by Rev. Dashiells. (BFG, 31 Oct.
1812)

MIDDLETON, William, died at Pools Island, 12th inst. in his 59th
year. (BFG, 17 April 1805)

MIERS, Major Stephen, member of the House of Delegates from Q. A.
Co., died yesterday. (BW, 26 Dec. 1811)

MIFFLIN, Thomas, late Governor of Penna., died 20 Jan. at Lancaster, Penna., in his 57th year. (BA, 24 Jan. 1800)

MIFFLIN, Warner, died 16th inst. at his res. in Delaware, from
the prevailing fever, which he supposedly caught at the
annual meeting of Friends in Phila. (BFG, 24 Oct. 1798)

MILDEWS, Aquila, of Fells Point, mourns the death of his 6 year
old dau., whose clothes caught fire. (BFG, 18 April 1800)

MARRIAGES AND DEATHS

MILES, Capt. Aquila, Balto. merchant, died last Thurs. in his 31st year. (BFG, 20 Feb. 1808)

MILES, Mrs. Elizabeth, died last Wed. in her 23rd year, wife of Aquila Miles. Interment at the Manor Chapel on Sat. (BA, 14 Jan. 1805)

MILES, John, and Miss Mary Dewees, both of Balto., were married Thurs. eve. by Rev. Richards. (BT, 28 Dec. 1799)

MILES, John, Sr., gunmaker of Phila., died there last Tues. (BEP, 27 May 1808)

MILES, Nathaniel, and Miss Elizabeth Cromwell, all of Balto. Co., were married last Sat., by Rev. Reese. (BA, 20 March 1816)

MILES, William, and Miss Mary Eliza Dailey, all of Balto., were married last Thurs. by Rev. Fenwick. (BA, 19 April 1816)

MILHAU, Michael C., died 19th inst., aged 53 years, a native of Hispaniola, who took refuge in the country at the start of the revolutionary disturbances on that island. He leaves a widow and 9 children.

MILHOLLAND, Robert D., and Miss Ann Day all of Balto. were wed last eve. by Rev. M'Keen. (BEP, 4 May 1810)

MILLAR, Edward, and Miss Mary Grimes both of Balto. Co. were wed last Sat. by Rev. Glendy. (BA, 10 June 1812)

MILLAR, James, of the house of Millar and Barklie of Balto., died on his passage from St. Thomas to Balto., on 2nd inst. (BFG, 20 Aug. 1799)

MILLAR, Walter M., and Miss Ann Maria Denny both of Balto. were married last Thurs. by Rev. Bartow. (BA, 6 Aug. 1816)

MILLEMON, George, of Balto., and Miss Mary Swampstead of A. A. Co., were married in the latter place last Thurs. by Rev. Robert Gillespie. (BEP, 6 March 1811)

MILLEMON, Mrs. Sarah, wife of George Millemon of Balto., died Sun., 18th inst., aged 26 years. (BEP, 23 March 1810)

MILLENGER, Mr., was found yesterday (23 Aug.) on the land of Mr. Harry D. Gough, about 12 miles from Balto., on the Belair Road. (BFG, 24 Aug. and 28 Aug. 1799)

MILLER, Adolphus, and Miss Eliza M'Glathery of Balto. were married at New Bremen on 5th inst. (BFG, 13 April 1798)

MILLER, Andrew, of Zanesville, Ohio, and Miss Charlotte Johnston of Fells Point, were married last Thurs. by Rev. Rattoone. (BA, 30 Sept. 1809)

MILLER, Dr. Edward, died in Balto. on Thurs. (BS, 21 March 1812)

MILLER, George, and Miss Martha Marshall, were married last eve. at Fells Point by Rev. Dr. Rattoone. (BFG, 7 Jan. 1804)

MILLER, George W., of Balto., and Miss Harriot Jacob of A. A. Co., were married last Thurs. by Rev. Rattoone. (BFG, 25 Feb. 1809)

MILLER, Jacob, of Balto., and Mrs. Elizabeth Swan, widow of Jacob Swan of Harf. Co. were married last eve. (BA, 13 May 1806)

MILLER, Jacob, Jr., died yesterday; funeral from his father's res. in Jones St., O. T. (BA, 19 March 1816)

MILLER, John, Jr., and Miss Catherine Frick both of Balto. were married last eve. by Rev. Kurtz. (BFG, 2 Jan. 1801)

MILLER, John, died yesterday in his 47th year; funeral from No. 20 Market St. (BA, 4 Nov. 1816)

MILLER, John N., and Miss Elizabeth Christine, both of Balto. were married last Thurs. by Rev. Dr. Baker. (BA, 15 Feb. 1812)

MILLER, John W., Balto. merchant, died Sat., 19th inst., in his 25th year at the seat of Edward Miller in Harf. Co. (BA, 23 Dec. 1813)

MILLER, Lewis C., and Miss Eliza Millard both of Fells Point were married last Thurs. by Rev. Kurtz. (BA, 15 July 1809)

MILLER, Matthew, and Miss Milcah Miller all of Balto. were married last eve. by Rev. Roberts. (BS, 8 May 1812)

MILLER, Major Samuel, U. S. Marine Corps, and Miss Maria Bedinger, dau. of Henry Bedinger of Berkley Co., Va., were wed in that county on 27th ult. (BA, 6 April 1816)

MILLER, Stephen, of Kent Co., and Anne Dunn of Kent Co. were wed last Thurs. week. (BA, 22 Nov. 1800)

MILLER, Walter Tolley of Kent Co., and Miss Sarah Scott, dau. of Solomon Scott of Q. A. Co., were married Tues., 9th inst. by Rev. Wallace. (BS, 17 June 1812)

MILLESS, William, and Miss Susanna Mathiot were married last eve. by Rev. John Glendy. (BPEA, 8 May 1816)

MILLION, Mrs., wife of Patrick of Balto., died last Thurs. (BT, 1 Feb. 1800)

MILLS, Capt. James, of the ship Catherine of Balto. died at Barcelona, Spain, on 9 July. He had been detained there upwards of five years by the Spanish government. (BFG, 28 Sept. 1804)

MILLWATER, Thomas, and Miss Henrietta M. Weedon all of Balto. were married last Sun. by Rev. Bartow. (BA, 18 June 1816)

MILTENBERGER, Anthony, and Miss Dorothy B. Warner all of Balto. were married last Thurs. by Rev. Dashiell. (BA, 12 Nov. 1811)

MILTENBERGER, George, of Balto., died yesterday; a loving husband and father; funeral from his late res. opposite the Lower Market. (BFG, 19 Oct. 1797)

MINCE, Daniel, and Miss Ellen Shaw both of Balto. Co. were wed last Thurs. by Rev. Guest. (BPE, 21 Dec. 1814)

MINCHEN, John, died Mon., 3rd inst., late wine merchant of Balto. (BFG, 5 May 1802)

MINCHIN, Humphrey, of Charleston, S. C., and Miss Margaret Guthrow of Balto. were married last eve. by Rev. Rattoone. (BFG, 3 June 1803)

MARRIAGES AND DEATHS

MINCHIN, Humphrey, formerly of Charleston, S. C., died in Balto. on 7th inst. (BEP, 23 Aug. 1805)

MINGALL, Robert P., and Miss Margaret Andrews were married 8th inst. by Rev. Glendy. (BEP, 20 Dec. 1808)

MINGHINY, Joseph, of Jefferson Co., Va., and Miss Mary Head, dau. of William Head of Fred. Co., were married last Tues. near Creagers Town by Rev. Dubois. (BFG, 24 Nov. 1807)

MINNICK, Michael, and Miss Mary Huel all of Balto. were married last Tues. by Rev. Kurtz. (BA, 12 Aug. 1814)

MINNIGDEN, Lewis, and Miss Susanna Ellmore all of Balto. were wed last Sun. by Rev. Glendy. (BA, 27 Nov. 1810)

MINOS, William, died Fri., 23 Nov., at Mt. Vernon Plantation, S. C., formerly of Centreville, Q. A. Co., aged 66 years, for the last 18 years a res. of S. C. (BFG, 16 Jan. 1805)

MINSKEY, Mrs. Mary Ann, died Sat., 29th ult., in her 68th year. (BFG, 1 Nov. 1803)

MINZIES, James, and Miss Susan Roberts were married 19 May by Rev. Glendy. (BA, 19 Aug. 1814)

MISKIMONS, Samuel, and Miss Elizabeth Carnaughan both of Balto. were married last eve. by Rev. Glendy. (BW, 30 June 1809)

MITCHEL, Capt. James, of Balto. died yesterday in his 63rd year. (BA, 3 Aug. 1807)

MITCHEL, James Rule, formerly a merchant of Balto., died last Sun., aged 33, leaving a wife, son and aged mother. (BA, 9 April 1816)

MITCHEL, Peter, died Thurs. in his 57th year, long an inhab. of Balto.; he leaves a wife and two children. (BFG, 21 Sept. 1805)

MITCHEL, Thomas, and Mrs. Rebecca Woods both of Balto. were wed by Rev. Mr. M'Combs. (BT, 28 May 1804)

MITCHELL, Dr. Abram, died 7th inst. at his res. in Cecil Co., in his 80th year. (Long obit.) (BFG, 19 Sept. 1816)

MITCHELL, Alexander, merchant, and Miss Eliza Torrence, dau. of Charles Torrance, all of Balto. were married last eve. by Allison. (BT, 20 Dec. 1799)

MITCHELL, Francis I., Balto. merchant, and Miss Eleanor Sewell, dau. of Robert Sewell of P. G. Co. were married 2nd inst. (BFG, 9 Jan. 1809)

MITCHELL, Col. George E., of U. S. Army, and Miss Mary Hooper of Dor. Co., Md., were married at Newark, Del., on Tues., 28th ult. by Rev. A. R. Russell. (BA, 5 June 1816)

MITCHELL, James, of Cumberland Co., Penna., and Miss Mary Scroggs of Balto. were married last Wed. by Rev. Glendy. (BEP, 27 Jan. 1808)

MITCHELL, James R., Balto. merchant, and Miss Jane Ann Wheland were married 1st inst. at Bower Hill, Som. Co., by Rev. John B. Slemmons. (BFG, 10 Sept. 1806)

MITCHELL, James Rule, formerly Balto. merchant, died 6th inst., aged 33 years, leaving a wife, son, mother, and many near relations. (BWA, 13 April 1816)

MITCHELL, Gen. John, died Sun., 11 Oct. at his farm in Charles Co. (BA, 2 Nov. 1812)

MITCHELL, Mr. John, died 3rd inst. at his res. in Dor. Co., at the advanced age of 105 years and 9 mos. (BFG, 15 June 1816)

MITCHELL, John Peter, died yesterday, aged 24; funeral from the res. of the widow Mitchell, Market Space. (BA, 22 June 1807)

MITCHELL, Joseph, of Kent, and Miss Ann M. Brent of Chas. Co. were married last Mon. by Rev. Fenwick. (BFR, 3 April 1812)

MITCHELL, Mrs. Sarah, died Mon., 9th inst., in her 29th year, wife of Francis I. Mitchell of Balto. (BFG, 11 June 1806)

MITCHELL, Mrs. Tacy, wife of John Mitchell, died 11th inst., in her 64th year. (BFG, 14 Sept. 1816)

MITTEN, William, and Miss Susanna Warner were married by Rev. Mr. Nelson. (BEP, 20 May 1811)

MIX, Lewis, and Miss Rebecca Patterson all of Balto. were married last Thurs. by Rev. Mr. Griffith. (BPEA, 15 April 1815)

MOALE, George Washington, son of the late John Moale, died last Tues. in his 20th year. (BFG, 21 March 1799)

MOALE, John, of Balto., died last Thurs. in his 67th year. (BTD, 11 July 1798)

MOALE, John, of Balto., died Fri., 3rd inst. in his 49th year. (BFG, 6 Nov. 1809)

MOALE, Mrs. Lucy, wife of John Moale, died 15th inst., aged 35. (BFG, 22 July 1802)

MOALE, Richard H., and Miss Armistead, both of Balto., were married last eve., by Rev. Ireland. (BFG, 17 April 1797)

MOALE, Richard H., Esq., died this morning after an illness of ten days; aged 36 years. He leaves a widow and two children. Interment in St. Pauls burying ground. (BFG, 22 June 1802)

MOALE, S., and Miss Ann Howard, dau. of S. H. Howard of Annap., were married last eve. (BFG, 23 Sept. 1796)

MOELLINGER, Jacob, and Susanna Augustine all of Balto. were wed last Tues. by Rev. Kurtz. (BFG, 11 April 1806)

MOHLER, William, and Miss Elizabeth Cook all of Balto. were wed 4th inst. by Rev. Aunan. (BEP, 16 Aug. 1806)

MOLLER, Adolphus, merchant, and Miss Eliza McGlathery of Balto. were married at New Bremen. (BI, 16 April 1798)

MOLTHROP, John, and Miss Mary Strang all of Balto. were married last Wed. by Rev. Healey. (BA, 22 June 1816)

MOLYNEUX, Rev. Robert, pres. of Georgetown College, died this morning, aged 72 years. "Georgetown - Dec. 2." (BFG, 14 Dec. 1808)

MONAT, James, and Jane Miles, both of Balto., were married last Thurs. at Fells Point by Rev. Rattoone. (BFG, 1 March 1806)

MONCRIEFF, Archibald, Esq., died Thurs., 6th inst., at the res. of Dr. Mackrell in Balto. Co.; late Secretary to the Balto. Insurance Co. (BFG, 7 Jan. 1803)

MONEY, Benjamin, died 28th ult. at his farm in Kent Co. (BEP, 9 April 1806)

MONEY, John, of Cecil Co., Md., and Miss Mary Hugg of St. George, New Castle Co., Del., were married 26th ult. by Rev. Henry L. Davis at the res. of Samuel Biddle in the latter place. (BFR, 3 Nov. 1809)

MONK, George, and Miss Ann Aitken were married last Tues. by Rev. Glendy. (BS, 21 May 1812)

MONKHOUSE, William, of the House of Bowerbank, Monkhouse, and Co., died in Phila., 29th ult. (BFG, 1 Dec. 1806)

MONKS, John, and Miss Lewis were married at Abingdon, Harf. Co. (BFG, 1 March 1805)

MONNOU, Mr. Laurent, died yesterday aged 70, formerly of St. Domingo. (BPEA, 17 March 1815)

MONROE, Richmond, and Miss Diana Edwards Dilworth all of Balto. were married last eve. by Rev. Hargrove. (BA, 2 Jan. 1816)

MONSARRET, David, and Miss Ann Weaver, all of Balto., were wed last eve. by Rev. Hargrove. (BFG, 8 July 1803)

MONTEITH, Mrs. Margaret, died Tues., 4th inst., aged 54. (BFG, 8 Feb. 1806)

MONTGOMERY, Alexander, carpenter, killed himself last Sat. by drowning himself. (BEP, 17 June 1805)

MONTGOMERY, George Washington, died 9th inst., in his 21st year, at Fells Point. (BT, 20 Sept. 1800)

MONTGOMERY, John, Assoc. Judge of the Court of Common Please for that county, died near Carlisle on 3rd inst. in his 87th year, a native of Ireland. (Long obit gives details of his career.) (BFR, 14 Sept. 1808)

MONTGOMERY, John, rep. in Congress from Md., and Miss Maria Nicholson of Balto. were married last Mon. by Rev. Abeel. (BA, 6 April 1809)

MONTGOMERY, Moses, died in Balto., yesterday. From Lancaster, he arrived three days ago from Charleston, S. C. Interment will be in the Presb. burial ground. (BFG, 8 April 1800)

MOODY, Isaac, and Mrs. Mary Ellicott both of Balto. were married last eve. by Bishop Kemp. (BFG, 28 July 1815)

MOODY, Robert, and Lucretia Butler both of Fells Point were wed last eve. by Rev. Bend. (BA, 7 June 1799)

MOON, Richard, and Miss Mary Bailey both of Balto. were married 21st ult. by Rev. Rattoone. (BFG, 8 April 1805)

MOON, William, and Miss Mary Starr were married at Phila. (BT, 7 Nov. 1804)

MOONEY, William, and Polly Slaymaker both of Balto. were married last eve. by Rev. Francis Beeston. (BFG, 29 June 1798)

MOOR, Thomas, and Miss Eleanor Kirkpatrick all of Balto. were married last Thurs. by Rev. Glendy. (BA, 18 Aug. 1813)

MOORE, Andrew, of the privateer Matilda, born in Md., aged 35 years, died at the Poor House and Hospital in Savannah on 16th ult. (BA, 14 Nov. 1812)

MOORE, Covington, and Miss Catherine Anderson all of Balto. were married. (BFG, 11 May 1807)

MOORE, David, died last Sat. in his 56th year, an old inhab. of Balto. (BFG, 9 May 1807)

MOORE, George, Jr., of Lancaster, Penna., died Sat., 15th inst.; funeral from his brother's res. in Great York St. (BA, 17 Oct. 1814)

MOORE, Mrs. Hannah, died at Effingham Co., Va., 26th ult. aged 111 years. (BFG, 5 June 1802)

MOORE, James, of the House of Dinsmore and Moore of Balto., died last Thurs. of consumption in his 33rd year. (BA, 19 June 1810)

MOORE, John, of Lancaster Co., Penna., and Miss Eliza Stump of Harf. Co., were married last Tues. at the res. of Abraham Jarrett, by Rev. William Stephenson. (BFG, 16 March 1814)

MOORE, Nathaniel, a native of Sicily, died 26th inst., leaving a wife and 5 children; funeral from his late res., 45 Bond St. (BFG, 27 Jan. 1816)

MOORE, Col. Nicholas Ruxton, former member of Congress, and commandant of a Cavalry Regt. attached to the 3rd Div., M. M., died yesterday in his 62nd year. (BFG, 8 Oct. 1816)

MOORE, Philip, of Balto., and Miss Delia Hall, second dau. of Aquila Hall of Harf. Co., were married last Tues. eve. by Rev. Coleman. (BFG, 2 May 1799)

MOORE, Dr. Robert, and Miss Belinda Slade both of Balto. were wed last Mon. by Rev. Bend. (BFG, 27 May 1801)

MOORE, Robert, died Thurs., 18th inst., in his 55th year, a native of Ireland. (BA, 19 June 1807)

MOORE, Samuel, merchant, and Peggy Hughes, dau. of Christopher Hughes, all of Balto., were married last eve. by Rev. Bend. (BFG, 10 June 1803)

MOORE, Mrs. Susannah, died last Thurs. aged 21 years and 8 mos., wife of Philip Moore, Balto. attorney. (BMJ, 21 March 1797)

MOORE, Thomas, carpenter, died last Mon., for over 40 years an inhab. of Balto. (BFG, 22 May 1813) (BA, 24 May 1813, gives his age as 82 years.)

MOORE, Thomas K., died last Fri., aged 23 years. (BFG, 1 May 1815)

MOORE, Thomas L., died in Phila., aged 55, a patriot of the Rev. War. (BPE, 11 Sept. 1813)

MOORE, William, Jr., of Balto., died 14 March at Jeremie. (BT, 7 April 1798)

MOORES, Dr. Daniel, M. D., died this morning. (BFG, 11 Sept. 1802)

MORANGES, Stephen, native of France, died last Fri., for 10 years past an inhab. of Balto. (BFG, 25 Jan. 1804)

MORDECAI, Manuel, and Miss Charlotte Wilson of Balto. were married Tues. by Rev. Rattoone. The groom was from England. (BFG, 6 June 1805, and BEP, 6 June 1805)

MORDECAI, Mrs. Zepporah, wife of Mordecai M. Mordecai, died Sat. leaving a numerous family. (BT, 8 April 1806)

MOREHEAD, Henry, and Miss Elizabeth, dau. of the late Samuel Worthington, of Balto. Co., were married Tues., 10th inst., by Rev. Mr. Davis. (BA, 14 Dev. 1816)

MOREHEAD, John, and Miss Mary Patterson all of Balto., were wed last Sat. by Rev. Glendy. (BT, 15 Feb. 1815)

MOREHEAD, Turner, Balto. merchant, and Miss Martha, dau. of Samuel Worthington of Balto. Co., were married 19th inst. by Rev. Fry. (BFG, 20 May 1812)

MORETON, John P., of the New Theatre, died Mon. at the house of Mr. Freeman, Front St., Phila. (BI, 6 April 1798)

MORGAN, Miss Amy, dau. of James Morgan of Fells Point, died on Thurs., 6th inst., in her 14th year. (BEP, 13 Sept. 1805)

MORGAN, Ann, of the Society of Friends died 13th inst. in Harf. Co. in her 93rd year. (BFG, 22 Jan. 1810)

MORGAN, Mr. Arthur, of New Orleans, and Miss Lacaze, dau. of the late Dr. Lacaze of Balto., were married yesterday by Rev. English. (BT, 8 June 1802)

MORGAN, Gen. Daniel, died at his seat in Fred. Co., Va., hero of the battle of Cowpens, and a member of Congress. (BT, 2 April 1799)

MORGAN, Major-Gen. Daniel, was buried on the 7th. Account of his funeral procession is given. "Winchester, July 14." (BFG, 28 July 1802)

MORGAN, James, Sr., died Wed. after a lingering illness, in his 62nd year. He leaves a wife and children. (BA, 23 June, 1806)

MORGAN, James, Jr., and Henrietta Ward, dau. of Col. John Ward, all of Sassafras Neck, Cecil Co., were married last Thurs. by Rev. Henry L. Davis. (BA, 12 Aug. 1806)

MORGAN, James Lee, and Miss Sophia Monks, dau. of John Monks, merchant, all of Harf. Co., were married at Abingdon on Thurs. eve. (BFG, 12 April 1802)

MORGAN, Jesse, Jr., merchant, and Miss Sarah Smith, dau. of Capt. Robert Smith, all of Balto.. were married last eve. by Rev. Richards. (BFG, 17 May 1811)

MORGAN, Miss Rebecca, dau. of the late James Morgan of Fells Pt., died 1 Aug. in Dorset Co., where she had been visiting. Six years ago her sister, then nearly her age, died at the same place. (BFG, 14 Aug. 1811)

MORGAN, Capt. Robert Clary, and Miss Martha B. Andrews, both of Conn., were married last eve. by Rev. Glendy. (BA, 15 Oct. 1816)

MORGAN, William, Fells Point merchant, and Miss Hannah Matthews of Balto. were married last Sun. by Rev. Mr. Bonsall. (BFG, 15 Dec. 1796)

MORGAN, Capt. William, of Balto. and Miss Mary Ann LeCompt dau. of Charles Lecompt of Dor. Co., dec., were married at Easton on 8 Dec. by Rev. Markland. (BFG, 18 Dec. 1813[

MORIARTY, Mrs. Jane, wife of John Moriarty, died near Hampton, Balto. Co., on 10th inst., aged 44 years. (BFR, 13 Sept. 1810)

MORILL, Rev. Thomas, and Miss Friser both of Elizabeth Town were married 24th inst. at that place by Bishop Asbury. (BFG, 4 June 1802)

MORRIS, Mrs. Elizabeth, wife of William Morris of Balto., died Tues. (BFG, 21 Nov. 1805)

MORRIS, Gouverneur, of Morrisania, and Miss Ann Carey Randolph, dau. of the late Thomas Randolph of Va., were married on Christmas Day by Rev. Wilkins. (BA, 1 Jan. 1810)

MORRIS, Jesse, and Miss Eleanor Sater both of Balto. were wed on last eve. by Rev. Coats. (BFG, 17 Feb. 1804)

MORRIS, John A., printer, and Miss Ann Field of Balto. were married last Mon. (BFG, 15 April 1797)

MORRIS, John B., of St. M. Co., and Miss Ann Ophelia Jenifer of Chas. Co. were married at Port Tobacco on Thurs., 12th ult. by Rev. Weems. (BFR, 20 April 1810)

MORRIS, Owen, one of the oldest theatrical performers of the American stage, died last Thurs. at Phila. (BFR, 16 Nov. 1809)

MORRIS, Rice, merchant of Staunton, Va., and Miss Catherine M. Yeiser, dau. of the late Englehard Yeiser, were married last Thurs. by Rev. Dashiell. (BEP, 14 Nov. 1808)

MORRIS, Robert, died at Phila. in his 72nd year. (Long obit has details of his activity in the Rev. War.) (BT, 14 May 1806)

MORRIS, Thomas, and Miss Margaret Shaffer both of Fells Point were married last eve. by Rev. Dashiell. (BFG, 2 March 1807)

MORRIS, Dr. William Winder, and Miss Mary Ridgely of Dover were married there on Thurs., 5th inst. (BFG, 10 Nov. 1807)

MORRISON, Mrs., wife of James Morrison, died; funeral from her husband's res. in Charles St. (BFG, 19 Feb. 1807)

MORRISON, I., merchant, and Miss Eliza Lowry, dau. of Col. Wm. Lowry of Balto., were married at Kaskaskias on 9th ult. (BT, 8 Sept. 1806)

MORRISON, Neal, and Mrs. Eleanor Durant all of Balto. were married last Wed. eve. by Rev. Glendy. (BFG, 2 Oct. 1812)

MORRISON, Peter V., and Miss Ann Liggett both of Balto. were married last Sat. by Rev. John Glendy. (BA, 8 May 1810)

MORRISON, William, and Margaret Cloud all of Balto. were wed on 28th ult. by Rev. Rattoone. (BFG, 6 May 1807)

MORROW, William, and Miss Barbara Cromwell were married 17th inst. by Rev. Glendy. (BFG, 28 Nov. 1812)

MORSE, Nathan, Esq., Attorney-at-Law of N. J., and Martha C. Nicholls formerly of Md. were married at New Iberie, New Orleans Terr., on 9 June by Father Isebaye. (BFG, 24 Aug. 1808)

MORSELL, Benjamin, died last Thurs. in his 54th year. (BFG, 3 July 1813)

MORSELL, John S., aged 22, son of James Morsell, Esq., of Cal. Co., died this morning at his lodging at Mrs. Cole's, Calvert St. (BFG, 17 Oct. 1801)

MORTIMER, John, and Miss Tamezine Thornberry both natives of Ireland were married last Sat. by Rev. Dr. Annon. (BT, 3 April 1804)

MORTON, Alexander, and Mrs. Martha Mathewson both of Balto. were married last eve. by Rev. Inglis. (BFG, 22 March 1808)

MORTON, John, and Mrs. Eleanor Hudson both of Balto. were married Mon. by Rev. Glendy. (BA, 29 Sept. 1813)

MORTON, Nathaniel, of Balto. and Miss Sally Copeland of Harf. Co. were married 1st inst. by Rev. Allen. (BFG, 3 March 1798)

MORTON, Nathaniel, died 22 Jan. in his 43rd year; res. at North Calvert St. (BFG, 23 Jan. 1808)

MORTON, Richard, died at Manchester, Va., on 7 Oct.; native of Va., and for some years past a res. of this city. (BFG, 13 Oct. 1802)

MOSHER, Miss Jane, dau. of Col. J. Mosher of Balto., died Fri., 10th inst., aged 19 years. (Long obit.) (BFG, 23 July 1812)

MOSS, Bryan, and Mrs. Bridget Carroll both of Balto. were married last Sun. by Rev. Moranville. (BW, 31 July 1810)

MOTAR, Rebecca, dau. of Richard Motar of Phila., died in that city. (BPE, 4 Jan. 1813)

MOTT, John, and Miss Rachel Griffith, both of Balto. Co., were married last Sun. by Rev. Fiddler. (BFG, 7 Aug. 1810)

MOULD, Mrs. Ann, wife of James Mould, a native of Eng., died last Thurs., aged about 50 years. (BFG, 27 Nov. 1811)

MOUND, John James, of Nomony Hall, died Tues., 26th ult., at Westmoreland Court House, where he had been pleading a case. (BT, 24 Nov. 1802)

MOWTON, James, and Miss Hannah Holland all of Balto. were married last eve. by Rev. Dr. Roberts. (BEP, 1 April 1811)

MOWTON, John, and Miss Rebecca Leahy both of Balto. were married Tues. eve. by Rev. Dr. Roberts. (BA, 16 Dec. 1815)

MOXLEY, Thomas, and Miss Elizabeth Johnson all of Balto. were wed last Tues. by Rev. Roberts. (BFG, 31 Dec. 1806)

MOXLEY, William, died last Mon. in his 25th year, a native of Alexandria. (BFG, 4 May 1808)

MOYLAN, Gen. Stephen, of Phila., died last Sat. in his 78th year; he was commissioner of loans for the Dist. of Penna. (BA, 19 April 1811)

MUHLENBERG, Mrs. Anna, wife of Gen. P. Muhlenberg, collector of the Port of Phila., died 28th ult. at the family res., banks of the Schuylkill. (BFG, 3 Nov. 1806)

MUHLENBERG, Frederick Augustus, receiver general of the Penna. Land Office, died last Thurs. at Lancaster. (BFG, 9 June 1801)

MUHLENBERG, Rev. Henry A., formerly of Lancaster, and Miss Mary Heister, dau. of Col. Joseph Heister of Reading, were wed at the latter place on 21st ult. (BA, 8 June 1805)

MUHLENBERG, Henry M., eld. son of the late Gen. Peter Muhlenberg, died last Thurs. at Marcus Hook. (BEP, 11 July 1808)

MUHLENBERG, Mrs. Mary, widow of the late Rev. Henry Muhlenberg, died at Norristown, Penna., 23rd ult., in her 78th year. (BFG, 3 Sept. 1802)

MUIR, John, Pres. of the Farmers Bank of Md., died yesterday. (BFG, 1 Sept. 1810)

MUIR, John, and Miss Eliza Spedden both of Dor. Co., were married Fri., 26th inst. by Rev. Mr. Parks. (BA, 27 Nov. 1816)

MULLEN, Samuel, merchant, and Rachel Botner, dau. of Elias Botner, all of Balto., were married last eve. by Rev. Bend. (BT, 7 March 1800) (BA, 7 March 1800, gives the groom's name as Muller.)

MULLER, Mrs. Charlotte Antoinette, wife of George Henry Muller of Balto., died at sea, 11th inst., in her 20th year on her passage to Balto. from the Havanna, on the brig *Eunice*. (BW, 27 April 1813)

MULLER, George C., merchant and Miss Matilda Owens Slade all of Balto. were married last eve. by Rev. Glendy. (BFG, 19 Dec. 1804)

MULLER, George Henry, of Havana, and Charlotte Antoinette Muller, dau. of Caspar Otto Muller of Balto., were married last Sat. by Rev. Kurtz. (BFG, 10 April 1810)

MULLER, George Henry, and Miss Theresa Muller both og Balto. were married last eve. by Rev. Kurtz. (BFG, 22 Dec. 1813)

MULLER, Mrs. Matilda, wife of George C. Muller, died Thurs., aged 26 years; res. at Albemarle Court. (BA, 4 Nov. 1809)

MULLIKIN, Mr. B. D., and Miss Eliza McElderry were married last eve. by Rev. Glendy. (BFG, 3 May 1815)

MULLIKIN, Richard D., and Miss Eliza Pannell all of Balto. were married Tues. by Rev. Dashiell. (BFG, 6 Dec. 1810)

MULLIKIN, Richard D., of the house of Wilson and Mullikin, died; res. on North Charles St. (BPEA, 18 Dec. 1815)

MULLIKIN, Rignal, and Mary Eleanor Croxall all of Balto. were married last Thurs. by Rev. Duncan. (BA, 2 Oct. 1815)

MUMMA, David, Sr., died Wed., 30th inst., in his 65th year; res. on York Road near the Hay Scales. (BA, 31 Oct. 1816)

MUMMA, Samuel, and Miss Mary Delshar both of Balto. were married last Sun. by Rev. Healey. (BA, 30 April 1811)

MUMMA, William, and Mrs. Christiana Renkert all of Balto. were married last eve. by Rev. Kurtz. (BA, 26 Oct. 1815)

MUMMERY, Thomas, of Hagers Town, and Kitty Fishburn of Balto., were married last eve. by Rev. Kurtz. (BT, 14 July 1797)

MUMMEY, John, died Sun., 14th inst., in his 63rd year; an old inhab. of Balto. Co. (BA, 19 Feb. 1813)

MUN, Capt. John, died last Sat. (BFG, 2 Oct. 1810)

MUNGAN, William, native of Ireland, died yesterday in his 25th year; funeral from 65 N. Gay St. (BW, 11 March 1811)

MUNNIKHUYSEN, John, and Miss Mary Howard, dau. of Thomas Gassaway Howard of Balto. Co., were married last Thurs. by Rev. Ireland, at the res. of Mr. Thomas Sadler. (BFG, 4 March 1799)

MUNNIKHUYSEN, John, died; res. on Granby St. (BT, 25 Oct. 1805)

MUNROE, Nathan W., aged 27, formerly of Boston, died last eve. Funeral from his brother's house in Dulany St., near Leaman's Gardens. (BFG, 9 April 1816)

MUNSON, Joel, died yesterday. (BA, 4 Oct. 1809)

MUNSON, Joel M., and Mrs. Ann Swan of Balto. were married last eve. by Rev. Richards. (BFG, 16 Aug. 1797)

MURDOCH, George, died 5th inst. in Frederick Town, where he had lived for over 40 years; interment in the Episcopal Cemetery. (BT, 14 May 1805)

MURDOCK, George W., of Frederick Town, and Miss Jacquelina Smith, dau. of Gen. John Smith of Winchester, were married Tues. at Hackwood near Winchester. (BPEA, 18 Nov. 1815)

MURPHY, Mrs. Ann Statia, died 1st inst. aged 31 years, wife of William Murphy of Balto., leaving a husband and one child. Interment in the Meth. Cem. (BFG, 6 July 1801)

MURPHY, Miss Eliza, died Fri., 7th inst., aged 19 years and 6 mos. (BPE, 12 Jan. 1814)

MURPHY, Francis, and Henna McClain, both of Balto., were married last eve. by Rev. Rattoone. (BA, 11 Feb. 1806).

MURPHY, William, died yesterday; for many years a merchant of Balto. (BFG, 28 March 1804)

MURRAY, Anthony, and Miss Mary Duke all of Balto., were married Sun. (BA, 23 Sept. 1806)

MURRAY, Archibald, died; res. in Old Town. (BA, 10 Nov. 1812)

MURRAY, Mr. D., of the U. S. Navy, and Miss Mary Dorsey of Balto. were married Thurs. by Rev. Bend. (BFG, 10 Dec. 1808)

MURRAY, Francis, of Balto., and Ann Shear of the precincts were married last Thurs. by Rev. Richards. (BA, 19 Aug. 1801)

MURRAY, George W., formerly of Alexandria, and Miss Elizabeth Higinbothom, were married last night at the house of D. Delozier, by Rev. Higinbothom of Annap. (BT, 11 March 1796)

MURRAY, John, of the House of John Murray and Son, died at New York on the 11th at his seat at Murray Hill, aged 70 years. (BFG, 14 Oct. 1808)

MURRAY, John, died last Thurs. in his 30th year, late a res. of Fells Point. (BW, 7 Dec. 1811)

MURRAY, John, printer, died last Thurs. in his 38th year, at Richmond, Va. (BA, 28 Dec. 1815)

MURRAY, John R., of New York, and Miss Harriet Rogers, dau. of Col. Rogers of Druid Hill, were married last eve. by Rev. Bend. (BFG, 18 Feb. 1807)

MURRAY, Dr. R. C., died yesterday, long an inhab. of Balto. (BT, 23 Sept. 1800)

MURRAY, Thomas, master cooper in the U. S. Navy Yard, and Mrs. Rachel Masters of D. C., were married last Sun. by Rev. McCormick. (BT, 16 Nov. 1804)

MURRAY, Capt. William A., U. S. Army, and Miss Frances Irwin of Phila., dau. of the late Matthew Irwin, dec., were married last Wed. by Rev. James P. Wilson. (BW, 18 Nov. 1808)

MURRAY, William Vans, died Sun., 11th inst. at his res. in Dor. Co., late minister from the U. S. to the Hague, and minister plenipotentiary to the French Republic. (BFG, 17 Dec. 1803)

MURRY, Alexander, and Miss Judith White both of Balto. were wed last Thurs. by Rev. Duncan. (BA, 14 April 1804)

MUSCHETT, John, of the House of Messrs. Walter and John Muschett of Balto., died 17th inst., aged 23 years. (BFG, 18 Sept. 1804; BA, 19 Sept. 1804)

MUSE, Mrs. Ann, died in Dorchester Town, a very old lady. (BFG, 9 Feb. 1803)

MUSKETT, John, and Mrs. Susanna Alexander both of Balto. were wed Sat. by Rev. Rattoone. (BFG, 8 April 1805) (BEP, 9 April 1805 gives the groom's name as Muschett.)

MUTTER, Mrs. Lucinda, wife of John Mutter of Richmond, Va., died Tues., 18th inst., aged 22 years, leaving a husband and a mother. (BA, 22 Oct. 1814)

MYER, Mrs. Barbara, died yesterday in her 66th year; res. in Conway St. (BFG, 2 May 1812)

MYER, John J., and Miss Susan Miller, dau. of Jacob Miller all of Balto., were married last Thurs. by Rev. Kurtz. (BFG, 21 May 1814)

MYER, Mrs. Mary, wife of Jacob Myer of J., died 14th inst. (BFG, 24 Dec. 1806)

MYERS, Mrs., wife of Mr. Myers, china merchant, died Sun., leaving 6 children. (BFG, 14 Oct. 1799)

MYERS, Mrs., wife of Jacob Myers of the Western precincts, died yesterday afternoon. (BA, 28 Feb. 1806)

MYERS, Miss Catherine, died yesterday. (BFG, 30 Sept. 1797)

MYERS, Charles, died Sun., in his 45th year, of a pulmonary consumption; res. at Hampstead Hill. (BA, 30 Dec. 1806)

MYERS, George, merchant, and Miss Maria Barry, dau. of Capt. Standish Barry, all of Balto., were married last Thurs. by Rev. Roberts. (BFG, 9 Jan. 1809)

MYERS, Henry, merchant, and Miss Mary Wehner both of Balto. were married last eve. by Rev. Dr. Roberts. (BA, 21 June 1816)

MYERS, Jacob, of Balto., and Miss Eliza Ross, eld. dau. of David Ross, of Cobbham, Cumberland Co., Va., were married 1st inst., by Rev. Dr. Hopkins. (BFG, 11 May 1797)

MYERS, Jacob, and Miss Sarah Warren both of Balto. were married last eve. by Rev. Mr. Morrell. (BFG, 6 Dec. 1800)

MYERS, Jacob, Esq., of Georgetown, S. C., and Miriant Etting, dau. of Solomon Etting of Balto., were married last eve. by Rev. Mr. Judah. (BFG, 1 Aug. 1806)

MYERS, John K., died at Havre de Grace on 9th inst., aged 54, leaving a family. (BW, 12 Feb. 1810)

MYERS, Joseph, tailor, and Catherine Small were married last Sun. by Rev. Otterbein. (BFG, 19 July 1796)

MYERS, Philip, of Balto. died last Tues. in his 56th year. (BA, 9 Oct. 1812)

MYERS, Mr. Stephen, and Miss Hannah Hepwell both of Balto. were married last eve. by Rev. Mr. Healy. (BA, 26 Aug. 1815)

MYERS, William, and Maria Hanson of Balto. were married Tues. eve. by Rev. Kurtz. (BA, 20 Nov. 1804)

MYERS, William, and Miss Eleanora Warren both of Balto. were wed Tues., 1st inst. by Rev. Dr. Roberts. (BFR, 8 Jan. 1811)

MYLES, Mrs., consort of Zachariah Myles, died Thurs. last, aged 32 years. (BFG, 17 July 1799)

MYLES, Zachary, Balto. merchant, and Miss Jane McMechen of Harf. Co., were married last eve. by Rev. Morrell. (BFG, 12 Sept. 1799)

NACE, Major William, and Miss Elizabeth Mury (Murray) both of
Balto. Co. were married last eve. by Rev. Butler. (BFG,
14 July 1797)

NAGOT, Rev. Francis Charles, first superior of the Catholic seminary, died this morning aged 82. (BFG, 9 April 1816)

NAILER, George, and Cecilia Jacobs both of Balto. were married
last Sat. by Rev. Roberts. (BW, 1 May 1809)

NATHAN, Isaiah, Phila. merchant, and Miss Judith Russel, dau. of
Philip Russel, Balto. merchant, were married yesterday eve.
4th March by Rabbi Mordecai M. Mordecai. (BFG, 5 March
1807)

NAUDAIN, Dr. Arnold, and Miss Mary M. Schee both of Delaware were
married at Phila. last Thurs. by Rev. James P. Wilson.
(BEP, 27 Nov. 1810)

NAYLOR, Capt. Samuel, formerly a lieut. in the U. S. Navy, will
be reinterred in Eng. Episcopal burial ground from the *
Potter's Field, where he had been interred by mistake.
(BEP, 3 June 1808)

NEAL, Abner, and Miss Barbara Reel both of Balto. were married
last Thurs. by Rev. Reed. (BFG, 3 July 1799)

NEALE, Bennett, died at Barbadoes, 4th March last, in his 23rd
year, Balto. merchant. (BFG, 8 April 1804)

NEALE, Edward, and Elizabeth Martin both of Balto. were married
last eve. by Right Rev. Dr. Carroll. (BT, 27 Jan. 1796)

NEALE, Edward, proprietor of the coffee house in Cumberland Row,
died Thurs. (BFG, 13 Sept. 1800)

NEALE, Capt. Edward Digges, died 20th inst. in St. M. Co. in his
26th year. (BFG, 5 Jan. 1798)

NEALE, Greenbury, died Thurs. (BFG, 31 Oct. 1800)

NEALE, J. G., of Balto. and Miss Louisa Humphreys of Kent Co.,
Md., were married Tues. by Rev. Turner. (BA, 21 Sept.
1815)

NEALE, John, and Miss Susanna Eisler both of Balto. were married
Tues. eve. by Bishop Carroll. (BA, 23 Oct. 1806)

NEALE, John B., died yesterday in his 31st year. (BFG, 10 Feb.
1804)

NEALE, Joseph, lieut. of marines, died on the U. S. ship Maryland
on her homeward bound passage, in his 27th year. (BFG,
14 Oct. 1800)

NEEDLES, John, of Balto., and Eliza Matthews of Balto. Co. were
married at Friends Meeting, Gunpowder, on 29th inst.
(BFG, 31 May 1811)

NEILL, John, and Miss Susanna Huisler all of Balto. were married
last eve. by Bishop Carroll. (BFG, 22 Oct. 1806)

NEILSON, Mrs., wife of William Neilson of Balto., died last eve.
aged 27 years. (BFG, 8 Jan. 1811)

NEILSON, David, died last Sat. in his 18th year. (BFG, 8 Oct. 1804)

NEILSON, Hugh, and Ann, dau. of Isaac Van Bibber, were married Tues. at Montpelier by Rev. Dashiell. (BFG, 19 July 1804)

NEILSON, James C., of Balto. and Miss Albertina Anna Backer, eld. dau. of Albertus Backer, former Gov. of Demerara, were married at Exeter, Eng., 31 Oct. 1809. (BFG, 15 Jan. 1810)

NEILSON, Mrs. Jane, died Sun., 3rd inst., in her 58th year. (BFG, 5 July 1814)

NEILSON, Mrs. Mary, wife of Thomas Neilson, Balto. merchant, died Tues. in her 27th year, leaving a husband and four children. (BA, 11 July 1816)

NEILSON, Robert, of Balto., and Miss D. Ridgely, dau. of D. Ridgely of Elk Ridge were married Thurs. by Rev. A. Dashiell. (BA, 14 Sept. 1816)

NEILSON, Thomas, merchant, and Miss Mary Honicomb both of Balto. were married Sat. eve. by Rev. Glendy. (BA, 17 March 1807)

NEILSON, William, and Miss Harriot Walsh were married on last Thurs. at Oak Hill, the res. of M. Eichelberger, by Rev. Otterbein. (BFG, 15 July 1809)

NELMS, Noah, merchant, and Miss Mary Ann Lemmon, both of Balto. were married Thurs., 15th inst., by Rev. Richards. (BFG, 19 Jan. 1801)

NELMS, Noah, of the House of Levering and Nelms of Balto., died last Sun. in his 33rd year. (BFG, 29 Nov. 1808)

NELSON, Basil, and Mrs. Rosanna Cunningham all of Balto. were married last eve. by Rev. Fenwick. (BA, 10 Oct. 1812) (BFG, 12 Oct. 1812, gives the bride's name as Finnigan.)

NELSON, John, and Mrs. Jean M'Cullough both of Balto. were married on Thurs. eve. by Rev. Richards. (BAP, 2 April 1803)

NELSON, John, died at his house in Tripolet's Alley. (BS, 18 Aug. 1810; BW, 11 Aug. 1810)

NELSON, Roger, revolutionary hero and member of Congress, died 7th ult. (BMG, 15 June 1815)

NESBIT, Alexander, and Miss Mary C. Owings were married last Thurs. by Rev. Inglis. (BFG, 26 Dec. 1807)

NESBIT, Dr. James, died 23 Feb. in his 34th year, of apoplexy, at Huntingdon, Penna. (BAP, 15 March 1803)

NESTOR, George, printer, formerly of Balto., died in Princess Anne, Va., on 10th inst., aged 32 years. (BA, 20 March 1811)

NEVILLE, Frederick, died last 25 Dec. in Northumberland Co., Pa., aged 100. (BEP, 16 Jan. 1806)

NEWMAN, Mrs., died yesterday, consort of Francis Newman of Port Tobacco. (BFG, 9 Aug. 1796)

NEWMAN, Daniel, and Miss Sarah Revell were married last 1 Sept.
by Rev. Glendy. (BW, 21 Nov. 1808)

NEWPORT, John, died last week at the Alms House of Phila., aged
100. (BFG, 29 Nov. 1808)

NEWTON, John, and Mrs. Eliza Townson all of Balto. were married
last Thurs. by Rev. Ryland. (BPE, 17 Nov. 1813)

NEWTON, Joseph James, died Thurs. morning in his 26th year, a
painter and glazier on Fells Point. He was interred the
same eve. in St. Pauls churchyard. (BMJ, 1 July 1797)

NIBLET, Solomon, native of Eng., died 15 Oct. in Lawrens Dist.,
S. C., aged 143. At age 19 he came to Md., where he lived
until he was age 55, and then moved to S. C. (BA, 11 Nov.
1815)

NICCOLLS, Richard, merchant, and Miss Hudson, both of Balto., were
married by Rev. Rattoone. (BFG, 23 May 1803)

NICHOLAS, Gen., native of Ireland, died yesterday in his 84th
year. He served in the Rev. War, and was the translator
of a French work on military tactics. "Alexandria paper."
(BFG, 13 Aug. 1807)

NICHOLAS, Dr. George, late of Centreville, Q. A. Co., and now of
the 14th U. S. Regt. of Infantry, died in Balto., 17th
inst., aged about 26 years. (BFG, 18 March 1813) His
only relation is a sister on the Eastern Shore, aged 14.
(BFG, 19 March 1813)

NICHOLAS, Lewis, and Eliza Zebne, were married by Rev. Rattoone.
(BA, 26 Sept. 1804; BFG, 25 Sept. 1804)

NICHOLAS, Philip N., of Richmond, VA., and Miss Mary Spear of
Balto. were married last eve. by Rev. Allison. (BFG, 19
Feb. 1799)

NICHOLS, Gen. Francis, died suddenly, 14th inst., at Pottstown,
Mont. Co., an officer of the U. S. Army during the Rev.
War. (BW, 21 Feb. 1812)

NICHOLS, Ninian, and Miss Barbara S. Hunt all of Balto. were wed
last eve. by Rev. Bend. (BFG, 22 Sept. 1806)

NICHOLS, Ninian K., Balto. merchant, died Fri., 26th inst., in
his 26th year, leaving a widow and two infant children.
(BA, 30 Oct. 1810)

NICHOLSON, Capt. Benjamin, native of Md., and aide-de-camp to
Brig.-Gen. Pike, died on board Comm. Chauncy's fleet on
the Lakes. (BFG, 27 May 1813)

NICHOLSON, Christopher, and Mrs. Mary James both of Balto. were
married Sun. (BFG, 29 May 1804)

NICHOLSON, George, died Mon. night at Phila., of the House of
Simmons and Nicholson, merchants, of Balto. (BFG, 13 Oct.
1800)

NICHOLSON, Commodore James, died last Sun. in New York in his 69th
year. Obit gives details of revolutionary service. (BA,
6 Sept. 1804)

NICHOLSON, James, and Miss Amy Thompson were married on Sun. by
    Rev. Healey. (BA, 12 March 1811)

NICHOLSON, Lieut. John, of the U. S. Navy, died Sat., 1 Sept. in
    Tal. Co. (BFG, 11 Sept. 1810)

NICHOLSON, Dr. John Ridgely, died last 29 April in his 28th year,
    on the U. S. Brig <u>Aurora</u>. He leaves a mother, widow, and
    two children. (Long obit.) (BFG, 18 July 1800)

NICHOLSON, Joseph H., Jr., of Centreville, and Charlotte Gibson
    of the same place were married Sun., 26th ult., by Rev.
    Simon Wilmer. (BA, 3 Sept. 1804)

NICHOLSON, Mrs. Rebecca, widow of the late Capt. John Nicholson,
    died last Tues., in her 43rd year, leaving several chil-
    dren. (BEP, 8 Oct. 1808)

NICHOLSON, Capt. Thomas, and Miss Sarah Harwood both of Balto.
    were married last Sun. by Rev. Richards. (BFG, 13 March
    1807)

NICKLIN, Philip, merchant of the House of Nicklin and Griffith,
    died last week at Phila. (BEP, 6 Nov. 1806)

NICODEMUS, Henry, and Miss Catherine Cassell were married Sun.,
    9th inst. by Rev. B. Nelson. (BEP, 18 Dec. 1810)

NICOLL, Thomas, and Miss Rebecca Taylor were married last Sun.,
    14 April, by Rev. Hargrove. (BFG, 18 April 1811)

NICOLS, Henry, of Balto., and Miss Sarah Holliday of Tal. Co.
    were married last Thurs. by Rev. Kemp at Radcliffe Manor,
    the res. of Henry Holliday, brother of the bride, near
    Easton. (BFG, 27 May 1812)

NICOLS, James, died yesterday, a Balto. merchant, leaving a widow
    and two children. (BFG, 3 Oct. 1796)

NICOLS, Mrs. Mary, died 1st inst. at Easton, wife of Samuel
    Nicols, merchant of that town. (BFG, 9 Dec. 1799)

NICOLS, Mrs. Rebecca, late consort of Henry Nicols, died yesterday
    8th inst. in her 39th year. (BFG, 9 Jan. 1809)

NICOLSON, Dr. George Digges, of Urbanna, and Miss Sarah Taylor
    Wormeley, dau. of the late Ralph Wormeley of Rosegill,
    Middlesex Co., Va., were married. (BFR, 12 Dec. 1811)

NILES, Mrs. Mary, died Sun. last at Wilmington, Del., mother of
    Hezekiah Niles, one of the editors of the <u>Evening Post</u>,
    aged about 60 years and 2 mos. (BA, 5 Nov. 1806)

NIND, Rev. William, and Miss Mary Cole were married last eve. by
    Rev. Dashiell. (BFG, 28 Feb. 1809)

NINDE, James, and Miss Catherine Blyth both of Fells Point were
    married last eve. by Rev. Richards. (BFG, 27 Feb. 1797)

NINDE, Mary Ann, dau. of James Ninde of Balto., died yesterday,
    aged about 8 years. (BFG, 26 Jan. 1807)

NIPPARD, George, and Julia Ann Smith all of Balto. were married
    last Sun. by Rev. D. E. Reese. (BA, 15 Nov. 1815)

NISBET, Rev. Charles, D. D., principal of Dickinson College, died
at Carlisle on 18 Jan. in his 68th year. When very young
he was ordained a minister of the Church of Scotland and
lived at Glasgow, and then Montrose until he came to America. (BT, 10 Feb. 1804)

NISBET, Charles, son of Alexander and Mary Nisbet, died Sun. at
Montrose, Balto. Co., aged 3 years and 7 mos. (BFG, 16
Dec. 1813)

NIXON, John, died at Phila. last Sat. aged 76, president of the
Bank of North America. (BEP, 3 Jan. 1809)

NIXON, Nicholas, and Miss Ann Borchall (Burchall) all of Balto.
were married last Thurs. by Rev. Healy. (BMG, 29 July
1815)

NOBLE, Alexander, and Miss Mary Burns all of Balto. were married
on Mon. by Rev. Glendy. (BS, 8 Jan. 1812)

NOBLE, Roswell, and Miss Elizabeth Barrow both of Balto. were
married last Sat. by Rev. Richards. (BPE, 29 Dec. 1813)

NOCQ (sic), Francis, and Miss Rebecca Reider were married last
Sat. by Rev. Glendy. (BFG, 21 Feb. 1814)

NOEGE, Francis, and Miss Rebecca Rider both of Balto. were wed
5th inst. by Rev. Greenfield. (BA, 25 Feb. 1814)

NOEL, Dr. Perry E., died at Cenreville, Q. A. Co., Thurs., 14th
Oct. A graduate of the University of Maryland in 1794, he
leaves a wife and children. (Long obit.) (BPE, 5 Nov.
1813)

NOELL, Jacob, and Mrs. Henrietta Coleman both of Balto. were
married last eve. by Rev. Dr. Baker. (BA, 16 June 1809)

NORRIS, Benjamin, and Miss Susan Cockey both of Balto. were wed
Tues., 20th inst., by Rev. Ryland. (BT, 30 Dec. 1814)

NORRIS, Benjamin Bradford, aged 12 years, son of William Norris
of Harf. Co., died yesterday; interment in the Friends
Burying Ground. (BFG, 10 Aug. 1805)

NORRIS, Benjamin Bradford, of Balto. died Sat., 21st inst., at
Norfolk, Va., leaving a mother. (BA, 27 Dec. 1816)

NORRIS, Mr. Cardis (sic), brother of Lloyd Norris of the House
of Whitney and Norris of Balto., died this morning. (BFG,
18 Nov. 1801)

NORRIS, Edward, and Rebecca Lee, both of Harf. Co., were married
last Sun., by Rev. Mr. Johnston. (BFG, 18 Dec. 1799)

NORRIS, Mrs. Elizabeth, relict of the late Edward Norris of Harf.
Co., died Mon., 19th inst., in her 53rd year. Interment
in the ancient family burying ground. (BFG, 22 Aug. 1805)

NORRIS, Miss Ellen, dau. of William Norris of Harf. Co., died
21st inst. in her 19th year. (BFG, 28 Dec. 1811)

NORRIS, Jacob, of the House of Richardson, Norris, and Co., and
Miss Harriott Frick, dau. of Peter Frick, all of Balto.,
were married last eve. by Rev. Kurtz. (BFG, 27 May 1803)

NORRIS, Jacob, died yesterday in his 26th year. (BFG, 25 Aug.
1807)

NORRIS, John, of Harf. Co., and Miss Mary Rooker were married last eve. by Rev. Dashiell. (BFG, 18 Sept. 1811)

NORRIS, John, died this morning at his res. in Balto. Co. in his 35th year, son of William Norris. Interment at his father's res. in Harf. Co. (BFG, 10 March 1814)

NORRIS, Lloyd, Balto. merchant, and Miss Jane Peterkin of Fells Point were married last eve. by Rev. Ireland. (BFG, 8 Nov. 1799)

NORRIS, Lloyd, died last Sun. in his 25th year. (BFG, 3 Oct. 1804)

NORRIS, Miss Martha, died 3rd inst. at her father's res. in Harf. Co. in her 27th year. (BFG, 5 Jan. 1814)

NORRIS, Miss Mary, died Fri., 5th inst., in Balto. aged 17; interment in the family burying ground in Harf. Co. (BFG, 9 Sept. 1806)

NORRIS, Miss Mary, aged 18, dau. of Wm. Norris of Harf. Co., died 30 Dec. Her sister died a week earlier. (BFG, 1 Jan. 1812; and BFR, 3 Jan. 1812)

NORRIS, Nelson, Balto. merchant, and Miss Sarah Carnan, dau. of Charles Carnan, dec., of Balto. Co., were married at Annandale last Tues. by Rev. Wells. (BFG, 17 June 1813)

NORRIS, Nelson, Balto. merchant, and Elizabeth Carnan, dau. of Charles Carnan, dec., were married Garrison Forest last Tues. by Rev. Bishop Kemp. (BA, 24 May 1816)

NORRIS, Oliver, and Miss Sarah Fairfax Herbert, dau. of William Herbert of Alexandria, were married last Tues. by Rev. Wilmer. (BFG, 3 June 1813)

NORRIS, Richard, Balto. merchant, and Miss Susan Fitzhugh Voss were married Thurs., 11th inst., at Bellmont near Fredericksburg, Va. (BFG, 20 May 1815)

NORRIS, Mrs. Sarah, consort of Nelson Norris, died Sat., 18th inst. in her 19th year. (BA, 22 June 1814)

NORRIS, Miss Susan, dau. of the late Benjamin Bradford Norris, of Harf. Co., died Mon. Interment in the Friends burying ground. (BFG, 6 Feb. 1799)

NORRIS, William, of Va., and Miss Sally Schaeffer, dau. of Baltzer Schaeffer a Balto. merchant, were married last eve. by Rev. Allison. (BFG, 27 Dec. 1799; BT, 27 Dec. 1799)

NORRIS, William, and Miss Rebecca Smith both of Balto. were wed last eve. by Rev. Roberts. (BFG, 17 March 1802)

NORRIS, William, Jr., of the House of Jacob and William Norris, and Sally H. Martin, dau. of Col. Martin of Snow Hill, were married last eve. by Rev. Bend. (BFG, 8 Aug. 1806)

NORRIS, William E., merchant, died last eve. of the House of Norris and Tyson, aged 32. Funeral from the house of Job Smith, western precincts near Lewis Pascault's. (BFG, 16 Feb. 1809)

NORRIS, Edward, and Prudence Wyles all of Balto. were married last eve. by Rev. Hargrove. (BFG, 27 July 1804)

NORTH, William, and Miss Polly Pritchard all of Balto. were wed last Tues. by Rev. Hargrove. (BFG, 28 Dec. 1807)

NORTON, Theophilus James, and Miss Elizabeth Ash both of Balto. were married last eve. by Rev. Birch. (BFG, 25 Aug. 1810)

NORVELL, John, and Mary Else Thurston all of Balto. were married last eve. by Rev. Glendy. (BFG, 6 Sept. 1811)

NORVELL, John, editor of the Baltimore Whig and Miss Catherine Cone were married at Phila. last Thurs. eve. (BFG, 8 Nov. 1813)

NORVELL, Mrs. Mary, wife of John Norvell, died yesterday in her 18th year. (BFG, 5 Dec. 1811)

NORWOOD, Col. Edward. a Revolutionary patriot, died at his seat in Elkridge, 25 Oct. at an advanced age. (BA, 28 Oct. 1815)

NORWOOD, Mrs. Sally, wife of Col. Edward Norwood of Elk Ridge, died yesterday aged 42, leaving a husband and many children. (BFG, 22 Dec. 1801)

NORWOOD, Miss Sally Odell, youngest dau. of Col. Edward Norwood, of Balto. Co., died 9 Jan. (BA, 16 Jan. 1815)

NORWOOD, Samuel, and Ann Wheeler both of Balto. Co. were married 4 June by Rev. Bloodgood. (BA, 5 June 1805)

NORWOOD, Samuel, and Henrietta Ridgely both of Balto. City were married 26 Dec. by Rev. Roberts. (BFG, 27 Dec. 1809)

NORWOOD, Samuel, of Balto. Co., died Wed. (BPE, 1 Feb. 1815)

NOWLAND, Dennis, of Balto., died last Wed. in his 34th year. (BFG, 29 June 1814)

NOWLAND, Mr. Elias, died Wed. (BFG, 9 April 1802)

NOWLAND, George, died 5th inst. on the Eastern Shore, a native of Phila. (BA, 11 March 1806)

NOWLAND, Lambert, and Miss Rachel Maria White all of Balto. were married last Thurs. by Rev. Dashiells. (BFG, 9 Sept. 1815)

OAKLEY, John, died at Georgetown (Col.), on Mon., 5th inst., collector of that port. (BFG, 13 May 1806)

OAR, Samuel, of Phila., and Miss Eliza Dennison of Balto. were married last Wed. by Rev. Dashiell. (BFG, 7 July 1808)

O'BRIEN, Mr. Henry, died last Fri., at Fells Point in his 19th year; a native of Ireland. (BFG, 19 Aug. 1800)

O'BRIEN, Rev. Matthew, died 20 Oct. in his 60th year. After his arrival from Ireland, he served in New York, Boston, Balto., and Norfolk. His funeral will be from St. Peter's Church, Alisanna St., to the R. C. cemetery beyond the western precincts of Balto. (BA, 21 Oct. 1815)

O'CONNOR, Francis, and Mrs. Elizabeth Kennedy were married on Thurs. by Rev. Glendy. (BA, 11 Aug. 1807)

O'CONNOR, Master John, aged 5 years, 9 mos., and 18 days, only son of John O'Connor, tavern keeper, Market Space, died yesterday. (BFG, 29 March 1806)

O'CONNOR, Dr. John, of Balto., and Miss Anne Hall of Harf. Co., were married last Thurs. by Rev. Mr. Eden. (BA, 21 June 1813)

O'DELL, Mr. Henry, and Miss Mary Sweeten were married last Tues. by Rev. Glendy. (BT, 20 Dec. 1804)

ODENHEIMER, Lieut. William H., late of U. S. navy, died 12 Nov. (BA, 16 Nov. 1815)

ODLE, William, and Miss Rachel Waters both of Balto. Co. were wed last eve. by Rev. Richards. (BFG, 10 Feb. 1797)

O'DONNEL, John, died 5th inst., at his country res. in the Balto. Barrens, aged 56. He was a colonel in the militia, and a delegate from Balto. to the state legislature. (Long obit.) (BFG, 7 Oct. 1805)

O'DONNELL, Columbus, and Miss Eleanor Pascault, dau. of Louis Pascault, all of Balto., were married Wed., 8th inst. (BFG, 10 Sept. 1813)

O'DONNELL, Hugh, and Miss Nancy Campbell all of Balto. were wed last eve. by Rev. Glendy. (BT, 13 Dec. 1805)

O'DONNELL, James, and Eliza Davis were married Thurs., 6th inst., by Rev. Glendy. (BEP, 22 April 1809)

OGDEN, David, and Miss Mary Deems all of Balto. were married last eve. by Dr. Roberts. (BFG, 12 Nov. 1810)

OGDEN, Jonathan, and Miss Eleanor M'Cann both of Balto. were wed last Sat. by Rev. Dr. O'Brien. (BFG, 13 Aug. 1810)

OGLE, Benjamin, late Gov. of Md., died the eve. of 6th inst. in his 61st year. (BEP, 11 July 1809)

OGLE, Benjamin, died aged 67. (BPE, 14 Sept. 1813)

OGLE, Clement, died yesterday, not more than 30 years old, native of Ireland. (BT, 28 Sept. 1802)

O'HARA, Anthony, and Miss Ann Ellis, both of Balto. were married last Sat. by Rev. Rattoone. (BFG, 26 Sept. 1806)

OKELY, John, Balto. merchant, and Miss Alisanna Wilson, dau. of Isaac Wilson, of Brighton, were married on Thurs., 13th inst., at Greensburg, Penna. (BFG, 28 Oct. 1808)

OLDEN, David, Phila. merchant, and Miss Susan Levy of Balto. were married Mon. eve. by Rev. Rattoone. (BFG, 28 July 1803)

OLDHAM, Nathan Giles, son of Nathan Oldham of Cecil Co., dec., died last 21 Sept. in Elkton, Cecil Co. (BEP, 8 Oct. 1807)

OLDHAM, Thomas, and Miss Ann Elizabeth Louch, both of Balto., were married Tues. eve. by Rev. Kurtz. (BA, 23 June 1809)

OLER, Peter, and Miss Margaret Maxwell all of Balto. were wed on Tues. eve. by Rev. Glendy. (BT, 14 April 1806)

OLIVER, Mr., rector of St. Thomas' Parish, died Wed. last at his house in Garrison Forest. (BMJ, 28 Jan. 1797)

OLIVER, ---, a carpenter, on last Sun. night on his way home from the point, mistook his way in the dark, and walked into the Falls, below the lower bridge and drowned. (BT, 24 Feb. 1802)

OLIVER, William G., Phila. merchant, and Miss Esther Ward, stepdau. of Abraham Steinberg, were married in Phila. on Sat. by Rev. Helfenstein. (BA, 10 May 1805)

OLYPHANT, David W. C., Balto. merchant, and Mrs. Ann Archer of N. Y. were married at the latter place last Tues. by Rev. Gardiner Spring. (BPEA, 6 May 1815)

O'NEAL, Clotworthy, of Balto., died a few days ago at GeorgeTown. (BA, 5 Sept. 1800)

O'NEALE, Bernard, and Miss Margaret O'Brien, both of Fells Point, were married Mon. by Rev. Beeston. (BMJ, 24 March 1796)

O'NEIL, Henry, of Balto. and Elizabeth Bickerton of Phila. were married last Sun. at Phila. by Rev. Dr. Rogers. (BFG, 29 March 1799)

O'NEIL, Terence Henry, late of Balto. died at Phila. on 11th inst. (BT, 17 Jan. 1799)

ONION, Thomas B., of Balto. died 16th inst. (BA, 19 Dec. 1812)

ORAM, John, and Miss Mary Duncan both of Balto. were married on Fri. by Rev. Richards. (BT, 25 May 1801)

ORD, George, of Phila. and Miss Margaret Biays, dau. of Joseph Biays of Balto., were married last eve. by Rev. Ingles. (BFG, 6 March 1804)

ORE, William, of Balto. and Miss Ruth Sutton of Balto. Co. were married by Rev. Rattoone on last Thurs. (BFG, 11 June 1808)

O'REILLY, J. C., and Mrs. Margaret Bussey all of Balto. were wed last Sun. by Rev. Dashiell. (BA, 15 Jan. 1805)

ORME, Rezin, of Georgetown and Miss Margaret Thomas of Balto. were married 13th inst. by Rev. Neal. (BFG, 16 July 1816)

ORMSBY, Henry, late of the Kingdom of Ireland, died 12th inst. at the house of Dr. De Butts, Sharpsburg, Wash. Co., aged 72 years. (BFG, 17 Aug. 1799)

O'ROURKE, Patrick, died yesterday aged 66. Interment in the Catholic burying ground. (BFG, 6 Nov. 1806)

ORR, James, died lately at Port-au-Prince, St. Domingo, aged 34, a native of Co. Wexford, Ireland, but recently of Balto. He was a British soldier but when the British invaded the U. S. he joined the American army. (Long obit.) (BA, 7 Nov. 1816)

ORR, Robert, died yesterday; res. at Wilkes St. and Strawberry Alley. (BA, 3 Aug. 1815)

ORRICK, Capt. Edward, and Miss Eliza Johnson, dau. of Hickman Johnson, all of Balto. Co. were married last Thurs. by Rev. Mr. Davis. (BA, 19 Jan. 1816)

ORRICK, Elijah, died 8th inst. in his 23rd year, late a student at law under the Hon. R. G. Haroer, and third son of John Orrick of Balto. Co. (BFG, 10 May 1803)

ORRICK, John, died 14 Nov. at his res. in Gunpowder Forest. (BFG, 17 Nov. 1810)

ORRICK, Mr. Nicholas, and Miss Susanna Keener were married last eve. at the res. of Christian Keener by Rev. Wells. (BFG, 18 Nov. 1803)

ORRICK, Mrs. Susan, wife of Nicholas Orrick, died; funeral will be Tues. from the res. of Christian Keener on Reisterstown Road. (BFG, 3 July 1809)

ORTH, Mr. Henry, died last Mon. in his 41st year. A Phila. merchant he leaves a wife and seven children. (BA, 17 March 1814)

OSBORN, Thomas, and Kitty Groundfield all of Balto. were married last eve. by Rev. Rattoone. (BFG, 16 Dec. 1808)

OSBORNE, Alexander, merchant, and Miss Martha James all of Balto. were married last eve. by Rev. Roberts. (BFG, 16 July 1813)

OSBORNE, George Jerry, died at Newburyport last Mon., 2nd inst., editor of the Republican Ledger. (Long obit.) (BA, 20 June 1800)

OSBORNE, James, and Miss Elizabeth Snowdey (sic) were married on 7th inst. by Rev. Glendy. (BA, 27 Aug. 1816)

OSGOOD, Henry, Balto. merchant and Miss Lydia Bryant, dau. of Capt. Timothy Bryant of Salem, Mass., were married in the latter place by Rev. Abbott. (BFG, 16 July 1816)

OTT, Dr. John, of Georgetown, and Miss Ann Ritchie were married last Mon. eve. at Frederick Town by Rev. Wagner. (BA, 4 Nov. 1806)

OTTERBEIN, Rev. William, died yesterday aged 87 and 5 mos.; for 60 years a minister, 40 of them in Balto. (BFG, 18 Nov. 1813)

OTTO, Anthony H., innkeeper, died last eve. in his 35th year. (BFG, 8 July 1800)

OULD, Robert, of Georgetown, and Miss Paulina Gaither of Mont. Co. were married by Rev. Reed at Washington on 27 Dec. by Rev. Reed. (BPEA, 4 Jan. 1815)

OUSLER, Alexander, deputy surveyor of Balto. Co., and Helen Daugharday of Balto. were married 1 April by Rev. Butler. (BT, 5 June 1804)

OUSLER, William, and Miss Rachel Keefer were married by Rev. Nelson. (BEP, 20 May 1811)

OVERY, Rowlin, and Miss Elizabeth Shepperd both of Balto. Co. were married last Thurs. by Rev. Hargrove. (BFG, 26 Dec. 1800)

OWEN, Kennedy, merchant, and Miss Agnes Riddell all of Balto. were married last eve. by Rev. Dr. Bend. (BFG, 19 Dec. 1806)

OWEN, Mrs. Rebecca, died yesterday in Hagerstown. "Hagerstown, Aug. 15." (BT, 27 Aug. 1806)

OWEN, Capt. William, and Miss Mary Ferguson all of Balto. were wed by Rev. Glendy last Tues. (BFG, 30 Nov. 1815)

OWENS, Joseph, and Miss Nancy Rutter both of Balto. were married last Wed. by Rev. John Hagerty. (BA, 22 April 1805)

OWENS, Thomas, and Miss Elizabeth Fass were married last eve. by Rev. Otterbein. (BFG, 2 Sept. 1808) (BEP, 2 Sept. 1808, gives the bride's name as Fays.)

OWENS, William, and Mrs. Mary Enright both of Balto. were married Sat. by Rev. Richards. (BFG, 14 Oct. 1799)

OWINGS, Mrs. Ann, wife of Dr. Thomas B. Owings, died 1st inst. in her 27th year. (BFG, 5 April 1804)

OWINGS, Beale, and Miss Eleanor B. Magruder all of Balto. were wed last eve. by Rev. Kemp. (BA, 12 Sept. 1814)

OWINGS, Beall, and Miss Ann Johnson both of Balto. Co. were wed last Thurs. eve. by Rev. Coleman. (BFG, 16 Aug. 1803)

OWINGS, Caleb, died at his farm in Balto. Co. on 26th inst. in his 84th year. (BA, 28 Feb. 1816)

OWINGS, Israel, and Miss Sarah Mummey both of Balto. Co. were wed last Thurs. by Rev. Kurtz. (BT, 21 Dec. 1802)

OWINGS, Capt. John, and Miss Long both of Balto. Co. were married last eve. by Rev. Richards. (BFG, 23 Oct. 1801)

OWINGS, Mr. John, only son of Caleb Owings, proprietor of Sulphur Springs, near Baltimore City, died 9th inst., in his 33rd year, leaving a wife and children. (BFG, 11 Oct. 1804)

OWINGS, John C., of Balto. Co., died Wed. eve. 28th April after a lingering illness. (BFG, 11 May 1813)

OWINGS, John Cockey, died last Sat. at his seat in Balto. Co. in his 75th year, a native of that county. (BFG, 6 Feb. 1810)

OWINGS, Joshua W., of A. A. Co., and Miss Elenor Worthington of Mont. Co. were married Tues., 24th inst. by Rev. Thomas Reed. (BW, 30 Dec. 1811)

OWINGS, Richard, son of Richard, and Miss Elizabeth Monro all of Balto. were married last Tues. by Rev. Richards. (BFG, 21 Dec. 1812)

OWINGS, Samuel, and Mrs. Mary Govane both of Balto. were married last Sat. eve. (BFG, 10 April 1797)

OWINGS, Samuel, died this morning at Balto. Co., aged 70 years. (BFG, 11 June 1803)

OWINGS, Samuel, died last Sun., one of the Judges of the Orphans' Court of Balto., and one of our most worthy citizens. (BA, 19 March 1816)

OWINGS, Capt. Samuel C., of Balto., and Miss Mary Yellott Willis, dau. of the late Rev. Willis, were married 3rd inst., at res. of Mrs. Ann Willis, Fred. Town, by Rev. Smith. (BFG, 10 Nov. 1814)

OWINGS, Miss Sarah, dau. of Samuel Owings of Balto., died last Mon. (BFG, 2 Oct. 1805)

OWINGS, Mrs. Susannah, wife of Caleb Owings, proprietor of the Sulphur Springs, died 8th inst. in her 71st year. (BA, 10 Sept. 1813)

OYSTON, Lawrence, died at his plantation in Patapsco Neck last Sat. in his 67th year. (BA, 24 Dec. 1799)

OZLOTTE, Peter, of Balto. and Sally Davis of Phila. were married there by Rev. Milldollar. (BA, 20 April 1801)

PACA, Hon. William, died Sun., 13th inst., at his seat in Talbot Co. (BFG, 16 Oct. 1799)

PACKET, John, and Mrs. Sidney Trownson, both of Balto., were wed Mon. by Rev. Rattoone. (BT, 7 Aug. 1805)

PAGE, Dr. James, and Miss Mary Coulter, dau. of Dr. John Coulter, all of Balto. were married last eve. by Rev. Glendy. (BFG, 9 June 1809)

PAGE, Col. John, died last Tues. at an adbanced age, commissioner of loans and late Gov. of the Commonwealth, representative of this state in Congress, one of our earliest Revolutionary patriots. (BA, 18 Oct. 1808)

PAGE, John, and Rebecca Humphreys all of Kent Co. were married 10th inst. by Rev. Simon Wilmore. (BW, 16 Aug. 1809)

PAGE, Mrs. Mary, wife of John Page of Kent Co., died 24th inst., leaving a husband and three small children. (BFG, 30 Aug. 1806)

PAGE, William B., of Loudon Co., and Miss Nancy Lee of Alexandria at Alexandria last Thurs. (BT, 16 Aug. 1797)

PAINE, William Osborne, merchant, formerly of Balto., died at New York, last Tues., 9th inst., aged 21 years and 9 mos. (BFG, 30 March 1804)

PALFRY, John, of Salem, and Miss Ann James of Balto. were married last Thurs. by Rev. Beasley. (BA, 18 March 1811)

PALMATARY, John H., and Miss Elizabeth T. Presbury all of Balto. were married last Sat., 11th inst., by Rev. Hargrove. (BEP, 13 June 1808)

PALMER, Edward, and Miss Catherine Cox all of Balto. were married last eve. by Rev. Dashiell. (BFG, 7 Sept. 1810)

PALMER, Elihu, noted apostle of atheism, died in Phila. last Mon. (BFG, 4 April 1806)

PALMER, Lieut. Loring, U. S. Army, died on his passage from Balto. to South America. (BA, 8 Oct. 1816)

PANNELL, Mrs., died last Sat. morning; wife of Edward Pannell, leaving a husband, and a numerous family. (BFG, 14 June 1802)

PANNELL, Edward, of Brandywine, Del., and Miss Deborah Jones, only dau. of Isaac Jones of Phila. were married in the latter place last Sun. by Rev. Abercrombie. (BEP, 4 Nov. 1807)

PANNELL, Edward, Jr., formerly of Balto., and Miss Caroline A.
Newton, dau. of Thomas Newton, a member of Congress from
Norfolk, were married there 12th inst. by Dr. Low. (BA,
19 Oct. 1816)

PANNELL, John, of Fells Point, died last Fri. (BFG, 7 Jan. 1799)

PANNELL, William, and Miss Sarah Pennock, dau. of William Pennock
of Norfolk, were married 13th ult. (BPEA, 27 March 1815)

PAPION, John, and Margaret Bradberry were married at Fells Point
on Thurs. by Rev. Dr. Rattoone. (BFG, 22 Sept. 1804)

PARISH, John, of Phila., member of the Soc. of Friends, died 21st
inst. at the house of Elias Ellicott. (BFG, 23 Oct. 1807)

PARK, James, merchant of Broadfield, King George Co., Va., died
last 21 Sept. (BFG, 4 Oct. 1802)

PARKER, Mrs. Elizabeth consort of Mr. George Parker, died 25th
inst. in her 45th year. (BEP, 30 Sept. 1807)

PARKER, Mrs. Elizabeth, long a res. of Balto., died yesterday.
(BW, 18 Feb. 1814)

PARKER, Gabiel (sic) John, and Mrs. Rachel Taylor of Balto. Co.
were married last Sat. by Rev. Healey. (BA, 20 March
1816)

PARKER, J. B., of Carlisle, and Miss Maria Veazey of Cecil Co.
were married at the latter place on 27th ult. by Rev. H.
L. Davis. (BFG, 11 May 1811)

PARKER, Peter, and Mrs. Elizabeth Chesney all of Balto. were wed
last eve. by Rev. Hargrove. (BFG, 16 July 1813)

PARKER, Robert, merchant, and Miss Margaret Millward both of Balto. were married last eve. by Rev. Reed. (BFG, 24 Aug.
1798) (BTD, 24 Aug. 1798, gives the bride's name as
Millford, and the minister's name as Hagerty.)

PARKER, Robert, and Mrs. Eleanor Mushberger both of Balto. were
married last eve. by Rev. Roberts. (BFG, 31 Oct. 1808)

PARKER, Thomas, Jr., of Eng., and Nelly, dau. of Samuel Owings,
Balto. merchant, were married last eve. by Rev. Joshua
Wells. (BFG, 22 Sept. 1802)

PARKER, Thomas, and Miss Elizabeth Foster both of Balto. were wed
Sun. eve. (BT, 5 June 1805)

PARKER, Thomas, and Miss Elizabeta Fowler all of Balto. were wed
Sun. eve. (BA, 5 June 1805)

PARKER, Thomas, merchant, of Charleston, S. C., and Miss Rachel
Wilkinson of Balto. Co. were married last eve. near this
Balto. (BFG, 25 June 1806)

PARKIN, Thomas, Balto, merchant, died yesterday. (BFG, 3 July
1797)

PARKS, David, and Mrs. Mary Brody all of Balto. were married
last Sun. by Rev. Bend. (BT, 20 Jan. 1801)

PARKS, Elizabeth Jane, dau. of John Parks, of Newburgh, N.Y.,
died Fri., 30th ult. at the res. of James Smith in Balto.
(BFG, 3 May 1813)

PARKS, James, late of Balto., died 4 July at Havana in his 21st year; of yellow fever. (BA, 2 Aug. 1805)

PARKS, Joshua, and Miss Mary Wheeler all of Balto. Co. were wed last Sun. by Rev. Healey. (BA, 28 July 1815)

PARKS, Mrs. Margaret, relict of the late John Parks, died 23rd inst. in her 70th year. (BFG, 26 April 1813)

PARKS, William, and Miss Sarah Franklin, both of Balto. Co., were married last Sun. by Rev. Neal. (BW, 18 Sept. 1811)

PARLETT, Benjamin, and Mrs. Elizabeth Wane of Balto. were married last Thurs. by Rev. D. E. Reese. (BA, 29 Oct. 1816)

PARMELE, James H., and Priscilla Horne both of Balto. were wed last eve. by Rev. Dr. Inglis. (BFG, 30 Sept. 1816)

PARR, David, and Miss Margaret McGowan both of Balto. were wed last Thurs. by Rev. Roberts. (BFG, 17 Aug. 1816)

PARR, Elisha, and Miss Eliza Preston all of Balto. were married by Rev. Glendy last Wed. (BA, 30 Dec. 1814)

PARROTT, Abner, printer, died yesterday in his 19th year. (Long obit.) (BFG, 22 June 1799)

PARSONS, Hiram W., of Boston, and Miss Ann Thompson of Balto. were married last Sun. eve. by Rev. Kemp. (BA, 13 Nov. 1816)

PARSONS, Thomas, and Mary Price of Balto. Co. were married at the Friends Meeting, Gunpowder, 29th inst. The groom was a merchant of Easton. (BFG, 31 May 1811)

PARSONS, Thomas, and Miss Margaret Kirkpatrick were married. (BS, 9 Nov. 1812)

PARTRIDGE, Daubner B., and Miss Harriot Willmor of Harf. Co. were married last Thurs. by Rev. Hagerty. (BS, 2 May 1812)

PARTRIDGE, James, Balto. merchant, and Miss Hannah Hollingsworth of Elkton were married there last Thurs. by Rev. Francis Hindman. (BFG, 7 May 1806)

PASCAL, Capt. Peter, of Balto. and Miss Elizabeth Nice of Easton were married there on 12th inst. by Rev. Edward Markland. (BEP, 25 May 1808)

PASCAULT, Lewis Charles, of Balto. and Miss Ann Goldsborough were married on Thurs., 30 May, at White Hall near Annapolis by Rev. Batuzy. (BFG, 3 June 1811)

PASSMORE, John, of Lancaster, Penna., and Mrs. Elizabeth Alexander of Balto. were married Mon., 18th inst., by Rev. Bend. (BEP, 27 Dec. 1809)

PASTEUR, Major Thomas, died at Bath, Buncomb Co., N. C., 29th ult., in the 46th year. He was a Revolutionary patriot. (BA, 20 Sept. 1806)

PATRICK, Daniel, died Sun., aged 49 years, leaving a widow and three children. (BA, 9 July 1816)

PATRICK, William F., merchant, and Mrs. Margaret Owens both of Balto. were married last eve. by Kurtz. (BT, 13 July 1802)

PATTEN, William, and Mrs. Ellen Conly both of Balto. were married on Sat. eve. by Rev. Roberts. (BFG, 21 July 1806)

PATTERSON, Benjamin, aged 35, died suddenly at his res. in Balto. Co., by the breaking of a blood vessel; he leaves a widow, six children, and his mother. (BEP, 16 May 1809)

PATTERSON, Mrs. Dorcas, wife of William Patterson, died Fri., 20th inst. in his 53rd year. (BPE, 23 May 1814)

PATTERSON, Edward, and Miss Sidney Smith, dau. of Gen. S. Smith, were married last eve. by Rev. Inglis. (BPEA, 21 April 1815)

PATTERSON, George, died last Fri. at Miles Hall, Harf. Co., in his 60th year. (BFG, 16 March 1808)

PATTERSON, George, and Miss Elizabeth Garman all of Balto. were married last Thurs. by Rev. Glendy. (BFG, 2 Nov. 1813)

PATTERSON, James, of Balto. died this morning. (BFG, 25 March 1806)

PATTERSON, John, of Balto. and Polly Nicholas, dau. of the Hon. Wilson Cary Nicholas of Va., were married at Warren, Va., on Sat., 31 May. (BA, 13 June 1806)

PATTERSON, John, and Miss Margaret Hinds both of Balto. were wed last Thurs. eve. by Rev. Dr. Roberts. (BFG, 12 April 1810)

PATTERSON, John, and Miss Joanna Smith both of Balto. were wed 23rd inst. by Rev. Healey. (BPEA, 24 March 1815)

PATTERSON, John W., and Miss Mary Brown both of Balto. were wed last Thurs. by Dr. Roberts. (BA, 7 Oct. 1816)

PATTERSON, Robert, of Balto., and Mary Ann Caton, dau. of Richard Caton, of Brooklandwood, were wed at Annapolis on Thurs., 1st inst. by Bishop Carroll. (BFG, 7 May 1806)

PATTERSON, Robert, and Miss Hannah Hill all of Balto. were wed by Rev. Glendy on 19th inst. (BA, 27 Aug. 1816)

PATTERSON, Thomas, and Mrs. Mary Morgan were married Thurs., 3rd inst. (BA, 25 April 1809)

PATTERSON, William, Jr., of Balto., and Miss Ann Gittings, dau. of James Gittings of Balto. Co. were married last eve. by Rev. Bend. (BFG, 22 Feb. 1804)

PATTERSON, William, died at Albany, 9th inst., one of the judges of the U. S. Circuit Court. (BFG, 18 Sept. 1806)

PATTERSON, William, Jr., died 20 Oct. in his 29th year; of the House of William and Patterson and Sons of Balto.; a husband and father. (BFG, 21 Oct. 1808)

PATTESON, Robert, of Phila. died at New Orleans, 3rd ult. (BEP, 3 Nov. 1808)

PATTON, Col. Robert, Post Master, died Sun., 2nd inst., in his 59th year. He served in the Rev. War. (BFG, 5 Jan. 1814)

PAUL, Peter, and Mrs. Elizabeth Merrell both of Balto. were wed last eve. by Rev. Rattoone. (BT, 16 March 1804)

PAULEY, James, merchant, and Miss Mary Ann Walter both of Balto. were married last eve. by Dr. Roberts. (BFG, 22 Oct. 1806)

PAULY, John, and Miss Martha Kilmer both of Balto. were married last Tues. by Rev. Otterbein. (BW, 17 March 1810)

PAWLING, Levi, of Norristown, and Miss Eliza Heister, dau. of Gen. J. Heister of Reading, were married there on Wed., 17th inst., by Rev. H. A. Muhlenberg. (BA, 27 Oct. 1804)

PAWSON, Capt. C., and Miss Eliza Graham all of Balto. were wed last Tues. by Rev. Glendy. (BA, 29 June 1815)

PAWSON, Capt. Matthew, and Miss Mary M. Brevitt, dau. of John Brevitt all of Balto. were married last Thurs. (BFG, 31 July 1807)

PAXTON, James, died at Washington on 19th ult. in his 53rd year; Commissary General of the U. S., for the State of New Jersey in the Rev. War; recently a clerk in the Treasury Dept. (BA, 27 Oct. 1804)

PAXTON, Samuel, of Balto. Co., died in his 49th year, one of the people called Quakers. (BT, 9 March 1803)

PAYSON, Miss Abigail, died Sun., 16th inst., aged 43 years. (BA, 19 Oct. 1814)

PEACH, Joseph, and Mary, dau. of Richard Peach all of P. G. Co., were married last week by Rev. Ralph. (BFG, 11 Jan. 1800)

PEALE, Mrs., of the museum in Phila., died last Sun. in Phila. (BT, 23 Feb. 1804)

PEALE, Mr. Raphaelle, and Miss M. M'Glathery both of Balto. were married on Thurs. eve. by Rev. J. B. Smith. (BFG, 31 May 1797)

PEARCE, Edward W., lawyer, native of Kent Co., Md., aged 29 years; was buried at Urbana, Ohio, on 19 Jan. (BFG, 14 Feb. 1814)

PEARSALL, John, a native of the state of N. Y., died Fri., 10th inst. (BA, 11 Jan. 1806)

PEARSON, Joseph, member of Congress from N. C., and Miss Eleanor Brent, dau. of Robert Brent of Washington, were married 3rd Oct. at the latter place by Rev. Plunket. (BFR, 4 Dec. 1811)

PECHIN, Eliza, dau. of the editor of the American, died Thurs. in her 3rd year. (BT, 30 Oct. 1802)

PECK, Mrs. Elizabeth, wife of Henry Peck, died Mon., 13 Aug., aged 18 years, leaving a husband, parents, and a 1 year old infant. (BFG, 16 Aug. 1810)

PECK, Henry, and Miss Elizabeth Culverwell all of Balto. were wed last Tues. by Dr. Roberts. (BFG, 10 Nov. 1808)

PECK, Henry, merchant, and Miss Rachel Lindenberger all of Balto. were married last Tues. by Dr. Roberts. (BFG, 24 July 1811)

PECK, John S., of Harf. Co., and Miss Ann Wilson of Balto. were married this morning by Rev. Richards. (BFG, 9 June 1803)

PEDERSON, Peter, Danish Consul-General to the U. S., and Miss
Maria Litchfield Scott, dau. of the late Lewis A. Scott
of New York, were married at Phila., 3rd inst., by Bishop
White. (BFG, 5 June 1812)

PEIRCE, Levi, of Boston, and Mary Elizabeth Williamson of Balto.
were married last eve. by Rev. Allison. (BFG, 13 Sept.
1798)

PEIRCE, William, of Phila., and Miss Ann Armstrong of Balto. were
married last Tues. by Rev. Wells. (BA, 2 Dec. 1815)

PELL, Gilbert, of Balto., died last Sat., of gout in his stomach
in his 63rd year. (BAP, 5 April 1803)

PELL, Jonathan, and Miss Mary Dwyer all of Balto. were married
last Thurs. by Rev. John Glendy. (BFG, 1 March 1816)

PENDLETON, Daniel, and Miss Lavinia Jane Ford all of Balto. were
married 27th inst. by Rev. Fectic. (BT, 5 May 1815)

PENDLETON, Edmund, of Martinsburg, Va., and Serena Catherine Purnell, dau. of Isaac Purnell of Balto., were married last
Thurs. (BFG, 2 April 1811)

PENDLETON, Major Philip, died 31 July at his seat in King and
Queen Co., Va., leaving a wife. He served in the Rev. War.
(Long obit.) (BT, 14 Aug. 1804)

PENFIELD, Ransom, died 17th inst., leaving a widow and three daus.
He was superintendent of the machine for deepening the
bason (sic) of Balto. (BA, 19 Sept. 1804)

PENN, Richard, foremrly Gov. of Penna., died in Richmond, Eng.,
on 27 May. (BA, 24 June 1811)

PENNINGTON, Mrs. Jemima, wife of Josiah Pennington, died last
night; res. near Dr. Stevenson's. (BFG, 17 April 1801)

PENNINGTON, Josias, died this morning in his 70th year. (BFG,
3 Nov. 1810)

PENNINGTON, Timothy Hanson, Balto. merchant, died 26 Sept. at
Sweet Springs, Va. (BFG, 15 Oct. 1805)

PENNY, Henry, and Miss Sarah Lowe were married 19th ult. by Rev.
George Rosewell at the seat of John Lowe in Balto. Co.
(BPEA, 7 Feb. 1815)

PENRICE, Capt. Thomas, and Mrs. Mary Ann Jones were married on
Sun., 13th inst., by Rev. Bend. (BA, 19 Aug. 1809)

PENSON, Mr., drowned near Phila. (BAP, 6 Aug. 1803)

PENTZ, Henry, Jr., and Miss Agnes Steuart, dau. of Robert Steuart,
were married last eve. by Rev. Kurtz. (BFG, 9 Feb. 1809)

PEPPLE, Peter, and Miss Rhoda Underwood of Balto. were married
last eve. by Rev. Dr. Roberts. (BEP, 24 Dec. 1806)

PERCY, Capt. Harman, and Miss Susan Henny, both of Balto., were
married last Thurs. by Rev. Glendy. (BEP, 12 July 1808)

PERHAM, Benoni, attorney at law of Balto., died 14th inst. in his
25th year; by suicide. A native of Chelmsford, Mass., he
graduated from Harvard. (Long obit.) (BFG, 15 May 1804)

MARRIAGES AND DEATHS

PERIGO, Daniel, and Miss Sophia Laurence both of Fells Point were married last Thurs. by Rev. McKane. (BEP, 31 Dec. 1808)

PERKINS, Capt. Benjamin, died this morning in his 30th year; res. in Old Town. (BFG, 1 Feb. 1799)

PERKINS, Isaac, Balto. merchant, died this morning aged 27; the funeral will be from Mrs. Way's, South St. (BFG, 6 Oct. 1812)

PERRY, Basil, and Miss Delilah Waters, dau. of Benjamin Waters of Mont. Co., were married. (BT, 14 Feb. 1801)

PERRY, Capt. Charles G., and Miss Frances L. Morris all of Fells Point were married last Thurs. by Rev. Dashiell. (BA, 2 March 1811)

PERRY, Capt. Herman, and Miss Susanna Henry both of Balto. Co. were married 5th ult. by Rev. Glendy. (BA, 2 Aug. 1808)

PERRY, Samuel, and Mary Nate were married in Portsmouth. (BPE, 20 Aug. 1813)

PERRY, Hon. William, died last Thurs. in Annapolis; president of the Senate of Md. "Annap., Jan. 17." (BFG, 21 Jan. 1799)

PETEE, James, and Miss Sarah Maddon all of Balto. were married last eve. by Rev. G. Hicks. (BA, 26 Feb. 1813)

PETER, David, and Miss Johns were married 17th inst. (BFG, 20 Sept. 1799)

PETER, Mrs. Eleanor, relict of John Peter, dec., died last Thurs. at Georgetown, Col. (BFR, 13 Feb. 1812)

PETER, Robert, died 15th inst. at Georgetown in his 81st year; he was the first Mayor of Georgetown. (BFG, 24 Nov. 1806)

PETERKIN, Capt., and Miss Spencer, were married last eve. by Rev. Rattoone. (BFG, 12 April 1803)

PETERKIN, Mrs. Eliza, died yesterday; funeral from her late res. in Market St. (BA, 5 Nov. 1816)

PETERKIN, Capt. William, died 19th inst., a shipmaster of the port and a husband and father. (BA, 23 Aug. 1816)

PETERS, Henry C., of Balto. and Miss Clarey Forrester of A. A. Co. were married last Thurs. by Rev. Swampsted. (BFG, 23 Dec. 1809)

PETERS, John, sailmaker of Balto., died yesterday. (BMJ, 14 Oct. 1796)

PETERS, Mr. Reese, and Miss Ann Walsh both of Balto. were married last eve. by Rev. Bend. (BFG, 4 April 1806)

PETERS, Lieut. William, U. S. Navy, died at St. Marys, 3rd inst. in his 27th year. (BS, 29 Nov. 1812)

PETTINGALL, Robert, and Miss Margaret Andrews were married Thurs. 8th inst. by Rev. Glendy. (BW, 21 Dec. 1808)

PETTINGALL, Robert, and Miss Sarah Shaw all of Balto. were wed last Tues., 24 Nov., by Rev. Glendy. (BFG, 28 Nov. 1812)

PETTIT, Charles, died at Phila., 4th inst., in his 70th year;
President of the Insurance Co. of North America. (BFG,
11 Sept. 1806)

PFEIFFER, Dr. George, died 6th inst. aged 35 years of dysentery,
at his res. in the Northern Liberties, leaving a wife and
five children. "Phil. paper." (BT, 14 Aug. 1804)

PHALZ, William, and Miss Dorothea Schrader, dau. of Mr. Schrader,
a tailor, were married Mon. by Rev. Kurtz. (BFR, 18 Oct.
1803)

PHELPS, Greenbury, and Kitty Poulet both of Balto. were married
last eve. by Rev. Rattoone. (BFG, 23 May 1804)

PHELPS, Joshua, and Mrs. Alicia Inglesby were married Tues., 16th
inst. by Rev. Moranvillier. (BFG, 24 April 1816)

PHENIX, Thomas, and Miss Jane Lowes Dawson, both of Balto., were
married Wed. by Dr. Wyatt. (BFG, 18 Nov. 1814)

PHILIPS, William, merchant, and Miss Eliza Robinson both of Balto. were married last eve. by Dr. Inglis. (BFG, 10 May
1805)

PHILIPS, William, of the U. S. N., and Miss Ann Parkinson of
Balto. were married Wed. at Fells Point by Rev. Rattoone.
(BFG, 14 Oct. 1808)

PHILLIPS, Abraham, and Miss Mary Ryan were married in Phila. (BT,
17 May 1799)

PHILLIPS, Benjamin Hammet, died in Curacao on last 14 March in
his 47th year; consul-general for the U. S. to that land.
(BFG, 17 May 1803)

PHILLIPS, Capt. Isaac, and Miss Ann Goldthwait, dau. of Samuel
Goldthwait of Balto., were married last Sat. by Rev. John
Ireland. (BFG, 9 June 1801)

PHILLIPS, James, died Tues., 14 June, at Chilberry, Harf. Co.,
in his 63rd year. (BFG, 2 July 1803)

PHILLIPS, James, died last Mon. at Chelsea, his seat in Harf. Co.,
who had just reached his 41st year. He leaves a widow and
infant dau., an aged mother and several sisters. (BFG, 15
Feb. 1812)

PHILLIPS, John, son of James Phillips, Esq., died Mon., 27th inst.
at Chilberry, Harf. Co. (BFG, 1 Oct. 1802)

PHILLIPS, Mrs. Sarah, wife of Capt. Isaac Phillips, died yesterday. Interment in the Meth. burying ground after a funeral
from her late res. in Bank St., opposite Mrs. Taylor's.
(BFG, 20 Aug. 1799)

PHILPOT, Bryan, died 11th inst., at his farm in Balto. Co., aged
57 years. He was an officer in the Maryland Line and he
leaves a widow and six children. (BFG, 15 April 1812)

PHILPOTT, Mrs. Mary, consort of late Thomas Philpott, died last
Mon. in her 22nd year. (BFG, 25 Feb. 1802)

PHILPOTT, Thomas, and Miss Maria Jacob both of Balto. were wed
last eve. by Rev. Hagerty. (BFG, 25 May 1799)

PHROW, John Lewis, of Charleston, S. C., and Miss Elizabeth Deaver of Balto. were married Sun. by Rev. Dr. Roberts. (BFR, 12 Dec. 1809)

PHYSICK, Edmund, died in Phila., 7th inst., aged 78 years, formerly receiver general and keeper of the great seals of the then province of Penna. (BT, 21 June 1804)

PICKERING, Jacob, and Miss Ann Conley both of Balto. were married Sat. by Rev. Kurtz. (BPEA, 27 June 1815)

PICKET, John, and Miss Elizabeth Rea both of Balto. were married last eve. by Rev. McCombs. (BFG, 28 May 1802)

PICKET, Levi, and Miss Mary Brown both of Balto. were married last eve. by Rev. Kurtz. (BEP, 21 Aug. 1808)

PICKETT, John, of Balto. and Miss Mary Taylor of Balto. Co. were married Thurs. by Rev. Dashiell. (BFG, 11 June 1808)

PIERCE, Levi, of Boston and Miss Mary Elizabeth Williamson of Balto. were married Wed. by Rev. Allison. (BTD, 15 Sept. 1798)

PIERCY, Capt. Henry, died last Sun. at Alexandria, aged 53; served in the Rev. War. (Long obit.) (BFG, 23 June 1809)

PIERCY, Henry, and Miss Hannah Duty all of Balto. were married Sun. eve., 1st inst., by Rev. Kurtz. (BFG, 3 March 1812)

PIERPOINT, Amos, died 20 Feb., aged 55 years and 9 days. (BPEA, 28 Feb. 1815)

PIERPOINT, Hannah, widow, died 19 Feb., aged 87 years and 21 days, in Balto. Co. (BPEA, 28 Feb. 1815)

PIERPOINT, Mrs. Mary, died yesterday in her 54th year; res. near Ellicott's Lower Mill. (BFG, 16 April 1816)

PIERPOINT, Mr. Misale, and Miss Mary Ann Williams, both of A. A. Co., were married in Balto. yesterday, by Rev. Dr. Kemp. (BA, 24 Dec. 1814)

PIERPONT, Mrs. Elizabeth, died last Tues., 8th inst., at Elk Ridge about 60 years old; member of the Society of Friends. (BFG, 14 Sept. 1802)

PIERREPOINT, Charles, died last Sun., aged 5 years and 10 days. (BT, 21 June 1804)

PIERREPOINT, Joseph, died 9th inst. at his res. at Elk Ridge, aged 86; for many years a preacher among the Society of Friends. (BFG, 12 April 1806)

PIERREPOINT, Thomas, died Tues. night, aged 27 years. He leaves a wife and 2 children. (BFG, 11 Sept. 1800)

PIKE, James, pilot of Balto., died Mon., 20th ult. on the brig Susan and Francis in Annapolis Roads. He was 49 years, 11 mos. and 2 days. Interment at Annapolis. (BW, 4 April 1809)

PILKINGTON, Thomas, and Miss Cyrene Dorset were married at Havre de Grace last Tues. by Rev. James W. Wilmer. (BS, 21 Nov. 1812)

PILLAR, William, of Balto., died this morning in his 63rd year. (BFG, 11 Sept. 1809)

PINDEL, Dr. Edward, of Balto. and Miss Frances T. Cockey were married last Tues. at "Cool Spring," by Rev. Richards. (BFR, 20 Dec. 1811)

PINDLE, James, and Henry Pindle, sons of Charles R. Pindle, were drowned yesterday in the Bason, near the mouth of Jones Falls. James was 12, and Henry was in his 8th year. (BFG, 3 Aug. 1810)

PINKERTON, William, and Miss Eliza Littig both of Balto. Co. were married last eve. by Rev. Armstrong. (BFG, 24 Nov. 1806)

PINKNEY, Jonathan, of Balto. and Mrs. Rebecca Davidson of Annapolis were married there by Rev. Higginbothom on 28th ult. (BFG, 5 Nov. 1804)

PINKNEY, Ninian, Secretary to the Governor and Council of Md., and Amelia Hobbs were married Thurs. eve. (BFG, 5 May 1806)

PINKNEY, William, Jr., and Miss Jane B. Hammond were married 29 Nov. by Rev. Dr. Kemp. (BFG, 30 Nov. 1813)

PIPER, James, Balto. merchant, died this morning in his 55th year. (BFG, 30 Oct. 1802)

PIPER, James, merchant, and Miss Jane Evans, dau. of Wm. Evans, all of Balto. were married last eve. by Rev. Dashiell. (BFG, 20 Nov. 1805)

PIPER, Mrs. Margaret, wife of James Piper of Balto., died leaving a husband and infant daughter. (BFG, 30 Sept. 1801)

PITT, Capt. Richard, and Ann Barry, dau. of Capt. Barry, all of Fells Point, were married last eve. by Rev. Bend. (BA, 15 April 1801)

PLEASANTS, Mrs. Ann Cleves, wife of John P. Pleasants, Balto. merchant, died last week at the res. of M. Bird, Berkley Co., Va. (BFG, 30 June and 1 July 1801)

PLEASANTS, John P., and Miss Mary Hall all of Balto. were married last eve. by Bishop Kemp. (BFG, 20 May 1816)

PLISTER, Stephen, and Miss Elizabeth Moore all of Fells Point were married last Thurs. by Rev. McCain. (BA, 4 May 1813)

PLOWDEN, Edmund, died last 20 April, of St. M. Co. (Long obit.) (BFG, 9 May 1804)

PLUMER, Joseph P., of South River, and Susanna Husband of Balto. were married yesterday at Friends Meeting. (BFG, 14 March 1806)

PLUMMER, Gerard, and Mary Hopkins, dau. of Richard Hopkins, were married Thurs., 25 Feb., in A. A. Co. (BFG, 5 March 1802)

POCHON, Charles Francis, and Miss Harriott Phillips, dau. of James Phillips, all of Balto. were married last eve. by Archbishop Carroll. (BFG, 17 Feb. 1815)

POE, Mrs., formerly Miss Arnold, late of the Phila. theatre, died 8th inst. at Richmond, Va. (BFR, 16 Dec. 1816)

POE, Mrs. Catherine, died last Thurs. at Havre de Grace; consort of George Poe of Balto., in her 65th year. Interment in the Presbyterian burying ground. (BFG, 20 Aug. 1806)

POE, David, native of Ireland, and for the last 40 years a resident of Balto., died yesterday in his 74th year. He was active in the Rev. War. (BFG, 18 Oct. 1816)

POE, George, of Balto., and Miss Maria Potts of Phila. were married there by Rev. Abercrombie. (BEP, 2 Jan. 1809)

POE, Jacob, merchant, and Miss B. Kennedy both of Balto. were wed last eve. by Rev. Inglis. (BFG, 5 Jan. 1803)

POGUE, James, died yesterday in his 37th year. (BFG, 19 April 1804)

POLE, Thomas, of Balto., and Miss Jane Gwynn of Balto. Co. were wed last Sun. by Rev. Dr. Roberts. (BEP, 10 Dec. 1807)

POLK, Dr., of the House of Polk and McHenry, merchants, died last Sat. morning. (BFG, 1 May 1804)

POLK, Dr. Gillis M. W. R., of Som. Co., and Miss Hetty Sitler of Balto. were married on Wed. by Rev. Richards. (BFG, 26 Feb. 1801)

POLK, Josiah, of Somerset, and Rebecca Troup of Easton, were wed 6th inst. at Easton. (BA, 21 July 1804)

POLK, William, died in Som. Co., on 2nd inst., Chief Judge of the Fourth Judicial Circuit of Md. (BFG, 11 Dec. 1812)

POLLARD, Seth, and Miss Maria Wheeler both of Balto. were wed last eve. by Rev. Shane. (BS, 20 April 1812)

POLLOCK, John, and Miss Esther Powell were married in Phila. (BPE, 4 Jan. 1813)

POLLOCK, John, and Miss Mary Warren were married 24th ult. by Rev. Healey. (BA, 20 Jan. 1814)

POLLOCK, Oliver, of Carlisle, Penna., and Mrs. Winefred Anne Deady of Balto. were married last Sat. by Bishop Carroll. (BFG, 5 Nov. 1805)

POLOCK, Elias, Balto. merchant, and Miss Rebecca Hart of Phila. were married there on 20th inst. by Rev. Cohen. (BT, 28 Aug. 1806)

POLSEN, Levin, and Caroline Lemont both of Balto. were married on Wed. by Rev. Rattoone. (BA, 31 May 1806)

POMPEY, a Black man, in Delaware, died Sat., 28th ult., in 120th year, near Dover. (BA, 6 Aug. 1804)

PONCET, L., and Miss Catherine R. Ducasse were married last Thurs. by Rev. Richards. (BA, 28 Dec. 1805)

PONEY, Samuel B., formerly of Balto., died 4th inst., near Newbern, N.E. (BA, 25 Aug. 1801)

PONTIER, Anthony, died yesterday, for many years an inhab. of Balto., leaving a wife and four children. (BFG, 2 Feb. 1816)

POOL, George Washington, and Miss Sarah Rowles all of Balto. were married last eve. by Rev. Shane. (BFG, 21 Aug. 1807)

POOL, James, and Miss Mary Ann McFadden of Balto. were married Thurs., 12th inst. by Rev. Hemphill. (BFG, 14 Dec. 1816)

POOL, Joseph, combmaker, died 30th ult. in Balto.; father and husband. (BT, 4 Oct. 1800)

POOL, Rezin, and Ann Hance both of Balto. were married Thurs. by Rev. Kurtz. (BFG, 28 April 1804)

POOLE, Edward, and Miss Jane Higginson both of Annapolis were wed Sun., 4th inst. (BFG, 7 June 1797)

POOR, Dudley, merchant, and Miss Deborah Hibernia O'Donnell, 2nd dau. of the late John O'Donnell all of Balto. were married last Sat. by Rev. Dr. Inglis. (BA, 16 May 1814)

POOR, John H., merchant, and Miss Jane Etting Taylor were married last eve. by Rev. Inglis. (BFG, 9 Aug. 1815)

POOR, Capt. Nathaniel, died at Newburyport, aged 65. (Long obit.) (BA, 19 Feb. 1806)

POOR, Capt. Samuel, and Mrs. Mary Naeton were married 21st inst. by Rev. Rattoone. (BA, 30 July 1808)

POPE, Folger, merchant, and Miss Ann Riley both of Balto. were married last eve. by Rev. Welch. (BFG, 25 Feb. 1808)

POPE, George C., died Thurs., aged 23. (BA, 6 Aug. 1799)

POPE, Henry, and Miss Maria Horn were married last eve. by Rev. Brown. (BFG, 7 June 1815)

POPE, John, U. S. Sen., and Miss Eliza J. D. Johnson, dau. of the late Joshua Johnson of Washington were married there on Sat., 11th inst. (BEP, 20 Feb. 1810)

PORTER, Alexander, of Del., and Miss Ann Porter, dau. of Capt. David Porter of Balto., were married last Thurs. at St. Georges, by Rev. Collins. (BT, 10 Nov. 1803)

PORTER, Major General Andrew, surveyor general of Penna., died on 16 Nov. at Harrisburg, Penna. in his 71st year. "Another hero of the Revolution gone." (BFG, 24 Nov. 1813)

PORTER, Capt. David, of Balto., died 24 June at New Orleans. (BA, 5 Aug. 1808)

PORTER, John, and Mrs. Elizabeth Commegys, all of Sassafras Neck Cecil Co., were married 1st inst. by Rev. Davis. (BA, 9 May 1806)

PORTER, Joshua, of Phila. fell from the wharf onto a spar and was killed immediately, leaving a wife and five small children. (BT, 3 March 1802)

PORTER, Mrs. Rebecca, wife of Capt. David Porter of The Observatory, died last Mon. in her 46th year. (BFG, 3 Sept. 1801)

PORTER, Thomas, and Mrs. Eleanor M'Neale all of Balto. were married by (Rev. Rattoone?).

PORTER, William, and Miss Jane Pannell, dau. of Edward Pannell, all of Balto. were married last Wed. by Rev. Inglis. (BFG, 23 July 1803)

PORTIOUS, William, merchant of Barbadoes, died yesterday at James Bryden's, of a liver complaint. (BT, 12 Oct. 1804)

POSEY, Adrian, and Mrs. Margaret Burns all of Balto. were wed last eve. by Archbishop Carroll. (BMG, 15 Aug. 1815)

POSEY, Alexander, aged 21, late officer on board the ship Thomas Wilson, of Balto., died 8 March in Chas. Co. (BA, 21 March 1808)

POST, Eve, died a few days ago, aged 106, a native of Germany. For the last seven years she lived in the Alms House and House of Employment. "Phil. paper." (BFG, 17 July 1811)

POTE, Anna Maria, died at Phila., 22nd ult. She was born in Germany on 20 Jan. 1702, and married Peter Pote by whom she had six children. She had 40 grandchildren, 45 great-grand children, and 7 great-great-grandchildren. On the 27th ult. she was interred in the burying ground at Kensington. (BFG, 3 March 1803)

POTEET, Jesse, and Nancy Taylor, both of Balto., were married on Sun. by Rev. Richards. (BA, 20 Nov. 1811)

POTT, Hon. John, U. S. Sen., and Miss Eliza J. D. Johnson, dau. of the late Joshua Johnson of Balto., were married Sun., 11th inst. (BA, 20 Feb. 1810)

POTTER, Capt. Charles, died at Richmond on 28th ult. Although he was blind, he commanded a packet to and from Phila. for many years. (BFG, 3 Jan. 1807)

POTTER, Dr. Nathaniel, and Miss Kitty Goldsborough were married Sun., 3 June in Tal. Co., at Belleair, the seat of Mrs. Catherine Goldsborough, by Rev. Bowie. (BFG, 22 June 1798)

POTTER, Samuel J., member of the U. S. Sen., died in Washington a few days ago. "Alexandria - Jan. 17." (BFG, 18 Jan. 1805)

POTTS, Isaac, of Cheltenham, Mont. Co., died 15th inst. at Germantown, aged 52 years; for many years a minister of the Gospel among the people called Quakers. (Long obit.) (BFG, 25 June 1803)

POTTS, Miss Rebecca, dau. of Richard Potts, died Tues., 21st inst. at Frederick Town. (BT, 28 Feb. 1804)

POTTS, Mrs. Susan, consort of William Potts, and dau. of William Campbell of this county, died at Frederick Town on 10th inst. in her 26th year. (BFR, 20 May 1812)

POTTS, William, Balto. merchant, and Miss Susannah Campbell, dau. of William Campbell of Fred. Co., were married Tues., 17th inst. by Rev. Mr. Bowers. (BEP, 31 March 1807)

POUDER, Mrs. Elizabeth, wife of Leonard Pouder of Balto., died 14th inst., aged 35 years. (BA, 23 March 1807)

POUDER, George, and Miss Mary Fouble all of Balto. were married Thurs., 15th inst., by Rev. Hoffman. (BA, 20 Feb. 1816)

POUDER, John, son of Jacob Pouder, died 10th inst. in his 24th
year at Westminster. (BFG, 14 Nov. 1814)

POULSON, Samuel, and Miss Polly Julia Gist, dau. of Col. Joshua
Gist both of Fred. Co. were married last eve. by Rev. Wm.
Dunken of Balto. (BFG, 4 June 1804)

POULSON, Zachariah, printer, father of the editor of the American Daily Advertiser, died at Phila. on Sat., 14th inst.,
in his 67th year. A native of Copenhagen, Denmark, he
emigrated with his father to this country in 1749. Interment in the Moravian Cemetery. (BT, 18 Jan. 1804)

POULTNEY, Anthony, member of the Society of Friends, died 24th
inst. at New Market. (BFG, 1 Aug. 1805)

POWELL, Mrs. Ann, died in Phila., aged 82. (BPE, 20 Aug. 1813)

POWELL, Thomas, and Miss Hannah Clarke, both of this county, were
married last Sun. by Rev. Glendy. (BA, 20 Jan. 1807)

POWELL, Thomas, and Miss Elizabeth Foster, all of Fells Point,
were wed last Thurs. by Rev. M'Caine. (BA, 22 Dec. 1807)

POWELL, William, and Miss Elizabeth Blake both of Fells Point
were married Thurs. eve. by Rev. Bend. (BW, 6 May 1809)

POWER, John, Balto. merchant, and Miss Ann H. Cruse, dau. of
Thomas Cruse of Alexandria, were married last Sat. by Rev.
Meade. (BA, 17 Dec. 1812)

POWERS, James, and Miss Rachel Floyd, dau. of Joseph Floyd, all
of Balto. Co., were married yesterday at Mt. Pleasant by
Rev. Lucas. (BFG, 4 Jan. 1809)

POWERS, John, of Phila., and Miss Elizabeth A. Sloan of Balto.
were married Sat. by Rev. Bend. (BT, 27 Jan. 1799)

POWERS, John, and Miss Helen Wheeler, all of Balto., were wed
last eve. by Rev. Fenwick. (BA, 3 Aug. 1813)

POWNALL, Mrs. Mary Ann, died 11th inst., in her 40th year, at
Charleston; a celebrated singer. (BFG, 3 Sept. 1796)

POYNTELL, William, for many years an inhab. of Phila., died there
last Tues. eve. (BFG, 14 Sept. 1811)

PRABSTING, Theodore, and Miss Frances Bohn, dau. of Charles Bohn,
Balto. merchant, were married last Thurs. by Rev. Kurtz.
(BFG, 5 Oct. 1811)

PRATHER, James, of Fred. Co., died. (BPEA, 24 March 1815)

PRATHER, Josiah, and Sarah Howard, both from P. G. Co., were wed
last Tues. eve. by Rev. Mr. McCormick. (BT, 11 April 1800)

PRATT, Mrs. Fanny, widow of the late Frederick Pratt, died Sat.,
28th inst., in her 52nd year. (BPEA, 2 May 1816)

PRATT, J. W., late Deputy Marshall of the District of Columbia,
died 5th inst. in Washington. (BFG, 11 April 1807)

PRATT, James Sylvester, formerly of Chelsea, Mass., but for some
years past a res. of Fells Point, died last Sat., in his
30th year. Interment in the Presbyterian burying ground.
He leaves a widow and a father. (BFG, 19 July 1796)

PRATT, John Horace, and Mrs. Martha Linvill, both of Balto. were married last eve. by Rev. Richards. (BT, 15 June 1804)

PRATT, Mrs. Susanna, consort of Henry Pratt, died yesterday in her 40th year. "Phila., June 15." (BFG, 17 June 1816)

PRATTEN, Mrs. Caroline Frances, dau. of the late Dr. Charles Frederick Wiesenthal, died yesterday morning in her 56th year; res. on Second St., near the Centre Market. (BFG, 13 April 1804)

PRENDEVILLE, Mr. Garrett, died last eve. in his 62nd year, an old inhab. of Fells Point; res. on Thames St. (BFG, 13 Feb. 1813)

PRENTISS, John M., Balto. merchant, and Miss Sarah Mackay Hunt, granddau. of the late Mungo Mackay, were married in Boston 14th inst. by Rev. Lowell. (BFG, 20 Sept. 1813)

PRESBURY, Mrs. Elizabeth, consort of George Presbury, died Thurs., 13th inst., aged 63 years. (BFG, 20 Dec. 1810)

PRESBURY, Mrs. Frances Gouldsmith, wife of Joseph Presbury of Fells Point, died yesterday in her 41st year. (BFG, 8 Oct. 1807)

PRESBURY, George G., of Middle River Neck, died last Wed. in his 51st year. (BFG, 3 Oct. 1810)

PRESBURY, Joseph, and Miss Frances Douglass all of Balto. were wed last eve. by Rev. Hargrove. (BFG, 23 Sept. 1808)

PRESBURY, Mr. Walter, son of George G. Presbury, and Mrs. Mary Galloway, both of Middle River Neck, Balto. Co., were wed last eve. by Rev. John Ireland. (BFG, 1 Sept. 1797)

PRESBURY, Walter Gouldsmith, son of George G. Presbury of Balto., died 5th inst. in his 27th year, in Middle River Neck. He leaves a wife and infant dau. (BFG, 6 Oct. 1801)

PRESSTMAN, Mrs. Frances, wife of George Presstman, died Sun. last in her 60th year; interment in the Baptist burying ground. (BFG, 23 Jan. 1805)

PRESSTMAN, Thomas, merchant, and Mrs. Phoebe Kelly both of Balto. were married Thurs. last by Rev. Richards. (BFG, 11 March 1797)

PRESSTMAN, William, died yesterday in his 50th year; res. in Goodman St. (BA, 2 Sept. 1816)

PREVAIL, John, and Miss Amelia Bursey both of Balto. were married last Thurs. by Rev. Bun. (BT, 4 Oct. 1806)

PRICE, Benjamin L., of St. M. Co., and Averilla J. Smith of Harf. Co. were married last Tues. by Rev. Greenbury Ridgely. (BFG, 17 Jan. 1807)

PRICE, Benjamin L., died this morning in his 29th year, leaving a widow and three small children; res. at No. 9 Market St., Fells Point. (BW, 13 April 1812)

PRICE, David, of Harford Town, drowned last Sat. while attempting to cross a stream near Stafford, leaving a wife and two children. (BFG, 1 Aug. 1810)

PRICE, Frederick, attorney-at-law of Balto., and Miss Penelope D. Owings, dau. of John C. Owings of Balto., were married on Sun. by Rev. Glendy. (BFG, 21 March 1809)

PRICE, Frederick, lawyer, died yesterday at his res. in Balto. Co. in his 34th year. (BFG, 9 Dec. 1813)

PRICE, James, died this morning in his 60th year; res. near Towson's Tavern, York Turnpike. (BFG, 31 March 1814)

PRICE, Jesse, of Balto. Co., and Miss Ellen Cooper of Balto. were married last Thurs. by Rev. Roberts. (BA, 4 March 1816)

PRICE, John, of the house of Messrs. T. Junno and J. Price of Charleston, S. C., died Sat. night at his lodging in the Indian Queen Hotel. (BFG, 8 Sept. 1807)

PRICE, John H., and Miss Rachel Jean all of Balto. were married on Thurs. by Rev. Roberts. (BFG, 14 May 1813)

PRICE, Joseph, and Mrs. Rhoda Hanes were married in Gunpowder Forest on 23rd ult. by Rev. Collister. (BT, 5 June 1805)

PRICE, Philip, Jr., of Phila., and Eliza Coale, dau. of Isaac Coale of Harf. Co., were married at Deer Creek Friends Meeting, Harf. Co. (BFG, 5 Sept. 1815)

PRICE, Richard, and Miss Phoebe Coates both of Balto., were wed last eve. by Rev. Otterbein. (BFG, 2 Dec. 1801)

PRICE, Samuel, and Elizabeth Pits, dau. of James Pits all of Balto Co., were married last Thurs. by Rev. Armstrong. (BFG, 13 Feb. 1806)

PRICE, Capt. William, and Margaret Pinder Sears all of Balto. were married on Sun. by Rev. Hargrove. (BA, 14 June 1806)

PRICE, William, died 26th ult. at his res. in Sassafras Neck, Cecil Co., in his 22nd year. (BEP, 4 Aug. 1807)

PRICE, William, and Mrs. Fanny Donaldson both of Balto. Co. were married last Sun. by Rev. Parks. (BPE, 5 Aug. 1813)

PRICE, William W., of the House of Clark and Price, auctioneers of Balto., died; interment in the family burying ground. (BFG, 27 Sept. 1805)

PRIESTLEY, Mrs., wife of Dr. Joseph Priestley, died at Northumberland, Penna., on 21st inst. (BFG, 6 Oct. 1796)

PRIESTLEY, Dr. Joseph, died 6 Feb. 1804 He would have been 71 next 24 March. "Pep. Argus." (BT, 18 Feb. 1804)

PRILL, Mrs. Elizabeth, widow of the late Frederick Prill of Balto., died Wed., 2nd inst., in her 52nd year, leaving six children. (BFG, 4 Sept. 1812)

PRINGLE, Mark, merchant, and Miss Lucy Stith, both of Balto., were married last eve. by Rev. Mr. Ireland, at "Willow Brook," the seat of Thorowgood Smith. (BFG, 7 July 1797)

PRINGLE, Mark Udny, merchant, and Miss Catherine James all of Balto. were married last Tues. by Rev. Bend. (BFG, 19 April 1809)

PRIOR, Joseph B., and Miss Mary Parker, both of Balto., were wed last Wed. by Rev. Shane. (BEP, 18 Aug. 1810)

PRITCHETT, Mr. Elijah, and Miss Ann Todd, all of Balto., were wed last Tues. by Rev. Fectic. (BA, 13 July 1816)

PROBERT, James, and Mrs. Mary Veal, both of Balto., were married last eve. by Rev. Bend. (BA, 14 June 1799)

PROCTOR, Isaiah P., died this morning, aged about 30 years, leaving a wife and four children. Masonic brethren are to attend funeral from his late res. in Liberty St., Old Town. (BEP, 11 Sept. 1807)

PROCTOR, Jesse, aged 10, son of Isaac, drowned yesterday in the Bason. (BFG, 3 Aug. 1810)

PROCTOR, Gen. Thomas, died at Phila., Sun. in his 68th year. (BFG, 19 March 1806)

PROCTOR, Thomas, of Balto., and Miss Maria Hakins of Harf. Co. were married on 13th inst. in Harf. Co. by Rev. Samuel Martin. (BA, 17 Aug. 1807)

PROCTOR, William, merchant, and Anna, dau. of John Wilson, all of Fells Point were married 16th inst. at Friends Meeting House in the Eastern Precinct. (BFG, 18 Nov. 1809)

PROSPER, Thomas, and Mrs. Elizabeth Binger both of Balto. were married Thurs. by Rev. Rattoone. (BFG, 2 Sept. 1806)

PROUD, Elizabeth, died last Mon., dau. of John Proud of New Bedford, Mass. (BFG, 15 July 1808)

PROUD, John G., merchant, and Miss Eliza Coale, dau. of the late Dr. Samuel Stringer Coale, were married last eve. by Rev. Bend. (BFG, 26 Oct. 1804)

PROUD, William T., and Miss Mary Coale were married last eve. by Rev. Kemp. (BFG, 10 Dec. 1813)

PROVINES, James, and Martha Wiley both of Balto. were married on Fri. by Rev. Annon. (BA, 6 Feb. 1805)

PRYON, Peter, and Mrs. Margaret Cole, both of Fells Point, were wed last Sat. (BMJ, 24 March 1796)

PUE, Dr. Arthur, and Miss Rebecca Ridgely Buchanan were married last Spring at Auburn. (BFG, 13 Nov. 1800)

PUE, Caleb, of Balto. Co., and Miss Emily Elizabeth Dorsey, dau. of Archibald Dorsey of Elk Ridge, were married at Elk Ridge on Sun. by Rev. Birch. (BA, 6 March 1816)

PUE, Edward, and Miss Sarah Rutter, dau. of Capt. Solomon Rutter, all of Balto. were married last Thurs. by Rev. Dashiell. (BFG, 23 May 1808)

PUE, Miss Priscilla, dau. of the late Dr. Pue, died last Tues. (BFG, 2 March 1799)

PUGH, David, and Miss Hetty Munday, all of Balto., were married last eve. by Rev. Kurtz. (BFG, 14 Sept. 1815)

PUGH, Mrs. Hetty, wife of David Pugh, and dau. of William Munday of Balto., died 12th inst., in her 25th yr. (BA, 15 May 1816)

PULCIFER, John H., of Mass., and Miss Margaret Blanch of Balto. were married Tues. eve. by Rev. Rattoone. (BFG, 9 Oct. 1806)

PULCIFER, John H., formerly of Mass., and lately a res. of Balto., died at Phila. on 20 May of small pox, leaving a wife and parents. (BA, 31 May 1808)

PURDIN, Mrs. Elizabeth, wife of Joseph Purdin of Balto., died last Sun., in her 51st year. (BFG, 16 Oct. 1804)

PURDIN, Joseph, died last eve. in his 54th year. (BFG, 20 April 1805)

PURKET, John, and Miss Sidney Trownson both of Balto. were married Mon. eve. by Rev. Rattoone. (BFG, 7 Aug. 1805)

PURNELL, Mrs., wufe of Isaac Purnell, died Sat., 2nd inst., in Caroline Co. (BA, 8 June 1805)

PURNELL, Lemuel, of Centreville, and Charlotte Wright Pratt, dau. of Henry Pratt, were married at Routhburg, Q. A. Co., on Tues., 28th ult., by Rev. Simon Wilmer. (BFG, 4 Sept. 1804)

PURVIANCE, Mrs. Eliza, died Sat.; wife of James Purviance. (BFG, 9 Aug. 1815)

PURVIANCE, Henry, died at Lexington Co., in Sept. (BW, 1 Oct. 1811)

PURVIANCE, Capt. Hugh, son of Robert Purviance of Balto., capt. of the schooner *Perseverance*, of Balto., died at Jacquemel on 4th ult., in his 19th year. (BFG, 10 Feb. 1797)

PURVIANCE, James, and Miss Eliza Young, both of Balto., were wed last eve. by Rev. Allison. (BT, 24 Nov. 1797)

PURVIANCE, John, and Miss A. Dugan, dau. of Cumberland Dugan, were married last eve. by Rev. Dr. Allison. (BFG, 4 Jan. 1799)

PURVIANCE, Miss Letitia, eld. dau. of the late Samuel Purviance, died last Wed. in her 34th year. (BFG, 13 Nov. 1802)

PURVIANCE, Robert, died yesterday in his 74th year. (BFG, 10 Oct. 1806)

PURVIANCE, Robert, and Miss Young, dau. of the late Hugh Young of Balto., were married Tues., 8th inst., by Rev. Inglis. (BFG, 15 Sept. 1812)

PURVIS, William, and Miss Hannah Kuyll, were married by Rev. Glendy on 19th ult. (BA, 5 Oct. 1809)

PUSSY, Thomas, and Miss Mary Wilde, dau. of Richard Wilde all of Balto. Co., were married last Tues. eve. by Bishop Carroll. (BFG, 23 July 1802)

PUTSER, David, aged 10, son of Mr. Martin Putsar of Liberty St., died Fri., 16th inst. (BFG, 20 Aug. 1816)

QUAIL, Capt., of the brig Saunders, died at Lisbon on 27 April. (BFG, 8 July 1811)

QUARTERMAS, John, native of Eng., died a few days ago in Hopewell Twp., York Co., Penna., aged 108 years. (BFG, 14 Jan. 1804)

QUINBY, Capt. Benjamin, and Mrs. Margaretta C. Brown all of Balto. were married last Thurs. eve. by Rev. Mr. Glendy. (BA, 13 May 1806)

QUINCY, Thomas Barton, son of Abraham, of Balto., died aged 3 years and 9 mos. (BPE, 23 Sept. 1813)

QUINLAN, Patrick, merchant, and Mrs. Mary Gamble of Fells Point were married Thurs. eve. by Rev. Moranville. (BW, 8 Oct. 1808)

QUINLEY, Benjamin, and Mrs. Margaret C. Brown both of Balto. were married last Thurs. eve. by Rev. Glendy. (BT, 10 May 1806)

QUISICK, Miss Mary, died Sat. eve., aged 13 years, dau. of John Quisick of Fells Point. She hand gone to a sand bank to obtain some sand, and the bank collapsed on her. (BFG, 3 March 1801)

QUYNN, Allen, died at Annapolis last Tues. morning in his 77th year, for 25 years a member of the House of Delegates of Maryland. (BFG, 14 Nov. 1803)

QUYNN, John, of Annapolis, and Miss Maria Leakin of Balto. were married last eve. by Rev. Bend. (BFG, 27 Aug. 1806)

RAATJES, Capt. Michael, died yesterday in his 59th year at the house of Paul Hartman. He was a native of Amsterdam and for many years was a merchant in St. Eustatia. (BFG, 29 Dec. 1796)

RABB, Adam Gotlieb, died this morning; res. at Saratoga and Liberty Sts. (BFG, 30 Oct. 1813)

RABB, William, merchant of Charleston, died. (BMJ, 8 Aug. 1796)

RABBA, Mr. Simon, put an end to his own existence yesterday eve. (BFG, 22 Sept. 1802)

RABORG, Christopher, Jr., of Balto., and Miss Ann Goddard of Phila. were married last Wed. by Rev. Dr. Green, in Phila. (BFG, 14 March 1806)

RABORG, Christopher, died this morning in his 70th year; res. in Water St. (BFG, 17 June 1815)

RABORG, Mrs. Eve M., wife of William Raborg, died 10th inst., in her 56th year. (BFR, 12 March 1812)

RABORG, John, son of Christopher Raborg, and Miss Rebecca Chandley, both of Balto., were married at Havre de Grace on 16th inst., by Rev. Mr. Stephenson. (BA, 31 July 1807)

RABORG, Samuel, of Balto. and Miss Henrietta Winemiller of Fred. Town were married last Tues. by Rev. Dashields. (BFR, 4 July 1811)

RABORG, William, and Mrs. Mary Eislen were married last eve. by Rev. Dashiells. (BFG, 2 Sept. 1812)

RABORG, William, died 19th inst., aged 66, native of Phila., but long an inhab. of Balto. (BFG, 21 Dec. 1815)

RACKE, Hieronimus, and Miss Dorothea Schrader all of Balto. were married last Fri. by Rev. Mr. Mertz. (BA, 22 Feb. 1812)

RAGAN, Col. John, died Sat., 4th inst., at his res. in Hagerstown, in his 86th year. (Long obit gives details of his military career. (BFG, 13 May 1816)

RAINES, David, and Miss Jane Phillips of Balto., were married on Tues. eve. last by Rev. Glendy. (BA, 17 Feb. 1807)

RALPH, Rev. George, professor of Rehtoric, University of Md., died at Pomona, Balto. Co., on 17th inst. in his 61st year. (Long obit.) (BFG, 22 May 1813)

RAMBO, Joseph, and Sarah Powell, were married last Thurs. by Rev. Ustick. (BA, 26 Aug. 1801)

RAMPLEY, James, and Miss Elizabeth Nelson both of Harf. Co., were married there on 9 Jan. by Rev. Rockland. (BA, 3 April 1812)

RAMSAY, Charles, and Miss Sarah Hutchinson were married last Sun. by Rev. Rattoone. (BFG, 27 July 1807)

RAMSAY, James, merchant, and Ann Neilson both of Balto. were wed last eve. at the seat of N. R. Moore by Rev. John Glendy. (BA, 11 April 1806)

RAMSAY, John, died Tues. at his house on the Little York Road, aged 57 years. He leaves a wife and nine children. (BFG, 29 Sept. 1803)

RAMSAY, Joseph, of Balto., and Miss Nancy Andrews of York, Penna., were married last Thurs. eve. by Rev. Glendy. (BA, 1 Oct. 1807)

RAMSAY, William, and Miss Sarah Brown all of Balto. were married last Wed. by Rev. D. E. Reese. (BA, 19 July 1816)

RAMSAY, William W., of Cecil Co. and Miss Eleanor Hall of Harf. Co. were married 5th inst. at Havre de Grace by Rev. Stevens. (BFG, 18 March 1816)

RAMSEY, Charles, died in Balto. on Fri., aged 28 years; res. at Frederick St. Dock. (BFR, 3 Nov. 1810)

RAMSEY, John, and Mrs. Elizabeth Barry all of Balto. were married last Sat. by Rev. Sinclair. (BT, 20 Nov. 1804)

RAMSEY, Capt. Stephen, died last 23 Nov. at Glasgow in Scotland, late of Balto. He was born in Ireland, and came to Balto. at an early age. He leaves a mother, widow, four sisters, and three brothers. (BEP, 26 March 1807)

RAMSEY, Thomas, and Miss Elizabeth Wallace were married last Wed. in Chanceford Twp., York Co., Penna., by Rev. Samuel Martin. (BFG, 26 Aug. 1807)

RAMSEY, William, dyer, died Thurs., 4th inst., in his 32nd year. (BFG, 16 Aug. 1806)

RANDALL, Israel, and Miss Delila Lee both of Balto. Town were married Sat. eve. by Rev. Bend. (BFG, 27 June 1796)

RANDALL, James, and Miss Mary Allworth were married last Tues. by Rev. Dr. Rattoone. (BFG, 24 May 1806)

RANDALL, John, and Caroline Killen were married last eve. by Rev. Coates. (BFG, 10 Dec. 1802)

RANDALL, Major Robert, the gentleman by whose enterprise the famous Bridgewaterworks near Chippewa were built, is among the unfortunate persons lately lost in the Washington on Lake Ontario. He was from this state. (BFG, 10 Jan. 1804)

RANDALL, Stephen, and Miss Harriet Campbell all of Balto. were married last Tues. eve. by Rev. Inglis. (BPE, 30 Sept. 1813)

RANDALL, Thomas Beal, and Martha Thomas both of Balto. were wed last Thurs. by Rev. Mr. Lisle. (BFG, 31 Dec. 1800)

RANDOLPH, John, of Chesterfield, was found dead in bed, shot through the head with a pistol. His son has since been committted to jail. (Peters. paper) (BT, 16 Jan. 1804)

RANKIN, Daniel J., died Sat., 25th inst., in his 47th year, leaving a wife and four small children. (BPEA, 30 March 1815)

RANKINS, Mr., was found dead in the meadows. (BFG, 1 Feb. 1806)

RAPP, Charles, son of the late Dr. Rapp of Balto. City, died at Demerara, last 1 Dec. (BFG, 19 March 1805)

RAPP, Master George, 3rd son of the late Dr. Rapp of Balto., died 15th inst. on his passage from Martinique to this port. (BFG, 29 July 1805)

RATCLIFF, James, of Dor. Co., and Miss Margaret Harris of Balto. City were married Sun. by Rev. D. E. Reese. (BA, 17 Dec. 1816)

RATCLIFFE, Luther, merchant, and Miss Eliza Welsh, dau. of Adam Welsh, all of Balto., were married last eve. by Rev. Mr. Hoffman. (BA, 25 May 1815)

RATTOONE, Rev. Dr., formerly of the city and Principal of the Charleston College, died at Charleston, 11th inst. (BFG, 22 May 1810)

RAUTHAUS, P. A., Balto. merchant, and Miss Maria Lee Warrington, dau. of Thomas Warrington of Wilmington, Del., were wed at Wilmington on 17th inst. (BMG, 22 Aug. 1815)

RAWLINGS, Aaron, died in this city, Mon., 23rd inst., an inhab. of Lower Marlboro, Cal. Co. (BFG, 24 April 1804)

RAWLINGS, Benjamin, and Miss Anna E. Sellman, dau. of John Sellman, all of Balto., were married Tues., 5th inst. by Rev. Bend. (BFG, 11 May 1807)

RAWLINGS, William, died last Fri. at his res. on Federal Hill, aged 63, leaving a widow and six children. (BFG, 4 Aug. 1812)

RAY, Miles, sailmaker of Balto., died yesterday morning; res. in Duke St. (BA, 13 Nov. 1815)

RAY, Samuel, and Miss Margaret Richards all of Balto. were married last Sat. night, 9 Feb., by Rev. M'Kean. (BFG, 11 Feb. 1811)

RAYMOND, Joseph H., merchant, and Miss Ann Cook, both of Dover, Del., were married 5th inst., by Rev. John Deboran. (BEP, 15 March 1810)

READ, Lieut. Benjamin Franklin, U. S., is dead at Balize, Miss.; son of Dr. J. R. Read of Norfolk, and a descendant of Dr. Franklin. He leaves a wife and infant child, and the only other relative is a widow of the late Gov. Geo. W. Smith of Va. (Long obit.) (BW, 19 March 1812)

READ, Charles, and Elizabeth Fisher both of Balto. were married yesterday at Friends Meeting House, Eastern District. (BFG, 17 March 1809)

READ, Dennis, and Miss Rachel Wells both of Balto., were married last eve. by Rev. Richards. (BFG, 2 Jan. 1801)

READ, John, and Ruth Underwood, both of Balto., were married last eve. by Rev. Mc Combs. (BFG, 28 July 1802)

READ, Mr. John, died at Frederick. (BPEA, 4 March 1815)

READY, John, of Balto., and Miss Elizabeth Rutter of Balto. Co., were married last eve. by Rev. Kurtz. (BFG, 18 Sept. 1801)

REAHM, Miss Mary, step-dau. of Mr. F. Prill of Balto., died yesterday in her 18th year; interment in the German Reformed burying ground, Howard's Hill. (BFG, 10 Sept. 1799)

REAM, Capt. George, of Balto., and Miss Catherine Elizabeth Stamman of Balto. Co., were married yesterday in Balto. Co. by Rev. Kurtz. (BFG, 22 Jan. 1813)

REAVES, Anthony, of Fells Point, a pilot, died last Fri. morning leaving a wife and several small children. (BFG, 19 Oct. 1802)

REAVES, Capt. John, and Miss Allen, both of Balto., were married last Tues. by Rev. Rattoone. (BFG, 14 July 1803)

RECHMAN, Henry, and Miss Mary Jones both of Balto. were married Thurs. eve. by Rev. Otterbein. (BFG, 2 Jan. 1808)

REDDING, John, and Mrs. Rebecca Livesay, were married last Thurs. eve. by Rev. Wells. (BA, 10 April 1813)

REDGRAVE, Mrs. Mary, wife of Isaac Redgrave of Kent Co., died 1st inst. in her 47th year. (BFG, 18 July 1803)

REDGRAVE, Samuel, and Miss Mary Foard both of Cecil Co. were wed last Thurs. by Rev. Sewell. (BEP, 15 Aug. 1806)

REED, George, and Miss Sarah Thomas all of Balto. were married 21st inst. by Rev. Glendy. (BFG, 23 Feb. 1813)

REED, Henry, and Miss Margaret Kiles all of Balto. were wed last Lord's Day by Rev. Glendy. (BS, 17 June 1812)

REED, Capt. James, shipmaster of Balto., died this morning; res. in Philpot St. (BFG, 2 July 1810)

REED, Joseph, and Miss Ann Carroll both of Balto. were married last Thurs. eve. by Rev. Dr. Roberts. (BW, 20 March 1810)

REED, William, died yesterday; res. in Pratt St., near the Lower Bridge. (BA, 25 Sept. 1812)

REEDER, Thomas A., of St. M. Co., died 14th inst., in his 66th year. (BFG, 29 Aug. 1806)

REESE, George, and Mrs. Margaret Webb all of Balto. were married on 2nd inst. by Rev. Kurtz. (BFG, 19 Dec. 1804)

REESE, John, and Miss Elizabeth Rusk all of this place were wed last eve. by Rev. Bend. (BFG, 4 Feb. 1799)

REESE, John, of Balto., and Miss Polly Zachariah, near Westminster, Fred. Co., were married last Thurs. by Rev. Hinch. (BFG, 30 Nov. 1799)

REESE, John S., and Miss Margaret Spindler were married last eve. in Harf. Co. by Rev. D. E. Reese. (BA, 9 Aug. 1816)

REESE, Thomas L., and Mary Moore, dau. of Thomas Moore of Balto. Co., were married 24th inst. at Friends Meeting, Elk Ridge. (BFG, 26 Nov. 1813)

REESE, William, died 19th inst. at Dublin Dist., Harf. Co., having reached the age of 108 years and 7 days. He was a native of Cecil Co. (BA, 28 Feb. 1816)

REEVE, George, of Phila. and Miss Grace Buckler of Balto. were married last eve. by Rev. Kurtz. (BFG, 7 June 1804)

REHN, Casper, merchant, and Miss Dorothea Lex, dau. of Peter Lex, of Phila. were married at that city last Thurs. by Rev. J. H. C. Helmuth. (BEP, 6 March 1809)

REIGART, John, of Penna., and Ann Mary Keener, dau. of Christian Keener of Balto. Co., were married yesterday by Rev. Altonier. (BFG, 12 April 1799)

REIGART, Philip, merchant of Lancaster, Penna., and Miss Sophia Diffenderfer, dau. of the late Michael Diffenderfer of Balto., were married last eve. by Rev. Baker. (BA, 14 May 1813)

REILEY, William R., and Miss Eliza Anderson, both of Balto. were married Wed. eve. at Fells Point by Rev. Rattoone. (BFG, 10 May 1805)

REINAGLE, Alexander, manager of the Phila. and Balto. theatres, and Miss Ann Duport, dau. of Peter Duport, were married last eve. by Rev. Inglis. (BFG, 21 Sept. 1803)

REINAGLE, Alexander, manager of the Balto. and Phila. theatres, died last Thurs. in his 62nd year. (BFG, 22 Sept. 1809)

REINECKER, Conrad, Balto. merchant, died last Sat. in his 44th year. (BFG, 17 April 1810)

REINECKER, George, Jr., died yesterday. (BFG, 11 Sept. 1805)

REINECKER, John, Balto. merchant, died 16th inst. (BFG, 18 Aug. 1815)

RENSHAW, James, and Nelly Coale, both of Balto., were married last Sun. eve. by Rev. Richards. (BT, 26 Jan. 1796)

RENSHAW, James, York merchant, and Miss Rebecca F. Shriver, dau. of Andrew Shriver of Union Mills, Md., were married at the latter place on Tues. by Rev. John Armstrong. (BFG, 22 May 1815)

REPOLD, George, of Reisterstown, died last Sun. aged 55. He came from Germany at the close of the Rev. (BFG, 13 Aug. 1811)

RETICKER, Jacob, of Balto., and Mrs. S. Amelia Clendenin, dau. of the late Rev. Chandler, were married at Frederick Town on Thurs. by Rev. Schaeffer. (BA, 4 Aug. 1815)

REVELL, John, and Miss Charlotte Frazier Shahanasey, all of Balto. were married last Thurs. by Rev. Inglis. (BA, 13 Oct. 1815)

REYNOLDS, Mr. George Edward Charles Frederick Meredith Rose, and Miss Ellen Hageman, dau. of Jacob Hageman, all of Balto., were married at New York on Sat. by Rev. Miller. (BA, 13 Dec. 1804)

REYNOLDS, Isaac, and Miss Mary M. Hoffman, dau. of Jacob Hoffman, all of Balto., were married last Tues. by Rev. Kurtz. (BFG, 26 Nov. 1807)

REYNOLDS, James, M. D., died at Phila. on Tues. (BEP, 28 May 1808)

RAYNOLDS, Joseph, and Ann Brown all of Balto. were married on Thurs. by Rev. Glendy. (BA, 1 Dec. 1810)

REYNOLDS, Samuel, and Miss Eliza Gantz, youngest dau. of Adam Gantz, all of Balto., were married last eve. by Rev. Kurtz. (BFG, 27 Sept. 1816)

RHOADS, Capt. George, late master of the brig Minerva of Bristol, Me., died 30th ult. on his passage from St. Barts. to Balto. (BFG, 23 June 1812)

RHODY, Mr. Henry, and Miss Maria Falsgraff, both of Balto., were married last eve. (BFG, 8 Oct. 1806)

RHULE, Eberhart, coachmaker, and Miss Mary Daugherty, all of Phila., were married last Thurs. at that city by Rev. Dr. Helmuth. (BEP, 22 Aug. 1809)

RIBBLE, Peter, and Margaret Clair, all of Balto., were married last Sat. by Rev. Rattoone. (BFG, 3 Feb. 1807)

RICAUD, Benjamin, Balto. merchant, and Mrs. Rebecca Hyatt were married 10th inst. at Swan Creek, Kent Co., by Rev. Armstrong. (BFG, 20 Sept. 1804)

RICAUD, Benjamin, Balto. merchant, died 22 Sept., leaving a wife and six children. (BFG, 23 Sept. 1815)

RICAUD, Richard, died at his res. in Kent Co., on 23rd inst., in his 60th year. (BPE, 30 Oct. 1813)

RICE, Arthur, and Elizabeth Connell of Balto. were married last Sun. by Rev. Bp. Carroll. (BA, 8 Aug. 1806)

RICE, Martha, dau. of James Rice, near Balto., died yesterday in a packet on her return from the Eastern Shore. (BA, 11 Sept. 1812)

RICE, William, of Christine, and Eliza Steele of New York, both now of Balto., were married last eve. by Rev. Rattoone. (BFG, 17 Jan. 1806)

RICE, William, and Mrs. Mary Scott, all of Balto., were married last Wed. by Rev. Hargrove. (BFG, 7 March 1812)

RICH, Charles, died suddenly on his passage from Liverpool, aged 25 years. (BFG, 10 Nov. 1809)

RICH, Mathias, Jr., died Thurs., aged 27 years. (BA, 14 Dec. 1816)

RICH, Peter, a delegate, died Wed. morning. (BA, 4 Feb. 1805)

RICHARD, Clement, an old Rev. soldier, died Sun., 14th inst., at Annap.; interred on Mon. with the honours of war. (BEP, 24 Aug. 1808)

RICHARDS, Mr., of Balto., and Miss Mary Vernon of Ashton Twp., Delaware Co., were married at Phila. last Thurs. by Rev. Greer. (BEP, 12 Sept. 1807)

RICHARDS, Mrs. Angelica, consort of Rev. Lewis Richards, pastor of the 1st Baptist Church, Balto., died 2 June in her 57th year. (BA, 5 June 1815)

RICHARDS, Mrs. Ann, consort of Rev. Lewis Richards, of Balto., died on Mon., aged 44 years; interment in the Baptist burial ground. (BFG, 23 May 1798)

RICHARDS, David, and Miss Ann Morton, all of Balto., were wed by Rev. Glendy yesterday. (BFG, 19 April 1816)

RICHARDS, John, and Mrs. Susanna Size, both of Balto. Co., were married last Fri. by Rev. John D. Evans. (BFG, 30 March 1803)

RICHARDS, John C., and Mary Thomas were married 15 Nov. by Rev. Richards. (BFG, 16 Nov. 1810)

RICHARDS, Rowland, and Miss Ann Price were married last Tues. by Rev. Glendy. (BA, 28 Dec. 1816)

RICHARDSON, Mr. A., Balto. merchant, and Polly Barry of Balto. were married 9 Sept. by Rev. Richards. (BA, 12 Sept. 1800)

RICHARDSON, Alexander, and Mary Ann Beal all of Balto. were wed yesterday by Rev. Glendy. (BT, 31 May 1803)

RICHARDSON, Arnold, died Sun., in his 28th year; funeral at his late country res. near Joseph Merryman's. (BA, 29 Nov. 1813)

RICHARDSON, Benjamin, and Miss Elizabeth Sharp both of this county were married Sat. eve. by Rev. Glendy. (BA, 25 Oct. 1804)

RICHARDSON, Daniel, and Miss Rebecca Jones all of Balto. were married last Sat. by Rev. Roberts. (BA, 27 Aug. 1805)

RICHARDSON, Daniel, died at Elkton yesterday. (BFG, 26 Dec. 1805)

RICHARDSON, Daniel, and Miss Ann D. Swartz, dau. of Peter Swartz, all of Balto., were married last Thurs. by Rev. M'Caine. (BFG, 8 Jan. 1813)

RICHARDSON, Patty W., dau. of Mr. Richardson, died last Mon. in Balto., aged 17 years and 17 days. (BW, 10 Sept. 1808)

RICHARDSON, Mrs. Rebecca, consort of David Richardson, died Tues. night. (BA, 22 Oct. 1812)

RICHARDSON, Robert R., merchant, and Eliza Ridgely, all of Balto., were married last Sun. eve. by Rev. Bend. (BT, 29 March 1796)

RICHARDSON, Thomas, clerk of Caroline Co., died last Wed. (BPEA, 28 Dec. 1815)

RICHARDSON, William, and Miss Charlotte Poteet, both of Harf. Co. were married last Thurs. by Rev. John Davis. (BT, 24 March 1803)

RICHARDSON, William, and Mrs. Jane Green, both of Balto., were married last eve. by Rev. Rattoone. (BA, 27 Nov. 1806)

RICHEY, Wm. W., and Miss Mary Hardister, all of Balto., were wed last Thurs. by Rev. Alexander M'Cane. (BEP, 16 Oct. 1807)

RICKARD, Mrs. Sarah, wife of Thomas Rickard, died Fri. in her 39th year. (BA, 27 Feb. 1809)

RICKARD, Thomas, died yesterday, leaving five orphans. (BA, 6 Jan. 1813)

RICKETTS, Levering, and Mrs. Violet Graham were married last Tues. by Rev. Glendy. (BS, 7 Feb. 1812)

RIDDELL, Alexander H., a son of the late Robert Riddell, died last Thurs., aged 22 years. (BA, 29 June 1814)

RIDDELL, Mrs. Mary, died Sat. morning last, 25th inst., in her 45th year, wife of Robert Riddell of Balto. (BFG, 27 Jan. 1806)

RIDDLE, Capt. Edward, and Miss Eliza Shahannasy, all of Balto., were married last Tues. by Rev. Glendy. (BA, 12 March 1810)

RIDDLE, Robert, and Mrs. Judith Carter Moale, all of Balto., were married last eve. by Rev. Dashiell. (BFG, 7 Jan. 1807)

RIDDLE, Robert, died 5th inst., in his 49th year, Balto. merchant, leaving a wife and children. (BFG, 10 May 1809)

RIDDLE, William, and Mrs. Margaret Marks, were married last eve. at Fells Point, by Rev. Rattoone. (BFG, 14 Sept. 1804)

RIDER, Arthur, and Miss Eliza Forsyth all of Balto. were wed on 23rd ult. (BEP, 4 Oct. 1809)

RIDGELY, Mrs. Ann, wife of Nicholas Ridgely of Balto. City, died Wed., 29th ult., in her 70th year. (BFG, 1 March 1804)

RIDGELY, C., of Balto., was drowned last Sat., 28th inst., when swept overboard from the Rock Hall Packet, Capt. Humphreys. (BA, 30 Sept. 1805)

RIDGELY, Mr. Charles, and Ruth Ingram Smith, were married last eve. by Rev. Richards. (BA, 3 Dec. 1800)

RIDGELY, Charles, of Wm., died 27 Sept. aged about 60, at his res. in Balto. Co. (BFG, 5 Oct. 1810)

RIDGELY, Charles Sterett, and Miss Eliza R. Hollingsworth, both of Balto., were married last eve. by Rev. Bend. (BFG, 12 April 1804)

MARRIAGES AND DEATHS

RIDGELY, Mrs. Eliza, died last Thurs. after a short illness; consort of Nicholas Ridgely, Balto. merchant. (BFG, 12 Feb. 1803)

RIDGELY, G., Jr., Balto. merchant, and Miss Harriett Talbott, dau. of Benjamin Talbott of Balto. Co., were married last Thurs. by Rev. Grice. (BFG, 8 Jan. 1814)

RIDGELY, Henry, of A. A. Co., Associate Judge of the second judicial district, died 22 June in his 48th year, leaving a numerous family. (BFG, 25 June 1811)

RIDGELY, James, died Sat., 6 Oct., aged about 28 years; interment in the Meth. burying ground. (Long obit.) (BFG, 9 Oct. 1804)

RIDGELY, John, and Prudence Gough Carroll, dau. of James Carroll, were married last eve. at Perry Hall by Rev. Beasley. (BFG, 16 Oct. 1812)

RIDGELY, Major John, died yesterday at his late res. Pomonean Grove, Balto. Co., in his 50th year. (BFG, 28 June 1814)

RIDGELY, Lott, son of Nicholas, died last Tues. (BFG, 19 Oct. 1804)

RIDGELY, Mordecai, of A. A. Co., and Miss Mary Wellmore of Balto. were married last eve. by Rev. Hagerty. (BFG, 14 Dec. 1798)

RIDGELY, Nicholas, aged 64, and Miss Rebecca Croxall, aged 51, were married last eve. by Rev. Geo. Roberts. (BFG, 5 Oct. 1804)

RIDGELY, Nicholas G., and Eliza Eichelberger, eld. dau. of Martin Eichelberger, of Balto., were married last eve. by Rev. Bend. (BFG, 31 July 1801)

RIDGELY, Nicholas Orrick, and Miss Anna Croxall, both of Balto., were married last Sat. (BA, 25 Sept. 1804)

RIDGELY, Mrs. Priscilla, wife of Gen. Charles Ridgely of Hampton, died last Sat., leaving a husband and a large family of children. (Long obit) (BA, 3 May 1814)

RIDGELY, Mrs. Rebecca, wife of Charles Ridgely of John, died last eve. in her 49th year. (BFG, 16 Nov. 1801)

RIDGELY, Mrs. Rebecca, relict of Capt. Charles Ridgely, died. Her funeral will be preached at Hampton on the 29th. (BFG, 23 Sept. 1812)

RIDGELY, W. H., Georgetown merchant, and Miss Sophia Plater, dau. of John R. Plater, were married 25th ult. at Sotterly, St. M. Co., by Rev. Wm. Drake. (BFR, 4 March 1812)

RIDGELY, William A., and Miss Eliza G. Dumeste, both of Balto. Co., were married Thurs., 1st inst., by Rev. Inglis. (BW, 7 March 1814)

RIDLEY, Miss Levy, died Mon. (BFG, 14 Aug. 1799)

RIGDEN, Mrs., wife of John E. Rigden, died Wed., 3rd March, leaving a husband and two infant children. (BFG, 6 March 1813)

RIGDEN, John E., merchant, and Miss Ann Orrick, dau. of John Orrick, of Balto. Co., were married Thurs. last by Rev. Mr. Rossell. (BFG, 22 Oct. 1808)

RIGDEN, William, and Miss Mary Gothrop, all of Balto., were wed Thurs. se'ennight by Rev. Shane. (BS, 30 April 1812)

RIGG, Rev. Elisha, died at Centreville, Md., formerly pastor of the Episcopal Church in Lancaster. (BT, 23 Feb. 1804)

RIGGEN, Rev. Benton, of the Methodist Congregation on Fells Point, died Sat. (BFG, 23 Sept. 1799)

RIGGING, Benton, and Mrs. Ann Bready were married last Thurs. by Rev. Glendy. (BFG, 29 Dec. 1815)

RIGGS, George, and Miss Mary Biggs of Balto. were married Thurs. eve. by Rev. Duncan. (BFG, 1 Feb. 1813)

RILEY, ---, a child of William Riley, tailor, fell through a hole in the Lower Bridge of Jones Falls yesterday eve. and was drowned. (BFG, 3 Aug. 1797)

RILEY, Joseph, and Miss Mary Driscol, both of Balto., were wed by Rev. Rattoone. (BEP, 15 May 1805)

RING, Capt. Thomas, and Mrs. Elizabeth Jones, both of Balto., were married last eve. by Rev. Rattoone. (BFG, 29 May 1806)

RINGGOLD, Benjamin, of Washington Co., died after a short illness. (BFG, 31 Aug. 1798)

RINGGOLD, Dr. Jacob, died Mon. last at an advanced age. (BA, 22 Dec. 1815)

RINGGOLD, Mrs. Maria, consort of Gen. Samuel Ringgold of Wash. Co., and dau. of the late Gen. Cadwallader of Phila., died at Fountain Rock last Thurs. (BFG, 12 Aug. 1811)

RINGGOLD, Samuel, Rep. in Congress from Md., and Miss Maria Antoinette Hay, dau. of George Hay of Richmond, were wed on Tues. in the city of Washington, by Rev. Mr. McCormick. (BFG, 18 Feb. 1813)

RINGROSE, John, and Miss Margaret McIntyre both of Balto., were wed last eve. by Rev. Reese. (BFG, 18 May 1812)

RISER, John, died yesterday, 8th inst., on Fells Point, in his 24th year; interment in the Protestant Episcopal burying ground. (BFG, 9 Sept. 1802)

RISINGSON, Henry, and A. Clark, both of Balto., were married 21 Nov. by Rev. Shane. (BA, 23 Nov. 1815)

RISTON, George, and Miss Margaret Hermange, both of Balto., were married last Tues. by Rev. Fenwick. (BA, 28 Nov. 1816)

RITCHIE, Miss Susanna, died 24th ult., in Frederick Town. (BT, 4 May 1799)

RITTENHOUSE, David, celebrated philosopher, died in Phila. on Sat. 25th ult., at an advanced age. (BMJ, 5 July 1796)

RITTER, John, co-editor of the Reading Eagle, and Miss Kitty Frailey, dau. of Col. Peter Frailey, were wed 5th inst. (BT, 20 Jan. 1804)

ROACH, Alexander, and Miss Mary Owings, all of Fells Point, were married last Sun. by Rev. Moranville. (BFG, 31 Aug. 1808)

ROADS, Ely, of Harf. Co. and Miss Priscilla Hobbs of Balto. were married last eve. (BFG, 20 Nov. 1812)

ROBB, Capt. John, died Sun. morning. (BFG, 3 Sept. 1805)

ROBB, William, native of Scotland, died yesterday. (BFG, 4 Aug. 1804)

ROBBINS, Luke, of the theatre, and Miss Harriet Beeston, all of Balto., were married last eve. at the house of John Gill by Rev. Sinclair. (BT, 11 Nov. 1803)

ROBERTS, Edward P., and Miss Elizabeth Davenport, all of Balto., were married last eve. by Rev. Glendy. (BA, 8 Nov. 1816)

ROBERTS, Mrs. Eliza, wife of John Roberts of Balto., died Sat., 24th inst., in her 23rd year. (BFG, 27 Oct. 1807)

ROBERTS, Capt. Francis, of Fells Point, and Miss Elizabeth Orrick of Balto., were married last eve. by Rev. Kurtz. (BFG, 15 July 1803)

ROBERTS, George, an old inhab. of Balto., died yesterday in his 51st year. (BFG, 11 Sept. 1797)

ROBERTS, George, and Miss Rachel Lellavant were married last Wed. by Rev. Bunn. (BW, 24 Oct. 1809)

ROBERTS, James, and Miss Catherine Strebach, all of Balto. Co., were married last Tues. by Rev. Glendy. (BPEA, 20 Nov. 1815)

ROBERTS, James, miller, son of lawyer Roberts of Balto., and Miss Mary James of Harf. Co., were married last Sun. by Rev. Cash. (BT, 17 Feb. 1802)

ROBERTS, James, Balto. merchant, and Mrs. Sarah Brinton of Wilmington, Del., were married at the latter place on Mon., 8th inst. by Rev. Price. (BFG, 11 Dec. 1806)

ROBERTS, John, merchant, and Miss Eliza Anthony were married last eve. by Rev. Glendy. (BA, 5 Aug. 1814)

ROBERTS, Dr. Jonathan, died 15th inst. at his farm in Kent Co., aged about 65 years. (BT, 27 July 1797)

ROBERTS, Hon. Jonathan, Penna. Sen., and Miss Elizabeth Bushby, dau. of the late Mr. Bushby of Wash., were married there on 21 April by Rev. Waugh. (BA, 26 April 1814)

ROBERTS, Peter, of Balto. Co., and Miss Jane Quinn of Fells Point were married last Thurs. by Rev. Green. (BA, 10 May 1813)

ROBERTS, Miss Sally, dau. of the late George Roberts, dec., of Balto., died at Winchester, Va., 4th inst. (BFG, 14 March 1809)

ROBERTS, Stephen, native of Dublin, lately arrived from N. Y., died last Fri. (BA, 6 Aug. 1799)

ROBERTS, Thomas, of Phila., and Mrs. Louvett Kemp, of Dorset (sic) Co., Md., were married last Thurs. eve. by Rev. Dr. Rattoone. (BFG, 18 May 1805)

ROBERTS, Thomas H., and Miss Jane Campbell all of Balto. were wed last eve. by Rev. Hargrove. (BFG, 17 July 1811)

ROBERTS, William, of Balto. Co., and Miss Frances Hanson of Harf. Co., were married at Abingdon on 26th ult. by Rev. Chalmers. (BEP, 10 April 1807)

ROBERTSON, James, of Balto., and Miss Amelia Edwards of Balto. Co., were married last eve. by Rev. Roberts. (BW, 9 March 1814)

ROBERTSON, John, Esq., died Thurs., 19th inst., at his res. in Charles Co., Md., aged about 54 years, leaving a wife and child. (BFG, 28 April 1810)

ROBERTSON, William, and Miss Elizabeth Hall, both of Balto., were married Sun. by Rev. Hagerty. (BFG, 6 July 1802)

ROBINSON, Mrs., wife of Andrew Robinson of York, Penna., died Sat. last in her 34th year, and was buried in the Presb. burying ground. (BFG, 5 July 1799)

ROBINSON, Alexander, Jr., aged 9, son of Alexander Robinson, Jr., died 1st inst., at Springwood, Va. (BFG, 9 Aug. 1804)

ROBINSON, Andrew, died 5th inst., in York, Penna., aged 52 years, assoc. judge of the civil court of York Co. (BFG, 9 Oct. 1805)

ROBINSON, Archibald, attorney-at-law, died 1st inst.; a young man in the prime of life. (BFG, 4 Sept. 1797)

ROBINSON, Caleb B., and Miss Elizabeth Johnson all of Balto., were married last Thurs., 1 May, by Rev. Glendy. (BA, 13 May 1806)

ROBINSON, Ebenezer, and Miss Margaret Catherwood, all of Wilmington, Del., were married Thurs., 22nd inst., by Rev. Reed. (BEP, 29 Dec. 1808)

ROBINSON, Miss Eliza L., died 7th inst. at her father's res. in the state of Delaware. (BA, 13 Sept. 1813)

ROBINSON, Ephraim, Balto. merchant, died Mon. (BFG, 23 July 1799)

ROBINSON, John, and Miss Sarah Sailer, both of Balto., were wed last eve. by Rev. Glendy. (BFG, 23 Dec. 1808)

ROBINSON, John, and Mrs. Sarah Taylor were married by Rev. Glendy. (BW, 16 Feb. 1809)

ROBINSON, John, and Miss Betsy Coleman all of Balto., were wed Sun. eve. by Rev. Hargrove. (BA, 25 April 1815)

ROBINSON, Jonathan, and Miss Martha Ady were married last Fri. in Harf. Co., by Rev. Richardson. (BA, 3 April 1812)

ROBINSON, Joseph, printer of the Federal Republican, and Miss Catherine Miller both of Balto. were married last eve. by Rev. Bend. (BFG, 14 Oct. 1808)

ROBINSON, Lyles B., of Jefferson Co., Va., and Mrs. Catherine W. Patterson, dau. of Dr. Richard Goldsborough of Cambridge were married at the latter place on 9th inst. by Rev. Stone. (BFG, 19 Nov. 1813)

ROBINSON, Nicholas N., and Miss Sarah H. Stewart, dau. of John
Stewart, all of Balto., were married Thurs., 21st inst.
by Rev. Wiatt. (BWA,30 March 1816)

ROBINSON, Samuel, died last Wed., leaving a widow and three small
children. (BFG, 15 Oct. 1802)

ROBINSON, Thomas, and Miss Sally Dickenson were married 21st May
by Rev. Glendy. (BA, 5 June 1807)

ROBINSON, Thomas, and Miss Mary Kelly all of Balto. were married
last Tues. by Rev. Moranville. (BA, 28 Sept. 1813)

ROBINSON, Thomas, merchant, and Miss Harriott Schaeffer, dau. of
Baltzer Schaeffer, all of Balto., were married last Tues.
by Rev. Roberts. (BFG, 24 Feb. 1815)

ROBINSON, Capt. William, and Deborah James both of Balto. were
married last eve. by Rev. Sinclair. (BFG, 11 Feb. 1802)

ROBINSON, William, and Miss Mary Fearson both of Balto. were married last eve. by Rev. M'Cain. (BA, 15 Feb. 1808)

ROCH, Joseph, and Secelia Haile both of Balto. were married last
Thurs. by Rev. Beason. (BA, 19 Sept. 1801)

ROCHE, Alexander, grocer, Market Place, Fells Point, died yesterday in his 41st year; interment in the Cath. burying
ground. (BA, 17 Aug. 1816)

RODENMEYER, George, and Miss Mary Bamberger all of Balto. were
married last Thurs. by Rev. Kurtz. (BW, 6 July 1810)

RODGERS, Major Alexander, died this morning in his 36th year;
res. in German Lane. (BFG, 27 Nov. 1810)

RODGERS, Commodore, John, and Miss Minerva Denison were wed on
Tues., 21st inst. at Sion Hill, Harf. Co., by Rev. John
Allen. (BFG, 31 Oct. 1806)

RODGERS, John, and Miss Mary Irvine both of Balto. were married
on 16th inst. by Rev. Glendy. (BA, 20 Aug. 1808)

RODGERS, Mrs. Mary, consort of John Rodgers of Balto., died Sat.,
18th inst., in her 25th year. (BFG, 23 Oct. 1800)

RODLEY, Robert, and Miss Elizabeth Swindal, both of Balto., were
married on Thurs. by Rev. Roberts. (BEP, 16 Oct. 1807)

RODNEY, Thomas, of Del., died 21st ult. at Washington, Mississippi Territory, 1st Judge of the Superior Court of that
territory and father of the Attorney General of the U.S.;
brother of Caesar Rodney. (BEP, 26 Feb. 1811)

RODRIGEZ, Don Michel Atalid, from Buenos Aires, S. A., and Miss
Aime Mary Frances Milhau, dau. of Michel Milhau of Balto.,
were married 24th inst. by Rev. Fenwick. (BFG, 27 July
1813)

ROE, James C., brother of Alexander S. Roe of Balto. died in Batavia. (BFG, 19 May 1797)

ROE, Mrs. Sarah, wife of Walter Roe of Balto., died Tues., after
a short illness in her 45th year. (BFG, 13 June 1806)

ROE, Thomas, formerly of Balto., died at St. Domingo in his 22nd year. (BMJ, 30 May 1796)

ROE, Thomas Lee, broker, died last night. (BFG, 27 April 1811)

ROE, Walter, merchant, died last Mon., 31 Oct., aged 60 years, leaving four sons and one dau. (BFG, 3 Nov. 1808)

ROESNER, John, of Fells Point, for the last eight years, died yesterday in his 46th year, leaving a widow. He was born in Hoof, Prussia. He served at Bladensburg and North Point and has been ill since his return. Res. on Bond St. (BA, 20 Oct. 1814)

ROGERS, Alexander, and Delia Christie, eld. dau. of the Hon. G. Christie (for several years a member of Congress), were married 15th inst. at Havre de Grace, by Rev. Wilmer. (BA, 21 Oct. 1801)

ROGERS, Andrew L., and Miss Margaret Hincks, both of Balto., were married on Tues. by Rev. Bend. (BFG, 4 Nov. 1803)

ROGERS, Charles, died last Sun. in his 64th year, at his res. near Balto. (BFG, 2 Jan. 1806)

ROGERS, Mrs. Eleanor, wife of Nicholas Rogers of Druid Hill, died on Sat. (BFG, 6 Jan. 1812)

ROGERS, Mrs. Elizabeth, died at Havre de Grace in her 75th year. (BA, 28 Sept. 1816)

ROGERS, George W., master commandant in the U. S. Navy, and Miss Ann M. Perry, dau. of Christopher R. Perry of Rhode Island, were married last Wed. in New York by Rev. Bowen. (BA, 11 July 1815)

ROGERS, Henry W., attorney-at-law, and Miss Mary Dulany, both of Balto., were married at Colebrook, near Washington, on Thurs., 24th inst. (BFG, 26 June 1813)

ROGERS, Major Hezekiah, died at Washington, a brave soldier of the Rev. (BW, 8 Sept. 1810)

ROGERS, James, attorney, and Miss Booth, dau. of the Hon. James Booth, were married at Newcastle, Del., last Thurs., by Rev. Robert Clay. (BEP, 23 April 1807)

ROGERS, John, and Miss Sarah Tilyard, all of Balto., were married last Tues. by Rev. Waugh. (BFG, 28 Oct. 1813)

ROGERS, John, and Miss Agnes Miskimon, all of Balto., were married last Thurs. by Rev. Glendy. (BA, 15 Oct. 1816)

ROGERS, John H., and Miss Julian Nagle, both of Balto., were wed last eve. by Rev. Dashiells. (BA, 26 May 1809)

ROGERS, Joseph, of Balto., and Miss Hannah Carlisle of Newcastle Co., Del., were married at Phila. on 17th inst. by Rev. Dr. Rogers. (BA, 21 March 1809)

ROGERS, Joseph, and Miss Mary Morgan were married in Harford Co. on 8th inst. (BA, 7 April 1813)

ROGERS, Nicholas Lowes, only son of Charles Rogers, died at his father's res. last night; leaving a wife. (BFG, 16 July 1803)

ROGERS, Richard, and Miss Phoebe Miller, all of Balto., were married last eve. by Rev. Rattoone. (BFG, 12 July 1803)

ROGERS, Samuel R., Balto. merchant, died in Jamaica on 18th ult. (BFG, 21 May 1805)

ROGERS, Miss Sarah, the celebrated painter, died at Phila. on 30th ult. (BFG, 3 Nov. 1813)

ROGERS, Dr. Thomas, died at Susquehanna Lower Ferry on 23rd of last month. (BFG, 6 Feb. 1797)

ROGERS, Thomas, Esq., Counsellor at Law, and Miss Elizabeth Howard of Balto. were married last eve. by Rev. Rattoone. (BFG, 26 Nov. 1802)

ROLES, John, and Miss Elizabeth Kerr both of Balto. were married last Thurs. eve. by Rev. Dr. Roberts. (BPEA, 4 March 1815)

ROLLS, John, and Miss Starling Lankford both of Fells Point were married last eve. by Rev. Beesley. (BS, 8 Sept. 1812)

ROLOSON, Richard, and Mrs. Margaret Pierpoint both of Balto. were married Thurs. by Rev. Kurtz. (BT, 6 Feb. 1804)

ROLLES, Rezin, and Miss Catherine Wilson, dau. of William Wilson of Balto. Co., were married yesterday at Ivy Hill by Rev. Glendy. (BFG, 2 Oct. 1807)

ROMAIN, Alexis, and Mrs. Ursules Poirie all of Balto. were wed last Sat. by Rev. Beeston. (BFG, 24 March 1803)

ROMER, Godfrey, and Miss Polly Barry were married on the 19th by Rev. Glendy. (BEP, 30 Nov. 1809)

RONEY, James, died 19th ult. at Phila., aged 64. (BT, 3 May 1804)

RONEY, William, and Miss Alice M'Blair all of Balto. were wed on yesterday eve. by Rev. Inglis. (BA, 13 Sept. 1809)

ROOF, Andrew, of Lexington, Va., and Miss Elizabeth Lannaway of Balto. were married last eve. by Rev. Roberts. (BEP, 25 March 1808)

ROOKER, Mrs. Mary, wife of James Rooker of Balto., died last Wed. night in her 52nd year. (BFG, 5 Jan. 1813)

ROPER, ---, son of Mrs. Mary Roper, died; funeral from her house on Hampstead Hill. (BA, 14 Jan. 1813)

RORAH, Abraham, and Miss Jane Dew of Balto. were married last eve. by Rev. Richards. (BT, 14 Jan. 1799)

RORE, John A., and Miss Kitty Vanderslice both of Phila., were married there last Tues. by Rev. Smith. (BA, 25 Sept. 1804)

ROSE, John P., of Balto., and Miss Caroline Hodge of Balto. were married Sat. by Rev. Richards. (BW, 30 Aug. 1808)

ROSE, R., and Charlotte Graham both of Balto. were married last eve. by Rev. Glendy. (BEP, 1 April 1808)

ROSENKILDE, Christian, died yesterday of the prevailing fever; a native of Norway, aged 17 years. (BFG, 18 Sept. 1800)

ROSENMILLER, Lewis, of York Co., and Miss Rebecca C. Porter, dau. of Capt. David Porter of Balto., were married last Tues. by Rev. Kurtz. (BFG, 4 May 1804)

ROSENMILLER, Mrs. Rebecca, wife of Louis Rosenmiller, of York, Penna., and dau. of Capt. Porter of Balto., died at York on 21st inst. (Long obit.) (BFG, 24 May 1815)

ROSENSTEEL, George, and Miss Barbara White both of Balto. were married last eve. by Rev. Beeton. (BFG, 1 Dec. 1797) (BT, 2 Dec. 1797, gives the bride's name as Isabella White.)

ROSENSTEEL, George, Jr., merchant, died yesterday, in his 31st year, leaving a wife and three children. (BFG, 18 Sept. 1805)

ROSENSTEEL, William, and Miss Eliza Graham both of Balto. Co. were married Mon. by Rev. Mertz. (BFG, 3 Jan. 1810)

ROSS, Mrs., died Tues., 29th Nov., wife of James Ross of Balto., and sister of the late Oliver Bond of Dublin. (BFG, 2 Dec. 1803)

ROSS, David, and Miss Eliza Dixon, were married last Sun. by Rev. Healey. (BA, 20 Jan. 1814)

ROSS, James, of Balto., died at Frankfort, Ky., on Thurs., 16th ult. "Kentucky paper." (BFG, 18 July 1808)

ROSS, John H., and Miss Mary Bradenbaugh all of Balto. were wed yesterday by Rev. Hargrove. (BFG, 20 Aug. 1807)

ROTE, John, and Miss Sarah Dauny both of Balto. were married on Thurs. eve., 16th inst., by Rev. Kurtz. (BFG, 17 July 1812)

ROTHROCK, Mrs. Barbara, consort of Mr. Jacob Rothrock, died last eve. in her 56th year. (BFG, 15 July 1802)

ROTHROCK, John, Jr., grocer, and Miss Lily Dun both of Balto., were married Sun. eve., 15th inst. (BFG, 23 April 1804)

ROTHROCK, Philip, died last Mon. at York, Penna., in his 90th yr. He took an active part in the Rev. War. (BFG, 4 March 1803)

ROUSSELL, Mrs. Sarah, died last Sun., in her 55th year. (BFG, 13 March 1810)

ROWE, Michael, and Miss Elizabeth Griffin, both of Balto., were married last eve. by Rev. Kurtz. (BEP, 30 March 1807)

ROWE, Philip, and Miss Charlottee Creusa Holcomb, dau. of the late Jonathan Holcomb of Hudson, N. Y., were married last Sat. by Rev. Bend. (BFG, 28 Dec. 1807)

ROWLES, Rezin, and Miss Sophia Myers, both of Balto., were wed last Sat. by Rev. Kurtz. (BFG, 13 June 1803)

ROWLES, Rezin, and Miss Catherine Wilson, were married 1st inst. at the country res. of W. Wilson, by Rev. Glendy. (BA, 23 Oct. 1807)

ROY, John, merchant, and Miss Slater, both of Balto., were wed Tues. by Rev. Rattoone. (BFG, 29 May 1806)

ROZANN, Dominock, and Miss Mary Ann Johnston all of Fells Point were married last Tues. by Rev. Moranville. (BW, 29 Oct. 1811)

RUCKLE, John, merchant, and Miss Eleanor Dorsey both of Balto. were married last eve. by Rev. Reed. (BT, 16 Nov. 1798)

RUCKLE, Thomas, painter, and Miss Mary Chambers were married last eve. by Rev. Read. (BFG, 28 Nov. 1798)

RUDOLPH, Ferdinand, of Balto., and Miss Mary Goff, lately from Va., were married last Sun. by Rev. Kurtz. (BEP, 26 July 1808)

RUDULPH, Tobias, of Elkton, and Miss Maria Hayes were married last Thurs. by Rev. Pryse. (BFG, 4 Jan. 1813)

RUFF, Rev. Daniel, died this morning, a native of Harf. Co., in his 64th year; a Meth. preacher for almost 35 years. He res. in South Charles St. (BFG, 2 May 1810)

RUMNEY, Miss Elizabeth, died last Sun. at Elk Ridge in her 65th year. (BFG, 28 Aug. 1811)

RUMSEY, Benjamin, died at Joppa, Harf. Co., on Mon., 7th inst.; for many years one of the Judges of the High Court of Appeals. (BFG, 17 March 1808)

RUSH, Richard, of Phila., and Miss Catherine E. Murray of Annapolis were married 29 Aug. in A. A. Co. (BFR, 7 Sept. 1809)

RUSK, John, plasterer, stepped over Peter's Bridge, where the railing is broken, and was drowned, Sun. (BT, 14 Aug. 1798)

RUSK, John, Jr., and Miss Barbara Kauffman, dau. of Abraham Kauffman, all of Balto., were married last eve. by Rev. Kurtz. (BEP, 17 Oct. 1808)

RUSK, Robert, and Miss Sally Murray all of Balto. were married last Thurs. by Rev. Glendy. (BW, 7 June 181)

RUSK, William, and Miss Margaret Stewart, dau. of Robert Stewart, were married last Wed. by Rev. Glendy. (BA, 24 May 1816)

RUSSEL, James, and Miss Milcah S. Browning both of Balto. were married last Thurs. by Rev. Stier. (BFG, 3 Feb. 1816)

RUSSELL, Rev. Andrew K., and Miss Catherine Whitery, dau. of Col. William Whitery were married in Caroline Co., 21st inst. by Rev. Bell. (BW, 1 Jan. 1814) (BA, 3 Jan. 1814 gives the bride's name as Whitely.)

RUSSELL, Capt. Charles, and Mrs. Margaret Guy were married on Sat. by Rev. Rattoone. (BFG, 23 Sept. 1806)

RUSSELL, James, Alexandria merchant, died there last Sat., aged 37. (BEP, 2 Nov. 1808)

RUSSELL, Joseph, merchant, died at Phila. on Mon., 9th inst., in his 70th year. (BFG, 16 March 1801)

RUSSELL, Thomas, died 20th inst., after a short illness, at his res. in North East, Cecil Co., in his 25th year, eld. son of Thomas Russell, dec.; formerly of Birmingham, Eng. He leaves a mother, brother, and three sisters. (BFG, 28 Oct. 1806)

RUSSELL, William, for many years an inhab. of Balto., died last Wed. in his 66th year. (BA, 11 April 1805)

RUSSUM, Mitchell, of Dor. Co., died last Wed. (BPEA, 18 Dec. 1815)

RUTH, Jacob, and Rachel Bull, all of Harf. Co., were married on Tues., 4th inst., by Rev. Richardson. (BA, 8 Feb. 1806)

RUTHERFORD, V., merchant, and Miss Mark, both of Berkley Co., Va., all were lately married at Shepherdstown. (BFG, 1 Feb. 1798)

RUTLEDGE, Nathaniel, and Ann Bateman were married last eve. by Rev. McCaine on Fells Point. (BFG, 21 Feb. 1806)

RUTTER, Capt. Josias, and Mary, dau. of Josias Pennington, both of Balto., were married last eve. by Rev. Bend. (BT, 25 May 1796)

RUTTER, Samuel, and Miss Catherine Peters, all of Balto., were married last Thurs. by Rev. Glendy. (BA, 13 April 1807)

RUTTER, Thomas B., and Miss Eliza M'Lure Rutter were married on Tues. eve. by Rev. Dr. Roberts. (BA, 29 Feb. 1816)

RUTTER, William, and Miss Elizabeth Drummond, all of Balto., were married last Wed. by Rev. Reese. (BA, 14 June 1816)

RYAN, Amos, and Miss Margaret Welsh, both of Balto., were married last eve. by Rev. John Welsh. (BEP, 30 Dec. 1807)

RYAN, Mrs. Elizabeth Burgess, wife of Timothy Ryan of Balto., died Sat. (BA, 8 July 1800)

RYAN, Jeremiah P., may have died in a fire last Thurs. (BFG, 23 Feb. 1805)

RYAN, Thomas, and Mrs. Nancy Hanna were married Thurs. by Rev. Richards. (BFG, 5 June 1813)

RYAN, Timothy, and Mrs. Pannell, both of Fells Point, were wed on Tues., 11th inst., by Rev. Ireland. (BA, 17 Feb. 1800)

RYAN, William Thomas Jefferson, only child of Michael Ryan, died 4th inst., about 6 years. His only sister aged about 7, died about 3 years ago. (BEP, 6 March 1806)

SABOTIER, Mme. Maria, died 4th inst., in her 50th year, a native of Bordeaux. (Long obit.) (BFG, 6 March 1806)

SACKRIDER, Daniel W., and Mrs. Mary Adair, all of Balto., were married last eve. by Rev. Hargrove. (BFG, 15 Feb. 1805)

SADLER, Leonard, brother of Thomas Sadler, Balto. merchant, died last Tues. (BFG, 1 Feb. 1798)

SADLER, Thomas, merchant, of Balto., died Sat. in his 40th year. (BFG, 27 April 1801)

SADTLER, Philip B., and Miss Catherine Sauerwein all of Balto. were married last eve. by Rev. Kurtz. (BFG, 9 Dec. 1812)

ST. CLAIR, Mr., and Miss Saunders were married lately in Harf. Co., by Rev. Wilmer. (BFG, 28 May 1802)

ST. JOHN, James, native of Upper Marlborough, died in New York of a pulmonary complaint on 21st inst. (BFG, 25 Jan. 1813) (BA, 26 Jan. 1813, states he was a printer, late of Washington, and died at the Baltimore Hospital.)

ST. VICTOR, Armand B., and Miss Ann Eliza Giles, both of Balto., were married last Thurs. by Rev. Wyatt. (BA, 13 May 1815)

SALES, Benjamin, and Miss Elizabeth Clarke, all of Balto., were married. (BFG, 27 July 1807)

SALISBURY, Capt. Daniel, and Miss Polly Hall, dau. of Isaac Hall, all of Fells Point, were married last Wed. by Rev. Riggen. (BA, 17 Aug. 1799)

SALMON, Mrs., consort of George Salmon, of Balto., died yesterday in her 47th year. (BFG, 22 Sept. 1797)

SALMON, Charles, merchant, and Miss Eliza Ann Wyant, all of Balto., were married Thurs. by Rev. Kurtz. (BFG, 2 Feb. 1816)

SALMON, Capt. George, of 2nd U. S. Regt., and son of George Salmon of Balto., died at Fort Wilkinson last 20 Dec. (BFG, 6 Oct. 1804)

SALMON, George, died; res. on Calvert St. (BA, 14 Sept. 1807)

SALMON, John, Jr., died at Phila., on Sat., 5th inst.; late of Balto. (BFR, 14 Jan. 1811)

SALTER, James, late Treasurer of New Jersey, died last Wed. at his res. in Nottingham. (BFG, 27 Dec. 1803)

SAMPSON, Mrs. Catherine, wife of George Sampson, died Thurs. eve., aged 29 years, leaving her husband, three small children, and her mother. (BFG, 11 Oct. 1800)

SAMPSON, David, and Mrs. Belinda Satiswait, both of Balto. Co., were married 30 July by Rev. Rattoone. (BFG, 31 July 1806)

SAMPSON, George, of Balto. Co., and Miss Rebecca of Balto. were married Sun., 26th inst., by Rev. Glendy. (BT, 28 April 1804)

SANDERS, Greenbury, and Mrs. Maria James, all of Balto., were married on Thurs. by Rev. Healy. (BA, 15 March 1806)

SANDERS, John, and Miss Elizabeth Fletcher, both of Fells Point, were married Sun. by Rev. M'Kean. (BFG, 14 April 1802)

SANDERS, Thomas, and Miss Elizabeth Morton, all of Balto., were married last Sun. (14 April) by Rev. Hargrove. (BFG, 18 April 1811)

SANDERSON, Mrs. Margaret, died Mon., aged 79, one of the oldest inhabitants of Balto. (BA, 28 Sept. 1816)

SANDS, John, of Balto., and Mrs. Ellen Rowland of A. A. Co., were married last Tues. at West River, by Rev. Compton. (BFG, 6 March 1809)

SANFORD, Capt. Lawrence, and Mrs. Isabella Phillips, all of Balto., were married Tues., 8th inst., by Rev. John Bloodgood. (BEP, 15 May 1810)

SANFORD, Samuel, Balto. merchant, died, in his 23rd year. (BT, 6 Sept. 1797)

SANGER, Seth, and Miss Mary Young, dau. of John Young all of Balto. were married last Tues. by Rev. Dashiell. (BFG, 14 June 1810)

SANGER, Capt. Seth, died yesterday; res. in the precincts, head of Fayette St. (BFG, 12 Feb. 1812)

SARGEANT, Wm. H., died 31 Oct. at his res. near Petersburg, Va. (BFG, 5 Nov. 1811)

SASSON, Martin, and Miss Mary Beard, all of Balto., were married last eve. by Rev. Roberts. (BFG, 23 Aug. 1816)

SAUKEY, William, and Miss Mary Hill, both of Balto., were married last Thurs. by Rev. Glendy. (BW, 7 June 1811)

SAUNDERS, Lieut. James, U. S. Navy, died at Norfolk on 7 Dec. (BA, 14 Dec. 1816)

SAUNDERS, Valentine, and Sophia Fien, both of Balto., were married last eve: by Rev. Kurtz. (BFG, 8 March 1802)

SAUNDERSON, Thomas, died suddenly on Sun., inspector of the port of Balto., and long an inhab. of the city. (BFG, 4 Aug. 1800)

SAVAGE, Dennis, died 17th inst., aged 55; res. on Federal Hill. (BA, 17 April 1814)

SAVAGE, Mrs. Elizabeth, wife of Patrick Savage of Balto., died last Thurs. in her 25th year, leaving a husband and one child. (BFG, 29 Nov. 1802)

SAVAGE, Hugh, and Miss Sarah Curran, all of Balto., were married last Thurs. by Rev. Fenwick. (BA, 30 Nov. 1816)

SAVAGE, Col. Littleton, died Wed., 9th inst., at Cherry Grove, his res. in Northampton Co., Va.; a husband and father. (BFG, 5 Feb. 1805)

SAVAGE, Patrick, and Miss Rachael Wise, both of Balto., were wed last eve. by Rev. Beeston. (BFG, 15 June 1804)

SAVAGE, Patrick, cordwainer of Balto., died last eve. of pulmonary complaint, in his 49th year; a native of Ireland. He res. in South St. (BFG, 13 April 1812)

SAVIN, Thomas, delegate from Cecil Co., died in his 32nd year, at Harford Town, Harf. Co., on his way to Annapolis. (BFG, 26 Dec. 1798)

SAVIN, Dr. William, died Wed., 7 Oct.; res. at Sassafras Neck, Cecil Co. (BA, 13 Oct. 1801)

SAY, Dr. Benjamin, died at Phila., last Fri. He was a member of the 10th or 11th Congress. (BA, 27 April 1813)

SAY, Mrs. Hellen, died Sat., 20th inst., in her 56th year. (BA, 23 July 1816)

SCANLON, James, and Miss Mary Pearson, both of Balto., were wed last Sat. by Rev. Kurtz. (BFG, 27 Nov. 1797)

SCARLETT, James, and Miss Mary Fowler both of Balto. were married by Rev. Healey. (BA, 1 Aug. 1810)

SCHADE, Martin G., of Hamburg, and Miss Mary Ann Miller of Balto. were married last Thurs. eve. by Rev. Bartow. (BA, 24 Aug. 1816)

SCHAEFFER, George, Jr., son of George Schaeffer, died this morning. (BFG, 4 Oct. 1797)

SCHAEFFER, George, died yesterday; inhab. of Balto. (BFG, 27 Sept. 1802)

SCHAEFFER, John, was found dead on Sun. in Bowley's Wharf. (BFG, 18 Sept. 1799)

SCHAEFFER, Samuel, aged 28, son of Baltzer Schaeffer, merchant, of Balto., died last Tues. (BA, 13 Jan. 1810)

SCHAEFFER, Rev. Solomon, pastor of the Lutheran Church of Hagerstown, died last Mon. (Long obit.) (BFG, 4 Feb. 1815)

SCHAEFFER, William A., Balto. merchant, and Miss Martha Ann Hyland, second dau. of the late Col. Stephen Hyland of Cecil Co., were married 25th inst. at Bohemia Manor, Cecil Co., the res. of Wm. Craig, by Rev. Chambers. (BFG, 31 Aug. 1816)

SCHAFFER, Mrs. Catherine, died yesterday, in her 40th year; consort of Mr. George Schaffer of Balto. (BFG, 13 Sept. 1800)

SCHAUBER, George, and Elizabeth Keller, dau. of John Keller all of Balto., were married last eve. by Rev. Kurtz. (BFG, 22 Aug. 1800)

SCHILLER, Christopher, and Rebecca Roschen (or Boschen) all of Balto. were married last eve. by Rev. Baker. (BFG, 27 Nov. 1812)

SCHINNICK, Jacob, and Miss Harriet Divers, all of this place, were married last Thurs. by Rev. Kurtz. (BEP, 15 Aug. 1808)

SCHISSNER, John, of Fredericktown, and Miss Catherine Smith of A. A. Co., were married last Tues. by Rev. Hood. (BA, 19 Feb. 1816)

SCHLEY, Mrs. Eliza Asbury, wife of Frederick Augustus Schley of Fredericktown, died 27th ult. (BA, 14 Dec. 1816)

SCHLEY, Frederick A., and Miss Eliza A. McCannon, all of Fred. Co., were married 28th ult. at the res. of James McCannon. (BFG, 9 May 1812)

SCHLOY (sic), John, died yesterday morning, aged 78 years, an old inhab. of this place. (BFG, 18 Nov. 1802)

SCHMIDT, Arnold, died last Mon. in his 47th year. (BFG, 24 Dec. 1813)

SCHMIDT, Rev. John Frederick, died last Sat. at Phila., in his 67th year, Pres. of the German Lutheran Clergy of Penna. and pastor of Zion and St. Michaels Congregation in an near Phila. (BFG, 19 May 1812)

SCHMIDT, William L., and Miss Maria Furnival, were married last eve. on Federal Hill by Rev. Rattoone. (BFG, 1 May 1805)

SCHMINKE, George, and Miss Ann Tschudy all of Balto. were wed last eve. by Rev. Becker. (BFG, 11 Nov. 1814)

SCHNAUBER, Mrs., wife of George Schnauber, died this morning; res. at Charles and Pratt Sts. (BFG, 22 April 1815)

SCHNEEMANN, John Andrew Christopher, and Mrs. Hannah Brache were married last eve. at Fells Point by Rev. Rattoone. (BFG, 22 April 1803)

SCHOELFIELD, Thomas S., and Miss Charlotte Bier of Balto. were married in Fredericktown last Sun. by Rev. Helfenstein. (BA, 19 Feb. 1816)

SCHRADER, John, and Mrs. Margaretta Roselle both of Balto. were married last Sun. by Rev. Hargrove. (BA, 9 March 1808)

SCHREIBER, John H., died last Tues. in his 34th year. (BA, 26 April 1810)

SCHREIBER, Mrs. Mary F., died last Wed., 17th inst., in her 34th year. (BFG, 23 Feb. 1813)

SCHREIER, Mrs. Mary F., died Wed., 17th inst., in her 34th year. (BA, 24 Feb. 1813)

SCHROEDER, Charles, letter carrier, and Miss Catherine Hauptmann from Penna., were married last eve. by Rev. Kurtz. (BT, 25 May 1799)

SCHROEDER, Henry, Jr., and Miss Henrietta Maria Ghequiere, dau. of Charles Ghequiere, all of Balto., were married last eve. by Rev. Beeston. (BFG, 18 Oct. 1809)

SCHROWDER, Capt. William, and Miss Hannah Gilbert both of this county were married last Tues. at Fells Point by Rev. Glendy. (BT, 21 Feb. 1806)

SCHWARTZ, Mr. Valentine, died at Fredericktown, 3rd inst., in his 77th year. (BFG, 10 March 1801)

SCHWARTZE, Dr. J. F., of Balto., died 7th inst., in his 60th year. (BA, 11 Jan. 1816)

SCHWARZAUER, Daniel, and Miss Elizabeth Heims both of Balto. were married last eve. by Rev. Kurtz. (BFG, 23 Sept. 1801)

SCHWEARER, George, and Miss Catherine Ann Watts both of Annapolis were married last Thurs. by Rev. Dr. Roberts. (BS, 13 July 1812)

SCHWITZER, Conrad, and Miss Mary Hindman, both of Balto., were married Thurs. by Rev. Kurtz. (BEP, 26 March 1808)

SCOFIELD, Mrs. Phebe, died last Mon.; long an inhab. of Balto. (BT, 14 Aug. 1805)

SCOT, John, and Miss Nancy Picket were married last eve. by Rev. Mr. Pitts. (BFG, 27 May 1807)

SCOTT, Mr. Ely, and Miss Elizabeth Cole, dau. of Abraham Cole, Jr., of Balto. Co., were married last Thurs. by Rev. Worton. (BA, 13 Feb. 1816)

MARRIAGES AND DEATHS

SCOTT, Gustavus, one of the commissioners of the city of Washington, died at his house at Rock Hill, the 25th inst. (BFG, 31 Dec. 1800)

SCOTT, Mrs. Hannah, wife of Joseph Scott of Balto., died Sat., 25th inst., in her 43rd year, leaving a husband and two children. (BFG, 31 May 1816)

SCOTT, Henry, merchant, and Mrs. Louisa Summers were married last eve. by Rev. Dr. Bend. (BFG, 8 Feb. 1811)

SCOTT, John, and Miss Elizabeth Key Bruce, dau. of Col. Bruce of Fred. Co., were married 7 Nov. by Rev. Bowers of Hagerstown. (BA, 14 Nov. 1805)

SCOTT, John, and Miss Rose Connell, were married Thurs. by Rev. John Carroll, Archbishop of Balto. (BPE, 13 March 1813)

SCOTT, John, chief justice of the court of oyer and terminer, Balto., died this morning in his 46th year, a native of Kent Co., Md. (BFG, 15 July 1813)

SCOTT, John, Attorney at law, and Miss Eliza M. Key, dau. of Philip Key of Chaptico, Md., were married 14th inst., at Montgomery Co. (BFG, 22 July 1816)

SCOTT, Mrs. Mary, died at Richmond, on 11th inst., wife of Richard M. Scott of Fairfax Co., and eld. dau. of the late Samuel Love of Salisbury. She died as a result of injuries received at a fire at the theatre. (BFR, 22 Jan. 1812)

SCOTT, Priscilla, died at Fredericktown on Mon., 17th inst., in her 60th year; formerly of Balto. (BA, 28 Jan. 1806)

SCOVIL, William, died Sun. near Balto. (BW, 18 Sept. 1810)

SCROGGS, John, of Balto., died yesterday, in his 32nd year, leaving a wife and four children. (BT, 13 June 1798)

SEABROOK, Mrs. Ann, died yesterday in her 43rd year, late wife of Richard Seabrook, merchant, leaving a husband and six children. (BFG, 4 March 1807)

SEABROOKS, Richard, merchant, of Balto., died 13th ult. at the Warm Springs. (BEP, 16 Sept. 1809)

SEALS, Mrs. Priscilla, died lately in Harf. Co., aged 85 years. (BT, 8 July 1802)

SEARS, Mr. George, died at Christiana Bridge, Delaware, on Wed., 17th inst.; merchant of Balto. (BFG, 18 Sept. 1800)

SEARS, Capt. John, formerly of Balto., died 29 Sept. at his res. in Havre de Grace, leaving a wife and several small children. (BT, 18 Oct. 1802)

SEATON, John Carson, of N. Y., and Miss Charlotte Gordon Gorham, widow of the late James Gorham, were married at Havanna on board H.B.M. ship *Vengeur*, 74, Capt. Ricketts, by Rev. Mr. Richards, chaplain. (BA, 25 April 1815)

SEAVER, Capt. Abraham, of the Norfolk line of packets, died 24th inst., leaving an aunt and two sisters. (BS, 27 Oct. 1812)

SEDARS, Samuel, and Miss Polly Coley all of this city were wed last eve. by Rev. Daniel Reese. (BFG, 13 Feb. 1808)

SEDDON, Capt. John, of Stafford Co., Va., was killed in a duel on Sat., 5th inst., with Peter V. Daniel. (BFG, 17 Nov. 1808)

SEEKAMP, Albert, and Miss Sophia Volkman, both of Balto., were married last Tues. by Rev. Kurtz. (BFG, 11 Sept. 1806)

SEEKAMP, Albert, merchant, died Sun., 27th inst., in his 48th year. (BFG, 1 Feb. 1811)

SEEKAMP, Mrs. Maria, wife of Albert Seekamp, died last Tues., in her 34th year. (BFG, 21 March 1806)

SEESNAP, Adam, and Miss Catherine Brown were married last Sun. by Rev. Doyer. (BT, 23 April 1806)

SEGUIN, John, formerly of Cap Francois, died Sun. in his 65th year. (BFG, 18 May 1803)

SEIXAS, Rev. Gershom Mandes, died a few days since in New York, minister of the Hebrew Congregation there, in his 71st year, and in the 50th of his ministry. (BFG, 21 Aug. 1816)

SELDEN, Dr., of Norfolk, and Miss Charlotte Colgate of Balto. were married last Mon. by Rev. Bend. (BFG, 25 Nov. 1802)

SELLERS, Francis, of Tal. Co., and Miss Anna Maria Hopper of Q. A. Co. were married 4th inst. by Rev. Soule. (BPE, 11 Feb. 1813)

SELLERS, William, printer, died at Phila. last Sat. night in his 79th year. (BFG, 8 Feb. 1804)

SELLMAN, George M., son of Johnzee Sellman, died last Fri., 20th inst., in his 29th year, leaving a wife and child. (BPE, 25 May 1814)

SELLMAN, John, died Thurs., 30 Sept. at his plantation on Morgan's Run, Balto. Co., in his 83rd year. (BT, 8 Oct. 1802)

SELLMAN, Gen. Jonathan, died last Mon. at his farm on Rhode River. "Annap. - May 23." (BFR, 28 May 1810)

SELLY, John, and Miss Ann McDonald were married last Tues. by Rev. Glendy. (BT, 22 Aug. 1804)

SENEY, Joshua, member elect to the represent the 7th dist. of Md. in the U. S. House of Reps., died Sat., 20th inst., at his res. in Q. A. Co., leaving a widow and three small children. (BFG, 29 Oct. 1798)

SERVER, Henry, and Miss Ann Leckey, all of Balto., were married Sun., 22nd inst., by Rev. Glendy. (BEP, 2 June 1808)

SETON, Angelina, 2]/2 years old, dau. of John Carson Seton of Balto., died last Mon. (BEP, 5 Nov. 1807)

SETON, John, died at Havanna, of the prevailing fever last July; he was a native of Scotland, and recently a res. of Balto. (BFG, 15 Aug. 1800)

SETON, John Curson, of Balto., and Miss Ann Wise of Summer Hill, near Alexandria were married at Georgetown last Sun. by Rev. M. Balch. (BFG, 9 Jan. 1800)

SEVEAR, Capt. Abraham, died Sat., 24th inst., in his 24th year; master of the Norfolk packet, he leaves an aunt and two sisters. (BA, 28 Oct. 1812)

SEVERN, Mr., merchant, and Miss Sarah Sanderson, both of Balto., were married last Thurs. by Rev. Dashiell. (BEP, 4 Oct. 1806)

SEWALL, Henry, of St. M. Co., died yesterday, at the house of John Ch. Kaminsky in Balto. (BA, 23 Nov. 1801)

SEWALL, Major James, and Miss Ann Maria Rudulph, dau. of Tobias Rudulph of Cecil Co., were married in Elkton on 14th inst. (BFG, 21 Feb. 1809)

SEWALL, William H., second son to Capt. John Sewall, and Miss Rebecca B. Lewis, all of Harf. Co. were married Thurs., 17th inst. (BT, 24 Feb. 1803)

SEWELL, Augustine, Sr., of A. A. Co., and Mrs. Nancy Swormstedt of Balto., were married 1st inst. by Rev. Macklefresh. (BFG, 3 Feb. 1816)

SEWELL, Charles E., of the Eastern Shore of Md., and Ann Catherine Keagg of Lancaster, Penna., were married 9th ult. at the latter place. (BFG, 17 Jan. 1805)

SEWELL, James H., and Miss Lucinda Johnson were married in Harf. Co. on last Thurs. by Rev. Johnson. (BW, 10 Jan. 1811)

SEWELL, John Young, aged 22 years, died 12th inst., at his father's res. in Harf. Co. (BFG, 16 Aug. 1803)

SEWELL, Richard, died at French Town, Cecil Co., the 18th inst. (BFG, 23 Dec. 1805)

SEWELL, Richard, and Miss Susan Hughes both of Balto. were wed last Thurs. by Rev. Ryland. (BT, 31 Dec. 1814)

SEWELL, Thomas, and Miss Elizabeth Hall, dau. of Edward Hall all of Balto. Co., were married Thurs., 19th inst. (BFG, 24 Aug. 1813)

SHAAF, Mrs. Mary, wife of Dr. John T. Shaaf of Balto., died at Annap. in her 34th year. (BFR, 10 Sept. 1810)

SHADE, John, and Miss Magdalina Walters both of Balto. were wed 9th inst. by Rev. Dashiell. (BA, 21 Nov. 1807)

SHAEFFER, Frederick George, and Louisa Clementina Kurtz were wed 21 Nov. (BA, 23 Nov. 1815)

SHAFFER, Capt. Casper, of Frederick, died Sat., 27 May, in that place in his 54th year. (BPEA, 5 June 1815)

SHAFFER, James, and Miss Eleanor Hall, all of Balto., were wed last eve. by Rev. M'Cain. (BPE, 24 Dec. 1813)

SHAKES, Capt. George, and Rachael Trimble, all of Balto., were wed last Sat. by Rev. Glendy. (BA, 5 Nov. 1806)

SHALCROSS, Thomas, merchant of Wilmington, Del., died yesterday in Balto. He was a member of the Society of Friends. (BFG, 9 Aug. 1805)

SHALLEY, John, and Elizabeth Haifleigh, both of Balto., were wed last eve. by Rev. Kurtz. (BFG, 9 Feb. 1801)

SHANE, Dennis, died yesterday, a mechanic of Balto. He is supposed to have died from a sudden fit of insanity. (BA, 20 March 1815)

SHANE, Henry, aged 70, and Mrs. Mary Almoney, aged 80, both of Balto. Co., were married last eve. by Rev. Ruchards. (BA, 12 Nov. 1805)

SHANGLE, John, aged 66, and Miss Eleanor Hilton, aged 45, both of Balto. Co., were married last Thurs. by Rev. McCombs. (BA, 31 Dec. 1804)

SHANKS, Mrs. Jane, died 7th inst. in Mont. Co., aged 83. "Fred. Town - 25 Jan." (BFG, 28 Jan. 1812)

SHANLEY, James, of Balto., and Miss Rosanna M'Cann of Balto. Co., were married last Sat. by Rev. Moranville. (BFG, 11 Sept. 1809)

SHANNARD, Edward, and Miss Harriet Wade, both of Balto., were married last Mon. by Rev. Bartow. (BA, 27 June 1816)

SHARDLE, William, and Martha Wilson, both of Balto., were married last eve. by Rev. Kurtz. (BFG, 30 Aug. 1800)

SHARP, David, of Elk Ridge, and Miss Henrietta Thomas of Annapolist were married last Wed. by Rev. Wyatt. (BT, 29 Aug. 1804)

SHARP, Capt. Peter, of Balto., died near Easton on Sat., 11th inst. (BFG, 25 June 1803)

SHARTEL, William, died last night in his 35th year, leaving a wife and a dau.; res. corner of Lexington and Liberty Sts. (BEP, 20 Nov. 1809)

SHAW, Capt., of Balto., and Miss Eliza Palmer, dau. of Thomas Palmer of Balto., were married at Phila. on Friday by Rev. Bishop White. (BFG, 13 Aug. 1798)

SHAW, Mrs. Catherine, died 30 Dec., aged 68 years, 10 mos. (BT, 7 Jan. 1815)

SHAW, Mrs. Elizabeth, died last Wed. in her 32nd year. (BFG, 8 Jan. 1813)

SHAW, James, a native of Md., was shot this afternoon in front of the Carolina Coffee House, by Richard Dennis, and Richard Dennis, Jr. The dec. was about 35 years old. "Charleston Times." (BT, 3 Sept. 1804)

SHAW, James, and Dorothy W. Whipple, all of Balto., were married last Thurs. by Rev. Glendy. (BFG, 29 Nov. 1814)

SHAW, Dr. John, native of Annapolis, died 10 Jan. last on board the British Schooner Polly, on her passage from Charleston S. C., to the Bahamas. (BFG, 15 March 1809)

SHAW, Capt. Pigot, and Miss Eliza Bigger were married last Sat. by Rev. Inglis. (BFG, 17 Sept. 1804)

SHAW, Mrs. Priscilla, relict of Archibald Shaw, died yesterday. Funeral will be from 90 Bond St., Fells Pt. (BFG, 29 Jan. 1803)

SHAW, William, and Miss Eliza Mince both of Balto. Co. were wed last eve. by Rev. Gest. (BA, 25 Jan. 1815)

SHEAFF, William, died at Phila., aged 58. (BFG, 17 Aug. 1803)

SHEARS, Michael, and Phebe Mail were wed Fri. eve. (BFG, 11 Sept. 1804)

SHEAVES, Robert, and Miss Jane Young, all of Balto., were married last eve. by Rev. Ryland. (BFG, 12 May 1813)

SHEDDEN, John, died Sun. in his 67th year. (BA, 27 April 1815)

SHEE, John, collector of the Port of Phila., died there on 5th inst. (BFG, 8 Aug. 1808)

SHEETZ, Joseph, merchant, and Ruth, dau. of Thomas Owings of Balto. Co., were married last eve. by Rev. Coleman. (BFG, 27 Nov. 1801)

SHEETZ, Mrs. Ruth, wife of Joseph Sheetz, died last Tues. (BFG, 7 Oct. 1805)

SHEFFER, Daniel, and Miss Naomi Wierman, dau. of John Wierman, near the Sulphur Springs, Adams Co., were married 6th inst. by Rev. Goering. "York - Nov. 20." (BFG, 25 Nov. 1806)

SHEFFEY, Daniel, member of Congress, and Miss Maria Hanson, dau. of Samuel Hanson of Washington, were married on Thurs., 30th ult. (BFR, 3 Feb. 1812)

SHEFFIELD, Mrs. Catherine, wife of Frederick Sheffield, died 27th inst., in her 50th year, leaving a husband and children; res. in Petticoat Alley, Fells Point. (BW, 29 Jan. 1814)

SHEPPARD, Mrs. Ann, consort of Major Thomas Sheppard, died yesterday in her 38th year. (BA, 19 Sept. 1816)

SHEPPARD, John, stepson of Wm. McDonald, merchant, died last Sun. aged 20 years. (BFG, 8 Sept. 1802)

SHERBERLY, William, and Miss Margaret Ballad, both of Fells Point, were married Sun., 24th inst., by Rev. Toy. (BT, 1 March 1799)

SHERBURN, Joseph, and Miss Mary Yates both of Chas. Co., were married 4th inst. by Rev. Contee. (BA, 12 April 1809)

SHEREDINE, Mrs. Eleanor, wife of Upton Sheredine, died Sat., 30th inst., at Midhill, Fred. Co. (BFG, 13 Jan. 1798)

SHEREDINE, Upton, died 14th inst. at Midhill, Fred. Co.; first commissioner under the law of the U. S. for the direct tax for Md. (BFG, 18 Jan. 1800)

SHERLOCK, John, Balto. merchant, and a native of Eng., died this morning. (BFG, 22 Dec. 1813)

SHERRER, George, of Balto., and Miss Ann Day of Balto. Co., were married last Thurs. by Rev. Haney. (BA, 11 June 1810)

SHERRER, Capt. John, died at Fells Point on Sat., 19th inst. (BFG, 30 Oct. 1805)

SHERWOOD, Philemon, and Miss Sarah Porter all of Balto. were wed last Sun. by Rev. M'Kane. (BEP, 4 Oct. 1809)

SHETTLEFORD, Lewis, and Miss Mary Curtain, both of Balto., were married last eve. by Rev. Ratoone. (BFG, 2 Aug. 1805)

SHIELDS, David, died last eve. in his 74th year; res. on Gay St. (BFG, 4 Oct. 1811)

SHIELDS, William, and Mrs. Kitty Waldron, both of Alexandria were married 1st inst. (BFG, 14 Dec. 1808)

SHIELDS, William, and Miss Harriet Butler, both of Balto., were married last eve. by Rev. Richards. (BFG, 27 Dec. 1811)

SHILLING, Philip, and Mrs. Abigail Omansetter were married Sun. by Rev. Rattoone. (BFG, 8 Oct. 1804)

SHINNICK, Elizabeth, wife of Jacob Shinnick, died 25th inst. in her 30th year; res. in Delany St. (BFG, 25 June 1807)

SHIPLEY, Benjamin, died 22 Feb. at his res. in Balto. Co., aged 61 years. His son Caleb Shipley, died one week before his father, in his 21st year. (BFG, 14 March 1812)

SHIPLEY, Johnzee, and Mrs. Ann Swan, both of Balto. Co., were wed last eve. by Rev. Hicks. (BA, 10 Nov. 1813)

SHIPLEY, Mr. Talbot, died 13th inst., leaving a wife and children. (BFG, 17 March 1800)

SHIPLEY, William, Jr., and Miss Sarah Ann Sellman, dau. of Johnzee Sellman of Balto. Co., were wed last Tues. at Green Hill by Rev. Bend. (BW, 24 May 1810)

SHIPPEN, Hon. Edward, late Chief Justice of the Penna. Supreme Court, died Tues., 15 April, in his 78th year. (BT, 22 April 1806)

SHIPPEN, Joseph, died at Lancaster on 11th inst., in his 78th year. (BEP, 3 March 1810)

SHIPPEN, William, died Mon. at his res. near Germantown, in his 75th year. (BEP, 13 July 1808)

SHOCK, Henry, and Miss Hannah Spicer, both of Balto., were wed last eve. by Rev. Willis. (BFG, 21 April 1797)

SHOEMAKER, David, bookbinder of Phila., and Nancy Bogle of Balto. were married last eve. by Rev. Glendy. (BA, 27 Feb. 1805)

SHOEMAKER, David, and Miss Mary Sumwalt, eld. dau. of Frederick Sumwalt, all of Balto. Co., were married last Thurs. by Rev. Dr. Innis. (BFG, 12 Oct. 1816)

SHOEMAKER, George, and Miss Rachel Walton were wed last Thurs. by Rev. Roberts. (BEP, 25 Nov. 1808)

SHOEMAKER, Joseph L., aged about 27, son of Jonathan Shoemaker of Penna., died this morning at the res. of Elisha Tyson on Sharp St. (BFG, 12 Feb. 1814)

SHORTRIDGE, John, and Miss Sarah Oram, all of Balto., were married on Sun. eve. by Rev. Dr. Roberts. (BA, 20 Jan. 1810)

SHREAGLEY, Michael, died Thurs., 4th inst., at Fells Point, aged 52 years. (BFG, 25 Sept. 1801)

SHRIM, Mrs. Barbara. died last eve., aged 63 years and 4 mos. (BFG, 18 June 1799)

SHRIM, Jacob, died this morning in his 33rd year; res. on North Frederick St. (BFG, 27 April 1803)

SHRIVER, Andrew, died this week last Wed., of the firm of Jacob and Andrew Shriver of this town, leaving a widow and parents. "Rep. Advocate." (BA, 25 Jan. 1805)

SHRIVER, Mrs. Ann Maria, died near Hanover, Adams Co., Penna., wife of the late Andrew Shriver, dec., on 8th inst., in her 92nd year. She was married for 66 years, and lived on the plantation where she died for 70 years. At the time of her death she had 126 descendants. (BT, 16 May 1801)

SHRIVER, Jacob, of Fred. Co., and Miss Eve Hoophert of Adams Co., Penna., were married Tues., 10 Sept., by Rev. Gobrecht. (BA, 18 Sept. 1805)

SHRIVER, John S., and Miss Henrietta Myer, all of Balto., were wed last Mon. by Rev. Glendy. (BA, 7 Aug. 1816)

SHRIVER, Mrs. Rebecca, consort of David Shriver of Fred. Co., died 24th ult., aged 71 years. (BS, 16 Dec. 1812)

SHROITER, Charles, letter carrier, and Miss Catherine Hauptmann from Hanover, Penna., were wed last eve. by Rev. Kurtz. (BFG, 25 May 1799)

SHROUD, Miss Elizabeth, died last Tues. in her 18th year. (BFG, 11 July 1805)

SHUTTLEFORD, Lewis, and Miss Mary Curtain, both of Balto., were wed last eve. by Rev. Dr. Rattoone. (BEP, 2 Aug. 1805)

SIEGFRIED, Mr. F. H., and Miss Charlotte Frazier of Balto., were married last Mon. by Rev. Ireland. (BFG, 29 March 1798)

SIEMSEN, John J., and Mrs. Eleanor McConnell, both of Balto., were married last eve. by Rev. Inglis. (BFG, 22 April 1816)

SIGIL, Milburn, printer, died at Annapolis last Mon. in his 41st year. (BEP, 4 March 1811)

SIM, Henry, of Fred. Town, and Catherine Bier, dau. of Philip Bier of Balto., were married last eve. by Rev. Otterbein. (BFG, 24 Nov. 1804)

SIMKINS, Eli, of Balto., and Miss Maria North Carnan, dau. of Robert North Carnan of Balto. Co., were married last eve. by Rev. Wells. (BFG, 15 Feb. 1815)

SIMMONS, Mrs., wife of William Simmons, an accountant in the War Dept., died Sat., 19th inst. (BEP, 25 Nov. 1808)

SIMMONS, Isaac, and Miss Mary Gittings, dau. of James Gittings of Long Green, Balto. Co., were married last Thurs. by Rev. Dashiell. (BFR, 13 Jan. 1812)

SIMMONS, Samuel, of Dor. Co., and Miss Mary Fisher of Balto. were married Sun., 16th inst. by Rev. Glendy. (BA, 18 Dec. 1810)

SIMMS, John D., and Miss Mary West, dau. of the late Roger West all of Alexandria, were married 7th inst. at the res. of Dr. James Craik. (BFR, 23 Sept. 1809)

SIMONSON, John, and Miss Margaret Keener, both of Balto., were wed last eve. by Rev. Kurtz. (BA, 3 June 1808)

SIMPSON, Basil, died Fri., 17th inst., at his res. on the Patuxent River, in his 47th year; a father. (BFG, 23 Aug. 1810)

SIMPSON, George, died Tues.; formerly a merchant of Balto. (BT, 18 March 1802)

SIMPSON, John, and Miss Jane Kuyt, all of Balto., were wed last eve. by Rev. Rattoone. (BFG, 16 Sept. 1809)

SIMPSON, Miss Sarah, died last eve. in her 18th year. (BFG, 2 Dec. 1803)

SINCLAIR. William, and Mrs. Jane Munroe, all of Balto., were wed 9th inst. by Rev. Glendy. (BA, 29 July 1807)

SINDALL, John, and Miss Mary Daughaday, all of Balto., were wed on Thurs. eve. by Rev. Dr. Styers. (BA, 27 Jan. 1816)

SINDLE, Abraham, and Miss Ann Burgan of Balto. Co., were married last Thurs. by Rev. Healy. (BA, 31 Oct. 1815)

SINGLETON, William, of Balto., died last Tues. in his 47th year. (BFG, 18 Aug. 1803)

SINLEY, Alexander, and Miss Margaret McDonnell, both of Balto., were wed last Sat. by Rev. Richards. (BA, 7 Oct. 1812)

SINNERS, James R., and Miss Mary Pollard, all of Balto., were wed Thurs., 14th inst., by Rev. Dr. Roberts. (BWA, 23 March 1816)

SINNET, James, and Mrs. Ann Doyle, both of Balto., were married last eve. by Rev. Moranville. (BEP, 13 June 1808)

SITLER, Abraham, died yesterday, after attending the funeral of George Washington; an old inhab. of Balto. (BFG, 2 Jan. 1800)

SITLER, Dr. Daniel, and Miss Tamer Hicks, both of Balto., were wed last Thurs. by Rev. Coats. (BT, 25 Sept. 1802)

SKELTON, John, and Mary M'Comas, all of Balto., were married on 25th ult. by Rev. Richards. (BFG, 9 Jan. 1806)

SKELTON, John, died Fri. se'ennight, in his 21st year. (BS, 13 Oct. 1810)

SKERRETT, Miss Maria, of Fells Point, died yesterday in her 20th year; the day was to have been her wedding day. (BFG, 17 Aug. 1802)

SKILLMAN, Robert, and Mrs. Sailors, both of Balto., were wed last Sun. by Rev. Allison. (BT, 27 Dec. 1797)

SKINNER, John S., of Annap., and Miss Elizabeth Glen Davies of Balto. were married last eve. by Rev. Glendy. (BS, 11 March 1812)

SKIPWITH, Col. William, died 6th inst. in Powhatan Co., an officer in the Rev. War. He was a husband and father. (BPEA, 27 Sept. 1815)

SKIRWAN, James W., supercargo and part owner of the schooner
Julia, of Balto., died at St. Thomas. (BA, 3 Dec. 1804)

SLATER, William, and Polly Evans were married last Thurs. (BA, 29 April 1806)

SLATER, William, died Tues., 27th inst. at the res. of Col. John Cromwell; for many years a Balto. merchant. He leaves a widow and children. (BFG, 31 July 1813)

SLAUCE, Charles, and Lydia Foster, both of Balto. Co., were married 4 July by Rev. Glendy. (BA, 6 July 1816)

SLEE, John, and Miss Mary Tipton all of Balto. were married last eve. by Rev. Dr. Roberts. (BFG, 30 March 1810)

SLEVERS, Augustus, chemist, native of Brunswick, Germany, died 29 June, aged about 30 years; his death was caused by bathing. (BFG, 7 July 1808)

SLOAN, Mrs. Ann, wife of James W. Sloan of Balto., died last Fri. in her 23rd year. Interment in St. Peter's Church. (BFG, 13 May 1805)

SLOAN, Jane, eld. dau. of James Sloan of Balto., died yesterday, aged 16 years. (BT, 5 Feb. 1796)

SLOVER, Isaac, and Miss Charlotte Mason of Balto. Co., were wed 5 March by Rev. Healey. (BA, 9 March 1816)

SLUBEY, Mrs. Rachael, wife of William Slubey of Chestertown, Md., died 24th ult. (BFG, 7 March 1798)

SMALL, George, died last Fri., in his 19th year, brother of Major Jacob Small of Balto. (BEP, 21 Aug. 1809)

SMALL, John, merchant, and Elizabeth Schaeffer, dau. of Baltzer Schaeffer, all of Balto., were married last eve. by Rev. Glendy. (BA, 24 April 1807)

SMALL, William, and Miss Priscilla Jackson, all of Balto., were married 5th ult. by Rev. Healey. (BW, 29 Aug. 1809)

SMALLWOOD, George, and Miss Julian Jarboe of St. M. Co., were married last Sat. by Rev. Inglis. (BA, 19 Sept. 1815)

SMALLWOOD, Nicholas, and Ruthy Beall, dau. of the late Capt. Richard Beall, were married last Thurs. eve. by Dr. Stephen B. Balch. (BFG, 11 March 1801)

SMALLWOOD, Mrs. Susanna, died yesterday afternoon. (BA, 26 Feb. 1805)

SMALLWOOD, William, of Balto., and Mrs. Anna Kauffman of Lancaster Co., Penna., were married last Thurs. by Rev. Kurtz. (BA, 8 Nov. 1806)

SMELSER, John, and Miss Rachel Norris, all of Fred. Co., were married Sun., 16th inst., of this month. (BEP, 18 Dec. 1810)

SMILEY, Mrs. Catherine, died; a member of the Catholic church. (BFG, 6 Nov. 1816)

SMILIE, John, rep. in Congress from Penna., died in Balto. yesterday, aged 74. A native of Ireland, he served in our Revolutionary War in both civilian and military capacities. (BA, 1 Jan. 1813)

SMILLEY, Peter, merchant, and Miss Catherine Walter, all of Balto., were married last Tues. eve. by Rev. Fenwick. (BA, 12 July 1816)

SMITH, Capt. Alexander H., of the ship Ardent of Balto., died 2 June in Algefiras, as a result of a wound received in an engagement with five French privateers. (BFG, 10 Aug. 1799)

SMITH, Alexander, of N. Y., and Miss Sarah (Pellom?) of Balto., were married last Sat. by Rev. Dr. Rattoone. (BFG, 6 Nov. 1806)

SMITH, Andrew, 51st R. M. M., and Miss Catherine Fontz, all of Balto., were married last eve. by Rev. Roberts. (BMG, 8 May 1815)

SMITH, Mrs. Ann, wife of Larkin Smith, collector of the Port of Norfolk, died there 17th inst. (BA, 28 Dec. 1812)

SMITH, Arnold, died 20th inst., in his 47th year. (BPE, 24 Dec. 1813)

SMITH, Lieut. Benjamin, first lieut. of the frigate Chesapeake, died at Norfolk. (BFG, 24 Oct. 1807)

SMITH, Capt. Benjamin B., and Miss Ann Thompson, all of Balto., were married last Thurs. by Rev. Glendy. (BFG, 15 March 1814)

SMITH, Caleb, died last eve. aged 52 years; res. in King George St. (BFG, 15 April 1812)

SMITH, Mrs. Cassandra, wife of Winston Smith of Balto. Co., died 7th inst., aged about 38 years; a wife and mother. (BPEA, 14 Nov. 1815)

SMITH, Mr. Charles, died at Trenton, 30th ult., in his 32nd year; he was a lieut. in a U. S. regt. (BT, 11 Feb. 1800)

SMITH, Chester C., printer, native of Springfield, Mass., died at Lancaster, Penna., in his 26th year. (BFG, 21 Jan. 1805)

SMITH, Clement, merchant of Georgetown, and Miss Margaretta Clare Brice, dau. of John Brice of Balto., were married last eve. by Rev. Whitehead. (BFG, 13 Nov. 1807)

SMITH, Daniel, of Balto., and Miss Ann Harvey of Washington were married Thurs., 2nd inst. (BWA, 11 May 1816)

SMITH, David, died this morning in his 35th year; funeral from the res. of his mother in Market St. (BFG, 18 Oct. 1810)

SMITH, David, register of wills for Cecil Co., died in Elkton, Md., last Wed. in his 74th year. (BFG, 20 Sept. 1813)

SMITH, Dennis A., of Balto., and Elizabeth T. Presbury, dau. of George G. Presbury, Jr., were married last eve. by Rev. Mr. Coates. (BFG, 24 Dec. 1802)

SMITH, Dennis, and Rebecca, dau. of Job Smith of Balto., were married last eve. at Poplar Grove by Rev. M'Kean. (BFG, 23 May 1806)

MARRIAGES AND DEATHS

SMITH, Edward, and Mrs. Catherine Webster were married in Phila. (BT, 17 May 1799)

SMITH, Edward, a native of Phila., and long-time res. of Fells Point, died in his 30th year, leaving a widow and two children; res. on Georges St. (BFG, 15 Oct. 1805)

SMITH, Miss Elizabeth, eld. dau. of Gen. Samuel Smith, died yesterday morning. (BFG, 12 May 1812)

SMITH, Mrs. Elizabeth, carver and gilder, died Wed., 10th inst., in her 38th year; interment in the Episcopal Cemetery. (BFG, 22 April 1816)

SMITH, Mrs. Elizabeth A., consort of Capt. John A. Smith, died at Fells Point on Sat., in her 35th year. (BFG, 2 Jan. 1804)

SMITH, Elizabeth Louisa, dau. of the Secretary of the Navy, died last eve. in her 14th year. Her bro., aged 3 years, died a few days ago. (BFG, 19 Feb. 1806)

SMITH, Mrs. Frances, of Balto. Co., died last Wed., in her 68th year. (BFG, 18 July 1807)

SMITH, Lieut. Frederick W., of the U. S. Navy, and Miss Marianne Parker of Balto. were married last Sun. by Rev. Bishop Kemp. (BPEA, 24 Feb. 1815)

SMITH, George, of Fells Point, died last Sat., after a painful illness, in his 29th year. (BT, 30 May 1802)

SMITH, George, and Miss Rebecca Howard both of Balto. were married Thurs. by Rev. Rattoone. (BFG, 31 Dec. 1807)

SMITH, George, of Balto., and Miss Frances Smith of P. G. Co., were married Thurs. by Rev. Dr. Roberts. (BA, 1 July 1816)

SMITH, Gilbert Hamilton, died last eve. at his res. in Gay St., in his 48th year. A res. of Balto. for only a short time, he leaves a large family. (BFG, 4 Sept. 1799)

SMITH, Mrs. Hannah, of Fells Point, died Fri., 28th ult. She survived her husband's death by only a few days. (BFG, 2 May 1797)

SMITH, Mr. Henry, son of Rev. Frederick Smith of Balto., died 30th ult., in the 18th year of his age; interment in the German Lutheran Cemetery. (BT, 6 Sept. 1800)

SMITH, Capt. Henry, and Miss Harriet Daniels, all of Balto., were married last Wed. by Rev. Bartow. (BFG, 2 Feb. 1816)

SMITH, Capt. Jacob, and Miss Mary Reese, all of Balto., were married last Sat. by Rev. Glendy. (BEP, 26 Jan. 1810)

SMITH, Jacob Giles, and Miss Sarah Evans, dau. of William Evans of Balto., were married last eve. by Rev. Rattoone. (BFG, 21 March 1804)

SMITH, Jacob J., and Miss Julia Ann Butler, all of Balto. Co., were married last Thurs. by Rev. Moranville. (BEP, 4 June 1810)

SMITH, James, of Balto., died this morning in his 29th year. (BFG, 19 Oct. 1797)

SMITH, James, died last Tues., 16th inst., aged 56 years, leaving a widow and a family. He had been supt. of the almshouse. (BFG, 20 Dec. 1800)

SMITH, Dr. James, and Miss Caldwell were married last Sun. by Rev. Alexander. (BFG, 19 Oct. 1801)

SMITH, James, merchant, died at Fredericktown on Mon., 2nd inst., in his 70th year. His only dau. married John McPherson. (BFG, 5 Jan. 1804)

SMITH, James, and Miss Rachel Glenville Honicomb all of Balto. were married on Thurs. by Rev. Bend. (BA, 16 Feb. 1811)

SMITH, James, and Miss Priscilla Clouden were married last Thurs. by Rev. J. Glendy. (BS, 4 March 1812)

SMITH, Jeremiah, member of Congress from N. H., and Miss Eliza Rose of Bladensburg were married 15th inst. (BWM, 26 March 1797)

SMITH, Job, and Mrs. Mary Presbury were married last eve. by Fev. Dashiell. (BFG, 27 Oct. 1809)

SMITH, Job, Jr., and Miss Rachel Stevenson both of Balto. were married last Thurs. by Rev. Roberts. (BA, 27 April 1815)

SMITH, Capt. John, of Balto., died last Fri., aged 43 years. Interment in St. Pauls Churchyard. (BMJ, 30 May 1796)

SMITH, Dr. John, and Miss Mary Ernest, both of Balto., were married Thurs. by Rev. Kurtz. (BT, 15 May 1802)

SMITH, John, and Miss Sarah Irvin both of Balto. were married on Thurs. by Rev. Coates. (BT, 4 Feb. 1804)

SMITH, John, Jr., and Frances Toon were married at Canton by Rev. Rattoone last Sat. (BFG, 16 Aug. 1804)

SMITH, John, carpenter, died last eve.; res. on Fish Market Space. (BS, 8 Sept. 1812)

SMITH, John, Post Captain in the U. S. Navy, died last Sun. at Phila. (BFG, 9 Aug. 1815)

SMITH, John Lane, died Mon., 25th inst., in his 21st year; of Patuxent. (BFG, 26 Sept. 1797)

SMITH, John Porter, son of the late Major Nathaniel Smith of Balto.. died at Aux-Cayes, last 13 June, aged 21 years; he leaves his mother. (BFG, 10 Aug. 1804)

SMITH, Joseph, and Miss Winifred McCarthy were married last eve. by Rev. Ireland. (BFG, 12 April 1799)

SMITH, Lieut. Joseph E., late of the U. S. Navy, and eld. son of Capt. Joseph Smith of Balto., died and was buried 1st inst. at Pittsburgh, Penna., with military honors. He was in his 24th year. (BPE, 15 Dec. 1813, gives a long obit.)

SMITH, Josiah, died at his res. in Harf. Co., at an advanced age; res. on Gunpowder Neck. (BW, 13 April 1812)

SMITH, Larkin, of Balto. Co., and Rachel Nicholson, dau. of Thomas Nicholson, of the Eastern Shore, were married a few evenings ago by Rev. Bend. (BFG, 12 July 1796)

SMITH, Louis B., eld. son of General Smith, died this morning. (BFG, 14 Oct. 1806)

SMITH, Mrs. Margaret, wife of Uriah Smith of Phila., died Wed. in her 22nd year. (BA, 29 Aug. 1801)

SMITH, Mrs. Margaret, died last Sat., wife of the late Conrad Smith, in her 82nd year. Interment in the German Reformed Evang. Church. (BFG, 12 Sept. 1804)

SMITH, Mrs. Margaret, wife of William R. Smith, died Tues., 10th inst., aged 26 years. (BFG, 12 April 1806)

SMITH, Mrs. Margaret, wife of Job Smith of the western precincts, died Sun., 20th inst. (BFG, 21 March 1808)

SMITH, Miss Margaretta, dau. of Gen. Samuel Smith, died Tues., aged about 10 years. (BA, 14 May 1807).

SMITH, Mrs. Maria, wife of Isaac Smith, and dau. of the late Judge Francis Hopkinson of Phila., died 17th inst., in her 32nd year. (BFG, 25 Oct. 1806)

SMITH, Martin, and Miss Elizabeth Simm, all of Fred. Co., were married at Fred. Town on 19th ult., by Rev. D. F. Schaeffer. (BPEA, 12 April 1815)

SMITH, Mathew, and Miss Betsy Barnett, both of Harf. Co., were wed by Rev. Glendy on 3rd inst. (BA, 12 Oct. 1811)

SMITH, Nicholas, and Miss Susannah Barnhart, both of Balto., were married last Sun. by Rev. Kurtz. (BEP, 20 May 1808)

SMITH, Pernel, and Miss Ann Gilberthorpe, all of Balto., were wed Fri. at Old Town. (BFG, 25 May 1805)

SMITH, Peter, died last Sat., in his 67th year, an old citizen of Balto. (BFG, 10 Oct. 1809)

SMITH, Peter M., late first officer on the ship Eutaw from Balto., died at St. Thomas on 26 Jan. (BFG, 13 March 1807)

SMITH, Ralph, Balto. merchant, and Miss Eliza Reigart, were wed at Lancaster, Penna., on 20th ult., by Rev. Mr. Lata. (BFG, 29 June 1805)

SMITH, Miss Rebecca, died 31st ult. in her 25th year. (BA, 14 June 1808)

SMITH, Mr. Richard, of Conn., and Miss Anne B. Clarke of Balto., were married Tues. eve. by Rev. Kurtz. (BT, 28 Jan. 1802)

SMITH, Capt. Robert, of Balto., and Miss Letitia Smith of St. M. Co., were married 29th ult. in the latter county by Rev. Deroshore. (BFG, 9 Nov. 1811)

SMITH, Mrs. Sally, native of Wor. Co., died yesterday, leaving five orphan children. (BPEA, 7 Nov. 1815)

SMITH, Mrs. Sally, died 29th inst., aged 38 years, leaving 3 orphan children. (BA, 31 Jan. 1816)

SMITH, Samuel, merchant, and Ann S. Sitler, both of Balto., were married last eve. by Rev. Richards. (BFG, 20 May 1796)

SMITH, Samuel S., of Washington Co., Penna., and Miss Ann Brown, dau. of William Brown of Balto., were married yesterday at Friends Meeting House. (BFG, 22 June 1804)

SMITH, Mrs. Sarah, consort of Capt. Joseph Smith, died last eve. in her 43rd year. (BFG, 21 Feb. 1799)

SMITH, Solomon, a carpenter of Balto., died today; res. in St. Pauls Lane. (BFG, 4 Sept. 1797)

SMITH, Thomas, of Fells Point, aged 57, died Tues., 18th inst. (BWM, 23 April 1797)

SMITH, Thomas, and Mrs. Sarah Robinson, all of Balto., were wed 22nd inst. by Rev. Hargrove. (BA, 27 Dec. 1816)

SMITH, Thorowgood, President of Baltimore Insurance Co., and late Mayor of Balto., died this morning in his 67th year. (BFG, 13 Aug. 1810)

SMITH, Major Walter, of Georgetown, and Miss Sarah Hoffman, dau. of Peter Hoffman of Balto., were married last eve. by Rev. Otterbein. (BFG, 2 Nov. 1808)

SMITH, Mrs. Walter, dau. of Peter Hoffman, of Balto., died at Georgetown last Sat. (BFG, 18 Sept. 1809)

SMITH, William, horse farmer of Balto., died last Sat. (BFG, 16 Nov. 1801)

SMITH, William, son of Robert Smith, Secretary of the Navy, died in Balto. on Tues. (BA, 30 Nov. 1801)

SMITH, William, died at Fells Point on last Fri., aged 19; son of James Smith, merchant of Old Town. (BT, 27 Sept. 1802)

SMITH, William, foreman of the Washington navy yard, and Miss Mary Murdock of the Dist. of Columbia, were married 22nd inst. at Washington by Rev. McCormick. (BT, 31 Jan. 1804)

SMITH, William, and Miss Betsy McComas, dau. of Col. James M'Comas of Harf. Co., were married last Sun. eve. by Rev. Harryman. (BA, 14 Aug. 1805)

SMITH, William, and Miss Catherine Adams, dau. of John Adams, merchant all of Balto., were married last Wed. by Rev. Glendy. (BFG, 27 Dec. 1806)

SMITH, William, and Mrs. Sarah Hete, all of Balto., were married last eve. by Rev. Hargrove. (BFG, 19 March 1813)

SMITH, William, died yesterday in his 86th year; res. in Calvert St. (BFG, 28 March 1814)

SMITH, William H., Balto. merchant, and Miss Mary C. B. Madison, dau. of the late Francis Madison of Madison Co., were wed near Orange Court House, Va., on 31st ult., by Rev. Cottom. (BFG, 12 Nov. 1804)

SMITH, Dr. William Kilty, of Balto. Co., died yesterday in his 2 26th year. (BFG, 27 Sept. 1811)

SMITH, William R., and Miss Margaret Dugan, dau. of Cumberland Dugan, were married last eve. by Rev. Ireland. (BFG, 3 Oct. 1798)

SMITH, Winston, and Miss Cassandra Dallam, both of Harf. Co., were married last Thurs. by Rev. Ireland. (BFG, 29 Oct. 1796)

SMITHSON, Daniel, and Miss Hannah Wright, both of Balto., were married last eve. (BEP, 3 Aug. 1810)

SMITHSON, Hon. William, of the Md. Senate, died a few days ago at his res. in Harf. Co. (BW, 30 Jan. 1809)

SMITHSON, William, and Miss Mary Yokeley, both of Balto., were married last eve. by Rev. Hagerty. (BEP, 10 April 1809)

SMOTHERS, Daniel, and Miss Maria M'Clain were married last Sun. by Rev. Hargrove. (BFG, 16 April 1805)

SMOTHERS, James, and Miss Leah Brown, all of Balto., were married by Rev. Glendy on Sat. (BFG, 17 Nov. 1812)

SNARES, William, of Strawberry Alley, died on the 6th. (BFG, 9 Aug. 1802)

SNAUBER, George, and Miss Elizabeth Keller, dau. of George Keller, all of Balto., were married last Sun. by Rev. Kurtz. (BA, 25 Aug. 1801)

SNAURER, George, died yesterday eve.; res. at Pratt and Charles Sts. (BA, 22 Aug. 1815)

SNEED, Capt. Griffin, of N. J., son of the late Brig.-Gen. Jackson, died in Balto. on Mon. (BA, 10 April 1816)

SNEEDEN, Sgt. Robert, U. S. Artillery, native of N. Y., died yesterday at Fort McHenry in his 25th year. (BPEA, 30 Aug. 1815)

SNIDER, John, Jr., and Harriott Webb, both of Balto., were married last Sat. by Rev. Richards. (BA, 4 Nov. 1806)

SNIDER, Matthias, and Miss Elizabeth Dayley, both of Balto., were married last eve. by Rev. Kurtz. (BFG, 8 Oct. 1800)

SNOUFFER, George, and Miss D. Thomas, all of Fred. Co., were wed 2nd inst. by Rev. D. F. Schaeffer. (BPEA, 12 April 1815)

SNOW, Jethro, and Miss Eliza Smith, were married by Rev. Dr. Rattoone at Fells Point on Thurs. (BFG, 20 Jan. 1808)

SNOW, Capt. John, and Miss Mary Bevins both of Balto. were wed on Tues. by Rev. Bartow. (BA, 17 Oct. 1816)

SNOW, Mr. Zedekiah, long an inhab. of Balto., died on his passage to Martinique, in his 39th year, leaving a wife and two children. (BA, 15 Oct. 1816)

SNOWDEN, Mrs. Eleanor, wife of the late Francis Snowden, died Sun., 7th inst., at her res. in Balto. Co., aged 63 years. (BFG, 15 June 1812)

SNOWDEN, Francis, died in Balto. Co., last Sun. in his 55th year. (BFG, 25 Feb. 1812)

SNOWDEN, John, died Tues., 1st inst., at his res. near Patuxent Iron Works, in his 71st year, the only survivor of several brothers. (BFG, 3 Nov. 1808)

SNOWDEN, Joseph, of Balto., and Miss Mary Ann Busey were married last Tues. at Springfield, the res. of Samuel Busey, Mont. Co., by Rev. Matthews. (BFG, 16 Oct. 1812)

SNOWDEN, Joseph, of Balto., died last Fri. in his 36th year. (BA, 22 Nov. 1816)

SNOWDEN, Richard, of P. G. Co., and Miss Eliza Warfield, dau. of Dr. Chas. A. Warfield, of A. A. Co., were married on Tues. last by Rev. Rees. (BFG, 19 Feb. 1798)

SNOWDEN, Samuel, editor of the Alexandria Advertiser, and Nancy Longden, were married Thurs. at Alexandria by Rev. Moffett. (BFG, 12 Jan. 1802)

SNOWDEN, Major Thomas, died last Thurs. at his seat in P. G. Co., in his 54th year. (BFG, 29 Oct. 1803)

SNUGGRASS, William, and Miss Catherine Hart, both of Balto., were married Thurs. by Rev. Allison. (BT, 9 Dec. 1797)

SNYDER, Mrs., consort of the Gov. of Penna., died 15th inst. (BFG, 22 March 1810)

SNYDER, Dr. Charles L., of Va., and Miss Elizabeth Ridgely Berry, dau. of Benjamin Berry of Balto., were married last eve. by Rev. Dr. Roberts. (BFG, 27 May 1812)

SNYDER, John, and Miss Hannah Marfield, both of Balto., were wed on Thurs. by Rev. Baker. (BA, 9 Nov. 1816)

SNYDER, Valentine, and Mrs. Jones, both of Balto., were married last eve. by Rev. Kurtz. (BT, 22 Dec. 1800)

SNYDER, Valentine, died this morning in his 61st year; res. in South Liberty St. (BFG, 1 Nov. 1803)

SOAPER, Nathan, and Miss Rutha Hill, both of P. G. Co., were wed last Sun. by Rev. Mr. Scott. (BT, 29 Jan. 1803)

SOLIMAN, Samuel, and Miss Ann Barton, both of Balto., were wed last eve. by Rev. Glendy. (BFG, 17 March 1812)

SOLLERS, Basil, and Susanna Owings, both of Balto. Co., were wed last Tues. by Rev. Coleman. (BT, 31 March 1800)

SOLLERS, Elisha, and Miss Sarah Partridge, both of Balto. Co., were wed last eve. by Rev. Richards. (BFG, 4 May 1798)

SOLLERS, John, and Miss Mary Anslow, both of Balto., were wed last Sun. eve. by Rev. M'Caine. (BFG, 1 July 1812)

SOLLOMON, Joseph, died this morning, aged near 21 years. (BFG, 29 July 1802)

SOLOMON, Mrs. Abigail, died yesterday, aged 51 years, leaving 5 children; res. on Pitt St. (BA, 26 Feb. 1812)

SOLOMON, Benjamin, and Miss Harriet Price, all of Balto., were wed last eve. by Rev. Richards. (BT, 1 Feb. 1802)

SOLOMON, George, drayman, died last Mon. when he mistook his way and drove his horse over the end of a wharf. (BFG, 6 March 1799)

SOLOMON, Isaac, Balto. merchant, died last Wed. in his 56th year. (BFG, 12 Jan. 1798)

SOLOMON, Mr. Myer, died last eve. after a short illness, an aged inhab. of Balto. (BFG, 1 Sept. 1800)

SOLOMON, Samuel, and Miss Ann Barton, both of Balto., were wed last Mon. by Rev. Glendy. (BFR, 18 March 1812)

SOMERVILLE, Henry Vernon, of Bloomsbury, Md., and Miss Rebecca M. Tiernan, 2nd dau. of Luke Tiernan of Balto., were wed Tues. eve. by Rev. Fenwick. (BA, 28 Dec. 1815)

SOMERVELL, James, Balto. merchant, died last Sat. in his 61st year. (BFG, 10 July 1806)

SOTHEREN, John, formerly of the Eastern Shore, died Mon., 7th inst., at the establishment of Richardson and Duff, near the Union Mfg. Co., Balto. Co. (BA, 21 June 1813)

SOUTHCOMB, Plummer, and Miss Elizabeth Ruth, all of Balto., were married last Sun. (BS, 31 March 1812)

SOUTHGATE, John, of Norfolk, and Miss Fanny P. McCausland, dau. of Marcus McCausland, were married Tues. eve. by Rev. Richards. (BFG, 4 Oct. 1810)

SOUTHWARD, Capt. William, of Balto., and Miss Emily Coffin of Salem, Mass., were married yesterday by Rev. Glendy. (BT, 27 Sept. 1805)

SOUTHWORD, Mrs. Mary, wife of Capt. William Southword of Balto., died at Salem, Mass., leaving children. (BA, 6 Oct. 1804)

SOWER, Brook W., printer, and Ruth Harriman, 3rd dau. of William Harriman, were married 20 Aug. at Middle River Neck by Rev. Hagerty. (BFG, 23 Aug. 1811)

SOWER, Christopher, died Wed., 3rd inst., at the house of Daniel Lammot; dec. was the late printer to H. M. from St. John, New Brunswick. (BT, 4 July 1799)

SPAFFORD, Capt. Samuel, of Boston, and Ann Alderson of Balto., were married at Fells Point on Tues. by Rev. Rattoone. (BFG, 27 March 1806)

SPALDING, Mrs. Mary, died yesterday morning. (BFG, 16 Dec. 1801)

SPALDING, Richard B., and Miss Maria Sower, all of Balto., were wed last Thurs. by Rev. Beasly. (BFG, 27 Jan. 1813)

SPALDING, William, aged 48, merchant, died 3rd inst., a loving husband and parent. (BFG, 5 Aug. 1803)

SPANHOF, Reinhardt, a native of Germany, and for some years a res. of Balto., died last Sun. at the horse of George Repold, aged 33 years. (BFG, 12 Dec. 1798)

SPARKS, J. B., native of Md., died 16th ult., at Sackett's Harbor, an officer in the U. S. Army. (BA, 6 Aug. 1813)

SPEAR, Col. John, of Balto., died at Surinam last 24 Jan. (BFG, 12 March 1796)

SPEAR, Joseph, and Miss B. Spear were married last eve. by Rev. Dr. Allison. (BFG, 11 Jan. 1798)

SPEAR, Joseph, Balto. merchant, died last Fri. in his 47th year. (BA, 1 Oct. 1810)

SPEAR, Capt. William, and Miss Leinora Creighton all of Balto. were married last Wed. by Rev. Glendy. (BA, 28 March 1810)

SPECK, Mr. Henry, of Balto., died yesterday in his 45th year. (BFG, 30 Jan. 1800)

SPECK, Henry, and Mrs. Ann Wright all of Balto. were married last Sun. by Rev. Curtz (sic). (BS, 27 Jan. 1812)

SPEDDEN, John, died last Sun. in his 67th year. (His name may be Shedden.) (BFG, 26 April 1815)

SPENCE, Capt. Peter, of N. Y., and Miss Eliza Jervis of Balto. were married last eve, by Rev. Ireland. (BA, 13 Nov. 1799)

SPENCER, Benjamin, bricklayer, a native of Delaware, but for the last 35 years an inhab. of Fells Point, died Fri., over 60 years old. (BFG, 28 Oct. 1805)

SPENCER, Joseph, and Miss Frances Matchett, dau. of George Matchett, all of Balto., were married last Thurs. by Rev. Dr. Roberts. (BA, 2 July 1814)

SPENCER, Robert, merchant of Easton, and Miss Susan M'Laughlin of Balto. were married last Wed. by Rev. Roberts. (BPEA, 25 Aug. 1815)

SPICER, Samuel L., and Rosanna A. Carrick, both of Balto., were married 23 Nov. by Rev. Fenwick. (BA, 24 Nov. 1815)

SPICER, Thomas, and Miss Mary Rutter, both of Balto., were wed last Thurs. by Rev. Dashiell. (BW, 13 April 1811)

SPICER, William Hall, and Miss Ediff (Edith?) Cole both of Balto. Co., were married last Thurs. at Abraham's Delight. (BW, 29 Feb. 1812)

SPICKNALL, Mrs. Ann, died this morning in her 56th year, wife of John Spicknall. (BFG, 16 Feb. 1813)

SPICKNALL, Frances Ann, dau. of John Spicknall, died 16th ult. in her 17th year. (BFG, 2 Nov. 1813)

SPICKNALL, Joseph, died 1st inst., in his 21st year. (BFG, 4 April 1812)

SPIES, Mr. I. P., and Miss Margaret Tschudy all of Balto., were married last Tues. by Rev. Dreyer. (BFG, 19 July 1805)

SPILMAN, James, and Miss Mary Ann Barrickman both of Balto., were married last Sun. by Rev. Mertz. (BFG, 1 Feb. 1815)

SPILMAN, P., and Dorcas Torrance, dau. of Charles Torrance of Balto., were married last eve. by Rev. Inglis. (BS, 22 May 1812)

SPIRES, Capt. Thomas, and Mrs. Ann Edwards both of Balto. were
married 1st inst., by Rev. Dashiell. (BA, 10 Jan. 1809)

SPOHN, William, and Miss Margaret Paris, dau. of the late Peter
Paris, were married at Phila. last Fri. by Rev. Dr. Helfenstein. (BA, 22 March 1805)

SPOTSWOOD, William, printer and bookseller of Phila., died Thurs.
morning in his 52nd year. (BFG, 17 April 1805)

SPRAGUE, Henry, and Miss Margaret Eaglestone Reese, all of Balto.,
were married last Wed. by Rev. Glendy. (BA, 25 Aug. 1810)
(BW, 25 Aug. 1810, gives the bride's name as Eaglestone.)

SPRAGUE, Jeremiah, painter, formerly of Boston, died in Balto.
(BPE, 26 Aug. 1813)

SPRIGG, Edward, and Mrs. Harriet Merriam, all of Balto., were wed
last Tues. by Rev. Hagerty. (BMG, 25 May 1815)

SPRIGG, Mrs. Elizabeth, wife of Gen. Thomas Sprigg, of Wash. Co.,
died 28 July. "Md. Herald." (BW, 4 Aug. 1808)

SPRIGG, Mrs. Harriet, wife of Capt. Thomas Sprigg of Balto., died
Sun. in her 20th year. (BFG, 25 Sept. 1804)

SPRIGG, Mrs. Margaret, wife of Richard Sprigg, died Wed., 13th
inst., at her res. at West River. (BMJ, 23 July 1796)

SPRIGG, Osborn, died at his seat in P. G. Co., the middle of last
month. (BPEA, 8 June 1815)

SPRIGG, Mrs. Rebecca, died 8th inst. (BFG, 11 Feb. 1813)

SPRIGG, Richard, died Sat., 24th inst., at his seat on West River.
(BFG, 27 Nov. 1798)

SPRIGG, Richard, died 15th of this month in Charleston, S. C.,
where he had gone for his health, in his 37th year; Chief
Justice of the First Judicial Circuit. Interment the
following day in the burying ground of the P. E. Church.
(BA, 3 April 1806)

SPRIGG, Capt. Thomas, and Miss Harriot Minsky were married last
eve. by Rev. Rattoone. (BFG, 27 April 1803)

SPRIGGS, George, and Mrs. Susannah Moore, all of Balto., were
married Thurs. eve. at John Shedden's, by Rev. Fidler.
(BW, 24 Oct. 1809)

SPROLE, William, and Miss Rebecca M'Connell, both of Balto., were
married last eve. by Rev. Annan. (BT, 30 Dec. 1803)

SPROLLS, Andrew, and Miss Mary Hill, all of Balto., were married
last Sat. (BT, 12 April 1802)

SPURRIER, Beale, and Miss Ann Askew all of Balto. were married on
Thurs. eve. by Rev. Rattoone. (BFG, 10 March 1804)

SPURRIER, John, of Elk Ridge, died 24th inst., a husband and
father. He was interred in the family burying ground, and
the sermon was delivered by Rev. Oliver Norris, of Queen
Caroline Parish. (BFG, 27 Jan. 1810)

SPURRIER, William, died Mon., at his place, 14 miles from Balto.,
for many years an inhab. of A. A. Co. (BA, 7 Jan. 1801)

SPURRIER, William, and Miss Sarah Dorsey, dau. of Benjamin Dorsey, all of Elk Ridge, were married last eve. by Rev. Bend. (BFG, 6 July 1810)

SPURRIER, William T., and Miss Juliet Spurrier, all of Balto., were married last Tues. eve. by Rev. Dr. Roberts. (BFG, 14 Sept. 1815)

STABLES, Mrs. Margaret, died last Tues., relict of William Stables. Both were natives of Scotland, and left three small children. (BFG, 9 Sept. 1808)

STABLES, William, died, and will be buried this afternoon. An upholsterer and a native of Scotland, he was a member of the Baltimore Independent Blues, who will attend the funeral. (BEP, 11 July 1808)

STACEY, Capt., and Mrs. Catherine Siddle of Fells Point, were married last Sun. (BA, 28 Dec. 1805)

STAFFORD, Capt. Patrick, native of Ireland, died Fri.; for many years an inhab. of Balto. (BA, 12 Dec. 1814)

STAHL, Dorothy, dau. of Godfrey Stahl, killed herself by hanging on 25th ult. She had been deprived of her reason since the age of 8. (BFG, 10 April 1807)

STALL, Andrew, and Mrs. Elizabeth Price, all of Balto., were wed on Thurs. by Rev. Healey. (BA, 4 May 1816)

STANARD, Edward C., editor of the "Spirit of Seventy-Six," a Randolph-like newspaper printed at Georgetown, D. C., died last Sat. at Leesburg, Va. (BW, 14 Dec. 1810)

STANLY, Capt. Robert, of the brig Lyon, died on his passage from the Ile of France, last 10 Sept. He leaves a widow and a family of small children. (BFG, 11 Nov. 1807)

STANSBURY, Rev. Daniel, and Miss Elizabeth Hunt, dau. of Job Hunt, were wed last Thurs. by Rev. Moore. (BA, 17 June 1816)

STANSBURY, Darius, and Miss Mary Holland, both of Balto., were wed on Thurs. by Rev. Kurtz. (BT, 4 Oct. 1803)

STANSBURY, David, and Miss Sarah Scott, dau. of R. Scott of Balto., were married on Thurs. by Rev. John Baxley. (BA, 25 Nov. 1815)

STANSBURY, Jacob, merchant, of Balto., died this morning at Oxford. (BFG, 22 Feb. 1812)

STANSBURY, Mrs. Mary, wife of Capt. Tobias E. Stansbury, died yesterday in her 49th year, leaving a husband and five children. (BFG, 22 April 1809)

STANSBURY, Tobias, and Miss Ariana Sollers, both of Balto. Co., were married last eve. by Rev. Richards. (BFG, 11 Dec. 1799)

STANSBURY, Gen. Tobias E., late Speaker of the House of Delegates, and Miss Nancy Dew of Green St., Old Town, were married on Tues. by Rev. Fidler. (BFG, 15 Jan. 1811)

STANSBURY, William, and Miss Susanna Deramit (Demmitt) of Balto. Co., were married last Tues. by Rev. Richardson. (BA, 15 May 1806)

STANSBURY, William, merchant, and Miss Ellen K. Gilder, dau. of the late Dr. Gilder, all of Balto., were married last eve. by Rev. Dr. Coate (BFG, 17 Feb. 1808)

STAPELS, Robert, coachmaker, and widow Ruth Jane Jalland, both of Balto., were married last eve. by Rev. Ireland. (BA, 21 Sept. 1801)

STAPLETON, Joshua, and Miss Harriot Dillon, all of Balto., were married last eve. by Rev. Coats. (BT, 13 April 1804)

STAPLETON, Thomas, of Balto., died yesterday, aged 55. Interment in the Friends Burying Ground. (BT, 24 March 1798)

STARCK, Capt. John, died 14th ult., at St. Thomas; a res. of Balto. (BFG, 15 June 1797)

STARK, John, for many years proprietor of the Indian Queen Tavern, died yesterday. (BFG, 4 April 1803)

STARR, Joseph, and Mrs. Margaret Nowers were married last Sat. eve. by Rev. Hargrove. (BT, 12 April 1802)

STARR, William, merchant taylor, and Miss Eunice Fisher, both of Fells Point, were married last eve. by Rev. Kurtz. (BA, 24 June 1799)

STARR, William, and Miss Rebecca Richardson, all of Balto., were married last eve. by Rev. Coats. (BT, 17 Dec. 1802)

STARRETT, Mrs. Mary, died in West Nantmeal, Chester Co., Penna., on 9th ult., at an advanced age. (BFR, 3 Sept. 1811)

STEAR, George, and Miss Nancy Shaney, both of Balto., were married Sun. eve. by Rev. Kurtz. (BEP, 1 Feb. 1806)

STEDIKORN, Mr. Samuel, died yesterday; funeral from the res. of William Billington, Market Space. (BA, 6 March 1813)

STEDMAN, John, merchant, died this morning after a short illness. Funeral from his res., 17 South Howard St. (BFG, 17 Sept. 1801)

STEEL, James, died at Boonsborough, Wash. Co., on Sat., 21st inst.; formerly of the Eastern Shore, but recently of Annapolis. (BFG, 30 Sept. 1816)

STEEL, John, and Nancy Payson, sister of Henry Payson, were wed last eve. by Rev. Bend. (BFG, 28 March 1797)

STEELE, Mrs. Henrietta, wife of Capt. John Steele of Fells Point, died last Mon., aged 53 years. (BFG, 19 Nov. 1800)

STEELE, John, died yesterday in his 71st year; res. in Pitt St., Fells Point. (BEP, 5 Sept. 1809)

STEELE, Capt. Robert, died at Phila., on 15th inst.; late of Balto., and formerly of New York. His wife Anna died near Balto. about 15 Sept. (BFG, 23 Oct. 1800)

STEELL, John, Balto. merchant, died this morning, leaving a wife and several children. (BEP, 19 Sept. 1806)

STEENE, Matthew, for many years an inhab. of Balto., died yesterday. (BPE, 14 May 1814)

STEENHUS, Henry, and Margaret Righter, both of Balto., were wed last eve. by Rev. Kurtz. (BFG, 28 Aug. 1801)

STEIGER, Matthias, of Balto., died last Thurs. (BT, 12 Sept. 1797)

STEIGER, Peter, and Miss Sally Duplessis, all of Balto., were wed last eve. (BFG, 21 Jan. 1807)

STEIGER, Mrs. Sarah, late consort of Peter Steiger, of Balto., died last eve. in her 21st year. (BFG, 18 June 1808)

STEINBECK, John C., died yesterday in his 52nd year; for 22 years a res. of Balto.; res. at 19 Fayette St. (BA, 23 May 1808)

STEINFORTH, John, and Miss Ann C hristen, both of Balto., were married last Sun. by Rev. Daniel Kurtz. (BPE, 9 Feb. 1813)

STEMMELL, Frederick, of Balto., died last eve. (BEP, 2 Oct. 1807)

STENSON, Mrs. William, of Balto. Co., died last Mon. at the Sulphur Springs in her 61st year. (BFG, 15 Aug. 1805)

STEPHENS, Horatio, and Miss Rebecca Rial were married on 5 May by Rev. Glendy. (BA, 19 Aug. 1814)

STEPHENS, James, died Tues., 21st inst., aged 48, ship carpenter, residing at the upper end of Charles St. (Long obit.) (BRAD, 26 July 1802)

STEPHENS, Thomas, and Miss Mary Hendrickson, dau. of the late Henry Hendrickson, all of Sassafras Neck, Cecil Co., were married on Mon., 27th inst. (BA, 2 March 1809)

STEPLETON, Mrs. Mary, died 21st inst., in her 52nd year. (BFG, 28 Nov. 1812)

STEPHENSON, Mrs. Rachel, of Harf. Co., died this morning in her 72nd year. Funeral from the res. of John Baxley, Jr., in Green St., a few doors south of Daniel Lamotte's. (BFG, 27 April 1804)

STEPHENSON, Uriah, and Miss Sarah Stephenson, both of Balto. Co., were married last Mon. by Rev. Coats. (BT, 28 Dec. 1803)

STERETT, Maj. Clement, Revolutionary officer, aged 70, died yesterday afternoon. (BFG, 19 May 1813)

STERETT, Mr. James, died yesterday at his res. in Gay St., aged 75 years. (BFG, 5 Nov. 1796)

STERETT, Capt. James, of U. S. Artillery, and Mrs. Charlotte Copperthwait, were married Sun., 2nd ult., at New Orleans. (BFG, 23 March 1805)

STERETT, James, and Miss Maria Harris, dau. of Edward Harris, all of Balto., were married last Thurs. by Rev. Inglis. (BFG, 16 Sept. 1809)

STERETT, John, died in Balto., on Fri. as a result of a fall from his horse. He leaves his mother. (BFG, 1 May 1809)

STERETT, Joseph, and Molly Harris, dau. of David Harris, were wed last eve. by Rev. Bend. (BFG, 17 Oct. 1800)

STERETT, Mrs. Juliet, died 23rd inst., a short time after her brother. (BFG, 25 May 1809)

STERETT, Mrs. Rebecca, consort of Samuel Sterett of Balto., died 1st inst., in her 42nd year. (BFG, 5 Feb. 1813)

STERLING, Aaron, and Miss Elizabeth Quisick, both of Balto., were married last Thurs. by Rev. Moranville. (BA, 9 June 1813)

STERLING, John, third son of James Sterling, died Wed. at his father's res. near Balto., in his 26th year. (BA, 6 Feb. 1816)

STETT, Jacob, and Miss Elizabeth Overy, both of Balto., were wed last Thurs. by Rev. Bend. (BFG, 11 April 1807)

STEUART, Robert, and Miss Sidney Slaten, all of Balto., were wed last Thurs. by Rev. Glendy. (BA, 29 Sept. 1810)

STEVENS, James H., and Miss Anna Owens, all of Balto., were married last eve. by Rev. Richards. (BFG, 8 Feb. 1813)

STEVENS, Timothy, and Elizabeth Healey, all of Balto., were wed last Wed. eve. by Rev. John Healey. (BFG, 20 Sept. 1816)

STEVENS, Vachel, examiner general of the western shore of Md., died last Sat. in his 58th year. (BFR, 14 Jan. 1811)

STEVENSON, Mrs. Ann, wife of Dr. Henry Stevenson of Balto., died last Thurs. in her 54th year. (BFG, 20 Oct. 1806)

STEVENSON, Dr. Cosmo Gordon, of Balto., and Miss Harriet Gore Handy, dau. of Col. Samuel Handy, were married at Snowhill last Tues. (BFG, 6 Nov. 1804)

STEVENSON, George P., and Miss Eliza Goodwin, all of Balto., were married last eve. by Rev. Glendy. (BS, 10 Jan. 1812)

STEVENSON, Dr. Henry, died Tues., aged 93. (BW, 31 March 1814)

STEVENSON, John, merchant, and Eleanor Hall, both of Fells Point, were married last eve. (BA, 26 Sept. 1799)

STEVENSON, John, and Miss Agnes Smith were married 25 Oct. by Rev. Glendy. (BA, 7 Nov. 1807)

STEVENSON, Col. Joshua, died suddenly last Mon., 20th inst., at his res. in Balto. Co., at an advanced age. He was an active officer in our late conflict with Great Britain, and at the time of his death was in public office. (BA, 25 May 1799, and BFG, 25 May 1799)

STEVENSON, Joshua, and Mary Spencer, both of Balto., were married last Sun. by Rev. Morrell. (BT, 20 May 1800)

STEVENSON, Joshua, died 3rd inst., aged 27 years, bro. of George Stevenson. (BFG, 14 March 1803)

STEVENSON, Capt. William, and Ann Foster both of Balto., were wed Thurs. (BA, 28 Feb. 1800)

STEVERS, Augustus, chemist of Fells Point, native of Brunswick, Germany, died 29th ult., aged about 30; partner of Henry Dorry. (BEP, 13 July 1808)

STEWARD, Joshua, and Miss Rachel Parrish, both of Balto., were
married last Thurs. by Rev. Roberts. (BFG, 21 June 1806)

STEWARD, William, and Miss Mary Jane Donaldson, dau. of the late
Stephen Donaldson, of Westminster, were married last week
by Rev. Forres. (BA, 23 Oct. 1816)

STEWART, Anne, aged 5, dau. of James Stewart, died last Sat. when
her shawl caught fire. (BA, 21 Dec. 1813)

STEWART, Charles, commander of the U. S. Frigate Constitution,
and Miss Delia Tudor, dau. of the Hon. William Tudor,
were married Thurs., 25th inst., by Rev. J. S. Gardiner.
(BFG, 3 Dec. 1813)

STEWART, David C., Balto. merchant, and Jane, dau. of Robert Purviance, were married Thurs. eve. by Rev. Allison. (BFG,
17 May 1799)

STEWART, David C., of Balto., and Miss Elizabeth Buchanan were
married Thurs. at Bladensburg, by Rev. Dr. Gantt. (BFG,
13 Aug. 1803)

STEWART, Mrs. Elizabeth, consort of James Stewart of the Richmond
Theatre, died last night, at the house of John Croxall.
(BFG, 10 March 1807)

STEWART, James, aged about 16 years, belonging to Capt. Campbell's
Frenchtown packet, fell overboard and was drowned yesterday. (BT, 8 Dec. 1798)

STEWART, James, of Fells Point, died last Fri. at Norfolk. (BFG,
13 Oct. 1802)

STEWART, James, and Miss Harriet Bankson were married 1 June by
Rev. Glendy. (BA, 16 June 1809)

STEWART, James, and Miss Ann Miller, both of Balto. Co., were wed
24th inst. by Rev. Edward Rockworld. (BW, 3 March 1814)

STEWART, James, and Miss Ann Shrote all of Balto. were married
last Thurs. by Rev. Kurtz. (BA, 4 Nov. 1815)

STEWART, Mrs. Jane, consort of David Stewart, Jr., died yesterday
suddenly. (BFG, 30 May 1801)

STEWART, John, and Miss Sarah Clark, both of Balto., were married
last Sun. (BT, 29 Nov. 1798)

STEWART, John, Balto. merchant, and Miss Hellen West, dau. of the
late William West of Phila., were married last Tues. by
Bishop White, at the res. of David H. Conyngham, Esq. (BA,
19 July 1799)

STEWART, John, second son of David Stewart, died last Fri., in
his 26th year. He was a husband and a father. (BFG, 10
May 1802)

STEWART, John, and Mrs. Mary Griffith, all of Balto., were married
last Thurs. by Rev. Bend. (BA, 18 Nov. 1807)

STEWART, John, and Miss Eliza Robinson, were married last eve. by
Rev. Roberts. (BFG, 22 April 1812)

STEWART, Joseph, and Miss Eliza Strebeck, all of Balto., were wed
Tues., 29th inst., by Dr. Roberts. (BA, 31 Oct. 1816)

STEWART, Mrs. Sarah, wife of John Stewart of Balto., died last Sun., in her 23rd year, leaving a husband and three small children. (BA, 19 Sept. 1804)

STEWART, Mrs. Susanna, wife of Peter Stewart, died at Owings' Sulphur Springs, last 28 Oct., aged 33 years, leaving a husband and 5 children. (BFG, 8 Nov. 1813)

STEWART, William, and Eliza Hagerty, were married last eve. by Rev. Richards. (BFG, 18 Sept. 1801)

STEWART, William, and Mrs. Greenfield, both of Balto., were wed last eve. by Rev. Roberts. (BEP, 16 June 1806)

STICKNEY, Miss Eliza, of Worcester, Mass., died in Balto. in her 20th year. (BFG, 23 Feb. 1805)

STICKNEY, Henry, merchant, and Miss Lydia Wells Fearson, second dau. of Capt. Jesse Fearson, all of Balto., were married last eve. by Rev. Dashiell. (BFG, 7 Sept. 1810)

STICKNEY, John, merchant, and Mrs. Mary Anne Grache were married 4th inst. by Bishop Carroll. (BFG, 6 Feb. 1804)

STILES, Mrs. Ann, wife of George Stiles, died at Harlem last Sat. in her 42nd year. (BA, 8 Oct. 1810)

STILES, Mr. Edward, and Mrs. Mary Angell, both of Havre de Grace, were married last Thurs. at that place by Rev. Dr. Allen. (BFG, 19 Jan. 1801)

STILES, John S., and Miss Emory Forman, both of Balto., were wed last Thurs. by Rev. Glendy. (BA, 15 Feb. 1813)

STINCHCOMB, Aquila, and Miss Sarah Martin, both of Balto., were married last eve. by Rev. Hunt. (BFG, 11 Oct. 1816)

STINCHCOMB, Beal C., and Miss Eliza Swann, both of Balto., were wed last Thurs. by Rev. Fechtig. (BA, 12 April 1816)

STINCHCOMB, Caleb, died last Sat. in his 19th year. Interment in the family burying ground at the res. of Samuel Merryman. (BT, 17 July 1797)

STINNECKE, Dr. Charles F., died last Mon. of the prevailing fever, formerly of Carlisle, Penna. (BFG, 18 Sept. 1800)

STITCHER, John, and Miss Sally Clemens, both of Balto., were wed last eve. by Rev. Kurtz. (BRAD, 26 March 1802)

STOCKETT, Capt. William S., and Miss Mary W. Rutter were married last Sun. by Rev. Dashiells. (BPEA, 4 Jan. 1815)

STOCKTON, Brig.-Gen. John, of Wilmington, Del., and Mrs. Sarah Hyatt of Del., were married Tues., 24th inst. by Rev. G. Farrall. (BEP, 28 May 1808)

STOCKTON, Mr. Richard G., and Miss Eliza P. Hughes, were wed at Havre de Grace last Thurs. by Rev. Allen. (BA, 17 May 1814)

STODDARD, Benjamin, late Secretary of the Navy, died last Fri. at his res. in Bladensburg. (BFG, 29 Dec. 1813)

STODDERT, Major David, died yesterday in his 58th year; res. at Harris Creek. (BFG, 1 Oct. 1806)

STODDERT, Mrs. Rebecca, died 10th inst. at Georgetown, wife of
Major Benjamin Stoddert, late Secretary of U. S. Navy.
(BFG, 19 Feb. 1802)

STODDERT, Richard, son of Benjamin Stoddert, died at Bladensburg
on 10th inst., aged about 18 years. (BFR, 16 Oct. 1810)

STOKES, William R., and Henrietta Maria C. Hughes, dau. of Capt.
J. Hughes, were married at Mt. Pleasant, the seat of
Hughes, on 28 June. (BFG, 6 July 1808)

STOLL, George, and Miss Mary Verner, both of Balto., were wed
last Sun. by Rev. Dr. Becker. (BA, 21 Dec. 1807)

STONALL, William, and Polly Ensor, both of Fells Point, were wed
last eve. by Rev. Bend. (BT, 14 March 1796)

STONE, Judge, and five other unnamed persons were killed last
Sat. eve. when the house of Samuel Wolfe of Cal. Co. was
blown down in a storm. (BFG, 30 April 1799)

STONE, Adam, and Miss Eliza Tilden, all of Balto., were married
last eve. by Rev. Hargrove. (BFG, 27 July 1803)

STONE, Erickson H., attorney-at-law, died at Frederick Town, on
24th ult. (BW, 6 Dec. 1810)

STONE, Gen. John Hoskins, died last Fri. in his 54th year. (BA,
15 Oct. 1804)

STONE, Richard, and Miss Margaret Mopps, dau. of Adam Mopps of
Balto., were married last Thurs. by Rev. Roberts. (BFG,
30 March 1816)

STONE, Robert Couden, and Miss Mary Mann of Annapolis were wed
on Tues. at that city by Rev. Higinbothom. (BFG, 27 July
1805)

STONER, Christian, a man in his 67th year, died at Frederick
Town last Sat. (BFG, 3 Jan. 1804)

STONER, Isaac, living near Woodensborough of this county, committed suicide last Mon. He leaves a wife. "Republican
Advocate." (BT, 14 June 1803)

STORCH, Mr. Luder, a native of Bremen, died at St. Thomas on 1st
inst. (BFG, 23 May 1798)

STORKE, Miss Catherine, dau. of William Storke of Belleisle, in
King George Co., died at the seat of Col. Bailey Washington in Stafford Co., Va., on Sun., 14th inst., in the
bloom of life. "Fred. Herald." (BA, 7 Aug. 1805)

STORM, Mr. John, of Stafford, died 14th inst. at his late res. on
Deer Creek in the (64th?) year of his age. (BA, 20 Feb.
1816)

STORY, Enoch, printer of Balto., died last Thurs. at James Armitage's. (BFG, 8 July 1807)

STORY, Robert, and Mrs. Margaret Bailey, all of Balto., were wed
last Tues. by Rev. Glendy. (BEP, 28 Sept. 1810)

STORY, Robert, died Tues. in his 36th year; res. near the foot
bridge. (BA, 22 Dec. 1814)

STOUFFER, Jacob, and Miss Ann C. Tinges, both of Balto., were married last Tues. by Rev. Dr. Roberts. (BA, 28 Nov. 1816)

STOUFFER, John, and Miss Ann Stitcher, both of Balto., were wed last eve. by Rev. Kurtz. (BA, 15 Nov. 1805)

STOUTSBERGER, Andrew, and Miss Ann Larrance, both of Balto., were married last Sun. by Rev. Haley. (BA, 21 Jan. 1810)

STOW, Thomas, and Miss Mary Shriver, all of Balto., were married Sun. by Rev. Healey. (BFG, 23 May 1815)

STRANDLEY, John, and Miss Rachel Stubbs, all of Balto., were wed 15th ult. by Rev. Healey. (BA, 9 Nov. 1816)

STRATTON, John, died at Norfolk, aged 35, late a representative in Congress. (BT, 21 June 1804)

STRAUGHAN, Sergeant, and Miss Patty Cross were married 3rd inst. at Fort Madison by Rev. Dr. Elliott. (BA, 5 Nov. 1816)

STRAW, Peter, trader from Wythe Co., Va., was killed in the fire at Mr. Fulton's Globe Inn on Sat. Interment in St. Paul's churchyard. (BFG, 19 Nov. 1810)

STREET, Dr. Saint Clair, and Miss Ariel Jarrett were married in Harf. Co. on 17th inst. by Rev. Stansbury. (BA, 25 Dec. 1816)

STREIBY, George, and Miss Ellen M'Cubbin, all of Balto., were wed last Thurs. by Rev. Pitts. (BFG, 13 Jan. 1812)

STREMMEL, Frederick, and Miss Capito, both of Balto., were wed last eve. (BT, 13 June 1803)

STRICKER, Col. George, formerly of Fred. Co., died 29th ult. at his res. in Ohio Co., Va., aged 78 years. Born in Winchester, Va., he leaves a son and two daus. (Long obit gives details of service in Rev. War.) (BFG, 18 Dec. 1810)

STRICKER, Mrs. Martha, consort of Gen. John Stricker, died yesterday, in her 53rd year. (BFG, 5 Nov. 1816)

STRINGER, Frederick, of Elk Ridge, and Elizabeth Martin were wed last eve. (BA, 25 Sept. 1801)

STRINGER, Frederick, of New Orleans, died at the res. of his father-in-law, Jas. Martin, Esq., last Sun. He had taken his family to New Orleans several years ago. He leaves a wife and three children, and was interred in the burying ground of the First Presbyterian Church. (BA, 25 Sept. 1811)

STRINGER, Dr. Samuel, died Mon., 9th inst., on Elk Ridge, in his 32nd year; son of the late Richard Stringer. (BA, 11 March 1801)

STROBEL, Peter, and Miss Barbara Bauder, both of Balto., were wed last Sun. by Rev. Kurtz. (BT, 20 July 1802)

STUART, Benjamin, late of Annapolis, died. (BA, 1 Nov. 1800)

STUART, Mrs. Eleanor, wife of David Stuart, of Ossian Hall, in Fairfax Co., Va., died at Tudor Place, the seat of Thomas Peter, near Georgetown, Potomac, in her 55th year. Her first husband was Mr. Custis, who died at the siege of York. (BFR, 10 Oct. 1811)

STUART, Mrs. Jane, consort of Richardson Stuart of Balto., died last Tues. (BFG, 1 Oct. 1805)

STUDDY, John, and Miss Nancy M'Caskey, both of Balto., were wed last eve. by Rev. Richards. (BFG, 8 May 1807)

STUDY, Dr., of Fred. Co., died 29th ult., aged 96 years. (BA, 16 Feb. 1811)

STUMP, Hannah, dau. of John Stump of Harf. Co., died last Fri., in her 16th year. (BFG, 30 June 1800)

STUMP, Herman, of Harf. Co., died in Phila. on Sun., 20 Sept. (BFG, 23 Sept. 1801)

STUMP, John, of Stafford, departed this life on 14th inst. at his late res. in Deer Creek, in his 64th year. (BWA, 24 Feb. 1816)

STUMP, John W., and Miss Sarah Biays were married last Thurs. eve. by Rev. Glendy. (BA, 15 Jan. 1814)

STUMP, William, and Miss Margaret Miller, all of Harford Co., were married Thurs., 10th inst., by Rev. Mr. Allen. (BFG, 17 Dec. 1807)

SUCKLEY, Mrs, Hannah, wife of George Suckley, merchant, died last Tues. night. Formerly of Sheffield, Eng., she was for a short time a res. of Balto. Funeral sermon will be preached in the Meth. Church. (BFG, 15 Sept. 1798)

SUELL, Reuben, and Mrs. Ann Boyle both of Balto. were married last eve. by Rev. William Duncan. (BFG, 18 June 1802)

SUET, John, mariner, aged 23 years, a native of St. Marys Co., died 10th inst. at Phila. of the small pox. (BFG, 17 Oct. 1808)

SUIRE, Joseph, and Eleanor Brooks, all of Balto., were married last Thurs. by Rev. Glendy. (BEP, 12 Dec. 1807)

SULIVAN(?), John, and Miss Abigail Robinson, both of Balto., were wed Tues. by Rev. Beverly Waugh. (BFG, 25 Feb. 1814)

SULLIVAN, Capt., and Miss Bridget Quisick, both of Fells Point, were married last Thurs. by Rev. Moranville. (BA, 4 July 1810)

SULLIVAN, Mrs. Bridget, died yesterday afternoon in her 20th year. Funeral from her late res. in Fleet St., Fells Point. (BW, 28 March 1812)

SULLIVAN, Mr. I. P., and Miss Harriot Lannaway were married on Sat. (BFG, 14 Oct. 1799)

SULLIVAN, John, and Miss Matilda Dorsey were married last eve. by Rev. Roberts. (BFG, 10 Feb. 1814)

SULTZER, Sebastian, and Susanna Dukehart, both of Balto., were wed 23 Nov. 1815, by Rev. Glendy. (BA, 25 Nov. 1815)

SUMAN, William, and Miss Rosanna Smith, both of Balto., were wed last Thurs. by Rev. Glendy. (BT, 30 June 1804)

SUMMERS, James, died Fri. in his 18th year. (BFG, 11 Jan. 1802)

SUMMERS, William S., and Louisa Fergusson, both of Balto., were wed last eve. by Rev. Dr. Rattoone. (BFG, 24 Oct. 1804)

SUMMERS, William S., late clerk of the court of oyer and terminer and gaol delivery, died. He was succeeded by Thomas Harwood. (BA, 26 Jan. 1807)

SUMWALT, John T., and Rachel Sparks, all of Balto., were wed on 22 Dec. by Rev. Hemphill. (BA, 25 Dec. 1816)

SUMWALT, Philip, and Maria Parsons, both of Balto., were married 22 Dec. by Rev. Wells. (BA, 31 Dec. 1816)

SUTER, John, and Miss Sally Dorsey, all of Balto., were married last Sun. by Rev. Kurtz. (BA, 18 Feb. 1807)

SUNENSHINE, Michael, and Miss Rebecca Dorney, both of Balto., were were married last Thurs. by Rev. Fry. (BW, 22 April 1812)

SUTER, Henry, and Miss Sarah Robinson, all of Balto., were wed on 11th inst. by Rev. Healey. (BA, 18 Nov. 1812)

SUTER, John. See above.

SUTER, John, died at Georgetown, Dist. of Col., on 26th ult. (BEP, 4 March 1808)

SUTHERLAND, John, merchant, and Miss Marian Stewart, dau. of Dr. William Stewart, all of Balto., were married last eve. by Rev. Glendy. (BFG, 6 July 1804)

SUTHERLAND, Mrs. Olivia, died Wed., wife of Mr. St. Clair Sutherland, aged 22 years. (BA, 12 Jan. 1816)

SUTHERLAND, St. Clair, and Miss Olivia Lowry, all of Balto., were married 1st inst. by Rev. Glendy. (BFG, 18 July 1814)

SUTHOD, Capt., of Boston, and Mrs. Speck of Balto. were married last Tues. by Rev. Ireland. (BFG, 26 June 1800)

SUTTON, Mrs. Alice, of Balto., a native of Great Britain, died 27th ult., aged 57 (?) years. (BA, 6 July 1808)

SUTTON, James A., son of John Sutton, died at Alexandria on the 27th inst. (BT, 30 Aug. 1805)

SUTTON, Thomas, was buried Sat. He had drowned about Christmas Eve on his passage from Annapolis. After three months his body was found on the south side of the Patapsco. (BEP, 21 April 1807)

SWAILS, Robert, of Mont. Co., and Ann Prather, dau. of Nathan Prather of P. G. Co., were married last week. (BFG, 19 Sept. 1800)

SWAIN, Freeman, and Mrs. Ellen Thorn all of Balto. were married. (BFG, 23 Sept. 1806)

SWAIN, John, and Miss Mary Newman, all of Balto., were married last Thurs. eve. by Rev. Glendy. (BW, 21 Nov. 1808)

SWAN, Caleb, died on 29 Nov. in Washington; Paymaster General of the U. S. Army, and officer in the Rev. War. (BFG, 6 Dec. 1809)

SWAN, Isaac, and Miss Ann Tasker, both of Balto., were married last Thurs. by Rev. Coats. (BT, 7 April 1804)

SWAN, John, merchant, and Miss Maria Smith, dau. of Walter Smith of Gettysburg, were married 15th inst. by Rev. Baxton. (BA, 19 Feb. 1816)

SWAN, Joseph, Balto. merchant, died yesterday. (BFG, 2 March 1803)

SEAN, William, Balto. merchant, and Miss Knox, dau. of Rev. Samuel Knox, Principal of Baltimore College, were married last Thurs. by Rev. Dr. Sinclair. (BA, 25 May 1816)

SWANN, William T., of Md., and Miss Frances Alexander, dau. of the late Charles Alexander of Preston, were married at Alexandria, on 12th inst. by Rev. Barclay. (BFG, 18 July 1810)

SWARING, Justus Gerardus, and Mrs. Elizabeth Toomes were married Wed. by Rev. Richards. (BFR, 13 March 1812)

SWART, David, of Harf. Co., and Miss Mary Lucas, all of Balto. Co., were married the eve. of 13th inst. by Rev. Lucas. (BFG, 14 April 1809)

SWARTOUT, Thomas, son of Col. Swartout of Balto., and midshipman aboard the U. S. Frigate Essex, was killed in a duel with another midshipman from the same ship at the Spanish port of Algeziras, near Gibraltar, last 13 April, aged 17. (BT, 26 June 1802)

SWEENY, Mr., and Miss Magnis were married 30th ult. in Harf. Co. by Rev. Wilmer. (BFG, 4 Jan. 1803)

SWEENY, Mrs., consort of E. Sweeny, died Thurs. morning at Fells Point. (BAP, 1 Oct. 1803)

SWEENY, Mr. Elias, mathematical instrument maker of Fells Point, died Sat. morning. (BFG, 16 June 1806)

SWEENY, Paul, and Miss Harriet Chester, both of Balto., were wed Thurs. night by Bishop Carroll. (BT, 7 June 1802)

SWEETING, Benjamin B., and Miss Mary Boyle, all of Balto. were wed last eve. by Rev. Galen Hicks, pastor of Trinity Ch. (BFG, 16 Oct. 1811)

SWEETING, Mrs. Caroline, wife of Thomas Sweeting, and dau. of Isaac Phillips, died this morning. Res. in King Tammany St. (BFG, 19 Aug. 1813)

SWEETING, Mrs. Catherine, consort of Thomas Sweeting of Balto., died Mon. in her 25th year. (BFG, 19 Sept. 1806)

SWEETING, Edward, died 16th inst. at his res. in Patapsco Neck, aged 80 years. (BFG, 19 June 1809)

SWEETING, Thomas, of Balto., and Miss Catherine Winneman of Balto. Co., were married last eve. by Rev. Allison. (BFG, 15 Nov. 1799)

SWEETING, Thomas, and Miss Caroline Phillips, dau. of Isaac Phillips, all of Balto., were married Sun. by Rev. Bend. (BFG, 27 March 1809)

SWEETSER, Samuel, and Miss Mary Ann Oldham, dau. of John Oldham, all of Balto., were wed last Thurs. by Rev. Fechtig. (BA, 3 June 1816)

SWIFT, Mrs. Ann, died yesterday, in her 29th year; funeral from the res. of Mrs. Yandel, in Ann St. (BFG, 5 March 1816)

SWIFT, William R., of the firm of Adams and Swift, and Miss Mary D. Harper, of Alexandria, were married there on Tues., 1st inst. by Rev. Muir. (BFG, 7 Aug. 1815)

SWITZER, John, died Sat. in his 62nd year, leaving a widow and twelve children. (BA, 12 Nov. 1810)

SYKES, George W., student of medicine, of Dover, Del., died at Phila., 25th inst., in his 28th year. (BEP, 2 March 1810)

SYLER, Frederick, and Miss Ann Seaver, all of Balto., were wed last Thurs. by Rev. Fenwick. (BFG, 1 May 1816)

SYLVESTER. Miss Sally, late of Balto., died 21 April at Cincinnati (Tennessee - sic!) (BA, 23 May 1808)

SYMONDS, Arthur, and Miss Susanna, dau. of Edward Stone of Balto., were married last Thurs. by Rev. Dashiells. (BT, 4 March 1806)

TAGGARD, William, employed in cutting the course of the water works, was killed in an explosion yesterday. (BT, 23 July 1805)

TAGUE, Daniel, of Fells Point, died yesterday. (BW, 12 Aug. 1809)

TALBERT, Elisha, of Balto. Co., and Mrs. Catherine Littig of A. A. Co., were married last eve. at Fells Point by Rev. Mr. Combs. (BFG, 23 Jan. 1804)

TALBOT, Benjamin, of Balto. Co., died 5th inst., in his 56th year, a member of the Baptist Church. (BA, 25 Jan. 1816)

TALBOT, Jesse, of ALexandria, and Hanna Little of Wash., D. C., were married at Friends Meeting in Wash. (BEP, 7 June 1808)

TALBOT, Ruth, dau. of Capt. Thomas Talbot, died Sun., 22nd ult., aged 11 mos., 22 days, of an overdose of laudanam given by a nurse. ("Cumberland Review") (BFG, 11 Feb. 1806)

TALBOTT, Sally, aged 12, only child of David Talbott of Canton, was ravished and murdered last Thurs. (BFG, 10 July 1804)

TALBOTT, Thomas, and Miss Mary Merryman, all of Balto. Co., were married last Sun. by Rev. Coleman. (BFG, 2 Feb. 1804)

TALBUT, John, and Miss Mary Slade, all of Balto., were married last Thurs. by Rev. Davis. (BT, 15 Nov. 1797)

TARBELL, Joseph, Post Capt. in the U. S. Navy, died in Phila. on 25 Nov. (BA, 2 Dec. 1815)

TAYLOR, Mrs. Ann F., consort of F. S. Taylor, died last Sat. at her own house a few days after her return from Balto. "Norfolk - 19 Aug." (BFG, 21 Aug. 1811)

TAYLOR, Benjamin, and Miss Sarah Eliza Howland, dau. of Capt.
Daniel Howland, all of Balto. Co., were married last eve.
by Dr. Roberts. (BFG, 18 Jan. 1815)

TAYLOR, Elijah, and Miss Sarah Hiss, all of Balto. Co., were wed
by Rev. Wells at the res. of Joseph Taylor. (BEP, 18 Oct.
1809)

TAYLOR, Miss Eliza, of Chas. Co. died at Elkton on 15th inst. in
her 21st year. (BA, 21 Aug. 1805)

TAYLOR, Capt. Giles, and Mary Ann Ridley of Balto. were married
last Tues. by Rev. Hargrove. (BFG, 12 Feb. 1802)

TAYLOR, Mrs. Hannah, wife of William Taylor of Balto. Co., died
last eve. (BFG, 24 Jan. 1812)

TAYLOR, Isaac, and Miss Lavinia Quail, 2nd dau. of Robert Quail
all of Balto., were married last Thurs. by Rev. Hemphill.
(BA, 13 April 1816)

TAYLOR, Capt. James, and Miss Phoebe Logan, all of Balto., were
married last eve. by Rev. Griffith. (BPEA, 17 Nov. 1815)

TAYLOR, Capt. Jesse, died last Tues. at Alexandria. (BT, 21 Oct.
1800)

TAYLOR, John, and Miss Sarah Walker, all of Balto., were wed last
Sat. by Rev. Glendy. (BA, 15 Sept. 1810)

TAYLOR, Capt. John B., and Miss Catherine L. Spalding, both of
Balto., were married on Sat. by Rev. Roberts. (BFG, 9
Jan. 1809)

TAYLOR, Dr. John B., and Miss Sarah Camp, all of Balto., were wed
last eve. by Rev. Glendy. (BS, 3 Dec. 1812)

TAYLOR, John E., and Mrs. Eleanor Evans, all of Balto. Co., were
married last eve. by Rev. Hagerty. (BFG, 18 Aug. 1809)

TAYLOR, Lemuel G., of Balto., and Miss Mary Merryman of Clover
Hill, were married at the latter place last Thurs. by Rev.
Birch. (BA, 22 April 1815)

TAYLOR, Lemuel G., merchant, and Miss Margaret Fowler, both of
Balto., were married last Thurs. by Dr. Roberts. (BA, 8
June 1816)

TAYLOR, Moses, of Balto., and Miss Mary Sheaff of Haverford Twp.,
Delaware Co., were married on Thurs. by Rev. Dr. Rogers.
(BA, 15 Sept. 1801)

TAYLOR, Polly, of 117 S. Water St., died. (BFG, 10 Aug. 1802)

TAYLOR, Richard, of Balto. Co., died last Wed. in his 40th year,
leaving a wife. (BFG, 29 Oct. 1805)

TAYLOR, Robert, and Miss Rachael Roney, both of Phila., were wed
in that city. (BT, 4 Oct. 1800)

TAYLOR, Lieut. Col. Robert, died last Mon., a husband and father.
(BFG, 16 March 1803)

TAYLOR, Samuel, and Miss Ann Chalmers, dau. of Mrs. Jas. Chalmers,
all of Balto., were wed last Thurs. by Rev. Stiers. (BPEA,
16 June 1815)

TAYLOR, Thatcher, a young gentleman, died last Sat. (BFG, 23 May 1796)

TAYLOR, Capt. Thomas, and Miss Ann White, both of Cecil Co., were married last Mon. by Rev. Rattoone. (BFG, 26 Dec. 1806)

TAYLOR, Thomas, and Miss Margaret Alexander, all of Balto., were married last Wed. by Rev. Glendy. (BFG, 19 Aug. 1814)

TAYLOR, Thomas, died yesterday in his 42nd year; res. at Pratt St., head of Smith's Wharf. (BA, 4 Oct. 1814)

TAYLOR, William, Jr., merchant of Shelburne, and Martha, dau. of Rev. Lewis Richards of Balto., were married last eve. by Rev. Davis. (BFG, 20 Aug. 1800)

TAYLOR, William, and Mrs. Mary Duffield, all of Balto., were wed last Tues. by Rev. Glendy. (BA, 1 March 1816)

TAYLOR, William Woodland, and Miss Mary Jones, both of Balto., were married last eve. by Rev. Richards. (BFG, 18 May 1801)

TAZEWELL, Henry, U. S. Sen. from Va., died 24th inst. in Phila. (BT, 29 Jan. 1799)

TEAGUE, Daniel, native of Omagh, Ireland, died yesterday aged 33; res. corner of Lancaster and Market Sts., Fells Point. (BA, 12 Aug. 1809)

TEAL, Archibald, and Susanna Whitelock, both of Balto., were married last Mon. by Rev. Kurtz. (BFG, 17 Oct. 1804)

TEMPLE, Peter, Esq., attorney-at-law, died at Sion House, Richmond Co., Va., on 7th inst. (BFG, 21 March 1808)

TESSANDIER, Mr., late organist of St. Marys and St. Peters Churches, died last eve.; res. in Ross St., near upper end of Eutaw St. (BPEA, 29 April 1816)

TESSON, Mrs. Mary, late consort of Pierre Tesson, died 12th inst. in her 27th year. (BFG, 14 Aug. 1812)

TESSON, Pierre, and Miss Mary M'Gauren, both of Phila., were wed last Sat. by Rev. Abercrombie. (BT, 8 Dec. 1804)

TESSON, Pierre, and Miss Eliza Le Blanc, both of Balto., were wed on Wed., 19th inst., by Rev. Fenwick. (BA, 28 Oct. 1814)

TEVIS, Capt. Benjamin, died at his plantation in Delaware Hundred on Mon., 18th inst., aged 47 years. He leaves a large family of orphans. (BFG, 27 Oct. 1802)

TEVIS, Joshua, of Balto., and Miss Rebecca R. Carnan, dau. of Robert North Carnan of Garretson (sic) Forest, were married last Thurs. by Rev. Joshua Wells. (BFG, 5 June 1813)

THARP, George, and Miss Susan M. Yeiser, dau. of Inglehart Yeiser, all of Balto., were married 19th April by Rev. Dashiells. (BW, 22 April 1817)

THAW, Joseph, and Miss Eliza Woodside, dau. of John Woodside, a clerk in the Treasury Dept., were married at Washington, 25th inst., by Rev. Sergeant. (BW, 3 Aug. 1808)

THEBAN, Henry, and Miss Eliza Gamble, were married last Sun. by Rev. Dr. Roberts. (BWA, 24 Feb. 1816)

THIEL, Gottlieb Henry, was found dead in bed yesterday morning. (BFG, 30 July 1802)

THOMAS, Mrs., died last Thurs. at Georgetown, aged 107 years. (BFG, 17 Oct. 1799)

THOMAS, A. J., of New Orleans, and Miss Mary Sophia Stump, dau. of the late Herman Stump, were married at Mount Friendship, Harf. Co., on Thurs., 29th ult. by Rev. Stevenson. (BFG, 4 Aug. 1813)

THOMAS, Mrs. Alice, wife of Benjamin Thomas of Fells Point, died yesterday morning. Her husband is currently traveling to some of the back settlements of N. Y. state. (BFG, 16 Nov. 1807)

THOMAS, Dr. Allen, and Miss Eliza Bradford Dall, dau. of the late James Dall of Balto., were married on Tues. eve. by Rev. Wyatt. (BA, 28 Nov. 1816)

THOMAS, Capt. Barton, and Miss Mary Probart, all of Balto., were married last Thurs. eve. by Rev. Glendy. (BT, 24 Nov. 1805)

THOMAS, Mr. E. S., of Providence, and Miss Ann Fonerden of Balto. were married at Charleston by Rev. Dr. Keith. (BFG, 9 Jan. 1806)

THOMAS, Gabriel, and Sophia Todd were married on Sun. by Rev. Rattoone. (BFG, 25 Sept. 1804)

THOMAS, George, and Miss Ann Maria Cooper, all of Balto., were married last Mon. eve. by Rev. M'Kean. (BS, 17 June 1812)

THOMAS, Capt. George, aged 23, son of Benjamin Thomas of Balto., died 6th ult. at Sunbury, Ga., where he commanded U. S. Gunboat No. 3. He leaves a young widow and an aged father. (BS, 16 Dec. 1812)

THOMAS, Hugh H., and Miss Margaret Fullerton of Fells Point were married last eve. by Rev. Dr. Annan. (BFG, 12 Dec. 1804)

THOMAS, Isaac, and Miss Patty Burkins, both of Balto., were wed last eve. by Rev. Wells. (BT, 2 Jan. 1804)

THOMAS, James, and Miss Mary Shaffer, all of Balto., were wed on Sun. eve. by Rev. Dashiell. (BA, 16 June 1812)

THOMAS, James S., only son of Luke Thomas of Balto., died 21st inst., in his 25th year. (BFG, 22 Dec. 1810)

THOMAS, Mrs. Jane, wife of Col. John Thomas, died 16 April aged 90. Her parents were named Black, from Penna. In 1779 when the Tories attacked her house to get to the powder magazine, she helped her son and son-in-law to defend it. "Charleston paper." (BA, 1 June 1811)

THOMAS, John, died Sun., 3rd inst., at West River, formerly of the State Senate, of which he was President. (BFG, 11 Feb. 1805)

THOMAS, John, and Miss Louisa Olar, both of Balto. Co., were wed last Sun. by Rev. Kurtz. (BA, 6 Aug. 1805)

MARRIAGES AND DEATHS

THOMAS, John Hanson, of Md., and Miss Mary I. Colston, dau. of
Rawleigh Colston, Esq., of Berkely Co., Va., were married
Thurs., 5th inst., by Rev. Ballman. (BFR, 11 Oct. 1809)

THOMAS, John Hanson, died in Frederick, of the typhus fever, on
Tues., 2nd inst., in his 39th year. (Long obit.) (BT,
5 May 1815, and BFG, 9 May 1815)

THOMAS, John W., of Cecil Co., and Miss Anna Webster, dau. of the
late John Lee Webster of Harf. Co., were married Thurs.,
7th inst., at Loch Eden, seat of John C. Weems, of A. A.
Co., by Rev. M. L. Weems. (BFG, 11 Jan. 1813)

THOMAS, Joseph, and Miss Eleanor Burton, all of Balto., were wed
7th inst. by Rev. Reese. (BWA, 18 May 1816)

THOMAS, Lambert, and Miss Jane Peters, both of Balto., were wed
yesterday by Rev. Sergent. (BFG, 5 Aug. 1805)

THOMAS, Lewis, and Miss Ann Pennington, all of Cecil Co., were
wed last Tues. by Rev. Mr. Bell. (BPE, 13 Feb. 1813)

THOMAS, Lewis, seaman, belonging to the ship Weymouth, died at
Carlsham, Sweden. His papers show that he had been some
time at Owings Mills, Md. (BFG, 1 Aug. 1815)

THOMAS, Luke, of the House of Thomas and Caldcleugh of Balto.,
died yesterday in his 64th year. (BFG, 4 Jan. 1816)

THOMAS, Moses, of Phila., and Miss Ann Dover, dau. of John Dover
of Frankford, were married 10 Oct. by Dr. Abercrombie.
(BFR, 8 Nov. 1811)

THOMAS, Owen, and Mrs. Catherine Lewis both of Balto., were wed
last Sat. by Rev. John Evans. (BA, 3 Nov. 1801)

THOMAS, Philip, Jr., and Miss Frances M. Ludlow of New York, were
married last Friday at New York by Rev. Hobart. (BEP, 2
Nov. 1807)

THOMAS, Philip, died last eve. at Rockland, Cecil Co. (BFG, 4
April 1809)

THOMAS, Dr. Philip, died last Tues. in Frederick Town in his 68th
year. "Fredericktown, April 29." (BFG, 2 May 1815)

THOMAS, Philip E., and Miss Eliza George of Piney Grove, Kent Co.,
Md., were married Mon., 20th inst. (BFG, 29 April 1801)

THOMAS, Richard, and Miss Mary Jane Fagg, all of Balto., were wed
Thurs. by Rev. Pitts. (BFG, 25 May 1811)

THOMAS, Richard Snowden, died 29th ult. in his 53rd year, in Kent
Co. (BFG, 16 Aug. 1814)

THOMAS, William, of Mont. Co., and Miss M. Patrick of Balto. were
married Fri., 15th inst., by Rev. Richards. (BFG, 22 Nov.
1799)

THOMAS, Hon. William, President of the Senate of Md., died Sun.,
1st inst., at his res. in St. M. Co. (BFG, 10 Aug. 1813)

THOMPSON, Amos, and Miss Nancy Deagen of Harf. Co. were married
last Tues. in Balto. by Rev. Richards. (BT, 31 Oct.
1799)

THOMPSON, Mrs. Elizabeth, died last Sat. in her 28th year, a res. of Balto., and wife of Capt. William Thompson of St. M. Co. (BFG, 27 Jan. 1800)

THOMPSON, Mrs. Elizabeth, wife of Hugh Thompson, of Balto., died Mon., 21st inst. (BFG, 23 Feb. 1814)

THOMPSON, Henry, of Balto., and Miss Bowly, dau. of Daniel Bowly of Furley, were wed last eve. (BFG, 30 March 1798)

THOMPSON, Henry, of Annap., and Miss West of Balto. were wed on last Sun. by Rev. Dr. Rattoone. (BFG, 15 Nov. 1803)

THOMPSON, James, Balto. merchant, and Anne Williamson were wed yesterday by Rev. Beeston at the country seat of David Williamson, Esq. (BFG, 14 Aug. 1804)

THOMPSON, James, and Miss Ann Stansbury, all of Balto., were wed by Rev. D. E. Reese last Thurs. (BA, 28 Sept. 1816)

THOMPSON, John, died in Petersburg, 25th ult., aged 23 years, author of "Curtius" and other essays. (BT, 6 Feb. 1799)

THOMPSON, John, cooper, died 18th inst. (BFG, 20 Oct. 1800)

THOMPSON, Capt. John, and Miss Mary Smith, both of Balto., were married last eve. by Rev. Roberts. (BFG, 25 May 1801)

THOMPSON, John, and Miss Margaret Kole of Balto. were married last Sun. eve. by Rev. Beasley. (BFG, 2 April 1811)

THOMPSON, John, and Mrs. Ann Strebeck were married last Thurs. by Rev. Glendy. (BS, 21 May 1812)

THOMPSON, John, died Tues., 16th inst., in his 45th year, leaving a wife and two children. His sister, Mrs. Mary Collins, died recently. His mother survives. (BFG, 20 Jan. 1816)

THOMPSON, Col. Mark, died last Wed. in Sussex Co., formerly a member of Congress from New Jersey. (BFG, 27 Dec. 1803)

THOMPSON, Col. Robert, died yesterday at Fells Point. (BA, 17 Sept. 1800)

THOMPSON, Robert, died last Sat. (BFG, 1 April 1805)

THOMPSON, Stephen I., and Miss Eveline Barney, all of Balto., were married last Mon. by Rev. Glendy. (BFG, 21 Sept. 1815)

THOMPSON, Capt. Thomas, and Miss Mary Fomes of Balto. were wed last eve. by Rev. Bend. (BFG, 6 Nov. 1801)

THOMPSON, William, and Miss Maria Miltenberger, both of Balto., were married last eve. by Rev. Kurtz. (BFG, 12 May 1797)

THOMPSON, Capt. William, and Mrs. Anderson, both of Balto., were married last eve. by Rev. Bend. (BFG, 11 Aug. 1797)

THOMPSON, William, died yesterday. (BFG, 18 Aug. 1802)

THOMPSON, William, and Sarah Button, both of Balto., were married last eve. by Rev. Dr. Rattoone. (BFG, 20 Sept. 1804)

THOMPSON, William, died yesterday in his 64th year, leaving a widow and several children. A carpenter, he res. in North Charles St. (BA, 10 April 1810)

THOMSON, Mrs., died Mon., relict of John Thomson of Balto., late from Eng. (BFG, 30 Oct. 1801)

THOMSON, Lawrence, of Balto., and Miss Maria E. Boller, of Phila., were married on Thurs. eve. by Dr. Kurtz. (BA, 23 Nov. 1816)

THOMSON, Reese, of the House of Reese, Thomson and Co., merchants, died in Mont. Co., aged 23 years. (BA, 19 July 1799)

THORNBURGH, Cassandra, wife of Joseph Thornburgh, died yesterday eve. at the family res. in Balto. Co. (BFG, 25 March 1812)

THORNBURGH, Joseph, merchant, and Cassandra Ellicott of Balto. Co., were married 21st inst. at Friends Meeting House on Elk Ridge. (BFG, 23 Nov. 1798)

THORNDICK, Mr., surgeon of the U. S. Frigate Congress, was found dead in his berth on Mon., 26th ult., having his throat cut in a shocking manner. (BFG, 3 June 1800)

THORNTON, Joseph, and Miss Ann Crabbin, both of Balto., were married on Wed., 14th inst. by Rev. Richards. (BT, 16 July 1802)

THRELFALL, Stephen, and Sarah Hunt of Balto., were married 20th inst. by Rev. Healy. (BFG, 25 April 1806)

THRELKELD, Mrs. Mary, died 9th inst. at the res. of her son John Threlkeld in the vicinity of Georgetown. (BFG, 12 Sept. 1801)

THURSTON, Lewis M., of the house of Proud and Thurston, merchants of Balto., son of John Thurston, Balto. merchant, died at Phila., 15th ult., aged 23 years. He was buried in the Friends burial ground of that city. "New York paper." (BFG, 4 March 1803)

TILDEN, John, son of Duke Tilden, and Eliza Angelica Barriere, were married last Thurs. eve. by Rev. Bend. (BFG, 24 Nov. 1800)

TILDEN, Mrs. Louisa Harvey, wife of Dr. Tilden of Kent Co., and 3rd dau. of Samuel Harvey Howard of Annap., died lately. (BFG, 1 May 1805)

TILDON, William, and Miss Mary Peck, were married last eve. by Rev. Daniel Coacker, pastor of the African Methodist Episcopal Church of Balto. (BFG, 28 Dec. 1810)

TILGHMAN, Hon. James, late Chief Justice of the Second District of Md., and one of the Judges of the Md. Court of Appeals, died Wed., 19th ult., in Chestertown. (BW, 12 May 1809)

TILGHMAN, John, of Tal. Co., and Miss Maria Gibson, of Annap., were married at the latter place by Rev. Judd on 22nd ult. (BEP, 6 Jan. 1808)

TILGHMAN, Matthew, Jr., of Kent Co., and Miss Eleanor M. Rozer of Q. A. Co., were married 10 Jan. last by Rev. Bolton. (BFG, 3 Feb. 1802)

TILGHMAN, Richard, IV, of Kent Co., died Tues., 28th ult., in Chestertown, Kent Co. (BA, 8 June 1805)

TILGHMAN, William, of Md., and Miss Anna Polk of Del., were wed at Wilmington, Del., last Tues., by Rev. Clay. (BEP, 20 Dec. 1808)

TILL, William, and Mary Foreman of Balto., were married last eve. by Rev. Kurtz. (BEP, 18 March 1808)

TIMANUS, John, and Miss Eliza Wall, all of Balto., were married last Thurs. eve. by Dr. Roberts. (BFG, 20 Oct. 1815)

TINGES, Charles, and Mary Hill, all of Balto., were married last Wed. eve. by Rev. Mr. Dashiell. (BA, 11 Jan. 1806)

TINGES, Charles, died Wed., in his 51st year, leaving a wife and ten children; res. at 9 Great York St. (BA, 16 Feb. 1816)

TINGES, Jacob, died last Tues. morning in his 27th year. (BFG, 15 April 1806)

TINGES, John, al old and respectable inhabitant of Balto., died in his 65th year; res. on Light St. (BFG, 2 Nov. 1801)

TINGES, Mrs. Rebecca, wufe of Charles Tinges, died last Tues., leaving a husband and six children. (BFG, 13 Sept. 1805)

TINGEY, Capt. Thomas, commandant of the U. S. Navy Yard, Wash., and Miss Ann Delany, dau. of Daniel Delany of Alexandria, were married. (BS, 16 Dec. 1812)

TINGSTROM, Peter, and Miss Catherine Haley, were married last eve. by Rev. Dr. Rattoone. (BFG, 22 April 1806)

TINKER, Mrs. Mary, died yesterday in her 80th year. A native of Phila. she had lived in Balto. for the last 45 years. She leaves offspring to the 3rd generation. (BA, 13 Feb. 1815)

TINKER, Thomas, died; funeral will be today in the Masonic Order. (BA, 7 Oct. 1807)

TINKER, William, died Sat., of Fells Point. (BFG, 16 Nov. 1801)

TIPPENS, James, mate of the Chestertown packet was stabbed last Fri. and died within 24 hours. (BFG, 26 May 1800) (BT, 26 May 1800 gives the victim's name as Isaac Tippens.)

TOBAN, Michael, died last Wed. as a result ofaccidentally cutting his wrist. (BFG, 29 June 1804)

TOBIN, Mrs. Jane, died at Fells Point yesterday, wife of John Tobin; res. in Ann St. Interment in the R. C. burying ground. (BA, 7 Oct. 1808)

TODD, Mr., overseer of the criminals confined at the wheelbarrow on the turnpike road, was murdered last Thurs. (BFG, 2 March 1799)

TODD, Archibald, died 10th inst., aged 20 years. (BFG, 11 Sept. 1800)

TODD, Mrs. Mary, died last Mon. at the res. of John Daughaday in her 80th year. (BFG, 21 March 1804)

TODD, Owen, son of James Todd, Esq., of Penna., and Nancy Bibell both of Balto., were married by Rev. Richards. (BT, 22 April 1800) (BT, 23 April gives her name as Besett.)

TODD, Thomas, Judge of the U. S. Supreme Court, and Mrs. Lucy Washington, sister of Mrs. Madison, were wed 22nd ult. at the res. of the Pres. of the U. S. by Rev. McCormick. (BFR, 1 April 1812)

TODHUNTER, Joseph, merchant, and Miss Eliza Onion, both of Balto., were married last Tues. by Rev. Otterbein. (BFG, 13 Dec. 1810)

TOELLE, Dr. Fred, and Miss Sarah Rous of Balto. were married last eve. by Rev. Kurtz. (BPE, 27 Jan. 1813)

TOLLEY, James W., died 8th inst. at his res. in Harf. Co. leaving a widow and a number of orphan children. (BFG, 18 June 1812)

TOLLY, Mrs. Martha, died at Long Green, 22 Aug., aged 81. (BFG, 23 Sept. 1801. In the issue of the previous day her name is wrongly given as Jolly.)

TOMBLINSON, Capt. Samuel, of Portsmouth and Hannah Fox of Balto. were married Sun. by Rev. Bend. (BFG, 22 March 1796)

TOMLIN, George, formerly of Balto., died 22nd ult., Commander of the U. S. Navy Gunboat # 153, aged 30 years. "Savannah paper." (BFG, 8 Sept. 1813)

TOON, Samuel, of Chelsea, and Miss Tennant of Canton were married last eve. by Rev. Bend. (BT, 25 March 1799)

TOON, Samuel, and Miss Elizabeth Bennet both of Balto. were wed Thurs. eve. by Rev. Rattoone. (BFG, 4 April 1807)

TOONE, Mrs., died yesterday morning, wife of John Toone of Chelsea Garden. (BT, 11 Feb. 1800)

TOOPE, Mrs. Elizabeth, died last Wed., aged 111 years last Christmas (old style). (BFG, 21 Sept. 1805)

TOOTELL, James, purser in the U. S. Navy, died at Annap. last Tues. (BW, 18 Sept. 1809)

TOOTLE, Mrs. Elizabeth, died last Sat. at the res. of Col. Richard Dallam, in Abingdon, aged consort of Dr. Tootle, formerly of Annap. Interment in the Paca family vault. (BFG, 26 Aug. 1802)

TOPKEN, Gerhard, merchant, and Mrs. Hannah Caroline Powley, both of Balto., were married last eve. by Rev. Dr. Baker. (BA, 7 Dec. 1808)

TOULSON, Joseph, died in Balto., on 24th inst., in his 18th year. (BPE, 28 Oct. 1813)

TOWERS, Capt. George, died Sun., 18th inst., leaving a wife and a number of relatives. (BFG, 21 Jan. 1801)

TOWERS, Capt. James, late sailing master of the Comet, died this morning. Funeral from his late res., 71 Albemarle St. (BFG, 8 April 1813)

TOWNSEND, James, Esq., attorney-at-law, of St. Marys, killed himself last Fri. (BT, 9 Jan. 1805)

TOWNSEND, Joseph, merchant of Balto., and Miss Esther Hallett of N. Y., were married at the Friends Meeting there on 3rd inst. (BFG, 8 June 1803)

TOWSON, Ezekiel, died Sat., 9th inst., at his res. on the York
Turnpike Road in his 70th year. He bore an active part
in the Rev. War. (BT, 13 Nov. 1805)

TOWSON, Henry H., and Priscilla Crane, both of Balto., were wed
7 Dec. by Rev. Styre. (BA, 14 Dec. 1815)

TOWSON, Joseph, of Balto., and Sarah Yundt, dau. of Leonard
Yundt, were wed in Balto. Co. on 28 April. (BA, 2 May
1814)

TOWSON, Martha, died 11 Nov. 1808 in her 24th year. (BFG, 16
Nov. 1808)

TOWSON, Lieut.-Col. Nathan, of U. S. Light Artillery, and Sophia
Bingham, dau. of Caleb Bingham, were married at Boston.
(BA, 16 April 1816)

TOWSON, Obadiah, and Miss Catherine O. Irvine, both of Balto.,
were married on Thurs. by Rev. Moranville. (BS, 4 Aug.
1812)

TOWSON, Parthanessa, died Fri., 11 Nov., in her 24th year. (BEP,
17 Nov. 1808)

TOWSON, Philemon, and Mrs. Catherine Cushman both of Balto. were
married 18 April by Rev. Shimer. (BA, 20 April 1811)

TOWSON, Mrs. Ruth, widow of Ezekiel Towson, died 1 Dec. in her
69th year. Funeral from Mrs. Rebecca Towson's near Towson's Tavern. (BFG, 3 Dec. 1808)

TOWSON, Mrs. Susannah, died Sat., 13 April, in her 62nd year.
(BA, 19 April 1811)

TOWSON, William, died 18th inst. at his house in Balto. Co. on
the York Road in his 40th year. His funeral sermon will
be preached at the burying ground near his late res. on
26th inst. by Rev. Richards. (BFG, 23 Sept. 1805)

TRAMER, Terry, of Balto. Co., died 19th inst. (BA, 26 Oct. 1809)

TRANER, Terry, native of Ireland, died Thurs., 19th inst., for
many years a res. of Balto. Co. (BEP, 26 Oct. 1809)

TRAPNALL, James, died at his seat in Harf. Co., on 25th inst. in
his 53rd year, leaving an only dau. (BFG, 1 June 1805)

TRAQUAIR, James, stonecutter of Balto., died at Phila. on 5th
inst. in his 55th year. (BEP, 12 April 1811)

TRAVERS, John, merchant of Lisbon, and Miss Susan Rebecca Moale,
youngest dau of Samuel Moale of Balto., were married last
Wed. eve. by Bishop Kemp. (BFG, 5 April 1816)

TRAVERS, Mrs. Louisa Ann, consort of the late Henry Travers, died
14th inst. in Dorset Co., in her 45th year. (BFG, 30 March
1814)

TRAVERS, Henry, died in Dorset Co., aged 55 years. (BFG, 19 Feb.
1814)

TRAVIS, John, Esq., merchant of Phila., died last night. (BFG,
11 Oct. 1803)

TREGO, Col. John, died a few days ago in Bedford Co., Va., a member of Congress. (BFG, 18 July 1804)

TRIGG, Guy S., merchant of Nashville, Tenn., and Fanny B. Jackson of Balto. were wed last Thurs. by Rev. Glendy. (BFG, 9 April 1808)

TRIGG, John, member of Congress, died a few days ago in Bedford Co., Va. (BA, 18 July 1804)

TRIMBLE, Mrs. Hannah, wife of William Trimble, died 24th inst., in her 74th year. (BA, 28 Dec. 1816)

TRIMBLE, Isaac, Jr., Balto. merchant, died in New Orleans on 13th Dec. last. (BFG, 20 Jan. 1813)

TRIMBLE, William, and Miss Elizabeth Zacharias both of Balto. Co. were married last Tues. by Rev. Glendy. (BS, 6 March 1812)

TRIPPE, Lieut., of U. S. Navy Commander of the brig Vixen, died at sea on his passage from Havanna to this port. He had signalized himself in the Mediterranean during the Tripolitan War. (BEP, 18 Aug. 1810)

TRISLER, George, editor of the Winchester Constitutional Gazette, and Rosanna Wetzell of Winchester, Va., were married at Frederickstown by Rev. Strait. (BA, 18 Jan. 1800)

TROLDENIER, John George, died 12th inst., aged 46, pastor of the German Reformed Congregation in Balto., leaving a widow. He was born in Anhalt-Goethen, Germany, in 1754, where his father was a pastor and teacher. In York he married Miss Elizabeth Steeg. Their four infant children died in inf. (Long obit.) (BFG, 16 Dec. 1800)

TROTH, Thomas, of Dor. Co., and Miss Ellen Hooper of Balto. were married last Tues. by Rev. Roberts. (BA, 25 Dec. 1812)

TROTTEN, Dr. John, died at his house on Patapsco Neck Thurs., 30 Nov., in his 39th year; a husband and a father. (BA, 9 Dec. 1809)

TROUP, Henry, died 13th inst., in his 36th year; a Balto. merchant. (Long obit.) (BFG, 20 June 1810)

TROXIL, Michael, of Gettysburg, Pa., and Miss Margaret Markle of Balto., were married Tues., 21st inst. by Rev. Kurtz. (BA, 24 May 1816)

TRUELOCK, John, cabinet-maker, and Miss Sidney Walker of A. A. Co., were married last eve. at Elk Ridge by Rev. Bend. (BTD, 31 Aug. 1798)

TRUEMAN, Capt. John, died at Annap., 4th inst., a gallant officer of the Rev. War. (BFG, 17 Feb. 1809)

TRUIT, George, and Mrs. Ann Rollins, both of Fells Point, were married Sun. eve. by Rev. Richards. (BFG, 22 March 1796)

TRULOCK, Emmarilles, dau. of Mrs. Lydia Trulock, Fells Point, died 21st ult. in her 19th year. (BPEA, 3 March 1815)

TRUMP, John, and Miss Lydia Branson, both of Balto., were married last eve. by Rev. Kurtz. (BT, 4 Dec. 1799)

TRUSTON, Samuel, and Miss Mary Flaneday both of Balto. were wed Tues. last by Rev. Dr. Roberts. (BFG, 3 Aug. 1815)

TSCHUDY, Nicholas, long an inhab. of Balto., died at Hanover, Penna., on 25th ult., leaving an aged widow. (BFG, 11 June 1810)

TUBBS, William, late captain's clerk on board the U. S. sloop of War Baltimore, died last Thurs. (BA, 17 Nov. 1800)

TUCKER, Abel, and Miss Mary Tydings were married last Sun. at South River by Rev. Mr. Lane. (BT, 31 July 1804)

TUCKER, Capt. George C., of Portland, Maine, and Miss Lenette Ann Martiacq, dau. of John Martiacq of Balto., were married last eve. by Archbishop Carroll. (BMG, 2 Sept. 1815)

TUCKER, James, and Harriot Wesly Day, eld. dau. of Edward Day, all of Balto. Co., were wed 24th inst. by Rev. Samuel Handy. (BFG, 28 July 1803)

TUCKER, Mrs. Joanna, relict of Col. Robert Tucker of Norfolk, died last Fri., aged 86. Married at the age of 17, she was the mother of 22 children, and had been a widow for 40 years. "Norfolk, 13 Feb." (BT, 24 Feb. 1804)

TUCKER, John, and Miss Ann Trumble Carter all of Long Green, Balto. Co., were married last eve. by Rev. McCain. (BFG, 21 Nov. 1805)

TUCKER, Richard, newly arrived in Balto. from Som. Co., lost his dau. when she drowned in the cellar of his house on Dugan's wharf, which flooded when the tide rose last Sat. night. (BFG, 25 April 1804)

TULL, Mrs., drowned yesterday. (BFG, 25 July 1803)

TUMBLESTONE, Mrs. Ann, died in Penna., aged 41. (BPE, 11 Sept. 1813)

TUNIS, Charles, and Miss Harriot Coale, dau. of the late Thomas Coale of A. A. Co., were married on Thurs. eve. by Rev. Bend. (BFG, 19 June 1802)

TULL, Joshua, and Miss Ann Dickenson, both of Balto., were wed on Sun. by Rev. Alexander M'Caine. (BEP, 29 April 1811)

TURNBULL, Mrs. Sarah, died last Sun. in her 64th year, long an inhab. of Balto. (BFG, 12 Nov. 1811)

TURNER, Mrs. Ann, widow, of Balto. Co., died at John Murray's last Wed. (BEP, 1 June 1810)

TURNER, Caleb, and Mrs. Elizabeth Davis, both of Balto., were married last eve. by Rev. Kurtz. (BEP, 3 June 1808)

TURNER, Isaac, and Miss Hetty Campbell, all of Balto., were wed 1st inst. by Rev. Glendy. (BFG, 13 July 1813)

TURNER, Dr. John B., and Miss Ann Stone, both of Port Tobacco, were married there on Sun., 20th inst., by Rev. Weems. (BFR, 31 May 1810)

TURNER, Joseph, Jr., and Rebecca Sinclair, dau. of John Sinclair, all of Balto., were married at Friends Meeting for the Western District on 21st inst. (BA, 27 Oct. 1812)

TURNER, Joshua, and Miss Margaret Speer, both of Balto. Co., were married last Sat. by Rev. Hargrove. (BT, 25 Jan. 1803)

TURNER, Col. Thomas, accountant of the navy dept., died 15th inst., at his seat in Georgetown. (BWA, 23 March 1816)

TUTTLE, William, and Miss Mary Norris, both of Balto., were wed last eve. by Rev. Roberts. (BFG, 15 Aug. 1808)

TWAITS, Mrs. Elizabeth, wife of William Twaits of the Broadway Stage, died at New York, 13th inst., in her 27th year. (BFG, 16 Dec. 1813)

TYLER, Miss Henrietta, died Mon., 7th inst., youngest dau. of Samuel Tyler of P. G. Co., Md. "Frederick-Town, 13 Jan." (BA, 25 Jan. 1805)

TYLER, Hon. John, Judge of the Federal Court for the Dist. of Va., died Wed., 6th inst., at his res. in Charles City Co. (BFG, 18 Jan. 1813)

TYLER, Samuel, of P. G. Co., died Tues., 1st inst., in his 68th year. (BA, 15 Oct. 1805)

TYLER, Samuel, Judge of the Chancery Court for Williamsburg, died there on Monday week. (BFG, 3 April 1812)

TYLER, Judge William, died 8th inst., of the Federal Court in Va. (BA, 21 Jan. 1813)

TYLYARD, William, died Wed., in his 51st year, an old and respected inhab. of Balto. (BA, 23 May 1806)

TYSON, Mrs. Elizabeth, wife of Isaac Tyson, died yesterday in her 33rd year. Funeral from her late res. in Sharp St. (BFG, 13 May 1812)

TYSON, George, merchant, and Miss Hannah Bull, both of Balto., were married last eve. by Rev. Roberts. (BFG, 29 March 1811)

TYSON, Henry, and Miss Mary Ann Mulberg, all of Balto., were wed last Thurs. by Rev. Dr. Rattoone. (BFG, 6 June 1806)

TYSON, Isaac, merchant of Balto., and Miss Eliza Thomas, dau. of Evan Thomas of Balto. Co., were married last Wed. (BFG, 11 Nov. 1797)

TYSON, Isaac, of Balto., and Patience Marshall, dau. of Charles Marshall of Phila., were married 8th inst. at Friends Meeting, Mulberry St., Phila. (BMG, 15 June 1815)

TYSON, Mrs. Margaret, wife of Jesse Tyson, Balto. merchant, died yesterday, leaving an aged mother, husband, and six small children. Interment in Friends Burying Ground. (BFG, 21 June 1804)

TYSON, Mrs. Mary, consort of Elisha Tyson, died yesterday in her 56th year; res. on Sharp St. (BFG, 17 April 1813)

TYSON, Mr. N., Jr., and Miss Martha Ellicott of Balto. Co. were married 27th year at Ellicott's Mills. (BA, 30 Sept. 1815)

TYSON, Nathan, merchant, and Miss Sally Jackson, both of Balto., were wed Thurs. by Rev. Dr. Allison. (BFG, 27 Jan. 1798)

TYSON, Nathan, and Mary Randall both of Balto. were married last eve. by Rev. Richards. (BFG, 30 Sept. 1801)

TYSON, Mrs. Sarah, wife of Nathan Tyson, Balto. merchant, died this morning. (BFG, 8 July 1800)

TYSON, Mrs. Sarah, wife of Jesse Tyson, died 13th Sept. in her 51st year. (BA, 21 Sept. 1816)

TYSON, William, and Elizabeth Ellicott, dau. of Jonathan Ellicott of Balto. Co., were married last Wed. at Elk Ridge Friends Meeting. (BFG, 1 Nov. 1803)

UFFINGTON, Thomas, and Miss Ann Hallett both of Balto. were wed last Mon. by Rev. Richard Moore. (BEP, 23 July 1810)

UHLER, Erasmus, died last eve., long an inhab. of Balto.; res. on South Hanover St. (BPE, 16 Aug. 1814)

UHLER, Erasmus, and Catherine Hoffman of Balto., were married 13 Sept. by Rev. Kurtz. (BA, 14 Sept. 1816)

UHLER, George, of Balto., and Miss Barbara Good of Va. were wed last Sun. by Rev. Kurtz. (BA, 23 July 1812)

UHLER, John, of Balto., and Miss Priscilla Gallaway of Balto. Co., were married Wed. eve. by Rev. Kurtz. (BA, 25 May 1816)

UNDERHILL, Benjamin T., of Balto., and Miss Eliza Weeks, dau. of James Weeks, were married at Oyster Bay, L. I., where the bride lived. (BPE, 31 Jan. 1814)

UNDERWOOD, William, and Miss Mary Roach, both of Balto. were wed last Sun. by Rev. Coats. (BFG, 14 March 1804)

USHER, James, died yesterday; merchant, in his 31st year. (BFG, 25 Nov. 1801)

USHER, Miss Mary, dau. of Mrs. Rachel Usher, died 21st inst. in her 18th year. (BFG, 25 Feb. 1814)

USHER, Noble Luke, and Mrs. Harriot Anna Snowden, both of the New Theatre, were married on Sat. by Rev. Richards. (BT, 30 April 1804)

USHER, Thomas, died last eve. of an apoplectic fit at his seat in the country, merchant. (BFG, 19 Aug. 1800)

USTICK, Rev. Thomas, A. M., pastor of the Baptist Church in that city, died at Phila., early last Mon. in his 50th year. He was a grad. of Rhode Island College in 1771, and settled in the ministry at Phila. in 1782. (BFG, 22 April 1803)

UTT, John F., and Miss Jemima Bradey both of Balto. were married last eve. by Rev. Dashiell. (BPE, 19 March 1813)

VAN BEUREN, Gol Beeckman M., of Balto. and Miss Ann Denyse, dau. of Denyse D. Denyse (sic), were married at New Utrecht, L. I., where the bride lived. (BPE, 31 Jan. 1814)

VAN BIBBER, Abraham, only son of Abraham Van Bibber, died last Tues. in his 5th year. (BFG, 9 Dec. 1801)

VAN BIBBER, Abraham, died this morning aged 61 at his res. near Balto. (BFG, 23 Aug. 1805)

VAN BIBBER, Mrs. Ann, died last Tues., wife of Isaac Van Bibber, in her 52nd year, leaving a husband and four children. Interment in St. Pauls Churchyard. (BFG, 19 May 1796)

VAN BIBBER, Elizabeth Ann, only dau. of Washington Van Bibber, died 11th inst. in her 8th year, at Avon Dale, her father's res. in Fred. Co. (BFG, 12 Jan. 1816)

VAN BIBBER, Washington, and Miss Lucretia Emory, all of Balto., were married last eve. by Rev. Bend. (BFG, 29 May 1807)

VAN BURGEN, William, and Miss T. Elliott, all of Balto., were wed last Thurs. by Rev. Glendy. (BFG, 16 March 1816)

VANCE, Mrs. Mary, wife of William Vance, died Mon., 12th inst., in her 23rd year. Interment in the Presb. burying ground on the 14th. (BFG, 16 March 1804)

VANCE, William, and Miss Ann Lowes were married last Thurs. eve. by Rev. Bend (or Bond). (BT, 19 June 1802)

VANCE, William, and Ann Hezlip both of Balto. were married last Thurs. eve. by Rev. Annan. (BFG, 20 Oct. 1804)

VANCE, William, and his eld. dau. Jane, in her 13th year, died on their passage from Jamaica. Interment in the Second Presbyterian Church. Mr. Vance was a member of Balto. society for 20 years, and leaves a widow and two daus. (BA, 23 May 1816)

VANCLEVE, John, Esq., died at Phila., on Sun., one of the newly appointed commissioners of bankruptcy for the district of Penna. (BFG, 24 July 1802)

VAN DE GRIFT, William, and Miss Christiana Monington, both of Bucks Co., Penna., were married last Tues. by Rev. Dr. Rogers. (BA, 16 Nov. 1801)

VANDERWALL, Marks, postmaster of Richmond, Va., died 12th inst. (BEP, 16 June 1808)

VAN DYKE, Mrs. Mary, died at Chestertown, Wed., 8th inst., relict of the late Dr. Thomas Van Dyke of that place. (Long obit) (BTD, 16 Aug. 1798)

VANECK, Mrs. Sarah, of Balto., died last Sat., aged 78. (BEP, 1 Feb. 1810)

VAN HARTEN, Mrs. Hester, second dau. of Anthony Kimmel, died last Sat., in her 35th year, leaving three children. (BFG, 5 Feb. 1816)

VAN HORN, Gabriel G., postmaster of Vansville, P. G. Co., died there 3 April aged 34 years. (BA, 8 April 1814)

VAN LEAR, Dr. Matthew Simms, died at the farm of Matthew Van Lear, near Williamsport, 1st inst., in his 28th year. "Hagerstown, Sept. 3." (BFG, 5 Sept. 1816)

VAN LEAR, Col. William, died Tues., 11th inst., in his 58th year a res. of Wash. Co., Md. (Long obit gives details of his military career.) (BFG, 17 Jan. 1815)

VANNELLE, Heinrich, and Miss Nancy Price, all of A. A. Co., were
  wed last Sun. by Rev. Toy. (BA, 24 Aug. 1808)

VANNESS, Hon. John P., member of Congress from the state of N. Y.,
  married Sun., 9th inst., at the city of Wash., to Miss
  Marcia Burns, an heiress. (BFG, 19 May 1802)

VAN SICKLE, Henry, and Miss Delia Chancey both of Harf. Co., were
  married last Thurs. by Rev. Allen. (BT, 6 Feb. 1804)

VAN WINKLE, William, and Miss Catherine Lawdenslager, all of
  Balto. Co., were married by Rev. Glendy on 22nd ult.
  (BW, 3 March 1810)

VANZANT, Christopher, and Miss Eliza Fenton, both of Balto., were
  married last Sun. by Rev. Dr. Bend. (BFR, 11 Dec. 1811)

VAN ZANT, William, and Miss Sarah Curley, both of Balto., were
  wed last eve. by Rev. Hagerty. (BFG, 4 May 1810)

VANZANT, John, and Mrs. Rhody Cruse, all of Balto., were wed
  last eve. by Rev. Dr. Roberts. (BFG, 31 July 1812)

VARICK, Mrs. Sarah, of Balto., died 27th ult., aged 78 years.
  (BFG, 1 Feb. 1810)

VARON, Peter, of Washington, D. C., and Miss Victoria Faussette
  of Balto., were married 24th inst. by Rev. Beasley. (BA,
  27 April 1813)

VAUGHAN, Rev. Joshua, pastor of the Baptist Church, Brandywine,
  Chester (sic) Co., Md., died Tues., 30th ult., leaving a
  widow and several children. (BEP, 10 Sept. 1808)

VAUGHAN, Lieut. Thomas V., commander of the Garrison at Savannah,
  Ga., died 30th ult. on the brig Botanie off the Va. capes
  on his passage to Balto. His friends are supposed to re-
  side near Balto. (BFG, 16 July 1811)

VEANER, Emanuel, and Mary Plummer, both of Balto. Co., were wed
  last Sun. by Rev. Parks. (BA, 6 Nov. 1816)

VEAUGHN, William, and Miss Louise Kline, granddau. of Daniel
  Diffenderfer, both of Balto., were married last Sat.
  (BPEA, 29 March 1815)

VEAZEY, Capt. Edward, and Miss Sophia Dieter, both of Fells Point,
  were married last eve. by Rev. Roberts. (BFG, 17 June
  1808)

VEAZEY, Sarah, eld. dau. of Col. Thomas W. Veazey of Cecil Co.,
  died at Judge Worrell's in Chester Town on Fri., 13th inst
  in her 16th year. Interment in the family burial ground
  in Cecil. (BW, 25 Sept. 1811)

VEAZEY, Col. T. W., and Miss Mary Wallace of Elkton were married
  last Thurs. at Dr. Groom's in that place. (BS, 29 Sept.
  1812)

VERNON, John, bootmaker, died last Sat., 6th inst., in his 37th
  year, leaving a widow and two children. (BFG, 11 June
  1812)

VEVERS, John, and Miss Mary Brannan both of Balto. were married
  last Thurs. eve. by Rev. Bend. (BEP, 29 Dec. 1807)

VICKERS, Capt. James, and Miss Sarah Christy, all of Balto., were married yesterday eve. by Rev. Glendy. (BFG, 11 Feb. 1814)

VICKERS, Samuel, of Kent Co., died 31st Aug. at Fells Point in his 25th year, leaving an aged mother. (BFG, 2 Sept. 1802)

VICKERY, Capt. Stephen, died last Sat. in his 44th year. (BA, 25 Sept. 1809)

VINCENT, John, and Miss Nancy Campbell, all of Balto., were married last Tues. by Rev. Inglis. (BA, 1 Oct. 1812)

VINING, Mrs. Anna Maria, died Fri., 8th inst., at Dover, Del., in her 27th year, consort of John Vining and four infant sons. (BFG, 19 Aug. 1800)

VINING, John, died at Dover, 4th inst., member of Delaware Senate. (BRAD, 16 Feb. 1802)

VIZE, William T., and Miss Britanne Smallwood, all of Balto., were married last Sat. by Rev. Beeston. (BEP, 13 June 1808)

VOGEL, Mr., and Miss Mary Fowble, both of Balto., were married on Wed. eve. by Rev. Kurtz. (BT, 18 Aug. 1797)

VOICE, John, and Miss Elizabeth Sherry, both of Balto., were wed last eve. by Rev. Dr. Roberts. (BEP, 2 Oct. 1807)

VOLKMAN, P. A., merchant, and Miss Sophia Amelung, dau. of J. P. Amelung, were married last Thurs. at New Bremen. (BFG, 16 Aug. 1797)

VOMIJIM, Jeremiah, and Miss Mary Kittleman, both of Balto., were married on Sun. eve. by Rev. Richards. (BT, 19 Nov. 1799)

VON HARTEN, Gerhard, merchant, and Miss Hetty Kimmel, both of Balto., were married on Tues. eve. by Rev. Kurtz. (BFG, 14 April 1802)

VON HIMESSEN, Andrew I., merchant, and Miss Catherine Yeiser, dau. of the late Frederick Yeiser of Balto., were married last eve. by Rev. Kurtz. (BFG, 21 May 1802)

VON KAPF, Bernard John, of the House of Von Kaph and (Boone?), and Miss Hetty Didier were wed last eve. at the res. of Henry Didier (called Montpelier) by Rev. Hargrove. (BFG, 30 May 1804)

VOWELL, John D., of Alexandria, and Miss Margaretta Brown, dau. of Stewart Brown of Balto., were wed last Thurs. by Rev. Inglis. (BA, 10 June 1815)

VOWLES, Major Henry, died 28th ult., at Bellieu, Stafford Co., Va., and one of the justices of that county, and an officer in the Rev. War. (BFG, 2 Feb. 1803)

WADE, Mrs. Dorothy, consort of Thomas Wade, and dau. of the late Enoch Bailey, died yesterday in her 27th year; res. at 38 Market Space. (BFG, 17 Dec. 1810)

WADE, Nelson, of Phila., and Susan Robinson of York Town, Penna., were married Wed., 11th inst., by Rev. Mr. Cathcart. (BFG, 19 Feb. 1801)

WADE, Philip, and Miss Harriet Davis, all of Fells Point, were wed on Wed. by Rev. Dr. Bond. (BFG, 22 Feb. 1812)

WADE, Thomas, of Phila., and Mrs. Dorothea Furlong of Balto. were married last Tues. by Rev. Rattoone. (BEP, 10 June 1808)

WAGAMAN, Thomas, of Balto., and Miss Martha Tyler, dau. of Judge Tyler, were wed 24th ult. in Charles City Co., Va., by Rev. John D. Blair. (BEP, 3 Jan. 1807)

WAGNER, Jacob, of Phila., and Rachel, dau. of Christopher Raborg of Balto., were married last eve. by Rev. Kurtz. (BFG, 8 Aug. 1798)

WAINWRIGHT, Samuel, of Easton, Tal. Co., and Matilda Matthews of Gunpowder, Balto. Co., were married Wed., 30th ult., at Friends Meeting House, Gunpowder. (BFG, 9 June 1810)

WAIRE, Luke, and Polly Bosley, dau. of James Bosley of Balto. Co.. were married last Thurs. by Rev. Healy. (BFG, 12 Oct. 1807)

WAITES, Richard, and Miss Elizabeth Bassett, all of Balto., were married last Tues. by Rev. Hargrove. (BFG, 24 Oct. 1811)

WALKER, Agness Ann, and Miss Sarah Walker, daus. of Charles Walker of Balto. Co., died 30 March and 14 April, both of pulmonary consumption. (BA, 20 April 1810)

WALKER, Mrs. Alice, consort of Joshua Walker of Balto., a carpenter, and late of Dublin, died this morning in her 28th year. (BFG, 12 March 1800)

WALKER, Rev. Arch., died 7th inst. in Hanover St., a native of Ireland, a clergyman of the Episcopal Church. He resided in this country for over 30 years, and taught Latin and Greek. He leaves a widow and five children. (BA, 9 Nov. 1815)

WALKER, Major Bennett, of St. M. Co., died 11th inst. at Washington, in his 39th year. He was a loving husband and son. (BFG, 19 Dec. 1809)

WALKER, Charles Arthur, died Fri., 27th ult., at his father's res. in Balto. Co., in his 20th year. (BA, 2 Nov. 1815)

WALKER, Ezekiel, and Mrs. Margaret Smallwood, both of Balto., were married last eve. by Rev. Kurtz. (BA, 31 Aug. 1801)

WALKER, Jacob, and Elizabeth Pumphrey, both of Balto., were married Thurs. (BT, 29 June 1802)

WALKER, Dr. James, a student of Dr. Allender, died last Sat., aged 22. (BA, 13 Jan. 1800)

WALKER, James, a native of Newcastle-on-Tyne, and member of the firm of Casenave and Walker, of Balto., died Fri., 3rd inst. (BFG, 17 Nov. 1809)

WALKER, John, equestrian, of Balto., died on Mon., at the house of Richard S. Kingsmore of Patapsco Neck, leaving a family. (BT, 13 Nov. 1799)

WALKER, Joseph, and Miss Ellen Stacy, all of Balto., were wed last eve. by Rev. Glendy. (BFG, 17 Nov. 1815)

WALKER, Lewis, died yesterday morning; funeral from his late res., Centre Market. (BA, 11 Nov. 1811)

WALKER, Capt. Robert, formerly of the Balto. Line of Packets, died 5th inst. at Norfolk. (BFG, 11 June 1816)

WALKER, Samuel P., of Balto., and Miss Caroline H. Lee of Va., were married last eve. by Rev. Beasley. (BFG, 6 Nov. 1812)

WALKER, Thomas B., and Mrs. Elizabeth Finlass, all of Balto., were married last Sat. by Rev. Richards. (BFG, 3 Feb. 1812)

WALKER, William, and Miss Elizabeth Kinsell were married last eve. by Rev. Cotes. (BFG, 2 May 1803)

WALL, John, Sr., died this morning in his 81st year; res. at 37 N. Howard St. (BFG, 30 Dec. 1805)

WALLACE, Andrew, Balto. merchant, died Mon. (BT, 20 July 1803)

WALLACE, Charles, died last Thurs. at the res. of Leonard Sellman, on South River, in his 34th year. (BFR, 24 Feb. 1812)

WALLACE, Dr. George, died 17th inst. at Elkton, in his 44th year, a husband and father. (BFG, 24 June 1796)

WALLACE, Col. Gustavus B., died at Fredericksburg, on Tues., 27th inst., in his 52nd year. He served in the Rev. War. Interment in the Masons Burying Ground. (BFG, 4 Sept. 1802)

WALLACE, James, and Miss Sarah Fowler, all of Balto., were wed by Rev. Healey. (BA, 1 March 1810)

WALLACE, John, a native of Scotland, inhabitant of Balto. Co., died Tues. morning, aged 54 years. (BPE, 23 Sept. 1813)

WALLACE, John T., died yesterday morning in his 25th year; res. on Lee St. (BPEA, 23 Dec. 1815)

WALLACE, Joseph, and Miss Margaret King, all of Balto., were wed last Thurs. by Rev. Glendy. (BEP, 3 Dec. 1808)

WALLACE, Mrs. Margaret, died suddenly at Elkton, Cecil Co., on Tues., 10th inst. (BFG, 13 March 1807)

WALLACE, Thomas, died 31st ult. at his mills in Cecil Co., "another spark of '76 is extinguished." (BW, 7 April 1812)

WALLACE, William, died 28th inst., a native of Ireland. (BW, 1 July 1808)

WALLACK, Richard, of York Co., and Miss Ann Simms, dau. of Charles Simms, Esq., of Alexandria, were married. (BPE, 5 March 1813)

WALLIS, John, Jr., Balto. merchant, and Miss Louisa Chew Jolly, dau. of William Jolly, were married in Harford Co., 28th ult., by Rev. William Stevenson. (BFG, 8 July 1815)

WALLIS, Thomas, of Balto. Co., and Miss Catherine Heck, dau. of Lewis Heck of Lancaster, Penna., were married there on 28th ult. by Rev. Dr. Muhlenberg. (BEP, 5 March 1810)

WALLS, Dr. William, and Miss Mary Ann Burneston, dau. of Mr. Burneston, were married Tues. eve. by Rev. Nelson Reed. (BA, 20 Oct. 1814)

WALMSLEY, Benjamin, formerly of Balto., and Miss Catherine Jimmerson of New Castle Co., Del., were wed Thurs., 18th inst., by Rev. Henry Lyon Davis at Mrs. H. Frazier's res. in the latter county. (BEP, 1 Sept. 1808)

WALMSLEY, Dr. T., of Hagerstown, died this morning. (BT, 27 Aug. 1806)

WALN, Jesse, Phila. merchant, died last Sat. (BEP, 1 April 1806)

WALRAVEN, John, merchant, died this morning in his 43rd year. (BFG, 24 March 1814)

WALRAVEN, William, merchant, formerly of Balto., died at New Orleans, on the 20th ult. (BFR, 24 Jan. 1812)

WALSH, Jacob, and Miss Margaret Yates, dau. of Thomas Yates, all of Balto., were married Thurs. at Springfield, by Rev. Bend (or Bond). (BFG, 26 June 1802)

WALSH, John, and Miss Mary Doyle all of Balto. were married last eve. by Rev. Beeston. (BFG, 22 June 1804)

WALSH, Philip, died yesterday morning. (BFG, 3 Dec. 1803)

WALSH, Robert, Jr., and Miss Anna Maria Moylan, only dau. of Jasper Moylan of Balto., were married at Phila. last Tues. by Rev. Dr. Egan. (BEP, 11 May 1810)

WALSTRUM, Peter, and Miss Mary Ann Louisa Craten, all of Balto., were married last Thurs. by Rev. Fenwick. (BPEA, 15 May 1815)

WALTER, Charles, merchant, and Mrs. Heidey, both of Balto., were married last Mon. by Rev. Ireland. (BFG, 2 Aug. 1799)

WALTER, Mrs. Elizabeth, consort of Charles Walter, dec'., died 5th inst., in her 42nd year. (BFG, 8 Jan. 1812)

WALTER, Jacob, and Miss Mary Deagle, all of Balto., were married last eve. by Archbishop Carroll. (BFG, 20 Nov. 1810)

WALTER, John, was found murdered yesterday within a mile from Elk Ridge, Md.; a tailor and lived on Howard St., leaving a wife and three children. (BFG, 22 Aug. 1797)

WALTER, John, and Miss Eleanor Jenkinson, both of Fells Point, were married last Thurs. by Rev. Beeston. (BT, 15 Dec. 1804)

WALTER, Philip, of Balto., and Miss Margaretha Krouze of Balto. Co., eld. dau. of George Krouze, formerly of Balto., were married last Thurs. by Rev. Kurtz. (BFG, 24 Sept. 1808)

WALTER, William, and Miss Margaret Boyd, both of Balto., were wed last Thurs. eve. by Archbishop Carroll. (BFG, 20 Oct. 1810)

WALTER, William, and Margaret Lamborn, dau. of Robert Lamborn of Kennett Twp., Chester Co., Penna., were married at Friends Meeting there on 26th day of 3rd mo. (BA, 1 April 1812)

WALTERS, Alexander, and Miss Elizabeth Worthington, were married last Thurs. by Rev. Davis. (BT, 27 March 1806)

WALTERS, Frederick, and Mrs. Elizabeth Ann Julian, all of Balto., were married 9th inst. by Rev. Roberts. (BPEA, 18 July 1815)

WALTHAM, Clement, and Miss Alisanna Webster were married last Thurs. in Harf. Co. by Rev. Wilmer. (BFG, 3 Feb. 1801)

WALTMAN, William, and Miss Sarah Beckwith, all of Balto., were married. (BFG, 21 April 1808)

WALTON, John, late a res. of Taylor's Island, E. Shore, died 6th Sept. at Balto. Prison. (BEP, 10 Sept. 1808)

WAMPLER, John, postmaster, and Miss Elizabeth Yingling, both of Westminster, were married there on Sat., 28th inst. by Rev. Mr. Clingan. (BFG, 30 June 1801)

WANTON, William B., and Miss Izabella Ramsey both of Balto. were married last Sat. by Rev. Glendy. (BFG, 18 April 1809)

WARD, Mrs. Arietta, wife of George Ward of Balto., died 6th inst., in her 26th year. (BFG, 8 April 1809)

WARD, George, and Arietta, eld. dau. of William Jessop, were wed last Tues. by Rev. Dashiell. (BFG, 26 Feb. 1806)

WARD, James, and Miss Elizabeth Finletter, all of Balto., were wed last eve. by Rev. Ryland. (BPEA, 27 Feb. 1815)

WARD, John, Sr., died 9 Sept., of Lunenberg Co., in his 104th year. (BT, 6 Oct. 1802)

WARD, Joseph, and Miss Mary Tellman, both of Balto. Co., were married last Tues. by Rev. Austen Shoate. (BEP, 12 Dec. 1808)

WARD, Patrick, and Mrs. Martha Murray, were married last Tues. by Rev. Glendy. (BFG, 11 Feb. 1814)

WARD, Mrs. Sarah, consort of Col. John Ward of Sassafras Neck of Cecil Co., died Sat., 9th inst. (BFG, 18 Aug. 1806)

WARD, William, and Mrs. Hannah Israel, all of Balto. Co., were married Fri. by Rev. Roberts. (BT, 14 April 1806)

WARD, William, of A. A. Co., and Mrs. Ann B. Carson, of Balto., were married last Thurs. by Rev. Stires. (BA, 26 April 1815)

WARDELL, Samuel, and Miss Maria Clarke, were married by Rev. Glendy on 12th inst. (BA, 27 Aug. 1816)

WARDEN, James, native of Ireland, died at his farm in Hamilton Twp., Franklin Co., on 7 Jan., in his 93rd year. He settled in that twp. when it was part of York Co. Interment in the Rocky Spring burying ground. (BEP, 11 March 1807)

WARFIELD, Mr. Basil H., and Elizabeth, dau. of Daniel Rieman, were married last Thurs. eve. by Rev. George Roberts. (BA, 4 Jan. 1806)

WARFIELD, Charles A., Jr., and Eliza Harris, dau. of Edward Harris, all of Balto., were married last Tues. by Rev. Dashiell. (BFG, 28 Feb. 1812)

WARFIELD, Dr. Charles Alexander, died Fri., 29th ult., at his res.
in A. A. Co., in his 62nd year. He espoused the cause of
independence, and practised medicine for 42 years. (BFG,
11 Feb. 1813)

WARFIELD, Dennis, died 9th inst. at Havana, Cuba, in his 22nd
year. (BFG, 31 Oct. 1806)

WARFIELD, Mr. Evan, died at Havanna on 15th ult., in his 19th
year, son of Lancelot Warfield of A. A. Co. (BFG, 12 Nov.
1803)

WARFIELD, Dr. Gustavus, of Md., and Miss Mary Thomas, dau. of
Evan Thomas, were married at Whitly Hall, near Phila. on
27th inst. by Right Rev. Bishop White. (BFG, 31 Oct.
1810)

WARFIELD, Dr. Peregrine, of A. A. Co., and Harriot Sappington,
dau. of Dr. Sappington of Liberty Town, Fred. Co., were
wed on Tues., 13th inst. (BA, 24 May 1806)

WARFIELD, Mrs. Susanna, relict of Azel Warfield of Elk Ridge,
died 30th ult. in her 80th year. (BFG, 3 April 1812)

WARING, Dr. Horatio S., of Charleston, S. C., and Miss Henrietta
Higinbothom of Balto. were married yesterday by Rev. Beasley. (BPE, 2 Feb. 1813)

WARK, Andrew, and Mrs. Sarah M'Intire, both of Balto. were married
on Sun. by Dr. George Roberts. (BW, 27 May 1811)

WARKING, George, died yesterday of wounds received from three con-
victs who were escaping. He leaves a mother, wife and
three small children. (BEP, 16 March 1808)

WARNER, Henry, and Mrs. Charlotte Arnolp (sic) of Balto., were
married last eve. by Rev. Kurtz. (BA, 12 March 1808)

WARMINGHAM, Mrs. Winifred, died Wed., 2nd inst., in her 70th year,
a native of Wales.

WARNER, Andrew E., of Balto., and Miss Dorothy Litzinger of Balto. Co., were married last Thurs. by Rev. Richards. (BW,
27 June 1812)

WARNER, Henry. See above.

WARNER, Thomas, and Mrs. Mary Ann Helm, all of Balto., were wed
last eve. by Rev. Beasely. (BFG, 26 Oct. 1810)

WARNER, William, and Miss Susan Miltenberger of Balto. were wed
last eve. by Rev. Kurtz. (BFG, 21 Nov. 1804)

WARRELL, Master Henry, son of Mr. and Mrs. Warrell of the New
Theatre, died last Mon. in his 8th year. (BFG, 30 Oct.
1799)

WARREN, Mrs. Ann, wife of Mr. Warren, manager of the Phila. and
Balto. Theatres, died at Alexandria on last Tues. (BFG,
1 July 1808)

WARREN, Capt. Nahum, of Maine, and Miss Martha Barney of Balto.
were married Thurs. eve. by Rev. Rattoone. (BFG, 16 Nov.
1808)

WARREN, William, and Mrs. Ann Wignell, both of the Balto. and
Phila. Theatres, were married this morning at James
Wharfe's. (BFG, 28 Aug. 1806)

WARRICK, William, and Achsa Tipton, of Balto. Co., were married
last Thurs. by Rev. John Healey. (BA, 21 Aug. 1815)

WASHINGTON, Corbin, of Fairfax Co., died 10th inst. at Bushfield,
Westmoreland Co., only surviving bro. of Judge Washington
and nephew of the late illustrious patriot of Mount Vernon.
(BA, 21 Dec. 1799)

WASHINGTON, George, died. (Long obit.) (BFG, 17 Dec. 1799)

WASHINGTON, George S., of Va., died 16th ult. in Augusta, nephew
of the late Pres. Washington, in his 37th year. Interment
in St. Pauls Churchyard. (BA, 14 Feb. 1809)

WASHINGTON, Mrs. Hannah, widow of Corbin Washington, died at Alexandria, Mon. se'ennight, in her 37th year. (BA, 8 Dec. 1801)

WASHINGTON, Mrs. Martha, died at Mt. Vernon, last Sat., relict of
the late illustrious George Washington. (BFG, 25 May 1802)

WASHINGTON, Col. William Augustine, died last Tues. at Georgetown
in his 53rd year. (BEP, 10 Oct. 1810)

WASHINGTON, William Henry, died suddenly on Tues. last at his farm
near Alexandria. (BT, 22 June 1803)

WATERHOUSE, William, and Mrs. Ann Butler, both of Balto., were
wed 17th inst. at Friends Meeting. (BT, 19 May 1798)

WATERHOUSE, William, a member of the Society of Friends, died 8th
inst. (BFG, 11 Sept. 1807)

WATERS, Dr., of one of the U. S. Regiments near Natches, committed
suicide by cutting his throat at Phila. (BI, 16 May 1798)

WATERS, Alexander, and Miss Elizabeth Worthington, were married
last eve. at the res. of John Worthington near Randallstown. (BFG, 26 March 1806)

WATERS, Miss Catherine, dau. of Mrs. Mary Waters (q.v.), died on
Sat., aged 19. (BFG, 23 Sept. 1800)

WATERS, David Rittenhouse, died in Penna., aged 22. (BPE, 11
Sept. 1813)

WATERS, Edward, merchant, and Sarah W. Brown, dau. of Wm. Brown,
all of Balto., were married today at Friends Meeting House.
(BFG, 21 Dec. 1815)

WATERS, Mrs. Elizabeth, consort of James Waters, merchant of Balto., died yesterday in her 20th year. (BFG, 14 May 1796,
and BT, 14 May 1796)

WATERS, Miss Esther, died at Cambridge, after a short illness,
dau. of Col. Richard Waters. (BFR, 25 Nov. 1811)

WATERS, Hezekiah, Jr., died at Fells Point on Sat., 30 May, aged
18 years. (BFG, 4 June 1801)

WATERS, Horatio, and Miss Margaret Meyerhofer, of Fred. Co., were
married last Thurs. by Dr. Roberts. (BA, 30 Dec. 1816)

WATERS, James, of Balto., drowned when the brig Kitty of Balto.,
Capt. Rogers, bound for Nantz was lost. Mr. Waters left
two children, who are the more to be pitied as their
mother died a short time ago. (BFG, 2 June 1796)

WATERS, John C., and Miss Rebecca Onion, were married at Ockney,
Harf. Co., on 12th inst. by Rev. Richardson. (BS, 19
Nov. 1812)

WATERS, Joseph, and Miss Sophia Easom, all of Balto., were wed
last eve. by Rev. Hargrove. (BFG, 18 Dec. 1810)

WATERS, Joseph G., and Mrs. Sarah Waters, both of Balto., were
married last eve. by Rev. Dashiell. (BFG, 11 Feb. 1815)

WATERS, Mrs. Mary, died Sun., aged 46, mother of Catherine Waters
(q.v.). (BFG, 23 Sept. 1800)

WATERS, Peter, and Miss Tabitha Franklin all of Balto. were wed
last eve. by Rev. Dr. Roberts. (BFG, 21 Jan. 1814)

WATERS, Capt. Philip, died yesterday, 20th inst., aged 55 years,
an inhab. of Balto. (BFG, 21 Sept. 1798)

WATERS, Richard, and Miss Louisa Thomas all of Balto. were wed
last eve. by Rev. Coker. (BFG, 11 Feb. 1813)

WATERS, Stephen, and Miss Polly Brown, all of Harf. Co., were
wed last Thurs. at the seat of Edward Day, by Rev. Wilmer.
(BFG, 2 April 1802)

WATERSON, Robert, and Jane Faris, both of Balto., were married
last Thurs. by Rev. Smith. (BA, 19 July 1800)

WATERSON, William, and Jane Faris, both of Balto., were married
Thurs. by Rev. Smith. (BT, 19 July 1800)

WATKINS, Archibald Washington, and Elizabeth Parsons both of
Fells Point, were married last eve. by Rev. Riggen. (BA,
28 June 1799)

WATKINS, Gassaway, and Mrs. Rebecca Thompson, both of Balto.,
were married last Thurs., 5th inst., by Rev. Hagerty.
(BA, 9 Sept. 1805)

WATKINS, James, and Miss Mary Chatterton both of Balto. were wed
Mon., 8 June, by Rev. Bend. (BFG, 20 June 1807)

WATKINS, Richard, and Elizabeth Beddo, dau. of Absalom Beddo, of
Mont. Co., were married last Thurs. (BFG, 18 March 1800)

WATKINS, Richard, and Mrs. Patience How, both of Balto., were
married in Sheppardstown on last Sat. by Rev. Welch.
(BFG, 21 Jan. 1804)

WATKINS, Thomas, and Elizabeth Spurrier, dau. of William Spurrier,
both of Elk Ridge, were married last Thurs. by Rev. Bend.
(BFG, 23 March 1799)

WATSON, Coleman, and Mrs. Elizabeth James, all of Balto., were
wed last Tues. by Rev. Hargrove. (BFG, 13 May 1813)

WATSON, Mrs. Harriet, consort of William Watson, aged about 28
years, died 27th inst. (BEP, 28 Dec. 1808)

WATSON, James, and Miss Margaret Watson, both of Balto., were
wed last Thurs. by Rev. Glendy. (BFG, 17 Feb. 1812)

WATSON, James, and Miss Elizabeth Spear, both of Franklin Co.,
Penna., were married 7th inst. by Rev. Glendy. (BA, 27
Aug. 1816)

WATSON, Robert, and Miss Rachel Price, dau. of Hezekiah Price,
were married Tues. eve. by Rev. Dr. Inglis. (BA, 20 April
1815)

WATSON, Sylvester, and Miss Louisa Georgiana Washington Furnival
of Balto. were married last Tues. by Rev. Duncan. (BA,
29 June 1815)

WATSON, Thomas, and Miss Rebecca Freeman, all of Balto., were wed
on Sat. by Rev. Glendy. (BA, 23 Nov. 1807)

WATSON, William, of Liverpool, Eng., and Miss Martha Jay of Harf.
Co., were married Thurs., 5th inst., at Friends Meeting
on Deer Creek. (BFG, 9 March 1801)

WATSON, William, and Mrs. Margaret Rogan, all of Balto., were wed
16th inst. by Dr. O'Brian. (BEP, 20 April 1810)

WATTS, Dixon, of Balto., and Miss Eleanor Bowen of Balto. Co.
were married last eve. by Rev. Armstrong. (BFG, 3 May
1809)

WATTS, Edward, of Port Tobacco, and Miss Elizabeth Aisquith, dau.
of William Aisquith of Balto., were married last eve. by
Rev. Ireland. (BFG, 10 July 1797)

WATTS, Edward, died last Tues. in Balto. Yesterday he was buried
in St. Pauls burial ground. (BFG, 14 Feb. 1799)

WATTS, Edward A., and Sarah Ellison both of Fells Point were wed
last eve. by Rev. Snethen. (BFG, 11 Sept. 1809)

WATTS, Josias, and Miss Sidney Wigley of Patapsco Neck were wed
by Rev. Healey. (BA, 1 March 1810)

WATTS, Richard, of Balto., formerly of St. M. Co., died last
Tues. (BFR, 16 Aug. 1811)

WATTS, Solomon, and Miss Nancy Jones, all of Balto. Co., were
wed yesterday by Rev. Stevens. (BPE, 20 May 1814)

WATTS, William, died. (Long obit.) (BEP, 18 Nov. 1808)

WAY, Andrew, Jr., printer, formerly of Phila., and now of Washington, and Mrs. Mary Pawson of Balto., were married on Mon.,
15th inst., by Rev. Roberts. (BEP, 23 May 1809)

WAY, Dr. Joseph, and Miss Sally Simpson, both of Balto., were wed
last Thurs. by Rev. Roberts. (BFG, 28 Feb. 1801)

WAYBELL, Adam, paper-maker, was found dead yesterday. His disappearance had been reported several weeks earlier. (BT,
29 April 1803)

WAYNE, John, printer, and Miss Elizabeth Ellicott, were married
last eve. by Rev. Rattoone. (BFG, 12 Dec. 1806)

WEAREY, William, and Miss Ann Merritt, both of Fells Point, were
married last eve. by Rev. Bend. (BA, 20 Sept. 1799)

WEATHERBURN, John, President of the Mechanics Bank, died yesterday, aged 61. He was born at Kenton, near Newcastle-on-Tyne, and in 1772 went to Alexandria, Va., and then came to Balto. He was a member of the Volunteer Independent Co. of militia in the Rev. (Long obit.) (BFG, 22 and 23 April 1811)

WEATHERFIELD, James, and Miss Ann Bane all of Balto., were wed 11th ult. by Rev. Waw (Waugh?). (BA, 10 Aug. 1813)

WEATHERLY, Capt. Jesse, and Mrs. Rachel Stapleton, both of Balto., were married last eve. by Rev. Dashiell. (BT, 14 March 1804)

WEATHERLY, Capt. Jesse, died at sea on 20 June, on his return from Cherbourg to Balto. (BFG, 16 July 1805)

WEATHERLY, Lyttleton, and Miss Sarah Jennith, both of Balto., were married Thurs. by Rev. Coates. (BT, 5 Feb. 1803)

WEAVER, Mrs. Ann, wife of Adam Weaver of Phila., died 19th inst., in her 40th year. (BT, 25 Sept. 1804)

WEAVER, Daniel, merchant, and Miss Elenor High, both of Balto., were married last eve. by Rev. Dr. Roberts. (BA, 30 Nov. 1810)

WEAVER, Isaac, Senator of Penna., and Miss Rachel Husbands of Deer Creek, were married Thurs., 26th ult. (BA, 3 Jan. 1812)

WEAVER, Jacob, and Miss Ruth Howard, dau. of Samuel Howard were married last Thurs. in A. A. Co., by Rev. Dorsey. (BT, 1 June 1802)

WEAVER, Capt. John, died Thurs. (BA, 17 Aug. 1799)

WEAVER, John, and Miss Rebecca Stinchcomb all of Balto. were wed last Mon. by Rev. Dr. Roberts. (BFG, 9 April 1811)

WEAVER, Capt. Joseph, and Miss Kitty Spinner of Milford Twp., Bucks Co., Penna., were married 18th ult. (BEP, 1 Sept. 1810)

WEAVER, P., and Miss Louisa Kline, dau. of George Kline, editor of the Carlisle Gazette, were married by Rev. Robert Birch on 18 July. (BEP, 8 AUg. 1809)

WEAVER, Thomas, captain of artillery, died yesterday eve. at Fells Point. Interment this afternoon in St. Pauls burying ground with the honors of war and Masonry. (BFG, 16 Aug. 1799)

WEAVER, William, and Miss Ann Heckman, dau. of the late Lawrence Heckman of Balto. Co., were married at Merry Hill last Sun. by Rev. Myers. (BT, 18 July 1804)

WEBB, Christina, died 21st ult. at Kennett, 10 miles from the borough of Wilmington, Del., in her 94th year. She was the last of the 17 children of Daniel and Jane Hoopes. (BFG, 18 April 1816)

WEBB, James, of Phila., and Miss Eliza Cullidon of Balto. were wed last eve. by Rev. Kurtz. (BA, 15 July 1811)

WEBB, John, and Miss Kitty Davis, both of Balto., were married last Thurs. by Rev. Dr. Rattoone. (BFG, 9 May 1806)

WEBSTER, John, druggist, died near Wilmington, aged 60 years, by a stroke of apoplexy. (BEP, 15 Aug. 1810)

WEBSTER, John A., capt., late of the U. S. Navy, and Miss Rachel Biays, dau. of Col. Joseph Biays, all of Balto., were wed Thurs. by Rev. Dr. Inglis. (BA, 10 Feb. 1816)

WEBSTER, John Skinner, and Elizabeth, dau. of Joseph Thornbury, merchant of Balto., were married yesterday morning by Rev. Ireland. (BT, 13 June 1800)

WEBSTER, Sarah, dau. of Richard Webster, died in Harf. Co., on 24 Dec. (BW, 28 Dec. 1809)

WEBSTER, Toppan, and Miss Martha Osborne, both of Balto., were wed last Tues. at Washington. (BEP, 1 Oct. 1807)

WEDERSTRANDT, Philemon C., and Miss Helen Smith, dau. of Judge A. Smith, were married yesterday at Poplar Grove, the res. of Judge Smith by Archbishop Carroll. (BFG, 26 Nov. 1813)

WEEDEN, Mrs. Elizabeth Scott, consort of Capt. Frederick Weeden, Matthews Co., Va., died Mon., 10th inst. (BA, 22 April 1815)

WEEMS, Dr., and Miss Eliza French of Georgetown were married on Tues., 14th inst. at Georgetown. (BWM, 26 March 1797)

WEEMS, George, of Cal. Co., and Miss Sarah Sutton of Fells Point were married last Tues. by Rev. Roberts. (BFG, 3 March 1808)

WEEMS, John, died 7 Sept. at his res. near Louisville, Ky., in his 77th year, late of A. A. Co. (BFG, 18 Oct. 1813)

WEEMS, John C., of West River, and Eliza, eld. dau. of John Lee Webster, were married Sat., 19th inst. by Rev. Mr. Bend. (BFG, 26 Jan. 1804)

WEEMS, Wm., of Cal. Co., Md., and Miss Mary Kinsey, dau. of the late Chief Justice Kinsey of Burlington, N. J., were wed at Phila., 31 May, by Rev. Dr. Wharton. (BAP, 9 June 1803)

WEESTON, William, Sr., died 13th ult., at Glouc. Co., Va., in his 45th year. (BA, 24 May 1811)

WEHNER, George, died last Tues., aged 30 years, leaving a wife and three children. (BW, 21 April 1814)

WEHRLY, Jonathan, and Miss Elizabeth Utz, all of Balto., were wed Tues., 28th ult., by Rev. Kurtz. (BFG, 5 April 1815)

WEIDENER, Mrs., died this morning; res. on Conway St. (BFG, 26 Nov. 1811)

WEIR, Charles, and Charlotte Fowler, both of Balto., were married last eve. by Rev. Richards. (BA, 16 July 1806)

WELCH, Edward, and Mrs. Hannah Henderson, both of Balto. Co., were married last Wed. by Rev. John Glendy. (BW, 27 March 1812)

WELCH, Peregrine, and Miss Lydia Richardson, all of Balto., were married last eve. by Rev. Dashiell. (BFG, 7 Oct. 1807)

WELCH, Robert, of Ben, of A. A. Co., and Miss Polly Sellman, 2nd dau. of Jonathan Sellman of this place, were married Tues. 3rd inst., by Rev. Bend. (BEP, 5 June 1806)

WELFORD, Robert Y., Balto. merchant, and Miss Louisa Gittings, dau. of Richard Gittings, were married at Berry Hill, Long Green, on last Tues. by Dr. Inglis. (BFG, 17 March 1815)

WELIMER, Mrs. Letitia, of Balto. Co., died in her 50th year. (BW, 15 March 1814)

WELLMORE, Peter C., died Fri., 31st ult. in his 41st year. (BPEA, 5 April 1815)

WELLMORE, William, and Miss Ann Ridgely, both of Balto., were wed last Thurs. by Rev. Hagerty. (BFG, 23 Nov. 1797)

WELLS, Benjamin, died last Sun., an old inhab. of Balto. (BFG, 19 Nov. 1801)

WELLS, Cyprian, died yesterday aged 65 years. (BW, 23 Feb. 1814)

WELLS, Mrs. Elizabeth, formerly widow of Mr. Edward Flanagan, died last Sun. in her 40th year; a wife, mother, and friend. (BFG, 18 Dec. 1799)

WELLS, Harrison V., and Miss Mary Jeffers, eld. dau. of Joseph Jeffers, all of Balto., were married last Thurs. by Rev. Richards. (BA, 25 May 1816)

WELLS, Rev. Joshua, and Mrs. Eve Reinecker, of Balto., were wed last eve. by Rev. Shinn. (BFG, 23 Sept. 1812)

WELLS, Miss Sally, dau. of the late Capt. William Wells of Fells Point, died Mon. Funeral from the res. of Capt. Matthew Kelly, 59 Market St., F. P. (BA, 21 May 1816)

WELLS, Mrs. Susan, consort of William Wells, merchant of Alexandria, Va., died 4th inst., in her 48th year. (BEP, 16 Feb. 1815)

WELLS, Thomas W., and Miss Elizabeth Pouder, dau. of Leonard Pouder of Balto., were wed last eve. by Rev. Otterbein. (BFG, 13 Jan. 1813)

WELSH, Capt. Enoch, died the morning of 26th inst., of Balto., in his 49th year. (BFG, 30 Jan. 1806)

WELSH, John, blockmaker of Fells Point, died last Sat., leaving a wife and two children. (BFG, 22 Feb. 1802)

WELSH, Philip, and Miss Elizabeth Lower, both of Balto., were wed last eve. by Rev. Wells. (BT, 15 Nov. 1802)

WELSH, Robert, of Va., and Miss Henrietta H. Cromwell of Balto. Co., were married last Sat. by Rev. Neal. (BA, 23 Dec. 1806)

WELTZHEIMER, Philip, died last Mon. night, aged 73. "Frederick Town, Jan. 14." (BFG, 18 Jan. 1803)

WENTWORTH, Joseph, died at Sandisfield, Mass., 17 Jan., aged 52, leaving a widow and seven children. (BA, 20 Feb. 1806)

WERNER, Daniel, and Miss Catherine Snyder, all of Fred. Co., were wed 26th ult. by Rev. D. F. Schaeffer. (BPEA, 12 April 1815)

WESSELS, Mr. I. F. F., Balto. merchant, and Sarah Shoemaker Johns, eld. dau. of the late Mr. Matthew Johnson of Phila., were married last Thurs. at Phila. by Rev. Dr. Joseph Hutchins. (BFG, 5 Nov. 1803)

WESSELLS, Mr. J. F. F., Balto. merchant, died last Mon. in his 43rd year, leaving a widow and four young children. (BFG, 9 APril 1812)

WEST, Capt., and Miss Sophia Frazer of Fells Point, were married last eve. by Rev. Rattoone. (BFG, 4 Aug. 1803)

WEST, Mrs., wife of the celebrated Benjamin West, Pres. of the Royal Academy, died 6 Dec. in London. (BA, 22 April 1815)

WEST, Mr. Amos, and Elizabeth Coats, youngest dau. of Jonathan Coats, all of Balto., were married Thurs. at Friends Meeting. (BFG, 17 April 1802)

WEST, Mrs. Elizabeth, wife of Capt. William West, died last eve.; res. at 55 Market St., Fells Point. (BFG, 13 May 1809)

WEST, James, and Margaret Whitaker, both of Annapolis, were wed in Annapolis on 31 March by Rev. Ralph Higginbothom. (BFG, 7 April 1796)

WEST, James, of Balto., and Miss Maria Blodget, dau. of Samuel Blodget of Phila., were married last Tues. in Phila. by Bishop White. (BFG, 10 Feb. 1798)

WEST, James, merchant, died 8th inst., aged 41. (BFG, 12 Dec. 1809)

WEST, James, formerly of Annap., and a res. of Balto., died Sat., 6th inst. in his 74th year. (BA, 19 June 1812)

WEST, James, died Mon., 16th inst., in his 35th year. (BA, 25 Dec. 1816)

WEST, Capt. Job, and Miss Isabella Smith, both of Balto., were married by Rev. Annon last Thurs. (BA, 11 Dec. 1810)

WEST, Joel, and Miss Julian Francisca Rapp, both of Balto., were married last eve. by Rev. Bend. (BFG, 20 July 1798)

WEST, John, board merchant of Balto., died last eve. (BT, 6 Sept. 1797)

WEST, John, and Miss Catherine Willingmyer, both of Balto., were married Thurs. eve. by Rev. Roberts. (BA, 14 Nov. 1815)

WEST, Mrs. Margaret, died at Norfolk, formerly an actress of the Virginia Company of Comedians, and late proprietor of the Norfolk Theatre. (BFG, 11 June 1810)

WEST, Mr. Stacy, and Miss Ann Whitaker, dau. of Joshua Whitaker, all of Harf. Co., were married there last Thurs. by Rev. Davis. (BFG, 9 March 1805)

WEST, William, and Elizabeth Fennell, all of Balto., were married last eve. by Rev. McCain. (BEP, 21 April 1809)

WEST, Wilmot, and Miss Elizabeth B. Miller, all of Balto., were married last Thurs. by Rev. Beasler. (BS, 24 March 1812)

WESTON, Clement B., sugar refiner of Alexandria, D. C., and Julia Day of this county, were married last Thurs. night by Rev. Sinclair. (BFG, 6 April 1816)

WESTON, John, died in Harf. Co., on 1 May, in his 67th year. (BFG, 8 May 1812)

WESTON, Joseph, of Balto., died last night in his 52nd year, leaving a numerous family. (BFG, 30 Dec. 1802)

WESTON, Mrs. Rebecca, relict of the late John Weston, died 22nd inst., at Orkney, Harf. Co., in her 67th year. (BFG, 24 Nov. 1812)

WESTROME, Andrew, of Balto., died yesterday in his 67th year; res. at #70 High St., Old Town. (BA, 19 July 1811)

WETHERED, Levin, and Miss Elizabeth Ellicott, dau. of Mr. Elias Ellicott, all of Balto., were married last Tues. by Rev. Bend. (BFG, 18 July 1805)

WHANN, William, and Miss Elizabeth Ewing, both of Cecil Co., were married last eve. by Rev. Dashiell. (BEP, 22 Jan. 1808)

WHARTNABY, Joseph, printer, and Mrs. Richardson, both of that city, were married at Phila., on Sat., 13th inst. by Rev. Dr. Rogers. (BA, 19 July 1799)

WHARTON, Charles, Jr., and Miss Ann Hollingsworth, dau. of J. Hollingsworth, Jr., were married last Thurs. in Phila. (BFG, 22 June 1815)

WHATCOAT, Rev. Richard, one of the Bishops of the M. E. Church, died at Dover, Del., on 5th inst. (BFG, 10 July 1806)

WHEATLEY, Richard P., and Miss Sarah Thatcher White of Balto., were married last Sat. by Rev. Dr. Rattoone. (BFG, 3 Feb. 1807)

WHEEDEN, James, ship-builder of Fells Point, and Eliza Spry Lambden, eld. dau. of Thomas Lambden of Fells Point, were wed last Thurs. by Rev. Hagerty. Immediately after, Mr. Lambden's youngest child was baptized only 4 mos. old, the last of 16 children in 16 and 1/2 years of marriage. (BFG, 8 Dec. 1804)

WHEEDEN, Mrs. Sarah, wife of James Wheeden of Fells Point, died last Tues, leaving a husband and children. Interment in the Meth, burial ground. (BFG, 28 June 1804)

WHEELER, Benjamin, aged 81 years, died last Thurs. at his res. in Gunpowder Forest, Balto. Co. (BA, 11 Aug. 1807)

WHEELER, Mrs. Clara, died yesterday in her 59th year. (BW, 17 March 1810)

WHEELER, Mrs. Elizabeth, died on Deer Creek, Harf. Co., last Mon. in her 41st year, consort of Benjamin Wheeler. (BFG, 12 Feb. 1802)

WHEELER, Jonathan, Balto. merchant, died at New York on the 3rd inst. (BFG, 6 Sept. 1811)

WHEELER, Philip, died last Sat., a husband and father. (BEP, 31 Aug. 1807)

WHEELER, Robert, of Balto., and Miss Polly Kepley of Penna., were married last eve. by Rev. Kurtz. (BS, 12 Feb. 1812)

WHEELER, Thomas, and Miss Alicia Blackburn were married last eve. by Rev. Rattoone. (BFG, 26 April 1805)

WHEELER, Thomas C., and Miss Hannah Donovan both of Balto. Co., were married last Thurs. by Rev. Grie. (BEP, 20 May 1809)

WHELAN, Bazel, and Kitty Riddlemoser, both of Balto., were wed last eve. by Rev. Carroll. (BA, 12 Feb. 1800)

WHELAN, David, merchant, of Balto., and Miss Sarah M'Cubbin, dau. of Zachariah MacCubbin of Balto. Co., were wed last eve. at Mt. Pleasant by Rev. Beeston. (BFG, 25 Feb. 1805)

WHELAN, David, died last Thurs. in his 34th year; a Balto. merchant. (BFG, 18 Oct. 1813)

WHELAN, Mathew, and Miss Ellen Vize, both of Balto., were married 1st inst. by Rev. Beeston. (BEP, 3 March 1808)

WHELON, Capt. Richard, died Fri., 24th inst., in his 74th year. (BFG, 23 April 1804)

WHETCROFT, James, died in Annap. last Wed. in his 80th year. (BFG, 25 Sept. 1804)

WHITCROFT, William, died in Annap. on Sat., aged 62 years. (BT, 8 Aug. 1799)

WHITE, Miss, only dau. of Dr. Campbell White of Balto., died Sun., 3rd inst. (Long obit.) (BFG, 4 June 1810)

WHITE, Alexander, died at his res. near Winchester, Va., last 28 Sept., aged 66. He represented Va. in the first Congress under the present government, and was commissioner of the Federal City. (BT, 10 Oct. 1804)

WHITE, Benjamin, and Mrs. Mary Miller, both of Fells Point, were married Sun. by Rev. Kurtz. (BA, 25 Feb. 1806)

WHITE, Benjamin, and Miss Hannah Wadsworth of Balto. Co., were wed last eve. by Rev. Haley. (BW, 20 Nov. 1811)

WHITE, Campbell P., of Balto., and Harriet Banyer Le Roy, eld. dau. of the late Jacob Le Roy, were married at New York on Wed. by Rev. Dr. Romeyn. (BA, 5 Feb. 1816)

WHITE, Dennis, and Rebecca Herrick, both of Balto., were married Thurs. by Rev. Bishop Carroll. (BFG, 13 April 1804)

WHITE, Miss Euphemia, dau. of the late Dr. Daniel White of Westchester, N. Y., died yesterday, 6th inst., at the res. of John B. Bernabeu, Spanish Consul. (BFG, 7 May 1810)

WHITE, Henry, and Miss Margaret Elder, both of Balto., were wed last eve. by Rev. Inglis. (BFG, 9 Aug. 1811)

WHITE, Henry, and Elizabeth Gissenderfer, both of Balto., were married last Thurs. by Rev. Inglis. (BA, 18 March 1816)

WHITE, Hugh, and Miss Ellen Nixon, all of Balto., were married last Thurs. by Rev. John Healey. (BA, 21 Aug. 1815)

WHITE, Hugh, and Miss Eleanor Lockerman, both of Balto., were wed last eve. by Rev. Healey. (BMG, 18 Aug. 1815)

WHITE, Jacob, of Balto., and Miss Elizabeth Bussey, dau. of Bennett Bussey, were married in Harf. Co. last Wec. by Rev. Mr. Mahon. (BFG, 31 Dec. 1804)

WHITE, Jehu, and Mary R. Rogers, were married 24th ult. by Rev. Hargrove. (BA, 2 Jan. 1816)

WHITE, John, died 25 April 1812, at the house of his father, Capt. James White, St. Jerome's Creek, St. M. Co., in his 29th year. (BFG, 19 May 1812)

WHITE, John, seaman, drowned last Thurs. on the Delaware on the U. S. frigate. (BA, 6 June 1799)

WHITE, John, merchant, and Miss Sarah Bahon, all of Balto., were married on Tues. by Bishop Carroll. (BT, 10 April 1806)

WHITE, John M., and Miss Ann Davis, both of Balto., were wed by Rev. Rattoone last eve. at Fells Point. (BFG, 12 Aug. 1805)

WHITE, Capt. John M., of Phila., and Mrs. Eliza Dew of Balto., were married last eve. by Rev. Rattoone. (BFG, 20 Sept. 1809)

WHITE, Capt. John M., and Miss Mary Ann Welch were married 17th inst. by Rev. Glendy. (BA, 28 May 1812)

WHITE, Capt. Joseph, and Miss Rosetta Landry, both of Balto., were married last eve. by Carroll. (BT, 15 Feb. 1799)

WHITE, Joseph, and Miss Margaret Faris, both of Balto., were wed last eve. by Rev. Dr. Roberts. (BEP, 14 Aug. 1810)

WHITE, Joseph, and Isabella Pinkney, dau. of Wm. Pinkney, all of Balto., were married by Bishop Kemp on 1 May. (BA, 3 May 1815)

WHITE, Joseph C., dry goods merchant of Balto., and Mary Jones, dau. of Mordica Jones of St. M. Co., were married Sun., 16th inst. in Balto. by Rev. Smoot. (BFG, 28 March 1805)

WHITE, Capt. K., and Miss Ann Hull, all of Balto., were married last Mon. by Rev. Glendy. (BA, 23 Oct. 1807)

WHITE, Mrs. Mary, consort of Joseph C. White, of Balto., died yesterday. (BFG, 17 Dec. 1805)

WHITE, Michael, and Miss Julian Leary of Balto., were wed last Tues. by Rev. Bend. (BT, 24 Feb. 1798)

WHITE, Orlando G., of A. A. Co., and Miss Rachel Musgrove of Mont. Co., were married last Sun. by Rev. Linthicum. (BEP, 2 Jan. 1810)

WHITE, Robert, died Wed. morning, aged 44 years, surgeon of Belfast, Ire.; bro. of Dr. White of Balto. He arrived in Balto. a few weeks ago for the benefit of his health. (BFG, 4 Sept. 1806)

WHITE, Robert, and Miss Mary Bond, all of Balto., were married Tues. by Rev. Hagerty. (BA, 4 July 1816)

WHITE, Samuel, U. S. Sen. from Delaware, died this morning. "Wilmington, Nov. 4." (BFR, 10 Nov. 1809)

WHITE, Capt. Samuel, and Miss Margaret Nichols, all of Balto., were married by Glendy on Sat. at the country seat of Major Biays. (BEP, 1 Sept. 1810)

WHITE, Capt. Stephen, and Miss Julia Martin, all of Balto., were married last eve. by Bishop Carroll. (BA, 17 Dec. 1806)

WHITE, William, and Mrs. Mary M'Donald were married by Rev. Glendy on 27 Aug. (BFG, 6 Oct. 1814)

WHITE, William J., and Miss Margaret Howard, all of Balto., were married last eve. by Rev. Dr. Roberts. (BA, 24 Dec. 1814)

WHITEFORD, David, and Miss Elizabeth Hoffman, both of Balto., were married last Thurs. by Rev. Kurtz. (BFG, 8 March 1814)

WHITEHEAD, Rev. James, D. D., died Sun., 21st inst. at Bath, Va., late assoc. pastor of St. Paul's Parish, Balto. (BFG, 31 Aug. 1808)

WHITELOCK, Charles, and Miss Jane M'Kinnel were married last Thurs. by Rev. Dashiell. (BS, 28 July 1810)

WHITELY, Col. William, of Caroline Co., Md., died at Newark, Del., 19th inst., aged 65 years. He served in the Rev. War, and for 10 years was in the Md. Senate. (BPEA, 26 Aug. 1815)

WHITESIDES, John, brewer, died last week at Phila. (BEP, 6 Nov. 1806)

WHITING, Col. John, U. S. Army, died lately at Washington. (BW, 8 Sept. 1810)

WHITLOCK, Mr., and Miss Montgomery, both of Balto., were married last Sun. by Rev. Ellison. (BA, 17 April 1800)

WHITMORE, Samuel, sgt. in the 1st Regt., U. S. Artillery, a native of Conn., died yesterday at Fort McHenry. (BFG, 26 Sept. 1811)

WHITNEY, Ephraim, merchant, and Miss Eliza Legrove, both of Balto., were married last eve. by Rev. Mr. Ireland. (BFG, 27 March 1801)

WHITTELSEY, Capt. Stephen, and Miss Nicey B. Pattison all of Balto. were married last eve. by Rev. Bend. (BEP, 27 April 1808)

WHITTINGTON, Thomas, and Miss Sally Taylor of Fair Lee, Kent Co., were married 8th inst. by Rev. William H. Wilmer. (BFR, 27 Oct. 1810)

WHITTINGTON, William, and Sarah Welch, dau. of Benjamin Whittington, were married last Sun. near the Head of South River, by Rev. Wyatt. (BFG, 23 Aug. 1804)

WHITTINGTON, William, of John, was knocked overboard and drowned 7th inst. on his passage from Balto. to Annapolis, leaving a wife and two small children. (BFG, 16 June 1810)

WHITTINGTON, William, and Miss Catherine White, both of Wor. Co., were married Tues., 10th inst. by Rev. Stuart Williamson. (BFR, 25 Oct. 1811)

WIATT, William, postmaster, died at Fredericksburg. (BFG, 23 April 1800)

WICKERSHAM, William, and Miss Mary Ann Roche, all of Fells Point, were married last eve. by Rev. Moranville. (BW, 16 Oct. 1811)

WICKES, Mrs. Milcah, consort of Major William Wickes of Kent Co., died Tues., 5th inst., leaving children. (BA, 12 Sept. 1815)

WICKES, Rev. William, of Snow Hill, Wor. Co., and Miss Sophia Price of Balto. were married last eve. by Rev. Roberts. (BFG, 21 Jan. 1812)

WIDROW, Samuel, and Miss Mary Roberts both of Balto. were married last Sun. by Rev. Roberts. (BFG, 10 Feb. 1808)

WIESENTHAL, Dr. Andrew, died yesterday in his 30th year. (BFG, 3 Dec. 1798)

WIESENTHAL, Mrs. Elizabeth, consort of the late Dr. Charles F. Wiesenthal of Balto., died yesterday morning. (BFG, 3 July 1805)

WIGAN, Andrew, of York-Town, Penna., and Miss Eliza Ann White of Harf. Co., Md., were married last Sat. by Rev. Kurtz. (BEP, 10 Sept. 1808)

WIGART, Henry C., and Mrs. Elizabeth Kalbfus, all of Balto., were married Tues. by Rev. Richard Hunt. (BA, 31 Oct. 1816)

WIGGONS, John, and Sarah Norton both of Harf. Co. were married Thurs. at Friends Meeting near Deer Creek. (BT, 5 Nov. 1803)

WIGLEY, Edward, and Miss Prudence Grimes, all of Balto., were wed on Sun. by Rev. Glendy. (BA, 7 May 1812)

WIGNELL, James, native of Lancashire, Eng., died 21st of this month in his 83rd year. (BFG, 22 March 1814)

WIGNELL, Thomas, manager of the new theatre in Phila., and Mrs. Ann Merry of the same theatre, were married in Phila. on Sat. by Rev. Abercrombie. (BFG, 5 Jan. 1803)

WILEY, Robert, and Ann Kennedy were married 9th inst. by Rev. Glendy. (BEP, 16 March 1809)

WILEY, Robert, died last afternoon; res. in Caroline St. (BS, 13 July 1812)

WILHELM, Henry, and Miss Mary Haney, both of Balto., were married last Thurs. by Rev. Kurtz. (BA, 5 Sept. 1808)

WILHELM, Peter, and Miss Susanna Thomson, both of Balto., were wed last eve. by Rev. Kurtz. (BA, 15 Nov. 1816)

WILK, Peter, and Catherine M'Guire, both of Balto., were married last eve. by Rev. Bend. (BT, 26 Feb. 1800)

WILKIE, Capt. Thomas, late of the American Navy, died at Phila. last Mon., aged 36. (BA, 13 Sept. 1804)

WILKINS, John, of Balto., and Miss Elizabeth Dorsey, dau. of Major Dorsey of A. A. Co., were married last Thurs. by Rev. Roberts. (BFR, 22 Oct. 1809)

WILKINS, Joseph, and Miss Mary Bedford, both of Balto., were wed last eve. by Rev. Glendy. (BFG, 15 Nov. 1811)

WILKINS, Mrs. Sarah, consort of William Wilkins, died this morning aged 72. (BFG, 23 April 1814)

WILKINS, William, of Pittsburgh, and Miss Catherine W. Holmes, dau. of John Holmes of Balto. were married at Carlisle on Tues., 13th inst. by Rev. Davidson. (BFG, 20 Oct. 1812)

WILKINSON, Benjamin, son of Gen. Joseph Wilkinson of Md., died a few days ago on his passage from New Orleans to Balto. (BEP, 6 Jan. 1810)

WILKINSON, Richard, and Miss Fanny Perriage of Balto. Co., were married last Thurs. by Rev. Mr. McCain. (BA, 2 Dec. 1813)

WILKINSON, Samuel, died this morning of the fever. (BFG, 24 Sept. 1802)

WILKS, Charles, and Miss Agnes L. Clagete (sic), all of A. A. Co., were married 25 Dec. by Rev. Linthicum. (BEP, 30 Jan. 1809)

WILLARD, Benjamin of Boston, Mass., died last Sun. at the house of Mr. John Miller, innkeeper of Balto. Interment in the Presbyterian burying ground. Dec. left a wife and four children in Boston. (BFG, 20 Sept. 1803)

WILLEMY, John Nicholas, and Mrs. Margaret Hartmer, both of Balto. Co., were married last Tues. by Rev. Reed. (BT, 31 Dec. 1803)

WILLESS, William, and Miss Sarah Griffen all of Balto. were wed last eve. by Rev. Bartow. (BFG, 1 Nov. 1815)

WILLET, John, and Deborah Butler both of Balto. were married last eve. by Rev. Richards. (BT, 16 July 1800)

WILLIAMER, Mrs. Ann Eleanor, died yesterday, aged 103 years, 3 mos., and 14 days. (BFG, 16 Feb. 1802)

WILLIAMS, Mrs. Amelia, wife of Samuel Williams, Jr., late of Del., died last Tues. in her 35th year. (BA, 2 Feb. 1817)

WILLIAMS, Andrew, and Miss Elizabeth Duncan all of Balto. were wed last eve. by Rev. Dr. Allison. (BFG, 1 April 1799)

WILLIAMS, Benjamin, and Miss Ann Seffel, both of A. A. Co., were married Thurs. by Rev. Hargrove. (BFG, 17 April 1802)

WILLIAMS, Benjamin, and Mrs. Sarah Morton all of Balto. were wed last eve. by Rev. Inglis. (BFG, 22 May 1811)

WILLIAMS, Benjamin, died; res. on North Charles St. (BFG, 20 June 1812)

WILLIAMS, Charles, and Miss Rachel Gooden, all of Balto., were married last Tues. by Rev. Robert R. Roberts. (BEP, 21 Feb. 1812)

WILLIAMS, Cumberland D., and Elizabeth Pinkney, eld. dau. of the
Hon. William Pinkney, were married last eve. by Bishop
Kemp. (BA, 16 Jan. 1816)

WILLIAMS, Capt. Dutton, native of Donegal, Ireland, died yesterday. For the last 15 years he was a ship-master of Balto.
Funeral will be from 37 Fleet St., Fells Point. (BA, 28
March 1814)

WILLIAMS, George, merchant of Balto., and Miss Elizabeth Hawkins
of Harf. Co., were married last Thurs. at Rangers Lodge,
Harf. Co., by Rev. Inglis. (BPEA, 3 June 1815)

WILLIAMS, Mrs. Hannah, died at Selby Mills, on 11th inst., wife
of Ension Williams. (BA, 25 Nov. 1815)

WILLIAMS, James, and Miss Elizabeth Savory both of Balto. were
married last Thurs. by Rev. Pitts. (BFG, 9 May 1807)

WILLIAMS, James, Balto. merchant, and Miss Mary Stump, dau. of
John Stump of Harf. Co., were married at Stafford, Harf.
Co., last Wed. by Rev. Stephenson. (BFG, 26 Sept. 1808)

WILLIAMS, James, and Miss Elizabeth Burrows, all of Balto., were
married last Sat. by Rev. Pitt. (BW, 30 Dec. 1811)

WILLIAMS, James, of Balto., seaman, died last month at the New
York Hospital of Pleuritis. (BS, 20 July 1812)

WILLIAMS, John, and Mrs. Sophia Drowan, both of Balto., were wed
20th inst. by Rev. Rattoone. (BFG, 25 July 1805)

WILLIAMS, John, and Elizabeth Green, both of Balto., were wed
last Mon. by Archbishop Carroll. (BW, 31 Aug. 1809)

WILLIAMS, John, and Miss Nancy Stevenson, all of Balto., were
married last eve. by Rev. Roberts. (BFG, 8 June 1810)

WILLIAMS, John, died yesterday; funeral from his late dwelling on
North Charles St. (BA, 7 Aug. 1812)

WILLIAMS, John, and Miss Mary Ann Cain, all of Balto., were wed
on Thurs. by Rev. Hagerty. (BA, 14 Dec. 1816)

WILLIAMS, Jonathan, and Miss Patty Whitaker, all of Balto., were
married Tues. eve. by Rev. Dr. Roberts. (BA, 18 Dec.
1813)

WILLIAMS, Joseph, and Mary Bedford, both of Balto., were married
on Tues. eve. by Rev. Glendy. (BW, 16 Nov. 1811)

WILLIAMS, Joseph, of Petersburg, Va., and Miss Mary Ann Moule of
Balto., were married last Thurs. by Rev. Hunt. (BA, 9
Oct. 1816)

WILLIAMS, Joseph S., of Annap., and Catherine Murray of Balto.
were married last Sun. by Rev. Beeson. (BW, 19 Sept.
1809)

WILLIAMS, Lemuel, of Balto., died last Mon. in his 22nd year.
(BFG, 5 Oct. 1797)

WILLIAMS, Lewis, and Miss Eleanor Thomas, all of Balto., were wed
last Wed. by Rev. Lewis Richards. (BFG, 16 Feb. 1805)

WILLIAMS, Mrs. Martha, mother of Nathaniel F. Williams of Balto., died at Brooklyn, Conn., in her 81st year on 11th inst. (BFG, 23 March 1815)

WILLIAMS, Mrs. Mary, consort of the late Gen. Williams, collector of this port, died last Sat. Interment in the Presbyterian burying ground. (BMJ, 21 Nov. 1796)

WILLIAMS, Mrs. Nancy, wife of Amos A. Williams, merchant of Balto., died 17th inst., aged 27 years. (BFG, 18 Sept. 1804)

WILLIAMS, Nathaniel, Balto. merchant, and Miss Elizabeth Redman Beck, dau. of Paul Beck of Phila., were married last eve. by Bishop White. "Phila., 19 Nov." (BFG, 21 Nov. 1808)

WILLIAMS, Nathaniel, attorney-at-law and Miss Caroline Barney, both of Balto., were married last Mon. by Rev. Glendy at Edward Stiles', Havre de Grace. (BA, 19 Oct. 1809)

WILLIAMS, Samuel, merchant, died yesterday, aged 44 years. (BFG, 14 Oct. 1813)

WILLIAMS, Stephen, and Miss Jane Creery, all of Balto., were wed last Thurs. eve. by Rev. Dashiell. (BEP, 26 Sept. 1807)

WILLIAMS, Thomas, and Eliza Fowell, both of A. A. Co., were wed last Sat. by Rev. Hargrove. (BFG, 9 June 1800)

WILLIAMS, Thomas, and Miss Ann Beadle, both of Balto., were wed last eve. by Rev. Rattoone. (BFG, 16 Dec. 1805. BA, 16 Dec. 1805 gives the bride's name as Readle.)

WILLIAMS, Thomas, and Miss Maria Ker, both of Balto., were wed last Thurs. by Rev. Roberts. (BA, 7 Oct. 1812)

WILLIAMS, Thomas S., and Miss Sarah Harlin, all of Balto., were married last Thurs. by Rev. Hunt. (BA, 4 May 1816)

WILLIAMS, William, and Miss Susan Ridgaway, both of Balto., were wed last eve. by Rev. Roberts. (BFG, 16 June 1800)

WILLIAMS, William E., and Miss Susan Cooke, dau. of William Cooke, all of Balto., were married last eve. by Rev. Bend. (BFG, 24 April 1812)

WILLIAMS, Capt. William N., of Balto., and Sally Hinson, dau. of Mary Hinson of Mount Ararat, Kent Co., were married Thurs., 23rd inst., by Rev. Dr. Ferguson. (BA, 31 May 1799)

WILLIAMSON, David, Jr., and Miss M. A. Tiernan, dau. of Luke Tiernan, all of Balto., were married last eve. by Archbishop Carroll. (BFG, 1 Feb. 1814)

WILLIAMSON, James, and Miss Maria Quynn, both of Balto. Co., were married 30th ult. by Rev. Glendy. (BT, 5 Jan. 1804)

WILLIAMSON, John, and Mrs. Mary Howland, all of Balto., were wed last Thurs., 24th inst. by Rev. Duncan. (BA, 28 Feb. 1814)

WILLIAMSON, Peregrine, and Miss Sarah Nowland, both of Balto., were married by Rev. Dashield. (BW, 30 June 1809)

WILLIAMSON, Thomas, died 7th inst. at Balto. He had been captured by the British. (Long obit.) (BA, 5 May 1800)

WILLING, Capt. Leonard, and Miss Margaret Anderson, both of Fells Point, were married last eve. by Rev. Beeston. (BT, 10 Nov. 1800)

WILLINGHAM, James, and Miss Sarah Garmin, all of Balto., were wed last Sun. by Rev. Reese. (BA, 19 July 1815)

WILLIS, George, merchant, native of Dublin and partner in the House of Medford and Willia of Phila., died yesterday eve. Interment in St. Pauls Burial Ground. (BFG, 31 Aug. 1799)

WILLIS, John, and Nancy Hill, both of Fells Point, were married yesterday by Rev. Allison. (BT, 13 Dec. 1798)

WILLIS, Robert, and Mrs. Burke both of Balto. were married yesterday by Rev. Dr. Roberts. (BT, 16 March 1805)

WILLOZ, Henry, and Miss Catherine Bain all of Balto. were married last Thurs. by Rev. D. E. Reese. (BA, 20 March 1796)

WILLS, Benjamin, died 6th ult., in his 18th year, of the meazles. (BA, 9 April 1813)

WILLS, Francis, and Miss Margaret Fisher were married last eve. by Archbishop Carroll. (BFG, 9 May 1810)

WILLSON, William, of A. A. Co., and Miss Aletha K. Britton, dau. of Richard Britton of Balto. Co. (BA, 28 May 1813)

WILMANS, Charles H., Balto. merchant, was lost with the ship Anthony Mangin, husband and father. (BFG, 10 March 1798)

WILMANS, John Herman, died yesterday in his 16th year, brother of Charles Wilmans. (BT, 22 Sept. 1797)

WILMER, Rev. J. J., and Mrs. Letitia Day, both of Balto. Co., were married last Sun. eve. by Rev. Richardson. (BFG, 24 March 1803)

WILMER, John, of the Eastern Shore of Md., and Miss Elizabeth Croxall, dau. of the late James Croxall of Balto., were married last eve. by Rev. Dashiell. (BFG, 23 Aug. 1809)

WILMER, Jonathan, late a member of the Executive Council of Maryland, and Miss Sarah Gibbs of Charleston, S. C., were wed there last 27 Jan. (BFG, 17 Feb. 1801)

WILMER, Jonathan, died last Thurs., a native of Md., back for a visit from Charleston, S. C. (BFG, 24 Aug. 1805)

WILMER, Lambert, died Sat., 3rd inst., at his res. in Harf. Co. (BFG, 10 Jan. 1801)

WILMER, Rev. Simon, and Miss Rebecca Frisby both of Kent Co. were married Tues., 20th inst., by Rev. William Stone. (BFG, 29 May 1806)

WILMOT, George, and Miss Rebecca Maria Howland, both of Balto., were married last Tues. by Rev. Roberts. (BFG, 21 Sept. 1815)

WILMOTT, Mrs. Hannah, of Balto. Co., died Sat., 4th inst., in her 50th year. (BPEA, 6 March 1815)

WILMS, Henry A., and Miss Elizabeth Grammer, Balto. merchant, were married last Sun. at Annapolis by Rev. Higginbothom. (BFG, 4 Nov. 1802)

WILSON, Abraham Ruxton, died last eve. at the seat of his father, Gittings Wilson in Balto. Co., in his 21st year. He had been a clark in the sheriff's office. (BFG, 29 Sept. 1802)

WILSON, Capt. Alexander, brother to the editor of this paper, was drowned 20th inst. in the Potomac on his way to Va., leaving a wife, child, mother, four bros., and a sister. "From the Sun." (BA, 1 Nov. 1811)

WILSON, Alexander, author of the American Ornithology, died in Phila. (BA, 26 Aug. 1813)

WILSON, Mrs. Ann, wife of William Wilson of Ivy Hill, died at the res. of Robert Cooke on Sun., 23rd inst. (BFG, 24 April 1809)

WILSON, Mrs. Ann, dau. of Dr. Samuel Carson, formerly of Armagh, Ireland, and consort of William Wilson, Jr., died 9th inst., leaving a father, husband, and two children. (BW, 14 Feb. 1814)

WILSON, Mrs. Ann, dau. of Robert S. Wilson, of Balto., died Fri., 8th inst. (Long obit.) (BFG, 14 Aug. 1816)

WILSON, Benjamin, and Mrs. Ann Cunningham, both of Balto., were married last eve. by Rev. Richards. (BT, 7 May 1804)

WILSON, Mrs. Elizabeth, died in Som. Co., on 13th inst., at Westover in her 28th year, wife of John C. Wilson, Jr., a delegate to the General Assembly. (BFG, 26 Dec. 1815)

WILSON, Ephraim K., and Miss Ann D. Gunby, dau. of the late Gen. Gunby, all of Snow Hill, were married 12th inst., by Rev. Stewart Williamson. (BFG, 24 Feb. 1812)

WILSON, George, ship-joiner, of Fells Point, died on Sun. eve, in his 47th year. (BA, 23 May 1816)

WILSON, Capt. George, and Mrs. Maria Wickham, both of Balto., were married last Wed. by Rev. Bartow. (BA, 16 Aug. 1816)

WILSON, Mr. Hall, and Miss Ann Kithcart, all of Balto., were wed last Mon. by Rev. Glendy. (BA, 21 Dec. 1814)

WILSON, Henry, Sr., died last eve. of the prevailing fever, at Fells Point, aged 56. (BFG, 4 Sept. 1800)

WILSON, Hosea, and Miss Elizabeth Coates, all of Balto., were wed 7th inst. by Rev. George Roberts. (BWA, 13 April 1816)

WILSON, James, and Mrs. Mary Davis, both of Balto., were married last eve. by Rev. Bend. (BT, 27 June 1800)

WILSON, James, and Miss Mary Shields, both of Balto., were married last eve. by Rev. Richards. (BFG, 31 Dec. 1800)

WILSON, James, and Miss Ebe Allen of Balto. were married last eve. by Rev. Coates. (BFG, 30 Sept. 1803)

WILSON, James, of the town of Walkill, died of hydrophobia, 7th ult., in his 17th year. (BT, 22 Feb. 1804)

WILSON, James, and Rebecca Cromwell, dau. of John H. Cromwell, all of Cecil Co., were married last Thurs. by Rev. Allen. (BFG, 5 April 1804)

WILSON, James, and Miss Eliza Cooper, both of Balto., were wed last eve. by Rev. Richards. (BW, 12 Jan. 1810)

WILSON, James, and Miss Henrietta Grays, all of Balto., were wed Thurs. eve. by Rev. Stiles. (BA, 25 Nov. 1815)

WILSON, James, died Sat. night, 9th inst., in his 50th year, long a respectable inhab. of Balto., leaving a widow and four children. Interment in the family burying ground of Gunpowder Forest. (BA, 12 Nov. 1816)

WILSON, James C., Balto. merchant, and Miss Anna E. B. Balch, dau. of the late Rev. S. B. Balch of Alexandria, were wed in Georgetown on Thurs. eve. by Rev. Dr. Muir of Alexandria. (BA, 20 Jan. 1816)

WILSON, James H., of A. A. Co., and Miss Julia Ann Mortimer of Balto., were married 16th inst. by Rev. Hunt. (BFG, 25 April 1816)

WILSON, Mrs. Jane, aged 48 years, consort of William Wilson, Balto. merchant, died last eve. (BFG, 11 June 1798)

WILSON, Mrs. Jane, wife of David Wilson, merchant, died 14th inst. (BA, 17 May 1816)

WILSON, John, who lived at Fells Point, took sick in Georgetown on the 14th, and died the 19th, two days after his return to his brother in East St. (BFG, 22 July 1802)

WILSON, John, of the Northern Liberties, and Miss Sarah Hergesheimer, dau. of Anthony Hergesheimer, of Germantown, were married at Germantown on Sun. eve. by Rev. Shaffer. (BA, 27 July 1804)

WILSON, John, merchant, and Miss Isabella Hutton, all of Balto., were married 3rd inst., by Rev. Glendy. (BW, 31 Aug. 1809)

WILSON, John W., son of John Wilson of Harf. Co., and Lucretia, dau. of Elisha Tyson of Balto., were married today at Friends Meeting House. (BFG, 15 May 1800)

WILSON, Mrs. Margaret, died last eve., wife of Henry Wilson, a Balto. merchant. (BFG, 26 June 1800)

WILSON, Nixon, of Balto., and Miss Mary Warner of Wilmington, Del., were married last Thurs. eve. (BFG, 9 April 1804)

WILSON, Richard, of Glouc., Eng., and Miss Mary Gardener of Va., were married last Sat. by Rev. Wyatt. (BA, 18 Sept. 1816)

WILSON, Robert, and Miss Maria Wilson, both of Balto., were wed on Sun., 13th inst. by Rev. Mr. Ryland. (BA, 15 Dec. 1812)

WILSON, Robert, and Miss Ann Maria McCausland, dau. of Marcus McCausland, all of Balto., were married last eve. by Rev. Richards. (BFG, 20 April 1814)

WILSON, Mrs. Sally K., consort of Ephraim K. Wilson of Snow Hill, died Tues., 13th Nov. (BFG, 8 Jan. 1805)

WILSON, Thomas, Balto. merchant, and Mary H. Cruse, dau. of Thomas Cruse of Alexandria, were married there on 6 May by Rev. Oliver Norris. (BA, 11 May 1815)

WILSON, William, and Susanna Wolf, both of Balto., were married yesterday eve. by Rev. Bend. (BFG, 15 Sept. 1800)

WILSON, William, Jr., son of William Wilson, merchant, of Balto., and Miss Ann Carson, dau. of Dr. Carson of Alexandria, were married at that place on Tues., 19th inst. (BFG, 26 Aug. 1806)

WILSON, William, Jr., and Miss Mary Knox, dau. of Rev. Samuel Knox of Balto., were married last Thurs. by Rev. Richards. (BPEA, 4 April 1815)

WILSON, William Ramsay, aged 21 years, 3 mos., and 3 days, son of William Wilson of Alexandria, died in that place on Wed. (BA, 21 June 1805)

WINAND, Jacob, and Sidney Brown, were married last Tues. by Rev. Dr. Bend. (BA, 11 Jan. 1805)

WINCHESTER, Charles, and Elizabeth Pannell, dau. of Edward Pannell, all of Balto., were married 23 Dec. by Rev. Wyatt. (BA, 25 Dec. 1816)

WINCHESTER, George, of Balto., and Miss Ann Owings of Balto., were married last eve. by Rev. Armstrong. (BEP, 12 May 1809)

WINCHESTER, Hon. James, died Sat., 5th inst., late Judge of the District Court of Md., at his res. at Shawan, Balto. Co., in his 34th year. (BFG, 9 and 11 April 1806)

WINCHESTER, Lycurgus, died 6th inst., in his 20th year. He studied under Judge John Cooper of Carlisle. (BFG, 8 April 1815)

WINCHESTER, Mrs. Lydia, died Sun. last at Westminster Town in Fred. Co. in her 84th year. (BFG, 23 Feb. 1809)

WINCHESTER, Mr. Samuel, merchant of Balto., and Miss Eliza Gover were married Thurs. eve. in Harf. Co. by Rev. Mr. Allen. (BFG, 29 Nov. 1803)

WINCHESTER, Miss Sarah, dau. of William Winchester, of Balto., died this morning in her 29th year. (BFG, 4 Aug. 1806)

WINCHESTER, Mrs. Sarah, relict of the late Judge Winchester, died Sun., in her 43rd year. (BA, 21 Sept. 1815)

WINCHESTER, Thomas C., and Miss Ann Page, both of Balto., were wed last Tues. by Rev. Dr. Roberts. (BA, 22 March 1816)

WINCHESTER, William, died today in his 62nd year; funeral from his late res., North Howard St. (BFG, 24 April 1812)

WINCHESTER, William, and Miss Hannah Saukey, all of Balto., were married by Rev. Glendy yesterday. (BPEA, 20 Nov. 1815)

WINDER, Charles H., died Thurs., 8th inst., at his res. near Princess Anne, in Somerset Co., after a tedious indisposition. (BFG, 17 Nov. 1804)

WINDER, William, died 28 June at his res. on the Eastern Shore. (BFG, 6 July 1808)

WINEGARDNER, Mrs. Anna Barbara, died 18th inst., native of Germany, res. of Balto., aged 78 years. (BT, 20 April 1802)

WINEMAN, Mrs. Ann B., relict of the late Henry Wineman, died Wed., 17th inst., in her 56th year. (BFG, 19 April 1811)

WINEMAN, Henry, died Fri., 11th inst. at his res. in Balto. Co., aged 68 years. (BFG, 14 Jan. 1811)

WINGATE, Joseph Ferdinand, and Miss Margaret Gay Tingey, dau. of Thomas Tingey, Commander of the Navy Yard, were married at Washington last Tues. by Rev. McCormick. (BEP, 2 Dec. 1808)

WINGATE, Levin, and Miss Harriet Forrester, all of Balto., were married Thurs. by Rev. Glendy. (BA, 26 Oct. 1816)

WINSTANDLEY, William H., and Miss Ann B. Fowler, both of Balto., were married last eve. by Rev. George Dashiell. (BA, 28 Sept. 1810)

WINTERS, Major John, and Miss Elizabeth Wampler were married Thurs., 13th inst. (BEP, 18 Dec. 1810)

WINTKLE, James, died yesterday in his 36th year. (BFG, 16 July 1810)

WINWOOD, Thomas, and Miss Elizabeth Hubball, both of Balto., were married Mon., 28th ult., by Rev. John Healey. (BA, 30 Sept. 1812)

WIRGMAN, Charles, Balto. merchant, and Sarah Stewart Bowly, dau. of Daniel Bowly of Furly, Balto. Co., were married last Thurs. eve. by Rev. Dr. Bend. (BFG, 22 Feb. 1805)

WIRGMAN, Peter, and Miss Rebecca Bowly, dau. of the late Daniel Bowly, were married last eve. by Rev. Beasley. (BFG, 7 June 1811)

WIRTS, Miss Susan, of Balto., died 4th inst. (BA, 16 Nov. 1801)

WISE, Augustus, confectioner of Balto., and Miss Susanna Louisa Kreider, of Phila., were married 29 Sept. in Phila. (BEP, 17 Oct. 1808)

WISE, Frederick A., and Miss Phoebe A. Kenny, all of Balto., were married last Tues. by Rev. Richards. (BFG, 20 July 1815)

WISE, William, and Ann Gordon, both of Balto., were married last Tues. by Rev. Dr. Roberts. (BFG, 31 July 1806)

WISNOR, John, and Miss Margaret Connelly, both of Balto., were married last eve. by Rev. Dr. Rattoone. (BA, 17 April 1805)

WITHERS, Michael, of Lancaster Co., Penna., and Miss Charlotte Calder of Balto. Co., were married last Sun. by Rev. Dashiell. (BFG, 13 June 1810)

WITMAN, William, died suddenly, a democratic candidate to represent the county of Berks., Penna., in the House of Representatives. (BFR, 31 Oct. 1808)

WOLF, Anthony, and Mrs. Catherine Newman, were married 5th inst., by Rev. Greenfield. (BA, 25 Feb. 1814)

WOLFE, John Michael, and Miss Dorothea Shrader, both of Boston, were married last Tues. by Rev. Kurtz. (BA, 27 April 1815) (BPEA, 26 April gives bride's name as Shroder.)

WOOD, Henry H., and Miss Rebecca Ruth, both of Balto., were wed by Rev. Dunken last Thurs. (BPE, 31 July 1813)

WOOD, John, and Miss Mary Halfpen, both of Balto., were married Sun. eve. by Rev. Whitehead. (BA, 24 March 1807)

WOOD, John, and Miss Barbara Miller, both of Balto., were married Thurs. by Rev. Kurtz. (BFG, 14 Nov. 1807)

WOOD, Capt. John H., and Miss Juliana Martin, all of Balto., were married last eve. by Rev. Fenwick. (BPEA, 6 June 1815)

WOOD, Luther, and Miss Susan Omenseter, all of Balto., were wed last Thurs. by Rev. Roberts. (BS, 1 Dec. 1812)

WOOD, Richard, and Miss Jemmison, only dau. of the Widow Jemmison, all of Harf. Co., were married there by Rev. Johnson. (BFG, 14 June 1802)

WOOD, Mrs. Sarah, widow of the late Charles Wood, died Sun., 12th inst., aged 87 years, at the seat of Basil Wood, near Liberty Town. "Fred. Town." (BFG, 28 Jan. 1812)

WOOD, William, late His Britannic Majesty's Consul for the State of Maryland, died Sat., 10 Oct. (BFG, 12 Oct. 1812)

WOOD, William B., and Miss Julia Westray, both of the New Theatre, were married last Mon. at Phila. by Rev. Abercrombie. (BT, 3 Feb. 1804)

WOOD, William H., of Balto., and Anna Maria Bond were married on last Tues., 30 Jan., at the res. of Thomas Bond of John. (BT, 6 Feb. 1798)

WOOD, William Haskin, died in Harf. last Sat., aged about 41 years and a preacher in the Methodist connection for about 20 years. He leaves a wife and six children. (BFG, 20 Jan. 1810)

WOODHOUSE, Dr. James, late Prof. of Chemistry at the University of Penna., died at Phila., on Sun. in his 39th year. (BFG, 7 June 1809)

WOODLAND, William, and Miss Mary Jones, both of Balto., were wed by Rev. Richards. (BT, 19 May 1801)

WOODLAND, William, merchant, and Miss Elizabeth Davis were married at Fells Point by Rev. Dr. Rattoone. (BFG, 11 Oct. 1808)

WOODLAND, Wilson, late sheriff of Kent Co., Md., died Mon., 6th inst. at Chestertown, Kent Co. (BFG, 10 April 1807)

WOODS, Jeptha, and Miss Harriet Lee, all of Balto., were married last eve. by Rev. Roberts. (BFG, 9 April 1813)

WOODS, Mrs. Mary, wife of William Woods, Balto. merchant, died today. Funeral from her late res. in Market St. A sermon will be preached at the new Methodist chapel on Sun. (BFG, 17 Aug. 1798)

WOODS, Samuel, and Miss Henrietta Gittens both of Balto. were wed last eve. by Rev. Richards. (BFG, 20 April 1805)

WOODS, Wesley, Balto. merchant, and Miss Mary Ann Hood of A. A. Co., were married last Thurs. by Rev. Waugh. (BA, 31 Dec. 1814)

WOODS, William, Jr., merchant, and Miss Elizabeth Gilbert, both of Balto., were wed last Thurs. by Rev. Bunn. (BW, 24 June 1809)

WOODS, William, and Miss Mary Kent were married last eve. (BA, 14 Oct. 1814)

WOODWARD, Thomas, Georgetown merchant, and Miss Octavia O. Rozzel, dau. of the late Rev. S. G. Rozzel of Balto., were wed last eve. by Rev. Hemphill. (BFG, 9 Oct. 1816)

WOODWORTH, Isaac, late a member of the "Balto. Carpenters' Society," died last Sat., aged 35, leaving a widow and four small children. Interment in St. Peter's burial ground. (BW, 27 Nov. 1809)

WOODYEAR, Edward G., of Balto., and Miss Elizabeth R. Newman, dau. of Col. Newman, were married Mon., 23rd inst., at The Grange, seat of Col. F. Newman in Chas. Co. (BFG, 27 May 1814)

WORK, Andrew, and Mrs. Sarah McIntire, both of Balto., were wed last eve. by Rev. Dr. Roberts. (BFG, 27 May 1811)

WORNKEN, Henry, and Mrs. Rachel Marrett, both of Balto., were wed 25th inst. by Rev. Bloodgood. (BA, 27 Jan. 1810)

WORRALL, Mrs. Abigail, wife of Thomas W. Worrall of Fells Point, died Wed. (BPEA, 10 March 1815)

WORRELL, Hon. Judge, and Miss Mary Clarkson, both of Chestertown, were married Tues., 11th inst., by Rev. Turner. (BA, 18 June 1816)

WORRELL, Mrs. Ann, wife of Thomas Worrell, died 21st inst. at Chestertown on the Eastern Shore of Md. (BA, 28 Oct. 1814)

WORTHINGTON, Charles, and Miss Mary Todd, both of Balto., were married last eve. by Rev. Bend. (BFG, 17 Sept. 1802)

WORTHINGTON, Miss Helen, died last Fri., 22nd inst., dau. of the late William Worthington of Balto. Co. (BPE, 27 July 1814)

WORTHINGTON, Dr. John, died last Thurs. in his 42nd year. (BW, 2 April 1814)

WORTHINGTON, John T. H., and Miss Mary T. Worthington were wed last eve. at the res. of John T. Worthington, by Rev. Ralph. (BFG, 27 Nov. 1811)

WORTHINGTON, Samuel, Jr., died 9th inst., at Montmorenci. (BFG, 12 Dec. 1811)

WORTHINGTON, Samuel, of Balto. Co., died 7th inst., in his 82nd year. (BT, 15 April 1815)

WOZENCROFT, John, and Hannah Jones, all of Balto. City, were wed Tues., 24th inst., by Rev. Healey. (BFG, 31 July 1806)

WRAY, Thomas R., aged 27, son of John Wray of Balto., died last Fri. in Adams Co., Penna., as a result of a fall from a horse. (BPE, 14 June 1813)

WRAY, William, died last Wed. in Phila. in his 45th year. (BFG, 6 April 1807)

MARRIAGES AND DEATHS

WRIGHT, Elizabeth, was found dead near the Marsh Market. (BEP, 7 Oct. 1809)

WRIGHT, Capt. James, of Balto., and Miss Anne Fowler of Annap. were married at the latter place last Tues. by Rev. Wyatt. (BA, 16 June 1807)

WRIGHT, John, and Miss Elizabeth C. Clarke, both of Balto., were married last eve. by Rev. Bend. (BT, 19 Aug. 1803)

WRIGHT, Capt. John, of the Port of Balto., died at Port-au-Prince last Sept., leaving a wife and three small children. (BFG, 19 Oct. 1805)

WRIGHT, John, Balto. merchant, and Miss Sarah Sollers of Balto. Co., were married last Tues. by Rev. Dashiells. (BA, 30 May 1809)

WRIGHT, Joseph, and Mary Rose, both of Balto. Co., were married last Thurs. by Rev. Mr. Bund. (BA, 19 July 1806)

WRIGHT, Mark, and Miss Ann Lowery, all of Balto., were married on Sat. by Rev. Dr. Roberts. (BEP, 25 Sept. 1810)

WRIGHT, Nathaniel, and Miss Elizabeth March?, all of Balto., were married last Thurs. (29 Oct.) by Rev. Dr. Moore. (BFG, 31 Oct. 1812)

WRIGHT, Richard, and Mrs. Martha Terry, all of Balto., were wed by Rev. Glendy last Thurs. (BW, 21 Dec. 1811)

WRIGHT, Samuel, late merchant of Balto., died last night. (BW, 20 April 1811)

WRIGHT, Samuel T., clerk of Q. A. Co., and Adjutant General of the State of Md., died Sat., 30 June. "Another hero of the Rev. gone." (BFG, 9 July 1810)

WRIGHT, Thomas, and Elizabeth Cooper, all of Balto., were wed last eve. by Rev. Rossell. (BFG, 3 June 1808)

WRIGHT, William E., and Mary Kite were married by Bishop White in Phila. on 18th inst. (BT, 24 March 1804)

WRIGHT, William T., died 17th ult. at Centreville, as a result of a fall from a horse. He was a member of a troop of horse commanded by Joseph H. Nicholson. (BEP, 25 April 1808)

WRITH, Henry, and Miss Maria Sewell, both of Q. A. Co., were wed there last Tues., by Rev. Meredith. (BAP, 21 June 1803)

WROE, Everitt, and Miss Mary Davis. all of Balto., were married by Rev. Rattoone. (BA, 30 July 1808)

WROE, Capt. Samuel, of N. Y., and Miss Maria Elizabeth Bowers, dau. of Martin Bowers, were wed on Mon. eve. by Rev. Kurtz. (BFG, 30 Nov. 1815)

WROTH, Dr. Peregrine, of Chestertown, and Miss Martha Page of Kent Co., were married last Thurs. (BFG, 2 Sept. 1807)

WYLIE, Nathaniel W., printer, died last Sat. in his 27th year. (BFG, 30 May 1808) He was a native of Phila., son of Capt. Wylie who served in the Rev., and who died when

Nathaniel was very young. His mother was a dau. of Nathaniel Irish of Pittsburgh. He leaves a wife and two small children. (BEP, 30 May 1808)

WYMAN, John B., and Miss Eliza Hiatt, both of Balto., were wed Sun. by Rev. Martz. (BEP, 7 Nov. 1809)

WYNARD, Jacob, of Balto., and Miss Ann Hoffman of Phila. were married at Phila., 5th inst., by Rev. P. F. Mayers. (BA, 10 March 1807)

WYNARD, Jacob, boot and shoemaker, aged 31, died this morning. (BEP, 5 April 1809)

WYNKOOP, Henry, aged 21, died at Phila. (BFG, 17 Aug. 1803)

WYTHE, George, Chancellor of the State of Va., died Sun., 7th inst., a Signer of the Declaration of Independence. (BFG, 17 June 1806)

WYVILL, Marmaduke, of Balto., and Miss Ellen M. Coe, of Annap., were married at Annap. last Thurs. eve. by Rev. Nind. (BFG, 8 April 1815)

YARNALL, Mordecai, died at Wheeling, Va., on 7th ult., magistrate of Ohio Co., Va. (BFG, 12 July 1811)

YARNALL, Samuel, member of the Soc. of Friends in Tal. Co., died last Fri. (BEP, 15 Sept. 1807)

YATES, Mrs., consort of Thomas Yates of Balto. (BFG, 20 Jan. 1802)

YATES, Charles, son of Major Thomas Yates of Balto., died yesterday at the res. of Samuel Chase, Jr., in his 21st year. He had recently returned from the West Indies. (Long obit.) (BFG, 14 July 1810)

YATES, Henry S., and Miss Eleanor H. Hungerford, both of Chas. Co., were married 14 Feb. by Rev. Contee. (BA, 12 April 1809)

YATES, Joseph, of Balto., died Mon., 8th inst., in his 61st year. (BFG, 10 Nov. 1810)

YATES, Mrs. Mary, died Mon. eve. at Springfield, near Balto., aged 37; consort of Col. Thomas Yates. (BFG, 14 Dec. 1796)

YATES, Col. Thomas, and Mrs. Mary Atkinson, both of Balto., were wed last eve. by Rev. Ireland. (BT, 8 Feb. 1799)

YATES, Major Thomas, died last eve. in his 64th year; an officer in the Rev. Army. (BFG, 17 Nov. 1815)

YATES, William, and Elizabeth Crowles, both of Balto., were wed last eve. by Rev. Dr. Rattoone. (BFG, 16 Jan. 1806)

YEAGER, John, and Miss Elizabeth Mary Matilda Hanson, all of Balto., were married Thurs. eve. by Rev. Inglis. (BA, 5 Oct. 1816)

YEAMAN, Mr., of Alexandria, and Miss Mary Evans of Balto., were maried last Thurs. by Rev. Richards. (BWM, 19 March 1797)

YEARLEY, Ann Elizabeth, dau. of Alexander Yearley of Balto., died last Wed., in her 3rd year. (BFG, 26 Oct. 1811)

YEARLY, Alexander, of Balto., and Miss Ann Frazier, dau. of John Frazier of Kent Co., were married on Thurs., 16th inst., by Rev. John Smith. (BFG, 18 April 1807)

YEARLY, John, and Miss Matilda Rogers, were married last Tues. at Rock Hall, Kent Co. (BFG, 27 April 1804)

YEATMAN, Mr., of Alexandria, and Miss Mary Evans of Balto. were married last eve. by Rev. Richards. (BFG, 17 March 1797)

YEISER, Mrs., relict of the late Frederick Yeiser, departed this life, aged 47, leaving a family. (BFG, 27 July 1807)

YEISER, Mr. Englehard, Jr., and Miss Margaret Swope, dau. of Mr. Benedict Swope, Jr., were married 3rd ult. near Danville. (BFG, 2 Nov. 1799)

YEISER, Engelhard, an old inhab. of Balto., died last Sat. (BFG, 9 March 1807)

YEISER, Frederick, died Tues.; res. near Griffith's Bridge. Interment in the Lutheran burying ground. (BFG, 29 March 1797)

YEISER, John, and Eleanor Addison Holliday, were married last eve. by Rev. Coleman. (BFG, 28 May 1802)

YEISER John M., only son of Englehard Yeiser, of Balto. Co., died Wed., 8th inst., at Staunton, Va., in his 26th year. (BFG, 15 Oct. 1806)

YELLOT, George, of Balto., and Miss Bethia Burrell, late of New York, were married 13th ult., near Lexington, Ky. (BT, 27 May 1815)

YELLOTT, Capt. Jeremiah, of Balto., died Sun. (BA, 6 Feb. 1805)

YELLOTT, Mrs. Mery, wife of Jeremiah Yellott, died yesterday in her 51st year. (BEP, 16 March 1811)

YERBY, Capt. William, of Lancaster Co., Va., and Elizabeth White, dau. of Capt. Joseph White of Balto., were married last Thurs. eve. by Rev. Beeston. (BT, 16 Aug. 1798)

YEWELL, John, and Margaret Salter, both of Balto., were married Sat. eve. by Rev. Coats. (BFG, 2 April 1804)

YEWELL, Samuel, and Miss Elizabeth Burk, all of Balto., were wed last Thurs. by Rev. Roberts. (BT, 16 Nov. 1804)

YOE, Benjamin, formerly of Balto., and Mrs. Mary Helm of Williamsport, were wed last Sun. by Rev. Rauhauser. (BFG, 29 March 1811)

YONER, Samuel, and Miss Polly Stover were married last Thurs. eve. by Rev. Otterbein. (BFG, 25 June 1796)

YOUNG, Charles B., Balto. merchant, died Fri., 16th inst. (BA, 23 June 1809)

YOUNG, Jacob, and Malinda Harden, both of Balto., were married last Sun. by Rev. Dashiell. (BFG, 28 Jan. 1806)

YOUNG, James, and Mrs. Elizabeth Neal of Balto., were married last Sat. by Dr. Whitehead. (BFG, 19 Aug. 1807)

YOUNG, James, and Miss Eleanor Scott, were married 1 April by Rev. Glendy. (BA, 19 Aug. 1814)

YOUNG, Jesse, of Fells Point, and Miss Jane M'Donogh were married Sat. by Rev. Dr. Allison. (BMJ, 1 Feb. 1796)

YOUNG, John, merchant, of Patch Landing, Hertford Co., died last week in Norfolk, Va., leaving a widow and one child. (BMJ, 29 Oct. 1796)

YOUNG, John, of Caroline Co., and Mary Turnbull of Annap. were wed at Annap. on 13th inst. (BFG, 21 Feb. 1798)

YOUNG, John, and Catherine Martin, both of Balto., were married last Thurs. by Rev. Rattoone. (BEP, 29 March 1808)

YOUNG, John, died Fri., 10th inst., in his 72nd year, formerly of Phila., but for many years an inhab. of Balto. (BFG, 13 Jan. 1812)

YOUNG, John H., of Fells Point, died Sun., 14th inst., aged 54 years. (BFG, 16 Feb. 1808)

YOUNG, John J., and Miss Cornelia Ensor, all of Balto., were wed by Rev. Wells last eve. (BFG, 26 Sept. 1816)

YOUNG, John R., M. D., of Hagerstown, died 8th inst. in his 22nd year. (BT, 20 June 1804)

YOUNG, Master John, died 12th inst. at Fells Point in his 16th year. (BFG, 17 April 1805)

YOUNG, Miss Martha, dau. of Dr. Samuel Young of Hagerstown, died 4th inst., in her 21st year. (BT, 18 April 1806)

YOUNG, Notley, died 22nd inst. at his res. in Washington City, one of the directors of the Bank of Columbia. (BFG, 26 March 1802)

YOUNG, Peter, died last Mon. in his 24th year. (BFG, 21 April 1804)

YOUNG, Peter, and Miss Nancy Haydock, all of Balto., were married Wed. eve. by Rev. Healey. (BA, 21 June 1811)

YOUNG, William, died last Thurs. in his 51st year, eld. son of the late Col. Young of Balto. Co., a dutiful son, affectionate bro., and good neighbor. (BFG, 11 May 1802)

YOUNG, William, and Miss Maria Leach, both of Balto., were wed on Tues., 1 May, by Rev. Healey. (BFG, 2 May 1810)

YOUNG, William Lewis, and Miss Elizabeth Potter, all of Balto., were married last Mon. by Rev. Glendy. (BFG, 20 Jan. 1810)

YOUNKER, Francis, and Miss Elizabeth Rose were married last Tues. eve. by Bishop Carroll. (BA, 12 Nov. 1807)

YUNDT, Leonard, Jr., and Miss Catherine Kalbfus of Balto. Co., were married last eve. by Rev. Otterbein. (BFG, 30 Sept. 1808)

MARRIAGES AND DEATHS

ZACHARIAS, Daniel, died suddenly, near Westminster Town last Mon. in his 62nd year. (BFG, 28 Aug. 1807)

ZANE, Joseph, of Balto., and Miss Eliza Hopkins of Phila. were wed last eve. by Rev. Rattoone. (BFG, 15 July 1808)

ZANE, Peter, and Miss Elizabeth Macbride, all of Balto., were married last eve. by Rev. MacCain. (BA, 10 Oct. 1809)

ZEIGLER, John, and Miss Mary Retig, all of Balto., were wed 4th inst. by Rev. Kurtz. (BEP, 21 Sept. 1808)

ZEIGLER, John, died last Sat. in his 79th year; for 55 years an inhab. of Balto. He emigrated from Germany. (BW, 6 March 1810)

ZEISBERGER, Rev. David, died 17th ult. at Goshen on the River Muskingum, state of Ohio, Senior Missionary of the United Brethren among the Indians; aged 87 years and nearly 7 mos. A native of Moravia in Germany, he came to this country in 1738, and landed in Georgia. (Long obit.) (BFG, 23 Feb. 1809)

ZEUMER, Augustus, of Balto., and Miss Margaret Alther of Hookstown, were married last eve., 22nd inst., by Rev. Mr. Kurtz. (BFG, 23 Dec. 1803)

ZIGLER, George, and Miss Eliza Roberts, all of Balto., were wed last Thurs. by Rev. Kurtz. (BT, 9 March 1801)

ZIGLER, Henry, and Rachel Roberts, both of Balto., were married 2 Nov. by Rev. Glendy. (BA, 6 Nov. 1815)

ZOLLER, Dr. Charles, died last Thurs., long a respectable physician. (BA, 20 Jan. 1816)

ZOLLICKOFFER, John Conrad, died at his house in Hanover St. yesterday, in his 54th year, leaving a widow and five small children. (BFG, 30 Jan. 1797)

ZOLLICKOFFER, John M. A., merchant, and Miss Louisa Ringgold, of Balto., were married Thurs. eve. by Rev. Otterbein. (BA, 17 April 1813)

ZWEILER, James, and Catharina Christina Gonderman, both of Balto., were married yesterday. (BA, 11 Aug. 1800)

ZWISLER, Mrs. Anne, died yesterday in her 29th year, wife of Mr. J. Zwisler, merchant, and mother of two children. Interment in Lutheran Burying Ground. (BFG, 26 Dec. 1799)

ADDENDA

BLAKELY, David, of Keady, Co. Armagh, Ireland, died 29th ult. in Balto. Interment in Second Presb. Burial Ground. (BW, 4 March 1812)

BRADENBAUGH, John, Jr., Balto. merchant, and Miss Priscilla Pew of Ashton, Penna., were married Thurs., 7 April. (BFG, 23 Dec. 1803)

GLENN, Harrison W., and Miss Martha Gardner, both of Balto., were married 28th ult. by Rev. Glendy. (BEP, 1 Jan. 1810) (BA, 1 Jan. 1810 gives his name as Hanson W. Glenn.)

KOONE, Daniel, and Miss Mary Wark, all of Balto., were married last eve. by Rev. Roberts. (BFG, 25 Nov. 1808)

LOVELL, William, and Miss Lilly Meekins, both of Balto., were wed Sat. eve. by Rev. Dr. Rattoone. (BA, 15 Oct. 1805)

MILHAU, Michael C., died 19th inst., aged 53 years, a native of Hispaniola who took refuge in this country at the start of of the first Revolutionary disturbances on that island. He leaves a widow and nine children. (BWA, 24 Feb. 1816)

RUSK, Robert, and Miss Sally Murray, all of Balto., were married last Thurs. by Rev. Glendy. (BW, 7 June 181)

SAMPSON, George, and Miss Rebecca -(?)-, of Balto., were wed on Sun., 26th inst., by Rev. Glendy. (BT, 28 April 1804)

SLEE, John, and Miss Mary Tipton, all of Balto., were married last eve. by Rev. Dr. Roberts. (BFG, 30 March 1810)

NOTES ON MARYLAND CLERGY

The following list of clergymen contains the names of some of the ministers mentioned in the text as having performed marriages. Clergymen who could not be further identified have not been included. Wherever possible, dates of birth and death, denomination, year of ordination and churches served have been included. A list of sources consulted is given following the notes.

ADDISON, Rev. Walter Dulany, d. 1848, aged 79; Prot. Ep.; 1799, ass't. minister of St. John's Par., P. G. Co.; 1805, rector of that parish; 1809, Georgetown Par., Wash., D. C., until 1821.

ALLEN, John, d. 1830, aged 70; Prot. Ep.; 1795-1815, rector of St. Geo. Par., Harf. Co.; 1800-1801, and 1803-1805, also served St. John's Par., Balto. and Harf. Cos.

ALLISON, Rev. Patrick, d. 1802; Presb.; 1763-1802, pastor of First Presb. Ch., Balto.

ANNAN, R.; 1803-1811, pastor of Associate Reformed Presb. Church of Balto.

ARMSTRONG, John; Prot. Ep.; 1804, St. Paul's Par., Kent Co.; 1806, St. Thomas' Par., Balto. Co.; 1810, moved to Penna.

ASBURY, Francis, d. 1816 in his 72nd year; Bishop of the Meth. Church.

BARCLAY, Rev. Francis; Prot. Ep.; 1805, St. Paul's Par., Q. A. Co.; 1806, All Hallows, A. A. Co.; 1808, William and Mary Par., St. M. Co.; 1810, went to Va.

BARTOW, John V., d. 1836; Prot. Ep.; 1815, Trinity Church, Balto.

BATUZEY. See Bitouzey.

BEASLEY, Rev. Frederick, d. 1845, aged 68; Prot. Ep.; 1810, Assoc. Rector, St. Paul's Par., Balto.; 1814, moved to Penna.

BECKER, Rev. Dr. Christian L., d. 1818; Germ. Ref.; 1806-1818, pastor First German Reformed Ch., Balto.

BEESTON, Rev. Francis, d. 1810; R. C.; c.1803-1810, rector of St. Peter's Ch., Balto.

BEND, Rev. Joseph J. G., .D D., d. 1812, aged 51; 1791-1812, rector of St. Paul's Par., Balto.

BIRCH. See Burch.

BITOUZEY, Germain; R. C.; by 1823 was at White Marsh plantation, which formerly belonged to the Jesuits, in Balto. Co.

BOWER, Rev. George; Prot. Ep.; in 1789 was rector of Frederick Par., Wash. Co., and All Saints Par., Fred. Co.; d. 1814.

BUDD, Rev. Thomas; Meth.; ord. 1803; d. 10 July 1810 in Phila., aged 28.

BUNN, Seely; Meth.; ord. 1792; d. 1834, aged 69.

BURCH, Rev. Thomas; Meth. Ep.; appears in records of First Meth. Ep. Church, Balto.

BUTLER, Absolom; Bapt.; preached at Chestnut Ridge (now Sater's) Bapt. Church at various times between 1756 and 1809.

CARROLL, John, R. C.; Bishop of Baltimore from 1789 until 8 April 1808 when he was made Archbishop of Balto.; b. 1735, d. 3 Dec. 1815.

CHALMERS, Rev. John; Meth.; ord. 1788, d. 3 June 1833 in Mont. Co., Md.

CHANDLER, John, Prot. Ep.; 1810, rector of St. Peter's Par., in Mont. Co.; 1813, St. Thomas, Balto. Co.; 1814, St. Mark's, Fred. Co.; d. 1814.

CLINGHAM, William; Bapt.; served Taneytown Bapt. Church from 1797 until 1803.

COACKER, Rev. Daniel; Pastor of the African Meth. Ep. Church in Balto. in 1810.

COATS, Rev, Samuel, in 1803 resided on Light St., Balto.

COKER, Abner; Meth. Ep.; native of Balto. Co., for many years a res. of Balto., died 8 Nov. 1833 in his 66th year, leaving a widow and 9 or 10 children.

COLEMAN, John; Prot. Ep.; 1787, St. John's Par., Balto. Co.; 1799, St. Thomas' Par.. Balto. Co.; 1806, St. James Par. in Balto Co. and Christ Church, Harf. Co.; d. 1816, aged 53.

COMPTON, John Wilson; Prot. Ep.; 1797, rector of St. James Par., A. A. Co.; 1806, added All Saints, Cal. Co.; d. 1813, aged 53.

CONTEE, Benjamin; Prot. Ep.; 1803, William and Mary Par., Chas. Co.; 1808, added Trinity Par., Chas. Co.; 1811, St. Pauls Par., P. G. Co.; d. 1816, aged 60.

CUDDY, Michael; R. C.; 1803-1804, pastor of St. Patrick's Ch., Balto.; d. 1804.

DASHIELL, George; Prot. Ep.; 1797, South Sassafras Par., Kent Co.; 1800, Chester Par., Kent Co.; 1804, St. Peter's Ch., in Balto.; 1816, renounced the church and organized the Evangelical Episcopal Church; d. 1852, aged 72.

DAVIS, Henry Lyon; Prot. Ep.; 1796, All Faith's Par., St. M. Co.; 1801, King and Queen Par., St. M. Co.; 1804, North Sassafras Par., Cecil Co.; 1816, St. Ann's Par., A. A. Co.; d. 1836.

MARYLAND CLERGY 369

DAVIS, John; Bapt.; organized Bapt. Ch. in Harf. Co.; from 1756 to 1809 preached at Sater's Bapt. Ch., Balto. Co.

DODGE, Daniel; Bapt.; b. 1777, d. 1851.

DRYER, John H.; Germ. Ref.; 1802-1806, pastor of First Germ. Ref. Church, Balto.

DUBOIS, John; R. C.; born in Paris, France, 1764: came to Va,; 1794, transferred from Norfolk, Va., to Frederick, Md.; founded Mt. St. Mary's, Emmittsburg; 1826, made Bishop of N. Y.

DUKE, William; Prot. Ep.; ord. 1785 and was rector of Queen Caroline Par., now Howard Co.; served many parishes (See Allen, p. 17); d. 1843, aged 43.

DUNCAN, John Mason; Assoc. Ref. Presb.; 1812-1822, pastor of Assoc. Ref. Church, Balto.

EMORY, John; Meth.; ord. 1810; in Tal. Co. by 1812; Bishop of the Meth. Ch., d. 1835.

FECHTIG, Lewis R.; Meth.; ord. 1812; d. 1823, aged 64; at time of his death was presiding elder of the M. E. Ch., Balto. Conf.

FENWICK, Rev. Enoch; R. C.; 1815, was rector of St. Peter's Ch., Balto.; res. at Saratoga near Charles.

FERGUSON, Colin, D. D.; Prot. Ep.; ord. 1785; served St. Pauls Par., Kent Co. until 1799 when he resigned; 1789-1805, Pres. of Washington College, Kent Co.; d. 1806.

FLOYD, John; R. C.; pastor of St. Patrick's Ch., Balto., from its opening until he died of yellow fever, 1797, aged 29.

FRYE, Joseph; Meth.; ord. 1809, d. 1845, aged 60.

GANTT, Edward, Jr.; Prot. Ep.; ord. 1784; was rector of All Saints Par., Cal. Co.; 1785, Christ Ch. Par.; 1796, resigned; in 1798, first missionary to Ky.; d. 1810, aged 51.

GARNIER, Anthony; R. C.; founder of St. Patrick's Ch., Balto., and rector, 1797-1803.

GIBSON, William Lewis; Prot. Ep.; 1806, St. Ann's Annap.; 1807 Alexandria, Va.; 1811, St. John's Par., Harf. Co.; 1812, Havre de Grace, Harf. Co.; 1813, St. Peter's Par., Mont. Co.; 1814, Queen Anne's Par., P. G. Co.; later became Meth. d. 1848.

GLENDY, John; Presb.; 1805-1826, pastor of Second Presb. Ch., Balto.

GREEN, Lemuel; Meth.; ord. 1783: d. 1831.

GRIFFITH, Alfred; Meth.; ord. 1806; d. 1871 in Va., aged 88.

GRUBER, Jacob; Meth.; ord. 1800; d. 1850 in Penna., aged 72.

GUEST, Job; Meth.; ord. 1806; d. 1857, aged 72.

HAGERTY, John; Meth.; d. 1823, having been a Meth. minister for almost 50 years; b. 1747.

MARYLAND CLERGY

HANDY, George Dashiell S.; Prot. Ep.; 1805, North Elk Par., Cecil Co.; 1808, St. Johns Par., Harf. Co.; 1812, Christ Church, Cal. Co.; 1816, All Saints Par., Cal. Co.

HANSON, James M.; Meth.; ord. 1809: d. 1860 at Reisterstown, Balto Co., aged 77.

HARGROVE, John; Swedenborgian; pastor of New Jerusalem Church, Balto., 1799 on.

HEALEY, Edmund; Meth.; ord. 1803; d. 1809 in S. C., aged 30.

HEALEY, John; Bapt.; pastor of Second Baptist Church, Balto., 1797-1848; d. 1848.

HEMPHILL, Andrew; Meth.; ord., 1803; d. 1837 at Carlisle, Penna.

HICKS, Galen; Prot. Ep.; 1812, rector of Trinity Church, Balto.; 1814, moved to Mass.

HIGGINBOTHOM, Ralph; Prot. Ep.; 1784, rector of St. Ann's Par., A. A. Co., where he served for over 20 years; d. 1813.

HARRYMAN, Hezekiah; Meth.: ord. 1795; d. 1818.

HORRELL, Thomas; Prot. Ep.; 1814, Addison Chapel, P. G. Co.; 1816, moved to Va.

INGLIS, James; Presb.; 1802-1819, pastor of First Presb. Church, Balto.

IRELAND, John; Prot. Ep.; 1796-1801, Associate rector, St. Pauls Par., Balto.; 1796-1801; in 1802 he returned to England.

JACKSON, Joseph; Prot. Ep.; 1796, St. Peter's Tal. Co.; 1811, William and Mary Parish, and St. Andrews Par., St. M. Co.: 1816, St. Johns Par., Hagerstown.

JUDD, Bethuel; Prot. Ep.; 1807, St. Ann's Annap.; 1811, returned to Conn.; d. 1858, aged 82.

KEMP, James; Prot. Ep.; 1812-1827, rector of St. Pauls Par., Balto.; 1814, Suffragan Bishop of Md.; 1816, Bishop of Md.; d. 1827, aged 62.

KURTZ, Daniel; Luth.; pastor of Lutheran Church, Balto., for over 50 years.

LANE, Nicholas; Prot. Ep.; 1794, ord., went to St. Peter's Par., Mont. Co.; 1798, All Saints Par., Cal. Co.; 1800, All Hallows Par., A. A. Co.; 1806, Christ Church Par., Cal. Co.; d. c.1813.

LEE, Jesse; Meth.; ord. 1783, d. 1816, aged 58, at Hillsboro, Md.

LEE, Wilson; Meth.; ord. 1799; d. 1804, A. A. Co., aged 57.

LUCAS, Thomas; Meth.; ord. 1791; d. 1819, aged 87.

LUCKEY, George; Presb.; served Bethel Presb. Church in Harf. Co., c. 1793-c.1803.

McCORMICK, Thomas; Prot. Ep.; ord. 1794, was assistant in Q. A. Par., P. G. Co.; 1788, Washington Par., Wash., D. C.; d. 1840, aged 70.

MAGRATH, Owen Fitzgerald; Prot. Ep.: 1793, St. Peters, Tal. Co.;
1804, King and Queen Par., St. M. Co.; 1805, Trinity Par.,
Chas. Co.· c.1808, moved to Va.

MATTHEWS, Lasley; Meth.; ord. 1786; d. 1813, aged 57.

MORANVILLE, J. F.: R. C.; came from France after that country's
revolution: 1804-1823, pastor of St. Patrick's Church,
Balto.; d. 1824.

NEALE, Leonard, R. C.; succeeded John Carroll as Archbishop of
Balto.; b. 1746, d. 1817.

NIND, William; Prot. Ep.; 1808, Westminster Par., A. A. Co.;
1812, St. Ann's Par., A. A. Co.; served other parishes;
d. 1822, aged 45.

OTTERBEIN, William; United Brethren; 1774-1813, pastor of the
United Brethren Church in Balto.; d. 1813.

PITTS, John; Meth.; ord. 1795; d. 1821 in Frederick Co., aged 51.

RALPH, George; Prot. Ep.; 1795, Washington Par., Washington, D.
C.; 1797, Queen Ann Par., P. G. Co.; 1800, Trinity Par.,
Chas. Co.; 1801, All Faiths Par., St. M. Co.; 1810,
Trinity Church, Balto.; d. 1813.

RATTOONE, Elisha Dunham; Prot. Ep.; 1802, Associate Rector, St.
Pauls Par., Balto.: 1807, Trinity Church, Balto.; 1809,
moved to S. C.

REED, Nelson; Meth.; ord. 1779; d. 1840, Balto., aged 89.

REIS, Edmund J.; Bapt.; 1815, came to First Baptist Church, Balto.;
later formed the Ebenezer Bapt. Church.

RICHARDS, Lewis; Bapt.: 1784-1818, pastor of First Baptist Church
in Balto.; d. 1°32.

RIGG, Elisha; Prot. Ep.; 1797, St. Pauls Par., Q. A. Co.: d. 1804.

RIGGEN, Benton; Meth.; ord. 1787; d. 1799 at Balto.

RILEY or REILEY, Tobias; Meth.; ord. 1810; d. 1843 at Cumberland,
Md., aged 55.

ROBERTS, Dr. George; Meth.; found in records of First Meth. Ep.
Church, Balto., prior to 1810; d. 1827 in his 63rd year.

ROBERTS, Robert R.; Meth.; ord. 1802; d. 1843 in Indiana, aged
65.

ROSZEL, Stephen George; Meth.; ord. 1789; d. 1841, aged 72.

RYLAND, William; Meth.; ord. 1802; preached at Stone Chapel Meth.
Church in Balto. Co. between 1802 and 1808; 1803 was appointed Chaplain to U. S. Navy; d. 1846, aged 76.

SARGENT, T. F.; Meth.; ord. 1795; d. 1823.

SHANE, Joseph; Meth.; preaching after 1806.

SNETHEN, Nicholas; Meth. Prot.; b. 1769, d. 1848.

STEPHENS, Daniel; Prot. Ep.; 1809, St. Luke's Par., Q. A. Co.;
1811, St. Paul's Par., Q. A. Co.; d. 1851 in Tennessee.

Stevens, David; Meth.; ord. 1796; d. 1825 aged 66, at Shippensburg, Penna.

Stevens, James; Meth.; ord. 1810; d. 1859, aged 84, in Penna.

Stone, Joseph; Meth.; ord. 1796; d. 1819 aged 76, in Fauquier Co., Va.

Stone, William Murray; Prot. Ep.; 1802, Stepney Par., Som. Co.; became third Bishop of Md.; d. 1840, aged 58.

Toy, Joseph; Meth.; ord. 1801; taught mathematics at Cokesbury College; d. 1826 in Balto., aged 79.

Troldenier, George; Germ. Ref.; 1791-1800, pastor, First German Reformed Church, Balto.; d. 1800.

Turner, Samuel Hulbeart; Prot. Ep.; 1812, Chester and St. Pauls Parishes, Kent Co.; 1817, went back to Penna.

Waugh, Beverly; Meth.; ord. 1809; d. 1858 at Balto., aged 69.

Wells, Joshua; Meth.; ord. 1789; served at Stone Chapel Meth. Church, Balto., 1809; d. 1862, aged 98 in Balto. Co.

Weems, John; Prot. Ep.; ord. 1787; 1787-1821 served Port Tobacco Par., Charles Co.; d. 1821.

Weems, Mason Locke; Prot. Ep.; ord. 1784; 1784, All Hallows Par., A. A. Co.; 1791, St. Margarets Par., A. A. Co.; 1793, went to Va.; d. 1825, aged 66.

Whitehead, James; Prot. Ep.; 1806-1807, Associate Rector of St. Pauls Par., Balto.; d. 1808.

Willis, Henry; Meth.; ord. 1778; d. 1808 at Pipe Creek.

Wilmer, James Jones; Prot. Ep.; 1801-1803, St. Johns Par., Balto. Co.

Wilmer, Simon; Prot. Ep.; 1802, North Sassafras Par., Kent Co.; 1806, St. Pauls Par., Kent Co.; 1808, moved to New Jersey; d. 1840.

Wood, William Haskin; Meth.; d. 1810, aged 41, having been a Meth. preacher for about 20 years.

Wyatt, William Edward; Prot. Ep.; 1814-1828, associate rector of St. Pauls Par., Balto.

SOURCES CONSULTED

Allen, Rev. Ethan. Clergymen in Maryland of the Protestant Episcopal Church Since the Independence of 1783. Baltimore: James S. Waters, 1860.

Minutes of the Baltimore Annual Conference of the Methodist Episcopal Church: Official Journal, 1929.

Dielman File, Maryland Historical Society.

INDEX

Abercrombie, 145
Ackinson, 193
Adair, 281
Adams, 7,58,64,140,143, 299
Aderson, 70
Adreon, 49,67
Ady, 275
Aiskey, 175
Aisquith, 340
Aitken, 226
Alderson, 302
Aldredge, 122
Aldridge, 23
Alexander, 26,111,233, 248,315,318
Alison, 54
Allan, 91
Allbright, 181
Allen, 72,99,138,267, 354
Allender, 215,333
Allison, 39,93
Allworth, 265
Almoney, 289
Alricks, 3,207
Alther, 364
Altherr, 89
Amelung, 187,332
Amey, 107
Amos, 86
Anderson, 141,152,227, 268,321,353
Andre, 21
Andree, 85
Andrews, 11,26,224,229, 252,265
Angell, 310
Anslow, 301
Anthony, 163,274
Apslay, 188
Archer, 243
Armistead, 82,225
Armitage, 108,141
Armstead, 211
Armstrong, 150,191,251
Arnold, 133,255
Arnolp, 337
Artz, 154
Ash, 241
Ashman, 135
Askew, 8,32,114,304
Atkinson, 69,361
Attwood, 67
Augustine, 78,225
Augustus, 73,130
Auiler, 217
Auld, 27,176,185
Austen, 4
Avenaux, 118

Bache, 96,148

Backer, 236
Bahan, 68
Bahon, 347
Bailey, 28,32,204,227, 311,332
Baily, 216
Bain, 353
Baker, 83
Balch, 355
Balderston, 97,150
Baldwin, 117,177
Ball, 13
Ballad, 290
Baltzell, 207
Bamberger, 276
Bane, 341
Banker, 51
Banks, 182
Bankson, 309
Bannerman, 208
Baptist, 175
Bare, 179
Barker, 96
Barklie, 222
Barkman, 149
Barnes, 4, 20,51,64,138, 168
Barnet, 298
Barnett, 60,166
Barney, 150,321,337, 352
Barnfield, 4
Barnhart, 298
Barr, 183
Barrett, 138
Barrickman, 303
Barriere, 322
Barroll, 118
Barron, 194
Barrow, 239
Barry, 183,234,255,265, 270,278
Barten, 206
Bartley, 46
Barton, 126,142,195, 301,302
Bartram, 51
Basse, 50
Bassett, 333
Bateman, 80,150,281
Battee, 133
Battery, 66
Bauder, 312
Baxley, 307
Bayard, 144
Bayles, 179
Bayly, 119
Beadle, 352
Beal, 270
Beall, 36,80,93,294
Beard, 191,283
Beck, 188,352
Beckley, 107

Beckwith, 336
Beddo, 339
Bedford, 350,351
Bedinger, 223
Beebe, 56
Beeks, 30
Beetson, 274
Beggs, 120
Bell, 90,144
Belt, 63
Bend, 136
Bennet, 324
Bennett, 47
Benson, 56
Benthime, 209
Bergeral, 105
Bernabeu, 346
Berry, 117,301
Besett, 323
Besse, 57
Betsworth, 143
Betts, 26
Bevans, 60
Bevins, 300
Bhaner, 112
Biays, 4,33,42,243,313, 342,348
Bibell, 323
Bickerton, 243
Bickham, 41
Biddison, 178
Biddle, 68,87,226
Bier, 285,292
Bigger, 289
Biggs, 273
Binger, 262
Bingham, 88,325
Binnix, 33
Birckhead, 31
Bird, 81,202,255
Birely, 113
Bishop, 70
Blachley, 130
Black, 159
Blackburn, 346
Blackney, 35
Blake, 139,258
Blakely, 365
Blakiston, 68
Blanch, 263
Blithe, 21
Block, 78
Blodget, 344
Bloodgood, 146
Bloomfield, 156
Blount, 120
Blundell, 155
Blunt, 88
Blyth, 238
Bodley, 6
Bogle, 291
Bohn, 258
Boller, 131,322

INDEX

Bond, 4,43,83,111,140, 149,163,181,211,279, 348,358
Boone, 38,217
Booth, 76,152,277
Bordley, 137
Borley, 173
Boschen, 284
Bose, 91
Bosley, 126,166,173,333
Botner, 231
Boudinot, 10
Boughen, 167
Bouldin, 182
Boulogne, 40
Bowen, 33,52,171,340
Bowers, 101,158,360
Bowie, 124
Bowly, 159,321,357
Bowne, 138
Bowyer, 70
Boyce, 218
Boyd, 36
Boyer, 127
Boyle, 20,313,315
Brache, 285
Bradberry, 247
Bradenbaugh, 279,365
Bradenhouse, 117
Bradey, 329
Bradley, 5
Bramble, 152
Brannan, 331
Branson, 326
Bray, 170
Bready, 158,273
Breidenbaugh, 195
Brent, 225,250
Brevitt, 144,250
Brice, 188,295
Bricker, 76
Brinton, 274
Briscoe, 27,60
Britain, 178,194
Briton, 220
Britten, 170
Britton, 353
Brody, 163,164,247
Bromfield, 17
Brooke, 58
Brooks, 140,313
Broom, 201
Broome, 164
Brown, 7,10,24,29,89,98, 101,,108,109,118,124, 142,145,167,168,177, 179,193,198,249,254, 264,265,269,287,299, 300,332,338,339,356
Browning, 4,12,155,280
Brownly, 18
Bruce, 286
Brumgart, 14
Brumingham, 82
Brumridge, 122
Brunton, 74
Bryan, 52,133
Bryant, 156,244
Bryden, 23,180
Bryson, 197
Buchanan, 49,64,109,176, 262,309
Buck, 115,173,220
Buckler, 268
Buckmen, 179
Buford, 50
Bull, 48,53,71,196,197, 204,281,328

Bunbury, 37
Buntz, 66
Burches, 20
Burgain, 114
Burgan, 293
Burgess, 26
Burk, 71,362
Burke, 108,113,122,353
Burkhead, 215
Burkins, 319
Burn, 7,204
Burneston, 334
Burnett, 52,153
Burnham, 175
Burns, 239,258,331
Burrell, 362
Burrows, 209,351
Burton, 189,320
Busch, 185
Busey, 301
Bushby, 274
Bussey, 216,243,260,347
Butler, 54,102,127,227, 291,296,338,350
Butt, 65
Butten, 170
Button, 46,160,321
Byerly, 20
Byus, 113

Cadored, 22
Cadwallader, 273
Cafrin, 78
Cain, 109,162,351
Calder, 196,357
Caldwell, 86,297
Calhoun, 139
Camp, 317
Campbell, 12,26,129,185, 208,209,211,213,242, 258,266,275,327,332
Candle, 181
Caney, 114
Cann, 218
Canter, 8
Capito, 29,37,312
Carback, 171
Carlbon, 107
Carlisle, 200,277
Carlson, 107
Carmichael, 29
Carnan, 240,292,318
Carnaughan, 224
Carnes, 37
Carnigham, 98,198
Carr, 27
Carre, 160
Carrell, 200
Carrick, 170,215,303
Carroll, 52,67,69,136, 145,147,211,230,267, 272
Carson, 6,18,134,336, 354,356
Carter, 44,162,327
Casenove, 121
Cassat, 55
Cassell, 238
Cassins, 60
Caswell, 85
Catherwood, 275
Caton, 211,249
Caughey, 131
Chalmers, 4,50,81,317
Chamberlain, 111,136, 162
Chambers, 54,69,280

Champlin, 122
Chancey, 331
Chandley, 148,264
Chaney, 219
Chase, 17,23,57,97,119, 142,184,361
Chateaudun, 215
Chatterton, 339
Chauncey, 72
Chavenes, 27
Chenoweth, 183
Chesney, 13,247
Chester, 315
Chew, 19,33,52
Childs, 211
Choice, 178
Christen, 307
Christie, 33,277
Christine, 223
Christy, 332
Church, 59,201
Churchman, 132
Clagete, 350
Clagett, 79,149
Claggett, 212
Clair, 269
Clapp, 28
Clark, 5,13,14,55,57,89, 191,206,212,273,309
Clarke, 9,31,42,72,108, 174,166,258,282,298, 336,360
Clarkson, 56,359
Claxton, 101
Claypoole, 23
Clayton, 107
Clemens, 310
Clemment, 53
Clendenin, 269
Clisroe, 206
Cloherty, 107
Cloris, 177
Cloud, 230
Clouden, 297
Coale, 91,261,262,268, 327
Coates, 261,354
Coats, 344
Cobb, 60
Cobuner, 7
Coburn, 7
Cochran, 28,72,152,169
Cockey, 166,255
Coe, 361
Coffin, 302
Coke, 50
Cole, 38,51,99,104,155, 177,201,230,238,262, 285,303
Coleman, 12,239,275
Coley, 287
Colgate, 287
Collins, 91,147,321
Colston, 320
Colver, 58
Colvin, 46
Commegys, 257
Commer, 135
Condle, 212
Cone, 241
Conkling, 146
Conley, 254
Conly, 249
Conn, 160
Connally, 178
Connary, 66
Connel, 286
Connell, 269

INDEX

Connelly, 357
Conner, 221
Connor, 90
Conroy, 212
Constable, 25
Conway, 173
Conyngham, 309
Cook, 74,100,133,146,
   200,225,266
Cooke, 125,352,354
Cooper, 114,143,153,200,
   261,319,355,360
Cope, 172
Copeland, 230
Copeman, 17
Copley, 133
Copperthwait, 307
Cornwall, 34
Corrick, 274
Coskery, 191
Coulson, 38,201
Coulter, 133,246
Courtenay, 96,218
Courtnay, 193
Cox, 116
Crabbin, 8,74,322
Craig, 10,27,37,112,139,
   140
Cralben, 9
Crane, 325
Craten, 335
Crawford, 6,100
Creek, 62
Creery, 352
Creighton, 303
Crist, 172
Crockett, 18
Cromwell, 222,230,294,
   343,354
Crosier, 185
Croskery, 172
Cross, 312
Crow, 149,160
Crowles, 361
Crowner, 101
Croxall, 232,246,272,353
Crozier, 49
Cruse, 25,258,331,355
Cullidon, 341
Culverwell, 178,250
Cuming, 101
Cumming, 218
Cummins, 10,93
Cunningham, 27,78,105,
   141,206,236,354
Curley, 331
Curran, 44,283
Curtain, 291,292
Cushman, 325
Custis, 312
Cyser, 147

Dabou, 99
Dailey, 222
Dall, 70,319
Dallam, 197,300,324
Dallas, 7,26
Dalrymple, 32
Daniels, 296
Danneman, 98
Dannie, 61
Danniels, 32
Danskin, 203
Dare, 57
Darlington, 21
Darrington, 218
Dashiell, 73,87
Daugharday, 244

Daughaday, 293,323
Daugherty, 269
Dauny, 279
Davenport, 274
Davey, 188
Davidson, 56,104,140,
   141,221,255
Davies, 293
Davis, 40,45,54,,83,108,
   140,,242,246,327,332,
   342,347,354,358,360
Davison, 119,198
Dawson, 253
Day, 163,222,290,327,
   339,345,353
Dayley, 300
Deady, 22,256
Deagan, 78
Deagen, 320
Deagle, 137,335
Deal, 35,38
Deale, 116
Dean, 138
Deas, 143
Death, 50
Deaver, 70,138,254
DeButts, 243
de Donjeur, 32
Deems, 242
Delany, 323
DelaRoche, 86
Delavet, 57
Delius, 136
Delozier, 81
Delshar, 232
Demmitt, 305
Denison, 276
Dennis, 135,289
Denny, 222
Dent, 146
Denyse, 329
Deramit, 305
Deschamps, 192
Detmar, 115
Devrickson, 72
Dew, 278,305,347
Dewees, 222
Dewitt, 34
Dewlin, 217
Dick, 111
Dickenson, 197,276,327
Dickey, 129
Dickins, 13
Didier, 200,332
Dieter, 331
Diffenderfer, 2,162,268,
   331
Diggs, 197
Dillon, 173,214,306
Dilworth, 226
Dimmitt, 115
Dinsmore, 187
Dinsmoore, 227
Divers, 28,159,203,284
Dixon, 208,279
Dobbin, 16,190
Dodds, 147
Dodge, 173
Dods, 98
Donaldson, 169,261,309
Donnally, 91,206
Donnell, 73
Donnelly, 87,108
Donovan, 346
Doran, 176
Dorney, 149,314
Dornin, 3
Dorset, 254
Dorsey, 7,25,58,66,92,
   109,113,126,128,143,
   150,159,164,233,262,
   280,305,313,314,350
Dougherty, 98
Douglas, 91
Douglass, 19,169,260
Dover, 320
Dowell, 88
Doyle, 293,335
Driscol, 273
Drowan, 351
Drugan, 95
Drummond, 281
Drury, 133
Drysdale, 125
Dubois, 102
Ducasse, 256
Ducate, 169
Dudley, 50
Duffie, 205
Duffield, 215,318
Dugan, 159,263,300
Duke, 38,233
Dukehart, 29,313
Dukes, 97
Dulany, 85,277
Duley, 78
Dumeste, 272
Dun, 279
Dunagan, 157
Dunant, 82
Dunbar, 177
Duncan, 19,57,74,113,243,
   350
Dunham, 1
Dunlavy, 3
Dunn, 102,188,223
Dunning, 19
Duplissis, 307
Duport, 268
Durang, 99
Durant, 230
Duty, 254
Dwyer, 251
Dyce, 81
Dyer, 91,97

Eagleston, 158
Eaglestone, 304
Eamorison, 63
Easom, 339
Edmonston, 178
Edwards, 4,129,151,177,
   275,304
Eichelberger, 63,236,272
Eiselen, 209
Eislen, 264
Eisler, 235
Elder, 41,148,346
Elleson, 340
Ellicott, 13,123,135,154,
   190,247,322,328,329,
   345
Elliott, 47,181,193,199,
   226,330,340
Ellis, 147,242
Ellmore, 224
Elvard, 202
Emmerson, 190
Emory, 195,330
Ennis, 66,108
Enright, 245
Ensor, 19,37,53,106,129,
   311,363
Ernest, 297
Eshelman, 170
Esminard, 39
Espey, 210

INDEX

Essendon, 96
Essex, 116
Estafv, 2
Etchberger, 124,177
Etting, 234
Evans, 32,49,82,128,154, 169,188,207,255,294, 296,317,361,362
Everett, 155,157
Everhard, 9
Everson, 55,114,202
Ewing, 184,345

Fagg, 320
Fakes, 18
Falconer, 186
Falls, 211
Falsgraff, 269
Faris, 12,339,347
Farmer, 97
Farnandis, 28
Farris, 216
Fass, 245
Fause, 61
Faussette, 331
Fearle, 103
Fearson, 276,310
Fenby, 18,79
Fendall, 18
Fennell, 344
Fenton, 331
Ferguson, 100,133,155, 245
Fergusson, 314
Fernandis, 57
Ferral, 123
Fetter, 165
Fetterling, 76
Fickie, 109
Field, 229
Fien, 283
Fifer, 145
Filbert, 110
Finch, 203
Finlass, 334
Finletter, 336
Finnigan, 236
Fishburn, 232
Fisher, 113,176,206, 215,267,292,306,353
Fishpaw, 64
Fit, 168
Fite, 202
Fitz, 82
Fitzgerald, 202
Fitzhugh, 78,97
Fitzpatrick, 67
Fizzrand, 81
Flanagan, 12,13,343
Flaneday, 327
Flannegin, 138
Flax, 106
Fleehart, 175
Fleming, 9,112,203
Fletcher, 282
Flin, 127
Flora, 112
Floyd, 208,258
Foard, 267
Focke, 30
Fomes, 321
Fonerden, 115,319
Fontz, 295
Ford, 67,90,98,137,161, 214,251
Foreman, 25,167,219,323
Forister, 217

Forman, 132,310
Forney, 136
Forrest, 186
Forrester, 252,357
Forsyth, 271
Foster, 44,101,190,201, 247,258,294,308
Fouks, 64
Fousdell, 22
Fowble, 258,332
Powell, 352
Fowler, 65,146,247,284, 317,334,342,357,360
Fox, 212,324
Foy, 39,195
Frailey, 273
Franciscus, 45
Franklin, 11,248,339
Frazer, 140,292,344,362
Freeman, 196,340
French, 100,342
Freshour, 12
Frick, 223,239
Frisby, 353
Friser, 229
Fromberger, 210
Fry, 218
Fryer, 25
Fulford, 73
Fuller, 28,204
Fullerton, 319
Fulton, 75
Funk, 176
Furlong, 71,333
Furnival, 5,7,285,340
Furnor, 119

Gabriel, 209
Gaddis, 131
Gaither, 244
Gallagher, 12
Gallaway, 329
Gallion, 122
Gallispy, 62
Galloway, 50,217,260
Galt, 146
Gamble, 57,264,319
Ganteaume, 80
Gantz, 110,114,269
Gardener, 355
Gardiner, 174
Gardner, 31,66,81,204, 365
Garman, 249
Garmin, 353
Garrett, 76
Gartner, 26
Garts, 137
Gassaway, 121
Gaston, 36
Gatch, 19
Gautier, 213
Gavin, 142
Geiger, 15,80
George, 320
Gest, 126
Ghequiere, 109,285
Gibb, 190
Gibbon, 53
Gibbons, 74
Gibbs, 353
Gibson, 29,76,87,89, 238,322
Gilbert, 285,359
Gilberthorpe, 298
Gilder, 55,306
Giles, 282

Gillmeyer, 172
Gilmor, 104,132
Gissenderfer, 346
Gist, 259
Gittens, 358
Gittings, 198,249,292,343
Glass, 167
Glen, 15
Glenn, 168,365
Glover, 166
Goddard, 264
Godman, 25
Goering, 146
Goff, 280
Gold, 172
Goldsborough, 248,258, 275
Goldthwait, 253
Godman, 364
Good, 329
Goodden, 144
Gooddens, 16
Gooden, 85,350
Gooding, 159
Goodwin, 94,308
Gordon, 15,101,124,128, 153,357
Gorham, 145,286
Gorner, 66
Gorsuch, 88,95,167
Gothrop, 273
Gough, 222
Gould, 73,123,132
Goulding, 23,150
Govane, 163,245
Gover, 202,356
Grache, 310
Grady, 24
Grafflin, 213
Graham, 12,35,250,271, 278,279
Grammer, 114,353
Grant, 104
Graves, 62,77
Gray, 21,138,174,182,207
Grays, 355
Green, 33,43,47,57,60, 122,,182,271,351
Greenfield, 75,310
Greenwood, 187
Greer, 21
Griffen, 350
Griffin, 131,279
Griffith, 39,77,110,171, 180,183,189,219,230, 309
Grimes, 4,14,154,205,222, 349
Groundfield, 161,244
Grover, 9
Grub, 85
Grubb, 155,179,181
Grundy, 51,124,174
Guffy, 66
Guiterr,165
Gumms, 109
Gun, 197
Gunby, 137,354
Guthrow, 223
Guy, 280
Gwinn, 140
Gwynn, 125,256

Hadley, 168
Hage, 136
Hagemen, 206,269
Hager, 34,194

INDEX 377

Hagerman, 189
Hagerty, 156,310
Hague, 2,137
Hahn, 204
Haiffligh, 289
Haile, 276
Hailer, 138
Hakins, 262
Haley, 82,323
Halfpen, 358
Halfpenny, 112
Hall, 44,62,85,120,127,
  134,138,139,155,158,
  164,174,175,183,194,
  208,217,220,227,242,
  255,265,275,282,288,
  308
Hallett, 324,329
Halverson, 117
Hambleton, 178
Hamer, 40
Hamilton, 47,109,150,
  198
Hammer, 22
Hammond, 54,61,92,93,
  113,178,255
Hampshire, 118
Hanaman, 156
Hance, 257
Hand, 15
Hands, 45
Handy, 219,308
Hanes, 45,261
Haney, 349
Hankey, 47
Hanna, 21,122,281
Hannaman, 151,192
Hans, 11
Hanson, 93,136,234,275,
  290,361
Hapke, 200
Harden, 129,362
Hardenbrook, 73
Hardester, 115,183
Hardister, 11,271
Hargrove, 22,105,117,
  146,163
Harkins, 67,74
Harlin, 352
Harlow, 55,147
Harman, 41
Harper, 81,198,316
Harps, 209
Harrion, 172
Harriman, 302
Harris, 131,266,307,
  336
Harrison, 77,189,198
Harryman, 218
Hart, 166,185,256,301
Hartmer, 350
Harvey, 185,220,295
Harwood, 88,164,288,
  314
Haskins, 74
Haslet, 210
Haslett, 32,219
Hassin, 121
Hatcheson, 149
Hauner, 35
Hauptmann, 285,292
Hawkins, 30,137,139,351
Hay, 15,79,109,273
Haydock, 363
Haydon, 71
Hayes, 280
Hays, 4
Hayward, 14

Hazel, 125
Hazell, 209
Head, 60,102,224
Healey, 308
Heath, 23
Hebb, 195
Heck, 334
Heckman, 341
Hegerty, 125
Heidey, 335
Heims, 285
Heislet, 125
Heister, 231,250
Helld, 129
Hellen, 151
Helm, 337,362
Hemings, 203
Hemsley, 100
Henderson, 91,127,342
Hendricks, 204
Hendrickson, 307
Henny, 251
Henry, 107,252
Hepwell, 234
Herbert, 135,240
Hergesheimer, 355
Herley, 152
Herman, 90
Hermange, 273
Herrick, 346
Herring, 60,203
Herrington, 104
Herron, 57
Hersey, 157
Hertick, 194
Hervey, 38
Heslip, 144
Hete, 299
Hewit, 162
Hezlip, 330
Hiatt, 361
Hickey, 136
Hickley, 207
Hicks, 132,293
Higginbothom, 48
Higginson, 257
High, 341
Higho, 148
Higinbotham, 81
Higinbothom, 233,337
Higson, 104
Hill, 71,145,180,249,
  283,301,304,323,353
Hillen, 121,166,172
Hilman, 81
Hilton, 289
Hincks, 277
Hindman, 17,285
Hinds, 249
Hinson, 352
Hiss, 76,317
Hitchborn, 215
Hobbs, 255,274
Hodge, 278
Hodgers, 124
Hodgson, 180
Hoffleigh, 108
Hoffman, 189,269,299,
  329,348,361
Hoges, 34
Hogg, 100
Holcomb, 279
Holland, 138,203,231,
  305
Holliday, 362
Hollenbach, 59
Holliday, 22,51,55,78,
  131,192,195,238,362

Hollingsworth, 33,58,124,
  248,271,345
Hollins, 33,210
Holmes, 48,199,350
Honicomb, 236,297
Hood, 358
Hook, 130,151
Hooper, 175,224,326
Hoopes, 341
Hoophert, 292
Hopkins, 15,36,106,171,
  255,364
Hopkinson, 298
Hopper, 287
Horn, 257
Horne, 248
Horstman, 182
Horton, 34
Houlton, 151
Houston, 71,157
How, 339
Howard, 7,73,101,160,197,
  225,232,258,278,296,
  322,341,348
Howland, 317,352,353
Hoyle, 186
Hubball, 357
Hubbs, 136
Hudgins, 120
Hudson, 93,230,237
Huel, 224
Huff, 147
Hugg, 188,226
Hughes, 3,8,61,115,138,
  196,227,288,311
Hughston, 16
Hugues, 310
Huisler, 235
Hull, 347
Humphreys, 196,235,246
Hungerford, 361
Hunt, 35,59,106,112,
  237,260,305,322
Hunter, 8,175
Husband, 255
Husbands, 341
Hussey, 90
Hutchings, 155
Hutchison, 265
Hutton, 355
Hyatt, 68,99,269,310
Hydorne, 116
Hyland, 284
Hynson, 52,197

Illingworth, 146
Immel, 114
Inglesby, 253
Inglis, 10
Ingram, 60
Inloes, 29,54,58,72,146
Innskeep, 35
Ireland, 102
Irvin, 152,291
Irvine, 276,325
Irwin, 233
Isaacke, 108
Isgrig, 133
Israel, 336

Jackson, 25,68,196,294,
  326,328
Jacob, 222,253
Jacobs, 32,235
Jalland, 306
James, 12,19,97,125,164,

INDEX

211,237,244,246,261,
274,276,282,339
Jamison, 9,128
Jarboe, 294
Jarrett, 227,312
Jay, 19,340
Jeames, 14
Jean, 261
Jeffers, 343
Jefferson, 6,51,105
Jemmison, 358
Jenifer, 229
Jenkins, 16,153,177
Jenkinson, 335
Jenning, 58
Jennings, 19
Jennith, 341
Jephson, 134
Jervis, 303
Jessop, 58,86,336
Jewett, 65
Jimmerson, 335
Job, 136
John, 171
Johns, 180,252,344
Johnson, 9,43,44,45,69,
  93,96,157,160,163,
  167,168,193,211,221,
  231,243,245,257,258,
  275,288
Johnston, 32,199,207,
  222,280
Joiner, 66
Jolly, 130,334
Jones, 13,51,78,105,
  106,150,152,180,185,
  199,201,246,251,267,
  270,273,301,318,340,
  347,358,359
Jordan, 5,44,109,181,
  205,206
Jordon, 69
Joyce, 84
Judge, 173
Julian, 336

Kabol, 213
Kalbfus, 349,363
Kantz, 193
Karthaus, 166,167
Karthous, 266
Kauffman, 280,294
Keagg,288
Kean, 16
Keefer, 244
Keener, 31,73,186,244,
  268,293
Keith, 173
Keller, 284,300
Kelley, 86
Kelly, 63,181,187,260,
  276,343
Kelso, 49
Kemp, 274
Kempe, 160
Kendal, 45,184
Kennedy, 23,192,197,198,
  221,241,256,349
Kenny, 357
Kensell, 334
Kent, 359
Kepley, 346
Kergin, 134
Kerr, 205,278,352
Key, 286
Keys, 44,100
Keyser, 25,167

Kilburn, 184
Kileholtz, 204
Kiles, 267
Killen, 265
Killum, 26
Kilmer, 250
Kilpatrick, 188
Kilty, 48
Kimmel, 17,184,330,332
Kincaid, 34
King, 4,30,49,97,179,
  334
Kingsmore, 333
Kinsell, 96
Kinsey, 68,342
Kintzing, 27
Kipp, 2,99
Kirby, 149
Kirk, 103,107
Kirkpatrick, 214,227,248
Kite, 360
Kithcart, 9,354
Kittleman, 332
Kline,331,341
Knowles, 26
Knox, 123,154,315,356
Koahl, 195
Kole, 321
Koone, 365
Kolhouse, 95
Konig, 79
Koone, 365
Koopson, 112
Kraber, 181,221
Kreider, 357
Krouze, 335
Kucher, 107
Kurnrich, 120
Kuyll, 263
Kuyt, 293
Kurtz, 288

Labbadie, 68
Lacaze, 228
Lacoste, 48
Ladson, 125
Lagge, 105
Lambden, 182,345
Lambert, 21
Lamborn, 335
Laming, 78
Lammot, 302
Lammott, 307
Landers, 45
Landeryoung, 178
Landry, 127,347
Lane, 42,168
Lanefelter, 45
Langdon, 69
Langford, 94,162,176
Lankford, 278
Lannaway, 278,313
Lannoy, 63
Larea, 121
Larere, 111
Larrance, 312
Larsh, 109
Lary, 148
Lauder, 129
Laurence, 252
Lavell, 17
Lawdenslager, 331
Lawrance, 192
Leach, 363
League, 167
Leahy, 17,143,231
Leake, 46

Leakin, 264
Leary, 178,347
LeBlanc, 318
LeCarre, 36
Leckey, 287
LeCompt, 229
Lee, 42,56,120,140,162
  239,246,265,334,358
Leeke, 80
Legard, 170
Legrove, 348
Lemmon, 236
Lemont, 256
Lemontier, 193
Lemott, 161
Lenaghan, 41
Lenum, 104
Leret, 204
LeRoy, 346
Levallunt, 274
Levely, 72,139,196
Levering, 62
Levy, 108,242
Lewis, 42,187,226,288,
  320
Lex, 268
Leydringham, 51
Leypold, 135
Lias, 218
Liddy, 181
Liggett, 230
Limes, 38
Lindenberger, 250
Linsdid, 82
Linvill, 260
Linville, 83
Littig, 255,316
Little, 1,135,190
Litzinger, 337
Livesay, 267
Livingston, 164
Locke, 92,219
Lockerman, 347
Loeffler, 190
Logan, 10,205,317
Long, 11,82,88,122,245
Longden, 301
Lord, 49
Louch, 242
Loudenslager, 187
Loughbridge, 42
Love, 198,286
Lovell, 365
Lowe, 251
Lower, 343
Lowerslyer, 78
Lowery, 360
Lowes, 330
Lowman, 85
Lown, 189
Lowndes, 169,176
Lowry, 92,112,175,201,230,
  314
Lucas, 26,315
Ludlow, 320
Luke, 20
Lusby, 83,108
Luttz, 165
Lux, 204
Lynch, 11,60,111
Lyon, 61,75

M'Allister, 190
McAtee, 47
M'Blair, 278
M'Bride, 203,364
M'Brune, 31

M'Cabe, 7,136
M'Cann, 242,289
McCannon, 64,66,97,284
M 'Carthy, 297
M'Caskey, 110,313
McCausland, 213,302,355
McCay, 24
McClain, 233,300
Maclay, 101
M'Clevery, 103
M'Colley, 75
McComas, 46,84,150,293, 299
McConkey, 214
McConnell, 72,186,292, 304
McCormick, 15,52,65,81, 83,119
McCoy, 131
McCreary, 46
Maccubbin, 14,34,36,52, 142,214,312,346
McCulloch, 36
McCullough, 45,152,236
McCumsey, 211
McCurdy, 63
McDaniel, 205
McDonald, 54,287,290, 348
McDonaugh, 4
McDonnell, 293
McDonogh, 65,200,363
McElderry, 95,232
McFadden, 257
McFadon, 110
M'Garven, 186
McGarvin, 210
M'Gauren, 318
M'Glathery, 211,222, 225,250
M'Gowan, 9,98,248
McGraw, 217
M'Guire, 208,349
M'Hard, 30
Machen, 211
M'Henry, 34
McIlvaine, 206
McIntire, 273,337,359
Mackay, 260
M'Kean, 15,43,100,157
Mackelfresh, 171
Mackenheimer, 15,86
M'Kenzie, 117,176
M'Kerlie, 83
Mackey, 104
M'Kim, 10,96,151
M'Kinnel, 348
M'Kinzie, 24,145
McKnight, 114
Mackrell, 226
Mackubin, 174
McLane, 16
M'Laughlin, 303
McMaster, 171,207
McMechen, 147,234
M'Millan, 60
McNamara, 207
M'Neale, 257
M'Neir, 156
M'Nelty, 57
M'Nulty, 86
M'Pherson, 125,171,297
Macrahon, 212
M'Rea, 187
M'Sherry, 63,133
Maddon, 252
Madison, 299,324
Magauran, 75,35

Magee, 218
Maggs, 102,194
Magillin, 79
Magnis, 315
Magruder, 35,245
Mags, 151
Mail, 290
Mallet, 202
Maloniere, 129
Malsby, 69
Manacrel, 213
Mankin, 35
Mann, 311
Manning, 127
Mansfield, 165
March, 83,99,202,360
Marfield, 301
Mark, 281
Markle, 326
Marks, 271
Marr, 107
Marret, 359
Marsden, 1
Marsello, 190
Marshall, 7,13,32,113, 189,222,328
Martiacq, 327
Martin, 11,40,83,88,154, 180,219,235,240,310, 312,348,358,363
Mashaw, 195
Mason, 19,23,47,163,215, 294
Massey, 201
Masters, 56,233
Mastin, 157
Matchett, 303
Mather, 144,179
Mathewson, 230
Mathiot, 223
Matthews, 54,95,155,229, 235,333
Mattison, 177
Mattocks, 196
Maxfield, 77
Maxwell, 15,28,76,98, 110,185,242
May, 117
Maynadier, 111
Mayns, 23
Mayo, 119
Meads, 39
Mears, 27
Meek, 76
Meekins, 199,365
Meissen, 182
Mercer, 63,183
Merin, 121
Merrell, 249
Merriam, 304
Merriken, 40
Merritt, 340
Merryman, 51,310,316, 317
Metcalf, 20
Meyerhofer, 338
Meyers, 279
Milbourne, 79
Miles, 53,165,226
Milhau, 276,365
Millar, 119
Millard, 223
Millemon, 222
Miller, 11,15,27,51, 79,114,117,135,167, 178,188,206,216,234, 275,278,284,309,313, 345,346,350,358

Milligan, 210
Milliman, 104
Millimon, 89
Million, 223
Mills, 4,107,151
Millward, 247
Miltenberger, 321,337
Mince, 290
Minchin, 73
Mines, 14
Minke, 121
Minsky, 304
Miskimon, 277
Mitchel, 54,63
Mitchell, 3,32,40,53,55, 61,103,115,135,221
Moale, 25,159,271,325
Mohler, 33,215,216
Mokebee, 14
Money, 218
Mongee, 192
Monington, 330
Monks, 229
Monro, 245
Monroe, 150
Montgomery, 43,204,348
Moody, 22
Moore, 2,16,149,204,255, 265,268,304
Mopps, 311
Moran, 34
Moren, 208
Moreton, 154
Morgan, 123,161,249,277
Morling, 53,208
Morris, 97,252
Morrison, 39,45
Morrow, 20,77,206,210
Mortimer, 355
Mortimore, 107
Morton, 202,270,282,350
Moule, 351
Mounticue, 147
Moylan, 335
Muhlenberg, 151
Muir, 29
Mulakin, 168
Mulberg, 328
Mullen, 35
Muller, 231
Muloniere, 96
Mummey, 245
Mummy, 56
Munday, 141,262
Munickeysen, 192
Munroe, 293
Murdock, 299
Murphy, 22,147,170,210
Murray, 23,27,95,112, 120,121,138,146,184, 235,280,327,336,351, 365
Musgrove, 347
Mushberger, 247
Myer, 42,55,212,292
Myers, 43,131,169,170, 179,183
Myring, 107

Naeton, 257
Nagle, 100,277
Nants, 34
Nate, 252
Neafe, 196
Neal, 363
Neale, 34,203
Nealy, 135

INDEX

Nearey, 110
Neaves, 135
Neilson, 119,182,189
Nelson, 265
Nesbit, 43
Nevets, 193
Newburn, 121
Newman, 314,357,359
Newton, 247
Nice, 248
Nicholas, 249
Nicholls, 230
Nichols, 131,135,166, 348
Nicholson, 200,209,226, 298,360
Nicoll, 66
Nind, 66
Ninde, 75
Nixon, 127,347
Norman, 127
Norris, 42,68,69,96, 106,189,215,294,304, 328
North, 96
Norton, 349
Norwood, 93,149
Nowers, 306
Nowland, 352
Nussear, 154

Obey, 99
O'Brien, 243
Oden, 28
O'Donnell, 6,25,257
Ogle, 26
Olar, 319
Oldham, 316
Oliver, 67,157
Omenseter, 358,
Omansetter, 291
Onion, 90,106,324,339
Oram, 291
Ore, 188
Orr, 84
Orrick, 40,175,273
Osborn, 203,214
Osborne, 122,145,342
Osmon, 129
Ostend, 51
Otto, 207
Overstreet, 173
Overy, 308
Owens, 248,308
Owings, 14,94,146,158, 173,236,247,261,274, 290,301,356
Oyster, 193

Paden, 54
Page, 28,356,360
Paints, 106
Palmer, 289
Pamphilion, 136
Pannel, 281
Pannell, 232,258,356
Paris, 304
Parish, 309
Parker, 6,26,199,262, 296
Parkinson, 253
Parks, 30,31,49,87, 247
Parsons, 314,339
Partridge, 301
Pascault, 242

Pasley, 202
Patrick, 10,38,96,145, 147,320
Patten, 86
Patterson, 30,38,119, 164,199,225,228,275
Pattison, 92,348
Patton, 121,186
Paul, 117
Pawson, 25,340
Payne, 85
Payson, 306
Peach, 121,250
Pearce, 18,143,172
Pearpoint, 218
Pearson, 283
Pebeto, 179
Pechin, 16
Peck, 322
Peers, 70
Peirpoint, 278
Pellom, 295
Pendleton, 79
Pennell, 101
Pennington, 170,281,320
Pennock, 247
Pentz, 129
Percey, 64
Peregoy, 20,50
Perigo, 125,133
Perkins, 43
Perriage, 350
Perry, 183,277
Perryman, 149
Pervail, 161
Peter, 312
Peterkin, 240
Peters, 37,121,144,281, 320
Peterson, 132
Petit, 99
Pettit, 170
Pew, 34,365
Philips, 18,114
Phillips, 8,78,106,124, 137,255,265,282,315
Phipps, 14
Pickering, 93,206
Picket, 55,285
Pickever, 66
Pierpoint, 84
Pierrepont, 134
Pindell, 184
Pindle, 26
Pine, 71
Pinkerton, 209
Pinkney, 347,351
Pinney, 190
Pitcher, 75
Pits, 261
Plater, 272
Plummer, 45,331
Pocock, 79
Poe, 63,89,153
Poirie, 278
Polk, 62,184,323
Pollard, 293
Pollock, 69,152,194
Poor, 141
Porter, 105,117,154, 204,210,257,279,290
Poteet, 191,271
Pottenger, 140
Potter, 111,127,363
Potts, 256
Pouder, 115,343
Poulet, 253
Powel, 153

Powell, 256,265
Powley, 324
Poyntell, 48
Prather, 163,314
Pratt, 263
Presbury, 21,140,155, 220,246,295,297
Preston, 21,105,141,167, 248
Prett, 200
Prian, 44
Price, 117,248,270,301, 305,331,340,349
Prill, 267
Primrose, 1
Prince, 118
Pritchard, 241
Probart, 319
Proctor, 73
Proud, 217
Pryce, 147
Pue, 93
Puel, 48
Pugh, 151
Pumphrey, 214,175,333
Purdin, 104
Purnell, 251
Purviance, 72,150,309

Quail, 185,317
Quay, 23,211
Quin, 211
Quinn, 274
Quirk, 89
Quisic, 65
Quisick, 308,313
Quynn, 352

Raab, 107
Raborg, 203,333
Radal, 9,186
Radel, 160
Rains, 28
Ramsay, 23,62,208
Ramsey, 226,336
Randal, 130
Randall, 106,138,329
Randolph, 229
Rapp, 344
Ratlin, 24
Rawlings, 149
Ray, 88
Rea, 254
Read, 40,51
Readle, 352
Rector, 73
Rediar, 46
Reeder, 2
Reel, 235
Reese, 99,170,182,296,301
Reider, 239
Reigart, 298
Reiley, 273
Reilly, 169
Reinecker, 343
Renaudet, 79
Renkert, 232
Renshaw, 118
Repold, 302
Retig, 364
Revell, 237
Revely, 210
Reynolds, 98,221
Rial, 307
Rice, 42,157
Richards, 83,123,134,174 196,266,318

Richardson, 30,63,111,
  122,306,343,345
Rickard, 56
Ricker, 6
Riddell, 1,52,244
Riddlemoser, 346
Rider, 239
Ridgaway, 173,352
Ridgely, 17,45,52,80,
  110,144,162,163,199,
  229,236,241,271,343
Ridley, 317
Rieman, 336
Rigby, 27
Righter, 307
Riley, 46,154,257
Ringgold, 146,158,364
Risteau, 159
Ritchie, 244
Ritter, 213
Roach, 77,202,329
Roache, 88
Robb, 109,137,183
Roberts, 192,224,349,
  364
Robertson, 23,148
Robinson, 1,21,47,98,
  141,151,169,172,253,
  299,309,313,314,332
Robison, 110
Roche, 206,349
Rodgers, 127,132,161,
  276
Rodney, 166
Roe, 6,46,276
Rogan, 340
Rogers, 21,55,56,89,
  158,217,233,347,362
Rollins, 326
Romney, 88
Roney, 20,317
Rooker, 240
Roper, 5
Roschen, 284
Rose, 31,99,297,360,363
Roselle, 285
Rosensteel, 40
Rosenstiel, 154
Ross, 46,90,234
Rothery, 152
Rour, 200
Rous, 324
Rowe, 46
Rowland, 282
Rowles, 257
Rozer, 322
Rozzel, 359
Rubert, 176
Rudulph, 288
Rusk, 77,103,132,268,
  365
Russel, 126,235
Russell, 125
Ruth, 302,358
Rutter, 144,245,262,
  267,281,303,310
Ryan, 168,204,253
Ryland, 132

Sadler, 232
Sagassar, 116
Sahner, 14
Sailer, 275
Sailors, 293
St. Clair, 61
Salsbury, 106
Salter, 362

Sampson, 114,184,365
Sanderson, 288
Sands, 217
Sanner, 20
Sapp, 47
Sappington, 337
Sater, 229
Satiswait, 282
Sauerwein, 281
Saukey, 356
Saunders, 76,281
Savage, 182,201
Savington, 78
Savory, 351
Scarf, 101
Schaeffer, 126,240,276,
  294
Schannaman, 220
Schee, 235
Schley, 214
Schrader, 253,264
Schultz, 103,218
Scoful, 9
Scott, 31,54,180,190,
  223,251,269,305,363
Scource, 71
Scroggs, 224
Sear, 65
Sears, 205,261
Seaver, 316
Seekamp, 5
Seffel, 350
Seger, 202
Sellman, 2,75,266,291,
  334,343
Selve, 187
Semans, 34
Sewel, 57
Sewell, 163,186,224,360
Shaeffer, 20
Shaffer, 229,319
Shahanasey, 269
Shahawnasy, 271
Shakes, 63
Shane, 71
Shaney, 306
Shannon, 156
Sharp, 6,270
Sharpe, 5
Shaw, 11,95,106,139,223,
  252
Sheaff, 317
Shear, 233
Shedden, 304
Sheeler, 89
Sheffy, 137
Shehanasey, 115
Shekell, 78
Sheldon, 137
Shepherd, 26
Sheppard, 5
Shepperd, 244
Sherry, 332
Sherwood, 9,32
Shields, 70,354
Shilling, 41
Shipley, 176,192
Shisler, 129
Shoate, 175
Shoemaker, 70
Shorb, 16
Shore, 153
Shrader, 357
Shriver, 118,268,312
Shroder, 357
Shrote, 309
Shugart, 221
Shultz, 187

Siddle, 305
Sidwell, 195
Silverdore, 66
Simm, 298
Simmons, 150,177
Simms, 334
Simonson, 179
Simpson, 169,171,340
Sinclair, 59,196,327
Sinners, 90,128,133
Sitler, 70,256,299
Size, 270
Skelton, 193
Skerett, 24
Skinner, 126
Slade, 46,227,231,316
Slaten, 308
Slater, 279
Slaughter, 215
Slaymaker, 227
Slee, 365
Sleppy, 219
Slett, 31
Sligh, 58
Sloan, 118,258
Slocum, 129
Slubey, 33,156
Small, 19,234
Smallwood, 3,332,333
Smith, 19,31,40,48,50,
  52,58,61,64,66,68,74,
  90,92,95,124,130,134,
  140,149,150,156,164,
  165,167,171,185,213,
  229,232,238,240,247,
  249,260,261,267,271,
  284,295,296,298,300,
  308,313,315,321,342,
  344
Snowden, 42,80,102,161,
  167,329
Snowdey, 244
Snyder, 80,344
Sollers, 305,360
Somers, 182
Sopp, 74
Sower, 15,302
Spalding, 172,219,317
Sparks, 41,314
Speak, 60
Speake, 59
Spear, 199,237,302,328,
  340
Speck, 314
Spedden, 191,231
Spence, 123
Spencer, 252,308
Spicer, 196,291
Spier, 11
Spindler, 268
Spingler, 113
Spinner, 341
Sprague, 119
Sprigg, 90,153
Springer, 195
Sprole, 195
Spurrier, 142,305,339
Stacy, 333
Stagers, 160
Stall, 212
Stamman, 267
Stanley, 186
Stanly, 8
Stansbury, 36,54,69,74,
  82,88,102,126,157,
  159,176,321
Staples, 55
Stapleton, 341

INDEX

Starck, 31
Starr, 104,227
Statzell, 74
Steeg, 326
Steele, 153
Stein, 36
Stephens, 166
Stephenson, 307
Sterett, 13
Steuart, 251
Stevens, 88
Stevenson, 52,88,153, 175,251,297,351
Steward, 147
Stewart, 22,30,31,41,43, 48,92,102,109,195, 276,280,314
Stiles, 70
Stinchcomb, 341
Stinnecke, 98
Stitcher, 116,151,312
Stith, 361
Stockard, 205
Stockett, 46,51
Stoddert, 49
Stone, 10,79,158,316, 327
Story, 170
Stouffer, 184
Stover, 362
Strachan, 163
Strahan, 14
Strain, 120
Stran, 170
Strang, 225
Strebach, 274
Strebeck, 309,321
Streimel, 216
Stretch, 121
Stricker, 8,212
Strimall, 216
Strough, 14
Strowbridge, 169
Stuart, 114
Stubbs, 312
Stump, 8,171,227,319, 351
Stutson, 142
Sugars, 41
Sullivan, 141,162
Sullivane, 148
Summers, 152,286
Sumwalt, 44,84,291
Sutherland, 162
Sutton, 243,342
Swampstead, 222
Swan, 222,232,291
Swann, 69,110,310
Swartz, 270
Swartzauer, 1
Swearingen, 28
Sweeten, 242
Swindal, 276
Swope, 362
Swormstedt, 288

Talbot, 71
Talbott, 272
Tankeley, 3
Tasker, 315
Tatnall, 12
Taylor, 75,90,91,99, .125,135,138,139,170, 191,192,238,247,254, 257,258,275,317,348
Teackle, 57
Tear, 65

Tellman, 336
Tennant, 324
Terry, 360
Tharp, 71
Thomas, 3,38,61,81,82, 88,103,116,128,141, 143,176,186,192,198, 212,243,266,267,270, 289,300,328,337,339, 351
Thompson, 7,61,89,116, 162,191,196,210,238, 248,295,339
Thomson, 9,349
Thorn, 314
Thornberry, 230
Thornburg, 342
Thornburgh, 87,203
Thornsbury, 92
Thornton, 26,210
Thrift, 65
Thurston, 241
Thryack, 123
Tier, 60
Tiernan, 302,352
Tilden, 37,142,185,311
Tilghman, 37,70
Tilyard, 277
Timons, 206
Tinges, 48,312
Tingey, 357
Tippins, 40
Tipton, 91,294,338,365
Tittle, 53
Tobel, 30
Todd, 39,181,262,319, 359
Toomes, 315
Toon, 297
Torrance, 303
Torrence, 63,224
Townsend, 172
Townson, 237
Towson, 6
Tracey, 69
Trapnell, 68
Travers, 59,82
Trenton, 82,188
Trimble, 26,123,133, 288
Trippolet, 213
Troltener, 103
Troth, 39
Trotten, 178
Troup, 256
Trownson, 246,263
Trulock, 326
Trumbo, 95
Trunstell, 145
Truxton, 27,73,141
Tschudy, 285,303
Tucker, 191
Tudor, 90,309
Tull, 192
Tunis, 103
Turnbull, 363
Turner, 65,71,109,155
Tydings, 327
Tyler, 67,333
Tyson, 60,143,291,355

Uhlring, 123
Ulrick, 24
Underwood, 38,72,251, 267
Utz, 342

Valck, 11
Vallette, 214
Van Bibber, 236
Vanderslice, 278
Van Horn, 186
Vanlear, 110
Van Noemer, 11
Van Wyck, 70,139
Veal, 262
Veazey, 65,247
Verner, 311
Vernon, 270
Vickers, 54
Vize, 346
Volckman, 5
Volkman, 287
Von Kapf, 7
Voss, 240

Wade, 289
Wadsack, 162
Wadsworth, 346
Wager, 199
Wagner, 217
Waldron, 291
Walker, 38,55,77,82,105, 134,317,326
Wall, 323
Wallace, 171,265,331
Wallis, 3,177
Walls, 10
Walsh, 36,236,252
Walter, 40,76,199,250, 295
Walters, 288
Walton, 291
Wampler, 357
Wane, 6,248
Ward, 200,228,243
Wardell, 7
Warfield, 301
Wark, 365
Wall, 148
Warner, 146,223,225,355
Warren, 74,234,256
Warrington, 266
Washington, 142,311,324
Waters, 6,108,174,193, 242,252
Watts, 90,127,155,285
Wayman, 64
Weary, 70,75,80
Weatherburn, 72,92,134, 148
Weatherington, 176
Weatherly, 121
Weaver, 38,166,226,341
Webb, 77,189,268,300
Webster, 78,296,320,336, 342
Weddrington, 164
Weedon, 223
Weeks, 44,68,329
Weems, 320
Wehner, 234
Weir, 166
Weis, 59
Weisenthal, 165
Welch, 281,347,348
Wellmore, 272
Wells, 47,130,161,173, 181,267
Welsh, 14,66,126,144, 173,266
Wesby, 126
West, 70,292,309,321
Westberry, 74

INDEX 383

Westray, 358
Wethered, 200
Wetzell, 326
Wharfe, 338
Whealer, 41
Wheaton, 45
Wheeler, 32,85,95,129,
  192,197,241,248,256,
  258
Whelan, 189
Wheland, 224
Whetcroft, 183
Whipple, 289
Whitaker, 344,351
White, 6,35,75,154,166,
  205,233,241,279,318,
  345,349,362
Whitelock, 318
Whitelsy, 119
Whitery, 280
Wickham, 354
Wierman, 290
Wiesenthal, 260
Wigley, 340
Wignell, 43,338
Wilcox, 172
Wilde, 263
Wiley, 79,262
Wilkes, 172
Wilkinson, 212,247
Willcox, 9
Willey, 34,37
Williams, 86,103,126,
  182,184,254
Williamson, 73,251,254,
  321
Willis, 37,120,156,204,
  245
Willmor, 248
Wilson, 5,13,37,40,55,
  71,73,87,99,108,130,
  159,161,176,185,191,
  207,211,228,242,250,
  262,278,279,289,355
Winchester, 8,50
Wineman, 315
Winemiller, 264
Winkes, 171
Winks, 44,46
Wise, 98,283,287
Wiseman, 6
Wisotzkey, 45
Wolf, 85,114,356
Wolfington, 20
Wollar, 105
Wolslager, 185
Woodland, 36
Woodrow, 63
Woods, 216,224
Woodside, 318
Woodward, 65
Woodyear, 156
Woollen, 199
Wormeley, 238
Worrell, 218
Worthington, 64,111,120,
  172,175,189,220,228,
  245,335,338
Wray, 101,133
Wright. 24,45,100,130,
  157,300,303
Wyant, 282
Wyles, 240
Wynn, 27

Yandel, 316
Yandell, 150
Yarnall, 13
Yates, 111,290,335
Yeiser, 31,79,98,180,
  185,229,318,332
Yellott, 9
Yingling, 336
Yokeley, 300
Young, 6,28,33,80,181,197,
  263,283,290
Younghusband, 38
Youse, 149
Yundt, 166,172,325

Zachariah, 268
Zacharias, 326
Zane, 46,54
Zebne, 237
Zigler, 119
Zinstack, 140
Zwisler, 2

www.ingramcontent.com/pod-product-compliance
Lightning Source LLC
Chambersburg PA
CBHW071143300426
44113CB00009B/1064